# Lecture Notes in Computer Science 3455

Commenced Publication in 1973
Founding and Former Series Editors:
Gerhard Goos, Juris Hartmanis, and Jan van Leeuwen

Helen Treharne   Steve King
Martin Henson   Steve Schneider (Eds.)

# ZB 2005:
# Formal Specification and
# Development in Z and B

4th International Conference of B and Z Users
Guildford, UK, April 13-15, 2005
Proceedings

 Springer

Volume Editors

Helen Treharne
University of Surrey
School of Electronics and Physical Sciences
Guildford, Surrey GU2 7XH, UK
E-mail: H.Treharne@surrey.ac.uk

Steve King
University of York
Department of Computer Science
Heslington, York, YO10 5DD, UK
E-mail: king@cs.york.ac.uk

Martin Henson
University of Essex
Department of Computer Science
Wivenhow Park, Colchester, Essex, CO4 3SQ, UK
E-mail: hensm@essex.ac.uk

Steve Schneider
University of Surrey
School of Electronics and Physical Sciences
Guildford, Surrey GU2 7XH, UK
E-mail: S.Schneider@surrey.ac.uk

Library of Congress Control Number: 2005923295

CR Subject Classification (1998): D.2.1, D.2.2, D.2.4, F.3.1, F.4.2, F.4.3

ISSN        0302-9743
ISBN-10     3-540-25559-1 Springer Berlin Heidelberg New York
ISBN-13     978-3-540-25559-8 Springer Berlin Heidelberg New York

Springer is a part of Springer Science+Business Media

springeronline.com

© Springer-Verlag Berlin Heidelberg 2005
Printed in Germany

Typesetting: Camera-ready by author, data conversion by Scientific Publishing Services, Chennai, India
Printed on acid-free paper        SPIN: 11415787        06/3142        5 4 3 2 1 0

# Preface

These proceedings record the papers presented at the 4th International Conference of B and Z Users (ZB 2005), held in the city of Guildford in the south-east of England. This conference built on the success of the previous three conferences in this series, ZB 2000, held at the University of York in the UK, ZB 2002, held at the *Laboratoire Logiciels Systèmes Réseaux* within the *Institut d'Informatique et Mathématique Appliquées de Grenoble* (LSR-IMAG) in Grenoble, France, and ZB 2003, held in Turku in Finland hosted by Åbo Akademi University and the Turku Centre for Computer Science (TUCS). ZB 2005 was held at the University of Surrey, Guildford, UK, hosted by the Department of Computing. The University has always placed particular emphasis on the applicability of its research and its relationship with industrial partners. In this context it is building up its formal methods activity as an area of strategic importance, with the establishment of a new group within the Department of Computing, and also with its support for this conference.

B and Z are two important formal methods that share a common conceptual origin; they are leading approaches in industry and academia for the specification and development (using formal refinement) of computer-based systems. At ZB 2005 the B and Z communities met once again to hold a fourth joint conference that simultaneously incorporated the 15th International Z User Meeting and the 6th International Conference on the B Method. Although organized logistically as an integral event, editorial control of the joint conference remained vested in two separate but cooperating programme committees that respectively determined its B and Z content, but in a coordinated manner.

All the submitted papers in this proceedings were peer reviewed by at least three reviewers drawn from the B or Z committee depending on the subject matter of the paper. For the first time for a ZB conference, reviewing, discussion and selection of papers were undertaken entirely electronically, with no face-to-face PC meeting. After an initial selection by each committee, a joint meeting of the chairs took place to finalize the selections and the conference programme.

The conference featured a range of contributions by distinguished invited speakers drawn from both industry and academia. The invited speakers addressed significant recent industrial applications of formal methods, as well as important academic advances serving to enhance their potency and widen their applicability. Our invited speakers for ZB 2005 were drawn from the UK, Australia and France.

Cliff Jones is a Professor of Computing Science at the University of Newcastle, UK. His career has been spent in both industry and academia, where his interests have been at the interface between research and application. He was behind the creation of the influential Vienna Development Method (VDM), one of the better-known formal methods (alongside Z and B!), during his time at

IBM in the 1970s. His interest in formal methods has now widened to encompass other aspects of dependability. Carroll Morgan is Australian Professorial Fellow at the School of Computer Science and Engineering, University of New South Wales, Australia. He has worked on Z, CSP, the refinement calculus, and probabilistic logic. He is the author of the seminal book on the refinement calculus 'Programming from Specifications,' and more recently (with Annabelle McIver) of 'Abstraction, Refinement and Proof for Probabilistic Systems.' His invited talk was sponsored by FME. Frédéric Badeau has been working on the B Method since 1994, and was part of the team that became ClearSy in 2001. He was involved in the development of the Atelier B tool, and has also worked on the B language. He has participated in a number of B software industrial projects within the railway industry. He has also been involved in some Event B projects in a research and development context. It was a pleasure to have three such eminent invited speakers at ZB 2005.

Besides its formal sessions the conference included tool demonstrations, exhibitions, a doctoral student poster session and tutorials. In particular, a Workshop on *Refinement* (REFINE 2005) was held on 12th April 2005, supported by the EPSRC RefineNet network, in association with the ZB 2005 meeting. In addition, the International B Conference Steering Committee (APCB) and the Z User Group (ZUG) used the conference as a convenient venue for open meetings intended for those interested in the B and Z communities respectively.

In one respect, the ZB 2005 meeting marked the end of an era, with the absence of a familiar face. Professor Jonathan Bowen, of London South Bank University, had been heavily involved in all three of the previous ZB conferences, and, prior to that, with Z User Group meetings since the first meetings in Oxford in the late 1980s. His contribution to the popularization of Formal Methods has been immense, both in conference organization and in his oft-cited website devoted to the subject. Both the Z and B communities are very grateful to him for his work, which continues in his activities with ZUG and with the BCS FACS group.

The topics of interest to the conference included: industrial applications and case studies using Z or using B; integration of model-based specification methods in the software development lifecycle; derivation of hardware-software architecture from model-based specifications; expressing and validating requirements through formal models; theoretical issues in formal development (e.g., issues in refinement, proof process, or proof validation, etc.); software testing versus proof-oriented development; tools supporting tools for the Z notation and the B Method; development by composition of specifications; validation of assembly of COTS by model-based specification methods; Z and B extensions and/or standardization.

The ZB 2005 conference was jointly initiated by the Z User Group (ZUG) and the International B Conference Steering Committee (APCB). The University of Surrey Computer Science Department provided all local organization, and financial backing was provided by ZUG. Without the great support from local staff at the University of Surrey and Royal Holloway, University of London, ZB 2005 would not have been possible. In particular, much of the local organization was undertaken by Helen Treharne, with the assistance of Sophie Gautier-O'Shea, Neil Evans and Rob Delicata. ZB 2005 was sponsored by the Atomic Weapons Establishment (AWE), BCS-FACS (the British Computer Society Formal Aspects of Computing Science specialist group), BCS Guildford Branch, FME (Formal Methods Europe), the University of Surrey, Royal Holloway, University of London, and ZUG (Z User Group). BCS-FACS specifically sponsored prizes for best papers at the conference, and AWE sponsored students to attend the poster session. We are grateful to all those who contributed to the success of the conference.

Online information concerning the conference is available under the following Uniform Resource Locator (URL): http://www.zb2005.org/
This also provides links to further online resources concerning the B Method and Z notation.

We hope that all participants and other interested readers benefit scientifically from these proceedings and also find it stimulating in the process.

February 2005

Helen Treharne
Steve King
Martin Henson
Steve Schneider

# Organization

## Programme and Organizing Committees

The following people were members of the ZB 2005 Z Programme Committee and reviewed papers for the conference:

*Co-chair:* Martin Henson, University of Essex, UK
*Co-chair:* Steve King, University of York, UK

Keijiro Araki, Kyushu University, Japan
Rob Arthan, Lemma 1, Reading, UK
Jonathan Bowen, London South Bank University, UK
Neville Dean, Anglia Polytechnic University, UK
John Derrick, University of Sheffield, UK
Jin Song Dong, National University of Singapore
Mark d'Inverno, University of Westminster, UK
Wolfgang Grieskamp, Microsoft Research, USA
Ian Hayes, University of Queensland, Australia
Rob Hierons, Brunel University, UK
Jonathan Jacky, University of Washington, USA
Randolph Johnson, National Security Agency, USA
Kevin Lano, King's College London, UK
Yves Ledru, LSR-IMAG, Grenoble, France
Andrew Martin, Oxford University, UK
Fiona Polack, University of York, UK
Steve Reeves, University of Waikato, New Zealand
Mark Saaltink, ORA, Ottawa, Canada
Thomas Santen, Technical University of Berlin, Germany
Graeme Smith, University of Queensland, Australia
Susan Stepney, University of York, UK
Ian Toyn, University of York, UK
Mark Utting, University of Waikato, New Zealand
Sam Valentine, York, UK

The following served on the ZB 2005 B Programme Committee and reviewed papers for the conference:

*Conference Chair:* Steve Schneider, University of Surrey, UK
*Chair:* Helen Treharne, University of Surrey, UK

Richard Banach, University of Manchester, UK
Juan Bicarregui, CLRC, Oxfordshire, UK
Dominique Cansell, LORIA, University of Metz, France

Daniel Dolle, Siemens Transportation Systems, France
Steve Dunne, University of Teesside, UK
Mamoun Filali, CNRS, IRIT, Toulouse, France
Marc Frappier, Université de Sherbrooke, Canada
Andy Galloway, University of York, UK
Henri Habrias, LINA, Université de Nantes, France
Adrian Hilton, Praxis Critical Systems, UK
Jacques Julliand, Université de Franche-Comté, Besançon, France
Régine Laleau, LACL, IUT Fontainebleau, France
Annabelle McIver, Macquarie University, Sydney, Australia
Luis-Fernando Mejia, Alstom Transport Information Solutions, France
Mike Poppleton, University of Southampton, UK
Marie-Laure Potet, LSR-IMAG, Grenoble, France
Ken Robinson, University of New South Wales, Australia
Emil Sekerinski, McMaster University, Canada
Véronique Viguié Donzeau-Gouge, CNAM, Paris, France
Marina Waldén, Åbo Akademi University, Finland

The following people helped particularly with the organization of the conference in various capacities:

| | |
|---|---|
| Conference Chair: | Steve Schneider, University of Surrey |
| Local Committee Chair: | Helen Treharne, University of Surrey |
| B Submissions: | Helen Treharne, University of Surrey |
| Z Submissions: | Martin Henson, University of Essex |
| Tools: | James Heather, University of Surrey |

| | |
|---|---|
| Posters: | Neil Evans, University of Surrey |
| Tutorials: | Ken Robinson, University of New South Wales |
| Proceedings: | Steve King, University of York |
| Local Arrangements: | Sophie Gautier-O'Shea & Neil Evans, University of Surrey |
| Website & CyberChair: | Rob Delicata, University of Surrey |

We are especially grateful to the above for their efforts in ensuring the success of the conference.

# External Referees

We are grateful to the following people who aided the programme committees in the reviewing of papers, providing additional specialist expertise:

Pascal André, University of Yamoussoukro, Ivory Coast

Christian Attiogbé, University of Nantes, France

Françoise Bellegarde, Université de Franche-Comté, Besançon, France

Didier Bert, LSR-IMAG, Grenoble, France

Jean-Paul Boidevex, IRIT, Toulouse, France

Pontus Boström, Åbo Akademi University, Finland

Michael Butler, University of Southampton, UK

Orieta Celiku, Åbo Akademi University, Finland

Frederic Gervais, CEDRIC (CNAM-IIE), GRIL, Université de Sherbrooke, Canada

Alain Giorgetti, Université de Franche-Comté, Besançon, France

Andy Gravell, University of Southampton, UK

Maritta Heisel, University of Magdeburg, Germany

Thai Son Hoang, University of New South Wales, Australia

Olga Kouchnarenko, INRIA Lorraine, Nancy, France

Michael Leuschel, University of Southampton, UK

Yuan Fang Li, National University of Singapore

Brian Matthews, CLRC, Oxfordshire, UK

Dominique Méry, LORIA, Université Henri Poincaré, France

Stephan Merz, INRIA Lorraine, Nancy, France

Jean François Rolland, IRIT, Toulouse, France

Marianne Simonot, CNAM, Paris, France

Bill Stoddart, University of Teesside, UK

David Streader, University of Waikato, New Zealand

Jun Sun, National University of Singapore

Raymond Turner, University of Essex, UK

Guy Vidal-Naquet, Supélec, Gif, France

Norbert Volker, University of Essex, UK

Frank Zeyda, University of Teesside, UK

## Support

ZB 2005 greatly benefited from the support of the following organizations

> The University of Surrey
> Royal Holloway, University of London

and sponsorship from

> AWE
> BCS-FACS
> BCS Guildford Branch
> FME
> The University of Surrey
> Royal Holloway, University of London
> Z User Group

## Tutorial Programme

The following tutorials were scheduled on the day before the main conference (April 12, 2005):

Expectation-Based Reasoning for Sequential Probabilistic Programs
*Carroll Morgan, University of New South Wales, Australia*

ProB: A Verification and Validation Tool for the B Method
*Michael Leuschel, Michael Butler and Stephane Lo Presti, University of Southampton, UK*

Case Study of a Complete Reactive System in Event-B: A Mechanical Press Controller
*Jean-Raymond Abrial, ETH Zurich, Switzerland*

Developing Z Tools with CZT
*Mark Utting and Petra Malik, University of Waikato, New Zealand*

Model-Based Testing Using Formal Models from Theory to Industrial Applications
*Bruno Legeard and Mark Utting, University of Waikato, New Zealand*

# Table of Contents

# Specification Before Satisfaction: The Case for Research into Obtaining the Right Specification
## —*Extended Abstract*—

Cliff B. Jones

University of Newcastle upon Tyne,
Newcastle, NE1 7RU, UK
`cliff.jones@ncl.ac.uk`

Model-oriented specification techniques like VDM [Jon80, Jon90], Z [Hay93] and B [Abr96] have an enormous amount in common (cf. [Hay92, HJN94]). Among other things that this formal methods community shares is the view that one can start with a formal specification and show that a design/implementation satisfies that specification. It is however obvious that, if a specification does not actually reflect the real need, proving a program correct with respect to it is somewhat pointless.

As computers have become more powerful and less expensive, they have become ever more deeply embedded in the way nearly everyone works. In their short sixty year history, computers have moved from batch processors in their own buildings to work tools on every desk (or lap); essential components of administration,retail trade, banking and vehicles; and are on their way to becoming invisible dust sprinkled on who-knows-what. This, in itself, has changed the task of understanding the *requirements* of a system. Above all, the close interaction of people with computer systems makes it essential that designers consider the whole system when formulating a specification of the technical parts.

It is often easiest to make the point by looking at accidents. Donald MacKenzie in [Mac94, Mac01] has traced the cause of just over 1100 deaths where computer systems appear to be implicated (up to 1994). Three percent of the lives lost appear to be attributed to bugs! Far more common causes of accidents appear to be where humans misunderstand what is going on in a control system or the object being controlled. This is a much deeper issue than the details of an interface; in many cases it is a fundamental question of the allocation of tasks between person and machine. Key questions include the visibility of the state of the system being controlled and the extent to which operations the user can perform are clumped together.

Although accidents are shocking and thus grab attention, there is also a significant penalty in the deployment of systems which make their users' lives more difficult than they need be. The enormous cost of systems which are so unusable that they are not even deployed is reported weekly in newspapers.

Of course, we should use formal specification techniques and we still need research to make them more widely usable. But it would appear to be worthwhile to see whether there is also a *technical* response to the question of how one arrives at a specification which does reflect the needs of the environment in which

H. Treharne et al. (Eds.): ZB 2005, LNCS 3455, pp. 1–5, 2005.

a system will be embedded. Does the formal methods community have a contribution to make here? I believe so. Dines Bjørner's forthcoming books [Bjø05] tackle "domain modelling". This paper sets out some further research challenges to which we might be able to offer useful responses.

This invited talk will review some suggestions which have arisen in the six year "Interdisciplinary Research Collaboration on Dependability" (DIRC) — see the WWW pages at [WWW04] for details. DIRC is focusing its research on how to design *Dependable*[1] computer-based systems. The phrase "computer-based systems" is intended to emphasize that most computer systems today are deeply embedded into an environment which also involves people. For example, the requirement in a hospital is for dependability of the overall system. Sometimes, humans will use a computer system to achieve objectives even where they know that it delivers less than perfect information; on other occasions, computers can be programmed to warn when errors made by humans. People are less good than computers at narrowly specified repetitive tasks but are much better at recognising and reacting to exceptional situations. To achieve overall system dependability, both humans and programs must be properly deployed.

Some insights from the DIRC project include:

- An approach being worked on with Ian Hayes and Michael Jackson [HJJ03] looks at determining the specification of, say, a control system by first specifying a wider system including the phenomena of the physical world which are to be influenced. To avoid having to build a model of the behaviour of all physical components, assumptions about their behaviour are recorded using *rely conditions* (cf. [Jon83]). This leaves a clear record of assumptions which need to be considered before the control system is deployed. Development from the derived specification of the control system is conducted in the standard (formal) way.
- The design of boundaries that limit the *propagation of failures* is better articulated for technical systems than for the human part of computer-based systems. This is odd because the intuition about limiting, say, accounting errors by auditors is long established. Many examples can be cited to suggest that most human systems are "debugged" rather than designed. The motivation for where to place containment boundaries ought come from an analysis of the frequency of minor faults and the the danger of their affecting a wider system. This analysis ought precede the allocation of tasks to computers which, in turn of course, must be done prior to their specifications being frozen.
- A major cause of near or actual accidents is a "cognitive mismatch"[2] between an operator's view of what is going on and the actual state of affairs in the

---

[1] The classic text on the terminology of dependability is [Lap92]; see also [Ran00]; an attempt to formalise the useful trichotomy between faults, errors and failures is given in [Jon03].

[2] Both of James Reason's books [Rea90, Rea97] look at relevant issues: the earlier reference looks at a division of the sort of errors that humans make; the second has insightful analyses of many system failures. Perrow in [Per99] talks of "Normal accidents".

system they are trying to control. This was a significant factor in the "Three Mile Island" reactor incident. John Rushby [Rus99] has looked at pilot errors on the MD-88: in simulators, they frequently breach the required altitude ceiling. Rushby's careful formal analysis builds a state model of the pilot's understanding of the system and explores its interaction with a model of the aircraft systems. It would be informative to compare this approach with rely conditions.

— The general way in which *processes* (or procedures) are used in the human parts of computer-based systems is interesting. If one contrasts a traditional car production line with the depiction in the film "Apollo-13" of the search for a solution to the need to improvise $CO_2$ scrubbers in the damaged capsule, one sees that processes both limit action and reduce the need for information. Designing processes which cope with all exceptions is in many cases impossible and one argument for relying on humans in computer-based systems is precisely that they notice when it is safer to violate a procedure than to slavishly follow one that does not cover an exceptional case. Clearly, either following an inappropriate process or deviating from a correct process can both lead to system failure. But it is absolutely mandatory that thought is given to processes in the design of a computer-based system. Interestingly, one can spot errors in legislation where an algorithmic rule is frozen into law: there have been several cases in financial legislation where a well-intentioned trigger has had (or nearly had) counter-productive effects.

— Within DIRC, the role of *advisory systems* has received particular attention: [SPA03] studies an image analysis prompter used in the analysis of mammograms. Surprising conclusions include statistically significant evidence that under the tested conditions the most accurate operators can offer less accurate conclusions with the help of the advisory system than without its use. It is clear that the role of such advisory systems has to be considered far more widely than just by looking at their technical specifications. In fact, even pure safety limiters (where one would believe they can only increase safety) have been used by operators in a way which supplants their normal judgment.

— Systems can create other things whose dependability is the goal. In the simplest case, a production line might manufacture silicon chips and faults in the manufacturing process might result in faulty components for computers. A software example is a compiler that, if faulty, could translate a perfect program into machine code which does not respect the formal semantics of the source language. In many cases, the creation process is human and, for example, a designer of a bridge which fails to withstand expected forces is at fault. The creation of computer software is just such a process and is not always fault free! DIRC has provided an opportunity to look at Gerry Weinberg's conjectures in [Wei71] that different psychological types might be more or less adept at different sub-tasks within the broad area known as programming. The implications of this research for building dependable systems might include steering people toward the tasks at which they are likely to perform best (and probably be most content).

– If the above list were not daunting enough (and it is far from complete even with respect to DIRC's findings) there is another overriding concern. The sort of computer-based system we have been studying will always *evolve*. Designing a system which can be modified in reaction to a reasonable class of evolutions in the environment is extremely challenging. One class of system which has been studied within the DIRC project is *generic systems*. The justification of this sort of system is that it can be instantiated for a range of applications: characterising this range is itself a technical problem. It is clear that issues around evolution will have a long-term impact on dependability. There are related questions of how data survives such evolution which are equally challenging.

DIRC has identified far more than the above set of issues; the selection here has been based on the ease with which this one member of a project (involving more than fifty researchers) could pull together the information.

One key experience from the first three quarters of the project is the invaluable role of interdisciplinarity. Looking at experiments on psychological type and debugging performance required wholehearted collaboration of psychologists and computer scientists; tackling the mammography advisory system involved interaction between statisticians, sociologists and psychologists. DIRC could list many more examples of how our combination of psychologists, statisticians, sociologists and computer scientists has made real progress that no one of these disciplines could have accomplished.

My own disposition is to seek technical approaches to problems and I hope that the list above indicates that this is a viable challenge. But the DIRC project has been a superb example of collaboration and if faced with a complex application area, I would now know how to call on the expertise of other disciplines. In particular, the painstaking gathering of observational data needs sociologists.

We have learned two general things in the DIRC project which are worth passing on to others who might wish to follow such a wide interdisciplinary approach. Collaboration has to be based on respect for the disciplines of other researchers: values differ and publication strategies vary between disciplines but if it is good research by the standards of the other discipline one should not –for example– argue that it is not presented in the style of one's own discipline. The other message is to tackle application problems together as a team. With an "operations Research" (OR) like team representing several disciplines terminology problems disappear, contributions become understood and something is achieved which no single discipline could have envisaged.

## Acknowledgments

My research acknowledgment is to the many colleagues involved in DIRC; it is a privilege to lead such an exciting project.

We are all grateful to EPSRC for the six year funding window which we feel was essential to foster such a wide interdisciplinary span.

# References

[Abr96]    J.-R. Abrial. *The B-Book: Assigning programs to meanings*. Cambridge University Press, 1996.

[Bjø05]    D. Bjørner. *Software Engineering (3 vols.)*. Springer-Verlag, 2005.

[Hay92]    I. J. Hayes. VDM and Z: A comparative case study. *Formal Aspects of Computing*, 4(1):76–99, 1992.

[Hay93]    Ian Hayes, editor. *Specification Case Studies*. Prentice Hall International, second edition, 1993.

[HJJ03]    Ian Hayes, Michael Jackson, and Cliff Jones. Determining the specification of a control system from that of its environment. In Keijiro Araki, Stefani Gnesi, and Dino Mandrioli, editors, *FME 2003: Formal Methods*, volume 2805 of *Lecture Notes in Computer Science*, pages 154–169. Springer Verlag, 2003.

[HJN94]    I. J. Hayes, C. B. Jones, and J. E. Nicholls. Understanding the differences between VDM and Z. *ACM Software Engineering News*, 19(3):75–81, July 1994.

[Jon80]    C. B. Jones. *Software Development: A Rigorous Approach*. Prentice Hall International, 1980. ISBN 0-13-821884-6.

[Jon83]    C. B. Jones. Specification and design of (parallel) programs. In *Proceedings of IFIP'83*, pages 321–332. North-Holland, 1983.

[Jon90]    C. B. Jones. *Systematic Software Development using VDM*. Prentice Hall International, second edition, 1990. ISBN 0-13-880733-7.

[Jon03]    Cliff B Jones. A formal basis for some dependability notions. In Bernhard K. Aichernig and Tom Maibaum, editors, *Formal Methods at the Crossroads: from Panacea to Foundational Support*, volume 2757 of *Lecture Notes in Computer Science*, pages 191–206. Springer Verlag, 2003.

[Lap92]    Jean-Claude Laprie. *Dependability: basic concepts and terminology—in English, French, German, Italian and Japanese*. Springer-Verlag, 1992.

[Mac94]    Donald MacKenzie. Computer-related accidental death: an empirical exploration. *Science and Public Policy*, 21:233–248, 1994.

[Mac01]    D. MacKenzie. *Mechanizing Proof: Computing, Risk, and Trust*. MIT Press, Cambridge, Mass., 2001.

[Per99]    Charles Perrow. *Normal Accidents*. Princeton University Press, 1999.

[Ran00]    B. Randell. Facing up to faults. *The Computer Journal*, 43(2):95–106, 2000.

[Rea90]    James Reason. *Human Error*. Cambridge University Press, 1990.

[Rea97]    James Reason. *Managing the Risks of Organisational Accidents*. Ashgate Publishing Limited, 1997.

[Rus99]    John Rushby. Using model checking to help discover mode confusions and other automation surprises. In *Proceedings of 3rd Workshop on Human Error*, pages 1–18. HESSD'99, 1999.

[SPA03]    L Strigini, A. Povyakalo, and E. Alberdi. Human machine diversity in the use of computerised advisory systems: A case study. In *DSN 2003-IEEE International Conference on Dependable Systems and Networks*, pages 249–258, San Francisco, USA, 2003.

[Wei71]    Gerald M. Weinberg. *The Psychology of Computer Programming*. Van Norstrand, 1971.

[WWW04]    WWW. www.dirc.org.uk, 2004.

# Visualising Larger State Spaces in PROB

Michael Leuschel[1,2] and Edd Turner[1]

[1] Department of Electronics and Computer Science,
University of Southampton,
Highfield, Southampton, SO17 1BJ, UK
[2] Institut für Informatik, Heinrich-Heine Universität Düsseldorf
{mal, ent03r}@ecs.soton.ac.uk

**Abstract.** PROB is an animator and model checker for the B method. It also allows to visualise the state space of a B machine in graphical way. This is often very useful and allows users to quickly spot whether the machine behaves as expected. However, for larger state spaces the visualisation quickly becomes difficult to grasp by users (and the computation of the graph layout takes considerable time). In this paper we present two relatively simple algorithms to often considerably reduce the complexity of the graphs, while still keeping relevant information. This makes it possible to visualise much larger state spaces and gives the user immediate feedback about the overall behaviour of a machine. The algorithms have been implemented within the PROB toolset and we highlight their potential on several examples. We also conduct a thorough experimentation of the algorithm on 47 B machines and analyse the results.

**Keywords:** Formal Methods, B-Method, Tool Support, Model Checking, Animation, Visualisation, Logic Programming.

## 1 Introduction

The B-method, originally devised by J.-R. Abrial [1], is a theory and methodology for formal development of computer systems. It is used by industries in a range of critical domains, most notably railway control. B is based on the notion of *abstract machine* and the notion of *refinement*. The variables of an abstract machine are typed using set theoretic constructs such as sets, relations and functions. The invariant of a machine is specified using predicate logic. Operations of a machine are specified as *generalised substitutions*, which allow deterministic and nondeterministic assignments to be specified. There are two main proof activities in B: *consistency checking*, which is used to show that the operations of a machine preserve the invariant, and *refinement checking*, which is used to show that one machine is a valid refinement of another. These activities are supported by industrial strength tools, such as Atelier-B [24] and the B-toolkit [5].

PROB [18] is an animation and model checking tool for the B method. PROB's animation facilities allow users to gain confidence in their specifications, and unlike the animator provided by the B-Toolkit, the user does not have to guess the right values for the operation arguments or choice variables. The undecidability

H. Treharne et al. (Eds.): ZB 2005, LNCS 3455, pp. 6–23, 2005.

of animating B is overcome by restricting animation to finite sets and integer ranges, while efficiency is achieved by delaying the enumeration of variables as long as possible. ProB also contains a model checker [9] and a constraint-based checker, both of which can be used to detect various errors in B specifications.

ProB shows the user a graphical view of the state space the model checker has already explored. For this ProB makes use of the Dot tool of the graphviz package [4]. This feedback is very beneficial to the understanding of the specification since human perception is good at identifying structural similarities and symmetries [10]. Such a feature works well for small state spaces, but in practice specifications under analysis often consume thousands of states, which severely limits the usefulness of the graph.

Take the following example machine (distributed with ProB).

```
MACHINE phonebook
SETS   Name   ; Code = {c1,c2,c3}
VARIABLES  db
DEFINITIONS    scope_Name == 1..3
INVARIANT
        db : Name +-> Code
INITIALISATION
        db := {}
OPERATIONS
  cc <-- lookup(nn) =  PRE nn : Name & nn : dom(db) THEN
                  cc:=db(nn) END;
 add(nn,cc) = PRE nn:Name & cc:Code & nn /: dom(db) THEN
                db := db \/ { nn |-> cc} END ;
 delete(nn,cc) = PRE nn:Name & cc:Code & nn: dom(db) &
                                cc: ran(db) & db(nn) = cc   THEN
                db := db - { nn |-> cc}  END
END
```

The full state space of this example (with Name set to cardinality 3) has 65 states and 433 transitions. As can be seen, the visualization of the state space in ProB is possible (depicted in Fig. 1; the reader is not expected to be able to read the labels, just get a general impression of the visualization) but is quite difficult to grasp by humans and certain "obvious" aspects of the state space are not be easy to identify in the visualization. For example, it is not obvious to spot what the actual enabled operations are or that one can do at most three consecutive calls to the add operation.

The question is whether the state space of B machines can be rendered in ways more suitable for human understanding. It turns out that there are surprisingly few tools and techniques that addressed this problem in general or for B in particular. In this paper we thus present various (complimentary) techniques to improve the visualisation of larger state spaces. These techniques have been implemented in the ProB toolset and we illustrate the performance of them on various examples. We also empirically evaluate the techniques on a large number of examples and show that the techniques can be surprisingly effective.

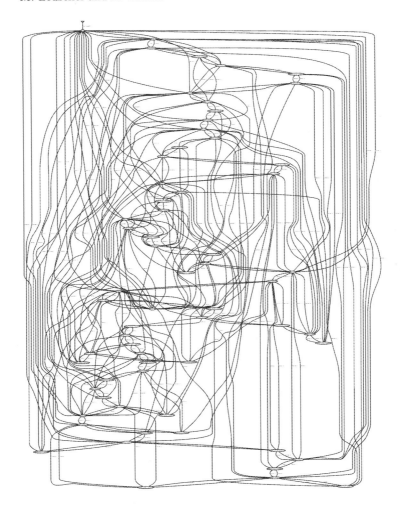

**Fig. 1.** Phonebook machine - Original State Space

## 2    The DFA-Abstraction Algorithm

The state space generated by PROB can be viewed as non-deterministic labelled transition system (LTS), where the edges are labelled with terms of the form $op(a_1, \ldots, a_n)$ and $op(a_1, \ldots, a_n) \to r_1, \ldots, r_k$, where $op$ is the name of the operation that has been applied and $a_1, \ldots, a_n$ are the arguments of the operation. The first form is used for operations that do not return values, whereas the second form is used for operations that do and where $r_1, \ldots, r_k$ are the returned values.

Formally, an LTS is a 4-tuple $(Q, \Sigma, q_0, \delta)$ where $Q$ is the set of states, $\Sigma$ the alphabet for labelling the transitions, $q_0$ the initial state and $\delta \subseteq Q \times \Sigma \times Q$ is the transition relation. By $q \to_a q'$ we denote that $(q, a, q') \in \delta$. As usual, we extend this to sequences of transitions so that $q \rightarrow_{a_1,...,a_k} q'$ denotes the fact that there exists a sequence of states $q_0, \ldots, q_k$ such that $q_0 = q$, $q_k = q'$ and $q_i \rightarrow_{a_i} q_{i+1}$. The set of *reachable states* of an automaton is defined to be the set $\{q \in Q \mid q_0 \rightarrow_\gamma q$ for some sequence of states $\gamma\}$. Finally, the *traces* of an automaton $L$ is the set of sequences $traces(L) = \{\gamma \in \Sigma^* \mid q_0 \rightarrow_\gamma q$ for some $q \in Q\}$.

One way to reduce the complexity of an LTS is to abstract away from certain details of the labelling function. For example, the user may not be interested in seeing (all) the arguments of (all) the operations. To this end we now define abstraction functions and a way to apply them to construct simplified LTS.

**Definition 1.** *An* abstraction function *for an LTS $(Q, \Sigma, q_0, \delta)$ is a function $\alpha$ from $\Sigma$ to some new alphabet $\Sigma'$.*

*The $\alpha$-abstraction of the LTS is then defined to be a new LTS $(Q, \Sigma', q_0, \delta')$ where $\delta' = \{(q, \alpha(a), q') \mid (q, a, q') \in \delta\}$.*

For the experiments later in the paper we have used $\alpha(op(a_1, \ldots, a_n)) = op/n$ for operations without return values and $\alpha(op(a_1, \ldots, a_n) \rightarrow r_1, \ldots, r_k) = op/n \rightarrow k$ for operations that return values, but any other abstraction (or even the identity function) can be used instead.[1] This encodes a common perspective where the user is interested in seeing which operations can be applied, but is not interested in the actual arguments.

Now, the $\alpha$-abstraction on its own is not yet very useful, as we have not yet diminished the number of states (even though we may have reduced the number of transitions). The first thing that comes to mind in that respect is the classical minimization algorithm for Deterministic Finite Automaton (DFA) [2, 14]. Indeed, a finite LTS can be viewed as a Non-Deterministic Finite Automaton (NFA) simply by marking all states as final states (basically the only difference between an NFA and an LTS is the notion of final states). We can then convert this NFA into a DFA using another classical algorithm [2, 14], to then apply the minimization algorithm. This is exactly what we have done in our first so-called *DFA-Abstraction* Algorithm, which we have implemented and integrated into the PROB toolset. In summary, the *DFA-Abstraction* Algorithm computes
  – the $\alpha$-Abstraction of an LTS
  – then determinizes the resulting intermediate LTS by converting sets of reachable states of the NFA into single states of the DFA,
  – before minimizing it by computing maximal equivalence classes of the DFA, yielding the result LTS.
The algorithm is shown on a small example in Fig. 2.

This algorithm was was primarily applied as a control: something to which other algorithms could be compared. We were also aware that it had the potential

---

[1] We have decided to show the number of arguments $n$ and the number of return values $k$ in our abstracted graphs. This is largely a matter of taste and $\alpha(op(a_1, \ldots, a_n) \rightarrow r_1, \ldots, r_k) = op$ could have been used instead (as one is not allowed to have two different operations with the same name anyway).

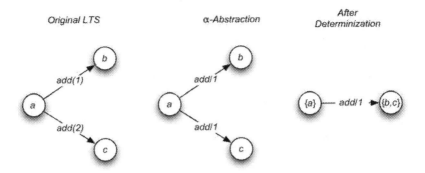

**Fig. 2.** Illustrating the DFA-Abstraction Algorithm

to collapse symmetrical subgraphs. It hence turns out to be very useful in some cases, while in other cases increasing the size of the graph (as is well-known, the NFA to DFA conversion can lead to an exponential blow-up, even though this is rarely observed in practice).

**How to Read DFA-Abstracted Graphs.** Every node in the graph corresponds to a set of states of the animated B machine. Obviously, we lose information from the $\alpha$-abstraction, i.e., we loose the operation arguments. The DFA conversion and minimization algorithms preserve the set of traces that can be performed. However, because of determinization, multiple B states are put together into a single node. Hence, if a node in the DFA-abstracted graph has an outgoing edge marked with $op/n$ this does not guarantee that the operation can be applied in *all* B states covered by this node. Thus, to make the graphs more informative, our LTS visualization algorithm checks whether an outgoing edge can be performed in all covered B states: if it does the edge is drawn solid, otherwise the edge is dashed.

In Fig. 3 you can see the effect of our algorithm on the full state space of Fig. 1. The reduction is considerable, and the graph can now be easily digested by a human. Furthermore, even though we have lost the operation arguments, the reduced graph still contains a lot of useful information (especially since all edges are solid). For example, one can see that it is only possible to add three entries into the phonebook. It is also clear that one can only perform a delete or lookup after something has been added to the phonebook. One can also deduce that add and delete are state changing operations.

An alternative approach to using a DFA-Abstraction would be to minimize the NFA – which is attractive considering that it is possible for an NFA to be exponentially smaller in size when compared to an equivalent DFA. However, the problem of minimizing NFAs is computationally intractable [16, 20], and we have hence decided not to go down this route.

Another approach, documented in [15], attempts to reduce, and not minimize, the size of an NFA while retaining language equivalence. Our experiments so far

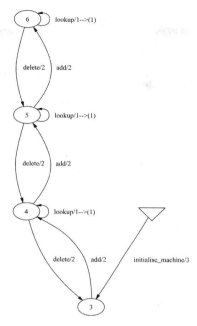

**Fig. 3.** Phonebook machine - DFA

have shown that the reductions gained are not as useful as our DFA-Abstraction or Signature Merge approach described in the next section.

# 3    Merge States with Same Outgoing Transitions

This technique was devised after studying a collection of graphs produced by ProB. It works by merging all states with the same enabled operations and so it may produce an automaton that is not equivalent (as far as the traces of possible operations are concerned) to the original one. However, the technique can achieve a big reduction in the size of the automaton while still preserving the information about which B operations are enabled in a particular state (i.e. the traces of length 1). To do this, we first introduce the concept of a signature of a state, which represents the operations (i.e., transition labels) that can be performed in that state.

**Definition 2.** *Let $(Q, \Sigma, q_0, \delta)$ be an LTS. We define the signature of a node $q \in Q$, denoted by signature(q), as follows: signature(q) $= \{a \mid q \rightarrow_a q'$ for some $q' \in Q\}$.*

If $signature(q) = \emptyset$ then we say that $q$ is *deadlocked*. An automaton is said to *deadlock* iff there is a reachable state that is deadlocked. If $a \in signature(q)$ then we say that $a$ is *enabled* in $q$. An automaton is said to be *quasi-live for transition a* iff there exists a reachable state where $a$ is enabled.

**Definition 3.** *Let $(Q, \Sigma, q_0, \delta)$ be an LTS. The* Signature-Merge *of the LTS is defined to be a new LTS $(Q^s, \Sigma, q_0^s, \delta')$ where $Q^s = \{signature(q) \mid q \in Q\}$, $q_0^s = signature(q_0)$, and $\delta^s = \{(signature(q), a, signature(q')) \mid (q, a, q') \in \delta\}$.*

Basically, the effect of a signature-merge is to merge all states which have a common signature. This ensures that at least for traces of length 1 we do not lose any precision. There are a few more properties that are preserved by the Signature-Merge:

**Proposition 1.** *3 Let $L = (Q, \Sigma, q_0, \delta)$ be an LTS and $L_S$ its Signature-Merge. Then $L$ deadlocks iff $L_S$ deadlocks. Also, for any $a \in \Sigma$, $L$ is quasi-live for a iff $L_S$ is quasi-live for a. Finally, $traces(L) \subseteq traces(L_S)$.*

The last property means that if a certain sequence is not possible in the Signature-Merge then it cannot be performed in the original LTS either.

The overall algorithm we have now implemented is to first compute the $\alpha$-abstraction of an LTS and then perform the Signature-Merge on the abstracted LTS.

**How to Read Signature-Merge Graphs.** As with the DFA-Abstracted graphs, every node in the graph corresponds to a set of states of the animated B machine. However, if a node has an outgoing edge marked with $op/n$ we are not sure that this particular edge can be taken in *all* B states covered by this node: we only know that there is at least one covered state where this edge can be followed. Hence, contrary to the DFA-conversion and minimization, signature merging does not preserve the set of possible traces. However, all the states associated with the node have the same signature: so we at least know that the operation *op* is possible in *all* B states covered by the node. We can also apply Proposition to deduce information about deadlocks and about traces that are not possible in the original machine.

To facilitate the interpretation of the Signature-Merge graphs, we will actually differentiate the edges according to whether an edge is definitely possible in all states that have been merged together. Such edges are called *definite*, as formally defined below, and will be drawn as solid lines, while edges which are not definite will be drawn as dashed lines. This gives the user clear visual feedback and allows to infer more properties about the underlying B machine.

**Definition 4.** *Let $(Q, \Sigma, q_0, \delta)$ be an LTS and $(Q^s, \Sigma, q_0^s, \delta')$ its Signature-Merge. A transition $(signature(q), a, signature(q')) \in \delta'$ is called definite iff $\forall p \in Q$ such that $signature(p) = signature(q)$: $\exists p'$ with $signature(p') = signature(q')$ and $(p, a, p') \in \delta$. In other words, for all other nodes $p$ that have been merged together with $q$, we can also perform the transition a leading to the same state (in the Signature-Merge graph).*

In Fig. 4 you can see the effect of this algorithm on the full state space of Fig. 1. The reduction is considerable, and the graph can now be easily digested by a human. Note that the reduced graph will not change even if we allow more entries to be added into the phonebook (e.g., by changing the cardinality

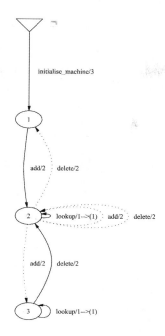

**Fig. 4.** Phonebook machine - Signature Merge

of the set Name). So, in principle, one could even visualise the machine for an unbounded set Name. This is not the case for the DFA (where if we allow 100 entries the DFA will have 100 nodes). However, some of the precision of the DFA visualization is lost: we can no longer spot how many entries can be added; all we can see is that we can add at least two entries, but not exactly how many. Still, the signature based approach has managed to keep relevant information. For example, it is still obvious from the graph that we can only lookup or delete entries after adding an entry, and we can see that it is possible to reach a state where it is no longer possible to add entries.

**Extending the Algorithm.** We can make the algorithm more precise by diminishing the $\alpha$-abstraction, e.g., by not abstracting away certain arguments. This could be guided by the user and also applies to the DFA-Abstraction algorithm. Second, the signature of a node basically corresponds to all the traces of length 1 that can be performed from that node. We could thus extend the notion of a signature and compare all the traces of length 2,3,... .[2]

On the other hand we can make the algorithm less precise and achieve more reduction in several ways. First, one could make $\alpha$ more aggressive, e.g., by mapping several operations together (e.g., maybe the user is not interested in some of the operations). Second, instead of merging nodes if they have exactly the same signature, we could merge them if the signatures are sufficiently close

---

[2] In the limit we obtain the classical equivalence preserving minimization algorithm.

(e.g., they are the same except for one element or we only look at the signature as far as a certain number of operations of interest is concerned).

In practice it may be good to combine both approaches: e.g. the user could type a certain number as a target for the ideal number of nodes (say 20) and then the graph is progressively made less or more precise to approach that number.

## 4    Two More Complicated Examples

Figures 5, 6, and 7 show the behaviour of our algorithms for the "scheduler" example taken from [7, 3]. Again, both algorithms perform very well, providing clear graphs about the overall behaviour of the system.

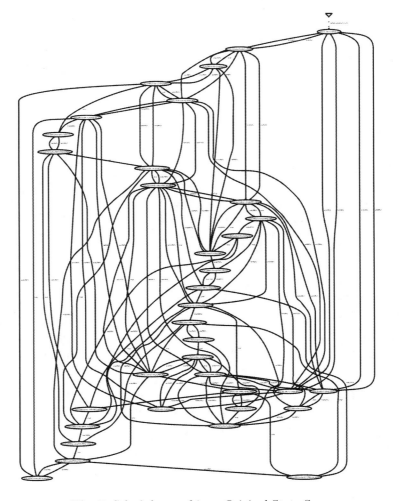

**Fig. 5.** Scheduler machine - Original State Space

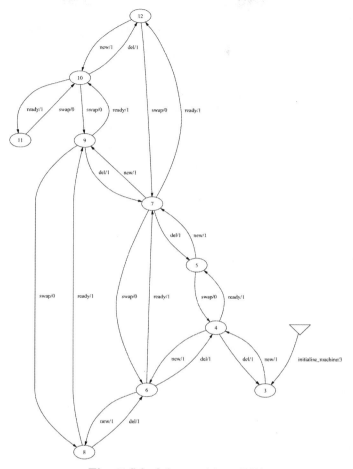

**Fig. 6.** Scheduler machine - DFA

Another example is taken from our ABCD[3] project where we have developed various B models for a distributed online travel agency, through which users can make hotel and car rental bookings. Here is one of the (partial) models where the DFA algorithm works extremely well: basically, the original graph is unreadable due to the large number of nodes and transitions, while Fig. 8 is quite clear and provides interesting feedback about the system.

## 5   Empirical Evaluation

The DFA-Abstraction and Signature-Merge algorithms described in this document have been implemented within PROB and are available in PROB 1.1 and later.

---

[3] "Automated validation of Business Critical systems using Component-based Design," EPSRC grant GR/M91013.

We have conducted both an empirical evaluation of our algorithms, with concrete numbers on the size reductions achieved, and a more informal evaluation. Some of the examples of the latter are found in the various figures of this paper (notably in the preceding section). A more extensive list of figures is presented in an accompanying technical report [19]. This informal evaluation suggests that the algorithms are often surprisingly efficient at deriving informative graphs. However, on some examples they fail to help the user, but overall they are a very useful addition to the PROB toolset. The precise numbers presented in the rest of this section underline this more informal evaluation.

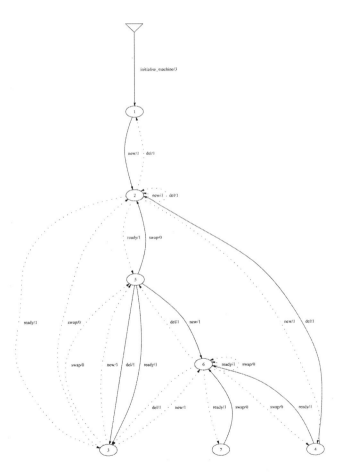

**Fig. 7.** Scheduler machine - Signature Merge

Tables 1 and 2 below show key statistics obtained after applying the *Signature-Merge* and the *DFA-Abstraction* algorithms on 47 arbitrary state spaces that had been previously model checked with the PROB model checker: Table 1 shows

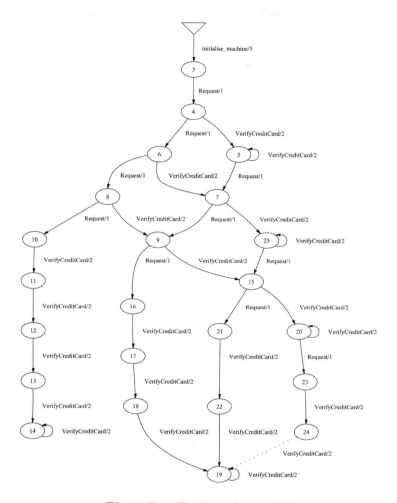

**Fig. 8.** TravelProB machine - DFA

percentages of states and transitions compared to the original state space[4] and Table 2 shows the overall statistics.

*Signature-Merge* produced the best results, reducing the number of states by at least 85% and the number of transitions by at least 87% in half of the state spaces tested. Moreover, 80% of the graphs had at least 43% fewer states and 59% fewer transitions than the original. The best case produced a graph with approximately 99% fewer states and transitions. The *DFA-Abstraction* technique

---

[4] Some of the machine names in Table 1 appear more than once, however their implementations differ.

**Table 1.** Size of state space compared to original (%)

| Machine Name | Sig. Merge States | Sig. Merge Transitions | DFA-Abstr. States | DFA-Abstr. Transitions |
|---|---|---|---|---|
| Ambulances | 0.24 | 0.02 | 0.86 | 0.10 |
| Baskets | 6.33 | 2.02 | 21.52 | 8.59 |
| B_Clavier_code | 100.00 | 42.11 | 133.33 | 42.11 |
| bibliotheque | 73.33 | 58.49 | 93.33 | 75.47 |
| B_Site_central | 60.00 | 12.50 | 80.00 | 12.50 |
| CarlaTravelAgency | 9.09 | 30.09 | 60.61 | 78.76 |
| CarlaTravelAgencyErr | 13.33 | 43.17 | 67.5 | 71.22 |
| countdown | 0.13 | 0.10 | 7.97 | 7.77 |
| Cruise | 29.54 | 18.19 | 1203.97 | 901.35 |
| CSM | 83.12 | 86.60 | 101.30 | 100.00 |
| DAB | 40.00 | 4.88 | 80.00 | 7.32 |
| dfa | 75.00 | 57.14 | 150.00 | 100.00 |
| dijkstra | 42.86 | 33.33 | 100.00 | 66.67 |
| DSP0 | 12.24 | 10.61 | 16.33 | 12.12 |
| Fermat | 11.76 | 3.70 | 58.82 | 20.99 |
| FinalTravelAgency | 0.93 | 0.57 | 7.69 | 6.12 |
| FunLaws | 1.95 | 0.63 | 14.79 | 6.49 |
| FunLaws | 4.28 | 2.45 | 20.23 | 15.39 |
| GAME | 8.97 | 5.30 | 32.79 | 20.45 |
| GSM_revue | 36.36 | 28.57 | 63.64 | 50.00 |
| Inscription | 25.93 | 16.03 | 33.33 | 19.08 |
| inst_adapted | 1.07 | 0.41 | 17.17 | 6.68 |
| Jukebox | 15.00 | 4.53 | 1225.00 | 616.83 |
| Level0 | 0.26 | 0.03 | 1.43 | 0.16 |
| m0 | 100.00 | 99.98 | 150.77 | 150.29 |
| Main | 100.00 | 100.00 | 150.00 | 100.00 |
| mm0 | 3.55 | 2.44 | 43.65 | 40.52 |
| monitor | 9.88 | 3.59 | 39.51 | 18.90 |
| phonebook7 | 6.15 | 1.62 | 9.23 | 2.31 |
| Queues | 42.86 | 22.22 | 57.14 | 22.22 |
| Results | 66.67 | 45.45 | 83.33 | 45.45 |
| Rubik2 | 0.09 | 0.10 | 100.03 | 100.00 |
| RussianPostalPuzzle | 2.04 | 1.71 | 27.21 | 22.33 |
| rw | 90.00 | 94.59 | 105.00 | 100.00 |
| scheduler | 22.22 | 14.05 | 33.33 | 20.66 |
| SensorNode | 60.00 | 18.18 | 80.00 | 18.18 |
| SeqLaws | 15.79 | 22.41 | 71.05 | 101.72 |
| SetLaws | 1.23 | 0.72 | 17.40 | 11.78 |
| station | 25.00 | 14.61 | 28.57 | 14.61 |
| Teletext | 16.00 | 5.71 | 48.00 | 35.71 |
| Teletext | 21.43 | 9.84 | 107.14 | 100.00 |
| TheSystem | 14.04 | 43.09 | 72.81 | 69.92 |
| TransactionsSimple | 16.79 | 33.33 | 76.34 | 83.01 |
| TravelAgency | 9.09 | 34.55 | 59.66 | 62.83 |
| TravelAgency_trace_check | 0.33 | 0.93 | 38.75 | 40.92 |
| TravelProB | 0.80 | 0.26 | 3.83 | 0.95 |
| UndefinedFunctions | 29.41 | 13.99 | 70.59 | 37.82 |

also gave good results; half of the graphs having at least 40% fewer states and at least 64% fewer transitions, and the best case again reduced the number of states and transitions by 99%. The worst case didn't follow the trend of producing a reduction, but in fact increased the size of the original graph by approximately ten times. A result like this should not come as a surprise since, after all, it is possible for a DFA to be exponentially greater in size than an equivalent NFA.

**Table 2.** Statistics of reductions on 47 arbitrary state spaces

| Statistic | Signature Merge States | Signature Merge Transitions | NFA to DFA States | NFA to DFA Transitions |
|---|---|---|---|---|
| Minimum | 0.09 | 0.02 | 0.86 | 0.10 |
| Maximum | 100.00 | 100.00 | 1225.00 | 901.35 |
| Median | 15.00 | 12.50 | 59.66 | 35.71 |
| Average | 27.77 | 22.23 | 107.76 | 73.33 |
| **80th Percentile** | **56.57** | **40.6** | **100.02** | **96.6** |
| Std. Dev. | 31.05 | 27.95 | 241.50 | 155.05 |

However, only a small proportion of the applications of this technique had this effect; approximately 80% of the tests produced a reduction.

## 6    Discussion and Related Work

Tables 1 and 2 show some encouraging results. The often considerable reduction of the original state space by the DFA-Abstraction algorithm can be explained by its ability of finding regular behaviour amongst abstracted transitions, and collapsing duplicated instances of it into a single path. A good example of this is shown in the original Phonebook example (Figure 1) and the DFA reduced Phonebook example (Figure 3).

The Signature-Merge algorithm gave better reductions than the DFA-Abstraction reduction, producing non-equivalent graphs to the original that do not show the exact behaviour. However, they remain useful since they can still be used to check many properties (e.g., to check whether a certain execution path may exist in the full state space).

The three algorithms, DFA minimization [2, 14], Computing Small NFAs [15] and the Minimal Unambigous $\varepsilon$-transition NFAs [17] were also tested but were found to be less effective than the two mentioned above. One reason for this is that they do not implement any $\alpha$-abstraction — hence future testing will attempt to incorporate this.

In addition to the two main algorithms, several other approaches for improving the visualization of state spaces were implemented and tested, and are documented in the following subsections.

**Integrated Java/Swing Visualizer.** Fig. 9 shows a version of PROB that has been developed using Java to take advantage of its cross platform compatability and rich graphical user interface library. Various panes in the main window present the user with information relating to the current state; including the variables and values of the current state, a history of operations executed, a hierarchical expansion of enabled operations (top left pane) and a state space visualization. There is also an integrated specification editor to facilitate any changes necessary. As can be seen in the central pane of the screenshot, the user has several choices of visualization to choose from – some of which allow

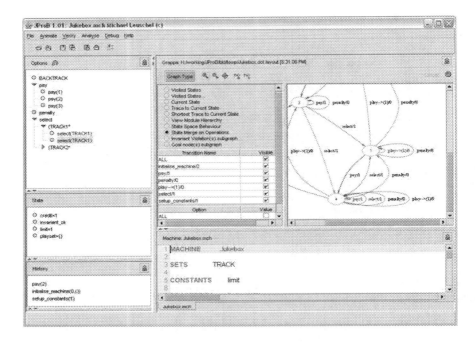

**Fig. 9.** Screenshot of Java version of ProB

operations to be selectively removed from the visualization e.g., to remove self loops and improve clarity.

**User Defined Constraints.** Through previous experience gained with model checkers, it was proposed that a better understanding of the system might be gained if the user were able to directly query the state space. Therefore we extended our tool by enabling the user to define constraints on system variables and on values of operation arguments, and to subsequently view a graph of all states in which these hold, and the relationship between them, if any. This is generally useful when the user is interested in exposing some subtle aspect of the state space, which a more general algorithm would be unlikely to reveal without user intevention. It should be noted that the effectiveness of reducing state spaces using this technique depends largely on the user's literacy in the specification language and their understanding of the system; however its potential makes it a feature worth keeping and extending in the future. As mentioned, it is also possible for the user to selectively turn off visible operations in the visualization, to further reduce the size of the graph: see the tick boxes in the middle of Figure 9.

**Subgraphs.** Another method of reducing the size of the graph is to show only part of it: a subgraph – hence our system has the option to view the subgraph that connects one or more states. This is particularly useful when one wants to view all paths that lead to a state that violates the system invariant.

**More Related Work**

In addition to considering algorithms and techniques that produce smaller graphs, with the goal of finding a more effective visualization, we must also consider the other aspects that affect this. These are outside the main scope of the present paper, but the interested reader is referred to [21], [8], [11], and [13].

The final aspect regards the influence of the size of a graph on the efficiency of the graph layout algorithm. This issue is somewhat orthogonal to the issues addressed in the present paper. Few layouting techniques can claim to deal effectively with thousands of nodes even though graphs of this size appear frequently in application domains, including model checking. The size of a graph can make a normally good layout algorithm completely unusable. Therefore many visualization techniques attempt to reduce the size of the graph to display. A large quantity of the important techniques are documented in [13], one of which appears particularly relevant to our overall goal: that of *clustering*. A clustering layout algorithm generally assigns nodes of a graph that satisfy some condition, into the same *cluster* (the condition may be an equivalence relation). Edges between clusters are displayed to represent the relation between the nodes of one cluster with those of another. Some good results have been witnessed and tested for large graphs containing thousands of vertices [12]. However, these graphs were representing deterministic protocols; it would be interesting to see if one could find a suitable clustering technique for the elements of the state space of a nondeterministic B model.

Finally, one can view the work in abstraction-based model checking, where abstractions are applied during exploration, as very related to our work. For example, the data abstraction of [9] is similar to our $\alpha$-abstraction. However, the purpose of all these model checking works (e.g., [22, 23, 6]) is to obtain more efficient model checking, and not visualization by humans.

## Acknowledgements

We would like to thank Michael Butler for stimulating discussions and feedback on the paper. We are also very grateful to anonymous referees of ZB'2005 for their very useful comments.

## References

1. J.-R. Abrial. *The B-Book*. Cambridge University Press, 1996.
2. A. V. Aho, R. Sethi, and J. D. Ullman. *Compilers — Principles, Techniques and Tools*. Addison-Wesley, 1986.

3. F. Ambert, F. Bouquet, S. Chemin, S. Guenaud, B. Legeard, F. Peureux, M. Utting, and N. Vacelet. BZ-testing-tools: A tool-set for test generation from Z and B using constraint logic programming. In *Proceedings of FATES'02, Formal Approaches to Testing of Software*, pages 105–120, August 2002. Technical Report, INRIA.

4. AT&T Labs-Research. Graphviz - open source graph drawing software. Obtainable at http://www.research.att.com/sw/tools/graphviz/.

5. B-Core (UK) Limited, Oxon, UK. *B-Toolkit, On-line manual.*, 1999. Available at http://www.b-core.com/ONLINEDOC/Contents.html.

6. S. Bensalem, Y. Lakhnech, and S. Owre. Computing abstractions of infinite state systems compositionally and automatically. In *Proceedings of CAV'98*, LNCS, pages 319–331. Springer-Verlag, 1998.

7. F. Bouquet, B. Legeard, and F. Peureux. CLPS-B - a constraint solver for B. In J.-P.Katoen and P.Stevens, editors, *Tools and Algorithms for the Construction and Analysis of Systems*, LNCS 2280, pages 188–204. Springer-Verlag, 2002.

8. S. Casner and J. Larkin. Cognitive Efficiency Considerations for Good Graphic Design. In *11th Annual Conf. of the Cognitive Science Society*, Ann Arbor, Michigan, August 1989.

9. E. M. Clarke, O. Grumberg, and D. Peled. *Model Checking*. MIT Press, 1999.

10. H. W. F. Ham and J. Wijk. Visualization of State Transition Graphs. In *IEEE Symposium on Information Visualization*, pages 59–63, San Diego, CA, USA, October 2001.

11. M. Fitter and T. Green. When Do Diagrams Make Good Programming Languages? *Int. Journal of Man-Machine Studies*, pages 235–261, 1979.

12. J. Groote and F. Ham. Large State Space Visualization. In *TACAS*, volume 2619 of *Lecture Notes in Computer Science*, pages 585–590. Springer, 2003.

13. I. Herman, G. Melanon, and M. S. Marshall. Graph Visualization and Navigation in Information Visualization: A Survey. *IEEE Transactions on Visualization and Computer Graphics*, 6(1):24–43, 2000.

14. J. E. Hopcroft and J. D. Ullman. *Introduction to Automata Theory, Languages and Computation*. Addison-Wesley, 1979.

15. L. Ilie and S. Yu. Algorithms for Computing Small NFAs. In *MFCS*, volume 2420 of *Lecture Notes in Computer Science*. Springer, 2002.

16. T. Jiang and B. Ravikunar. Minimal NFA Problems are Hard. *SIAM Journal on Computing*, 22(6):1117–1141, 1993.

17. S. A. John. Minimal Unambigous ε-NFA. In *9th International Conference on Implementation and Application of Automata (CIAA-2004)*, Kingston, Ontario, Canada, July 2004.

18. M. Leuschel and M. Butler. ProB: A model checker for B. In K. Araki, S. Gnesi, and D. Mandrioli, editors, *FME 2003: Formal Methods*, LNCS 2805, pages 855–874. Springer-Verlag, 2003.

19. M. Leuschel and E. Turner. Visualising larger states spaces in ProB. Technical report, School of Electronics and Computer Science, University of Southampton, January 2005.

20. A. Malcher. Minimizing Finite Automata is Computationally Hard. *Springer-Verlag Berlin Heidelberg*, 2710:386–397, August 2003.

21. N. L. N. Dulac, T. Viguier and M.-A. Storey. On the use of Visualization in Formal Requirements Specification. In *IEEE Joint International Conference on Requirements Engineering*, pages 71–81, Essen, Germany, September 2002.

22. V. Rusu and E. Singerman. On proving safety properties by integrating static analysis, theorem proving and abstraction". In *Tools and Algorithms for the Construction and Analysis of Systems TACAS '99*, LNCS. Springer-Verlag, 1999.
23. H. Sadi and N. Shankar. Abstract and model check while you prove. In *Proceedings of CAV'99*, LNCS, pages 319–331, Trento, Italy, July 1999. Springer-Verlag.
24. Steria, Aix-en-Provence, France. *Atelier B, User and Reference Manuals*, 1996. Available at http://www.atelierb.societe.com/index_uk.html.

# Non-atomic Refinement in Z and CSP

John Derrick[1] and Heike Wehrheim[2]

[1] Department of Computing, University of Sheffield, Sheffield, UK
`J.Derrick@dcs.shef.ac.uk`
[2] Universität Paderborn, Institut für Informatik, 33098 Paderborn, Germany
`wehrheim@uni-paderborn.de`

**Abstract.** In this paper we discuss the relationship between notions of non-atomic (or action) refinement in a state-based setting with that in a behavioural setting. In particular, we show that the definition of non-atomic coupled downward simulation as defined for Z and Object-Z is sound with respect to an action refinement definition of CSP failures refinement.

## 1 Introduction

In this paper we investigate the relationship between definitions of non-atomic (or action) refinement in a state-based setting with that in a behavioural setting. In particular, we show that the definition of non-atomic coupled downward simulation as defined for Z and Object-Z in [8] is sound with respect to non-atomic refinement on CSP failures sets. This work fits into two strands of work in the formal specification community. The first is that of integrating formal specification notations, and the second of relating notions of refinement across different paradigms.

Work on integrating formal specification languages is being driven by the desire and need to tackle the design of systems which cross paradigm boundaries, for example, those needing explicit notions of communication as well as state, as well as providing some formality to informal languages such as UML. Work in this sphere typically shows how existing languages can be combined in a useful and meaningful way, whilst preserving their original syntax and semantics. Examples include combinations of Object-Z and CSP as defined by Smith [21], Fischer [9] and Mahony and Dong [16]. Other combinations of process algebras with Z or B include those investigated by Galloway [11] and Treharne [23]. A survey of some of these approaches is given in [10].

Work on relating notions of refinement typically compares the relative strengths of the refinement relations in different semantic domains. This, of course, links into work on integrating formal specification languages since it opens the way for uniform methods of refinement to be defined for integrated notations. Our particular interest here is that provided by state-based languages such as Z and Object-Z and the process algebra CSP. Refinement in state-based languages is based upon data refinement, and downwards and upwards simulations are the standard way to verify such refinements. This contrasts with a

H. Treharne et al. (Eds.): ZB 2005, LNCS 3455, pp. 24–44, 2005.

behavioural setting such as CSP where process refinements are used to compare implementations and specifications, and, in particular, we are interested here in CSP failures-divergences refinement. There are two facts relevant to this paper: downwards simulations are sound with respect to failures-divergences refinement, and both notions of refinement assume the granularity of the refinement is unchanged.

The latter means that operations and events are assumed to be *atomic*, and thus indivisible upon refinement. This is well known to be an unrealistic assumption in a general software development setting, and consequently there has been work on non-atomic or action refinement, whereby the granularity of the operations or events can be broken in a refinement. Work in a state-based setting includes [5, 8]. The latter, which builds upon relevant work for process algebras [17, 18], is our starting point. Specifically this paper takes the definition of non-atomic refinement as given in [8] and shows that it is sound with respect to a notion of non-atomic refinement defined on failure sets, that is, defined for a behavioural context.

The structure of the paper is as follows. In Section 2 we define non-atomic refinement in Z. In Section 3 we provide the corresponding definition for CSP, and in Section 4 we show the state-based definition is sound with respect to the process algebraic version. We also show the monotonicity of parallel composition with respect to non-atomic refinement. In Section 5 we then generalise our results by considering the role of input and output. We conclude in Section 6.

## 2    Non-atomic Refinement in Z

This section deals with the state-based part of non-atomic refinement. It defines non-atomic coupled downward simulations (as presented in [8]) which are used to verify non-atomic refinements between Z specifications. A Z specification $A = (AState, AInit, \{AOp_i\}_{i \in I})$ consists of a state space with an initialisation condition and a set of operations performing transformations on the state space. We assume a blocking model for operation executions, i.e. an operation can only be executed when its precondition evaluates to true. This fits well with the failure semantics of CSP and is therefore most often assumed in integrations of Z or Object-Z and CSP.

Refinement in formal methods is used to compare an implementation with an abstract specification: the implementation should only exhibit behaviour which is also present in the specification. The technical tools for showing refinement relationships in state-based languages are *simulation relations* (viz. downwards or upwards simulation relations, see [25, 6]) which allow one to verify refinements on a step-by-step basis. In contrast to standard refinement, non-atomic refinement assumes that operations in the abstract specification may be split into a number of concrete operations in the implementation. The purpose of simulation relations is thus to show that an abstract operation $AOp$ is simulated by a sequence of concrete operations $COp_1 \mathbin{\S} COp_2 \mathbin{\S} \ldots \mathbin{\S} COp_n$ (for simplicity $n$ will in the following always be two).

Before giving a formal definition we explain the general concept behind non-atomic refinement by means of a small example. The example will be used throughout the whole paper and later be enhanced with inputs. The abstract specification contains operations to translate and multiply coordinates $x, y, u$ and $v$: operation *Translate* shifts $x$ and $y$ by 4 and 2 respectively, and operation *Multiply* multiplies $u$ and $v$ by 10. The constants will later be replaced by values of input variables.

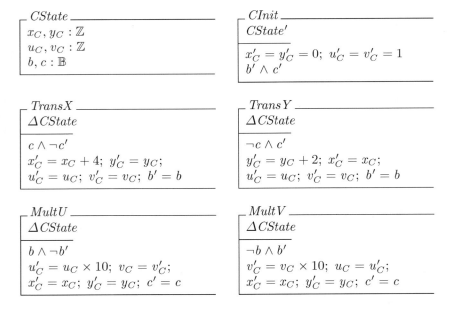

The abstract specification is refined into a concrete specification in which both *Translate* and *Multiply* are split such that the two coordinates are modified in two consecutive steps. Boolean flags $b$ and $c$ are used to control the ordering of the steps: *TransX* has to occur before *TransY* and *MultU* before *MultY*.

―――― *CState* ――――
$x_C, y_C : \mathbb{Z}$
$u_C, v_C : \mathbb{Z}$
$b, c : \mathbb{B}$

―――― *CInit* ――――
*CState'*
$x'_C = y'_C = 0;\ u'_C = v'_C = 1$
$b' \wedge c'$

―――― *TransX* ――――
$\Delta CState$
$c \wedge \neg c'$
$x'_C = x_C + 4;\ y'_C = y_C;$
$u'_C = u_C;\ v'_C = v_C;\ b' = b$

―――― *TransY* ――――
$\Delta CState$
$\neg c \wedge c'$
$y'_C = y_C + 2;\ x'_C = x_C;$
$u'_C = u_C;\ v'_C = v_C;\ b' = b$

―――― *MultU* ――――
$\Delta CState$
$b \wedge \neg b'$
$u'_C = u_C \times 10;\ v_C = v'_C;$
$x'_C = x_C;\ y'_C = y_C;\ c' = c$

―――― *MultV* ――――
$\Delta CState$
$\neg b \wedge b'$
$v'_C = v_C \times 10;\ u_C = u'_C;$
$x'_C = x_C;\ y'_C = y_C;\ c' = c$

To show that $C$ is a non-atomic coupled downward simulation of $A$ we augment the standard non-atomic conditions with further conditions relating to the necessity for the two specifications to be coupled. In the sequel we always assume that an abstract operation $AOp$ is split into the sequence $COp_1 \, \mathbin{\mathring{\,}} COp_2$. Generalising standard downward simulation conditions to the non-atomic case leads to the following requirements as introduced in [5].

**Definition 1.** *Non-atomic downward simulation without IO transformations A specification $C$ is a non-atomic downward simulation of the specification $A$ if there is a retrieve relation $R$ such that every abstract operation $AOp$ is recast into a sequence of concrete operations $COp_1 \, \mathbin{\mathring{\,}} COp_2$ and the following hold.*

$\forall \, CInit \bullet (\exists \, AInit \bullet R)$

$\forall \, AState; \; CState; \; CState' \bullet (COp_1 \, \mathbin{\mathring{\,}} COp_2) \wedge R \Rightarrow \exists \, AState' \bullet R' \wedge AOp$

$\forall \, AState; \; CState \bullet R \Rightarrow (pre \, AOp \iff pre \, COp_1)$

$\forall \, AState; \; CState; \; CState' \bullet R \wedge COp_1 \Rightarrow (pre \, COp_2)'$

This already covers a range of aspects: similar to the non-atomic case a retrieve relation $R$ is used to relate abstract and concrete state space and every concrete initial state has to be linked with an abstract initial state. Furthermore, the execution of a sequence $COp_1 \, \mathbin{\mathring{\,}} COp_2$ has to be matched by an abstract operation $AOp$, and in related states $COp_1$ is enabled if and only if $AOp$ is enabled (blocking model). The last condition guarantees that immediately after a $COp_1$ the refinement can be completed by a $COp_2$.

Looking at our example the following relation $R$ shows that $C$ is a non-atomic downward simulation of $A$.

---
$R$
$AState; \; CState$

$x_A = x_C; \; y_A = y_C; \; u_A = u_C; \; v_A = v_C; \; c \wedge b$

---

Nevertheless, this is not yet sufficient: it allows a number of undesirable behaviours of the concrete system. For instance, the concrete system can execute $COp_2$ without ever having performed a $COp_1$, and it might, once a third operation $DOp$ has been executed after $COp_1$, never be able to complete the sequence. This can be ruled out by using *coupled simulations*: the retrieve relation $R$ is completed by a family of relations $R^S$ which allow for a closer comparison of concrete and abstract system. Intuitively, $R^S$ is used to relate abstract states with *intermediate* concrete states, i.e. states in which a refinement sequence has only been partly executed. $S$ is a sequence of concrete operations which records which decompositions have been started but not finished. On idle states (i.e., states where all refinement sequences have been completed, $S = \langle \rangle$) $R^S$ has to agree with $R$. This is the coupling condition C which gives the definition its name.

**Notation.** The notation $S \backslash \langle COp_1 \rangle$ stands for removing $COp_1$ from the sequence $S$, i.e., is shorthand for $S \upharpoonright (ran \, S \setminus \{COp_1\})$. We also write $COp_1 \in S$ for $COp_1 \in ran \, S$.

**Definition 2.** *Non-atomic coupled downward simulation without IO transformations A specification $C$ is a non-atomic coupled downward simulation of the* specification $A$ (denoted $A \sqsubseteq_{na} C$) if there is a retrieve relation $R$ showing that $C$ is a non-atomic downward simulation of $A$, and there is a family of simulation relations $R^S$ such that the following hold.

**C** $R^{\langle\rangle} = R$

**S1** $\forall\, AState,\, CState,\, CState' \bullet R^S \wedge COp_1 \Rightarrow \exists\, AState' \bullet \Xi\, AState \wedge (R^{S^{\frown}\langle COp_1\rangle})'$

**S2** $\forall\, AState,\, CState \bullet R^S \wedge COp_1 \in S \Rightarrow pre\, COp_2$

**S3** $\forall\, AState,\, CState,\, CState' \bullet R^S \wedge COp_2 \Rightarrow COp_1 \in S \wedge \exists\, AState' \bullet AOp \wedge$
$(R^{S \backslash \langle COp_1\rangle})'$

Condition S1 is used to record the started but not yet finished refinements in $R^S$, condition S2 guarantees that started refinement may always be completed and S3 rules out that refinements can be started "in the middle", i.e. a $COp_2$ occurs with no previous (uncompleted) $COp_1$. In our example, we could use the following relations $R^S$.

---

$R^{\langle TransX\rangle}$

$AState$
$CState$

$x_A = x_C - 4;\ \neg c \wedge b$
$y_C = y_A;\ u_C = u_A;\ v_C = v_A$

---

$R^{\langle MultU\rangle}$

$AState$
$CState$

$u_A \times 10 = u_C;\ c \wedge \neg b$
$x_C = x_A;\ y_C = y_A;\ v_C = v_A$

---

$R^{\langle TransX, MultU\rangle}$

$AState$
$CState$

$x_A = x_C - 4;\ u_A \times 10 = u_C$
$\neg c \wedge \neg b;\ y_C = y_A;\ v_C = v_A$

---

One relation is still missing, $R^{\langle MultU, TransX\rangle}$, which in fact we take to equal $R^{\langle TransX, MultU\rangle}$. As can be seen by the execution traces of the concrete and abstract specification in Figure 1, this definition also allows for an *overlap* of refinements: the refinements of *Translate* and *Multiply* can be executed in an interleaved manner. This is, however, only allowed if there is a (sequential) abstract counterpart of this interleaved execution. For example, it would not be possible if the operations manipulate a common part of the state space.

In fact, starting with a given relation $R$ there is a canonical way of finding (the smallest) family of relations $R^S$ (if they exist at all). They can be inductively computed by the following set of equations:

$$R^{\langle\rangle} \,\hat{=}\, R \tag{1}$$

$$R^{S^{\frown}\langle COp_1\rangle} \,\hat{=}\, (R^S[CState'/CState] \, \raise.3ex\hbox{$\scriptstyle 9$} \, COp_1)[CState/CState'] \tag{2}$$

where $[CState'/CState]$ represents the obvious global substitutions.

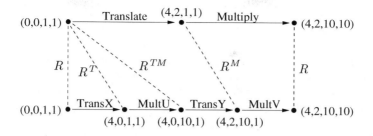

**Fig. 1.** A concrete and the matching abstract trace

With this definition, conditions C and S1 automatically hold by construction. In $R^{S^\frown\langle COp_1\rangle}$ the abstract state remains unchanged (compared to $R^S$) and is related to the concrete state reached after executing $COp_1$. Condition S2 then still requires checking (which is easy) as does S3 (in which lies some complexity). To check S3 we define the effect of finishing a concrete non-atomic operation as follows.

$$R^S \blacktriangledown \langle COp_1\rangle \ \widehat{=}$$
$$\Big(\big((R^S[CState'/CState]\ \mathring{,}\ COp_2)[AState'/AState]\ \mathring{,}\ AOp\big)$$
$$[AState'/AState,\ CState'/CState]\Big)$$

Condition S3 is equivalent to checking that $R^S \blacktriangledown \langle COp_1\rangle$ equals[1] $R^{S\backslash\langle COp_1\rangle}$.

## 3   Non-atomic Failures Refinement

We are interested in the interplay between state-based and behavioural refinements, and thus we now transfer these ideas to a behaviour-oriented setting like the process algebra CSP, where *process refinement* is used to compare implementations and specifications. For this, we assume that the specification and implementation are built over two distinct alphabets, $\alpha$ for the abstract and $\gamma$ for the concrete level: $\alpha$ contains all abstract operations $AOp_i, i \in I$, and $\gamma$ all concrete operations $COp_1^i, COp_2^i, i \in I$.

In CSP, refinement compares processes according to their *failure sets*: failures record the traces a process may execute together with the refusals, i.e. the set of operations (or events) that can be refused after a certain trace. CSP has two different semantic models based around the stable failures and the failure-divergence model which differ in the way they treat internal ($\tau$) operations. Since the operational semantics of Z we use here generates no $\tau$ transitions at all, we restrict ourselves to comparing failures only, and thus the two models coincide. Thus abstract and concrete processes $A$ and $C$ are represented by failure sets $\mathcal{F}_A$ and $\mathcal{F}_C$, respectively:

---

[1] [8] contains an example of its calculation.

$$\mathcal{F}_A \subseteq \alpha^* \times \mathbb{P}\,\alpha$$
$$\mathcal{F}_C \subseteq \gamma^* \times \mathbb{P}\,\gamma$$

Due to absence of internal actions we can define the traces of $A$, $\mathcal{T}_A$, to be the set $\{(tr, X) \in \mathcal{F}_A \bullet tr\}$ (and similarly $\mathcal{T}_C$). In order to transfer the state-based definition to a failures context we first define what it means for all refinements to have been completed.

**Definition 3.** *A trace $tr \in \gamma^*$ is completed iff for all pairs $COp_1$ and $COp_2 \in \gamma$ we have $\#\langle i \mid tr[i] = COp_1 \rangle = \#\langle j \mid tr[j] = COp_2 \rangle$. The set of all completed traces of $C$ is denoted $Comp(C)$.*

The completed traces are those which have to have an abstract counterpart. We also define an abstraction operator on completed traces and their refusals.

$$tr\!\uparrow = (tr \upharpoonright \{COp_2^i \mid i \in I\})[COp_2^i \mapsto AOp_i, i \in I]$$
$$X\!\uparrow = (X \setminus \{COp_2^i \mid i \in I\})[COp_1^i \mapsto AOp_i, i \in I]$$

The abstraction operator on traces removes all $COp_1$s and then replaces $COp_2$s by $AOp$s, similarly, the abstraction operator on failures removes all $COp_2$s and then replaces $COp_1$s by $AOp$s. The abstraction operator on traces could also be applied to divergences when a semantic model of CSP with divergences is needed (which is not the case here).

For the proof of soundness we will need one more definition on traces: the *non-completed* part of a trace $tr$ is $tr^\lhd \,\hat{=}\, squash(tr \rhd \{tr[i] = COp_1 \wedge \neg \exists j > i \bullet tr[j] = COp_2 \bullet i\})$. For instance, $\langle COp_1, DOp_1, COp_2, EOp_1 \rangle^\lhd = \langle DOp_1, EOp_1 \rangle$.

We are now in a position to define a non-atomic version of failures refinement for processes. In it the ordering on the abstract level is determined by the ordering of completions on the concrete level, and the definition coincides with standard failures refinement when there are no non-atomic decompositions.

**Definition 4.** *A set of failures $\mathcal{F}_C$ is a non-atomic coupled refinement of a set of failures $\mathcal{F}_A$ (denoted $\mathcal{F}_A \sqsubseteq_{fna} \mathcal{F}_C$) if the following hold:*

1. $\forall (tr, X) \in \mathcal{F}_C \bullet tr \in Comp(\mathcal{T}_C) \Rightarrow (tr\!\uparrow, X\!\uparrow) \in \mathcal{F}_A$
2. $\forall (tr, X) \in \mathcal{F}_C, \forall i \in I \bullet$
   $$\forall tr_1, tr_2 \bullet tr = tr_1 \,^\frown \langle COp_1^i \rangle \,^\frown tr_2, COp_2^i \notin ran\, tr_2 \Rightarrow COp_2^i \notin X$$
3. $\forall i \in I, tr \,^\frown \langle COp_2^i \rangle \in \mathcal{T}_C \Rightarrow \exists tr_1, tr_2 \bullet tr = tr_1 \,^\frown \langle COp_1^i \rangle \,^\frown tr_2 \wedge COp_2^i \notin ran\, tr_2$

The second condition is the analogue of S2: as long as the refinement sequence is not completed $COp_2$ may never be refused. The third condition is the analogue of S3: a refinement may not be started in the middle. Both the coupling condition and S1 are incorporated in the first condition: since we are comparing traces here, we still have the whole execution history present in the comparison and do not have to record it in a relation $R^S$.

The following example gives two CSP processes describing the behaviour of an abstract and a concrete system performing translate and multiply operations.

$$P_A = Multiply \rightarrow Translate \rightarrow P_A \ \square \ Translate \rightarrow Multiply \rightarrow P_A$$
$$P_C = MultU \rightarrow (TransX \rightarrow TransY \rightarrow Skip \ ||| \ MultV \rightarrow Skip); \ P_C$$

In the failure set of $P_C$ there are, for instance, the following three failures with completed traces:

$$(tr_1, X_1) \cong (\langle \rangle, \{TransY, MultV\}),$$
$$(tr_2, X_2) \cong (\langle MultU, TransX, MultV, TransY \rangle, \{TransY, MultV\}),$$
$$(tr_3, X_3) \cong (\langle MultU, MultV \rangle, \{MultU, MultV, TransY\}),$$

a non-completed trace is $\langle MultU, TransX, MultV \rangle$. Using the abstraction operators we get $tr_1 \uparrow = \langle \rangle$, $X_1 \uparrow = \varnothing$, $tr_2 \uparrow = \langle Multiply, Translate \rangle$, $X_2 \uparrow = \varnothing$ and $tr_3 \uparrow = \langle Multiply \rangle$, $X_3 \uparrow = \{Multiply\}$. Obviously, $P_C$ is a non-atomic coupled refinement of $P_A$.

# 4    Integration

We are ultimately interested in using the notion of non-atomic refinement in an integrated specification formalism combining a state-based specification language such as Z or Object-Z with a process algebra such as CSP. Integrations of this type include CSP-OZ [9] and Object-Z/CSP [21] which both use a failures semantics. The semantics is obtained by giving a failure semantics to the (Object-)Z part and composing it with the CSP part using CSP parallel composition. This poses the question of correspondence between the two notions of non-atomic refinement: if two Z specifications are related by a non-atomic coupled downwards simulation is there also a non-atomic process refinement relationship between them? This question has been intensively studied in the standard atomic case (see [4, 7, 3, 15, 12, 4]) and will now be answered for the non-atomic setting.

In the atomic case, data refinement in a state-based system is verified by a combination of upward and downward simulations. To investigate the relationship with failures refinement a correspondence is set up between operations and events, and under this correspondence downward simulation is sound with respect to failures-divergences refinement. That is, if $C$ is a downward simulation of $A$ then $C$ is a failures-divergences refinement of $A$ under this interpretation of operations as events. This is the result we will generalise to the non-atomic case. (The corresponding result for upward simulations is left for future work.)

To verify the result we establish the correspondence between a state-based system and its failures by deriving a failure semantics for Z specifications in two steps: first, we define an operational semantics by means of transition systems, and then we derive the failures from the transition system. A transition system $T = (Q, In, \rightarrow)$ labelled over $A$ has the usual components: $Q$ is a set of states, $In \subseteq Q$ are the initial states and $\rightarrow \subseteq Q \times A \times Q$ is the transition relation.

**Definition 5.** *Let* $S = (State, Init, \{Op\}_{i \in I})$ *be a Z specification. The operational semantics of* $S$, $T(S)$, *is given by a transition system* $(Q, In, \rightarrow)$ *labelled over* $\{Op_i \mid i \in I\}$ *such that* $Q = State, In = Init$ *and* $q \xrightarrow{Op_i} q'$ *iff* $(q, q') \in Op_i$.

Note: In this definition we are explicitly using the fact that the semantics of an operation is taken to be a set of bindings [25]. Thus $(q, q') \in Op_i$ means that $q$ and $q'$ are the before and after states, respectively, of the operation $Op_i$.

We also need the following, standard, definition. Note that we are assuming to have no internal (i.e., unobservable) actions in the transition system.

**Definition 6.** *Let* $T = (Q, In, \rightarrow)$ *be a transition system labelled over some alphabet* $A$, $q, q' \in Q$, $a_i \in A$ *and* $tr \in A^*$.

1. $q \xrightarrow{a_1 \ldots a_n} q'$ *iff there are states* $q_0, q_1, \ldots, q_n$ *such that* $q = q_0$, $q_i \xrightarrow{a_{i+1}} q_{i+1}$ *and* $q_n = q'$.
2. *The (maximal) set of events refused in a state* $q \in Q$ *is* $refs(q) \hat{=} A \setminus \{a \in A \mid q \xrightarrow{a}\}$.
3. *The set of failures of* $T$ *is*

$$\mathcal{F}(T) \hat{=} \{(tr, X) \in A^* \times \mathbb{P} A \mid \exists q \in Q, q_0 \in In : q_0 \xrightarrow{tr} q \wedge X \subseteq refs(q)\}$$

With these definitions at hand we can formulate the following correspondence result: a non-atomic coupled downward simulation between Z specifications induces a non-atomic coupled refinement on their failure sets.

**Theorem 1.** *Let* $A, C$ *be Z specifications. Then the following holds:*

$$A \sqsubseteq_{na} C \Rightarrow \mathcal{F}(T(A)) \sqsubseteq_{fna} \mathcal{F}(T(C))$$

We prove this theorem in two steps: first, we define a notion of non-atomic coupled simulation on transition systems and show a correspondence result for Z specifications and transition systems (which is, in fact, straightforward). In the second step we prove correspondence between non-atomic refinement on transition systems and on their failure sets (which is less straightforward).

**Definition 7.** *A transition system* $T_C = (Q_C, In_C, \rightarrow_C)$ *is a non-atomic coupled downward simulation of a transition system* $T_A = (Q_A, In_A, \rightarrow_A)$ *(denoted* $T_A \sqsubseteq_{tna} T_C$*) if there is a relation* $R \subseteq Q_A \times Q_C$ *satisfying the following*

1. $\forall q_0 \in In_C \bullet \exists q'_0 \in In_A \bullet (q'_0, q_0) \in R$,
2. $\forall (q_1, q_2) \in R \bullet \forall q'_2 \in Q_C \bullet q_2 \xrightarrow{COp_1 COp_2} q'_2 \Rightarrow \exists q'_1 \in Q_A \bullet q_1 \xrightarrow{AOp} q'_1$ *and* $(q'_1, q'_2) \in R$,
3. $\forall (q_1, q_2) \in R \bullet q_1 \xrightarrow{AOp}$ *iff* $q_2 \xrightarrow{COp_1}$
4. $\forall q_1 \in ran R \bullet \forall q'_1 \in Q_C \bullet q_1 \xrightarrow{COp_1} q'_1 \Rightarrow q'_1 \xrightarrow{COp_2}$,

*and there is a family of relations $R^S \subseteq Q_A \times Q_C$, $S \in \gamma^*$, such that, in addition, we have:*

**C** $R^{\langle \rangle} = R$,

**S1** $\forall (q_1, q_2) \in R^S \bullet \forall q_2' \in Q_C \bullet q_2 \xrightarrow{COp_1} q_2' \Rightarrow (q_1, q_2') \in R^{S \frown \langle COp_1 \rangle}$,

**S2** $\forall (q_1, q_2) \in R^S \bullet COp_1 \in S \Rightarrow q_2 \xrightarrow{COp_2}$,

**S3** $\forall (q_1, q_2) \in R^S \bullet \forall q_2' \in Q_C \bullet q_2 \xrightarrow{COp_2} q_2' \Rightarrow COp_1 \in S \wedge \exists q_1' \in Q_A \bullet$
$q_1 \xrightarrow{AOp} q_1' \wedge (q_1', q_2') \in R^{S \setminus \langle COp_1 \rangle}$.

**Theorem 2.** *Let $A, C$ be Z specifications. Then*

$$A \sqsubseteq_{na} C \Leftrightarrow T(A) \sqsubseteq_{tna} T(C) .$$

**Proof:** Easily follows by the definition of the operational semantics (see Definition 5) of a Z specification. □

**Theorem 3.** *Let $T_A, T_C$ be transition systems.*

$$T_A \sqsubseteq_{tna} T_C \Rightarrow \mathcal{F}(T_A) \sqsubseteq_{fna} \mathcal{F}(T_C) .$$

**Proof of Theorem 3:** Let $T_A = (Q_A, In_A, \rightarrow_A)$, $T_C = (Q_C, In_C, \rightarrow_C)$ be the transition systems and $R, R^S \subseteq Q_A \times Q_C$ be the relations proving $T_A \sqsubseteq_{tna} T_C$.

1. Let $(tr, X) \in \mathcal{F}_C$. Then by definition of failures there are states $q_1, \ldots q_n$ such that $q_1 \in In_C$, $q_i \xrightarrow{tr[i]}_C q_{i+1}$, $X \subseteq refs(q_n)$. We inductively construct a sequence $p_1, \ldots p_n \in Q_A$ with $p_1 \in In_A$, $(p_i, q_i) \in R^S$, $S = tr[1 \ldots i-1]^\lhd$:
   - Choose $p_1$ such that $p_1 R q_1$ (possible by initialisation condition), then $tr[1 \ldots 0] = \langle \rangle, \langle \rangle^\lhd = \langle \rangle$.
   - If $q_i \xrightarrow{COp_1} q_{i+1}$ then set $p_{i+1}$ to $p_i$, then $tr[1 \ldots i]^\lhd = tr[1 \ldots i-1]^\lhd \frown \langle COp_1 \rangle$ and by S1 $(p_{i+1}, q_{i+1}) \in R^S$ with $S = tr[1 \ldots i]^\lhd$.
   - If $q_i \xrightarrow{COp_2} q_{i+1}$ then choose $p_{i+1}$ such that $p_i \xrightarrow{AOp} p_{i+1}$ (by S3), then $tr[1 \ldots i]^\lhd = tr[1 \ldots i-1]^\lhd \setminus \langle COp_1 \rangle$, hence by S3 $(p_{i+1}, q_{i+1}) \in R^S$ with $S = tr[1 \ldots i]^\lhd$.

   We need to show that $tr \in Comp(\mathcal{T}_C) \Rightarrow (tr \uparrow, X \uparrow) \in \mathcal{F}_A$. Let $tr$ be a completed trace. Then $(p_n, q_n) \in R^{\langle \rangle}$ and by construction $p_1 \xrightarrow{tr \uparrow} p_n$. Concerning the refusals: if $COp_1 \in X$ then $q_n \xrightarrow{COp_1} \!\!\!\!\!/\,$, hence $p_n \xrightarrow{AOp} \!\!\!\!\!/\,$ (by condition 3 of Definition 7) which implies $AOp \in refs(p_n)$. It follows that $X \uparrow \subseteq refs(p_n)$ and hence $(tr \uparrow, X \uparrow) \in \mathcal{F}_A$.

2. Let $(tr, X) \in \mathcal{F}_C$, and $tr_1, tr_2$ be traces with $tr = tr_1 \frown \langle COp_1 \rangle \frown tr_2$ such that $COp_2 \notin ran\, tr_2$. We have to show that $COp_2 \notin X$. A construction analogous to (1) gives us the existence of pairs $(p_1, q_1), (p_n, q_n)$ such that $q_1 \xrightarrow{tr} q_n, p_1 \xrightarrow{tr \uparrow} p_n, q_1 \in In_C, p_1 \in In_A$ and $(p_n, q_n) \in R^S$ where $S = tr^\lhd$. Hence $COp_1 \in S$ and by S2, $q_n \xrightarrow{COp_2}$. It follows that $COp_2 \notin X$.

3. Let $tr \frown \langle COp_2 \rangle \in \mathcal{T}_C$. Again we can construct pairs of states $(p_1, q_1)$, $(p_{n-1}, q_{n-1}), (p_n, q_n)$ such that $p_1 \in In_A, q_1 \in In_C, q_1 \xrightarrow{tr} q_{n-1} \xrightarrow{COp_2} q_n, p_1 \xrightarrow{tr\uparrow} p_{n-1}, (p_{n-1}, q_{n-1}) \in R^S, S = tr^\lhd$. By S3 it follows that $COp_1 \in S$, and hence by definition of $\lhd$ there are traces $tr_1, tr_2$ such that $tr = tr_1 \frown \langle COp_1 \rangle \frown tr_2$ and $COp_2 \notin \text{ran } tr_2$.                           $\square$

When using non-atomic refinement in an integrated specification formalism the above correspondence theorem is not the only result of interest. The main question is whether a separate non-atomic refinement of the state-based and the behaviour-oriented part gives a non-atomic refinement of the combination. Theorem 1 only partly answers this question. Additionally, we need to know whether non-atomic refinement is preserved under parallel composition (the operator used for combining the semantics of the separate parts), or, rephrased whether parallel composition is monotone with respect to non-atomic refinement.

Parallel composition in CSP, denoted $\|_A$, requires the joint execution of all events in $A$ and an arbitrary interleaving of the remaining events [20]. When composing a Z and a CSP part of an integrated specification parallel composition often requires synchronisation on the intersection of the alphabets of both parts. We therefore formulate the monotonicity of parallel composition with respect to non-atomic refinement as follows.

**Theorem 4.** *Let $\mathcal{F}_P, \mathcal{F}_Q$ be failure sets over the abstract alphabet $\alpha$, $\mathcal{F}_{P'}, \mathcal{F}_{Q'}$ over the concrete alphabet $\gamma$ and let $A \subseteq \gamma$ be a synchronisation set which is the intersection of the alphabets of $P'$ and $Q'$. Furthermore, let $COp_1 \in A$ iff $COp_2 \in A$ hold for all pairs of concrete operations $COp_1, COp_2$. Then the following holds:*

$$\mathcal{F}_P \sqsubseteq_{fna} \mathcal{F}_{P'} \text{ and } \mathcal{F}_Q \sqsubseteq_{fna} \mathcal{F}_{Q'} \text{ implies } \mathcal{F}_P \|_{A\uparrow} \mathcal{F}_Q \sqsubseteq_{fna} \mathcal{F}_{P'} \|_A \mathcal{F}_{Q'} .$$

Due to lack of space the proof is not given here.

# 5   Adding IO Transformers

We now turn our attention to generalising the results in Sections 2 to 4 to deal with the transformations necessary in the presence of input and output. The structure of what follows is identical to that above: we use a running example to motivate the definition of a non-atomic coupled downward simulation with IO transformations, the definition of non-atomic coupled refinement between failure sets and the proof of soundness of the former with respect to the latter via a transition system definition.

## 5.1   State-Based Definition

We begin by generalising the translate/multiply example. Now the values to translate and multiply by are given as inputs, so the abstract operations become

┌─ *Translate* ────────────────────
│ $\Delta AState$
│ $val? : \mathbb{Z} \times \mathbb{Z}$
├──────────────────────────────────
│ $x'_A = x_A + first\ val?$
│ $y'_A = y_A + snd\ val?$
│ $u'_A = u_A;\ v'_A = v_A$
│ $(first\ val? < 0 < snd\ val?)\vee$
│ $\quad (snd\ val? < 0 < first\ val?)$
└──────────────────────────────────

┌─ *Multiply* ─────────────────────
│ $\Delta AState$
│ $m? : \mathbb{Z}$
├──────────────────────────────────
│ $u'_A = u_A \times m?;\ v'_A = v_A \times m?$
│ $x'_A = x_A;\ y'_A = y_A$
└──────────────────────────────────

To make the example more interesting *Translate* does not accept any input but just those where the two values in the pair *val?* have different signs. As before, in the concrete system we split *Translate* into *TransX* and *TransY*, and *Multiply* into *MultU* and *MultY*. The variable $n$ is used to asure the different signs of $x_C?$ and $y_C?$.

┌─ *CState* ───────────────────────
│ $x_C, y_C, u_c, v_C : \mathbb{Z}$
│ $b, c : \mathbb{B}$
│ $m, n : \mathbb{Z}$
└──────────────────────────────────

┌─ *CInit* ────────────────────────
│ $CState'$
├──────────────────────────────────
│ $x'_C = y'_C = 0;\ u'_C = v'_C = 1$
│ $b' \wedge c'$
└──────────────────────────────────

┌─ *TransX* ───────────────────────
│ $\Delta CState$
│ $x_C? : \mathbb{Z}$
├──────────────────────────────────
│ $c \wedge \neg c'$
│ $x'_C = x_C + x_C?;\ y'_C = y_C;$
│ $u'_C = u_C;\ v'_C = v_C;\ b' = b$
│ $m' = m \wedge (n'\ \text{iff}\ x_C? < 0)$
└──────────────────────────────────

┌─ *TransY* ───────────────────────
│ $\Delta CState$
│ $y_C? : \mathbb{Z}$
├──────────────────────────────────
│ $\neg c \wedge c'$
│ $y'_C = y_C + y_C?;\ x'_C = x_C;$
│ $u'_C = u_C;\ v'_C = v_C;\ b' = b$
│ $m' = m \wedge (n\ \text{iff}\ y_C? > 0)$
└──────────────────────────────────

┌─ *MultU* ────────────────────────
│ $\Delta CState$
│ $m? : \mathbb{Z}$
├──────────────────────────────────
│ $b \wedge \neg b'$
│ $u'_C = u_C \times m?;\ v_C = v'_C;$
│ $x'_C = x_C;\ y'_C = y_C;\ c' = c$
│ $m' = m?;\ n' = n$
└──────────────────────────────────

┌─ *MultV* ────────────────────────
│ $\Delta CState$
├──────────────────────────────────
│ $\neg b \wedge b'$
│ $v'_C = v_C \times m$
│ $u_C = u'_C;\ x'_C = x_C;\ y'_C = y_C;\ c' = c$
│ $n' = n$
└──────────────────────────────────

As discussed in [8] Definition 1 now needs to be augmented with IO transformers in order to verify a non-atomic downward simulation. IO transformers are a mechanism to alter the input and output in an IO refinement. IO refinement [6, 2, 22] generalises the standard simulation rules, which require identities between the concrete and abstract operations' inputs and outputs. In order to allow the types of inputs and outputs to change, IO refinement replaces these identities with arbitrary relations $IT$ and $OT$ between the input and output elements respectively. $IT$ and $OT$ can be seen as retrieve relations between the inputs and outputs, thus allowing these to change under a refinement in a similar way to changing the state space.

$IT$ and $OT$ are written as schemas and called *input and output transformers*. An input transformer for a schema is an operation whose outputs exactly match the schema's inputs, and whose signature is made up of input and output components only; similarly for output transformers. These are applied to the abstract and concrete operations using piping ($\gg$). In addition, Definition 8 uses an overlining operator, which extends componentwise to signatures and schemas: $\overline{x?} = x!, \overline{x!} = x?$. Thus $\overline{IT}$ denotes the schema where all inputs become outputs with the same basename, and all outputs inputs.

To use IO transformers in a non-atomic setting we use mappings from an abstract input to a sequence of concrete inputs representing the inputs needed in the decomposition. The first part of the definition of non-atomic downward simulation with IO transformation given next differs from the previous definition in the following aspects:

- The sequence of concrete operations $COp_1 \, \S \, COp_2$ now has to be matched by an abstract operation $AOp$ with inputs and outputs of $COp_1 \, \S \, COp_2$ transformed according to $IT$ and $OT$,
- the preconditions of $AOp$ and $COp_1$ are also compared via transforming the inputs,
- the third condition requiring the possibility of completing a started refinement now has to take into account that a completion might only be possible for *some* inputs of $COp_2$. In the definition this is captured by *hiding* the input of $COp_2$ (assumed to be $Inp_2$) in the precondition of $COp_2$.

**Definition 8.** *Non-atomic downward simulation with IO transformations A specification $C$ is a non-atomic IO downward simulation of the specification $A$ if there is a retrieve relation $R$ such that every abstract operation $AOp$ is recast into a sequence of concrete operations $COp_1 \, \S \, COp_2$, and for every $COp_1 \, \S \, COp_2$ there is an input transformer $IT$ which is total on the abstract inputs, for every $AOp$ there is a total injective output transformer $OT$, and, in addition to initialisation, the following hold.*

$$\forall \, AState; \; CState; \; CState' \bullet$$
$$R \, \wedge \, (COp_1 \, \S \, COp_2) \Rightarrow \exists \, AState' \bullet R' \wedge (\overline{IT} \gg AOp \gg OT)$$
$$\forall \, AState; \; CState \bullet R \Rightarrow (pre(\overline{IT} \gg AOp) \Longleftrightarrow pre \, COp_1)$$
$$\forall \, AState; \; CState; \; CState' \bullet R \wedge COp_1 \Rightarrow ((pre \, COp_2) \setminus Inp_2)'$$

(The necessity of these conditions on $IT$ and $OT$ are discussed in [2]. In addition, $OT$ being injective ensure that the abstraction operator $\uparrow$ on refusals is well-defined, in particular, a single abstract output cannot be mapped to two or more concrete outputs.)

Now, using the same retrieve relation $R$ as before, we use input transformers to verify the refinement (the necessary output transformers are all the identity). For *Multiply*, an identity input transformer is sufficient, whilst for *Translate* we use

$$
\begin{array}{|l}
\hline
\_IT \underline{\hspace{8cm}} \\
\hline
val? : \mathbb{Z} \times \mathbb{Z};\ x_C!, y_C! : \mathbb{Z} \\
\hline
(x_C!, y_C!) = val? \\
\hline
\end{array}
$$

Definition 8 can be applied, checking, for example,

$$\forall\, AState;\ CState;\ CState' \bullet$$
$$R \wedge (TransX \,\mathbin{\raise0.3ex\hbox{$_9^o$}}\, TransY) \Rightarrow \exists\, AState' \bullet R' \wedge (\overline{IT} \gg Translate)$$

The purpose of the input transformer is clear in this example: $\overline{IT}$ takes in the inputs $x_C?$ and $y_C?$ of *TransX* and *TransY* and turns them into an output *val!* to be used as input for *Translate*. The necessity of hiding the inputs of $COp_2$ in the precondition is also clear in the example: after *TransX* operation *TransY* is only enabled for some inputs, namely either those below or above zero depending on the input to *TransX*.

We now need to generalise Definition 2 (the second part with coupled simulations) to incorporate IO transformers in an analogous fashion. This is described in [8], and as noted requires only a small change in the definition. Essentially there are two differences: the first concerns the relations $R^S$ which now have to record the inputs and outputs of the operations in $S$ (and thus this affects S2). The second is a change in the formulation of condition S3: the input and output transformers have to be applied when completing a sequence and matching it with the abstract operation $AOp$.

**Definition 9.** *Non-atomic coupled downward simulation with IO transformationA specification $C$ is a non-atomic coupled downward simulation of the specification $A$ if there is a retrieve relation $R$ and there are input and output transformers $IT$ and $OT$ showing that $C$ is a non-atomic downward simulation of $A$, and there is a family of simulation relations $R^S$ such that the following hold.*

**C** $R^{\langle\rangle} = R$

**S1** $\forall\, AState, CState, CState' \bullet R^S \wedge COp_1 \Rightarrow \exists\, AState' \bullet \Xi AState \wedge (R^{S^\frown\langle COp_1\rangle})'$

**S2** $\forall\, AState, CState \bullet R^S \wedge COp_1 \in S \Rightarrow (pre\ COp_2) \setminus Inp_2$

**S3** $\forall\, AState, CState, CState' \bullet R^S \wedge COp_2 \Rightarrow$
$$COp_1 \in S \wedge \exists\, AState' \bullet (\overline{IT} \gg AOp \gg OT) \wedge (R^{S \setminus \langle COp_1\rangle})'$$

Now $R^S$ records the effects of part of the concrete operation. With inputs in the concrete operation this necessitates the input being part of the coupled simulation. We can see this in our running example, where the coupled simulations are now:

$R^{\langle TransX \rangle}$ _____
> $AState$; $CState$
> $x_C? : \mathbb{Z}$
>
> ---
>
> $x_A = x_C - x_C?$
> $y_A = y_C$; $u_A = u_C$; $v_A = v_C$
> $\neg c \wedge b$
> $n$ iff $x_C? < 0$

$R^{\langle MultU \rangle}$ _____
> $AState$; $CState$
> $m? : \mathbb{Z}$
>
> ---
>
> $u_A \times m? = u_C$
> $c \wedge \neg b$
> $x_C = x_A$; $y_C = y_A$; $v_C = v_A$
> $m = m?$

$R^{\langle TransX, MultU \rangle}$ _____
> $AState$; $CState$
> $x_C?, m? : \mathbb{Z}$
>
> ---
>
> $x_A = x_C - x_C?$; $u_A \times m? = u_C$; $y_C = y_A$; $v_C = v_A$
> $\neg c \wedge \neg b$; $m = m?$; $n$ iff $x_C? < 0$

Then, to check S2, we would need to check, for example, that

$$R^{\langle TransX, MultU \rangle} \wedge TransX \in \langle TransX, MultU \rangle \Rightarrow (\text{pre } TransY) \setminus (y_C?)$$

and upon calculation we find that $(\text{pre } TransY) \setminus (y_C?) = [\, CState \mid \neg c \,]$ which is in fact implied by $R^{\langle TransX, MultU \rangle}$. Similarly, for S3, we need to check

$$R^{\langle TransX, MultU \rangle} \wedge TransY \Rightarrow$$
$$TransX \in \langle TransX, MultU \rangle \wedge \exists AState' \bullet (\overline{IT} \gg Translate) \wedge (R^{\langle MultU \rangle})'$$

thus we calculate

$R^{\langle TransX, MultU \rangle} \wedge TransY$ _____
> $AState$; $\Delta CState$
> $x_C?, y_C?, m? : \mathbb{Z}$
>
> ---
>
> $x_A = x_C - x_C?$
> $u_A \times m? = u_C$
> $\neg c \wedge \neg b \wedge c'$
> $y_C = y_A$; $v_C = v_A$; $y_C' = y_C + y_C?$
> $x_C' = x_C$; $u_C' = u_C$
> $b' = b$; $m = m?$
> $n$ iff $(y_C? > 0)$; $n$ iff $(x_C? < 0)$

$(\overline{IT} \gg Translate) \wedge (R^{\langle MultU \rangle})'$
> $\Delta AState$; $CState'$
> $x_C?, y_C?, m? : \mathbb{Z}$
>
> ---
>
> $x_A' = x_C' = x_A + x_C?$
> $y_A' = y_C' = y_A + y_C?$
> $u_A' \times m? = u_C'$; $u_A' = u_A$
> $v_A' = v_A = v_C'$
> $(x_C? < 0 < y_C?) \vee$
> $\quad (y_C? < 0 < x_C?)$
> $c' \wedge \neg b'$
> $m' = m?$

Applying $\exists AState'$ to the right schema we see that the implication required by S3 holds.

## 5.2   Transition Systems and Failures Definition

With this definition in place we then need to generalise the definition of non-atomic refinement on failure sets and transition systems. We start with the latter.

We thus amend Definition 7 to include IO transformers. To do so we must first adapt Definition 5 (semantics of Z specifications). The purpose of Definition 5 was to motivate our definition of traces and failures of a specification in order to prove the soundness of non-atomic refinement. In a specification without input or output this is straightforward, but is less so when we have, specifically, non-deterministic outputs. Therefore we first generalise Definition 5, which is straightforward, we then discuss how the failures (and traces) can be derived. The transition system definition is straightforward since a state change between $q$ and $q'$ due to an operation $Op$ with input $i$ and output $o$ is modelled as a transition $q \xrightarrow{Op.i.o} q'$. Thus we change the set the transition system is labelled over, and to do so we assume for simplicity that all operations have input of type $Input$ and output of type $Output$. The update to Definition 5 is thus.

**Definition 10.** *Let $S = (State, Init, \{Op\}_{i \in I})$ be a Z specification. The operational semantics of $S$, $T(S)$, is given by a transition system $(Q, In, \rightarrow)$ labelled over $\{Op_i.in.out \mid i \in I, in \in Input, out \in Output\}$ such that $Q = State$, $In = Init$ and $q \xrightarrow{Op_i.in.out} q'$ iff a state change between $q$ and $q'$ occurs due to $Op_i$ with input $in$ and output $out$.*

Note: the wording *a state change between $q$ and $q'$ occurs due to $Op_i$ with input in and output out* can, if necessary, be formalised in terms of changes to the state alone by embedding input and output into that state. Such an approach is detailed in [25, 7], however, it is not necessary to use that level of formality here.

The traces of the system will simply be the traces arising from the transitions. The refusals are slightly more complicated. A consequence of including outputs in the events is that the traditional Z precondition, which excludes outputs, does not tell us whether a particular event is possible – only whether an event with *some* output value is possible for a particular input and before-state.

The obvious case is easy: for a given input $i$ and state $q$, if these lie outside the precondition of an operation $Op$, then $Op.i.o$ will be refused for all possible outputs $o$. However, if an operation is applied in a state and input inside its precondition, there can also be refusals if the operation contains non-deterministic choice of outputs. In particular, since the environment cannot influence the output, there are refusals of "possible" output values due to another output value being chosen. Thus the process can refuse all but one of the possible outputs. So $Op.i.o$ will be in a refusal set $E$ if there is another possible output $o_2$ ($\neq o$) which is not in $E$. Hence the refusals (in a particular state $q$) are characterised by:

$$Op.i.o \in E \Rightarrow \neg \exists\, q' \bullet q \xrightarrow{Op.i.o} q' \vee$$
$$(\exists\, q'' \bullet q \xrightarrow{Op.i.o} q'' \wedge (\exists\, o_2 \neq o;\ q' \bullet \xrightarrow{Op.i.o_2} q' \wedge Op.i.o_2 \notin E))$$

And this characterisation defines the failures of a specification. For a further discussion of this issue see [21].

At the level of transition systems, IO transformers are best viewed as sets of bindings, and we write $((i_1, i_2), i) \in IT$ whenever $IT$ as a schema transforms an abstract input $i$ into $i_1$ and $i_2$ for consumption by the concrete operations. Similarly for the output transformers.

**Definition 11.** *A transition system $T_C = (Q_C, In_C, \rightarrow_C)$ is a non-atomic coupled downward simulation of a transition system $T_A = (Q_A, In_A, \rightarrow_A)$ (denoted $T_A \sqsubseteq_{tna} T_C$) if there is a relation $R \subseteq Q_A \times Q_C$ satisfying the following*

1. $\forall q_0 \in In_C \bullet \exists q_0' \in In_A \bullet (q_0', q_0) \in R$,
2. $\forall (q_1, q_2) \in R \bullet \forall q_2' \in Q_C \bullet \forall i_1, i_2, , o_1, o_2 \bullet q_2 \xrightarrow{COp_1.i_1.o_1 \, COp_2.i_2.o_2} q_2' \Rightarrow$
   $\exists q_1' \in Q_A \bullet \exists i, o \bullet q_1 \xrightarrow{AOp.i.o} q_1'$ *and* $(q_1', q_2') \in R \wedge ((i_1, i_2), i) \in IT$,
   $((o_1, o_2), o) \in OT$,
3. $\forall (q_1, q_2) \in R \bullet \forall i_1, i_2, i \bullet$
   $(\exists o_1 \bullet q_2 \xrightarrow{COp_1.i_1.o_1}) \Longleftrightarrow (\exists o, i_2 \bullet q_1 \xrightarrow{AOp.i.o} \wedge((i_1, i_2), i) \in IT)$
4. $\forall q_1 \in ran\, R \bullet \forall q_1' \in Q_C \bullet \forall i_1, o_1 \bullet q_1 \xrightarrow{COp_1.i_1.o_1} q_1' \Rightarrow \exists i_2, o_2 \bullet$
   $q_1' \xrightarrow{COp_2.i_2.o_2}$,

*and there is a family of relations $P^T \subseteq Q_A \times Q_C$, $T \in \gamma^*$, such that, in addition, we have:*

**C** $P^{\langle\rangle} = R$,
**S1** $\forall (q_1, q_2) \in P^T \bullet \forall q_2' \in Q_C \bullet \forall i_1, o_1 \bullet$
   $q_2 \xrightarrow{COp_1.i_1.o_1} q_2' \Rightarrow \exists q_1' \bullet q_1 = q_1' \wedge (q_1', q_2') \in P^{T^\frown \langle COp_1.i_1.o_1 \rangle}$,
**S2** $\forall (q_1, q_2) \in P^T \bullet \forall i_1, o_1 \bullet COp_1.i_1.o_1 \in T \Rightarrow \exists i_2, o_2 \bullet q_2 \xrightarrow{COp_2.i_2.o_2}$,
**S3** $\forall (q_1, q_2) \in P^T \bullet \forall q_2' \in Q_C \bullet \forall i_2, o_2 \bullet q_2 \xrightarrow{COp_2.i_2.o_2} q_2' \Longrightarrow$
   $\exists i_1, o_1 \bullet \exists q_1' \in Q_A \bullet \exists i, o \bullet COp_1.i_1.o_1 \in T \wedge q_1 \xrightarrow{AOp.i.o} q_1' \wedge$
   $(q_1', q_2') \in P^{T \backslash \langle COp_1.i_1.o_1 \rangle} \wedge ((i_1, i_2), i) \in IT \wedge ((o_1, o_2), o) \in OT$.

Notice that in this definition, relations $P^T$ are between states only, whereas in the schema calculus formulation, the coupled simulations $R^S$ contain input and output in their signature. This apparent difference is resolved by noting the values used for input and output are recorded in $T$, this prevents the need for complicated technicalities in defining $P^{T^\frown \langle COp_1 \rangle}$ in terms of $P^T$. We now state Theorem 2 in the context of operations containing input and output (proof omitted due to lack of space).

**Theorem 5.** *Let $A$, $C$ be Z specifications. Then*

$$A \sqsubseteq_{na} C \Leftrightarrow T(A) \sqsubseteq_{tna} T(C) .$$

We now generalise the definition of non-atomic failures refinement to incorporate i/o and their transformations in order to prove Theorem 3 in the context of i/o. (The theorem is given for one operation, the quantifiers over $i$ being used for quantification over input.) We assume here that the input transformer $IT$ is total on the abstract inputs, and the inverse of $IT$ is a partial, surjective function, and $OT$ is an injective function.

**Definition 12.** *A set of failures $\mathcal{F}_C$ is a non-atomic coupled refinement of a set of failures $\mathcal{F}_A$ (denoted $\mathcal{F}_A \sqsubseteq_{fna} \mathcal{F}_C$) if the following hold:*

1. $\forall (tr, X) \in \mathcal{F}_C \bullet tr \in Comp(\mathcal{T}_C) \Rightarrow (tr\!\uparrow, X\!\uparrow) \in \mathcal{F}_A$,

2. $\forall (tr, X) \in \mathcal{F}_C \bullet \forall i_1, o_1 \bullet \forall tr_1, tr_2 \bullet tr = tr_1 \frown \langle COp_1.i_1.o_1 \rangle \frown tr_2 \wedge \forall i_2, o_2 \bullet COp_2.i_2.o_2 \notin ran\, tr_2 \Rightarrow \exists i_2, o_2 \bullet COp_2.i_2.o_2 \notin X$,

3. $\forall i_2, o_2 \bullet tr \frown \langle COp_2.i_2.o_2 \rangle \in \mathcal{T}_C \Rightarrow \exists tr_1, tr_2 \bullet \exists i_1, o_1 \bullet tr = tr_1 \frown \langle COp_1.i_1.o_1 \rangle \frown tr_2 \wedge COp_2.i_2.o_2 \notin ran\, tr_2$.

Where the abstraction operators are defined by (again the definition is given for single decomposition to aid readability) the following.

$$tr\!\uparrow = (tr \restriction \{COp_2.i_2.o_2\})[COp_2.i_2.o_2 \mapsto AOp.i.o \text{ iff}$$
$$\exists l, k \bullet l \le k \wedge tr[k] = COp_2.i_2.o_2 \wedge \exists i_1, o_1 \bullet ((i_1, i_2), i) \in IT$$
$$\wedge((o_1, o_2), o) \in OT \wedge tr[l] = COp_1.i_1.o_1 \wedge$$
$$\forall p \bullet l \le p \le k, \forall i, o \bullet tr[l] \ne COp_1.i.o]$$
$$X\!\uparrow = (X \setminus \{COp_2.i_2.o_2\})[COp_1.i_1.o_1 \mapsto AOp.i.o \text{ iff}$$
$$\exists i, i_2 \bullet ((i_1, i_2), i) \in IT \wedge \exists o, o_2 \bullet ((o_1, o_2), o) \in OT]$$

and the definition of completed traces remains as before. Given these definitions the analogue of Theorem 3 holds.

**Theorem 6.** *Let* $T_A$, $T_C$ *be transition systems.*

$$T_A \sqsubseteq_{tna} T_C \Rightarrow \mathcal{F}(T_A) \sqsubseteq_{fna} \mathcal{F}(T_C) \,.$$

The proof follows that of Theorem 3 but is - due to lack of space - omitted here.

Our running example illustrates some of the components defined above. For example, the coupled simulation $R^{\langle TransX, MultU \rangle}$ defines coupled simulations on the transition system with, e.g., $((0, 0, 1, 1), (-3, 0, 7, 1)) \in P^{\langle TransX.-3, MultU.7 \rangle}$. S3 can be illustrated on the transition system by noting that

$$\forall q_2' \bullet (-3, 0, 7, 1) \xrightarrow{TransY.i_2} q_2' \Longrightarrow$$
$$TransX. - 3 \in T \wedge \exists q_1' \bullet q_1 \xrightarrow{Translate.(-3, i_2)} q_1' \wedge (q_1', q_2') \in P^{\langle MultU.7 \rangle}$$

We can also calculate some of the failures. For example, $(\langle TransX. - 3, MultU.7, TransY.4, MultV \rangle, \{TransY.2, MultV\}) \in \mathcal{F}_C$ and we note that

$$\langle TransX. - 3, MultU.7, TransY.4, MultV \rangle \uparrow = \langle Translate.(-3, 4), Multiply.7 \rangle$$
$$\{TransY.2, MultV\} \uparrow = \varnothing$$

and find as expected that $(\langle Translate.(-3, 4), Multiply.7 \rangle, \varnothing) \in \mathcal{F}_A$.

Finally, Theorem 4 without change carries over to the case of input/output transformers since the proof is independent of the particular alphabet of events used (thus it makes no difference whether the events carry parameters or not).

# 6    Conclusions

In this paper we have related notions of non-atomic refinement in a state-based setting with that in a behavioural setting. In doing so, we took the definition of coupled simulation as defined in [8] and proved it was sound with respect to a definition of non-atomic failures refinement defined in Section 3. This proof of soundness was subsequently extended to the most general case of input and output and their transformations.

Of course there have been numerous attempts to define non-atomic refinement (viz. *action refinement*) in a process algebraic setting. The general difference between process algebraic definitions and our work is that in process algebras action refinement is an *operator* of the language (like choice or parallel composition) whereas here we define a *relation* between specifications. Instead of constructing the refinement out of an abstract process we only check whether two processes are in a refinement relationship.

While a lot of approaches in process algebras do not allow overlapping of refinements of sequential abstract actions (e.g. [1, 24]) there are also proposals for non-strict action refinement [19, 13]. Out of these the work closest to us is [19] where the possible overlaps are determined by apriori given *action dependencies*: independent actions are allowed to overlap in refinements. In our setting action dependencies could be derived from the operation schemas: two operations are independent if the set of variables they change are disjoint. Similarly to [19] such operations are allowed to commute in the refinement; this is - however - not defined via dependencies but via the existence of a coupled simulation and the requirement of finding a matching operation in the abstract specification.

Work relating state-based and behavioural notions of refinement are also not new. Work in this vein goes back to [15, 14, 26]. More recent work includes [21, 3, 7, 4]. The latter looks at some of the issues explicit in integrating formal specification languages. The standard result [7] which we extend in this paper is the soundness of downward simulation with respect to failures-divergences refinement. The full result is that data refinement (as given in, e.g., [7]) is sound and complete with respect to failures-divergences refinement under a correspondence between data types and processes which relates the two in an obvious fashion (e.g., relating operations to events). This gives two obvious directions that our work could be extended in. The first is to incorporate internal events into our discussion, and thus treat divergence and CSP in its entirety. The second is to define non-atomic coupled upward simulations, and demonstrate its soundness and, with downwards, its joint completeness. These are left as future work.

# References

1. L. Aceto. *Action Refinement in Process Algebras*. CUP, London, 1992.
2. E. A. Boiten and J. Derrick. IO-refinement in Z. In A. Evans, D. J. Duke, and T. Clark, editors, *3rd BCS-FACS Northern Formal Methods Workshop*. Springer-Verlag, September 1998. http://www.ewic.org.uk/.
3. C. Bolton and J. Davies. A Singleton Failures Semantics for Communicating Sequential Processes. *Formal Aspects of Computing*, 2002. Under consideration.
4. C. Bolton and J. Davies. Refinement in Object-Z and CSP. In M. Butler, L. Petre, and K. Sere, editors, *Integrated Formal Methods (IFM 2002)*, volume 2335 of *Lecture Notes in Computer Science*, pages 225–244. Springer-Verlag, 2002.

5. J. Derrick and E. Boiten. Non-atomic refinement in Z. In J. Woodcock and J. Wing, editors, *FM'99, World Congress on Formal Methods*, number 1709 in LNCS, pages 1477–1496. Springer, 1999.
6. J. Derrick and E. A. Boiten. *Refinement in Z and Object-Z*. Springer-Verlag, 2001.
7. J. Derrick and E.A. Boiten. Relational concurrent refinement. *Formal Aspects of Computing*, 15(2-3):182–214, November 2003.
8. J. Derrick and H. Wehrheim. Using coupled simulations in non-atomic refinement. In *ZB 2003: Formal Specification and Development in Z and B*, number 2651 in LNCS, pages 127–147. Springer, 2003.
9. C. Fischer. CSP-OZ - a combination of CSP and Object-Z. In H. Bowman and J. Derrick, editors, *Second IFIP International conference on Formal Methods for Open Object-based Distributed Systems*, pages 423–438. Chapman & Hall, July 1997.
10. C. Fischer. How to combine Z with a process algebra. In *ZUM'98: The Z Formal Specification Notation*, volume 1493 of *Lecture Notes in Computer Science*, pages 5–23. Springer-Verlag, September 1998.
11. A. Galloway and W. Stoddart. An operational semantics for ZCCS. In M. G. Hinchey and Shaoying Liu, editors, *First International Conference on Formal Engineering Methods (ICFEM'97)*, pages 272–282, Hiroshima, Japan, November 1997. IEEE Computer Society Press.
12. Jifeng He. Process simulation and refinement. *Formal Aspects of Computing*, 1:229–241, 1989.
13. Wil Janssen, Mannes Poel, and Job Zwiers. Actions systems and action refinement in the development of parallel systems. In J. C. M. Baeten and J. F. Groote, editors, *Concur '91*, volume 527 of *LNCS*, pages 298–316. Springer, 1991.
14. He Jifeng. Process refinement. In J. McDermid, editor, *The Theory and Practice of Refinement*. Butterworths, 1989.
15. M. B. Josephs. A state-based approach to communicating processes. *Distributed Computing*, 3:9–18, 1988.
16. B.P. Mahony and J.S. Dong. Blending Object-Z and timed CSP: An introduction to TCOZ. In K. Futatsugi, R. Kemmerer, and K. Torii, editors, *20th International Conference on Software Engineering (ICSE'98)*. IEEE Press, 1998.
17. J. Parrow and P. Sjödin. Multiway Synchronisation Verified with Coupled Simulation. In R. Cleaveland, editor, *CONCUR '92, Concurrency Theory*, number 630 in LNCS, pages 518–533. Springer, 1992.
18. A. Rensink. Action Contraction. In C. Palamidessi, editor, *CONCUR 2000 - Concurrency Theory*, number 1877 in LNCS, pages 290–304. Springer, 2000.
19. Arend Rensink and Heike Wehrheim. Dependency-based action refinement. In P. Ruzicka, editor, *MFCS'97 Mathematical Foundations of Computer Science*, number 1295 in LNCS. Springer, 1997.
20. A. W. Roscoe. *The Theory and Practice of Concurrency*. 1998.
21. G. Smith and J. Derrick. Specification, refinement and verification of concurrent systems - an integration of Object-Z and CSP. *Formal Methods in Systems Design*, 18:249–284, May 2001.
22. S. Stepney, D. Cooper, and J. C. P. Woodcock. More powerful data refinement in Z. In J. P. Bowen, A. Fett, and M. G. Hinchey, editors, *ZUM'98: The Z Formal Specification Notation*, volume 1493 of *Lecture Notes in Computer Science*, pages 284–307. Springer-Verlag, September 1998.
23. H. Treharne and S. Schneider. Using a process algebra to control B operations. In K. Araki, A. Galloway, and K. Taguchi, editors, *International Conference on Integrated Formal Methods 1999 (IFM'99)*, pages 437–456, York, July 1999. Springer.

24. R. van Glabbeek and U. Goltz. Equivalence notions for concurrent systems and refinement of actions. In A. Kreczmar and G. Mirkowska, editors, *Mathematical Foundations of Computer Science 1989*, volume 379 of *LNCS*, pages 237–248. Springer, 1989.

25. J. C. P. Woodcock and J. Davies. *Using Z: Specification, Refinement, and Proof.* Prentice Hall, 1996.

26. J. C. P. Woodcock and C. C. Morgan. Refinement of state-based concurrent systems. In D. Bjorner, C. A. R. Hoare, and H. Langmaack, editors, *VDM'90: VDM and Z!- Formal Methods in Software Development*, volume 428 of *Lecture Notes in Computer Science*. Springer-Verlag, 1990.

# Process Refinement in B

Steve Dunne and Stacey Conroy

School of Computing, University of Teesside,
Middlesbrough, TS1 3BA, UK
{s.e.dunne, s.conroy}@tees.ac.uk

**Abstract.** We describe various necessary and sufficient conditions with which to augment B's existing refinement proof obligations for forward and backward refinement in order to capture within the B Method a variety of CSP process refinement relations, including most significantly that of failures-divergences which provides the standard denotational semantics of CSP processes.

## 1 Introduction

In recent years there has been increasing interest in combining state-based formalisms with process algebras. This is exemplified inside the B community particularly by the work of Schneider and Treharne *et al* [36, 31, 37, 32] integrating B [1] with CSP [20, 27]. Over the same period researchers in the theoretical underpinnings of refinement like Bolton and Davies [6, 5] and Derrick and Boiten [11, 12, 13], have been exploring the semantic relationship between data refinement in a state-based formalism such as Z [35, 40] and the various notions of process refinement in a process algebra formalism such as CSP.

However, Z has certain disadvantages in comparison to B as a state-based formalism in this sort of work. The main one is that traditionally when using Z to specify an abstract data type the operations are described simply by operation schemas, where such a schema is essentially just an alphabetised before-after relation. This means an *a priori* decision has to be made, between the so-called "blocking" and "non-blocking" (*i.e.* aborting) interpretations, about how to interpret the invoking of such an operation outside its domain. In B we can formulate operations with both guards and preconditions so we face no such decision about interpretations. Indeed since guards and preconditions can coexist in the same operation, B operations are capable of simultaneously bearing both interpretations.

One of the factors inhibiting an investigation of B refinement *versus* process refinement till recently was a recognition that B's refinement theory was incomplete since it was based only on forward simulation, but this obstacle has now been overcome by [16]. In this paper we capitalise on [16] to derive necessary and sufficient conditions for modelling in B a variety of process refinement relations, but most significantly, perhaps, the standard refinement relation for CSP of failures-divergences. In Section 2 we review the semantic connections variously

H. Treharne et al. (Eds.): ZB 2005, LNCS 3455, pp. 45–64, 2005.

established over the last 18 years or so between state-based and process-algebraic descriptions of system behaviours. In Section 3 we summarise CSP refinement concepts. In Section 4 we discuss the interpretation of abstract machines in B as abstract systems and thence as CSP processes, and in Section 5 we present a complete theory of data refinement for B. In Section 6 we at last reach our key results establishing the various particular extra pairs of refinement conditions by which in B we can model the different varieties of CSP process refinement described in Section 3.

We should note that all three anonymous reviewers of the draft version of this paper justifiably criticised it for providing only informal proofs of all its main propositions. We confess we have not found it possible to develop formal proofs within the timescale for preparing the final camera-ready version, and that this deficiency therefore remains in it. Even an informal proof can have some utility, though, providing the argument it makes is in some degree convincing. We hope the reader will entertain our informal proofs in such a spirit, as at least providing some measure of justification of the likely validity of our propositions.

## 2   Processes Versus Abstract Data Types

A duality has long been recognised between the algebraic description of the behaviour of a concurrent process in a formalism such as CSP, and its alternative state-based description, for example as a labelled transition system (LTS) [38], action system [4], abstract data type (ADT) [11, 30] or Object-Z class [33]. Among the first explicit state-based characterisations of a behavioural process to achieve prominence were those of Josephs [23] describing how a non-divergent CSP process could be represented as an LTS, and of He [18, 19] who developed a similar state-based relational process model which did accommodate divergence. The motivation in both cases was to provide a state-based process model in respect of which it would be possible to adapt He *et al*'s ADT refinement proof methods of forward and backward simulation [22] to the failures-divergences refinement of processes.

Soon afterwards Morgan [25] showed how to interpret an action system as a CSP process by describing precisely how to derive its failures and divergences from its wp semantics. What is particularly striking about Morgan's approach is the way the phenomenon of divergence is embraced so uniformly by it; the wp semantics handles divergence at no extra cost, so to speak. This is in marked contrast to the approaches for example in [11] and [30] whereby divergence is accommodated within the relational semantics of an ADT only by introducing an artificial 'bottom' element $\perp$ into its state space, which compromises the homogeneity of that space and thus considerably complicates the model.

Woodcock and Morgan [41] used the action-system representation of processes in [25] to formulate wp-based sound and jointly complete proof obligations for failures-divergences refinement by exploiting the same proof methods from [22] as Josephs and He each had done. But while they are certainly theoretically significant [41]'s proof obligations have limited utility for practical system development, since they are formulated as higher-order conditions involving quantification over all postconditions and thus in most cases intractable.

Until quite recently the accepted but mistaken wisdom among many researchers, as seen for example in [7, 11, 17, 34], was that Josephs' results in [23] imply that, for blocking[1] ADTs at least, a complete notion of ADT refinement based on both forward (downward simulation) and backward (upward simulation) refinement equates to failures refinement.

The misapprehension was finally exposed by Bolton and Davies [5, 6] and subsequently acknowledged by other recanters [12, 13, 14]. The error arose from a mistranslation into the context of ADTs of one of Josephs' LTS upward simulation conditions which was mistakenly taken to be required only respectively of each corresponding concrete/abstract operation pair, whereas Josephs' condition in question is actually a single global one simultaneously involving all abstract and concrete operations.

## 3    Process Refinement in CSP

CSP processes have a standard denotational semantics based on *failures* and *divergences*.[2]

A *trace* of a process $P$ is a finite sequence of events of its alphabet in which after its inception it is observed to engage. The set of all traces of $P$ is denoted traces($P$). In particular, for any process $P$ the empty trace $\langle \rangle$ belongs to traces($P$).

We consider that a process $P$ evolves after its inception as it engages in successive events. A *refusal set* of $P$ at any stage of its evolution is a set of events in all of which it is observed at that stage to decline to engage. Refusal sets are subset-closed in the sense that in any situation where $X$ is a refusal set of $P$ then any $Y$ where $Y \subseteq X$ is also a refusal set of $P$. In particular, a process can always refuse an empty set of events, so $\{\}$ is always a refusal set of $P$.

A *failure* of $P$ is a pair $(tr, X)$, where $tr$ is a trace of and $X$ a refusal set of $P$, such that $P$ is observed to engage after its inception in the events of $tr$ and then decline to engage in any event in $X$. The set of failures of $P$, denoted failures($P$), is therefore a relation between traces and refusal sets. The domain of this relation is traces($P$). In particular, for any $tr$ where $tr \in$ traces($P$) we have that $(tr, \{\}) \in$ failures($P$).

A *divergence* of $P$ is a trace of $P$ after engaging in which $P$ may descend into irretrievably pathological behaviour, so that it may engage in or decline any event of its alphabet, or even livelock by engaging in an indefinite sequence of internal actions and so fail to reach any further stable observable state at all. The set of divergences of $P$ is denoted divergences($P$).

---

[1] That is, ones whose partial operations are interpreted as being disenabled, or blocked, outside the domains of their characterising relations.

[2] If unbounded nondeterminism is admitted then *infinite traces* are also required to differentiate certain processes, but we ignore such distinctions in this paper.

**Traces Refinement.** The coarsest notion of refinement in CSP is traces refinement $\sqsubseteq_T$. A process $P$ is traces-refined by process $Q$ if every trace of $Q$ is also a trace of $P$:

$$P \sqsubseteq_T Q \quad \Leftrightarrow \quad \text{traces}(Q) \subseteq \text{traces}(P)$$

**Failures Refinement.** Traces refinement is adequate for distinguishing between deterministic processes, but for distinguishing between nondeterministic ones, even in the absence of divergence, we need the finer notion of failures refinement $\sqsubseteq_F$. A process $P$ is failures-refined by process $Q$ if every failure of $Q$ is also a failure of $P$:

$$P \sqsubseteq_F Q \quad \Leftrightarrow \quad \text{failures}(Q) \subseteq \text{failures}(P)$$

**Failures-Divergences Refinement.** If we admit divergent processes we must also take into account the divergences of each process when distinguishing between them, giving failures-divergences refinement $\sqsubseteq_{FD}$. A process $P$ is failures-divergences-refined by process $Q$ if every failure of $Q$ is also a failure of $P$, and every divergence of $Q$ is also a divergence of $P$:

$$P \sqsubseteq_{FD} Q \quad \Leftrightarrow \quad \text{failures}(Q) \subseteq \text{failures}(P) \ \wedge \ \text{divergences}(Q) \subseteq \text{divergences}(P)$$

Milner [24] points out that the failures model [and hence by extension to divergent processes, the failures-divergences model too] "...has a special place in concurrency theory; it is, precisely, the weakest congruence which respects deadlock." Clearly, traces, failures and failures-divergences refinement make successively finer distinctions between processes.

**Traces-Divergences Refinement.** We can define other refinement relations intermediate between those above. For example, [30] features traces-divergences refinement $\sqsubseteq_{TD}$, whereby a process $P$ is traces-divergences-refined by process $Q$ if every trace of $Q$ is also a trace of $P$, and every divergence of $Q$ is also a divergence of $P$:

$$P \sqsubseteq_{TD} Q \quad \Leftrightarrow \quad \text{traces}(Q) \subseteq \text{traces}(P) \ \wedge \ \text{divergences}(Q) \subseteq \text{divergences}(P)$$

Clearly, $\sqsubseteq_{TD}$ is strictly intermediate between $\sqsubseteq_T$ and $\sqsubseteq_{FD}$, although it is incomparable with $\sqsubseteq_F$.

**Singleton-Failures Refinement.** Bolton and Davies [5] introduce the notion of the *singleton failures* of a process. A singleton failure is a failure $(tr, X)$ such that the refusal set $X$ is either empty or a singleton. The singleton failures of a process $P$, which we denote singletonfailures$(P)$, are therefore a subset of its failures. They define singleton-failures refinement $\sqsubseteq_{SF}$ as follows: a process $P$ is singleton-failures-refined by process $Q$ if every singleton failure of $Q$ is also a singleton failure of $P$:

$$P \sqsubseteq_{SF} Q \quad \Leftrightarrow \quad \mathrm{singletonfailures}(Q) \subseteq \mathrm{singletonfailures}(P)$$

Clearly, $\sqsubseteq_{SF}$ is strictly intermediate between $\sqsubseteq_T$ and $\sqsubseteq_F$.

**Completed-Traces Refinement.** We may be particularly interested in knowing which traces of a process $P$ may lead to deadlock. We can identify such traces, called the *complete traces* of $P$, by examining $P$'s failure relation for failures of the form $(tr, \Sigma)$ where $\Sigma$ is the entire alphabet of $P$. Any trace $tr$ which appears in such a failure is in this sense a complete trace. We denote the set of complete traces of $P$ by completetraces($P$). Then completed-traces refinement $\sqsubseteq_{CT}$ is defined as follows: a process $P$ is completed-traces-refined by process $Q$ if every trace of $Q$ is also a trace of $P$, and every complete trace of $Q$ is also a complete trace of $P$:

$$P \sqsubseteq_{CT} Q \quad \Leftrightarrow \quad \mathrm{traces}(Q) \subseteq \mathrm{traces}(P) \ \wedge$$
$$\mathrm{completetraces}(Q) \subseteq \mathrm{completetraces}(P)$$

Clearly, $\sqsubseteq_{CT}$ like $\sqsubseteq_{SF}$ is also strictly intermediate between $\sqsubseteq_T$ and $\sqsubseteq_F$, although it isn't comparable with $\sqsubseteq_{SF}$.

**Failuretraces Refinement.** Even in the absence of divergence we can still define other notions of refinement strictly finer than failures refinement. Failuretraces refinement [38] compares processes on the basis of observations of their behaviour which involve testing for refusals before every event the process engages in, as well as after the final event in the course of the observation. It essentially captures the *refusals testing* semantics of processes [26]. Interestingly, this rather than failures semantics underlies the semantics of timed CSP [29], in the sense that if time is disregarded the latter reduces to refusals-testing semantics.

We define a *failuretrace* is as a pair $(X_0, ftr)$ where $X_0$ is a refusal set and $ftr$ is a finite sequence of pairs of the form $(a, X)$ where $a$ is an event and $X$ is a refusal set. A failuretrace can therefore be pictured as a pseudo-sequence of the form $\langle\!\langle X_0, a_1, X_1, a_2, X_2, a_3, X_3, \ldots, a_n, X_n \rangle\!\rangle$ where the $X_i$ are refusal sets and the $a_i$ are events. It represents an observation of behaviour of a process in which immediately after its inception the process has refused the events $X_0$, then engaged in $a_1$, then refused $X_1$, then engaged in $a_2$, then refused $X_2$, and so on. We denote the set of failuretraces of a process $P$ by failuretraces($P$). We say a process $P$ is failuretraces-refined by $Q$, written $P \sqsubseteq_{FT} Q$, if the failuretraces of $Q$ are a subset of those of $P$. That is,

$$P \sqsubseteq_{FT} Q \quad \Leftrightarrow \quad \mathrm{failuretraces}(Q) \subseteq \mathrm{failuretraces}(P)$$

Every ordinary failure $(\langle a_1, a_2, a_3, \ldots, a_n \rangle, X)$ of a process is represented in its failuretraces by the failuretrace $\langle\!\langle \{\}, a_1, \{\}, a_2, \{\}, a_3, \{\}, \ldots, a_n, X \rangle\!\rangle$. Hence failuretraces refinement implies failures refinement.

**Failuretraces-Divergences Refinement.** We can extend failuretraces refinement in the obvious way to encompass divergence, by defining failuretraces-divergences refinement $\sqsubseteq_{FTD}$ so that

$$P \sqsubseteq_{FTD} Q \quad \Leftrightarrow \quad \text{failuretraces}(Q) \subseteq \text{failuretraces}(P) \ \wedge$$
$$\text{divergences}(Q) \subseteq \text{divergences}(P)$$

In Fig. 1 we summarise the relativities between these various notions of process refinement.

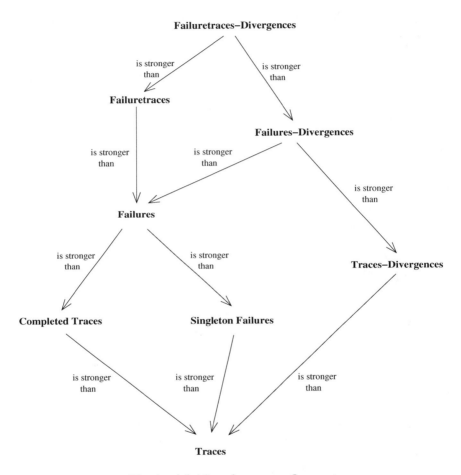

**Fig. 1.** A lattice of process refinements

## 4    Event B

If an abstract machine is to be implementable in conventional B all its operations need to be feasible, but Abrial [2] and Butler and Waldén [10] show that abstract machines with infeasible (*i.e.* non-trivially guarded) operations can nevertheless be useful in modelling the behaviour of distributed systems. Abrial coined the term *abstract system* for such a machine, redesignating its operations as *events*.

The theory of Event B, as this event-driven interpretation of B machines as abstract systems has come to be known, has been subsequently further developed, supported and exploited in [8, 3, 39, 9].

In effect a B abstract system is a species of action system. In Abrial's original formulation of an abstract system the operation preconditions of an ordinary B machine are entirely replaced by event guards, so the system cannot behave abortively because there are no preconditions to be contravened. However, there is no reason in principle why guards and preconditions cannot coexist in an event of an abstract system, as indeed they do in other formulations of action systems, and we will therefore allow this. For us then, an abstract system is just an abstract machine whose operations may be infeasible, which is not intended to be implemented in conventional B terms but rather whose purpose is to model event-driven process behaviour, the operations of the machine being identified with the events of the process being modelled. Moreover, since we interpret an abstract machine as an abstract system, which is itself just a species of action system, we can by virtue of [25] also interpret it as a CSP process. In particular, the abortive behaviour of an abstract machine provoked by invoking any of its operations outside its termination precondition would manifest as divergence in the corresponding CSP process.

Let $S$ be the generalised substitution which constitutes the body of an operation $e$ of such an abstract machine. Then the event $e$ is only enabled when $S$ is feasible, and will provoke divergence if it occurs outside $S$'s realm of guaranteed termination. That is, the guard of the corresponding event $e$ will be fis($S$) and its realm of non-divergence characterised by trm($S$)[3].

## 4.1    How to Interpret a B Abstract Machine as a CSP Process

Here we adapt the formulation of traces, divergences and failures of an action system given in [25] in terms of our B concepts of trm and fis of operations. This enables us to describe exactly how to deduce the traces, divergences and failures of a B abstract machine.

**Traces of an Abstract Machine.** A sequence $\langle e_1, e_2 \ldots e_n \rangle$ of operations of an abstract machine $M$ with initialisation *init* is a trace of $M$ if the sequential composition of $M$'s initialisation with this sequence of operations is feasible: that is, precisely if

$$\text{fis}(\mathit{init} \; ; \; e_1 \; ; \; e_2 \; ; \ldots ; \; e_n)    \text{holds.}$$

**Divergences of an Abstract Machine.** A divergence of an abstract machine $M$ is a sequence $\langle e_1, e_2 \ldots e_n \rangle$ of operations of $M$ such that the sequential composition of $M$'s initialisation with this sequence of operations may not terminate: that is, precisely if

---

[3] Recall if $[S]Q$ denotes the weakest precondition for $S$ to establish the postcondition $Q$, then, as defined in [1, 15], fis($S$) $=_{df} \neg [S]$false and trm($S$) $=_{df} [S]$true.

$\neg\,\mathrm{trm}\,(\,init\,;\,e_1\,;\,e_2\,;\,\ldots e_n\,)$      holds.

Note that since in B the initialisation $init$ of an abstract machine must always be a drastic wp predicate transformer, in that $[init]\,Q$ must be either identically true or false for each postcondition $Q$, our definitions of trace and divergence of a machine $M$ are absolute, not contingent on its state. In particular, as long as its initialisation $init$ is feasible, the empty sequence $\langle\,\rangle$ will be a trace of any machine $M$. And should the initialisation $init$ of a machine $M$ not be guaranteed to terminate, then $M$ would have the empty trace as one of its divergences and thus correspond to the immediately divergent process **div**. Also, note that if $M$ is an B abstract machine whose initialisation and operations are all always guaranteed to terminate, then $M$ will correspond to a CSP process with no divergences.

**Refusal Sets of an Abstract Machine.** A set $\{f_1, f_2 \ldots f_m\}$ of operations of an abstract machine $M$ will be a refusal set of any state of $M$ where none of these operations are feasible: that is, $\{f_1, f_2 \ldots f_m\}$ is a refusal set of any state of $M$ where

$\neg\,\mathrm{fis}\,(f_1\;[]\;f_2\;[]\;\ldots\;[]\;f_m\,)$      holds.

In particular the empty set of operations will be a refusal set of any state of any machine, since an empty choice of operations is equivalent to magic and $\neg\,\mathrm{fis}\,(\mathrm{magic})$ always holds because magic is nowhere feasible.

**Failures of an Abstract Machine.** For any sequence $\langle e_1, e_2 \ldots e_n\rangle$ and set $\{f_1, f_2 \ldots f_m\}$ of operations of an abstract machine $M$ with initialisation $init$, the pair $(\langle e_1, e_2 \ldots e_n\rangle, \{f_1, f_2 \ldots f_m\})$ is a failure of $M$ if $\langle e_1, e_2 \ldots e_n\rangle$ is a trace of $M$ which might lead to a state where $\{f_1, f_2 \ldots f_m\}$ is a refusal set. Recall that for a substitution $S$ and postcondition $Q$, the conjugate weakest precondition $\neg\,[S]\neg\,Q$ defines those states from where $S$ might establish $Q$, so the above pair is a failure of $M$ if

$\neg\,[init\,;\,e_1\,;\,e_2\,;\,\ldots\,;\,e_n]\;\mathrm{fis}\,(f_1\;[]\;f_2\;[]\;\ldots\;[]\;f_m\,)$      holds.

## 4.2   Operation Inputs and Outputs

Morgan [25] does not discuss actions with inputs and/or outputs, but Derrick and Boiten [13] and Schneider [30] show that these can accommodated in the CSP interpretation of an ADT by regarding an operation as a two-way channel for passing input and output values in opposite directions. Thus an operation of a B machine whose signature is $y \longleftarrow op(x)$ is associated with a set $Op$ of events, where $T_x$ and $T_y$ are the respective types of $x$ and $y$, such that

$$Op \quad =_{df} \quad \{\,op.x.y \mid x \in T_x \,\wedge\, y \in T_y\}$$

# 5    Data Refinement in B

The refinement theory underpinning the B method, as developed by Abrial [1] and mechanised in both currently available B support environments, is based on the refinement proof method of forward simulation, one of the two refinement proof methods originally proposed by He, Hoare and Sanders [22]. There the methods were applied only to ADTs all of whose operations are modelled as total relations, but later He and Hoare [21] proved the same methods were sound and jointly complete in the more general context of ADTs whose operations are modelled as possibly partial relations. These correspond to B abstract systems with nontrivially guarded events.

Crucially, Abrial provided a *first-order* wp predicate-transformer formulation of the forward simulation proof obligations, which made their generation and discharge for the first time amenable to the sort of mechanisation which lies at the heart of the B method. Yet on its own this forward simulation refinement theory is incomplete since, as Rouzaud [28] points out, there exist certain semantically valid refinements which cannot be proved correct in terms alone of its rules.

To illustrate this we borrow the following example from [16], which models the spinning of a roulette wheel in a casino. The first machine in Fig. 2 represents a forward-thinking roulette wheel which always decides nondeterministically but in advance what the outcome of its next spin will be. The second represents a more impulsive roulette wheel which nondeterministically decides the outcome of each spin only as it occurs.

It should be intuitively clear that these machines would be indistinguishable to any importing implementation, and so should represent mutual refinements of each other. Yet using B's ordinary refinement rules we can only prove refinement between them in one direction: the *thinking_wheel* can certainly be proved by them to refine the *impulsive_wheel*, but not *vice versa*.

```
MACHINE      thinking_wheel
VARIABLES    ii
INVARIANT    ii ∈ 0..36
INITIALISATION    ii :∈ 0..36
OPERATIONS
    rr ⟵ spin  ≙  BEGIN  rr := ii  ||  ii :∈ 0..36  END
END


MACHINE      impulsive_wheel
OPERATIONS
    rr ⟵ spin  ≙   rr :∈ 0..36
END
```

**Fig. 2.** A forward-thinking and an impulsive roulette wheel

**Table 1.** Strongest postcondition semantics of generalised substitutions

| $S$ | $R[S]$ |
|---|---|
| $skip$ | $R$ |
| $x := E$ | $\exists x' . \ R(x'/x) \ \wedge \ x = E(x'/x)$ |
| $P \,\vert\, S$ | $(\forall s . \ R \Rightarrow P) \ \Rightarrow \ R[S]$   where $s$ is frame($S$) |
| $P \Longrightarrow S$ | $(P \wedge R)[S]$ |
| $S \,[]\, T$ | $R[S] \ \vee \ R[T]$ |
| $@z.S$ | $\exists z . \ R[S]$ |
| $S \,;\, T$ | $R[S][T]$ |

This imcompleteness in B's ordinary refinement theory was addressed by one of the current authors in [16] by providing a corresponding *first-order* predicate-transformer formulation of *backward* simulation proof obligations for B, thus endowing B for the first time with two tractable and jointly complete refinement theories which together are sufficient for proving any valid refinement.

These backward simulation proof obligations are formulated in terms of strongest postcondition (sp) rather than the more familiar wp predicate transformer. We recap the characterisation of sp originally given in [16]: for a substitution $S$ we adopt the postfix notation $R[S]$ to signify the strongest postcondition established by $S$ from the precondition $R$. Thus $R[S]$ characterises precisely the set of after-states reachable after execution of $S$ from any before-state satisfying $R$. Table 1 gives the sp characterisation of all the basic constructs of the Generalised Substitution Language (GSL).

**Precedence.** Our convention is that the precedence of each of our wp and sp predicate transformers is greater than that of any ordinary logical connective, even $\neg$ . Hence, for example, $[S]Q \wedge R$ means $([S]Q) \wedge R$ and $\neg R[S]$ means $\neg (R[S])$ .

### 5.1   Forward Refinement

Fig. 3 shows an abstract machine $M$ and its supposed forward refinement $MF$, together with the necessary proof obligations (POs), as per [1], which must be discharged to establish the correctness of this refinement.[4] In these POs $C_n'$ denotes the substitution $C_n$ modified to refer to fresh variable $y_n'$ in place of $y_n$. Those marked * have to be proved in respect of each operation of $M$, these being indexed by $n$.

---

[4] For brevity we omit any reference to the properties and constraints of our machine $M$ and its refinement $MF$. The refinement POs we present here would therefore need adapting to accommodate these static aspects before being useable in practice.

MACHINE $\quad\quad$ $M$ $\quad\quad$ REFINEMENT $\quad$ $MF$

VARIABLES $\quad\quad$ $a$ $\quad\quad$ (Fwd)REFINES $\quad$ $M$

INVARIANT $\quad\quad$ $I$ $\quad\quad$ VARIABLES $\quad\quad$ $c$

INITIALISATION $\quad$ $AI$ $\quad\quad$ INVARIANT $\quad\quad$ $J$

OPERATIONS $\quad\quad\quad\quad\quad\quad$ INITIALISATION $\quad$ $CI$

$\quad\quad$ $y_n \longleftarrow \mathbf{op_n}(x_n) \ \ \widehat{=} \ \ A_n$ $\quad\quad$ OPERATIONS

END $\quad\quad\quad\quad\quad\quad\quad\quad\quad$ $y_n \longleftarrow \mathbf{op_n}(x_n) \ \ \widehat{=} \ \ C_n$

$\quad\quad\quad\quad\quad\quad\quad\quad\quad\quad\quad$ END

(Fwd.init) $\quad$ $\forall\, a, c\ .\ \ [CI]\,\neg\,[AI]\,\neg\,J$

(Fwd.trm)* $\quad$ $\forall\, a, c, x_n\ .\ \ I \wedge J \wedge \mathrm{trm}(A_n) \ \Rightarrow\ \mathrm{trm}(C_n)$

(Fwd.corr)* $\quad$ $\forall\, a, c, x_n, y_n, y_n'\ .\ \ I \wedge J \wedge \mathrm{trm}(A_n) \ \Rightarrow\ [C_n{'}]\,\neg\,[A_n]\,\neg\,(J \wedge y_n{'} = y_n)$

**Fig. 3.** Abstract machine $M$ and its forward refinement $MF$, plus POs

Note that a refinement such as $MF$ is not in itself a concrete machine, because in B we never actually write the concrete machine $N$ which simulates the given abstract machine $M$. Instead $MF$ is what Abrial [1–ch. 11] calls the *differential* which can be combined syntactically with $M$ to yield $N$. Given that the invariant of $M$ is $I$ and that of $MF$ is $J$ then the invariant of the implied concrete machine $N$ is $\exists\, a\ .\ I \wedge J$. We say that the concrete machine $N$ is *deducible* from our refinement $MF$.

## 5.2 Backward Refinement

Fig. 4 shows the same abstract machine $M$ again but this time with its supposed backward refinement $MB$. Again the necessary proof obligations, as derived in [16], which must be discharged to establish the correctness of this backward refinement, are also shown[5]. Those marked * have to be proved in respect of each operation of $M$, as indexed by $n$. As with the forward refinement $MF$, the backward refinement $MB$ is only a differential, but the actual concrete machine $N$ it represents is deducible from it.

## 5.3 A General Refinement Relation for B Abstract Machines

We know from [22, 21] that forward and backward refinement jointly provide a complete refinement theory for ADTs, in the sense that a "concrete" ADT $C$ simulates an "abstract" ADT $A$ if and only if there exists an intermediate ADT $B$ such that $B$ backward-refines $A$ and is itself forward-refined by $C$. We can therefore define a general refinement relation $\sqsubseteq$ between abstract machines $M$

---

[5] In fact, the proof obligation Bwd.init1 appearing here in Fig. 4 was mistakenly omitted in [16].

and $N$ such that $M \sqsubseteq N$ if and only if $M$ is backward-refined by some backward refinement $MB$, which is in turn forward-refined by some forward refinement $MF$ from which $N$ is deducible. This is exactly the sense in which He *et al* [21, 22] show their two proof methods are jointly complete with respect to one ADT arbitrarily simulating another. Thus $\sqsubseteq$ captures precisely our intuitive notion of one abstract machine simulating another, which is that the result of executing any finite sequence of operations on the simulating machine is compatible with what might have happened had that same sequence of operations been executed on the simulated machine instead. This exemplifies the principle of substitutivity: a user who is restricted to running finite sequences of operations on his machine wouldn't be able to detect if his machine has been substituted by another which simulates it in this way. Forward and backward refinement are themselves two special cases of this general refinement, in each of which one the two intermediate refinements is a trivial identification.

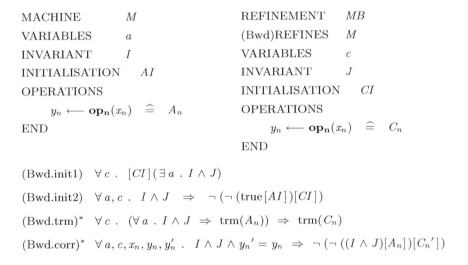

(Bwd.init1)    $\forall c \ . \ [CI](\exists a \ . \ I \wedge J)$

(Bwd.init2)    $\forall a, c \ . \ I \wedge J \ \Rightarrow \ \neg\,(\neg\,(\text{true}\,[AI])[CI])$

(Bwd.trm)$^{*}$    $\forall c \ . \ (\forall a \ . \ I \wedge J \ \Rightarrow \ \text{trm}(A_n)) \ \Rightarrow \ \text{trm}(C_n)$

(Bwd.corr)$^{*}$    $\forall a, c, x_n, y_n, y_n' \ . \ I \wedge J \wedge y_n{}' = y_n \ \Rightarrow \ \neg\,(\neg\,((I \wedge J)[A_n])[C_n{}'])$

**Fig. 4.** Abstract machine $M$ and its backward refinement $MB$, plus POs

Of course, what a user might detect is dependent on just what he can observe. In the most basic case, we might imagine our user is just a passive observer of the sequences of events his abstract system engages in. In particular, he cannot actively probe it at any stage to determine which events it might at that stage notionally be willing to engage in. For such an observer an abstract system which never engages in any event is an effective substitute for any other, since our observer will thereby never observe it engaging in any event which would lead him to conclude it isn't that other system.

# 6    Data Refinement as Process Refinement

In Section 4.1 we showed how any B abstract system can be interpreted as a CSP process. The question therefore naturally arises: does a data refinement between abstract systems correspond to any recognisable refinement between processes? Also, can B's forward and backward proof methods be augmented with further proof obligations to provide finer distinctions between abstract systems which mirror the finer distinctions which can be made between CSP processes by the various process refinement relations described in Section 3. In the following subsections we address these important questions.

## 6.1    Traces and Traces-Divergences Refinement

The following proposition establishes that the general B refinement relation between abstract machines we defined in Section 5.3 equates to traces-divergences refinement between processes.

**Proposition 1.**    Let $P_M$ and $P_N$ be the respective CSP process interpretations of the B abstract systems $M$ and $N$ as defined in Section 4.1. Then

$$M \sqsubseteq N \quad \Leftrightarrow \quad P_M \sqsubseteq_{TD} P_N$$

Proof:  Since $\sqsubseteq$ embodies arbitrary simulation, any sequence of operations executable on $N$ must also be executable on $M$ with similar results. Thus any trace of $P_N$ is also a trace of $P_M$. Moreover, any abortive behaviour exhibited by $N$ during the execution of such a sequence would have to be mirrored by similar abortive behaviour of $M$. Thus any divergence of $P_N$ is also a divergence of $P_M$.
                                                                                                    □

**On Schneider's Result for Non-blocking ADTs.**  Schneider [30] shows that ADT refinement for "non-blocking" ADTs –that is, ADTs whose partial operations abort rather than block when invoked outside the domains of their characterising operations– equates with traces-divergences refinement. Our Proposition 1 extends Schneider's result to cover the wider category of ADTs represented by B abstract systems, whose operations can accommodate coexisting blocking guards and termination preconditions. It therefore renders Schneider's restriction to non-blocking ADTs unnecessary.

**On Bolton and Davies' Result for Blocking ADTs.**  An immediate corollary of Proposition 1 is that for non-aborting abstract machines[6] $M$ and $N$, interpreted respectively as non-divergent CSP processes $P_M$ and $P_N$, we have that

$$M \sqsubseteq N \quad \Leftrightarrow \quad P_M \sqsubseteq_T P_N$$

---

[6] That is, ones whose initialisation and operations are always guaranteed to terminate.

This seems *prima facie* to contradict Bolton and Davies' [5, 6] conclusion that ADT refinement under the "blocking" (*i.e.* non-aborting) interpretation of ADTs equates with singleton-failures rather than traces refinement. However, to model their "blocking" interpretation of an ADT with partial operations Bolton and Davies totalise such partial operations so that invoking a blocked operation leads to an irretrievable "undefined" state which is incorporated in their formulation of their forward and backward refinement proof obligations. Thus their refinement proof obligations implicitly contain information about such blocked states denied to an ordinary passive observer, who can never detect that an operation is blocked because he is restricted to observing successful operation invocations. Our refinement proof obligations in Figs 3 and 4, in contrast, encapsulate only the observations of which such an observer is capable.

**Traces Refinement.** For processes that do exhibit divergence, pure *traces* (as opposed to *traces-divergences*) refinement is not usually considered a useful relation between them. Nevertheless, we are still entitled to ask what notion of data refinement between two B abstract systems $M$ and $N$ would equate to such pure traces refinement between their corresponding CSP processes $P_M$ and $P_N$. It is in fact the weaker form of refinement between B abstract systems which would ensue from discarding the proof obligations Fwd.trm and Bwd.trm in Figs 3 and 4. These particular obligations address the aborting behaviour of the abstract and concrete operations of a refinement, and such behaviour corresponds to divergence in the CSP process interpretations of the abstract systems concerned.

## 6.2 Completed-Traces and Singleton-Failures Refinement

In this subsection we confine our attention to non-aborting B abstract machines and refinements. For such forward refinements the forward refinement termination proof obligation Fwd.trm in Fig. 3 is of course superfluous, and likewise the backward refinement termination proof obligation Bwd.trm in Fig. 4 for such backward refinements.

**Proposition 2.** If the forward and backward refinement POs in Figs 3 and 4 are respectively augmented with the following pair of conditions, where quantification over $n$ signifies quantification over all the operations of abstract machine $M$,

(Fwd.CT)    $\forall\, a, c\ .\ I \wedge J \wedge (\forall\, n, x_n\ .\ \neg\, \mathrm{fis}(C_n)) \quad \Rightarrow \quad \forall\, n, x_n\ .\ \neg\, \mathrm{fis}(A_n)$

(Bwd.CT)    $\forall\, c\ .\ (\forall\, n, x_n\ .\ \neg\, \mathrm{fis}(C_n)) \quad \Rightarrow \quad \exists\, a\ .\ I \wedge J \wedge \forall\, n, x_n\ .\ \neg\, \mathrm{fis}(A_n)$

then the resulting strengthened refinement relation restricted to non-aborting B abstract machines equates to completed-traces refinement.

Proof: The forward condition Fwd.CT guarantees that in any concrete state where all the concrete operations are blocked, then in any valid abstract state related to that concrete state by the abstraction relation $J$ all the abstract operations will be blocked too. This is what we require to ensure that any completed trace of a forward refinement of $M$ is also a completed trace of $M$.

Meanwhile the backward condition Bwd.CT guarantees that for any concrete state where all the concrete operations are blocked, there exists at least one valid abstract state related to that concrete state by the abstraction relation $J$ where all the abstract operations will be blocked. This is what we require to ensure that any completed trace of a backward refinement of $M$ is also a completed trace of $M$.    □

In the following proposition, as often in the succeeding ones, the conditions we present are qualified by *. As in Figs 3 and 4, this signifies that the condition in question must be proved "for each $n$": that is, for each of the abstract machine's operations.

**Proposition 3.** If the forward and backward refinement POs in Figs 3 and 4 are respectively augmented with the following pair of conditions

$$(\text{Fwd.SF})^* \qquad \forall\, a, c, x_n \;.\; I \wedge J \wedge \neg\, \text{fis}(C_n) \quad \Rightarrow \quad \neg\, \text{fis}(A_n)$$

$$(\text{Bwd.SF})^* \qquad \forall\, a, c, x_n \;.\; \neg\, \text{fis}(C_n) \quad \Rightarrow \quad \exists\, a \;.\; I \wedge J \wedge \neg\, \text{fis}(A_n)$$

then the resulting strengthened refinement relation restricted to non-aborting B abstract machines equates to singleton-failures refinement.

Proof: The forward condition Fwd.SF guarantees that in any concrete state where a concrete operation is blocked, then in any valid abstract state related to that concrete state by the abstraction relation $J$ the corresponding abstract operation will be blocked too. This is what we require to ensure that any singleton failure of a forward refinement of $M$ is also a singleton failure of $M$.

On the other hand the backward condition Bwd.SF guarantees that for any concrete state where a concrete operation is blocked, there exists at least one valid abstract state related to that concrete state by the abstraction relation $J$ where the corresponding abstract operation will be blocked. This is what we require to ensure that any singleton failure of a backward refinement of $M$ is also a singleton failure of $M$.    □

## 6.3 Failures Refinement

The task of formulating an appropriate pair of rules with which to augment the basic B forward and backward refinement rules to provide a refinement relation equivalent to failures-divergences refinement of processes, is complicated by the presence of operation outputs. This is because outputs are demonic in the sense that the environment of the machine has no influence over the choice of output value. Moreover, when an operation $op$ outputs the value $p$ it is engaging in the event $op.p$ while simultaneously refusing all similar events $op.y$ where $y$ is of appropriate type and $y \neq p$. We call such refusals *output-simultaneous* ones.

To help us in characterising such output-simultaneous refusals we first identify the following characteristic predicate of an operation with inputs and outputs. For an operation $op$ defined by $\quad y \longleftarrow op(x) \quad \widehat{=} \quad S \quad$ then the predicate

$\neg [S] y \neq p$ characterises those before-states and input values $x$ for which invoking $op$ could result in output of the value $p$. We are now in a position to formulate our main results.

**Proposition 4.** If the forward and backward refinement POs in Figs 3 and 4 are respectively augmented with the following pair of conditions

(Fwd.FD)*    $\forall a, c, x_n \ . \ I \wedge J \wedge \neg \operatorname{fis}(C_n) \ \Rightarrow \ \neg \operatorname{fis}(A_n)$

(Bwd.FD)    $\forall c \ . \ \exists a \ . \ I \wedge J \ \wedge \ \forall n, x_n, y_n \ . \ \operatorname{fis}(A_n) \ \Rightarrow$
$\operatorname{fis}(C_n) \ \wedge \ \forall p \ . \ \neg [C_n] y_n \neq p \ \Rightarrow \ \neg [A_n] y_n \neq p$

then the resulting strengthened refinement relation on abstract machines equates to failures-divergences refinement.

Proof: The forward condition Fwd.FD guarantees that in any concrete state where a concrete operation is blocked, then in any valid abstract state related to that concrete state by the abstraction relation $J$ the corresponding abstract operation will be blocked too. Furthermore, the basic forward operation-correctness condition Fwd.corr (see Fig. 3) ensures that in any concrete state where a concrete operation can execute to yield output $y$, then in any valid abstract state related to that concrete state by the abstraction relation $J$ the corresponding abstract operation can execute to yield the same output, so all output-simultaneous refusals of the refinement are matched by similar output-simultaneous refusals of the abstract machine. Thus Fwd.FD is sufficient as it stands to ensure that any failure of a forward refinement $MF$ of $M$ is also a failure of $M$.

In contrast we have to take output-simultaneous refusals explicitly into account when formulating Bwd.FD. In fact Bwd.FD guarantees that for every concrete state there is at least one abstract state where each abstract operation with input is blocked unless the equivalent concrete operation and input is unblocked and furthermore every output that may arise from executing the concrete operation is also possible from executing the abstract operation. This ensures that any failure of a backward refinement $MF$ of $M$ is also a failure of $M$.    □

## 6.4    Failuretraces-Divergences Refinement

The B proof obligations for failuretraces-divergences refinement are obtained from those we saw in the last subsection for failures-divergences by a strengthening the latter's backward-refinement proof obligation. This is done by simply changing its existential quantification over the abstract state $a$ into a universal quantification. The result is embodied in our next and final proposition.

**Proposition 5.** If the forward and backward refinement POs in Figs 3 and 4 are respectively augmented with the following pair of conditions

(Fwd.FTD)*    $\forall a, c, x_n \ . \ I \wedge J \wedge \neg \operatorname{fis}(C_n) \ \Rightarrow \ \neg \operatorname{fis}(A_n)$

$(\text{Bwd.FTD})^* \quad \forall\, a, c, x_n, y_n \;.\; I \wedge J \wedge \neg\, \text{fis}(C_n) \;\Rightarrow\;$
$$\neg\, \text{fis}(A_n) \;\wedge\; \forall p \;.\; \neg\, [C_n]\, y_n \neq p \;\Rightarrow\; \neg\, [A_n]\, y_n \neq p$$

then the resulting strengthened refinement relation on abstract machines equates to failuretraces-divergences refinement.

Proof: The only difference between these conditions and the previous ones for failures-divergences refinement is in the Bwd conditions. The $\exists\, a$ which occurred in Bwd.FD has effectively been replaced by $\forall\, a$ here in Bwd.FTD. This ensures that at every stage, rather than merely at the end of the overall observation, every refusal of the concrete system will also be a refusal of the abstract system.  □

# 7  Conclusion

We have seen that by augmenting the basic forward and backward refinement proof obligations of B with another suitable pair of conditions a variety of different process refinements can be achieved. What is interesting is that in most cases it is the backward refinement conditions which determine the particular variety of process refinement expressed by the the overall conditions. For example the conditions Fwd.SF, Fwd.FD and Fwd.FTD are identical, but Bwd.SF, Bwd.FD and Bwd.FTD are all distinct. The varieties of process refinement we have explored for B are therefore much more critically dependent on the precise backward refinement conditions deployed than they are on the forward ones.

It is important to stress that the various extra pairs of proof obligations we have presented in Section 6 to augment B's basic refinement proof obligations in order to mirror the various finer process refinement relations of Section 3, are all presented in a *first-order* form. That is to say, none of them involve quantification over arbitrary postconditions or preconditions. This means they could easily be generated machanically by B's support tools in a concrete form which is amenable to fully mechanised or tool-supported interactive proof.

# Acknowledgements

We are grateful for the comments of the three anonymous reviewers on the draft version of this paper.

# References

1. J.-R. Abrial. *The B-Book: Assigning Programs to Meanings.* Cambridge University Press, 1996.
2. J.-R. Abrial. Extending B without changing it (for developing distributed systems). In H. Habrias, editor, *Proceedings of the First B Conference*, pages 169–190. IRIN, Nantes, 1996.

3. J.-R. Abrial and L. Mussat. Introducing dynamic constraints in B. In D. Bert, editor, *B'98: Recent Advances in the Development and Use of the B Method; Proceedings of the 2nd International B Conference*, number 1393 in Lecture Notes in Computer Science, pages 83–128. Springer-Verlag, 1998.
4. R.J.R. Back and R. Kurki-Suonio. Decentralisation of process nets with centralised control. In *2nd ACM SIGACT-SIGOPS Symposium on Principles of Distributed Computing*, pages 131–142, 1983.
5. C. Bolton and J. Davies. A comparison of refinement orderings and their associated simulation rules. In John Derrick, Eerke Boiten, Jim Woodcock, and Joakim von Wright, editors, *REFINE' 02 Proceedings*, Electronic Notes in Theoretical Computer Science, 70. Elsevier, 2002. http://www.elsevier.nl/locate/entcs.
6. C. Bolton and J. Davies. Refinement in Object-Z and CSP. In M.Butler, K.Sere, and L.Petre, editors, *Integrated Formal Methods, IFM 2002 Proceedings*, number 2335 in Lecture Notes in Computer Science, pages 225–244. Springer, 2002.
7. C. Bolton, J. Davies, and J.C.P. Woodcock. On the refinement and simulation of data types and processes. In K. Araki, A. Galloway, and K. Tagushi, editors, *IFM'99, 1st International Conference on Integrated Formal Methods*, pages 273–292. Springer, 1999.
8. M. Butler. An approach to the design of distributed systems with B AMN. In Jonathan P. Bowen, Michael Hinchey, and David Till, editors, *ZUM '97: The Z Formal Specification Notation; 10th International Conference of Z Users*, number 1212 in Lecture Notes in Computer Science, pages 223–241. Springer, 1997.
9. M. Butler. csp2B: a practial approach to combining CSP and B. In J.M. Wing, J. Woodcock, and J. Davies, editors, *FM'99 - Formal Methods*, number 1708 in Lecture Notes in Computer Science, pages 490–508. Springer-Verlag, 1999.
10. M. Butler and M. Waldén. Distributed system development in B. In H. Habrias, editor, *Proceedings of the First B Conference*, pages 155–168. IRIN, Nantes, 1996.
11. J. Derrick and E. Boiten. *Refinement in Z and Object-Z*. Springer, 2001.
12. J. Derrick and E. Boiten. Unifying concurrent and relational refinement. In John Derrick, Eerke Boiten, Jim Woodcock, and Joakim von Wright, editors, *REFINE' 02 Proceedings*, number 70 in Electronic Notes in Theoretical Computer Science. Elsevier, 2002. http://www.elsevier.nl/locate/entcs.
13. J. Derrick and E. Boiten. Relational concurrent refinement. *Formal Aspects of Computing*, 15:182–214, 2003.
14. J. Derrick and G. Smith. Structural refinement of systems specified in Object-Z and CSP. *Formal Aspects of Computing*, 15:1–27, 2003.
15. S.E. Dunne. A theory of generalised substitutions. In D. Bert, J.P. Bowen, M.C. Henson, and K. Robinson, editors, *ZB2002: Formal Specification and Development in Z and B*, number 2272 in Lecture Notes in Computer Science, pages 270–290. Springer, 2002.
16. S.E. Dunne. Introducing backward refinement into B. In Didier Bert, Jonathan P. Bowen, Steve King, and Marina Walden, editors, *ZB2003: Formal Specification and Development in Z and B*, number 2651 in Lecture Notes in Computer Science, pages 178–196. Springer, 2003.
17. C. Fischer. *Combination and Implementation of Processes and Data: from CSP-OZ to Java*. PhD thesis, University of Oldenburg, 2000.
18. He Jifeng. Process refinement. In *Refinement Workshop, University of York*, 1988.
19. He Jifeng. Process refinement. In J. McDermid, editor, *The Theory and Practice of Refinement*. Butterworths, 1989.
20. C.A.R. Hoare. *Communicating Sequential Processes*. Prentice-Hall, 1985.

21. He Jifeng and C.A.R. Hoare. Prespecification and data refinement. In *Data Refinement in a Categorical Setting*, Technical Monograph PRG-90. Oxford University Computing Laboratory, 1990.

22. He Jifeng, C.A.R. Hoare, and J.W. Sanders. Data refinement refined. In B. Robinet and R.Wilhelm, editors, *Proceedings ESOP'86*, number 213 in Lecture Notes in Computer Science, pages 187–196. Springer-Verlag, 1986.

23. M. B. Josephs. A state-based approach to communicating processes. *Distributed Computing*, 3:9–18, 1988.

24. A.J.R.G. Milner. Foreword. In A.W. Roscoe, editor, *A Classical Mind: essays in honour of C.A.R. Hoare*. Prentice-Hall, 1994.

25. C.C. Morgan. Of wp and CSP. In W.H.J. Feijen, A.J.M. van Gasteren, D. Gries, and J. Misra, editors, *Beauty is our business: a birthday salute to Edsger W. Dijkstra*, pages 319–326. Springer, 1990.

26. I.C.C. Phillips. Refusals testing. *Theoretical Computer Science*, 50:241–284, 1987.

27. A.W. Roscoe. *The Theory and Practice of Concurrency*. Prentice-Hall, 1998.

28. Y. Rouzaud. Interpreting the B-Method in the Refinement Calculus. In J.M. Wing, J. Woodcock, and J. Davies, editors, *FM'99 - Formal Methods*, number 1708 in Lecture Notes in Computer Science, pages 411–430. Springer-Verlag, 1999.

29. S. Schneider. *Concurrent and Real-time Systems: the CSP approach*. Wiley, 1999.

30. S. Schneider. Non-blocking data refinement and traces-divergences semantics. Technical report CS-04-09, Department of Computing. University of Surrey, 2004.

31. S. Schneider and H. Treharne. Communicating B machines. In Didier Bert, Jonathan P. Bowen, Martin C. Henson, and Ken Robinson, editors, *ZB2002: Formal Specification and Development in Z and B*, number 2272 in Lecture Notes in Computer Science, pages 416–435. Springer, 2002.

32. S. Schneider and H. Treharne. Verifying controlled components. In Eerke Boiten, John Derrick, and Graeme Smith, editors, *Integrated Formal Methods, IFM 2004 Proceedings*, number 2999 in Lecture Notes in Computer Science, pages 87–107. Springer, 2004.

33. G. Smith. *The Object-Z Specification Language*. Advances in Formal Methods. Kluwer Academic Publishers, 2000.

34. G. Smith and J. Derrick. Specification, refinement and verification of concurrent systems - an integration of Object-Z and CSP. *Formal Methods in System Design*, 18:249–284, 2001.

35. J.M. Spivey. *The Z Notation: a Reference Manual (2nd edn)*. Prentice Hall, 1992.

36. H. Treharne and S. Schneider. How to drive a B machine. In Jonathan P. Bowen, Steve Dunne, Andy Galloway, and Steve King, editors, *ZB2000: Formal Specification and Development in B and Z*, number 1878 in Lecture Notes in Computer Science, pages 188–208. Springer, 2000.

37. H. Treharne, S. Schneider, and M. Bramble. Composing specifications using communication. In Didier Bert, Jonathan P. Bowen, Steve King, and Marina Walden, editors, *ZB2003: Formal Specification and Development in Z and B*, number 2651 in Lecture Notes in Computer Science, pages 58–78. Springer-Verlag, 2003.

38. R.J. van Glabbeek. The linear time - branching time spectrum I: the semantics of concrete sequential processes. In J.A. Bergstra, A. Ponse, and S.A. Smolka, editors, *Handbook of Process Algebra*. Elsevier, 2001.

39. M. Waldén. Layering distributed algorithms within the B method. In D. Bert, editor, *B'98: Recent Advances in the Development and Use of the B Method; Proceedings of the 2nd International B Conference*, number 1393 in Lecture Notes in Computer Science, pages 243–260. Springer-Verlag, 1998.

40. J. Woodcock and J. Davies. *Using Z: Specification, Refinement and Proof.* Prentice Hall, 1996.

41. J.C.P. Woodcock and C.C. Morgan. Refinement of state-based concurrent systems. In Dines Bjørner, C. A. R. Hoare, and Hans Langmaack, editors, *VDM '90, VDM and Z - Formal Methods in Software Development, Third International Symposium of VDM Europe*, number 428 in Lecture Notes in Computer Science, pages 340–351. Springer, 1990.

# CZT: A Framework for Z Tools

Petra Malik and Mark Utting

The University of Waikato, Hamilton, New Zealand
{petra, marku}@cs.waikato.ac.nz

**Abstract.** The Community Z Tools (CZT) project is an open-source Java framework for building formal methods tools for Z and Z dialects. It also includes a set of tools for parsing, typechecking, transforming and printing standard Z specifications in LaTeX, Unicode or XML formats. This paper gives an overview of the CZT framework, including an introduction to its visitor design pattern that makes it possible to write new Z transformation tools in just a few lines of Java code. The paper also discusses several problems and challenges that arose when attempting to build tools based on the ISO Standard for Z.

## 1 Introduction

The Z specification language was adopted as an ISO standard in 2002 [1]. It can be used to precisely specify the behaviour of systems, and analyse it via proof, animation, test generation etc. However, one of the biggest barriers to the widespread use of the Z standard is the issue of tool support.

There are several industry-quality Z tools available that offer parsing and typechecking facilities (FuZZ[1], ZTC[2]) and some that also offer proof facilities (Z/EVES[3], CadiZ[4], ProofPower[5]). However, most of them do not support the ISO Standard for Z (CadiZ is the only one that supports almost all of the ISO Standard for Z). Furthermore, they use different versions of Z[6] or require different LaTeX macros, and there is little integration between the tools.

Other Z tools have been constructed as academic experiments or student projects, but these are typically not robust enough or complete enough for widespread use. Many good ideas and tools that were developed to prototype stage are no longer maintained or available now, because the project has finished or people have moved on.

---

[1] See http://spivey.oriel.ox.ac.uk/mike/fuzz.
[2] See http://se.cs.depaul.edu/fm/ztc.html.
[3] See http://www.ora.on.ca/z-eves.
[4] See http://www-users.cs.york.ac.uk/~ian/cadiz.
[5] See http://www.lemma-one.com/ProofPower/index.
[6] A quote from the ProofPower web page illustrates the challenge: *"The [ProofPower] ASCII mark-up is similar in spirit to the e-mail mark-up of the ISO Standard, but not in the details. There is no automatic way of transferring specifications between the ProofPower dialect of Z and other Z support tools at the moment. Now the standard has been finalised we hope that there will be more convergence."*

H. Treharne et al. (Eds.): ZB 2005, LNCS 3455, pp. 65–84, 2005.

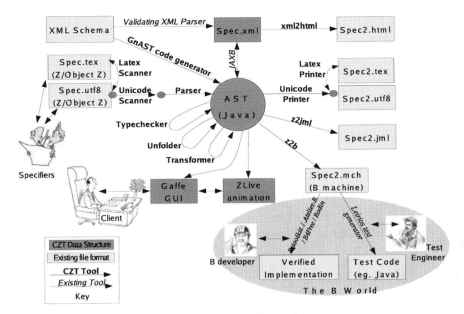

**Fig. 1.** Overview of the CZT architecture

The Community Z Tools (CZT) project was proposed by Andrew Martin in 2001[7], with the goal of providing an open Internet-based community project that survives individuals, research projects, companies, etc. In 2003, the authors created the CZT project on Sourceforge[8], the world's largest open-source software development web-site.

Meanwhile Java core libraries for the ISO Standard for Z and some Z dialects have been designed and implemented. Alpha versions of several tools (parsers, printers, typechecker and a variety of transformers to and from different Z markups and other languages) are now available. People from all over the world have joined the project, and are either improving existing software or building new tools on top.

Figure 1 gives an overview of the CZT software, and provides an idea how it can be used. The XML Schema in the top left-hand corner of the diagram, which is introduced in Sect. 2, defines an XML file format for Z specifications. It can be used as an interchange format between different sessions and between external Z tools. In addition, the XML Schema has been used to generate Java interfaces and classes for annotated syntax trees (AST) for Z, as described in Sect. 3. These classes provide a convenient, markup-independent way to access the syntactic objects of a Z specification. Most of the tools provided either create, modify, or traverse an AST. All the tools in Fig. 1 that take an AST as input use our *CZT visitor* design pattern described in Sect. 4 to traverse the AST.

---

[7] See http://web.comlab.ox.ac.uk/oucl/work/andrew.martin/CZT.

[8] See http://czt.sourceforge.net.

The CZT parser can transform Z specifications in various formats into an AST representation. Once available as an AST, a wealth of options for further processing are possible. Using the XML file format, it can be passed on to other tools. Alternatively, the specification can be typechecked, animated, or translated into a variety of formats such as, for instance, B, HTML, JML, or another markup language. Section 5 gives an overview of the CZT tools available.

In Sect. 6, the paper discusses some problems that arose while designing and implementing CZT. Finally, Sect. 7 contains some concluding remarks.

## 2   ZML—XML Markup for Z

The heart of CZT is an XML Schema that describes the XML markup for Z specifications (ZML). It is an interchange format that can be used to exchange parsed and even typechecked specifications between sessions and tools. It was first described in [2] and has been enhanced since then. To allow for evolution of the ZML format, version numbers have been introduced. Each ZML specification should specify which version of the ZML format it is using. The original proposal has version number 1.0, which is also the default when no version number is given. At the time of writing, the current version number is 1.3. A list of changes can be found at the web-site http://czt.sourceforge.net/zml.

ZML was designed in a way to capture sufficient information to rebuild the constructs from which it was originally parsed and, at the same time, to minimise the number of cases a tool needs to deal with. This has been achieved by adding a type hierarchy—parts of it are shown in Fig. 2—to reflect commonalities, and by using common XML tags for similar constructs. Attributes are then used to distinguish between the similar constructs.

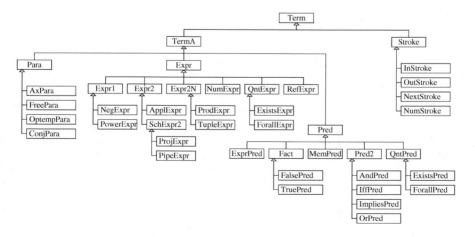

**Fig. 2.** Part of the inheritance hierarchy

```
<AxPara Box="SchBox">
  <SchText>
    <ConstDecl>
      <DeclName><Word>BirthdayBook</Word></DeclName>
      <SchExpr>...</SchExpr>
    </ConstDecl>
  </SchText>
</AxPara>
```

**Fig. 3.** ZML snippet

A ZML snippet for the Z schema given by the following LaTeX markup

\begin{schema}{BirthdayBook}...\end{schema}

can be seen in Fig. 3. As described in the ISO Standard for Z, a schema definition is semantically equivalent to an axiomatic description associating the name of the schema with the schema text. In ZML, the `AxPara` is used to represent axiomatic descriptions, generic axiomatic descriptions, schema definitions, generic schema definitions, horizontal definitions, generic horizontal definitions, and generic operator definitions. The attribute `Box` distinguishes between the different types of paragraphs and ensures that the original construct can be restored. `SchBox` is short for schema box and indicates that we are dealing with a schema definition.

The XML Schema definition for `AxPara` is given in Fig. 4. The `AxPara` element defines the XML tag `AxPara`. The attribute `substitutionGroup` is used to define the inheritance hierarchy (see Fig. 2). `AxPara` is in the substitution group of `Para`, that is, it is a special paragraph. The complex type `AxPara` is used to define the children and attributes of the element `AxPara`. The `AxPara` element contains, in addition to the elements defined in `Para`, a possibly empty list of generic parameters (`DeclName`) followed by a schema text (`SchText`).

## 3   AST—Annotated Syntax Tree

The *annotated syntax tree* (AST) provides a tree view of a parsed Z specification using Java interfaces and classes. This allows easy access to syntactical objects like, for instance, paragraphs, predicates, and expressions, from within Java programs. Currently, CZT contains AST interfaces and classes for Z [1], Object Z [3], and TCOZ [4]. Support for other extensions is conceivable.

The AST interfaces reflect the XML markup defined in ZML very closely. In fact, the AST interfaces and classes were automatically generated from the XML Schema describing ZML using our code generator *GnAST* (GeNerator for AST). For each element defined in the XML Schema, a corresponding interface and implementing class is generated. A user of the AST should always use references to the interfaces instead of references to concrete classes. This protects the user from changes to the underlying implementation and allows the use of different implementations of the AST interfaces.

```
<xs:element name="AxPara" type="Z:AxPara" substitutionGroup="Z:Para">
  <xs:annotation>
    <xs:documentation>
      A (generic) axiomatic paragraph, (generic) schema definition,
      or (generic) horizontal definition.
    </xs:documentation>
  </xs:annotation>
</xs:element>

<xs:complexType name="AxPara">
  <xs:complexContent>
    <xs:extension base="Z:Para">
      <xs:sequence>
        <xs:element ref="Z:DeclName"
            minOccurs="0" maxOccurs="unbounded"/>
        <xs:element ref="Z:SchText"/>
      </xs:sequence>
      <xs:attribute name="Box" type="Z:Box"
          use="optional" default="AxBox"/>
    </xs:extension>
  </xs:complexContent>
</xs:complexType>
```

**Fig. 4.** XML Schema definition for `AxPara`

The *abstract factory pattern* [5] is used to provide a way to create AST objects without any knowledge of their concrete classes. For example, a Z tool that creates a new `AxPara` object should *never* call the constructor of an `AxPara` implementation, instead it should use `factory.createAxPara()`, where `factory` is an interface that has methods for creating each kind of AST node. Different implementations of this interface can then be used to create instances of different concrete AST classes. By passing the tool an alternative factory object, one can control which implementations of the AST interfaces it will create. The CZT software provides a standard factory that creates instances of the implementation classes supplied within CZT. A user is free to use their own classes that implement the AST interfaces by providing an alternative factory.

The inheritance hierarchy of AST interfaces and classes—parts of it are shown in Fig. 2—is the same as the element inheritance hierarchy defined in the XML Schema. The leaves of this tree represent concrete classes, which can be instantiated via the factory mentioned above, while the inner nodes represent abstract classes, which cannot be directly instantiated.

For each child and attribute defined for a ZML element, the corresponding Java interface provides getter and setter methods. For example, the Java interface `AxPara` given in Fig. 5 is automatically generated from the `AxPara` element definition given in Fig. 4, which is taken from the XML Schema that describes ZML. The `AxPara` element is defined to extend `Para` and to contain, in addition to the elements defined in `Para`, a possibly empty list of declaring names (`DeclName`) followed by a schema text (`SchText`). There is also an attribute called `Box`.

Accordingly, the `AxPara` interface extends `Para` and contains, in addition to the methods defined in the interface `Para`, the following getter methods: `getDeclName` returning a list, `getSchText` returning a schema text (`SchText`),

```
/**
 * A (generic) axiomatic paragraph, (generic) schema definition,
 * or (generic) horizontal definition.
 *
 * @author GnAST code generator
 */
public interface AxPara extends Para
{
    /** Returns a list of declaring names (formal parameters). */
    ListTerm getDeclName();

    /** Returns the schema text. */
    SchText getSchText();

    /** Sets the schema text. */
    void setSchText(SchText schText);

    /** Returns the Box attribute. */
    Box getBox();

    /** Sets the Box attribute. */
    void setBox(Box box);
}
```

**Fig. 5.** AST interface for `AxPara`

and `getBox` returning a `Box`, which is an enumeration used to indicate whether this was parsed from a schema text, axiomatic definition, or horizontal definition. In addition to getter methods, setter methods are provided. Note that there is no setter method for `DeclName` since the getter returns a list, and the `List` interface can be used to add and remove elements.

The getter and setter methods defined by the AST interfaces provide a convenient way to access and manipulate individual AST objects. However, it is often necessary to manipulate a whole AST in a certain way. The following section shows how complete trees can be handled with just a few lines of code.

## 4   The CZT Visitor Design Pattern

The visitor design pattern [5] provides a way to separate the structure of a set of objects from the operations performed on these objects. This allows a new operation to be defined without modifying the AST classes. To define a new operation, all you need to do is to implement a new visitor class. An example of a visitor class is given in Fig. 6. It traverses an AST and prints the word-parts of all declaring names (`DeclName`).

A variety of variants [6] of the visitor design pattern have been proposed, all having different advantages and disadvantages. The visitor design described in this section is the result of a lot of experimentation and redesign. We discussed many variants and implemented three or four different designs before we found a design that met all our requirements.

The standard visitor pattern described in [5] is based on a double dispatch mechanism. The set of objects on which new operations are to be defined must

```
import net.sourceforge.czt.base.ast.Term;
import net.sourceforge.czt.base.visitor.TermVisitor;
import net.sourceforge.czt.base.visitor.VisitorUtils;
import net.sourceforge.czt.z.ast.DeclName;
import net.sourceforge.czt.z.visitor.DeclNameVisitor;

public class DeclNamePrintVisitor
  implements TermVisitor, DeclNameVisitor
{
  public Object visitTerm(Term term)
  {
    VisitorUtils.visitTerm(this, term);
    return null;
  }

  public Object visitDeclName(DeclName declName)
  {
    System.out.println(declName.getWord());
    return null;
  }
}
```

**Fig. 6.** A simple visitor

support this pattern by providing an `accept(Visitor v)` method. The `Visitor` is an interface that defines `visit` methods for each class of object that is to be visited (like `visitDeclName` in Fig. 6). The `accept` method of an object calls back the correct `visit` method for its class. This allows different implementations of the `Visitor` interface to perform different operations on the objects.

The disadvantage of this approach is that it is difficult to add new AST classes, because each new AST class implies that a new method needs to be added to the `Visitor` interface, which in turn requires modifications to all its existing implementations. Within CZT, we want to support extensions like Object Z, TCOZ, etc, and therefore need to be able to easily extend the AST classes. Another disadvantage is that each visitor class needs to implement a fixed set of methods, one for each AST class—and there are a large number of AST classes defined in CZT. While it is possible to provide default `Visitor` implementations, then use inheritance to override just the desired methods, the lack of multiple inheritance in Java often makes this a clumsy or undesirable solution.

The CZT visitor incorporates the advantages of the *acyclic visitor* [7] pattern and the *default visitor* [8] pattern, as well as some new twists. The *acyclic visitor* pattern allows new AST classes to be added without changing the existing visitor classes. This is done by defining a visitor interface for each object and using a dynamic cast in the AST `accept` methods. The *default visitor* pattern adds another level of inheritance to the visitor pattern, making it possible to implement default behaviour by taking advantage of the AST inheritance relationships. That is, the visitor classes of the default visitor pattern define a visit$AAA$ method for each *abstract* AST class $AAA$, in addition to the usual visit$CCC$ methods for each concrete AST class $CCC$. Visitors can then define default behaviour within these extra (abstract) `visit` methods. If not overridden, a concrete visit$CCC$ method typically just calls the visit$AAA$ method which corresponds to its closest superclass.

```
public interface AxParaVisitor extends Visitor
{
 /** Visits an AxPara. */
 Object visitAxPara(AxPara axPara);
}
```

**Fig. 7.** The AxParaVisitor interface

```
public class AxParaImpl extends ParaImpl implements AxPara
{
  ...

  /** Accepts a visitor. */
  public Object accept(Visitor visitor)
  {
    if (visitor instanceof AxParaVisitor) {
      AxParaVisitor axParaVisitor = (AxParaVisitor) visitor;
      return axParaVisitor.visitAxPara(this);
    }
    return super.accept(v);
  }
  ...
}
```

**Fig. 8.** The `accept` method of AxPara

Now we describe the CZT visitor pattern. In CZT, a visitor interface is defined for every AST class, including abstract superclasses. As an example, the visitor interface for AxPara is given in Fig. 7. If a visitor implements this interface, then any AxPara AST nodes that it visits will call the visitor's visitAxPara method. However, if the visitor does not implement the AxParaVisitor interface, then the AxPara AST nodes will search up though their superclasses and call the first visit$AAA$ method that the visitor implements (for example, visitPara or visitTermA or visitTerm). Figure 8 illustrates how the accept method for AxPara implements this semantics. With this approach, the AST classes themselves take care of calling the closest (with respect to the inheritance hierarchy) visit method implemented by the visitor.

```
public interface Term
{
  /** Accepts a visitor. */
  Object accept(Visitor visitor);

  /** Returns an array of all the children of this term. */
  Object[] getChildren();

  /** Creates a new object of the implementing class
   * with the objects in args as its children. */
  Term create(Object[] args);
}
```

**Fig. 9.** The `Term` interface

```
import net.sourceforge.czt.base.ast.Term;
import net.sourceforge.czt.base.visitor.TermVisitor;
import net.sourceforge.czt.z.ast.DeclName;
import net.sourceforge.czt.z.util.Factory;
import net.sourceforge.czt.z.visitor.DeclNameVisitor;

/** A visitor that copies a given AST (except for annotations)
 *   into one where all strokes are removed from each DeclName.
 */
public class StrokeKiller
  implements TermVisitor, DeclNameVisitor
{
  private Factory factory_ = new Factory();

  public StrokeKiller()
  {
  }

  public StrokeKiller(Factory factory)
  {
    factory_ = factory;
  }

  public Object visitTerm(Term term)
  {
    Object[] args = term.getChildren();
    for (int i = 0; i < args.length; i++) {
      if (args[i] instanceof Term) {
        args[i] = ((Term) args[i]).accept(this);
      }
    }
    return term.create(args);
  }

  public Object visitDeclName(DeclName declName)
  {
    return factory_.createDeclName(declName.getWord(), null);
  }
}
```

**Fig. 10.** Another simple visitor

The `Term` interface given in Fig. 9 is the base of all AST objects and must therefore be implemented by every AST class. The two additional methods defined in the `Term` interface provide a convenient way to handle AST classes generically within visitors. The `getChildren` method provides a generic alternative to the getter methods by returning all children of a term as an array. This allows us to write a single `visitTerm` method that recurses through the entire AST tree (see `visitTerm` in Fig. 10). This default `visitTerm` method is so common that it is supplied in the `VisitorUtils` library class, which has been used to implement the `visitTerm` method in Fig. 6.

Similarly, the `create` method is a convenient way for default `visit` methods to change the contents of a tree node, while retaining its original type. The `create` method is similar to a clone, but allows new children to be provided. These children are typically returned by the `visit` calls to the original children.

Figure 10 shows a visitor that copies an AST into one where all decorations, i.e. strokes, are removed from `DeclName` elements.[9]

The visitor needs to traverse the tree to find all `DeclName` objects. This traversal is handled in the `visitTerm` method, which is called for all AST classes except `DeclName`. It makes sure that all children are visited. Furthermore, the results of visiting the children are used to create a new object of the same type containing the new children. When a `DeclName` accepts this visitor, the `visitDeclName` method is called. In this case, a new `DeclName` is created with the same name as the one that is visited, but no decorations are added.

This visitor demonstrates the use of the `getChildren` and `create` methods, as well as the use of a factory to create new `DeclName` objects. Note that this visitor has no reference to concrete implementations of the AST interfaces; only references to AST interfaces are used. The visitor uses the standard factory provided within CZT if no factory is given. It can also be configured to use alternative factory implementations.

Visitors are extensively used throughout CZT. Virtually all of the tools that access or manipulate an AST, like the typechecker, printers, etc., are visitors or use visitors to achieve their functionality. The advantage of the CZT visitors is that the amount of code that needs to be written is directly proportional to the AST nodes that need to be transformed or accessed—recursion through all the other AST nodes is done by the default `visitTerm` method. This makes it easy to write visitors that transform Z in some new way. It is simple to combine such a visitor with the existing Z parsers and printers in CZT, to quickly obtain a new Z tool.

## 5    CZT Tools

The CZT software also includes a set of tools as shown on the diagram in Fig. 1. At the time of writing, the scanners, parsers, printers and typechecker are quite robust and well-tested.[10]

Figure 11 gives an overview of the different parser components. The components responsible for parsing specifications in Unicode are given on the right side. As described in the ISO Standard for Z and in [9], scanning and parsing is performed in several steps. The first step is the scanning phase carried out by the `Unicode Scanner`. In fact, the scanner itself consists of several components: the `Context-Free Scanner`, the `Keyword Scanner`, the `Smart Scanner`, and the `Operator Scanner`.

The `Context-Free Scanner` is an implementation of the context-free lexis described in the ISO Standard for Z [1–§7.2]. JFlex[11], a Java scanner generator,

---

[9] Note that annotations are not copied. If we wanted to retain annotations as well, the `TermAVisitor` interface could be implemented in a way that also copies annotations.

[10] The typechecker is the newest addition and has checked only about 2000 lines of Z so far.

[11] See `http://www.jflex.de`.

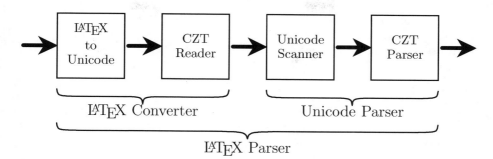

Fig. 11. The parser architecture

is used to generate this class. The context-free lexis is followed by the context-sensitive lexis implemented by the Keyword and Operator Scanner. The Smart Scanner resolves one of the context-sensitive ambiguities in the Z grammar that is discussed in the ISO Standard for Z [1–§8.4, Note 4]. For example, in $\{x, y, z...\}$, if the $x, y, z$ is followed by ':', then it is part of a declaration (a set comprehension) and declares new names. Otherwise it is a set extension, and $x, y, z$ must already have been declared somewhere else. The Smart Scanner performs lookahead to resolve this ambiguity.

The scanning phase is followed by the parsing phase. The CZT Parser is a look-ahead LR parser (LALR parser) generated by the Cup[12] Java parser generator. See Sect. 6 for a description of some problems that we encountered while writing this parser.

In order to parse a specification in LaTeX markup, it is first converted into Unicode using the LaTeX markup to Unicode Converter shown on the left side, and subsequently parsed by the Unicode Parser described above. One requirement on the parser is that it retains the original line and column positions from the file that is parsed. This location information is added to the AST nodes as LocAnn annotations, so that tools can later provide error messages that contain accurate location information pointing to the original specification document. It is difficult to preserve this location information when a specification in LaTeX markup is converted into Unicode before it is parsed since we want to preserve the location within the LaTeX document, not within the temporary Unicode document.

Our solution to this problem is to design the LaTeX markup to Unicode converter so that it returns a token stream (with line and column number information) rather than just a sequence of Unicode characters. Then a special reader, called CZT Reader, accepts these tokens and passes the Unicode characters into the Unicode Parser. In addition to the usual methods provided by the Java class Reader, the CZT Reader class provides special methods to access line and column number information. Those methods are then used by the Unicode

---

[12] See http://www.cs.princeton.edu/~appel/modern/java/CUP.

`Scanner` to obtain location information for the tokens. This is an elegant way of retaining the original LATEX line and column positions, even though the LATEX input briefly becomes Unicode as described in the ISO Standard for Z. This solution is far simpler than writing a completely separate set of scanners specifically for LATEX input.

In addition to a parser for Z, an Object Z parser is provided, and a TCOZ parser is under development. The Object Z parser and scanner extend the Z parser and scanner by some more tokens and grammar rules. Unfortunately, it is quite difficult to reuse code from an automatically generated scanner or parser, and Cup does not provide means to do so. To avoid duplicated code, XML templates are used that contain the different parser and scanner variants. From this, the different input files for JFlex and Cup are generated. This maximises the commonality between the parsers and minimises versioning and maintenance problems.

A parsed Z specification can be typechecked using the `CZT Typechecker`. The type inference rules are defined in the ISO Standard for Z [1–§13] and explained in [10]. The `CZT Typechecker` is implemented as an AST visitor. It visits every term in the tree to determine its type (if any) and detects typing errors. If there are no typing errors in an expression, a `TypeAnn` annotation is added to the term, recording the expression's type. If there are type errors, a `TypeErrorAnn` annotation is added to the term. Each `TypeErrorAnn` records the position of the typing error in the original specification document using `LocAnn` annotations, and contains an error message describing the problem.

The typechecker also maintains a list of references to all `TypeErrorAnn` instances for easy printing of error messages. As defined in the ISO Standard for Z [1–§10.2], the typechecker also adds an annotation containing the signature of a paragraph (the empty signature for paragraphs that contain no global declarations), as well as a `SectTypeEnvAnn` annotation, which records the global declarations and their types visible in this section (including declarations for parent sections).

The `Unfolder` tool (which unfolds schema calculus operators and some other Z constructs) and the `Transformer` tool (which transforms ASTs by applying user-defined rewrite rules) are still under development. The `zml2html`, `z2jml` and `ZLive` animator tools are preliminary prototypes only. The `z2b` tool handles the Birthday Book example [11], but does not yet translate all Z constructs. The aim behind developing this Z-to-B translator is to give Z users access to the excellent refinement tools available in the B world (such as the B-Toolkit[13], Atelier-B[14] and the forthcoming Rodin tools[15]) and also to the BZ-TT automatic test generation tools [12] for B, which are being released commercially.[16]

---

[13] See http://www.b-core.com.

[14] See http://www.atelierb.societe.com/index_uk.html.

[15] See http://rodin-b-sharp.sourceforge.net.

[16] See http://www.leirios.com.

# 6     Challenges and Problems

This section describes some of the difficulties that we have encountered in trying to build a 'strongly conforming' Z tool as defined in the ISO Standard for Z [1–§5.2.5] (one that accepts all correct Z specifications, and rejects all incorrect specifications). We describe the solutions that we have adopted, and make some suggestions for how the ISO Standard for Z could be changed in the future to avoid some of the difficulties.

## 6.1     Grammar Complexities

The grammar in the ISO Standard for Z is intentionally ambiguous, and needs significant modification before it can be used as the basis for a parser. For example, there is ambiguity between schemas as expressions (sets of bindings) and predicates [1–§8.4]. Fortunately, Ian Toyn showed us some elegant strategies for obtaining an LALR(1) grammar[17] by merging expressions and predicates, thus parsing a larger set of inputs than desired. We use Java runtime typing (`instanceof`) to 'fix up' the types of the AST after parsing. That is, inputs that are definitely predicates are parsed into `Pred` objects, inputs that are definitely expressions are parsed into `Expr` objects, and ambiguous inputs, which could be interpreted as either expressions or predicates, are also initially parsed as `Expr` objects, because expressions are a subset of predicates in the ISO Standard for Z. If one of these ambiguous `Expr` objects is later placed into the AST in a context which requires it to be a predicate, it is then converted into a `Pred` object by wrapping it in an `ExprPred` object.[18] Conversely, if we have an AST context that requires an expression, but we find that the parsed subexpression is actually an instance of `Pred`, we throw an exception to report a syntax error.

## 6.2     Multiple Passes

The Z standard allows Z sections, operator definitions and LaTeX markup definitions to appear in almost any order. For example, operators can be used before they are defined. This means that, in general, it is necessary to make several passes over the input. In this subsection, we describe what passes are necessary and which ones we have currently implemented.

Firstly, the Z standard states that a Z specification is comprised of a sequence of Z sections, but suggests that tools should not require sections to appear in order. That is, tools should allow a section to appear prior to one of its parent sections. The Z standard does not define any relationship between *files* and section or specifications. In CZT, we allow a specification to be split over several files, and allow each file to contain one or more sections. The *parent* dependencies

---

[17] The 1 means one token of lookahead. But note that this is *after* the smart scanner has done unbounded lookahead to resolve the syntactic ambiguities described in [1–§8.3, Note 4].

[18] The CZT AST hierarchy currently separates expressions and predicates, as shown in Fig. 2, for clarity of programming and to obtain stronger typechecking in Java.

between sections means that it may be necessary to reorder sections *within* a file, as well as handle dependencies *between* files. The Z standard does not allow circular dependencies between sections. The CZT tools do not allow circular dependencies between files either.

Secondly, the scope of an operator template includes the whole section in which it appears. That is, a user defined operator can be used before its definition, making it impossible to parse a specification without reordering the paragraphs so that operator definitions are parsed before all other paragraphs. Thirdly, the same scope problem arises with LATEX markup directives; a user defined LATEX command might be used before its rendering information is given via a markup directive.

Thus in the general case, it seems necessary to make five character-level passes over the input file of a LATEX Z specification (while retaining the line and column positions of the original source file!):

1. to reorder the sections into parent-before-child order,
2. to collect the LATEX markup directives within each section,
3. to convert the LATEX input into Unicode characters,
4. to parse the operator template definitions,
5. to parse the Unicode and build the AST.

To simplify this, the CZT tools currently assume that sections are already in the correct order within each file and that LATEX markup directives and operator templates appear before they are used. This is the case in most specifications. It even seems desirable for human readability that operators are defined before they are used. These restrictions mean that pass 1 is unnecessary and allows the CZT tools to perform all the remaining passes within a single pipeline, which is simple and efficient. However, we intend to provide alternative modes and tools that will perform the reordering and additional passes when the user desires.

## 6.3    Operator Templates

Z provides a way to define new operators using so called *operator templates*. For example, the operator template

generic 30 leftassoc $(\_ \, a \, \_ \, b \, \_)$

defines a ternary operator with *name* "$\_ \, a \, \_ \, b \, \_$", with *precedence* 30, and *associativity* left. The ISO Standard for Z [1–§8.3] allows the same *word* to appear in several different operator templates, but with quite complex restrictions on which kinds of reuse are 'acceptable'. For instance, the operator template

generic 30 leftassoc $(\_ \, a \, \_ \, c \, \_)$

reuses the word "$a$" acceptably, but

generic 40 leftassoc $(\_ \, a \, \_ \, c \, \_)$

would be in conflict because both templates use the word *"a"* and have different precedence.

Each operator template also defines an association between operator words and so-called *operator tokens* [1–§7.4.4]. The context-sensitive lexis makes sure that operator names are lexed as the corresponding operator tokens. This implies that the association between word and token must be a function.

Thus, a Z tool needs to check for each Z section that its templates

- that share the same word have the same precedence,
- that share the same precedence have the same associativity, and
- that share the same word associate it with the same operator token.

When a section inherits multiple parent sections, the tool must detect any inconsistencies between the parents. Although these rules are complex, they seem necessary to prevent users defining ambiguous sets of operators. The CZT parser maintains the following data structures for each Z section to check these rules:[19]

$[OpName, OpWord, OpToken, OpTemplate]$

$Assoc ::= leftAssoc \mid rightAssoc$

```
┌─ OpTable ──────────────────────────────────────────┐
│  operators : OpName ⇸ OpTemplate                    │
│  operatorWords : OpWord ⇸ OpToken                   │
│  operatorPrecedence : OpWord ⇸ ℕ                    │
│  associativity : ℕ ⇸ Assoc                          │
└─────────────────────────────────────────────────────┘
```

The ISO Standard for Z does not answer some questions about user-defined operator precedences. For example, it does not specify what range of precedence numbers is allowed, which presumably means that any non-negative integer is allowed. This means that all 'strongly conforming' Z tools must accept an operator template definition whose precedence numeral is one million digits long. This seems unnecessarily complex. To improve interoperability between Z tools, and to make it easier to build strongly conforming tools, we recommend that future versions of the ISO Standard for Z specify a fixed range of operator precedences, such as $0 .. 1000$ (the CZT tools currently allow any integer in the range $0 .. 2^{31} - 1$).

Allowing user-defined operators with thousands of precedence levels makes parsing more difficult, as noted in the ISO Standard for Z. A fixed LL(k) or LALR(k) grammar is not sufficient, instead we parse all user-defined operators at the same precedence level, then add a post-processing phase that rotates adjacent levels of the AST to respect the user-defined precedences. The transformation

---

[19] This little Z specification has been checked with the CZT parser and typechecker. Our first try gave a syntax error on the 'leftassoc' word because it is a reserved word in standard Z! After we renamed it to 'leftAssoc' (similarly for 'rightAssoc'), it parsed and typechecked correctly.

rules for this post-processing are described in the ISO Standard for Z [1–§8.3, Note 3]. For example:

$$(e_1 \; infix_1 \; e_2) \; infix_2 \; e3 \Longrightarrow e_1 \; infix_1 \; (e_2 \; infix_2 \; e_3)$$

It was not initially clear to us whether these rules apply only to binary infix operators (like "_ + _"), or to all infix operators (for example, a user could define the ternary operator "_ ♣ _ ♠ _"). It turns out that the latter is the case. Similarly, the prefix and postfix operators mentioned in these rules may be operators with more than one argument, like the postfix relational image operator "_ (| _ |)".

Overall, operator templates are one of the most complex aspects of the ISO Standard for Z (they account for over 50% of the Z grammar!), but give Z users enormous flexibility in defining new mathematical notation.

## 6.4    Newlines and White Space

There are some unclear issues related to which Unicode characters should be used for line breaks, paragraph breaks etc. These have been addressed in a "Draft Technical Corrigendum 1" [13] to the ISO Standard for Z. This says that the NLCHAR mentioned throughout the ISO Standard for Z is in fact the Unicode character U+2028 (Line Separator). However, in practice, Unicode files are likely to continue using the platform-specific line terminator characters (LF for Linux, CRLF for Windows etc.) and the algorithm for translating these into Z characters is left somewhat vague, stating only that it should follow the Unicode standard.[20] In CZT, we currently treat all line termination sequences (LF, CR, CRLF) as equivalent to the Unicode Line Separator (U+2028) which is NLCHAR in the ISO Standard for Z.

Even after one has decided which Unicode characters correspond to newlines, the handling of newlines is very complex. It is described in the ISO Standard for Z [1–§7.5] where *newline categories* for tokens are defined. The newline category of a newline depends on the newline categories of the closest tokens. However, it also depends on the context where it appears. Quoting from the ISO Standard for Z: "*All newlines are soft outside of a DeclPart or a Predicate*". But newlines are supposed to be handled in the scanning phase where nothing is known about grammatical objects like DeclPart or Predicate. Furthermore, it is not clear to us what "outside" actually means. Is a newline after the formal parameters of a schema definition (which is just before the DeclPart) *outside* the DeclPart or not? According to the newline categories rule, a newline between formal parameters and declaration would be hard and therefore result in a parse error. Since it makes sense to allow newlines at this position, we conclude that it is outside the DeclPart and therefore soft. To handle this case, we had to modify the grammar of the parser to allow newlines there.

---

[20] See http://www.unicode.org/reports/tr13/tr13-9.html for an overview of the issue.

The handling of white space is very complex and fragile, particularly when translating to and from LaTeX markup. White space is meaningful in Unicode ("x'" is different from "x '"—and see [1–§8.4, Example 1] for a lovely example!), but not in the LaTeX markup, where explicit spacing commands must be used instead. The LaTeX input "f a" meant to be an application of function f to a is interpreted as the single word "fa", which usually results in interesting type errors. It must be written as "f~a" or using any other spacing command. A more tricky example is the following: the LaTeX inputs "[a_1, b_1]" and "[a_1 , b_1]" are both wrong. They result in parse errors since "a_1," is treated as one word (note the comma at the end). The reason for this is that the corresponding Unicode representation of "a_1" ends with a "word glue" character that glues the following comma on the word. It must therefore be written as "[a_1~, b_1]". To ease the problem, the CZT parser makes use of the nice idea from FuZZ to print a warning whenever it finds a suspicious word like, for instance, one that contains spaces or newlines in its LaTeX markup.

## 6.5   Retaining LaTeX Markup Directives

LaTeX markup directives contain rendering information and specify the conversion of user defined LaTeX commands to the corresponding sequences of Z characters [1–§A.2.3]. A typical directive is, for example,

```
%%Zchar \Delta U+0394
```

stating that the LaTeX command "\Delta" is rendered as the Unicode character with code point U+0394. When converting LaTeX markup to Unicode, this information is used but not retained in the resulting Unicode markup. This is problematic since the scope of a markup directive is the section in which it appears and any sections of which it is an ancestor. This implies that the parents of a section written in LaTeX markup should also be given in LaTeX markup.

ZML is intended to retain as much of the layout of the original specification as possible. If a specification is given in LaTeX markup, we want to retain the LaTeX markup directives in ZML. This also makes it possible for a LaTeX Z section to have a ZML section as a parent. So we extended ZML by a new kind of paragraph, LatexMarkupPara, which contains LaTeX markup directives. These paragraphs are added directly to the AST by the LaTeX to Unicode converter (the parser does not see them, since they do not appear in the Unicode markup).

## 6.6   Unicode to LaTeX Conversion

The translation from Unicode to LaTeX markup turned out to be more difficult than we expected. The ISO Standard for Z describes scanning and parsing of Z specifications on the basis of Unicode markup. In Annex A, LaTeX and e-mail markup are introduced and its conversion to Unicode is described. However, no algorithm for the translation of Unicode to LaTeX or e-mail markup is given.

Initially we thought that a simple character or token translater would be sufficient for translating specifications in Unicode into LaTeX markup. However, the task turned out to be quite difficult and a kind of parser is required to do this task. The reason for this is that the Unicode character '|' (U+007C), must be translated into different LATEX tokens depending on the context where it appears. In top-level paragraphs like axiomatic definitions and vertical schema definitions it must be translated into "\where" see [1–§A.2.7], but within predicates and expressions (including horizontal schema definitions) it is left as the character '|'. In future versions of the ISO Standard for Z, it might be nice to use separate Unicode characters to represent these rather different separators. For example, '├' (U+251C Box Drawings Light Vertical and Right) would look nicer as the separator within top-level paragraphs than '|'.

CZT provides a LATEX printer for parsed specifications. Thus, in order to convert Unicode to LATEX markup, a specification must be parsed before it can be printed as LATEX markup. This means that only syntactically correct specifications can be converted. CZT also provides a token converter from Unicode to LATEX markup that does not require parsing, but is affected by the '|' problem described above. The current workaround is to translate the Unicode character '|' (U+007C) to "\where" when '|' is on a line on its own, otherwise it is translated to '|'. Thus, the converter works only for specifications that obey this formatting rule.

### 6.7   Summary

Overall, we conclude that, partly for historical reasons, Z is a very complex language to scan and parse. It took us about 1 person-year to implement the scanners and parsers (Tim Miller developed most of the current Z and Object-Z parsers), with many iterations of finding increasingly complex syntax examples that required redesign of our architecture. If it was not for the fact that both authors of this paper are perfectionists and enjoy the challenge of getting every last case to work (elegantly), we probably would not have finished. In spite of these difficulties and the above comments, we note that the ISO Standard for Z does an excellent job of describing most of the complexities. Some very important implementation considerations are just briefly mentioned in notes and examples, but it is obvious that a great deal of care was taken in getting these right.

## 7   Conclusions and Future Work

The CZT Java framework and XML format have been developed in order to improve tool support for the Z specification language, particularly for the ISO Standard for Z. It allows developers to easily develop new Z tools and to integrate existing tools via the XML interchange format. The CZT software is available from the Sourceforge web-site http://czt.sourceforge.net under an open source license.

Currently, we are developing a *rewrite rule* mechanism for user-defined AST transformations and for unfolding schema operators. We are also working on a central *section manager* subsystem, which will manage all the Z objects, the dependencies between them and the commands that transform them.

In the future, we would like people to develop many more translators from the CZT AST (standard Z) into older dialects of Z to give access to the existing Z provers, and into Alloy[21] for performing simple animations and counter-example generation.

We would also like to integrate the CZT tools with an integrated development environment, to provide a full WYSIWYG editing and analysis environment for Z. We have developed an experimental plug-in for JEdit[22] that does this, but a better long-term alternative may be the Eclipse environment,[23] or the ZEUS[24] system, which is an extension of Adobe Framemaker.

## Acknowledgements

Thanks to Andrew Martin for proposing the CZT project, and to the dozen or more people who have contributed expertise and code over the last two years[25], particularly Jin Song Dong and his students at National University of Singapore, who have been working on the TCOZ extensions. Thanks to Ian Toyn for his XML DTD for Z, and for answering numerous questions about the ISO Standard for Z. Especial thanks to Tim Miller, who has implemented most of the Z and Object Z parser and typechecker.

## References

1. ISO/IEC 13568: Information Technology—Z Formal Specification Notation—Syntax, Type System and Semantics. First edn. ISO/IEC (2002)
2. Utting, M., Toyn, I., Sun, J., Martin, A., Dong, J.S., Daley, N., Currie, D.: ZML: XML support for standard Z. In: ZB 2003: Formal Specification and Development in Z and B: Third International Conference of B and Z Users, Turku, Finland, June 4-6, 2003. Proceedings, Springer-Verlag Heidelberg (2003) 437–456
3. Smith, G.: The Object-Z Specification Language. Advances in Formal Methods. Kluwer Academic Publishers (2000)
4. Mahony, B., Dong, J.S.: Timed communicating Object Z. IEEE Transactions on Software Engineering **26** (2000) 150–177
5. Gamma, E., Helm, R., Johnson, R., Vlissides, J.: Design Patterns: Elements of Reusable Object-Oriented Software. Addison Wesley, USA (1995)
6. Mai, Y., de Champlain, M.: A pattern language to visitors. In: The 8th Annual Conference of Pattern Languages of Programs (PLoP 2001), Monticello, Illinois, USA. (2001)

---

[21] See http://alloy.mit.edu.

[22] See http://www.jedit.org.

[23] See http://www.eclipse.org.

[24] See http://www.cs.virginia.edu/~zed/zeus.

[25] See http://czt.sourceforge.net/people.html.

7. Martin, A.C.: Acyclic visitor. In Martin, R.C., Riehle, D., Buschmann, F., eds.: Pattern Languages of Program Design 3, Addison-Wesley Longman Publishing Co., Inc. (1997)

8. Nordberg III, M.E.: Default and extrinsic visitor. In Martin, R.C., Riehle, D., Buschmann, F., eds.: Pattern Languages of Program Design 3, Addison-Wesley Longman Publishing Co., Inc. (1997)

9. Toyn, I., Stepney, S.: Characters + mark-up = Z lexis. In: ZB 2002: Formal Specification and Development in Z and B: 2nd International Conference of B and Z Users, Grenoble, France, January 23-25, 2002. Proceedings. Volume 2272 of LNCS., Springer-Verlag Heidelberg (2002) 100–119

10. Toyn, I., Valentine, S.H., Stepney, S., King, S.: Typechecking Z. In Bowen, J.P., Dunne, S., Galloway, A., King, S., eds.: ZB 2000: First International Conference of B and Z Users, York, UK, August 2000. Volume 1878 of LNCS., Springer (2000) 264–285

11. Spivey, J.M.: The Z Notation: A Reference Manual. Second edn. International Series in Computer Science. Prentice-Hall International (UK) Ltd (1992)

12. Legeard, B., Peureux, F., Utting, M.: Automated boundary testing from Z and B. In Eriksson, L.H., Lindsay, P., eds.: Formal Methods Europe, FME 2002. Volume 2391 of LNCS., Springer-Verlag (2002) 21–40

13. Toyn, I.: Information technology – Z formal specification notation – Syntax, type system and semantics. DRAFT TECHNICAL CORRIGENDUM 1, Corrections to use of Unicode. Available from `http://www-users.cs.york.ac.uk/~ian/zstan/IS.html` (2004) This draft has yet to be submitted for official ballot.

# Model Checking Z Specifications Using SAL

Graeme Smith and Luke Wildman

School of Information Technology and Electrical Engineering,
The University of Queensland 4072, Australia
{smith, luke}@itee.uq.edu.au

**Abstract.** The Symbolic Analysis Laboratory (SAL) is a suite of tools
for analysis of state transition systems. Tools supported include a simulator and four temporal logic model checkers. The common input language
to these tools was originally developed with translation from other languages, both programming and specification languages, in mind. It is,
therefore, a rich language supporting a range of type definitions and expressions. In this paper, we investigate the translation of Z specifications
into the SAL language as a means of providing model checking support
for Z. This is facilitated by a library of SAL definitions encoding the Z
mathematical toolkit.

**Keywords:** Z, model checking, SAL, tool support.

## 1   Introduction

The Symbolic Analysis Laboratory (SAL) [1] is aimed at allowing different verification tools, such as various types of model checkers and theorem provers, to
be combined. The input language shared by the tools was originally proposed as
a target for translation of a variety of specification and programming languages
and provides a broad range of features to support them. In this paper, we describe the translation of Z [18] to SAL for the purpose of taking advantage of the
variety of verification tools that SAL supports, as well as those it will support
in the future.

Currently SAL provides a suite of four model checkers and a simulator. The
SAL simulator is a customisable environment for manipulating state transition
systems and their traces, and it is a significant advance on Z animators such as
Possum [9]. The model checkers are also customisable. There are two symbolic
model checkers for checking linear time temporal logic (LTL) and branching
time temporal logic (CTL) properties [5]. There are also two *bounded* LTL model
checkers, one of which supports infinite types in the model's state space. Bounded
model checking involves a state space search to a given depth, rather than of
the entire state space. This is a way of finding counter-examples in large models
(proving a property, however, still involves a complete state space search). SAL
also supports a technique called *k-induction* [14] which allows the bounded model
checkers to be called iteratively to search further into the state space when a
counter-example is not yet found.

H. Treharne et al. (Eds.): ZB 2005, LNCS 3455, pp. 85–103, 2005.

Applying temporal logic model checking to Z allows us to check both invariant and behavioural properties of specified systems. The latter include liveness properties (e.g., *eventually* some state is reached, or some property remains true *until* some state is reached) which are valid under the assumption that operations continue to occur. Using CTL one can also check properties about the *possibility* of certain behaviours (e.g., it is possible, but not guaranteed, that some state can be reached).

Applying temporal logic model checking to Z, however, involves significant challenges. Z is a very expressive language supporting a range of datatypes and complex predicates which are difficult to compile into a representation suitable for model checking. Such challenges have meant that Z specifications have had to be rewritten in another notation in order to model check them. A Z specification writer may not, however, want to give up the expressiveness of Z (which aids in understandability, separation of concerns, etc.) for a less expressive model-checkable language.

SAL helps to solve this dilemma. Its compilation routines, based on the ICS decision procedure library [6], enable expressive mathematics to be used. In addition, the module mechanism of SAL is quite similar to the concept of a Z state transition system. In this paper, we explore the similarities between Z and SAL by defining a translation which enables (most) Z specifications to be accepted by the model checkers.

We model Z operations in SAL as having a *blocking* semantics, i.e., where operations are unable to occur outside their calculated preconditions. Under a blocking semantics, most temporal logic properties on states written in LTL are preserved by refinement, and all are preserved under simple restrictions on the refinement retrieve relation [3]. Similar results can be shown to hold for CTL.

This does not preclude model checking Z specifications with the conventional non-blocking semantics, i.e., where operations may occur outside their preconditions resulting in arbitrary state changes. All non-trivial temporal properties that hold for such specifications include an assumption that operations are not applied outside their preconditions. Hence, if properties are formulated correctly, what happens outside the precondition of operations (both in the specification and any refinement) is not important. As discussed by Smith and Winter [17], to prove arbitrary temporal properties of such specifications, operations must be *totalised*, i.e., have a true precondition.

Our translation scheme is straightforward, preserving Z-style predicates where primed and unprimed variables may be mixed freely, and following the Z approach of modelling relations, functions, sequences and bags as sets of tuples. The translation scheme has not yet been implemented; although we believe this is possible. Also, we have not yet fully considered optimising the encoding for efficient analysis. The paper presents a "proof of concept" (that Z *can* be model checked); issues such as optimising model checking efficiency and automation of the translation are areas of future work.

The paper is structured as follows. In Section 2, we give an overview of the SAL language. In Section 3, we show how *minimal* Z specifications, those not involving the use of datatypes from the Z mathematical toolkit nor advanced use of schemas, can be translated into SAL. In Section 4, we describe how the datatypes of the Z mathematical toolkit may be encoded as a library of SAL definitions and, hence, how our translation scheme may be extended. We then look at uses of schemas as predicates and types, and the schema calculus in Section 5. In Section 6, we close with a discussion of related work, an evaluation of the results of our translation, and our plans for further development.

## 2    The SAL Language

The common input language to the SAL tools was originally developed with translation from other languages, both programming and specification languages, in mind. It is a rich language supporting a range of type definitions and expressions. The former include basic types such as integers and naturals, tuple (or Cartesian product) types, total functions, enumerated types, recursive datatypes, array and record types, and subtypes of any other type defined in terms of set comprehensions. Expressions in the language may involve lambda abstractions and set comprehensions. Predicates (i.e., Boolean-valued expressions) may involve universal and existential quantification.

A complete syntax of the type and expression sublanguages of SAL can be found in the SAL language manual [2]. Syntax relevant to the work in this paper will be introduced as it is required. Below we describe the main structuring mechanisms of the SAL language: *contexts* and *modules*.

### 2.1    Contexts

A SAL context groups together a number of definitions and properties. The definitions include types, constants and modules for describing state transition systems. The properties, expressed in LTL or CTL, refer to modules and are intended to be checked by the model checking tools. Contexts may have both type and value parameters. Type parameters are treated as uninterpreted types, and value parameters as uninterpreted constants. For example, a context with type parameters $X$ and $Y$ and value parameter $N$ of type natural number is defined as follows.

$mycontext\{X, Y : TYPE;\ N : NATURAL\} : CONTEXT =$
$BEGIN$

$\quad \ldots$
$END$

where the ... represents the elided definitions and properties.

Contexts may refer to definitions in other contexts. In this way a SAL specification can be structured across several contexts, and contexts can be used to create libraries of commonly used definitions. The context above, for example, may be instantiated within another context. We could instantiate it with the type $NATURAL$ for $X$ and $Y$ and the value 3 for $N$ as follows.

$$mc : CONTEXT = mycontext\{NATURAL, NATURAL;\ 3\}$$

Then, given a definition *def* in *mycontext*, we can refer to *def* by *mc*!*def*.

Alternatively, we could have referred to *def* without the declaration of *mc* via *mycontext*$\{NATURAL, NATURAL;\ 3\}$!*def*.

## 2.2    Modules

Modules appear in contexts and are used to describe state transition systems. A module comprises the declaration of a set of variables representing the state of the module, and optional sections describing state invariants, module initialisation and possible transitions. An example of a module can be found at the end of Section 3.

The variables may be input variables, output variables, global variables or local variables. Input variables are not under the control of the module and are nondeterministically assigned a value in their type before each transition. All other variables are controlled by the module. Global variables may be controlled by more than one module within the same context.

There are also means of composing modules. These, however, are not discussed in this paper.

## 3    Basic Translation Approach

In this section, we show how *minimal* Z specifications can be encoded in the SAL language. By minimal, we mean specifications which do not make use of datatypes from the Z mathematical toolkit nor the advanced use of schemas (including the use of schemas as predicates and types, and the operators of the schema calculus). The encoding of the former will be detailed in Section 4 and the latter in Section 5.

Our translation scheme between Z and SAL requires the Z specification to be syntactically correct and type correct. To simplify the translation, we also assume some simple syntactic simplifications are made first. Specifically, schema references in the declaration part of schemas and quantified expressions are expanded, and predicates involving the quantifier $\exists_1$ are rewritten in terms of the quantifiers $\exists$ and $\forall$. Also, set comprehensions of the form $\{d \mid p \bullet e\}$ are converted to the simpler $\{d \mid p\}$ form. For example, $\{n : \mathbb{N} \mid n < 10 \bullet 2 * n\}$ is converted to $\{m : \mathbb{N} \mid \exists n : \mathbb{N} \bullet n < 10 \land m = 2 * n\}$. Similarly, $\mu$-expressions of the form $(\mu\, d \mid p \bullet e)$ are converted to the simpler $(\mu\, d \mid p)$ form.

## 3.1    Types and Constants

SAL supports the basic types *NATURAL* of natural numbers, and *INTEGER* of integers[1]. These types however can only be used with one of the four model

---

[1] It also supports the types *REAL* of real numbers, and *BOOLEAN* of Boolean values which are useful for certain extensions of Z.

checkers (the infinite-bounded model checker). In general, the model checkers work only with finite types. Therefore, subranges of *NATURAL* and *INTEGER* need to be used. For example, we could define the type *NAT* as the natural numbers between 0 and 100 as follows.

$$NAT : TYPE = [0..100]$$

The actual subrange required to perform effective checks will depend on the particular specification. Setting of the maximum value for the natural numbers (and minimum value for the integers) is therefore a task for the user. It requires a detailed understanding of the specification, or the use of abstraction techniques, and is not discussed further in this paper.

**Given sets** are used in Z when we want to abstract away from the actual values of a type. For example, the type *NAME* representing people's names can be specified as

[*NAME*]

In SAL, we need to give values for all types. Hence, such a type is represented by an enumerated type as follows

$$NAME : TYPE = \{NAME1, NAME2, NAME3\};$$

The cardinality and elements of this type are again the responsibility of the user. He or she needs to ensure that enough values are available to perform effective checks (either via his or her understanding of the specification, or the use of abstraction techniques).

**Free types** in Z enable the definition of types whose values are either constants or *constructors*. The latter construct values of the free type from other values. For example, the type of a process identifier may be *null* when no identifier has been allocated, and a natural number, otherwise.

$$PID \ ::= \ null \mid id\langle\!\langle \mathbb{N} \rangle\!\rangle$$

SAL supports a similar type definition facility. The above is represented in SAL as

$$PID : TYPE = DATATYPE$$
$$null,$$
$$id(nat : NAT)$$
$$END;$$

The label *nat* above is necessary and provides access to the number allocated to a process, i.e., if $p$ is a non-null process identifier then $nat(p)$ returns the number. Hence, an expression in Z which returns the number allocated to a process, i.e., $id^\sim(p)$, is translated as $nat(p)$.

In Z, the values used in a constructor may also be of the free type being defined. This allows recursive type definitions. Although this is also supported by SAL, it results in infinite types and hence disallows the use of most of the model checking tools.

**Abbreviation definitions** can be used to introduce types via expressions. For example, the type of all prime numbers could be specified as follows.

$$Primes == \{n : \mathbb{N} \mid \forall m : \mathbb{N} \bullet n \bmod m = 0 \Rightarrow m = n \vee m = 1\}$$

This is represented in SAL as a subtype of the type $NAT$ defined above.

$$Primes : TYPE = \{n : NAT \mid FORALL\ (m : NAT) :$$
$$n\ MOD\ m = 0\ =>\ m = n\ OR\ m = 1\};$$

Note the close mapping between the Z and SAL predicates. Of the primitive constructs used in Z predicates and expressions only $\mu$ (used for selecting a unique value satisfying a predicate) and $\mathbb{P}$ (used for denoting an arbitrary subset of a set) are not directly supported in SAL. We will delay the discussion of $\mathbb{P}$ until Section 4. With $\mu$-expressions, assuming our specification is correct Z, the predicate of the expression will guarantee a unique value. Hence, there is no need for SAL to check this. A predicate $x = (\mu\, n : \mathbb{N} \mid n * 1 = 3)$ can be represented in SAL by $x * 1 = 3$. When the predicate is not a simple equality, for example, $(\mu\, n : \mathbb{N} \mid n * 1 = 3) < y$ then we introduce an existentially quantified variable to denote the unique value defined by the $\mu$-expression. That is, the above is represented in SAL by $EXISTS\ (n : NAT) : n * 1 = 3\ AND\ n < y$.

Abbreviation definitions can also be used to define constants. For example, a constant $max$ could be specified as

$$max == 100$$

This is represented in SAL as

$$max : NAT = 100$$

**Axiomatic definitions** are also used in Z to define constants. For example,

$$
\begin{array}{|l}
n : \mathbb{N} \\
p : \mathbb{N} \times \mathbb{N} \\
\hline
n < 10 \\
\mathit{first}(p) = n
\end{array}
$$

In SAL, we declare them using set comprehensions in order to capture the predicate of the axiomatic definition.

$$n : \{n : NAT \mid n < 10\};$$
$$p : \{p : [NAT, NAT] \mid p.1 = n\};$$

Z generic constants can also be translated by making the generic type a parameter of the SAL context in which the constant is declared. Since we may require more than one instantiation of a generic constant, it should be declared in its own context and its definition imported and instantiated as required.

## 3.2    Schemas

The main use of schemas in Z is in the definition of state transition systems. Typically, a specification has a single state schema, an initial state schema and a number of operation schemas. Such a specification can be represented by a SAL module.

The variables of the state schema become local variables of the module, and inputs and outputs of the operations become input and output variables of the module respectively. The output variables need to be renamed since ! is not allowed as part of a variable name in SAL. We choose to translate an output $x!$ in Z to an output variable $x\_$ in SAL.

The key to representing the schema predicates is a powerful *guarded command* facility supported by SAL for defining the initialisation and transition sections of a module. Guarded commands are of the form

$$Guard \;\; \longrightarrow \;\; Assignment \;;$$
$$\vdots$$
$$Assignment$$

A guard is an arbitrary predicate which may refer to values of primed (post-state) variables. The assignments they guard may be nondeterministic, i.e., each variable is assigned a value from a set of potential values. For example, a variable $x$ can be assigned a value from the set of natural numbers less than 10 as follows.

$$x' \; IN \; \{n : NAT \mid n < 10\}$$

Any variables which are not assigned a value remain unchanged.

To support such guarded commands, SAL checks the guard after the assignments are made and, if it is false, undoes the assignments and makes new assignments when possible. The guarded command is enabled only when a set of assignments satisfying the guard can be found.

A Z predicate referring to a variable $x : \mathbb{N}$

$$x' = 3 * x$$

can hence be represented in SAL as the guarded command

$$x' = 3 * x \; \longrightarrow \; x' \; IN \; \{x : NAT \mid TRUE\}$$

Note that the guard can be any predicate and hence if the above predicate were instead

$$x = 3 * x'$$

it could be represented in SAL as

$$x = 3 * x' \; \longrightarrow \; x' \; IN \; \{x : NAT \mid TRUE\}$$

This approach allows the flexibility required to *directly* translate Z predicates into SAL. Some care must be taken with quantified variables, however, as discussed after the example below.

Guarded commands may be used in the initialisation and transition sections of a SAL module. The initialisation section of a SAL module may comprise a single guarded command. The transition section may comprise a choice between several guarded commands separated by the syntax []. These guarded commands may be labelled to aid the understanding of counter-examples generated by the SAL model checkers. Normally, a counter-example is given as a sequence of states; labels in the counter-example indicate which branch of the transition fired between consecutive states.

Guarded commands may not be used in a state invariant section of a SAL module. This is not a problem, however, given the syntactic simplifications we have assumed. Specifically, uses of schema inclusion are expanded before the translation to SAL. Hence, in the Z specification which we translate to SAL, the state schema's predicate will be included in the initial state schema, and in both unprimed and primed form in each operation schema. Hence, it will be true initially and after each operation as required.

In the translation from Z to SAL, the initial state schema's predicate becomes the guard of the initialisation section of the module. The operations' predicates become the guards of the transition section. In each guarded command representing initialisation or an operation, all state variables are assigned values non-deterministically from their types. For operations with outputs, the corresponding output variables are additionally assigned values nondeterministically from their types. For such operations, we need to refer to the output variable in primed form in SAL.

Finally, SAL's model checkers may produce unsound results when a module being checked can deadlock. It is therefore necessary to ensure that the transition relation is total. This can be ensured by a final guarded command in the transition section of the form

$ELSE \quad -->$

This guard will evaluate to true only when all other guards evaluate to false. There are no assignments, so the state will remain unchanged.

As an example, consider the following Z specification.

| ┌─ *State* ─────────── |
| :--- |
| $x : \mathbb{N}$ |
| ─────────── |
| $x < 10$ |

| ┌─ *Init* ─────────── |
| :--- |
| *State* |
| ─────────── |
| $x = 0$ |

| ┌─ *Increment* ─────────── |
| :--- |
| $\Delta State$ |
| $x! : \mathbb{N}$ |
| ─────────── |
| $x' = x + 1$ |
| $x! = x'$ |

| ┌─ *Choose* ─────────── |
| :--- |
| $\Delta State$ |
| $x? : \mathbb{N}$ |
| ─────────── |
| $\exists x : \mathbb{N} \bullet x < x? \wedge x' = x$ |

Its SAL translation is

$state : MODULE =$
    $BEGIN$
        $INPUT\ x? : NAT$
        $LOCAL\ x : NAT$
        $OUTPUT\ x_- : NAT$
        $INITIALIZATION\ [x = 0\ AND\ x < 10$
                      $--> \ x\ IN\ \{n : NAT\ |\ TRUE\}]$
        $TRANSITION\ [\ Increment :\ x' = x + 1\ AND\ x_-' = x'\ AND$
                          $x < 10\ AND\ x' < 10$
                        $--> x'\ IN\ \{n : NAT\ |\ TRUE\};$
                            $x_-'\ IN\ \{n : NAT\ |\ TRUE\}$
              $[]\ Choose :\ (EXISTS\ (x0 : NAT) :$
                        $x0 < x?\ AND\ x' = x0)\ AND$
                        $x < 10\ AND\ x' < 10$
                        $--> \ x'\ IN\ \{n : NAT\ |\ TRUE\}$
              $[]\ ELSE\ --> \ ]$
    $END$

Note that the quantified variable in the transition corresponding to *Choose* is renamed to a fresh variable $x0$. This is because SAL regards the prime symbol as an operator on a state variable rather than a decoration on a name. If we left the quantified variable as $x$, it would not be possible to refer to $x'$ in its scope since $x$ would no longer refer to the state variable, but instead to the quantified variable. For similar reasons, it is not possible to translate a predicate $\forall x' : NAT \bullet \ldots$ directly; $x'$ is not a name but an expression involving the prime operator. We translate this predicate to $\forall x1 : NAT \bullet \ldots$ where $x1$ is a fresh variable.

# 4    Z Mathematical Toolkit

The Z mathematical toolkit [18] is a library of definitions of types and operators used commonly in Z. It includes operators for sets and natural numbers, and types and operators for relations, functions, sequences and bags. The encoding of these definitions in SAL are, for the most part, relatively straightforward. Complications arise for those definitions given for Z in terms of the $\mu$ operator since this is not supported by SAL. The affected definitions are those for function application and set size, #. Complications also arise from our use of a finite subrange of natural numbers. The affected definitions are those for sequence concatenation and bag union.

## 4.1    Sets

As mentioned in Section 3, SAL does not support an operator equivalent to the $\mathbb{P}$ operator of Z. However, the standard SAL installation comes with a context *set* which defines a type which is an arbitrary subset of another type given as a type parameter. A part of this context is shown below.

$set\{ T : TYPE; \} : CONTEXT =$
$BEGIN$
$\quad Set : TYPE = [T \rightarrow BOOLEAN];$
$\quad \vdots$
$END$

The type *Set* defined in *set* maps all elements in the parameter type $T$ to a Boolean value (the notation $[X \rightarrow Y]$ denotes a total function). The variables which are mapped to *TRUE* are regarded as being in the set whereas those mapped to *FALSE* are not. This is also the representation underlying SAL's set comprehensions. Hence, it is legal, for example, to write predicates of the form $s = \{x : X \mid \ldots\}$ when $s$ is declared to be of type $set\{X; \}!Set$.

Given this representation of sets, the basic set operators are defined in context *set*. For example, set membership is defined as

$contains?(s : Set, e : T) : BOOLEAN = s(e);$

which is a short-hand for writing

$contains? : [[Set, T] \rightarrow BOOLEAN] = LAMBDA\ (s : Set, e : T) : s(e);$

Similarly, set union is defined as

$union(s1 : Set, s2 : Set) : Set = LAMBDA\ (e : T) : s1(e)\ OR\ s2(e);$

We have extended *set* with additional set operators that are used in Z. For example, we defined subset, $\subseteq$, as[2]

$subset?(s1 : Set, s2 : Set) : BOOLEAN =$
$\quad FORALL\ (e : T) : contains?(s1, e) => contains?(s2, e);$

The other set operators can be defined similarly except for the size operator, #, which is defined using the $\mu$ operator in Spivey [18] as follows.

$$\#S = (\mu\, n : \mathbb{N} \mid (\exists f : 1 \ldots n \rightarrowtail S \bullet \operatorname{ran} f = S))$$

In SAL, we encode it as a function which takes a set and a natural number as arguments and returns *TRUE* when the number is the size of the set.

$size?(s : Set, n : NATURAL) : BOOLEAN =$
$\quad (EXISTS\ (f : [[1..n] \rightarrow T]) :$
$\quad\quad (FORALL\ (x1, x2 : [1..n]) : f(x1) = f(x2) => x1 = x2)\ AND$
$\quad\quad (FORALL\ (y : T) : s(y) <=> (EXISTS\ (x : [1..n]) : f(x) = y)));$

---

[2] We have adopted the convention used in the *set* context that functions which return a Boolean value have names ending in '?'.

The first conjunct ensures that the total function $f$ is an injection, and the second that its range is equal to the set $s$.

A Z predicate of the form $n = \#s$ could, therefore, be translated to $size?(s, n)$. However, in the general case where we do not have a simple equality, an existentially quantified variable needs to be introduced. For example, $\#s < 5$ is translated to $EXISTS\ (n : NAT) : size?(s, n)\ AND\ n < 5$.

## 4.2    Relations

Relations are modelled, as they are in Z, as sets of tuples. This allows set operators to be used directly on relations. We define a context *relation* which has two type parameters $X$ and $Y$ corresponding to the domain and range types respectively.

$relation\{X, Y : TYPE;\ \} : CONTEXT =$
$BEGIN$
$\quad xset : CONTEXT = set\{X;\ \};$
$\quad yset : CONTEXT = set\{Y;\ \};$
$\quad tset : CONTEXT = set\{[X, Y];\ \};$

$\quad dom(r : tset!Set) : xset!Set =$
$\quad\quad \{x : X \mid EXISTS\ (t : [X, Y]) : tset!contains?(r, t)\ AND\ t.1 = x\};$
$\quad ran(r : tset!Set) : yset!Set =$
$\quad\quad \{y : Y \mid EXISTS\ (t : [X, Y]) : tset!contains?(r, t)\ AND\ t.2 = y\};$
$\quad image(r : tset!Set, xs : xset!Set) : yset!Set =$
$\quad\quad \{y : Y \mid EXISTS\ (t : [X, Y]) : tset!contains?(r, t)\ AND$
$\quad\quad\quad\quad\quad xset!contains?(xs, t.1)\ AND\ t.2 = y\};$
$\quad\quad \vdots$

$END$

This context instantiates the *set* context three times: with type $X$, type $Y$ and the tuple type $[X, Y]$. Hence, it can refer to operators on sets of these types. This is needed in the definitions of the operators for domain (*dom*), range (*ran*) and relational image (*image*) shown. Other operators, for example, relational composition, domain and range restriction and subtraction, and relational inverse, can be defined similarly.

## 4.3    Functions

Although total functions are supported as a primitive in SAL, partial functions are not. To encode partial functions, we have simply followed the approach of Z, i.e., partial functions are appropriately restricted relations. This approach has the advantage that relational operators defined in the *relation* context can be used directly on partial functions, as can set operators defined in the context *set*.

**Aside.** An alternative approach would be to encode partial functions as SAL total functions. This would require introducing an 'undefined' element to all partial function range types (which could be done using the SAL datatype facility), and additional definitions of the set and relational operators. These definitions would be complicated by the fact that their argument and result types could be a combination of sets and SAL total functions. Investigating the comparative efficiency of such an approach is an area of future work.

$$function\{X, Y : TYPE; \} : CONTEXT =$$
$$BEGIN$$
$$\quad tset : CONTEXT = set\{[X, Y]; \};$$
$$\quad rel : CONTEXT = relation\{X, Y; \};$$

$$\quad pfun : TYPE = \{f : tset!Set \mid$$
$$\qquad\qquad FORALL\ (x : X, y1, y2 : Y) :$$
$$\qquad\qquad\qquad tset!contains?(f, (x, y1))\ AND$$
$$\qquad\qquad\qquad tset!contains?(f, (x, y2))\ =>$$
$$\qquad\qquad\qquad y1 = y2\};$$
$$\quad tfun : TYPE = \{f : pfun \mid rel!dom(f) = \{x : X \mid TRUE\}\};$$
$$\qquad \vdots$$

$$END$$

The context *function* introduces a type *pfun* of partial functions. A type for total functions *tfun* is also shown. Similar types can be given for the other kinds of functions (injections, surjections and bijections) in Z. The functional override operator can be defined as in Spivey [18].

Function application is defined using the $\mu$ operator in Spivey [18] as follows.

$$f(x) = (\mu\, y : Y \mid (x, y) \in f)$$

In SAL, we encode it (within context *function*) as a function which takes a (partial) function $f$ and a domain value $x$ and range value $y$ of $f$ as arguments and returns *TRUE* when $f(x) = y$.

$$apply?(f : tset!Set, x : X, y : Y) : BOOLEAN = tset!contains?(f, (x, y));$$

Its use is similar to that of the *size?* function defined for sets. A Z predicate of the form $y = f(x)$ could be translated to $apply?(f, x, y)$. However, in the general case where we do not have a simple equality, an existentially quantified variable needs to be introduced. For example, $f(x) < 5$ is translated to *EXISTS* $(y : NAT) : apply?(f, x, y)\ AND\ y < 5$.

Note that *apply?* takes a tuple set, rather than a partial function, as its first argument. This is for reasons of efficiency. Since we assume that the Z specification is correct Z, function application will only be used on variables which are functions. Therefore, it is not necessary for SAL to check the type of such a variable, i.e., check that it is a partial function, each time function application occurs.

## 4.4    Sequences and Bags

Sequences and bags are specified, as in Z, as appropriately restricted partial functions. In this section, we will focus on sequences; bags can be defined in SAL in a similar manner.

As well as a parameter $X$ for the range type, the context *sequence* requires a variable parameter $N$ of type $NATURAL$ to represent the maximum number of elements in a sequence. When instantiating the context *sequence*, we set this number to be equal to the maximum natural number (selected by the user as described in Section 3.1). It is used to ensure the type *seq* of sequences is finite; specifically, sequences can have at most $N$ elements.

$$sequence\{X : TYPE;\ N : NATURAL\} : CONTEXT =$$
$$BEGIN$$
$$\qquad nat : TYPE = [0..N];$$
$$\qquad nat1 : TYPE = [1..N];$$
$$\qquad nset : CONTEXT = set\{nat1;\ \};$$
$$\qquad tset : CONTEXT = set\{[nat1, X];\ \};$$
$$\qquad rel : CONTEXT = relation\{nat1, X;\ \};$$
$$\qquad fun : CONTEXT = function\{nat1, X;\ \};$$

$$\qquad seq : TYPE = \{s : fun!pfun \mid EXISTS\ (n : nat) :$$
$$\qquad\qquad\qquad\qquad\qquad rel!dom(s) = \{x : nat1 \mid x\ <=\ n\}\};$$

$$\qquad cat(s1 : tset!Set, s2 : tset!Set) : tset!Set =$$
$$\qquad\qquad LET\ s : tset!Set =$$
$$\qquad\qquad\qquad \{t : [nat1, X] \mid EXISTS\ (n : nat) :$$
$$\qquad\qquad\qquad\qquad\qquad rel!dom(s1) = \{x : nat1 \mid x\ <=\ n\}\ AND$$
$$\qquad\qquad\qquad\qquad\qquad (EXISTS\ (t2 : [nat1, X]) :$$
$$\qquad\qquad\qquad\qquad\qquad\qquad tset!contains?(s2, t2)\ AND$$
$$\qquad\qquad\qquad\qquad\qquad\qquad (t2.1 + n < N => t.1 = t2.1 + n)\ AND$$
$$\qquad\qquad\qquad\qquad\qquad\qquad (t2.1 + n >= N => t.1 = N)\ AND$$
$$\qquad\qquad\qquad\qquad\qquad\qquad t.2 = t2.2)\}$$
$$\qquad\qquad IN\ tset!union(s1, s);$$
$$\qquad\qquad \vdots$$
$$END$$

The context defines two types $nat$ and $nat1$ which represent the natural numbers and strictly positive natural numbers, respectively, up to $N$. The latter set is used for the domain of the sequence type $seq$. The predicate in the set comprehension defining this type ensures that the actual domain of any sequence is a contiguous set of numbers up to a maximum value less than or equal to $N$.

The definition of concatenation is shown above. Again we have used tuple sets as the types of the arguments for reasons of efficiency. The definition uses a $LET \ldots IN$ clause to introduce a set $s$ which corresponds to the second argument of the operator ($s2$ above) with each of its domain values increased by the length of the first argument ($s1$ above), except when the new value would exceed $N$, in which case the domain value is set to $N^3$.

The result of concatenation is the union of $s1$ and $s$. Note that this tuple set will not be a sequence when the combined length of $s1$ and $s2$ exceeds $N$. In this case, there will be more than one tuple with $N$ as its domain value.

In the translation of a Z specification, however, the result of sequence concatenation will be restricted to also be a sequence, i.e., of type $seq$. Hence, trying to concatenate a pair of sequences which together have more than $N$ elements will not be possible; the result would not be of type $seq$. That is, the guard in SAL will not be able to be satisfied by any assignment of values and the branch of the transition in which the concatenation occurs will not fire. This ensures that the domain of a sequence does not extend beyond our subrange of natural numbers.

Other sequence operators such as head, tail, front and last are readily defined as in Spivey [18].

## 4.5    Extending the Basic Translation Approach

To translate Z specifications using the Z mathematical toolkit, we simply import the definitions required from the appropriate contexts defined above. When a state variable is declared to be a relation, function, sequence or bag, it is declared to be a tuple set in the corresponding SAL. For example, a Z declaration $s : seq\ T$ is translated to $s : set\{[[1..N], T];\ \}!Set$, where $N$ is the maximum natural number. To ensure that $s$ is indeed a sequence, we also make sure its assignment initially and after each operation is restricted to sequences. That is, the assignments are of the form $s\ IN\ \{s : sequence\{T;\ N\}!seq\ |\ TRUE\}$.

This approach is more efficient than declaring the SAL variable to be of the more complex type. When the latter is done, the tools spend a significantly larger amount of time converting the specified state transition system into the internal Binary Decision Diagram (BDD) representation on which analysis is performed.

## 5    Schemas Revisited

Z allows the use of schemas to define other schemas via their use as predicates and types and via the operators of the schema calculus. Most of this is peculiar to Z, and hence it is not directly supportable in SAL. Our translation scheme is extended to support these uses of schemas as follows.

A schema occurring as a predicate is translated to the SAL translation of its predicate. A schema occurring as a type is translated to a subtype of a SAL record type whose indices correspond to the names of the schema's variables. For example, given the following Z schema

---

[3] The addition operator is defined on the integer type and may return any value of this type, despite its arguments belonging to particular subranges of integers.

$$\begin{array}{|l}\hline S \\\hline x, y : \mathbb{N} \\\hline x \leqslant y \\\hline\end{array}$$

the predicate $S$ is translated to $x <= y$. The variable declaration $a : S$ is translated to the more general declaration $a : [\# \ x : NAT, \ y : NAT \ \#]$ and the value of $a$ restricted by assignments (occurring in the initialisation and transitions of its module) of the form $a \ IN \ \{s : [\# \ x : NAT, \ y : NAT \ \#] \ | \ s.x <= s.y\}$. The notation $[\# \ldots \#]$ denotes a SAL record type.

The Z notation $\theta S$ constructs a schema binding of schema type $S$ with values taken from common-named variables in the current scope. It can be translated to the SAL record literal $(\# \ x := x, \ y := y \ \#)$, i.e., the record whose $x$ index maps to the value of $x$ in the current scope, and whose $y$ index maps to the value of $y$ in the current scope.

All expressions involving the operators of the schema calculus can be flattened to a single equivalent schema [18]. Our approach is to perform this flattening as part of the translation process. For example, given $S$ above and

$$\begin{array}{|l}\hline T \\\hline y, z : \mathbb{N} \\\hline z = y \\\hline\end{array}$$

we flatten the schema expression $S \Rightarrow T$ to

$$\begin{array}{|l}\hline S \Rightarrow T \\\hline x, y, z : \mathbb{N} \\\hline x \leqslant y \Rightarrow y = z \\\hline\end{array}$$

and translate this resulting schema as before. Some schema calculus operators, for example the precondition operator, pre, involve quantification over state variables. The flattening process needs to be defined such that fresh variables are used instead of the state variables as described at the end of Section 3.

## 6   Discussion

Although Z has been encoded in a number of theorem provers including PVS [19], Isabelle/HOL [12] and EVES [15], there have been no full encodings in a model checking tool. The Alloy approach of Jackson [10] brings "Z-style specification the kind of automation offered by model checkers." However, the Alloy language, although quite elegant and expressive in its own right, is significantly different to Z. Furthermore, the Alloy analyser is not a temporal logic model checker and is predominantly used for checking system invariants. We see it as being complementary to our approach.

The closest work to ours is that of encoding the Z extensions, CSP-OZ, CSP-Z and Object-Z, in the CSP model checker, FDR [7, 13, 11]. The input language to FDR is quite expressive allowing a straightforward translation of many Z predicates. Although FDR lacks direct support for some constructs supported by SAL, such as quantification, it includes direct support for others, such as sequences and sequence concatenation, which SAL does not.

The main difference between the two approaches is the way the model checkers are used. FDR is not a temporal logic model checker. Rather, it checks that a refinement relation holds between two models. Therefore, to check a property holds for a given model $M$, we need to state the property itself as a model: one that is refined by $M$. This can be difficult for a novice user. Also, since FDR was developed for a process algebra, rather than a state-based notation, encoding Z in it is arguably more difficult; to date, there is no full encoding of Z in FDR.

As with the FDR approaches, our approach has certain limitations. Firstly, all types must be finite (unless the infinite bounded model checker is used). This rules out the use of the types $\mathbb{N}$ and $\mathbb{Z}$, given sets and recursive type definitions in Z specifications. Furthermore, even finite types need to be small. As well as causing the state-explosion problem, large types can result in the conversion process from the input language to the analysable BDD representation becoming a bottleneck.

As an indication of the time required for model checking, the table below presents some figures for an Alternating Bit Protocol (ABP) specification adapted from the Object-Z specification in Duke and Rose [4]. The translated SAL specification has 7 state variables, including 2 which are sequences (1 of these is a sequence of tuples), and 8 operations. The property proved was an LTL encoding of the obvious one for this protocol: when there is no indefinite loss of messages on the message channel, all transmitted messages will eventually be received. The property was checked on a PC with a 3GHz Intel Pentium 4 processor and 512MB of RAM.

| Max. natural number (N) | Verification time (seconds) | Total time (seconds) |
|---|---|---|
| 4 | 0.18 | 8.39 |
| 8 | 3.43 | 22.72 |
| 12 | 27.48 | 151.31 |

For N greater than 12, the model checker did not return after 30 minutes due to the limits of the available memory being reached and the need for extensive swapping. This is due to the large BDD representation to cater for the sequences, especially the sequence of tuples. Although any of the above values of $N$ are sufficient to check the property for this case study, other case studies of similar complexity may require larger values for $N$.

There are a number of ways to improve on these results. Firstly, our encoding of Z in SAL is only one possible encoding. Some improvement in the above results could be made by a more efficient encoding. We have already discovered it is more efficient to declare variables by their base types (sets of tuples for functions, sequences and bags) and constrain them when assignments are made. In the ABP case study, this resulted in a five-fold decrease in total model checking time.

Secondly, the model checking tools support many optimisation features (including control of BDD variable ordering) which we have not utilised. Thirdly, they also support a variable abstraction facility which can be used to effectively ignore variables not influencing a property we wish to prove. In addition to this, future versions of SAL are expected to support predicate abstraction [8].

Our future work will investigate all of the above options, as well as developing our own abstraction techniques. The latter will be based on recent work on data abstraction [20] and predicate abstraction [17] in the Z context.

Regarding other future work, an obvious next step is to automate our translation scheme and pretty print the SAL output to make it more familiar to Z users. These tasks should not prove too onerous given that both Z and SAL have XML representations, and the SAL tools have explicit support for pretty printing. Our approach could also be adapted to variants of Z. We are particularly interested in additionally developing support for Object-Z[16]. As well as abstraction, decomposition of specifications based on the modular structure of Object-Z may be beneficial for this work [21].

## 7   Conclusion

We have presented an approach for translating between Z specifications and the input language to the SAL tool suite. This makes it possible to simulate and model check Z specifications. The latter includes both LTL and CTL model checking including bounded LTL model checking with infinite types. Our approach enables the conventional use of arbitrary predicates to describe operations in Z, and also supports the flexible "everything is a set" construction of the Z mathematical toolkit. Our future work will focus on automating the translation process and extending the limits on the size and complexity of types in Z specifications that can be supported by the approach.

## Acknowledgements

Thanks to Leonardo de Moura and John Rushby for their help with our use of SAL. Thanks to John Derrick and Kirsten Winter for discussions on aspects of this work, and to the anonymous referees for their comments which helped to improve the paper. Luke Wildman was supported by an Australian Research Council Discovery grant, DP0343877: *Practical Tools and Techniques for the Testing of Concurrent Software Components*.

# References

1. L. de Moura, S. Owre, H. Rueß, J. Rushby, N. Shankar, M. Sorea, and A. Tiwari. SAL 2. In R. Alur and D. Peled, editors, *International Conference on Computer Aided Verification (CAV 2004)*, volume 3114 of *LNCS*, pages 496–500. Springer-Verlag, 2004.

2. L. de Moura, S. Owre, and N. Shankar. The SAL language manual. Technical Report SRI-CSL-01-02 (Rev. 2), SRI International, 2003.

3. J. Derrick and G. Smith. Linear temporal logic and Z refinement. In C. Rattray, S. Maharaj, and C. Shankland, editors, *Algebraic Methodology and Software Technology (AMAST 2004)*, volume 3116 of *LNCS*, pages 117–131. Springer-Verlag, 2004.

4. R. Duke and G. Rose. *Formal Object-Oriented Specification using Object-Z*. Cornerstones of Computing. MacMillan, 2000.

5. E.A. Emerson. Temporal and modal logic. In J. van Leeuwen, editor, *Handbook of Theoretical Computer Science*, volume B, pages 996–1072. Elsevier Science Publishers, 1990.

6. J.-C. Filliâtre, S. Owre, H. Rueß, and N. Shankar. ICS: integrated canonizer and solver. In G. Berry, H. Comon, and A. Finkel, editors, *International Conference on Computer Aided Verification (CAV 2001)*, volume 2102 of *LNCS*, pages 246–249. Springer-Verlag, 2001.

7. C. Fischer and H. Wehrheim. Model-checking CSP-OZ specifications with FDR. In K. Araki, A. Galloway, and K. Taguchi, editors, *International Conference on Integrated Formal Methods (IFM '99)*, pages 315–334. Springer-Verlag, 1999.

8. S. Graf and H. Saïdi. Construction of abstract state graphs with PVS. In *International Conference on Computer Aided Verification (CAV '97)*, volume 1254 of *LNCS*, pages 72–83. Springer-Verlag, 1997.

9. D. Hazel, P. Strooper, and O. Traynor. Possum: An animator for the SUM specification language. In W. Wong and K. Leung, editors, *Asia Pacific Software Engineering Conference (APSEC '97)*, pages 42–51. IEEE Computer Society, 1997.

10. D. Jackson. Alloy: A lightweight modelling language. Technical Report 797, MIT Laboratory for Computer Science, 2000.

11. G. Kassel and G. Smith. Model checking Object-Z classes: Some experiments with FDR. In *Asia-Pacific Software Engineering Conference (APSEC 2001)*, pages 445–452. IEEE Computer Society Press, 2001.

12. Kolyang, T. Santen, and B. Wolff. A structure preserving encoding of Z in Isabelle/HOL. In J. von Wright, J. Grundy, and J. Harrison, editors, *Theorem Proving in Higher Order Logics (TPHOLs '96)*, volume 1125 of *LNCS*, pages 283–298. Springer-Verlag, 1996.

13. A. Mota and A. Sampaio. Model-checking CSP-Z: strategy, tool support and industrial application. *Science of Computer Programming*, 40:59–96, 2001.

14. H. Rueß and L. de Moura. Bounded model checking and induction: From refutation to verification. In W. Hunt and F. Somenzi, editors, *International Conference on Computer Aided Verification (CAV 2003)*, volume 2725 of *LNCS*, pages 14–26. Springer-Verlag, 2003.

15. M. Saaltink. The Z-Eves system. In J. Bowen, M. Hinchey, and D. Till, editors, *International Conference of Z Users (ZUM '97)*, volume 1212 of *LNCS*, pages 72–85. Springer-Verlag, 1997.

16. G. Smith. *The Object-Z Specification Language*. Advances in Formal Methods. Kluwer Academic Publishers, 2000.

17. G. Smith and K. Winter. Proving temporal properties of Z specifications using abstraction. In D. Bert, J.P. Bowen, S. King, and M. Waldén, editors, *International Conference of Z and B Users (ZB 2003)*, volume 2651 of *LNCS*, pages 260–279. Springer-Verlag, 2003.

18. J.M. Spivey. *The Z Notation: A Reference Manual.* Prentice Hall, 2nd edition, 1992. http://spivey.oriel.ox.ac.uk/~mike/zrm/.

19. D. Stringer-Calvert, S. Stepney, and I. Wand. Using PVS to prove a Z refinement: A case study. In J. Fitzgerald, C. Jones, and P. Lucas, editors, *Formal Methods Europe (FME '97)*, volume 1313 of *LNCS*, pages 573–588. Springer-Verlag, 1997.

20. H. Wehrheim. Data abstraction for CSP-OZ. In J. Woodcock and J. Wing, editors, *World Congress on Formal Methods (FM '99)*, volume 1709 of *LNCS*. Springer-Verlag, 1999.

21. K. Winter and G. Smith. Compositional verification for Object-Z. In D. Bert, J.P. Bowen, S. King, and M. Waldén, editors, *International Conference of Z and B Users (ZB 2003)*, volume 2651 of *LNCS*, pages 280–299. Springer-Verlag, 2003.

# Proving Properties of Stateflow Models Using ISO Standard Z and CADiZ

Ian Toyn and Andy Galloway

Department of Computer Science, University of York,
Heslington, York, YO10 5DD, UK
{ian, andyg}@cs.york.ac.uk

**Abstract.** This paper focuses on the use of ISO Standard Z and CADiZ in the formal validation of Stateflow models against requirements-oriented assumptions. It documents some of what the Simulink/Stateflow Analyser tool does in support of the Practical Formal Specification method. The tool aims to automate the formal validations of the method, so that users of Simulink/Stateflow can benefit from them. The Z exploits some notations that are particular to ISO Standard Z. The automation is aided by quite terse tactics interpreted by CADiZ.

## 1   Introduction

This paper focuses on the use of ISO Standard Z and CADiZ in the formal validation of Stateflow models against requirements-oriented assumptions. CADiZ [1, 2] is a typechecker and theorem prover for ISO Standard Z [3] specifications. Stateflow [4] is an editor and animator of statechart models [5], which works in the context of Simulink in the Matlab development environment.

The formal validation is performed with the aim of answering the question "Is this the intended model?", not the more usual "Has this model been correctly implemented?". An example of the latter is provided by the ClawZ tool for Simulink models [6]. These formal validations are similar in that they both have abstract and concrete specifications, with healthiness conditions generated to ensure that the concrete is consistent with the abstract. They differ in that the Simulink model is the abstract specification for ClawZ, whereas the Stateflow model is the concrete specification for the analysis presented in this paper. Ensuring that a model is as intended before implementing it may reduce the overall cost of software development.

The validation is done by the Simulink/Stateflow Analyser (SSA) tool [7], based on the healthiness conditions specified by Galloway's Practical Formal Specification (PFS) method [8, 9, 10]. PFS combines statecharts with assumptions. Its statecharts are a subset of Stateflow statecharts; its assumptions make explicit the requirements on each state. The SSA tool ensures that the Stateflow model is in the PFS subset, translates relevant aspects of the model and assumptions to Z, generates healthiness conditions as Z conjectures, and attempts

H. Treharne et al. (Eds.): ZB 2005, LNCS 3455, pp. 104–123, 2005.
© Springer-Verlag Berlin Heidelberg 2005

to prove those healthiness conditions automatically. This automation is important in making the method usable without much mathematical expertise. SSA's validation of Simulink models [11] is outside the scope of this paper.

Tool support for the PFS method could have been based on other technologies. Matlab/Simulink/Stateflow was chosen instead of alternative model construction tools because it is widely used by aerospace companies (who are amongst our sponsors) and Simulink is readily customisable. CADiZ was chosen as the theorem prover because of the authors' familiarity with it. Z was chosen because of the ISO Standard and CADiZ's support for that.

This paper is structured around two perspectives: first that of the user of the SSA tool, and second that of the underlying Z. Each perspective considers the model, the assumptions, the healthiness conditions and the proofs. Explanations of the PFS method and the SSA tool are given largely from the first perspective. Comments on the use of ISO Standard Z and CADiZ, which are the main aim of the paper, are given from the second perspective. Some measurements and conclusions end the paper.

## 2    The User Perspective

The SSA tool uses the existing Stateflow statechart editor and associated dialogues for creation of the statechart and associated aspects of the model. It offers a separate new dialogue for entering of assumptions and consideration of healthiness conditions. The mathematical analysis is intended to be automatic and hidden, but some indication of progress is needed to fill the time that takes.

### 2.1    Model

Fig. 1 shows a Stateflow statechart that will be used as an example throughout this paper. It is from a simplified model of a jet engine starting process, derived from that of a real helicopter engine. How the model relates to the real engine is explained after a brief review of the PFS subset of Stateflow notation.

A statechart is a convenient model for a function whose output values depend on previous values of its inputs. The input values determine transitions between states. There are a finite number of states. The destination state of each transition determines the output values.[1]

The states are the nodes of the chart, and are labelled with their names. Some states are nested within other states: they are children of parent states. Only one child of a parent can be active at any time.[2] A state with no children is called a basic state; a state with children is a non-basic state. At any time, a configuration of states is active, all nested within one another. Most transitions

---

[1] Stateflow can alternatively have transitions (and even source states) determine the output values, but PFS cannot, so that is ignored in this paper.

[2] All children of a Stateflow AND state are active concurrently, but AND states are not supported by PFS.

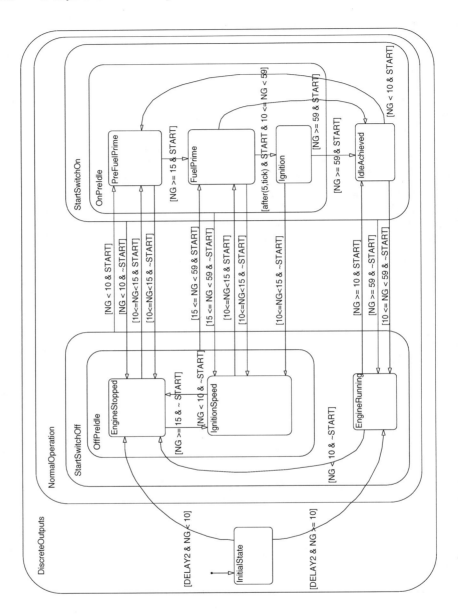

**Fig. 1.** Example statechart

(the directed lines) connect a source state to a destination state. The initial configuration is determined by the transition without a source state.

The transitions are labelled with conditions expressed in terms of the inputs to the model. A transition between states is triggered (taken) when its source state is active and the values of the inputs make its condition *true*. A transition whose source is a non-basic state abbreviates a set of similar transitions, each from a child of that source state. The PFS method decrees, and the SSA tool ensures, that no inputs can simultaneously trigger more than one transition from the same source state.

The inputs to the example statechart are as follows:[3] *START* represents whether the pilot is requesting that the engine start; *NG* represents the compressor's rotational speed expressed as a percentage of its maximum; and *DELAY2* abstracts a period needed for initialisation. The outputs from the statechart are as follows: *STARTR* disables mechanical assistance to rotate the compressor; *FUELON* allows fuel into the manifold; and *IJVIEU* actuates the fuel ignition system (the Ignitor Jet Valve and Ignitor Exciter Unit). Stateflow allows the output values to be specified in the state labels. For clarity here, these specifications are elided from Fig. 1, instead being shown in the assumptions dialogue below (Fig. 2), where there is more space.

The statechart starts in state *InitialState*. When *DELAY2* becomes *True*, the compressor speed determines the relevant next state. Whenever the *START* input is toggled, a transition is taken between *StartSwitchOff* and *StartSwitchOn*. With *START* equal to *True*, the starting of the engine proceeds from mechanical assistance (*PreFuelPrime*) through priming sufficient fuel (*FuelPrime*) and igniting fuel (*Ignition*) to having achieved idle speed (*IdleAchieved*).

## 2.2   Assumptions

The PFS method encourages recording of the following information on each state in a statechart.

**Last Assumptions** — for any state, constraints on what the last values of the inputs should have been for the state to be active.

**Initial Assumptions** — for a non-basic state, constraints on what the values of the inputs should have been for the state to have become active.

**Next Assumptions** — for any state, constraints on what the next values of the inputs should be while in the state.

**State Preservation Condition** — for a basic state, constraints on what the next values of the inputs should be while the state persists.

This information should all be known to the user of Stateflow. Moreover, it can all be expressed using the language of Stateflow conditions, with which the user is already familiar. This is not to say that it is easy: careful thought is needed to position information in the appropriate places, and some practice is necessary before the method becomes familiar.

---

[3] This explanation is intended to illuminate the example; detailed understanding of jet engines is not expected.

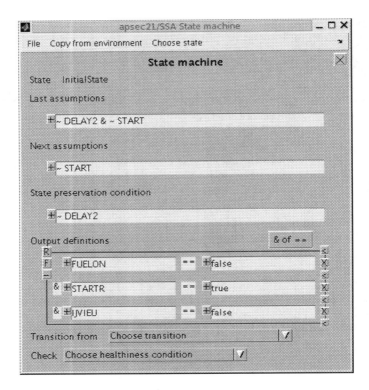

**Fig. 2.** Example state assumptions

As examples of assumptions, consider those on state *InitialState* in the example model, as presented by the SSA tool in the dialogue shown in Fig. 2. Statecharts rarely explicitly specify behaviour in all circumstances. Assumptions document intentionally implicit behaviour, e.g. the persistence of a state when no transition is taken. The assumptions are expressed as Stateflow conditions, which are simple propositions written using &, | and ~ for conjunction, disjunction and negation respectively.

Fig. 2 also shows output definitions using a tabular form, the rows being equalities that are conjoined together. Large formulae can be easier to read as tables than as straight text. Tabular forms may be used for any assumption, a variety of combinators for their fields being available.

In expressing assumptions, constants such as upper and lower bounds are often needed. Having names for such constants makes them easier to read and to maintain. The lexicon is provided to associate the names and values of constants. The engine starting model has a lexicon containing constants for the maximum compressor speed achievable by mechanical assistance, *NGmax1fromstarter*, and for the maximum compressor speed below which mechanical assistance will increase the compressor speed, *NGmax2fromstarter*.

## 2.3    Healthiness Conditions

The assumptions provide a basis for validating that the Stateflow model does what it is intended to do. Healthiness conditions can be formulated to check that the model conforms to the assumptions, and that the assumptions are mutually consistent. The necessary healthiness conditions are determined by the PFS method. Failure to prove healthiness conditions reveals mistakes such as inappropriate trigger conditions, missing transitions, and contradictory and missing assumptions. (Several of the transitions in Fig. 1 were introduced as results of attempts to validate earlier versions of the model.) The method ensures that all the assumptions made by the model on its surrounding environment become explicit assumptions of the root state. This is one of the beneficial results of applying the PFS method. Validation of the assumptions on the environment is not considered in this paper.

At the bottom of Fig. 2 is a button that pops-up a menu of relevant healthiness conditions, as shown in Fig. 3. Choosing a named healthiness condition from that menu changes the dialogue to show that particular healthiness condition. As an example, Fig. 4 shows the *Exiting transitions complete* healthiness condition for state *InitialState*. All the healthiness conditions are formed by combining assumptions. The dialogue shows the logical operators that combine the assumptions, while still allowing the individual assumptions to be revised. The implication (could be turnstile $\vdash$?) operator is the only new notation needing to be explained to the user.

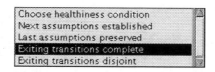

**Fig. 3.** Healthiness conditions menu for state *InitialState*

Some understanding of what a healthiness condition checks is useful in determining any mistake to be corrected. This is discussed from the Z perspective below (Section 3).

## 2.4    Proofs

When presented with a healthiness condition, such as that in Fig. 4, the user wants to determine whether it is valid (provable). By inspection of the healthiness condition of Fig. 4, it can be seen that the state preservation condition covers all circumstances in which neither transition can be taken, so this healthiness condition is valid regardless of *InitialState*'s *last* and *next* assumptions. So thinking about a healthiness condition as presented may be effective, but there are so many healthiness conditions that a user quickly tires of resolving them mentally.

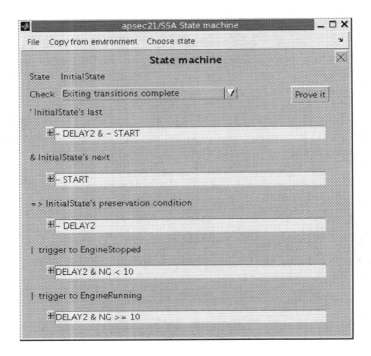

**Fig. 4.** Example healthiness condition

Even if the user is able to decide the validity of a healthiness condition, reassurance from an alternative proof may be desirable. (Also, certification authorities might wish to see particular forms of proof.) Pressing the *Prove it* button causes the SSA tool to search for a proof. Finding a proof may take SSA some time, so some indication of progress is provided in the Matlab command window, as shown in Fig. 5. If the model is unchanged since the last search for a proof, all steps bar the last are skipped.

```
Command Window
Checking well-formedness...
Running Simulink compiler...
Translating model...
Typechecking formalisation...
Generating healthiness conditions...
Typechecking healthiness conditions...
Proving healthiness condition...
Proved Complete_InitialState
>>
```

**Fig. 5.** Progress of analysis messages

Fig. 5 shows that SSA claims to have found a proof of this healthiness condition. In cases where the SSA tool fails to find a proof, it proceeds to search for a counterexample, then displays that if found. Such counterexamples can illuminate mistakes. If no counterexample is found, *Undecided* is displayed.

Thus far, the only mathematics seen by the user is the many small assumptions written in the notation of Stateflow conditions, and the logical operators that combine them to form healthiness conditions. If the user wishes to see details of any proof found automatically, or—in the *Undecided* case—wishes to search for a proof interactively, the *File* menu offers the *Try proof* command to invoke CADiZ. A user who is uncomfortable with large quantities of mathematics would pass that obligation on to another user. A key purpose of this paper is to explain how the search for a proof is automated, so it is time to see large quantities of mathematics...

# 3    The Z Perspective

Enough has to be formalised about the model and its assumptions to be able to generate the healthiness conditions, but not everything. For example, the nesting of states needs to be formalised, but not their co-ordinates in the diagram.

## 3.1    Model

The inputs and outputs of a Stateflow model are of types such as $uint32$ and $boolean$. ISO Standard Z's empty schema representation of Booleans is used, as explained in [12]. The definition of $boolean$ is expressed here in a way that is easier for proof than the one given there. These definitions are common to the formalisations of all Stateflow models, so appear in a separate ISO Standard Z section.

section *stateflow_toolkit* parents *standard_toolkit*

$$
\begin{array}{|l}
uint32 == 0 \ .. \ 4294967295 \\
boolean == \mathbb{P}[] \\
True == [|\ true] \\
False == [|\ false]
\end{array}
$$

The formalisation of a particular model is expressed in terms of this parent.

section *engine_starting_model* parents *stateflow_toolkit*

The inputs and outputs of the engine starting model are its signature, as formalised in the *Sig_Statechart* schema. The usual Z convention of decorating names with ? for an input and ! for an output is followed (though no use is made of the schema composition and schema piping notations that depend on this convention).

```
┌─ Sig_Statechart ─────────────────────────────────────────────┐
│ START? : boolean                                              │
│ DELAY2? : boolean                                             │
│ NG? : 0 .. 100                                                │
│ STARTR! : boolean                                             │
│ FUELON! : boolean                                             │
│ IJVIEU! : boolean                                             │
└───────────────────────────────────────────────────────────────┘
```

The states of the model can be active only in certain configurations, as formalised in the *Config* schema. If a child state is active, its parent state shall be active. If a parent state is active, exactly one of its child states shall be active. These constraints are given for the outermost states, the rest being elided for brevity.[4]

```
┌─ Config ──────────────────────────────────────────────────────┐
│ DiscreteOutputs, NormalOperation, InitialState, StartSwitchOn, │
│ StartSwitchOff, OnPreIdle, IdleAchieved, OffPreIdle,           │
│ EngineRunning, PreFuelPrime, FuelPrime,                        │
│ Ignition, EngineStopped, IgnitionSpeed : boolean               │
├───────────────────────────────────────────────────────────────┤
│ NormalOperation ⇒ DiscreteOutputs                              │
│ InitialState ⇒ DiscreteOutputs                                 │
│ DiscreteOutputs ⇒                                              │
│     NormalOperation ∧ ¬ InitialState ∨                         │
│     ¬ NormalOperation ∧ InitialState                           │
│                              [More constraints elided...]      │
└───────────────────────────────────────────────────────────────┘
```

The empty schema representation of Booleans enables particularly terse and readable forms for the constraints. The logical operations can be read as predicate or schema operations, as the whole predicate part of the schema has the same meaning regardless of this choice.

The transitions of a model have their *sources*, *destinations* and *trigger* formalised using binding extension expressions. As an example, here is the formalisation of the initial transition.

$$Trans\_Init ==$$
$$\langle\!\vert\ sources == [Config \mid true],$$
$$destinations == [Config\,' \mid InitialState' \land DiscreteOutputs'],$$
$$trigger == [Sig\_Statechart \mid true]\ \vert\!\rangle$$

Specifying the parent state *DiscreteOutputs* here is redundant, as it is already implicit in the *Config* schema, but here may be more convenient for analysis. A more traditional Z formalisation could be defined in terms of the binding.

─────────────

[4] The comment is not ISO Standard Z.

$$
\begin{array}{|l}
\hline
\;\_\_Trans\_Init\_Schema_____ \\
\Delta Config \\
Sig\_Statechart \\
\hline
Trans\_Init.sources \\
Trans\_Init.destinations \\
Trans\_Init.trigger \\
\hline
\end{array}
$$

Such a schema representation may be convenient for testing the feasibility of the transition, perhaps using an existing test case generation tool. For an analysis tool wishing to extract the sources, destinations and trigger information, having the binding representation is more convenient than just an unfolded schema representation.

These definitions formalise the transitions as they appear in the statechart diagram; the expansion of transitions from non-basic sources is done later, as a first step in healthiness condition generation. Basing as much as possible of the analysis on the Z formalisation allows as much as possible to be reused when switching to—or offering an alternative—statechart editor.

## 3.2   Assumptions

Assumptions can refer to constants, so the lexicon has to be formalised first. The traditional Z formulation would be as follows.

$$
\begin{array}{|l}
\hline
\;\_\_Lexicon_____ \\
NGmax1fromstarter : uint32 \\
NGmax2fromstarter : uint32 \\
\hline
NGmax1fromstarter = 40 \\
NGmax2fromstarter = 50 \\
\hline
\end{array}
$$

In ISO Standard Z, this can be abbreviated using constant declarations.

$$
\begin{array}{|l}
\hline
\;\_\_Lexicon_____ \\
NGmax1fromstarter == 40 \\
NGmax2fromstarter == 50 \\
\hline
\end{array}
$$

Using a schema when there is only one binding seems clumsy. ISO Standard Z allows a simpler formulation using a binding extension expression.

$$
BLexicon == \\
\quad \langle\!| \; NGmax1fromstarter == 40, NGmax2fromstarter == 50 \; |\!\rangle
$$

SSA allows more general forms of definition into its lexicon. Expressions that are common to several assumptions can be named, and they can refer to the inputs and outputs of the model and to other definitions in the lexicon. A formulation that would be able to cope with such definitions follows.

```
┌─ Lexicon ──────────────────────────────────────────────────────────┐
│  Sig_Statechart                                                     │
│  NGmax1fromstarter : uint32                                         │
│  NGmax2fromstarter : uint32                                         │
│ ────────────────────────────                                       │
│  NGmax1fromstarter = 40                                             │
│  NGmax2fromstarter = 50                                             │
└─────────────────────────────────────────────────────────────────────┘
```

This generality is not needed by the example, so the rest of this paper refers to the *BLexicon* form.

Stateflow conditions are easily formalised as Z predicates, mapping & to $\wedge$, | to $\vee$ and ˜ to $\neg$ . They can be given mnemonic names by first turning them into schemas and then using a binding extension expression, as in the following binding that contains the assumptions on state *InitialState*.[5]

```
│  InitialState_Anns ==
│      ⦇ last ==
│          [Sig_Statechart | ¬ DELAY2? ∧ ¬ START?],
│        next ==
│          [Sig_Statechart | ¬ START?],
│        spc ==
│          [Sig_Statechart | ¬ DELAY2?],
│        outputs ==
│          [Sig_Statechart | STARTR! ∧ ¬ FUELON! ∧ ¬ IJVIEU!],
│        trigger_EngineRunning ==
│          [Sig_Statechart | DELAY2? ∧ NG? ≥ 10],
│        trigger_EngineStopped ==
│          [Sig_Statechart | DELAY2? ∧ NG? < 10],
│        inittrigger ==
│          [Sig_Statechart | true] ⦈
```

This binding also contains transition triggers, to ease access to them during healthiness condition generation. The formalisations of non-basic states are similar, but the bindings contain an *initial* assumption in place of the state preservation condition *spc*.

As an example of references to constants in the lexicon, consider the *next* assumptions of state *DiscreteOutputs*, which are formalised as follows.

---

[5] There is no need to worry about the meanings of these assumptions; their form is what is important here.

$DiscreteOutputs\_Anns ==$
$\langle\!|\ next ==$
$\quad [Sig\_Statechart\ '\ ;\ Sig\_Statechart\ |$
$\qquad (\neg\ DELAY\,2?' \Rightarrow \neg\ START?) \wedge$
$\qquad (DELAY\,2?' \wedge \neg\ START?' \wedge$
$\qquad\qquad NG?' > BLexicon.NGmax1fromstarter \Rightarrow$
$\qquad\qquad\qquad NG? \leq NG?') \wedge$
$\qquad (DELAY\,2?' \wedge \neg\ START?' \wedge$
$\qquad\qquad NG?' \leq BLexicon.NGmax1fromstarter \Rightarrow$
$\qquad\qquad\qquad NG? < 59) \wedge$
$\qquad (START?' \wedge$
$\qquad\qquad NG?' < BLexicon.NGmax2fromstarter \Rightarrow$
$\qquad\qquad\qquad NG? \geq NG?') \wedge$
$\qquad (START?' \wedge$
$\qquad\qquad NG?' \geq BLexicon.NGmax2fromstarter \Rightarrow$
$\qquad\qquad\qquad NG? \geq 10) \wedge$
$\qquad (DELAY\,2?' \wedge NG?' < 15 \Rightarrow NG? < 59) \wedge$
$\qquad (DELAY\,2?' \Rightarrow DELAY\,2?)]$

[Other assumptions elided...]

$\quad |\!\rangle$

These *next* assumptions on the root state are interesting for two more reasons. First, they express the assumptions made by the model on its surrounding environment. They were not written by the user in advance, but are a consequence of the PFS analysis: next assumptions can be added by the user to parent states as needed to make healthiness conditions valid, eventually leading to these assumptions on the root state. Second, they relate the expected next values of the inputs with the previous (primed) values of the inputs. Thus the inputs' rates of change can be constrained as well as their ranges. This use of priming is the opposite of the usual Z convention, the latter not being needed in this formalisation. Primes meaning previous are more mnemonically written as prefixes in names rather than postfixes, but Z does not allow prefix primes in names. The SSA tool expects the user to write primes in prefix position, and moves them to postfix position in the translation to Z.

## 3.3   Healthiness Conditions

This section says informally what the various healthiness conditions check for, and shows how specific healthiness conditions related to the *InitialState* of the example statechart are formalised.

**Next Assumptions Established** — for any child state, are its next assumptions established by its configuration's last assumptions and the next assumptions of its parent? For example...[6]

---

[6] The conjecture name is not ISO Standard Z.

Next_InitialState ==

> ⊢? ∀ *Sig_Statechart* ′ ; *Sig_Statechart* |
> *DiscreteOutputs_Anns.last* ′ ∧ *InitialState_Anns.last* ′ ∧
> *DiscreteOutputs_Anns.next* •
> *InitialState_Anns.next*

This mnemonic formulation is quite readable—it is easy to verify that it has been formulated correctly—and the binding selections are easily unfolded by a prover. Each selects a schema from a binding and uses it as a predicate (exploiting schemas as expressions in ISO Standard Z); all of its variables are bound by the universal quantification in the healthiness condition. The last assumptions need to be primed for this healthiness condition, but not in some others; assumptions are expected to be prepared using the minimum of primes.

The rest of this section discusses the other healthiness conditions. As they all take a similar Z form, a reader interested only in the use of Z may prefer to skip over the rest of this section.

The last assumptions of a state implicitly include those of its parent, since all healthiness conditions refer to the last assumptions of the state's configuration. In contrast, the next assumptions of a state need to be made fully explicit.

**Last Assumptions Established** — for any transition between states, are its destination configuration's last assumptions established by its trigger in combination with its source state's next assumptions and its source configuration's last assumptions? For example...

Last_EngineRunning_InitialState ==

> ⊢? ∀ *Sig_Statechart* ′ ; *Sig_Statechart* |
> *DiscreteOutputs_Anns.last* ′ ∧ *InitialState_Anns.last* ′ ∧
> *InitialState_Anns.next* ∧
> *InitialState_Anns.trigger_EngineRunning* •
> *DiscreteOutputs_Anns.last* ∧ *NormalOperation_Anns.last* ∧
> *StartSwitchOff_Anns.last* ∧ *EngineRunning_Anns.last*

Also, for any initial transition, are its destination configuration's last assumptions established by its trigger in combination with its destination state's parent's initial assumptions? For example...

Last_InitialState_DiscreteOutputs ==

> ⊢? ∀ *Sig_Statechart* ′ ; *Sig_Statechart* |
> *DiscreteOutputs_Anns.initial* ′ ∧ *InitialState_Anns.inittrigger* ′ •
> *DiscreteOutput_Anns.last* ∧ *InitialState_Anns.last*

**Last Assumptions Preserved** — for any basic state, are its configuration's last assumptions preserved by its next assumptions in combination with its state preservation condition? For example...

Last_InitialState_SPC ==

$\vdash$? $\forall$ _Sig_Statechart_ ' ; _Sig_Statechart_ |
 _DiscreteOutputs_Anns.last_ ' $\wedge$ _InitialState_Anns.last_ ' $\wedge$
 _InitialState_Anns.next_ $\wedge$ _InitialState_Anns.spc_ $\bullet$
  _DiscreteOutput_Anns.last_ $\wedge$ _InitialState_Anns.last_

**Initial Assumptions Established** — for any transition to a non-basic destination state, are its destination state's initial assumptions established by its trigger in combination with its source configuration's last assumptions and its source state's next assumptions? For example...

Initial_EngineRunning_InitialState ==

$\vdash$? $\forall$ _Sig_Statechart_ ' ; _Sig_Statechart_ |
 _DiscreteOutputs_Anns.last_ ' $\wedge$ _InitialState_Anns.last_ ' $\wedge$
 _InitialState_Anns.next_ $\wedge$
 _InitialState_Anns.trigger_EngineRunning_ $\bullet$
  _EngineRunning_Anns.initial_

Also, if the transition is an initial transition, are its destination state's initial assumptions established by its trigger in combination with its destination state's parent's initial assumptions? For example...

Initial_InitialState_DiscreteOutputs ==

$\vdash$? $\forall$ _Sig_Statechart_ |
 _DiscreteOutputs_Anns.initial_ $\wedge$ _InitialState_Anns.inittrigger_ $\bullet$
  _InitialState_Anns.initial_

**Transitions Complete** — for any basic state, do the triggers of its exiting transitions in combination with its state preservation condition cover all situations permitted by the combination of its configuration's last assumptions and its next assumptions? For example...

Complete_InitialState ==

$\vdash$? $\forall$ _Sig_Statechart_ ' ; _Sig_Statechart_ |
 _DiscreteOutputs_Anns.last_ ' $\wedge$ _InitialState_Anns.last_ ' $\wedge$
 _InitialState_Anns.next_ $\bullet$
  _InitialState_Anns.trigger_EngineRunning_ $\vee$
  _InitialState_Anns.trigger_EngineStopped_ $\vee$
  _InitialState_Anns.spc_

**Transitions Disjoint** — for any basic state, are the triggers of its exiting transitions and its state preservation condition pairwise disjoint in all situations permitted by the combination of its configuration's last assumptions and its next assumptions? For example...

Disjoint_InitialState ==

$\vdash?\ \forall\ Sig\_Statechart\ '\ ;\ Sig\_Statechart\ |$
$\quad DiscreteOutputs\_Anns.last\ '\ \land\ InitialState\_Anns.last\ '\ \land$
$\quad InitialState\_Anns.next\ \bullet$
$\qquad \neg\ (InitialState\_Anns.trigger\_EngineRunning\ \land$
$\qquad\qquad InitialState\_Anns.trigger\_EngineStopped)\ \land$
$\qquad \neg\ (InitialState\_Anns.trigger\_EngineRunning\ \land$
$\qquad\qquad InitialState\_Anns.spc)\ \land$
$\qquad \neg\ (InitialState\_Anns.trigger\_EngineStopped\ \land$
$\qquad\qquad InitialState\_Anns.spc)$

## 3.4    Proofs

Automatic proof of the healthiness conditions is desirable. If the healthiness conditions were arbitrary Z conjectures, this would be unachievable, but fortunately they have a simple form that should usually be decidable. The following CADiZ tactic aims to automate the proofs of conjectures of this form.

```
1      CheckTactic goal g  |
2          !pat_cons pred p | 1 •
3              !( "normalization" p ∨ skip) ;
4              match p
5              :: decls ds; pred p2 | ∀ ds • p2 •
6                  "apply tactic" p2 "expandAssumptions" ;
7                  "apply tactic" p2 "expandLexicons" ;
8                  "apply tactic" ds "expandInclusions" ;
9                  "apply tactic" p "expandPred"
10             :: . ;
11             ( "linear decision" p ∨ "model check" p ∨
12             "heuristic decision" p ∨ "simplification tac" p ∨ skip)
```

The line numbers are used in subsequent explanation; they are not part of the tactic. This tactic is used for proofs of all Stateflow models, so is best placed for CADiZ in section *stateflow_toolkit*.

Line 1 gives the name of the tactic and lists its parameters. If the argument to which the tactic is applied is not a goal (conjecture paragraph), the tactic immediately fails. Suppose for example that tactic *CheckTactic* is applied to healthiness condition *Next_InitialState*. Line 1 associates $g$ with the whole conjecture.

Next_InitialState ==

$\vdash?\ \forall\ Sig\_Statechart\ '\ ;\ Sig\_Statechart\ |$
$\quad DiscreteOutputs\_Anns.last\ '\ \land\ InitialState\_Anns.last\ '\ \land$
$\quad DiscreteOutputs\_Anns.next\ \bullet$
$\qquad InitialState\_Anns.next$

Line 2 of the tactic associates $p$ with the first consequent of the current goal. Every tactic application has a current goal, which is the goal in which all the arguments appear. It is coincidental that in this tactic the sole argument is the whole goal. However, the current goal might not have any consequents: goals in CADiZ can have antecedents (predicates to the left of the ⊢?) as well as or instead of consequents. If there are no consequents, this tactic would fail. The association of $p$ remains in scope to the end of the tactic, unless an inference rule produces sub-goals in which nothing corresponds to what was associated with $p$. Line 2 also has a cut operator (!), which says not to evaluate any more than the first success of the following tactic. In the example, line 2 associates $p$ with the universal quantification, keeping $g$ associated with the whole conjecture.

Line 3 says to normalize the consequent or else (!) to do nothing (*skip*). If the consequent is a universal quantification, normalization applies the following inference rule, where $p1$ is not *true*.

$$\forall\, ds \mid p1 \bullet p2 \implies \forall\, ds \bullet p1 \Rightarrow p2$$

The *skip* is there in case normalization is not applicable ($p1$ is *true*, or $p$ is not a quantified predicate). For the healthiness conditions considered in this paper, $p1$ is always a conjunction, but the tactic is applicable more generally. In the example, the *normalization* inference rule applies, producing the following sub-goal.

⊢? $\forall\, Sig\_Statechart\,'\,;\; Sig\_Statechart \bullet$
    $DiscreteOutputs\_Anns.last\,' \land InitialState\_Anns.last\,' \land$
    $DiscreteOutputs\_Anns.next \Rightarrow$
    $InitialState\_Anns.next$

The $p$ is now associated with the normalized universal quantification, and $g$ is associated with the whole sub-goal.

Line 4 says to try matching the normalized universal quantification against following patterns, with line 10 marking the end of the *match* construct and denoting sequential composition with what follows.

Line 5 starts the only pattern in this particular *match* construct; if this pattern doesn't match, then the tactic fails. It declares $ds$ and $p2$, and associates these with specific parts of $p$. These associations remain in scope until the end of the *match* construct. In the example, $ds$ is associated with the two schema inclusions, $p2$ is associated with the implication, $p$ remains associated with the universal quantification, and $g$ with the whole goal.

Line 6 applies an auxiliary tactic *expandAssumptions*, whose purpose is to replace the mnemonic selections of assumptions by the corresponding mathematics. In the example, tactic *expandAssumptions* produces the following sub-goal.

⊢? ∀ *Sig_Statechart* ' ; *Sig_Statechart* •
   *true* ∧ (¬ *DELAY*2?' ∧ ¬ *START*?') ∧
   (¬ *DELAY*2?' ⇒ ¬ *START*?) ∧
   (*DELAY*2?' ∧ ¬ *START*?' ∧
        *NG*?' > *BLexicon.NGmax1fromstarter* ⇒ *NG*? ≤ *NG*?') ∧
   (*DELAY*2?' ∧ ¬ *START*?' ∧
        *NG*?' ≤ *BLexicon.NGmax1fromstarter* ⇒ *NG*? < 59) ∧
   (*START*?' ∧
        *NG*?' < *BLexicon.NGmax2fromstarter* ⇒ *NG*? ≥ *NG*?') ∧
   (*START*?' ∧
        *NG*?' ≥ *BLexicon.NGmax2fromstarter* ⇒ *NG*? ≥ 10) ∧
   (*DELAY*2?' ∧ *NG*?' < 15 ⇒ *NG*? < 59) ∧
   (*DELAY*2?' ⇒ *DELAY*2?) ⇒
        ¬ *START*?

In expanding each assumption, the tactic applies a composition of inference rules, each producing an intermediate goal. These goals exploit ISO Standard Z's syntax that allows use of any schema as an expression, and any schema expression as a predicate.

Line 7 applies the auxiliary tactic *expandLexicons*, whose purpose is to replace all mnemonic selections of constants by their values. In the example, tactic *expandLexicons* produces the following sub-goal.

⊢? ∀ *Sig_Statechart* ' ; *Sig_Statechart* •
   *true* ∧ (¬ *DELAY*2?' ∧ ¬ *START*?') ∧
   (¬ *DELAY*2?' ⇒ ¬ *START*?) ∧
   (*DELAY*2?' ∧ ¬ *START*?' ∧ *NG*?' > 40 ⇒ *NG*? ≤ *NG*?') ∧
   (*DELAY*2?' ∧ ¬ *START*?' ∧ *NG*?' ≤ 40 ⇒ *NG*? < 59) ∧
   (*START*?' ∧ *NG*?' < 50 ⇒ *NG*? ≥ *NG*?') ∧
   (*START*?' ∧ *NG*?' ≥ 50 ⇒ *NG*? ≥ 10) ∧
   (*DELAY*2?' ∧ *NG*?' < 15 ⇒ *NG*? < 59) ∧
   (*DELAY*2?' ⇒ *DELAY*2?) ⇒
        ¬ *START*?

Line 8 applies the auxiliary tactic *expandInclusions*, whose purpose is to expand the inclusions of *Sig_Statechart* to declarations of the inputs and outputs, appropriately decorated. In the example, tactic *expandInclusions* produces the following sub-goal.

⊢? ∀ *START*?' : *boolean*; *DELAY*2?' : *boolean*;
   *NG*?' : 0 .. 100; *STARTR*!' : *boolean*;
   *FUELON*!' : *boolean*; *IJVIEU*!' : *boolean*;
   *START*? : *boolean*; *DELAY*2? : *boolean*;
   *NG*? : 0 .. 100; *STARTR*! : *boolean*;
   *FUELON*! : *boolean*; *IJVIEU*! : *boolean* •

$$true \land (\lnot\, DELAY2?' \land \lnot\, START?') \land$$
$$(\lnot\, DELAY2?' \Rightarrow \lnot\, START?) \land$$
$$(DELAY2?' \land \lnot\, START?' \land NG?' > 40 \Rightarrow NG? \leq NG?') \land$$
$$(DELAY2?' \land \lnot\, START?' \land NG?' \leq 40 \Rightarrow NG? < 59) \land$$
$$(START?' \land NG?' < 50 \Rightarrow NG? \geq NG?') \land$$
$$(START?' \land NG?' \geq 50 \Rightarrow NG? \geq 10) \land$$
$$(DELAY2?' \land NG?' < 15 \Rightarrow NG? < 59) \land$$
$$(DELAY2?' \Rightarrow DELAY2?) \Rightarrow$$
$$\lnot\, START?$$

Line 9 applies the auxiliary tactic *expandPred*, whose purpose is to unfold those notations in the given predicate that are unknown to one or more of the decision procedures. In the example, it merely replaces every occurrence of *boolean* by $\mathbb{P}[]$. (Recall that *boolean* is defined in section *stateflow_toolkit*, which is unknown by the built-in decision procedures.)

Lines 11 – 12 then try various decision procedures, each of which might or might not be applicable. The *linear decision* procedure uses a SUP-INF procedure [13] to decide linear arithmetic problems. The *model check* procedure tries to pass the problem to NuSMV [14], which works for some finite problems. The *heuristic decision* procedure uses simulated annealing to solve some non-linear problems. The *simplification tac* procedure works for some predicates that are expressed purely in terms of the Z core language (no toolkit operators). The final *skip* is beneficial for users wishing to see how far an otherwise failed application of *CheckTactic* got. In the example, *linear decision* is not applicable (empty schemas are not arithmetic), but *model check* is (empty schemas are finite, as is $0\,..\,100$), and it decides that the goal is valid.

To find a counterexample, the healthiness condition is negated and then a variant of *CheckTactic* is used, in which the decision procedures are replaced by solution finders. For example, in an earlier version of the engine starting model, the transition from *FuelPrime* to *Ignition* was labelled [*after*(5, *tick*) & *START* & $15 <= NG <= 59$]. Analysis of the healthiness condition for completeness of the transitions exiting *FuelPrime* gave the counterexample $NG = 11, 'NG = 31, START = True, tau = 5$, where *tau* is a measure of ticks (and with all unmentioned variables taking arbitrary values from their types). This drew attention to the lack of an exiting transition not just in that circumstance but also for any value of $NG$ between 10 and 15, and hence the change was made.

More information on the CADiZ tactic language has been published [15] and up-to-date details may be found in the CADiZ documentation [2].

# 4    Measurements

The Z formalisation of the engine starting model is about 35 pages as typeset. There are 83 healthiness conditions typeset over a further 24 pages. This is all generated in about 13 seconds on a 1900MHz Pentium running Linux.

The tactics, with all their auxiliaries, are about 7 pages as typeset. Tactic *CheckTactic* successfully proves all the healthiness conditions for the engine starting model (having corrected the model and assumptions) in about 10 minutes. Some counterexamples were found during the development.

Since *CheckTactic* searches for proofs, it is to be expected that it should take longer than replaying scripts of previously found proofs. However, 7 seconds on average per healthiness condition is annoyingly slow. This performance is largely due to exponential behaviour in the tactic interpreter, and partly due to the fixed order of invocation of the decision procedures being sometimes unfortunate. Much better performance would be possible with further work.

These measurements are for thorough analysis of a single statechart. In a system modelled by many statecharts, the method can be applied selectively, typically to the most critical statecharts.

## 5    Conclusions

Within the specific context of Stateflow models, this paper has presented a formal method that is based on Z yet can be applied without users needing any special mathematical expertise. The focus has been on the use of ISO Standard Z and CADiZ. Much good use has been made of the empty schema representation of Booleans, and of binding extensions for naming the components of structures. The healthiness conditions exploit schemas as expressions not only in their proofs but also in the formulation of their conjectures. Sections have assisted the reuse of common definitions. Without these notations, the Z specifications would have been much less clear. A CADiZ tactic has been outlined that co-ordinates the application of inference rules, auxiliary tactics and decision procedures to produce an inference capability greater than any one decision procedure (though the integration of the decision procedures is shallow).

Although the PFS method was developed in collaboration with aerospace engineers, that involved pencil-and-paper exercises: no engineers have yet used the SSA tool. The engine starting model used as an example in this paper was first done as a pencil-and-paper exercise, revealing some mistakes in the original model. Application of the SSA tool to the example revealed incompleteness in the pencil-and-paper analysis and further mistakes in the model.

The chief barrier to immediate usage of the SSA tool in industry is its lack of support for some Stateflow notations, e.g. junctions, AND states, supertransitions, and local variables. Further work on the SSA tool should focus on these, as required by more case studies. It will require further research on the PFS method.

## Acknowledgements

Funding for this work was provided by the UK MoD, the EPSRC (MATISSE project, GR/R/70590/01), the High Integrity Systems Engineering group at the Department of Computer Science, University of York, and by NATEC. John

McDermid, Frantz Iwu and anonymous referees provided helpful comments on earlier drafts.

# References

1. Toyn, I., McDermid, J.: CADiZ: An architecture for Z tools and its implementation. Software — Practice and Experience **25** (1995) 305–330
2. Toyn, I.: CADiZ on-line documentation (2005) http://www-users.cs.york.ac.uk/~ian/cadiz/.
3. ISO/IEC: Information Technology—Z Formal Specification Notation—Syntax, Type System and Semantics. http://www.iso.org/iso/en/ittf/PubliclyAvailableStandards/c021573_ISO_IEC_13568_2002(E).zip (2002) International Standard 13568:2002.
4. The MathWorks: Matlab and Simulink for technical computing (2005) http://www.mathworks.com/.
5. Harel, D.: Statecharts: A visual formalism for complex systems. Science of Computer Programming **8** (1987) 231–274
6. Arthan, R., Caseley, P., O'Halloran, C., Smith, A.: ClawZ: Control laws in Z. In: ICFEM 2000: 3rd IEEE International Conference on Formal Engineering Methods. (2000) 169–176
7. Toyn, I.: Simulink/Stateflow Analyser user's manual. Technical report, Dept of Computer Science, University of York (2005)
8. Galloway, A., Cockram, T., McDermid, J.: Experiences with the application of discrete formal methods to the development of engine control software. In: Proceedings of Distributed Computer Control Systems (DCCS), IFAC (1998)
9. McDermid, J., Galloway, A., Burton, S., Clark, J., Toyn, I., Tracey, N., Valentine, S.: Towards industrially applicable formal methods: Three small steps, and one giant leap. In: International Conference on Formal Engineering Methods, IEEE Press (1998) 76–88
10. Iwu, F., Galloway, A., Toyn, I., McDermid, J.: Practical Formal Specification for embedded control systems. In: INCOM'04: 11th IFAC Symposium on Information Control Problems in Manufacturing. (2004)
11. Blow, J., Galloway, A.: Generalised substitution language and differentials. In: ZB2002: Formal Specification and Development in Z and B. Volume 2272 of Lecture Notes in Computer Science., Springer (2002) 396–415
12. Toyn, I.: Innovations in the notation of Standard Z. In: ZUM'98: The Z Formal Specification Notation. Volume LNCS 1493., Springer-Verlag (1998) 193–213
13. Shostak, R.: On the SUP-INF method for proving Presburger formulas. JACM **24** (1977) 529–543
14. Cimatti, A., Clarke, E., Giunchiglia, F., Roveri, M.: NuSMV: a new Symbolic Model Verifier. In N. Halbwachs, D. Peled, eds.: Proceedings Eleventh Conference on Computer-Aided Verification (CAV'99). Number 1633 in Lecture Notes in Computer Science, Trento, Italy, Springer (1999) 495–499
15. Toyn, I.: A tactic language for reasoning about Z specifications. In: 3rd Northern Formal Methods Workshop, BCS Electronic Workshop in Computing http://www.ewic.org.uk/ewic/workshop/view.cfm/NFM-98 (1998)

# A Stepwise Development of the Peterson's Mutual Exclusion Algorithm Using B Abstract Systems

J. Christian Attiogbé

LINA - FRE CNRS 2729,
University of Nantes, France
`Christian.Attiogbe@univ-nantes.fr`

**Abstract.** We present a stepwise formal development of the Peterson's mutual exclusion algorithm using Event B. We use a bottom-up approach where we introduce the parallel composition of subsystems which are separately specified. First, we specify subsystems as B abstract systems; then we compose the subsystems to get a first abstract solution for the mutual exclusion. This solution is improved to obtain the Peterson's algorithm. This is achieved by refinement and composition of the former abstract subsystems. Therefore the result is formally proved on the basis of correctness (safety) properties added to the invariant. Atelier B (a B prover) is used to check completely the development.

**Keywords:** Event B, Parallel Composition, Refinement, Mutual Exclusion.

## 1 Introduction

The B method [1] resides in the category of formal techniques which deal with correct system development starting from (abstract) model-oriented specifications. Stepwise refinement is undertaken until more concrete specifications are obtained or code generated. The refinement steps are formally proved by theorem proving. Consequently, one may build a correct system provided that the initial abstract specification is judiciously captured from the analysis of the informal requirements of the problem at hand. The event-based approach of B [6, 2] allows the specification of *abstract systems* which may be used for developing distributed and concurrent systems.

However, the B approach is a top-down approach and its application may be tedious for large system development. In [8] we propose a bottom-up approach to complement the top-down one; our approach provides parallel composition of B abstract systems in order to build large interacting systems by combining their components. This copes well with the practical need to focus on one subsystem at time (without omitting the global identified properties) when developing large systems. Practically it is difficult to formally reason on a very large system; but a solution is to do it through decomposition and reasoning on the subsystems.

H. Treharne et al. (Eds.): ZB 2005, LNCS 3455, pp. 124–141, 2005.

Thereby this requires compositionality property in order to have correct system built from the composition of correct and separately built subsystems.

The current paper addresses the development of a system to control the accesses to *critical sections* by processes or subsystems which run concurrently. This topic is a well-studied one; it is known as the mutual exclusion of accesses to critical sections. It is more generally related to the development of a concurrent system from its subsystems. Therefore we concentrate on the illustration of our approach instead of the problem details. The contribution of the paper is a bottom-up technique to build, within Event B, correct interacting systems with access to shared variables.

In the paper we focus on one aspect which concerns global shared variables but our approach of abstract system composition is general; it also deals with message passing (not discussed in the current paper), which is a more general technique in distributed environments. Indeed, techniques of message passing generalise to systems without common memory.

The paper is structured as follows. In Section 2 we present the technique that we use for the parallel composition of B abstract systems. The Section 3 is devoted to the application to the mutual exclusion algorithm: we present a stepwise construction (refinement and composition) of Peterson's algorithm. In Section 4 we discuss some related works and we finish by the Section 5 where we give some concluding remarks.

# 2     Communicating B Abstract Systems: The Technique

In this section, we begin with the presentation of the working hypothesis and then we present our approach (CBS: Communicating B Systems) through the composition operator introduced to structure abstract systems and to make them communicate. We examine the composition based on the classical communication mechanism of shared state variables.

## 2.1     Fundamental Preliminaries

**Proposition 1.** *An abstract system involving several events which cooperate to achieve the same task may be split into several abstract (sub)systems on the basis of the global state variables and the local variables used by these events.*

**Variables and Invariant Distribution.** The variables and the invariant of an abstract system may be distributed over two or more abstract (sub)systems on the basis of the variables used by its events. Some variables are shared by all events, other variables are not. A common part (made of the shared variables and the associated invariant part) of the abstract system is then shared by all events. Accordingly, the remaining variables and invariant may be split to form the desired distribution.

This constitutes a *distribution policy* which is an important working hypothesis in what follows. We define a specific *composition operator* which composes the abstract subsystems in such a way that the result is an abstract system.

**Shared Variables and Multiple Substitutions.** Simultaneous composition of generalized substitutions $(S \,\|\, T)$ was initially defined when the generalized substitutions $S$ and $T$ have disjoint space of variables [1]. Here, for the composition of abstract systems, we need the composition of substitutions with non-disjoint space of variables. Therefore, we use the extension of $\|$ proposed by Dunne [18, 19]. Several authors have dealt with this concern [14, 18, 19]. Dunne [18] extends the domain of the multiple composition operator $\|$ and calls it parallel composition of substitutions. He adds the following rule to the initial rewrite rules of Abrial [1]

$$x := E \,\|\, x := F \ \ \widehat{=} \ \ E = F \Rightarrow x := E$$

Dunne points out that when the substitutions share the same variable space[1], the generalized composition $\|$ corresponds to the more general[2] *fusion* operator of Back and Butler[11]. Moreover, Dunne's $\|$ parallel composition of substitutions can have an arbitrarily overlapping variable spaces; It is not the case for the fusion operator. The practical issues involved in adopting this approach are: shared variables can be introduced in the specification of abstract systems; concurrent composition is then tractable.

**Working Structure of Abstract System.** We follow the approach presented for abstract machines in [14] by considering the *signature* and the *body* of an abstract system. The signature *signature*$(\mathcal{S})$ of an abstract system $\mathcal{S}$ is the set of the identifiers appearing in the static part (constants, variables) and in the dynamic part of an abstract system (event names). Consequently, the identifiers are gathered together according to their category (constant, variable, event). A concrete shape of a signature with these features is:

$$\{\langle \texttt{constant}, \{\mathit{consId\_list}\}\rangle, \langle \texttt{variable}, \{\mathit{varId\_list}\}\rangle, \langle \texttt{event}, \{\mathit{evtId\_list}\}\rangle\}$$

where *consId_list*, *varId_list* and *evtId_list* are respectively the list of constant identifiers, the list of variable identifiers and the list of event identifiers.

The signature is required for practical reasons: it is the interface for renaming and comparison of systems. The body *body*$(\mathcal{S})$ is made of the variables ($V$), the invariant ($Inv$), the initialisation ($U$) and the set of events ($E$) of the abstract system. We introduce auxiliary functions $sets(\mathcal{S}_i)$, $var(\mathcal{S}_i)$, $inv(\mathcal{S}_i)$, $init(\mathcal{S}_i)$, $events(\mathcal{S}_i)$ to denote respectively the set of sets appearing in the SETS clause, the set of variables, the invariant, the initialisation and the set of events of an abstract system $\mathcal{S}_i$. We simplify the constituents[3] and the notation by considering $\mathcal{S} = \langle \Sigma, B \rangle$ with $\Sigma$ representing *signature*$(\mathcal{S})$ and $B = \langle V, Inv, U, E \rangle$ representing $body(\mathcal{S}) = \langle var(\mathcal{S}), inv(\mathcal{S}), init(\mathcal{S}), events(\mathcal{S}) \rangle$.

---

[1] It is called *frame* by Dunne.

[2] It is defined in the general context of all monotonic predicate transformers.

[3] We do not consider all the clauses of an abstract system, however the extension is trivial.

Thus, an abstract system $\mathcal{S}_i = \langle signature(\mathcal{S}_i), body(\mathcal{S}_i) \rangle$ is simply given by $\langle \Sigma_i, B_i \rangle$ or equivalently $\langle \Sigma_i, \langle V_i, Inv_i, U_i, E_i \rangle \rangle$. Moreover, for each event $ee$ member of $events(\mathcal{S}_i)$, $guard(ee)$ denotes the guard part of $ee$ and $subst(ee)$ denotes the generalized substitution which describes the action of $ee$.

**Abstract System Renaming.** A renaming of an abstract system $\mathcal{S} = \langle \Sigma, B \rangle$ is a consistent syntactic replacement of some identifiers used in $\mathcal{S}$ by other given identifiers. Consequently, the renaming is defined on the signature $\Sigma$ and extended to $B$. Let $\Sigma_i$ and $\Sigma_j$ be signatures (with $\Sigma_i \subseteq \Sigma$) and $\alpha \in \Sigma_i \rightarrow \Sigma_j$ be an injective signature mapping such that the types of the identifiers are preserved; $\alpha$ can be extended easily to $B$ in such a way that each free identifier $idt$ in $\Sigma_i$ used within $B$ is replaced by its value $\alpha(idt)$ in $\alpha(B)$.

$$\texttt{rename}(\langle \Sigma, B \rangle, \alpha) \mathrel{\widehat{=}} \langle \alpha(\Sigma), \alpha(B) \rangle$$

On this basis and following [14], other auxiliary operations can be defined on abstract systems.

**Asynchronous Versus Synchronizing Communication.** Communication involves first the simultaneous evolution of two or more systems, and then the exchange of data. For this purpose, we need composition and communication mechanisms for abstract systems. Above all the involved systems are asynchronous: there is no global clock. From a practical point of view, a simple communication involves a receiver and a sender. Two points of view are generally accepted for communication mechanisms. The communication can be synchronizing (and blocking until completion). This is referred to with the rendez-vous paradigm à la CSP where one considers the final act of communication involving the communicating systems, provided that all the systems reach the communication point. From asynchronous communication point of view, any time duration may pass between the starting of the communication (by one of the involved systems) and its completion (the other involved system participates). It means that systems involved are not blocked before completion. In the scope of the event-driven B approach, events are considered as atomic. Their occurrences are asynchronous, and they do not consume time. They may be synchronizing when the effect of one affects the guard of another one. This is explained in more detail below.

## 2.2    Composition and Communication with Shared State Variables

A composition operator may permit communication between several abstract systems so as to achieve a common task. We begin with the definition of a composition operator that makes abstract systems communicate through shared state variables. The working hypothesis is that this composition should be compatible with the top-down approach. That means, following on from the result of the composition, it may be possible to use refinement and decomposition[3]. The subsystems to be composed may share some common state variables $gv$ and the associated global invariant properties $I(gv)$. However if the subsystems do not

```
SYSTEM S₁                          SYSTEM S₂
SETS CS, SS₁                       SETS CS, SS₂
VARIABLES  gv, lv₁                 VARIABLES  gv, lv₂
INVARIANT Inv₁                     INVARIANT Inv₂
INITIALISATION U₁(gv, lv₁)         INITIALISATION U₂(gv, lv₂)
EVENTS                             EVENTS
   ee1 ≙                              ee2 ≙
      ANY bv₁ WHERE                      ANY bv₂ WHERE
         P₁(lv₁, bv₁, gv) ∧ P₂(gv)          Q₁(lv₂, bv₂, gv) ∧ Q₂(gv)
      THEN                               THEN
         S(gv, lv₁, bv₁)                    T(gv, lv₂, bv₂)
      END                               END
END                                END
```

**Fig. 1.** Abstract systems $\mathcal{S}_1$ and $\mathcal{S}_2$

share state variables, the composition results in a pure interleaving. Additionally, each subsystem $\mathcal{S}_i$ may have its own local variables ($lv_i$). The initialisation operates on $gv$ and $lv_i$. In the following we use $\mathcal{S}_1$ and $\mathcal{S}_2$ for illustration (Fig. 1). Note that the invariant $Inv_i$ of $\mathcal{S}_i$ is rewritten with local and common state variables of $\mathcal{S}_i$ as: $I_i(gv) \wedge L_i(lv_i) \wedge K_i(gv, lv_i)$.

$L_i(lv_i)$ deals with the local properties, $K_i(gv, lv_i)$ relates local variables and global ones and expresses the associated properties. As already stated, $I_i(gv)$ is the common part of the invariant shared by the abstract systems under consideration. If $K_i(gv, lv_i)$ is not explicit in a given invariant, it is interpreted as the *true* predicate.

The shape of events in Figure 1 is used as a canonical form of the event. Each abstract systemmay have several events. The guard *guard*(ee) of an event ee is made of two predicate parts. The first one is expressed using local state variables $lv$, bound variables $bv$ (variables bound by ANY) and global variables $gv$ of the event: $P_1(lv_1, bv_1, gv)$. The second one is uniquely based on global state variables: $P_2(gv)$. A before-after predicate $BA(v, v')$ is associated to each event and describes it as a predicate relating the values of the state variables before ($v$) and after ($v'$) the event occurrence.

An event is *enabled* if its guard holds otherwise the event is *disabled*. An event $ee_i$ enables another event $ee_j$ if the action of $ee_i$ contributes in enabling the guard of $ee_j$. Event guards depend on the state variables. Some events of one of the composed abstract systems may be affected by the action of certain events of the other abstract systems. That means the guard of a particular event may hold after the effect of the other event on the common variables. These events which depend on each other are called *related* events. On the other hand, *unrelated* events are events whose guards do not depend on the actions of the others and vice versa.

**Parallel Composition with Asynchronous Communication.** Asynchronous communication generally refers to the fact that a communication between two or more subsystems is non-blocking; an arbitrary time duration may pass between the starting of an exchange and its effective completion. It may be contrasted with the rendez-vous paradigm which is blocking and used in the synchronizing case. The asynchronous parallel composition of two abstract systems $S_1$ and $S_2$ is denoted by $S_1]|[S_2$. This composition defines an abstract system $AS$ obtained by computing its state and event parts from those of $S_1$ and $S_2$. The notation $AS \cong S_1]|[S_2$ is then used. A procedure *asynchronousMerging* is used for the computation of the composition result. The procedure is described by the forthcoming inference rules which formalize the computation of each clause of the resulting abstract system.

For the state part, the SETS clause of the resulting abstract system is obtained by merging the SETS clauses of the composed abstract subsystems with a set union: $\{CS, SS_1\} \cup \{CS, SS_2\}$. This is formalized with the **AsyncSetsRule** rule.

$$\frac{sS_1 = sets(S_1) \qquad \begin{array}{c} AS = S_1]|[S_2 \\ sS_2 = sets(S_2) \end{array} \qquad sS = sS_1 \cup sS_2}{sets(AS) = sS} \textbf{AsyncSetsRule}$$

In the same way we formalize using similar inference rules the computation of the other clauses of the composed abstract systems. The VARIABLES clauses of $S_1$ and $S_2$ are merged with a set union to form the variables of $S$: $\{gv, lv_1\} \cup \{gv, lv_2\}$.

$$\frac{vS_1 = var(S_1) \qquad \begin{array}{c} AS = S_1]|[S_2 \\ vS_2 = var(S_2) \end{array} \qquad vS = vS_1 \cup vS_2}{var(AS) = vS} \textbf{AsyncVarsRule}$$

The initialisation of $AS$ is defined with the merging (parallel composition of substitutions Ă la Dunne) of the initialisations of $S_1$ and $S_2$: $U_1 \| U_2$. We adopt a simplification, the shared variables are not repeated.

The invariant of the resulting $AS$ abstract system is the conjunction of the $S_1$ and $S_2$ invariants: $Inv_1 \wedge Inv_2$ (**AsyncInvRule**). To avoid inconsistency, we require that the invariants of subsystems do not express contradictory requirements. That means one does not imply the negation of the other and vice versa. We note $notContradict(Inv_1, Inv_2)$ for: $K_1(gv, lv_1) \wedge K_2(gv, lv_2)$

$$\frac{iS_1 = inv(S_1) \qquad \begin{array}{c} AS = S_1]|[S_2 \\ iS_2 = inv(S_2) \qquad notContradict(Inv_1, Inv_2) \\ iS = iS_1 \wedge iS_2 \end{array}}{inv(AS) = iS} \textbf{AsyncInvRule}$$

The result of this stage of the procedure is presented in the Figure 2 (a).

As far as the event part is concerned, the events of $S_1]|[S_2$ are obtained by the union of all the events of the abstract systems $S_1$ and $S_2$ (**AsyncEvtRule**). The operator $\uplus$ denotes such a union of event sets (**MergeEvtRule**).

$$\frac{ee \in events(S_1) \vee ee \in events(S_2)}{ee \in events(S_1) \uplus events(S_2)} \textbf{MergeEvtRule}$$

SYSTEM $\mathcal{S}_1$]|[$\mathcal{S}_2$

SETS
$$CS, SS_1, SS_2$$
VARIABLES
$$gv, lv_1, lv_2$$
INVARIANT
$$Inv_1 \wedge Inv_2$$
INITIALISATION
$$U_1 \| U_2$$

(a) State Part

SYSTEM $\mathcal{S}_1$]|[$\mathcal{S}_2$ (Cont'd)
. . .
EVENTS

  **ee1** $\widehat{=}$
   ANY $bv_1$ WHERE
     $P_1(lv_1, bv_1, gv) \wedge P_2(gv)$
   THEN
     $S(gv, lv_1, bv_1)$
   END
; **ee2** $\widehat{=}$
   ANY $bv_2$ WHERE
     $Q_1(lv_2, bv_2, gv) \wedge Q_2(gv)$
   THEN
     $T(gv, lv_2, bv_2)$
   END
END

(b) Event Part

**Fig. 2.** Abstract system corresponding to $\mathcal{S}_1$]|[$\mathcal{S}_2$

In case of event names conflict, a renaming should be performed before the composition of the abstract systems.

$$\frac{\begin{array}{c} \mathcal{AS} = \mathcal{S}_1\text{]|[}\mathcal{S}_2 \\ events(\mathcal{S}_1) \cap events(\mathcal{S}_2) = \emptyset \\ e\mathcal{AS} = events(\mathcal{S}_1) \uplus events(\mathcal{S}_2) \end{array}}{events(\mathcal{AS}) = e\mathcal{AS}} \textbf{AsyncEvtRule}$$

The subsystems should be proved to be consistent with respect to their invariant. Therefore, The events of $\mathcal{S}_1$ (resp. $\mathcal{S}_2$) preserve the part of the invariant involving the free variables used in $\mathcal{S}_1$ (resp. $\mathcal{S}_2$) due to variable distribution. The resulting abstract system $\mathcal{AS}$ evolves by one of the observable transition denoted by the events of $\mathcal{S}_1$ or by the events of $\mathcal{S}_2$. The event part of the resulting abstract system has the shape shown in Figure 2 (b). From the observational point of view, the behaviour of $\mathcal{AS}$ is a non-deterministic interleaving of events from $\mathcal{S}_1$ and $\mathcal{S}_2$. Since $\mathcal{S}_1$ and $\mathcal{S}_2$ share global variables, the actions of some events coming from one abstract system may enable (a part of) the guards of some other events coming from the other abstract system. An occurrence of an event is then followed (non-deterministically) by any event (of $\mathcal{S}_1$ or of $\mathcal{S}_2$) whose guard is true. There is a non-deterministic choice if several guards are simultaneously enabled.

To sum up, given $\mathcal{S}_1 = \langle \Sigma_1, \langle V_1, Inv_1, U_1, E_1 \rangle \rangle$ and $\mathcal{S}_2 = \langle \Sigma_2, \langle V_2, Inv_2, U_2, E_2 \rangle \rangle$, the parallel composition of $\mathcal{S}_1$ and $\mathcal{S}_2$ is defined using the previous rules as follows:

$$\mathcal{S}_1\text{]|[}\mathcal{S}_2 \widehat{=} \langle \Sigma_1 \cup \Sigma_2, \langle V_1 \cup V_2, Inv_1 \wedge Inv_2, U_1 \| U_2, E_1 \uplus E_2 \rangle \rangle$$

This formalizes the procedure we called *asynchronousMerging* which is the combined use of the rules computing each part.

**Algebraic Properties of the Composition.**

$$\mathcal{S}_1][\mathcal{S}_2 \equiv \mathcal{S}_2][\mathcal{S}_1$$

$$(\mathcal{S}_1][\mathcal{S}_2)][\mathcal{S}_3 \equiv \mathcal{S}_1][(\mathcal{S}_2][\mathcal{S}_3)$$

The parallel composition is commutative and associative. Indeed, firstly the invariant of the composition is the conjunction of the invariants of the components; secondly, the parallel composition of substitutions ($\|$) is used for the initialisation part; finally, for the event part, the composition results in a set of events.

Because of these two properties, the parallel composition of a finite set of abstract systems $\mathcal{S}_i$ is written $][_{i \in 1 \cdots n} \mathcal{S}_i$. The result is the successive (pairwise) application of $][$. Therefore the notation is generalized as follows:

$$][_{i \in 1 \cdots n} \mathcal{S}_i \; \hat{=} \; \langle \cup_{i \in 1 \cdots n} \Sigma_i, \, \langle \bigcup_{i \in 1 \cdots n} V_i, \, \bigwedge_{i \in 1 \cdots n} Inv_i, \, \|_{i \in 1 \cdots n} U_i, \, \biguplus_{i \in 1 \cdots n} E_i \rangle \rangle$$

We emphasize that our composition approach remains in the initial B framework. We have just temporarily worked on the abstract specification level with composition, nevertheless the B process will continue with refinement (and decomposition).

## 2.3 Modelling Style with Event B

From a methodological point of view, the presented technique permits a specification style close to the one widely used in the context of process algebra and of action systems. To build larger systems we may specify several subsystems, prove their consistency and compose them gradually. Therefore, this may also help for mastering large systems development. The availability of concurrent communication operators will facilitate the translation from existing related formalisms, based on such operators, into B. Consequently, the B tools may be used following a first specification step based on process algebra and action systems for instance.

Practically, one has to identify interacting subsystems, identify shared resources and specify them in the same way in the subsystems. The interaction between events should then be made explicit (using the composition operator). This is a common working approach already used for programming concurrent processes in operating systems for instance.

# 3 Development of the Mutual Exclusion Algorithm

We present a development of the well-known bakery algorithm for distributed mutual exclusion. The development is based on the technique introduced in the previous section. In the discussion we use the term "subsystem" instead of "process" as is often encountered in the literature on the topic of mutual exclusion.

SYSTEM $\mathcal{P}_1$
VARIABLES
$\quad$ $cs1, cs2$ /* global variables*/
$\quad$ $pc1$ $\quad$ /* local variables*/
INVARIANT
$\quad$ $pc1 \in 0..2$ $\quad$ /* this is $L_1(v_1)$ $\quad$ */
$\quad$ $\wedge$ $cs1 \in 0..1$ $\quad$ /* and now $I_1(gv)$ */
$\quad$ $\wedge$ $cs2 \in 0..1$
INITIALISATION
$\quad$ $cs1, cs2 := 0, 0 \parallel pc1 := 1$
EVENTS
$\quad$ askCS1 $\widehat{=}$
$\quad\quad$ SELECT $pc1 = 1$
$\quad\quad$ THEN $cs1 := 0 \parallel pc1 := 2$ END
; $\quad$ inCS1 $\widehat{=}$
$\quad\quad$ SELECT $pc1 = 2 \wedge \neg (cs2 = 1)$
$\quad\quad$ THEN $cs1 := 1$ END
; $\quad$ outCS1 $\widehat{=}$
$\quad\quad$ SELECT $(cs1 = 1) \wedge (pc1 = 2)$
$\quad\quad$ THEN $cs1 := 0 \parallel pc1 := 1$ END
END

SYSTEM $\mathcal{P}_2$
VARIABLES
$\quad$ $cs1, cs2$ /* global variables*/
$\quad$ $pc2$ $\quad$ /* local variables*/
INVARIANT
$\quad$ $pc2 \in 0..2$ $\quad$ /* this is $L_2(v_1)$ $\quad$ */
$\quad$ $\wedge$ $cs1 \in 0..1$ $\quad$ /* and now $I_2(gv)$ */
$\quad$ $\wedge$ $cs2 \in 0..1$
INITIALISATION
$\quad$ $cs1, cs2 := 0, 0 \parallel pc2 := 1$
EVENTS
$\quad$ askCS2 $\widehat{=}$
$\quad\quad$ SELECT $pc2 = 1$
$\quad\quad$ THEN $cs2 := 0 \parallel pc2 := 2$ END
; $\quad$ inCS2 $\widehat{=}$
$\quad\quad$ SELECT $pc2 = 2 \wedge \neg (cs1 = 1)$
$\quad\quad$ THEN $cs2 := 1$ END
; $\quad$ outCS2 $\widehat{=}$
$\quad\quad$ SELECT $(cs2 = 1) \wedge (pc2 = 2)$
$\quad\quad$ THEN $cs2 := 0 \parallel pc2 := 1$ END
END

**Fig. 3.** Concurrent subsystems to be composed

## 3.1 Quick Overview on Mutual Exclusion: Abstract Solution

The bakery's mutual exclusion algorithm was studied in many works[21, 25]. In [21] for example, the study is done within the context of temporal logic. We begin with a very abstract version of the mutual exclusion algorithm and then we give a more precise version named Peterson's algorithm following its author's name.

The general problem is that of accesses of the critical sections of code statements, where resources are used or updated by several subsystems. The goal of the algorithm is to avoid simultaneous accesses to these critical sections. In the abstract version one considers two subsystems $\mathcal{P}_1$ and $\mathcal{P}_2$. We specify the B abstract system corresponding to each subsystem. The B specification is quite straightforward. The subsystems to be composed are depicted in the Figure 3.

Each subsystem $i$ has a variable $pc_i$ which indicates if the subsystem is inside (value 0) or outside (value 1) its critical section or interested in entering it (value 2). The accesses to the critical section are protected by the use of Boolean variables $cs_1$ and $cs_2$. They respectively indicate that the subsystem $\mathcal{P}_1$ (resp. $\mathcal{P}_2$) is within its critical section. Initially the $cs_i$ are set to 0 and the $pc_i$ are set to 1. Each subsystem desiring to enter its critical section sets its $cs_i$ to 0 and additionally its $pc_i$ to 2 (that means its it is ready to enter). A subsystem enters its critical section if it asked for it and if the other subsystem is not within its critical section. In this case the variable $cs_i$ is set properly. On leaving the critical section, the corresponding $cs_1$ and $pc_i$ are respectively set to 0 and 1.

SYSTEM
  $\mathcal{P}_{12}$
VARIABLES
        /* global variables*/
    $cs1$
,   $cs2$
        /* local variables*/
,   $pc1$
,   $pc2$

INVARIANT
    $pc1 \in 0..2$      /* this is $L_1(v_1)$   */
$\wedge$   $pc2 \in 0..2$      /* this is $L_2(v_2)$   */
$\wedge$   $cs1 \in 0..1$      /* and now $I(gv)$   */
$\wedge$   $cs2 \in 0..1$
INITIALISATION
    $cs1, cs2 := 0, 0$
$\|$   $pc1 := 1$
$\|$   $pc2 := 1$

EVENTS
  askCS1 $\widehat{=}$
      SELECT $pc1 = 1$
      THEN   $cs1 := 0 \| pc1 := 2$ END
; inCS1 $\widehat{=}$
      SELECT $pc1 = 2 \wedge \neg (cs2 = 1)$
      THEN   $cs1 := 1$ END
; outCS1 $\widehat{=}$
      SELECT $(cs1 = 1) \wedge (pc1 = 2)$
      THEN   $cs1 := 0 \| pc1 := 1$  END
; askCS2 $\widehat{=}$
      SELECT $pc2 = 1$
      THEN   $cs2 := 0 \| pc2 := 2$ END
; inCS2 $\widehat{=}$
      SELECT $pc2 = 2 \wedge \neg (cs1 = 1)$
      THEN   $cs2 := 1$ END
; outCS2 $\widehat{=}$
      SELECT $(cs2 = 1) \wedge (pc2 = 2)$
      THEN   $cs2 := 0 \| pc2 := 1$ END

END

**Fig. 4.** Mutually exclusive resulting system

## 3.2    The Asynchronous Composition of the Subsystems

The desired system is simply obtained by applying the parallel composition operator to the already defined subsystems (Fig. 3):

$$\mathcal{P}_{12} \ \widehat{=} \ \mathcal{P}_1 \| \mathcal{P}_2$$

The abstract system resulting from this composition is depicted in Figure 4. It is computed by applying the rules which formalize the procedure *asynchronous-Merging* (section 2.2).

From the composition point of view, this first solution works well and illustrates the idea of asynchronous parallel composition we have presented. The main desired property for the system is mutual exclusion:

  *at most one subsystem is in its critical section at the same time*

$$\neg ((cs1 = 1) \wedge (cs2 = 1))$$

This safety property can be introduced into the invariant of the composed system and completely proved using Atelier B [17].

However, the solution itself is not satisfactory for that it has some drawbacks. For example it is not fair for the composed subsystems; a given event can be observed many times (even infinitely) repeatedly (without allowing other events to occur). We shall go beyond the composition and improve this abstraction by using a refinement. This refinement results in the algorithm of Peterson.

## 3.3     Refinement: Peterson's Algorithm

To overcome the drawbacks of the previous abstract solution, we consider the Peterson's policy and we show how it can be constructed within the B approach augmented with parallel composition. We also study the correctness of the system by strengthening the invariant after the composition. This leads to correctness proofs that establish the soundness of the solution. Here, the main mechanism to protect accesses to the critical section is based on the use of the (new) Boolean variables $y_1$ and $y_2$. They are set to *True* by each subsystem desiring to enter its critical section, and which is ready to do it. Additionally, a variable $ss$ is used to record the number ($i$) of the process which is the latest to request the access. The other abstract variables $pc1, pc2, cs1, cs2$ are respectively refined by the concrete ones $pc1c, pc2c, cs1c, cs2c$. As with the previous abstract solution, $y_1$, $y_2$ and $ss$ are system variables shared by the two subsystems and may be considered as internal to the system. Therefore a subsystem $i$ enters its critical section if its request is not the latest ($ss \neq i$), or the other subsystem (say $j$) does not request for its critical section: $ss \neq i \vee \neg (y_j = True)$.

Consequently, a subsystem $i$ is within its critical section if its variable $y_i$ is set and, the other subsystem is not within its critical section ($\neg (y_j = True)$), and if $i$ is not the latest: $((cs_i = 1) \Rightarrow ((y_i = True) \wedge \neg (y_j = True) \wedge \neg (ss = i)))$.

**Refining the Previous B Abstract Subsystems.** We build the new solution by refining the abstract system $\mathcal{P}_i$. The B refinement process of an abstract system may introduce new variables and new events in the resulting (less) abstract system. The guards of the new system events may be strengthened. The abstract system and its refinement are related by a gluing invariant. The refinement should be proved correct by discharging some proof obligations [5, 6, 22]: *i)* each introduced new event refines *skip*; *ii)* each abstract event is correctly refined by its corresponding concrete form; *iii)* the introduced new events do not take control for ever; this is achieved by decreasing a variant (included in the refinement) by each occurrence of a new event; *iv)* deadlock-freedom is preserved; considering the disjunction of the event guards.

Consider an abstract system $A$ with variables $av$ and invariant $I(av)$ which is refined by a concrete system $C$ with variables $cv$ and a gluing invariant $J(av, cv)$. Consider $BAA(av, av')$ and $BAC(cv, cv')$ respectively as the abstract and concrete before-after predicates of the same event, for the correctness of event refinement we have to prove that under the conjunction of the abstract and the concrete invariant, a concrete event (described with $BAC(cv, cv')$) can be simulated ($\exists av'$) by an abstract one (described with $BAA(av, av')$) in such a way that the gluing invariant is preserved. Formally

$$I(av) \wedge J(av, cv) \wedge BAC(cv, cv') \Rightarrow \exists av'.(BAA(av, av') \wedge J(av', cv'))$$

In the following, we specify an abstract system $\mathcal{P}et_1$ (Fig.5) which refines $\mathcal{P}_1$; this is noted $\mathcal{P}_1 \sqsubseteq \mathcal{P}et_1$. We introduce the new variables $ss, y1, y2$. The invariant of the new system states the type properties of the three new variables. The old variables are retained. The new initialisation trivially establishes the new invariant. We introduce one new event `readyP1`; it refines *skip*. The other events `askCS1`, `inCS1` and `outCS1` are the new specifications of their abstract counterparts. The guard of the event `askCS1` does not change. Its body is updated using the new variables $y1$ and $ss$ following the request policy explained above. The event `inCS1` is refined by changing slightly its guard according to the considered policy. The new guard uses the link between abstract variables and the new concrete ones.

The deadlock-freedom is stated by proving that:

*i)* the guard of each event ee implies that its substitutions is feasible; it does not establish *False*. (this is proved from $\mathsf{fis}(v := E) = TRUE$ where $v$ is a variable and $E$ is an expression):

$$guard(ee) \Rightarrow \mathsf{fis}(subst(ee))$$

*ii)* one of the event guards is always true: $(pc1c = 0) \vee (pc1c = 1) \vee ((pc1c = 2) \wedge ((y2 = FALSE) \vee (ss = 2))) \vee (cs1c = 1)$
This is true at the outset because on the initialisation we have $pc1c = 0$; from then and cyclically, the event `readyP1` is enabled. Then it establishes $pc1c = 1$ which in turn is the guard of the event `askCS1`. This one enables the events `inCS1` since $y2$ has not been changed; the body of `outCS1` implies $pc1c = 0$ and the cycle continues.

To sum up, each of the two concurrent subsystems to be composed has the specification (upto a variable renaming) given in the Figure 5. The variables related to $\mathcal{P}_1$ (resp. $\mathcal{P}_2$) are subscripted with 1 (resp. 2).

**Composition.** Now we build the Peterson's algorithm by the composition of the components. First we compose two instances of the subsystem depicted in the Figure 5. Note that the second instance may be obtained by our renaming technique (see Section 3). Then, the asynchronous parallel composition is performed in the same way as in the section 3.2.

$$Peterson\_Alg \,\, \widehat{=} \,\, \mathcal{P}et_1 \| \mathcal{P}et_2$$

The result of the composition is given in the Figure 6.

We may be confident in this result since it is exactly that of the widely known Peterson's algorithm. However, another advantage of our approach is that we can formally state and prove the correctness properties of the obtained algorithm. This is the subject of the following section.

**Correctness of the Algorithm.** The mutual exclusion property proved on the abstract version should be maintained: *at most one subsystem is in its critical section at the same time*:

$$\neg \, ((cs1c = 1) \wedge (cs2c = 1))$$

REFINEMENT $\mathcal{P}et_1$
REFINES $\mathcal{P}_1$
VARIABLES
        /* global variables*/
    $cs1c, cs2c, ss, y1, y2$
        /* local variables*/
    $pc1c$
INVARIANT
    $pc1c \in 0..2$        /* this is $L_1(v_1)$ */
$\wedge$  $cs1c, cs2c \in 0..1$  /* $I_1(gv)$ */
$\wedge$  $ss \in 1..2$
$\wedge$  $y_1, y_2 \in BOOL$
$\wedge$  $((cs1c = cs1) \vee (cs1c = 0))$
        /* glue */
$\wedge$  $((cs2c = cs2) \vee (cs2c = 0))$
$\wedge$  $((pc1c = pc1) \Rightarrow \neg (pc1 = 0))$
INITIALISATION
    $cs1c, cs2c, ss := 0, 0, 1$
$\|$  $pc1c := 0$
$\|$  $y1, y2 := FALSE, FALSE$

EVENTS
    readyP1 $\widehat{=}$
        SELECT $pc1c = 0$ THEN
            $cs1 := 0 \| y1 := FALSE$
        $\| pc1c := 1$
        END
;   askCS1 $\widehat{=}$
        SELECT $pc1c = 1$ THEN
            $y1 := TRUE \| ss := 1$
        $\| pc1c := 2$
        END
;   inCS1 $\widehat{=}$
        SELECT $(pc1c = 2) \wedge$
            $((y2 = FALSE) \vee (ss = 2))$
        THEN  $cs1c := 1$ END
;   outCS1 $\widehat{=}$
        SELECT $(cs1c = 1)$
        THEN  $cs1c := 0 \| pc1c := 0$
        END
END

**Fig. 5.** Refinement of $\mathcal{P}_1$ with Peterson's policy

Additionally, we should verify that each subsystem respects the defined conditions when it is within its critical section:

$$(cs1c = 1) \Rightarrow ((y1 = TRUE) \wedge ((y2 = FALSE) \vee (ss = 2)))$$

$$\wedge (cs2c = 1) \Rightarrow ((y2 = TRUE) \wedge ((y1 = FALSE) \vee (ss = 1)))$$

Therefore in order to guarantee this within B, we augment the invariant of the abstract system with the conjunction of these properties:

$(\neg (cs1c = 1) \wedge (cs2c = 1))$
$\wedge (cs1c = 1) \Rightarrow ((y1 = TRUE) \wedge ((y2 = FALSE) \vee (ss = 2)))$
$\wedge (cs2c = 1) \Rightarrow ((y2 = TRUE) \wedge ((y1 = FALSE) \vee (ss = 1)))$

**Monotonicity of the composition.** We prove that: *the refinement of the composition is the composition of the refinement.*

$$\mathcal{P}_1 \| [\mathcal{P}_2 \sqsubseteq \mathcal{P}et_1 \| [\mathcal{P}et_2$$

This confirms a general result established for our approach. Formally we have

$$\frac{\mathcal{S}_1 \sqsubseteq \mathcal{S}_1' \qquad \mathcal{S}_2 \sqsubseteq \mathcal{S}_2'}{\mathcal{S}_1 \| [\mathcal{S}_2 \sqsubseteq \mathcal{S}_1' \| [\mathcal{S}_2'}$$

SYSTEM *Peterson_Alg*
VARIABLES
      /* global variables*/
   $cs1c, cs2c, ss, y1, y2$
      /* local variables*/
   $pc1c, pc2c$
INVARIANT
   $pc1c, pc2c \in 0..2 \land cs1c, cs2c \in 0..1$
$\land\ ss \in 1..2$
$\land\ y1, y2 \in BOOL$
$\land\ ((cs1c = cs1) \lor (cs1c = 0))$
      /* glue */
$\land\ ((cs2c = cs2) \lor (cs2c = 0))$
$\land\ ((pc1c = pc1) \Rightarrow \neg (pc1c = 0))$
$\land\ ((pc2c = pc2) \Rightarrow \neg (pc2c = 0))$
INITIALISATION
   $cs1c, cs2c, ss := 0, 0, 1$
$\|\ pc1c, pc2c := 0, 0$
$\|\ y1, y2 := FALSE, FALSE$

EVENTS
                    /* they are unchanged */
      readyP1 $\,\widehat{=}\,$
         ...
;   askCS1 $\,\widehat{=}\,$
         ...
;   inCS1 $\,\widehat{=}\,$
         ...
;   outCS1 $\,\widehat{=}\,$
         ...
;   readyP2 $\,\widehat{=}\,$
         ...
;   askCS2 $\,\widehat{=}\,$
         ...
;   inCS2 $\,\widehat{=}\,$
         ...
;   outCS2 $\,\widehat{=}\,$
         ...
END

**Fig. 6.** Peterson's algorithm: result of the composition

Consider the context implicitly indicated by the subscripts for each abstract system; by instantiating the refinement proof obligations given above (see 3.3), we have:

$$I_1(av_1) \land J_1(av_1, cv_1) \land BAC(cv_1, cv_1') \Rightarrow \exists av_1'.(BAA(av_1, av_1') \land J_1(av_1', cv_1'))$$

$$I_2(av_2) \land J_2(av_2, cv_2) \land BAC(cv_2, cv_2') \Rightarrow \exists av_2'.(BAA(av_2, av_2') \land J_2(av_2', cv_2'))$$

The composed systems shared the variables $gv$ only; therefore $av_1 \cap av_2 = gv$.

For an event originating from one of the composed systems, it follows from the definition of $]|[$ (conjunction of invariants), the union of events (of composed systems), and that *the shared variables are refined in the same way* in the composed systems, that its concrete description ($BAC(cv_1, cv_1')$) simulates the abstract one ($BAA(av_1, av_1')$):

$$I_1(av_1) \land I_2(av_2) \land J_1(av_1, cv_1) \land J_2(av_2, cv_2) \land BAC(cv_1, cv_1') \Rightarrow$$
$$\exists av_1'.(BAA(av_1, av_1') \land J_1(av_1', cv_1'))$$

This holds for the other events.

Several authors already establish this general result on the monotonicity of composition in various contexts: [10] for the refinement calculus, [16] for action systems, [21, 25] for logical frameworks.

**Experiment Report.** We use Atelier B to check all the abstract systems and their refinements. The management of shared variables (naming and initialisation) are achieved manually. Note that Atelier B does not manage *abstract* *systems* directly. But using an encoding into abstract machines, we generate the proof obligations and completely prove the development. As far as this encoding is concerned, the composition is first performed; the new events introduced in refinements are first specified with *skip* in earlier machines; proving the correctness is then straightforward. There is a prototype tool (evt2b) originally developed within the Matisse project [22] which may assist in a systematic translation from B abstract systems into abstract machines.

## 4    Discussion

Composing systems in a bottom-up manner in B event systems is not a new topic. It has been studied by several authors in the context of process algebra and Action Systems for example. Our approach is therefore very close to the Action Systems view as shown hereafter.

**Action Systems View.** The *Action System* formalism of Back and Kurki-Suonio [12] permits the description of parallel or distributed systems. Actions are guarded statements and are executed atomically. An action $A_i$ has the shape $g_i \rightarrow S_i$ where $g_i$ is the guard and $S_i$ is the statement or the body. The statement can be a non-deterministic choice (noted []) between several other statements $S_i$. Bottom-up composition has been introduced for action system in [9].

An *action system* enables one to specify the behaviour of a system by a collection of actions. It takes the form:

$$\mathcal{A}_i \; \widehat{=} \; |[\, \mathbf{var}\, x_i; \; u_i; \; \mathbf{do}\, A_i \, \mathbf{od}\,]| : z$$

where $x$ and $z$ are (state) variables; $x$ stands for local variables; $z$ stands for global variables which are used to interact with the environment; $u_i$ stands for the initialisation condition.

The action system formalism provides a parallel composition operator to model concurrent system. The parallel composition of two action systems is achieved if they share some global variables but use disjoint local variables. The composition results in another action system. The latter has the same global variables and the union of the local variables. Its initialisation is the conjunction of the initialisations of the component systems and its action part is made of the choice ([]) of the action part of the component systems.

$$\mathcal{A}_1 \| \mathcal{A}_2 \; \widehat{=} \; |[\, \mathbf{var}\, x_2, x_2; \; u_1 \wedge u_2; \; \mathbf{do}\, A_1 \, [] \, A_2 \, \mathbf{od}\,]| : z$$

These composition ideas have also been studied in [16] and within B by Butler et al [15]; they adapt the action systems view (for expressing distributed systems) to the B formalism. Whilst, in [15] an experimental translation from action systems to B machines is given, the specific formal rules for the composition are not given. But these rules are now quite standard for the related formalisms; further developments on these aspects are presented in [22].

We provide a similar composition approach using Event B (with abstract systems instead of abstract machines). But the composition is here completely defined within B. Moreover, the practical advantage of our B approach is the tool availability to assist in the proof steps.

**Abrial's Decomposition Approach.** Abrial is also working on the *decomposition approach* of abstract systems to split a large system into smaller ones using shared variables [4]. The ideas are similar in that the global system is a composition of several interacting subsystems. However he deals with the top-down approach going from the global system to the subsystems. Moreover there is not an explicit composition operator. In our bottom-up approach, the shared variables and the associated invariant are effectively elements of the top level. The shared variables should be refined in the same manner; this is also a constraint of the decomposition approach. We have an explicit composition operator (Å la Process Algebra) expandable to explicit message passing. Therefore the approaches are not orthogonal, they are complementary.

As far as the B method is concerned, there are some works related to composition and interaction between specifications. An example is the work by Schneider and Treharne [24, 23] on composing CSP and B. CSP processes [20] are used to describe controllers for B machines. The controllers handle the control flow of machine operations without sharing machine states. The machine model and the controller model are developed separately. The composition of B machines is done here through the CSP controllers of the involved B machines. This approach is highly CSP-driven even if the machines part may be developed within the B framework. In our approach B systems are used and the control part is incorporated in the event guards.

The *Assumption-Commitment* approach (also called *Rely-Guarantee*) [27, 26] has been proposed for the composition of concurrent systems with shared state variables. Briefly, it consists for each system involved in the composition, to establish correctness properties by making some assumptions about the other systems which constitute its environment. Therefore, the design of the component systems are not really independent and this makes the structuring of specifications tedious. The *Assumption-Commitment* approach does not permit independent refinement. Our composition approach does not constrain the composed systems to reason about their environment. The components are independent but the correctness properties are treated with proof obligations during the composition. This simplifies the structuring of the global system and also the independent refinement of the subsystems. Indeed, the interference between global variables are considered only during the composition.

## 5    Concluding Remarks

In this paper, we presented a complete development of a concurrent system by combining composition techniques, refinement and tools. First, a composition approach (bottom-up) to build interacting concurrent systems within Event B is presented. Then it is used for a development: the construction of Peterson's algorithm by refinement from an earlier abstract version. Currently, we use global variables to ensure the communication between the interacting subsystems. Atelier B is used to prove the complete development. Only safety properties are considered here; but we have investigated liveness properties in [7] for a subset of Event B, by combining B and the Spin Model checker.

As far as composition is concerned, in [16] Butler deals with the refinement of communicating action systems. We share some features with his work: a compositional approach. But the main difference is that Butler's approach is based on communication with shared events (occurrences of system transitions which are commonly named) instead of shared variables as we presented here.

The contribution of our work can be underlined through several points. First, the systematic construction of software systems using well-defined techniques: composition (bottom-up approach), refinement and theorem proving. Second, the effective use of available tools to support this construction.

Some aspects of the presented work are the subject of ongoing development; for example some dedicated interfaces in front of the B tools (including evt2b), and the development of many other real size case studies to assess and improve the proposed approach. Other communication operators are needed. Yet we have experimented a technique for message passing; we use specific variables to handle messages; but more work on this technique of message passing is necessary, to make the development of large distributed systems practical. Besides, we are working on a procedure to translate from process algebra specifications into Event B systems.

**Acknowledgments.** Many thanks to my colleagues and to the anonymous referees for their valuable comments on the current work.

# References

1. J-R. Abrial. *The B Book.* Cambridge University Press, 1996.
2. J-R. Abrial. Extending B without Changing it (for developping distributed systems). *Proc. of the 1st Conference on the B method, H. Habrias (editor), France,* pages 169–190, 1996.
3. J-R. Abrial. Event Driven Distributed Program Construction. MATISSE project, August 2001.
4. J-R. Abrial. Discrete System Models. Internal Notes (available at www-lsr.imag.fr/ B, B Working Group), February 2002.
5. J-R. Abrial, D. Cansell, and D. Mery. Formal Derivation of Spanning Trees Algorithms. In D. Bert et al., editor, *ZB'2003 – Formal Specification and Development in Z and B*, volume 2651 of *Lecture Notes in Computer Science*, pages 457–476. Springer-Verlag, 2003.
6. J-R. Abrial and L. Mussat. Introducing Dynamic Constraints in B. In *Proc. of the 2nd Conference on the B method, D. Bert (editor)*, volume 1393 of *Lecture Notes in Computer Science*, pages 83–128. Springer-Verlag, 1998.
7. C. Attiogbé. A Mechanically Proved Development Combining B Abstract Systems and Spin. In *Proceedings of the 4th International Conference on Quality Software (QSIC 2004)*. IEEE Computer Society Press.
8. C. Attiogbé. Communicating B Abstract Systems (CBS). Technical Report 02.08, IRIN, University of Nantes, December 2002.

9. R. J. Back and K. Sere. From Action Systems to Modular Systems. *Software - Concepts and Tools*, 17(1):26–39, 1996.

10. R-J. Back and J V Wright. *Refinement Calculus: A Systematic Introduction*. Graduate Texts in Computer Science. Springer, 1998.

11. R. J. R. Back and M. J. Butler. Fusion and Simultaneous Execution in the Refinement Calculus. *Acta Informatica*, 35(11):921–949, 1998.

12. R.J. Back and R. Kurki-Suonio. Decentralisation of Process Nets with Centralised Control. In *Proc. of the 2nd ACM SIGACT-SIGOPS Symposium on Principles of Distributed Computing*, pages 131–142. ACM, 1983.

13. D. Bert, J. P. Bowen, M. C. Henson, and K. Robinson, editors. *ZB'2002: Formal Specification and Development in Z and B, 2nd International Conference of B and Z Users, France*, volume 2272 of *Lecture Notes in Computer Science*. Springer-Verlag, 2002.

14. D. Bert, M-L. Potet, and Y. Rouzaud. A Study on Components and Assembly Primitives in B. *Proc. of the 1st Conference on the B method, H. Habrias (editor), France*, pages 47–62, November 1996.

15. M. Butler and M. Walden. Distributed System Development in B. *Proc. of the 1st Conference on the B method, H. Habrias (editor), France*, pages 155–168, 1996.

16. M. J. Butler. Stepwise Refinement of Communicating Systems. *Science of Computer Programming*, 27(2):139–173, 1996.

17. ClearSy. *Atelier B V3.6*. Steria, Aix-en-Provence, France.

18. S. Dunne. The Safe Machine: A New Specification Construct for B. In *Proceedings of FM'99: World Congress on Formal Methods*, pages 472–489, 1999.

19. S. Dunne. A Theory of Generalised Substitutions. In Bert et al. [13], pages 270–290.

20. C. A. R. Hoare. *Communicating Sequential Processes*. Prentice-Hall, NJ, 1985.

21. Y. Kesten, Z. Manna, and A. Pnueli. Temporal Verification of Simulation and Refinement. In *REX Symposium A Decade of Concurrency*, volume 803 of *Lecture Notes in Computer Science*, pages 273–346. Springer-Verlag, 1994.

22. MATISSE. Handbook for Correct Systems Construction. Technical Report IST-1999-11345, EU-Project MATISSE: Methodologies and Technoloies for Industrial Strength Systems Engineering,University of Southampton, April 2003.

23. S. Schneider and H. Treharne. Verifying Controlled Components. In E. Boiten, J. Derrick, and G. Smith, editors, *Proc. of the Integrated Formal Methods (IFM'2004)*, volume 2999 of *Lecture Notes in Computer Science*, pages 87–107. Springer-Verlag, 2004.

24. S. Schneider and H. Treharne. Communicating B Machines. In Bert et al. [13], pages 416–435.

25. Q. Xu. On Compositionality in Refining Concurrent Systems. In J. He, J. Cooke, and P. Wallis, editor, *Proceedings of the BCS FACS 7th Refinement Workshop*. Springer-Verlag, 1996.

26. Q. Xu, W. P. de Roever, and J. He. The Rely-Guarantee Method for Verifying Shared Variable Concurrent Programs. *Formal Aspects of Computing*, 9(2):149–174, 1997.

27. Q. Xu and M. Swarup. Compositional Reasoning Using the Assumption-Commitment Paradigm. *Lecture Notes in Computer Science*, 1536:565–583, 1998.

# An Extension of Event B for Developing Grid Systems

Pontus Boström and Marina Waldén

Åbo Akademi University, Department of Computer Science,
Turku Centre for Computer Science (TUCS),
Lemminkäisenkatu 14 A, 20520 Turku, Finland
{Pontus.Bostrom, Marina.Walden}@abo.fi

**Abstract.** Computational grids have become widespread in organizations for handling their need for computational resources and the vast amount of available information. Grid systems, and other distributed systems, are often complex and formal reasoning about them is needed, in order to ensure their correctness and to structure their development. Event B is a formal method with tool support that is meant for stepwise development of distributed systems. To facilitate the implementation of grid systems we here propose extensions to Event B that take grid specific features into account. We add new constructs to model the client-server architecture of grid systems, as well as important features like communication and synchronisation. We introduce the extensions in such a manner that the necessary proof obligations are automatically generated and the system can be implemented in a straightforward manner.

## 1   Introduction

Organizations need the ability to efficiently utilise existing hardware and be able to effectively share information with each other. Computational grids have become a popular approach to enable organizations to handle the vast amount of available information. These grids are also used for solving problems in, e.g., biology, nuclear physics and engineering. Grid computing [9, 14] is a distributed computing paradigm that differs from traditional distributed computing in that it is aimed toward large scale systems that even span organizational boundaries.

The development of correct grid systems is difficult with traditional software development methods. Hence, formal methods are needed in order to ensure their correctness and structure their development from specification to implementation. The Action Systems formalism [5] is a formal method that is well suited for developing large distributed systems, since it supports stepwise development. However, it lacks good tool support. The B Method [1], on the other hand, is a formal method provided with good tool support, but originally developed for construction of sequential programs. The B Method can be combined with Action Systems in order to formally reason about distributed systems as in the related methods B Action Systems [20] and Event B [3]. B Action Systems

H. Treharne et al. (Eds.): ZB 2005, LNCS 3455, pp. 142–161, 2005.

models Action Systems in the B Method, while Event B also extends original B with new constructs. We mainly use Event B in this paper.

With generic formal languages like Event B, specifications are often unintentionally constructed in such a way that they cannot be implemented or are very difficult to implement efficiently. The problem becomes especially apparent when developing distributed systems with complicated synchronization and communication patterns. Therefore, we propose new extensions to Event B in order to be able to construct models of grid systems that can be implemented and to verify their correctness in a convenient way. The language obtained by the extensions will be referred to as Distributed B in the rest of the paper.

The language Distributed B is targeted towards Grid systems using the Globus Toolkit [11] middleware. Grid systems usually have a client-server architecture. This means that there is a client that initiates communication with the server, which only responds to the clients' requests. Distributed B supports client-server architectures with multiple concurrent accesses by the same client to several servers. The main communication mechanism of the grid middleware is remote procedure calls. However, the grid middleware also supports asynchronous notifications sent from a server to a client. Both these communication primitives are used in Distributed B. The constructs are introduced in such a manner that they ensure that the system will be implementable and all needed proof obligations can be automatically generated.

In Section 2 we describe formal development of systems in Event B. In Section 3 we give an overview of the grid technology and discuss how the grid features are incorporated into Event B. The new constructs, grid service machine and grid refinement machine, are presented in Sections 4 and 5, respectively. In Section 6 we discuss implementation issues and in Section 7 we conclude.

## 2    Formal Development with Event B

In order to be able to develop correct grid systems and other distributed systems, we need to reason about these systems in a formal manner. Furthermore, it is important that the formal reasoning is facilitated by good tool support. Action Systems is a well established formalism for reasoning about distributed systems [5]. However, it lacks good tool support. Event B [3] is a formalism that is based on Action Systems and is an extension of the B Method for developing distributed systems. This formalism is also provided with tool support currently in the form of a translator to original B. Because of this we have chosen Event B as the formalism within which we develop our framework for specifying and implementing grid systems.

### 2.1    Abstract Specifications

An abstract model of a system within Event B is encapsulated in a *system*-machine identified by a unique name. Let us study the abstract model $\mathcal{C}$.

SYSTEM $\mathcal{C}$
**VARIABLES**
  $x$
**INVARIANT**
  $I(x)$
**INITIALISATION**
  $x := x_0$
**EVENTS**
  $E_1 \; \hat{=} \; S_1;$
  $E_2 \; \hat{=} \; S_2;$
   ...
**END**

Each variable $x$ in the *variables*-clause is associated with some domain of values. The set of possible assignments of values to the state variables constitutes the state space. The data invariant $I(x)$ in the *invariant*-clause defines the state space of the variables and their invariant properties. In the *initialisation*-clause initial values are assigned to these variables. The *events*-clause contains events describing the behaviour of the system. Each event in the *events*-clause is a substitution statement, where the substitution, for example, can be a *skip*-substitution, a simple substitution, a multiple substitution, a sequential substitution, a preconditioned substitution, a conditional substitution, a guarded substitution or a non-deterministic guarded substitution. The semantics of these substitution statements is given by the weakest precondition calculus developed by Dijkstra [8].

$$\begin{aligned}
\text{wp}(skip, Q) &= Q \\
\text{wp}(x := e, Q) &= Q[x := e] \\
\text{wp}(x := e \parallel y := f, Q) &= Q[x, y := e, f], \text{ where } x \cap y = \emptyset \\
\text{wp}(x := e; \; y := f, Q) &= (Q[y := f])[x := e] \\
\text{wp}(\textbf{PRE } G \textbf{ THEN } S \textbf{ END}, Q) &= G \wedge \text{wp}(S, Q) \\
\text{wp}(\textbf{IF } G \textbf{ THEN } S \textbf{ ELSE } T \textbf{ END}, Q) &= (G \Rightarrow \text{wp}(S, Q)) \wedge (\neg G \Rightarrow \text{wp}(T, Q)) \\
\text{wp}(\textbf{SELECT } G \textbf{ THEN } S \textbf{ END}, Q) &= G \Rightarrow \text{wp}(S, Q) \\
\text{wp}(\textbf{ANY } x \textbf{ WHERE } G \textbf{ THEN } S \textbf{ END}, Q) &= \forall x.G \Rightarrow \text{wp}(S, Q)
\end{aligned}$$

Here, $Q$ and $G$ are predicates, $x$ and $y$ are variables, $e$ and $f$ are expressions, while $S$ and $T$ are arbitrary substitution statements.

An event is considered to consist of a guard and a body. For example, for event $E \; \hat{=} \; \textbf{SELECT } G \textbf{ THEN } S \textbf{ END}$ the guard, $\text{gd}(E)$, is $(G \wedge \text{gd}(S))$. When the guard of an event evaluates to *true* in a given state, the event is said to be enabled. Only enabled events are considered for execution. If several events are enabled, they are executed in random order. Events that do not share variables can be executed in parallel. When there are no enabled events the system terminates. The events are considered to be atomic and, hence, only their input-output behaviour is of interest.

In grid systems remote procedures play an important role. Remote procedures [18] are, however, not supported in Event B. The reason for this is that a model in Event B is closed, i.e., the system is modeled as a whole without relying on outside information. For reasoning about remote procedures we rely on the formalism B Action Systems [20], another formalism applying Action Systems within the B Method and related to Event B. Remote procedures are discussed in more detail elsewhere [18, 7].

## 2.2  Decomposing Event Systems

Grid systems are often very complex systems. Therefore, it is beneficial to split these systems into several smaller ones during the development [6]. Let us study how an event system $\mathcal{C}$ can be decomposed into two components $\mathcal{C}_1$ and $\mathcal{C}_2$. System $\mathcal{C}$ contains the variables $x$, $y$ and $z$, where the event $E_1$ refers to $x$ and $z$, and event $E_2$ to $y$ and $z$. We assume that $E_1$ does not modify $z$. The parallel decomposition of system $\mathcal{C}$ into the components $\mathcal{C}_1$ and $\mathcal{C}_2$ is then defined by splitting the variables and events as follows.

| SYSTEM $\mathcal{C}$ | | SYSTEM $\mathcal{C}_1$ | SYSTEM $\mathcal{C}_2$ |
|---|---|---|---|
| **VARIABLES** | | **EXTENDS** | |
| $x, y, z$ | | $\mathcal{C}_2$ | |
| **INVARIANT** | decomp. | **VARIABLES** | **VARIABLES** |
| $I_{C1}(x, z) \wedge I_{C2}(y, z)$ | $\longrightarrow$ | $x$ | $y, z$ |
| **INITIALISATION** | | **INVARIANT** | **INVARIANT** |
| $x := x_0 \;\|$ | | $I_{C1}(x, z)$ | $I_{C2}(y, z)$ |
| $y := y_0 \;\| \; z := z_0$ | | **INITIALISATION** | **INITIALISATION** |
| **EVENTS** | | $x := x_0$ | $y := y_0 \;\| \; z := z_0$ |
| $E_1 \;\hat{=}\; S_1;$ | | **EVENTS** | **EVENTS** |
| $E_2 \;\hat{=}\; S_2$ | | $E_1 \;\hat{=}\; S_1$ | $E_2 \;\hat{=}\; S_2$ |
| **END** | | **END** | **END** |

Here we say that system $\mathcal{C}_1$ *extends* system $\mathcal{C}_2$ indicating that $\mathcal{C}_1$ is composed in parallel with $\mathcal{C}_2$, $\mathcal{C}_1 \;\|\; \mathcal{C}_2$. Note that the *extends*-clause is as defined in original B. After the decomposition the variables $x$ are located in $\mathcal{C}_1$ while $y$ and $z$ are in $\mathcal{C}_2$. The invariant, the initialisation, as well as the events referring to the variables $x$ are included in $\mathcal{C}_1$, while the ones referring to $y$ and $z$ are given in $\mathcal{C}_2$. In $\mathcal{C}_2$ the variables $z$ are global variables, since they are referenced also in system $\mathcal{C}_1$. The decomposition rule can be applied in reverse and is then called parallel composition [6, 7]. We can note that the composed system terminates when all its sub-systems have terminated.

## 2.3  Refinement

In Event B we can refine an abstract specification in a stepwise manner to a more concrete and detailed specification. New variables can be introduced and the old variables can be refined to more concrete ones. This is reflected in the substitutions of the events, as well. Furthermore, new events that only assign the new variables may be introduced. In a refinement step we can also merge several events into one event, as well as refine one event by several events. The merging and splitting of events should be stated explicitly in the Event B specification and the rules for these operations are described in more detail in [2, 3].

Let us assume that we have two event systems $\mathcal{C}$ and $\mathcal{C}_1$ as below. The variables $x$ in $\mathcal{C}$ are refined to $x'$ in $\mathcal{C}_1$, while $y$ are the new variables introduced in $\mathcal{C}_1$. The events $E_i$ are refined by the corresponding events $E_i'$ to also take $y$ into account. The events $F_j$ are introduced in this refinement step and refer only to the new variables $y$.

SYSTEM $C$

VARIABLES
$x$
INVARIANT
$I(x)$
INITIALISATION
$x := x_0$
EVENTS
$E_1 \; \hat{=} \; S_1;$
$\cdots$
$E_n \; \hat{=} \; S_n$
END

REFINEMENT $C_1$
REFINES $C$
VARIABLES
$x', y$
INVARIANT
$J(x, x', y)$
INITIALISATION
$x' := x_0' \parallel y := y_0$
EVENTS
$E_1' \; \hat{=} \; S_1';$
$\cdots$
$E_n' \; \hat{=} \; S_n';$
$F_1 \; \hat{=} \; T_1;$
$\cdots$
$F_m \; \hat{=} \; T_m$
END

When invariant $J(x, x', y)$ is a relation between the abstract variables $x$ and the concrete variables $x'$ and $y$, we write $E \sqsubseteq_J E'$ to denote that the abstract event $E$ is data refined by the concrete event $E'$ under $J$ [5]. If $I$ is an invariant of event $E$, event $E'$ is guaranteed to terminate when $E$ is, and $E'$ establishes a situation where $E$ cannot fail to maintain the abstraction invariant $J$:

$$I \wedge J \wedge \mathrm{wp}(E, true) \Rightarrow \mathrm{wp}(E', true) \wedge \mathrm{wp}(E', \neg\mathrm{wp}(E, \neg J))$$

then $E \sqsubseteq_J E'$. In order to show in Event B that system $C_1$ is a refinement of $C$ under abstraction invariant $J$, $C \sqsubseteq_J C_1$, the following proof obligations should hold [3]:

1. $\mathrm{wp}((x' := x_0' \parallel y := y_0), \neg\mathrm{wp}(x := x_0, \neg J))$
2. $E_i \sqsubseteq_J E_i'$, for $i \in 1..n$
3. $skip \sqsubseteq_J F_j$, for $j \in 1..m$
4. $J \wedge \neg(\mathrm{gd}(E_1') \vee \ldots \vee \mathrm{gd}(E_n') \vee \mathrm{gd}(F_1) \vee \ldots \vee \mathrm{gd}(F_m)) \Rightarrow \neg(\mathrm{gd}(E_1) \vee \ldots \vee \mathrm{gd}(E_n))$
5. $J \Rightarrow V \in \mathbb{N}$
6. $\mathrm{gd}(F_j) \Rightarrow \mathrm{wp}(n := V, \mathrm{wp}(F_j, V < n))$, for $j \in 1..m$

The initialisation in the refined system maintains the behaviour of the abstract system under abstraction invariant $J$ (1). Every event $E_i$ in the abstract system is refined by an event $E_i'$ in the concrete system (2). New events $F_j$ should only refer to the new variables and should not change the behaviour of the abstract system (3). The refined event system must not terminate more often than the abstract one (4). The behaviour of the abstract system should be preserved and, hence, the new events should terminate when executed in isolation (5 and 6). Here, $V$ is a variant that is decreased by every new event $F_j$. All these proof obligations can be automatically generated by the tools for Event B.

For the remote procedures we rely on the proof obligations for B Action Systems [7]. Let us assume that we have procedure $P_k$ in $C$ that is refined by $P_k'$ in $C_1$. When considering procedures in event systems the following additional proof obligations should hold.

7. $P_k \sqsubseteq_J P_k'$, for $k \in 1..h$
8. $J \wedge \mathrm{gd}(P_k) \Rightarrow \mathrm{gd}(P_k')$, for $k \in 1..h$

The abstract remote procedure $P_k$ should be refined by the corresponding procedure $P'_k$ in $C_1$ (7). Furthermore, the guards of the procedures may not be changed (7 and 8). Proof obligation (7) can be automatically generated via Event B, while proof obligation (8) requires some extra constructs corresponding to the ones in [20].

# 3     Grid Systems in Event B

Relying on Event B we can formally specify correct grid systems. However, it is not straightforward to develop the specification in such a manner that it can be automatically implemented. This is due to the difficulties in synchronizing distributed components and maintaining atomicity of events. We propose an extension of Event B, Distributed B, that enable us to create implementable specifications of grid systems in a convenient way.

## 3.1     Grid Systems

The purpose of grid systems is to share information and computing resources even over organizational boundaries. This requires security, scalability and protocols that are suited for Internet wide communication. The Open Grid Service Architecture (OGSA) [10] aims at providing a common standard to develop grid based applications. This standard defines what services a grid system should provide. A technical infrastructure specification defined by Open Grid Service Infrastructure (OGSI) [12] gives a precise technical definition of what a grid service is. The Globus Toolkit 3.x [11], an implementation of the OGSI specification, has become defacto standard toolkit for implementing grid systems. This is also the toolkit we use as grid middleware for Distributed B in this paper.

Grid systems usually have a client-server architecture, where the client initiates communication with the server that only responds to the client's request. A client may access several servers concurrently. A server is referred to as a grid service in Globus Toolkit, since it provides services to other grid components. Grid services as implemented in Globus Toolkit provide features such as remote procedures, notifications, services that contain state, transient services and service data. The main communication mechanism of grid services is remote procedure calls from client to grid service. By using notifications a grid service can asynchronously notify clients about changes in its state. The state of grid services are preserved between calls and grid service instances can be dynamically created. Service data adds structured data to any grid service interface. Thus, not only remote procedures, but also variables are available to clients. Furthermore, Globus Toolkit contains an index service for managing information and keeping track of different types of services in the grid.

## 3.2     Extending Event B

The main purpose of the language Distributed B is to be able to specify, verify and implement correct grid systems in a convenient way. As for grid systems the

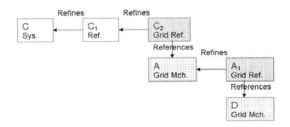

**Fig. 1.** The structure of the Distributed B development

most common communication mechanism in Distributed B is remote procedure calls. However, in order to support concurrent accesses by the same client to multiple grid services, Distributed B also takes into account notifications.

In order to meet the requirements above, we propose to extend Event B with two types of machines, a *grid service machine* modelling abstract grid service features and a *grid refinement machine* for refining an ordinary Event B model by introducing grid features or for refining a grid service machine. A grid service machine is a template of which a client (a grid refinement machine) can obtain instances. Using terminology from object oriented programming, the grid service machine can be viewed as a class and the instances as objects of the class. This new composition mechanism is expressed with the *references* construct in the grid refinement machine. Several instances of the same grid service machine can be controlled by the same client as a master can control several identical worker nodes. A grid service machine contains specifications of remote procedures, events and notifications. The grid refinement machine, on the other hand, has clauses for refined remote procedures and events, as well as a clause for handling notifications. The clients and the grid services use remote procedure calls and notifications to communicate and synchronize with each other. For example, a client can make a request to a grid service with a remote procedure call and when the request has been carried out a notification is sent back to the client.

The development of the grid system shown in Figure 1 starts with an initial specification, $C$, in Event B that is refined in a number of steps, $C_1$. The specification is then split up into a client, $C_2$, and a number of grid services, $A$. The grid services can in turn be independently refined in a stepwise manner, $A_1$, and reference new grid services, $D$. For simplicity we assume that each grid service machine can only be referenced from one grid refinement machine.

Throughout the development of the system the grid constructs are translated to ordinary B machines for verification purposes. Note that we translate the Distributed B specifications to B and not to Event B. The reason for this is that the current tool support also translates Event B specifications to B for verification. The translation of the Event B constructs in Distributed B to B is performed as in the current tools for Event B.

# 4   Grid Service Machines

In Distributed B an abstract model of a grid service is given as the construct *grid service machine*. Grid service machines extend Event B with clauses for specifying remote procedures and notifications. A grid service can wait for a remote procedure call from a client. Upon the call it performs the requested task. When the task has been completed, i.e., when all the events in the grid service machine has become disabled, a notification is sent. By choosing to send the notification only after the task has been completed, the notification mechanism can be implemented using the Globus Toolkit in a straightforward manner.

## 4.1   Grammar for the Grid Service Machine

The grammar for the grid service machine is an extension of the grammar for an abstract system in Event B. Here only the differences between the grammars are shown.

```
gridservice ::= "GRID_SERVICE" Name
                Clause_gridservice+
                "END"
Clause_gridservice ::=
   Clause_system_abstract |
   Clause_rpcs |
   Clause_notif
Clause_rpcs ::= "REMOTE_PROCEDURES" Rpc_oper+;
Rpc_oper ::= Header_operation "=" NG_Substitution
Clause_notif ::= "NOTIFICATIONS" Notif+;
Notif::= Name "=" "GUARANTEES" Predicate "END"
```

The grid service machine grammar contains all the constructs present in abstract systems of Event B, such as constants, sets, variables and events. Additionally, the grid service has a number of remote procedures that other services can access. A remote procedure is an implementable operation in the B Method, i.e., it only contains non-guarded substitutions (here called *NG_Substitution*) of the set of substitutions in Event B. The *notifications*-clause contains *guarantees*-statements with conditions indicating when the notifications can be sent to the client. A notification is sent when none of the events in the *events*-clause are enabled and the predicate in its *guarantees*-statement holds.

## 4.2   Mapping the Specification to B

An abstract grid service machine contains clauses which do not exist in an Event B specification. In order to be able to use tool support for verifying the consistency of the grid service machine, we need to translate the grid service machine to an abstract machine specification in B.

**Translation of the Grid Service Machine to B.** In a system developed within Distributed B it is assumed that all available instances of all the grid services are created upon initialisation of the system. The index service of Globus Toolkit then provides references to available grid service instances of correct type. In the B Method, a model of the set of instances that can be obtained from the index service first has to be defined. This dynamic management of instances of machines has to be explicitly modeled in the B Method [4, 17].

Let us assume that we have a grid service machine $\mathcal{A}$. The set of instances of $\mathcal{A}$ that can be obtained from the index service is then given as the set $A\_INSTANCES$. The constant $A\_null$ models an empty instance of grid service machine $\mathcal{A}$. Upon a request for a new instance from the index service, the value $A\_null$ is returned when no non-empty instance is available.

$$\textbf{SETS}$$
$$A\_INSTANCES$$
$$\textbf{CONSTANTS}$$
$$A\_null$$
$$\textbf{PROPERTIES}$$
$$A\_null \in A\_INSTANCES$$

The variable $A\_Instances$ models the set of non-empty instances of $\mathcal{A}$ currently in use by the client. They are obtained dynamically from the index service.

$$\textbf{VARIABLES}$$
$$A\_Instances$$
$$\textbf{INVARIANT}$$
$$A\_Instances \subseteq A\_INSTANCES \wedge$$
$$A\_null \notin A\_Instances$$

All the variables in a grid service machine are translated to functions from the set of instances in use to the variable types. Assume that grid service machine $\mathcal{A}$ has a variable $x$ of type $X$. When $\mathcal{A}$ is translated to original B the type of $x$ is defined as $x \in A\_Instances \rightarrow X$.

When we translate remote procedures to B to take an instance $inst$ into account, we introduce the instance for which it is called as an additional parameter. For example, procedure $Proc(p) \mathrel{\widehat{=}} P$ becomes $Proc(inst, p) \mathrel{\widehat{=}} P(inst)$ upon translation. The events are translated to non-deterministic guarded substitutions ($any$-substitutions) to take instances into account. The event $E \mathrel{\widehat{=}} S$ in the grid service machine becomes:

$$E \mathrel{\widehat{=}} \textbf{ANY}\ inst\ \textbf{WHERE}\ inst \in A\_Instances\ \textbf{THEN}\ S(inst)\ \textbf{END}$$

Hence, there is an event $E_{inst}$ for every instance $inst$ of grid service machine $\mathcal{A}$ in use. As a result of this $\mathcal{A}$ can be considered to be a parallel composition of its instances, $\mathcal{A} = \|_{inst} \mathcal{A}_{inst}$. Since at least one of the notifications should be enabled when the events of the grid service machine have become disabled, we add the following predicate to the invariant of the abstract machine upon translation:

$$\forall inst.(inst \in A\_Instances \wedge \neg \mathrm{gd}(\mathcal{A}_{inst}) \Rightarrow Q_1(inst) \vee ... \vee Q_n(inst))$$

where $Q_i$ is the predicate of the *guarantees*-statement in notification $i$ in $\mathcal{A}$. The predicate states that one of the notifications is enabled when all events of $\mathcal{A}$ are disabled.

In order for a client to be able to obtain new instances for a grid service machine via the index service, a procedure *GetNew* is automatically generated in the translated abstract B machine. This procedure can be viewed as the constructor of instances.

$$z \leftarrow A\_GetNew \; \widehat{=}$$
**IF** $A\_Instances \neq A\_INSTANCES$
**THEN**
    **ANY** $inst$ **WHERE**
      $inst \in A\_INSTANCES - A\_Instances \wedge inst \neq A\_null$
    **THEN**
      $A\_Instances := A\_Instances \cup \{inst\} \parallel$
      $x(inst) := x_0 \parallel z := inst$
    **END**
**ELSE** $z := A\_null$
**END**

The procedure ensures that the instance returned is not already in use and returns $A\_null$ if no non-empty instance is available. If variable $x$ is assigned $x_0$ in the *initialisation*-clause of grid service machine $\mathcal{A}$, variable $x$ for the returned instance *inst* is assigned $x_0$, $x(inst) := x_o$, in $A\_GetNew$.

Grid services allocated by a client may need to be returned to the index service. Hence, a procedure *Destroy* is automatically generated for each grid service machine upon translation to B to return an instance no longer in use.

$$A\_Destroy(inst) \; \widehat{=}$$
**PRE** $inst \in A\_INSTANCES$
**THEN**
    **IF** $inst \in A\_Instances$
    **THEN**
      $x := \{inst\} \lessless\mid x \parallel$
      $A\_Instances := A\_Instances - \{inst\}$
    **END**
**END**

The operation $A\_Destroy$ in $\mathcal{A}$ deletes the instance, *inst*, from the set of instances in use and marks the instance as available in the index service. This procedure can be viewed as the destructor of instances.

**Example of a Grid Service Machine.** As an example of translating grid service machines in Distributed B to B, let us study grid service machine *ADDER* that computes the sum of all values it receives. The machine has two remote procedures, *SetNewData* and *GetResult*. The new value to be added to the sum is given via procedure *SetNewData*. The result of the latest computation can be obtained via procedure *GetResult*. The variable *sum* gives the current result of the sum computation, while *param* contains the latest value received via *SetNewData*. The variable *state* ensures that all the received values are added once and only once to *sum*. The actual computation of the sum is performed in event *Comp*. A notification is sent after the initialisation, *InitNotif*, as well as after a new sum has been computed, *DoneNotif*.

The grid service machine *ADDER* is translated to the abstract B machine *ADDER_VERIFICATION* for verification as follows:

**GRID_SERVICE**
*ADDER*

**VARIABLES**
*sum, param, state*
**INVARIANT**
$sum \in \mathbb{N} \wedge$
$param \in \mathbb{N} \wedge$
$state \in STATE$

**INITIALISATION**
$sum := 0 \parallel param := 0 \parallel$
$state := init$
**REMOTE_PROCEDURES**
$SetNewData(p) \;\hat{=}$
  **PRE** $p \in \mathbb{N}$
  **THEN**
    $param := p \parallel$
    $state = start$
  **END** ;
$z \leftarrow GetResult \;\hat{=}$
  **BEGIN** $z := sum$
  **END**


**EVENTS**
$Comp \;\hat{=}$
  **SELECT** $state = start$
  **THEN**
    $sum := sum + param \parallel$
    $state := done$
  **END**
**NOTIFICATIONS**
$InitNotif \;\hat{=}$
  **GUARANTEES** $state = init$ **END** ;
$DoneNotif \;\hat{=}$
  **GUARANTEES** $state = done$ **END**
**END**

**MACHINE**
*ADDER_VERIFICATION*
. . .
**VARIABLES**
*sum, param, state, ADDER_Instances*
**INVARIANT**
$ADDER\_Instances \subseteq ADDER\_INSTANCES \wedge$
$A\_null \notin ADDER\_Instances \wedge$
$sum \in ADDER\_Instances \to \mathbb{N} \wedge$
$param \in ADDER\_Instances \to \mathbb{N} \wedge$
$state \in ADDER\_Instances \to STATE \wedge$
$\forall inst.(inst \in ADDER\_Instances \wedge$
    $\neg(state(inst) = start) \Rightarrow$
    $state(inst) = init \vee state(inst) = done)$
**INITIALISATION**
$sum := \emptyset \parallel param := \emptyset \parallel state := \emptyset \parallel$
$ADDER\_Instances := \emptyset$
**OPERATIONS**
$SetNewData(inst, p) \;\hat{=}$
  **PRE** $p \in \mathbb{N} \wedge inst \in ADDER\_Instances$
  **THEN**
    $param(inst) := p \parallel$
    $state(inst) = start$
  **END** ;
$z \leftarrow GetResult(inst) \;\hat{=}$
  **PRE** $inst \in ADDER\_Instances$
  **THEN** $z := sum(inst)$
  **END** ;
$y \leftarrow ADDER\_GetNew \;\hat{=}$ ... ;
$ADDER\_Destroy(inst) \;\hat{=}$ ... ;

$Comp \;\hat{=}$
  **ANY** $inst$ **WHERE** $inst \in ADDER\_Instances$
  **THEN**
    **SELECT** $state(inst) = start$
    **THEN**
      $sum(inst) := sum(inst) + param(inst) \parallel$
      $state(inst) := done$
    **END**
  **END**
**END**

The types of the variables in the grid service machine are translated to functions from instances of the grid service machine to data values. For example, the variable *sum* has type $\mathbb{N}$ in *ADDER*, while it is a total function from the instances *ADDER_Instances* to $\mathbb{N}$ in *ADDER_VERIFICATION*. Instances are created and deleted by the procedures *ADDER_GetNew* and *ADDER_Destroy* introduced in *ADDER_VERIFICATION*. The remote procedures *SetNewData* and *GetResult* also take the instances into account. An additional parameter is introduced to denote for which instance the procedure is called. Event *Comp* is translated to an *any*-substitution for a non-deterministically chosen instance *inst* of *ADDER*. Hence, there is an event *Comp* for every instance of *ADDER* in use. The notifications *InitNotif* and *DoneNotif* are not translated directly to B, although the invariant should explicitly say that the *guarantees*-predicate in at least one of the notifications holds when event *Comp* is not enabled.

# 5  Refinement in Distributed B

We introduce a new type of refinement machine in Distributed B to deal with remote procedure calls and notification handlers in Event B. The *grid refinement machines* refine Event B systems, grid service machines, as well as other grid refinement machines. In a refinement step in Distributed B variables and events can be refined in the same way as in Event B. The substitutions in the remote procedures and the notification handlers are also refined as the events to reflect the changes of the variables. Note that the variables of the abstract grid service machines are global variables and may not be refined.

A grid refinement machine contains a new structuring mechanism in B that enables the grid refinement to obtain instances of the grid service machines via the index service. When the grid refinement machine has obtained a grid service instance, it can perform a remote procedure call to this instance and then wait for a notification from it. The grid service machine can in turn be refined into a grid refinement machine to reference new grid service machines.

## 5.1  Grammar for Refinements of Grid Services

The grammar of a grid refinement machine is an extension of the grammar of the refinement machine in Event B. For brevity we concentrate on the differences from the refinement machine.

```
Ref_gridservice ::= "GRID_REFINEMENT" Name
                    "REFINES" Name
                    Clause_ref_gridservice+
                    "END"
Clause_ref_gridservice ::=
   Clause_refinement |
   Clause_references |
   Clause_rpcs |
   Clause_notif_handlers
Clause_references ::= "REFERENCES" Name+,
Clause_rpcs ::= "REMOTE_PROCEDURES" Rpc_oper+;
Rpc_oper ::= Header_operation "=" NG_Substitution
Clause_notif_handlers ::= "NOTIFICATION_HANDLERS" Notif_handler+;
Notif_handler ::= Name "=" "NOTIFICATION" Name
                  "SOURCE" Name ":" Name
                  "THEN" NG_Substitution "END"
```

In the *references*-clause we give the names of the grid service machines that the grid refinement machine can access and obtain instances of. The refined remote procedures are given in the *remote_procedures*-clause. Notifications are handled by special events, *notification*-substitutions, in the *notification_handlers*-clause. There should be one notification handler event for each notification in the referenced grid service machines. The source of the notification is given as *<instance>:<grid service machine>*. The notification handlers and the remote procedures should be implementable and not contain guarded substitutions. The *notifications*-clause that we introduced for grid service machines is not included in the refinement, since the *guarantees*-predicate of a notification should not be refined.

## 5.2    Translation of the Refinement to B

In order to be able to show that the grid refinement machine is a correct refinement of another machine, e.g., an Event B specification or a grid service machine, both the grid refinement machine and its referenced grid service machines need to be translated to B. Note that when we refine a grid service machine, we actually refine the instances of the grid service. In the translation from Distributed B to B the instances of grid refinement machines are treated in the same way as the ones of the grid service machines.

In Figure 2a grid refinement machine $C_2$ refines Event B specification $C_1$ and references grid service machine $\mathcal{A}$. The grid refinement $C_2$ is translated to the refinement machine $C_2\_V$ and $\mathcal{A}$ is translated to the abstract machine $\mathcal{A}\_V$. The *references*-relation between $C_2$ and $\mathcal{A}$ is translated to an *includes*-relation between $C_2\_V$ and $\mathcal{A}\_V$.

**Managing Instances of Grid Service Machines.** In the grid refinement machines we give instances of referenced grid service machines as ordinary variables. The instance $aa$ of grid service machine $\mathcal{A}$ is declared as variable $aa$ of type $A$, $aa \in A$. This type declaration is translated to the predicate $aa \in A\_Instances \cup \{A\_null\}$ in B.

The grid refinement machines refer to the variables and remote procedures of the instances of a grid service machine with the notation $<instance>.<variable>$ and $<instance>.<procedure>$, respectively. The variables of the grid service machine can be referred to only in the invariant of the grid refinement machine.

The remote procedure calls need to be translated to match the corresponding procedure definitions of the translated grid service machine. A call to a remote procedure $Proc(p)$ in instance $aa$, $aa.Proc(p)$, is translated to procedure call $Proc(aa, p)$ in B, where the instance $aa$ is given as an additional parameter.

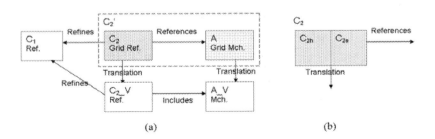

**Fig. 2.** Translation to Event B

**Notifications.** Notifications in a grid service machine inform the client that all the events in the grid service machine instance have become disabled. A notification handler in the client ensures that proper actions are taken for each notification. In the grid refinement machine a notification handler is expressed with the *notification*-substitution:

$$Handler \mathrel{\widehat{=}}$$
**NOTIFICATION** $Notif$
**SOURCE** $inst \in A$
**THEN** $T(inst)$
**END**

Here *Notif* is the name of the notification to be handled, the source $inst \in A$ stands for the instance *inst* of the grid service $A$ that sent the notification, and $T(inst)$ is a non-guarded substitution that refers to instance *inst*. Note that $T$ can only make read-only remote procedure calls to instances of $A$. A notification handler in a client is only enabled when all the events in the corresponding grid service have become disabled and the *guarantees*-predicate of the corresponding notification holds. Hence, we consider the events in instance *inst* of grid service machine $A$ to have higher priority than the corresponding notification handlers in $C_2$ [13]. Moreover, since a notification handler should only be executed once for each notification, it must disable itself.

Let us assume that we have an Event B specification $C_1$ that is refined by the composition of grid refinement machine $C_2$ and its referenced grid service machine $A$, $C_2$ *references* $A$, as in Figure 2a. We denote the composition of $C_2$ and $A$ with $C_2'$, $C_2' \mathrel{\widehat{=}} C_2 \parallel A$. Furthermore, let $C_2$ be the composition of the event systems $C_{2h}$ containing the notification handlers (*notification*-substitutions) and $C_{2e}$ containing the rest of the events in grid refinement machine $C_2$, $C_2 = C_{2h} \parallel C_{2e}$ (Figure 2b). In order to ensure the correct behaviour of the notification handling in $C_2'$, the following conditions should hold for each notification handler $C_{2h}$ of $C_{2h}$:

$$\forall inst.(\mathrm{gd}(C_{2h(inst)}) \;\Rightarrow\; \neg\mathrm{gd}(A_{inst})) \tag{1}$$

$$\forall inst.(\mathrm{gd}(C_{2h(inst)}) \Rightarrow \mathrm{wp}(C_{2h(inst)}, \neg\mathrm{gd}(C_{2h(inst)}))) \tag{2}$$

Condition (1) states that all events from instance *inst* of grid service machine $A$ are disabled when notification handling event $C_{2h}$ is enabled for that instance. A notification handler $C_{2h}$ for instance *inst* can only be executed once for each notification that $C_2$ receives and, hence, it must disable itself as stated in condition (2).

In the event system $C_{2e}$ we focus on the local events that do not make remote procedure calls. A local event $C_{2loc}$ in system $C_{2e}$ should not interfere with the notification handlers in $C_{2h}$ by enabling or disabling them as stated by conditions (3) and (4).

$$\mathrm{gd}(C_{2loc}) \wedge \mathrm{gd}(C_{2h}) \Rightarrow \mathrm{wp}(C_{2loc}, \mathrm{gd}(C_{2h})) \tag{3}$$

$$\mathrm{gd}(C_{2loc}) \wedge \neg\mathrm{gd}(C_{2h}) \Rightarrow \mathrm{wp}(C_{2loc}, \neg\mathrm{gd}(C_{2h})) \tag{4}$$

The conditions (1) - (4) above are fulfilled by introducing extra features upon translating the grid refinement $C_2$ to B. Firstly, we introduce a boolean variable $A\_notification$ for each referenced grid service machine $\mathcal{A}$:

$$A\_notification \in A\_Instances \rightarrow BOOL$$

When the variable $A\_notification(inst)$ has the value $true$, the grid refinement $C_2$ is prepared to receive a notification from instance $inst$ of $\mathcal{A}$. The notification handler $Handler$ is translated to take variable $A\_notification$ into account:

$Handler \,\hat{=}\,$
**ANY** $inst$ **WHERE**
    $inst \in A\_Instances \wedge$
    $\neg gd(\mathcal{A}_{inst}) \wedge Q_{Notif}(inst) \wedge$
    $A\_notification(inst) = TRUE$
**THEN** $T(inst) \parallel A\_notification(inst) := FALSE$
**END**

The guard of the translated notification handler $Handler$ states that the events of the grid service machine $\mathcal{A}$ for the instance $inst$ should be disabled when $Handler$ is enabled, $\neg gd(\mathcal{A}_{inst})$, ensuring that condition (1) is fulfilled. Predicate $Q_{Notif}$ is obtained from the *guarantees*-statement of the corresponding notification *Notif* in $\mathcal{A}$ and gives the condition for this notification to be sent. The condition $A\_notification(inst) = TRUE$ in the guard of the translated notification handler states that the grid refinement is prepared to receive a notification. In order to ensure condition (2) stating that a notification handler is executed only once for each notification, the assignment $A\_notification(inst) := FALSE$ is also added to $Handler$ upon translation. In the events of $C_2$ the assignment $A\_notification(inst) := TRUE$ is added after the remote procedure calls to procedures in instance $inst$ of $\mathcal{A}$ to prepare the notification handlers to receive a notification. Note that this assignment is also added after a call to $A\_GetNew$ for a new instance of $\mathcal{A}$.

The guards of the notification handlers, $gd(C_{2h})$, refer to the variables of $\mathcal{A}$, as well as the variable $A\_notification$. Since, an event $C_{2loc}$ in the event system $C_{2e}$ does not modify these variables, conditions (3) and (4) hold trivially.

**Example of a Grid Refinement Machine.** Let us give an example of a grid refinement machine and its translation to B. The grid refinement machine *CLIENT1* below sums up a number of sub-sums (here 100), $(\sum_{counter=1}^{100} \sum_{j=0}^{counter} j)$. It refines the abstract system CLIENT that computes this sum in one step. The sub-sums from 0 to *counter* are computed in the grid service machine *ADDER* presented in the example in Subsection 4.2. The instance of grid service machine *ADDER* used for the sum computation is given by variable *adder*. The variable *counter* keeps track of the number of calls made to instance *adder*, while *total* gives the current result of the sum computation. The variable *rpc* states whether there is a computation in progress in *adder* or not. Event *Evt* of *CLIENT1* initiates the computation of the inner sum $(\sum_{j=0}^{counter} j)$ by a call to procedure *SetNewData* in instance *adder*. The event *Comp* in *adder* performs the computation by adding *counter* to the previously computed sub-sum, *sum*. *CLIENT1* waits for a notification to update variable *total* with the new sub-sum computed by *adder*. This process is repeated until the value of *counter* is 100.

The grid refinement machine *CLIENT1* in Distributed B is translated to the refinement machine *CLIENT1_VERIFICATION* in B as follows:

**GRID_REFINEMENT**
  *CLIENT*1
**REFINES**
  *CLIENT*
**REFERENCES**
  *ADDER*

**VARIABLES**
  *counter, total, rpc, adder*
**INVARIANT**
  *counter* $\in \mathbb{N} \wedge$ *total* $\in \mathbb{N} \wedge$
  *rpc* $\in BOOL \wedge$
  *adder* $\in ADDER$
  . . .

**INITIALISATION**
  *counter* := 0; *total* := 0;
  *rpc* := *FALSE*;
  *adder* $\leftarrow ADDER\_GetNew$

**EVENTS**
  . . .
*Evt* $\hat{=}$
  **SELECT** *adder* $\neq A\_null \wedge$
    *rpc* = *FALSE* $\wedge$ *counter* < 100
  **THEN**
    *counter* := *counter* + 1; *rpc* := *TRUE*;
    *adder.SetNewData(counter)*
  **END**

**NOTIFICATION_HANDLERS**
*Handler* $\hat{=}$
  **NOTIFICATION** *DoneNotif*
  **SOURCE** *inst* $\in ADDER$
  **THEN**
    **VAR** *val* **IN**
    *val* $\leftarrow inst.GetResult$;
    *total* := *total* + *val*;
    *rpc* := *FALSE*
    **END**
  **END**
**END**

---

**REFINEMENT**
  *CLIENT*1_*VERIFICATION*
**REFINES**
  *CLIENT*
**INCLUDES**
  *ADDER_VERIFICATION*
**PROMOTES**
  *Comp*
**VARIABLES**
  *counter, total, rpc, adder*
**INVARIANT**
  *counter* $\in \mathbb{N} \wedge$ *total* $\in \mathbb{N} \wedge$
  *rpc* $\in BOOL \wedge$
  *adder* $\in ADDER\_Instances \cup$
    $\{ADDER\_null\}$
  . . .

**INITIALISATION**
  *counter* := 0; *total* := 0;
  *rpc* := *FALSE*;
  *adder* $\leftarrow ADDER\_GetNew$;
  *ADDER_notification(adder)* := *TRUE*

**OPERATIONS**
  . . .
*Evt* $\hat{=}$
  **SELECT** *adder* $\neq A\_null \wedge$
    *rpc* = *FALSE* $\wedge$ *counter* < 100
  **THEN**
    *counter* := *counter* + 1; *rpc* := *TRUE*;
    *SetNewData(adder, counter)*;
    *ADDER_notification(adder)* := *TRUE*
  **END** ;

*Handler* $\hat{=}$
  **ANY** *inst* **WHERE**
    *inst* $\in ADDER\_Instances \wedge$
    $\neg(state(inst) = start) \wedge$
    *state(inst)* = *done* $\wedge$
    *ADDER_notification(inst)* = *TRUE*
  **THEN**
    **VAR** *val* **IN**
    *val* $\leftarrow GetResult(inst)$;
    *total* := *total* + *val*;
    *rpc* := *FALSE*
    **END** ;
    *ADDER_notification(inst)* := *FALSE*
  **END**
**END**

During the translation variable *adder* is transformed into an instance type of the grid service machine *ADDER*, *adder* $\in ADDER\_Instances \cup \{ADDER\_null\}$. In the remote procedure call *SetNewData* the instance *adder* is introduced as a parameter, *SetNewData(adder, counter)*. The notification handler *Handler* is translated to a new notification handling event for every instance *inst* of *ADDER*. The notification *DoneNotif* is taken into account by adding the condition $(state(inst) = done)$ from its *guarantees*-clause to the guard of the notification handling event. The variable $ADDER\_notification$ is included in the notification handler and after every remote procedure call in the events, in order to ensure that notification handler is executed once for each notification.

## 5.3    Proofs

In order to show that the grid refinement is a correct refinement of a more abstract system the proof obligations given in Subsection 2.3 need to be generated and discharged. The proof obligations concerning the refinement of the initialisation, the procedures, as well as the events are generated automatically by the tools of the B Method. Furthermore, the proof obligation for showing that the refined system does not terminate more often than the abstract system can also be directly generated by these tools (via Event B). In order to show that the new events terminate when executed in isolation, a variant that is decreased upon execution of each new event is needed in the grid refinement machine. Note that the notification handlers are introduced as new events. For the notification handlers dealing with notifications from grid service machine $\mathcal{A}$ the variant is the number of instances for which the notification has not yet been sent:

$$\mathrm{card}(\{inst|inst \in A\_Instances \land A\_notification(inst) = TRUE\})$$

This variant requires that new events do not call procedures in $\mathcal{A}$. The proof obligation ensuring that a refined remote procedure is enabled when the corresponding abstract remote procedure is enabled is *true* by construction, since the remote procedures contain only non-guarded substitutions. Hence, all the proof obligations for proving the correctness of a refinement step in Distributed B can be automatically generated with the tool support for the B Method (via Event B). These proof obligations can then be automatically or interactively discharged with the help of these tools.

## 6    Implementation

The grid system development in Distributed B continues until all the non-determinism has been removed and all the used constructs can be implemented, i.e., they belong to the implementable subset of B, B0. When all substitutions of the system belong to the B0 language, they can be translated to Java. The remote procedures and notification handlers are constructed in such a way that they can be directly translated [19]. Furthermore, translation of all the variables except for instances of grid service machines is straightforward [19]. The instances are translated to objects encapsulating the grid specific features. Finally, all the events in an *events*-clause are merged into a single event [2]. The composed event is translated to a while-loop in Java as follows:

| | |
|---|---|
| **SELECT** $G1$ **THEN** $S1$<br>...<br>**WHEN** $Gn$ **THEN** $Sn$<br>**END** | ```while (true) {``` |

```
while (true) {
  if(G1) S1;
  ...
  else if(Gn) Sn;
  else break;
}
```

Note that the event can only be implemented, if all the guards $Gi$ and the substitutions $Si$ belong to the B0 language.

When the grid system has been translated to Java, grid specific features of Distributed B need to be attended to. Each notification handler need to be registered with the Globus Toolkit grid middleware to automatically execute it each time a notification is received. The handling of grid service instances is set up via the API's for grid services and for service data provided by Globus Toolkit. This grid specific code can be inserted into the Java code concerning the initialisation of the grid services, as well as the procedures *GetNew* and *Destroy*. After we have translated the Distributed B code to Java and all the grid specific features have been handled, we have implemented the grid system in a formal manner where the implementation is proved correct with respect to its specification.

# 7   Conclusions

In this paper we have proposed a language Distributed B that extends Event B for designing and implementing correct grid systems. Grid systems are large distributed systems and standard development tools cannot guarantee their correct implementation. We introduced two new types of machines, *grid service machine* and *grid refinement machine,* for handling grid specific issues in Event B. We proposed a method where the development of a grid system starts with refinement within Event B. After a number of refinement steps the system is split up into a grid refinement machine that references a number of grid service machines in Distributed B. The grid refinement machine manages instances of the grid service machines dynamically and can access these instances concurrently. The grid service machines can in turn be further refined and decomposed. Throughout the development in Distributed B the grid constructs are translated to machines in original B for verification purposes. The machines are introduced in a manner that allows automatic generation of the necessary proof obligations. Furthermore, the concrete specifications can be automatically translated to executable code, since the grid constructs have been introduced in such a way that they ensure that the system will be implementable. Hence, we have introduced a method for implementing grid systems where the implementation can be proved correct with respect to its specification.

The B language has earlier been successfully used for modelling distributed systems, e.g., in [20]. These examples do, however, not consider implementation issues of the developed specification. Implementation of distributed systems using the B Method has also been considered for the combination of B and

CORBA by Rolland et al. [16]. Though, their paper does not consider concurrent behaviour and dynamic management of instances of distributed components. Other formal methods have also been extended previously to enable implementation of distributed systems using different application domains. For example, the DisCo formalism has been used for designing and implementing systems that were translated to Enterprise Java Beans (EJB) [15]. Grid specific features were not considered in that extension.

The architecture of the systems developed with Distributed B forms a tree of grid services. Even if this is a very common architecture for grid systems, it might be too restrictive in some cases. Hence, we plan to investigate also other architectures. In the modelling of grid systems in Distributed B we have made the assumption that no network failures occur. In future versions of Distributed B also network failures and node failures will be taken into consideration in remote procedure calls and notifications. Moreover, we consider development of tool support for grid systems in Distributed B.

The language Distributed B that we proposed in this paper can provide a convenient formal development process for grid systems. The systems will by construction have an architecture that is implementable. Furthermore, specifications of grid systems constructed in this language will be clear to understand, since the systems are modeled in terms of grid primitives with a precise meaning. We believe that our approach to adapt Event B to the Globus Toolkit middleware can also be useful for other types of middleware for distributed systems.

## Acknowledgements

The authors would like to thank the anonymous referees for their useful comments. ·

## References

1. J. R. Abrial. *The B-Book: Assigning Programs to Meanings*. Cambridge University Press, 1996.
2. J. R. Abrial. Event Driven Sequential Program Construction, 2001. `http://www.atelierb.societe.com/ressources/articles/seq.pdf`. (accessed 13.01.2005)
3. J. R. Abrial and L. Mussat. Event B Reference Manual, 2001. `http://www.atelierb.societe.com/ressources/evt2b/eventb_reference_manual.pdf`. (accessed 13.01.2005)
4. N. Aguirre, J. Bicarregui, T. Dimitrakos and T. Maibaum. Towards Dynamic Population Management of Abstract Machines in the B Method. In D. Bert, editor, *Proceedings of the Third international conference of B and Z users: ZB2003*. LNCS 2651. Turku, Finland, pp. 528-545. Springer-Verlag, 2003.
5. R. J. R. Back and R. Kurki-Suonio. Decentralization of process nets with centralized control. In *Proceedings of the 2nd ACM SIGACT-SIGOPS Symposium of Principles of Distributed Computing*, pp. 131-142, 1983.

6. R. J. R. Back and K. Sere  From modular systems to action systems. In *Software - Concepts and Tools*, 17:26-39, 1996.
7. M. Butler and M. Waldén  Parallel programming with the B Method. Chapter 5 in E. Sekerinski and K. Sere  (eds.) *Program Development by Refinement - Case Studies Using the B Method*, pp. 183-195. Springer-Verlag, 1998.
8. E. W. Dijkstra  *A Discipline of Programming.* Prentice-Hall International, 1976.
9. I. Foster, C. Kesselman and S. Tuecke. The Anatomy of the Grid: Enabling Scalable Virtual Organizations. *The International Journal of Supercomputer Applications*, 15(3), 2001.
10. I. Foster, C. Kesselman, J. Nick and S. Tuecke. The Physiology of the Grid: An Open Grid Services Architecture for Distributed Systems Integration. Technical report, Argonne National Laboratory, 2002. `http://www.globus.org/research/papers/ogsa.pdf`. (accessed 13.01.2005)
11. Globus Toolkit. The Globus Alliance, 2004. `http://www.globus.org/`. (accessed 13.01.2005)
12. K. Czajkowski, et. al. Open Grid Services Infrastructure, 2003. `http://www-unix.globus.org/toolkit/draft-ggf-ogsi-gridservice-33_2003-06-27.pdf`. (accessed 13.01.2005)
13. E. J. Hedman, J. N. Kok and K. Sere. Coordinating Action Systems. *Theoretical Computer Science*, 240:91-115. Elsevier Science, 2000.
14. G. Mair and A. Villazón. Implementing a Distributed Master/Slave Grid Service with Globus Toolkit 3 (GT3). `http://dps.uibk.ac.at/~gregor/mandel.pdf`, 2003. (accessed 13.01.2005)
15. R. Pitkänen. A Specification-Driven Approach to Development of Enterprise Systems. In *Proceedings of NWPER'2004 - 11th Nordic Workshop on Programming and Software Development Tools and Techniques*, TUCS General Publication 34. Turku, Finland, 2004.
16. O. Rolland and T. Muntean. Refining Open Distributed Systems to CORBA. In *Proceedings of RCS'02- International workshop on refinement of critical systems: methods, tools and experience.* Grenoble, France, 2002.
17. C. Snook and M. Waldén. Use of U2B for specifying B action systems. In *Proceedings of RCS'02- International workshop on refinement of critical systems: methods, tools and experience.* Grenoble, France, 2002.
18. K. Sere and M. Waldén. Data Refinement of Remote Procedures. *Formal Aspects of Computing*, 12(4):278-297, 2000.
19. J. C. Voisinet, B. Tatibouet and A. Hammand. JBTools: An experimental platform for the formal B Method. In *Proceedings of the inaugural conference on the principles and practice of programming and Proceedings of the second workshop on intermediate representation engineering for virtual machines.* National University of Ireland, 2002
20. M. Waldén and K. Sere. Reasoning About Action Systems Using the B-Method. *Formal Methods in Systems Design*, 13:5-35, 1998.

# The Challenge of Probabilistic *Event B*
## —*Extended Abstract*—

Carroll Morgan[1], Thai Son Hoang[1], and Jean-Raymond Abrial[2]

[1] Dept. Eng. and Comp. Sci., Univ. New South Wales,
Sydney 2052, Australia
[2] Dept. Comp. Sci., ETH Zürich,
ETH Zentrum RZ H 7 8092 Zürich, Switzerland

**Abstract.** Among the many opportunities offered by computational semantics for probability, the challenge of probabilistic Event B (*pEB*) is one of the most attractive.

The *B* method itself is now almost 20 years old, and has been much improved and adapted over that time by the many projects to which it has been applied, and by its philosophy —right from the start— that it must be practical, effective and amenable to tool support.; more recently, *Event B* has extended it and altered its style of use. The probabilistic-program semantics we appeal to is even older (in Kozen's original form), but has only recently been "revived" in the context of *B*-style abstraction and refinement.

The especial attraction of putting the two together is the likely interplay between the probabilistic theory, on the one hand, and the decades of practical experience that have by now been built-in to the *B* approach, on the other.

In particular, there are areas where a full theoretical treatment of probability, concurrency, abstraction and refinement —all at once— seems prohibitively complex; and yet in practice either the complexities seldom occur, or the exigencies of *B*'s having been so-often applied to real, non-toy problems has forced it to evolve styles for avoiding such complexities. In short, we want to use (event) *B* to guide us towards the issues that truly are important.

Rabin's *randomized mutual-exclusion algorithm* is used as a motivating case study.

## 1   Theoretical Framework

We summarise separately the theory behind *B* (very briefly) and behind our treatment of probability, and then we comment on how they are brought together.

### 1.1   *B* and Event *B*

The *B* Method is based ultimately on Dijkstra's *predicate transformers* [6] for its semantics, but has its own distinctive approach:

H. Treharne et al. (Eds.): ZB 2005, LNCS 3455, pp. 162–171, 2005.

- Rather than highlighting the two levels of programs, syntax and semantics, instead the program text is regarded simply as a specialised notation for logical substitutions (into post-conditions to yield pre-conditions); thus the "programming language" is known as *Generalised Substitutions* [1].
- The substitutions are broken into smaller pieces than in Dijkstra's *guarded command language* [6], on which they are based, in particular giving independent meanings —as substitutions— to the individual guarded commands within an **if-fi** construct. This required abandoning Dijkstra's *Law of the Excluded Miracle* [23, 24, 19].
- The structuring of (large) systems into modules, and the way they are combined, is based on principles of abstraction and (data-) refinement. For the proofs of refinement, a first-order formulation is used [7] which has been shown to be equivalent to the common second-order formulations [5].
- In *Event B* specifically, the miraculous semantics of "naked" guarded commands is used to interpret their guards as *enabling conditions*, thus providing a simple treatment of (interleaving) concurrency [20, 3, 4].
- *Event B* does not impose any fairness conditions on the (repeated) scheduling of enabled substitutions; rather it is in the *B* style to elaborate (and possibly refine) such conditions explicitly.

## 1.2   Probabilistic Predicate Transformers

Dijkstra's interpretation of programs as "transformers of desired post-conditions into the weakest pre-conditions sufficient to attain them" [6] was adapted by Kozen to transform (what we call) "post-expectations" into "pre-expectations" [13]; this was based on an underlying operational model of programs as functions from initial state to final distribution of states [12].

Described informally, a *post-expectation* is a non-negative real-valued function of the (final) state that tells you how much quantitative benefit will accrue should the program finish in that state. A *pre-expectation* on the other hand is a function of the initial state, and estimates *before the program is run* how much you can reliably expect to gain by running the program from this state.[1]

Kozen's work is a generalisation of Dijkstra's in the sense that it replaces a simple-but-coarse good/bad (Boolean) judgement —whether or not the postcondition is achieved— by a finer valuation in which the original true/false judgements can still be embedded (win \$1 if the postcondition is achieved; win \$0 otherwise). But in another sense it is not a generalisation, since the ability to handle nondeterminism, and hence abstraction/refinement, has been lost: demonic choice was replaced by, not combined with, probabilistic choice.

---

[1] For a fruit/slot/poker machine, the post-expectation is the function from fruit-triples to payout; it is usually written on the front of the machine. The pre-expectation is the average —weighted by the probabilities implemented in the machine's hardware— of the outcomes you can expect *before* pulling the handle; it is (or easily could be) a function of the initial state.

More recent work has combined probability and demonic nondeterminism by synthesising a combination of the Dijkstra- (sets of final states) and the Kozen- (distributions of final states) approaches: the result is that programs take initial states to sets of distributions of final states [9, 21, 16], and the programming logic of expectations is correspondingly generalised.

### 1.3     Probability and $B$

Because both approaches above are predicate-transformer based, it is tempting (and rewarding) to put them together, and some experiments have already been carried out [18, 17, 11, 10]. The issues raised included the following: [2]

- Probabilistic substitutions do not satisfy conjunctivity, the property that allows multiple "conceptual" invariants of a machine to be treated as a single object (their conjunction) by the $B$ proof-engine; thus a $B$ machine might need to have several invariants.
- Machines' invariants need to be given initial values. (Non-probabilistic machines also need "initialised" invariants, in theory, but there are only two possible initialisations: false and true. Since false is pointless, the rules are specialised so that true is assumed and an initialisation need not be written.)
- The proof [5] that the first-order definition of refinement [7] is equivalent to the standard second-order versions fails without conjunctivity, so that a new formulation must be found.
- The interaction between probability and demonic choice is subtle and treacherous, particularly when the latter is implicit, as in for example in the choice between possible invocation order of machines' operations if several guards are simultaneously enabled.

## 2     The Mutual-Exclusion Algorithm

As a case study we chose an example where intricate reasoning seems to be required to achieve a goal that is nevertheless simple to state; it involves concurrency, probability and adversarial (i.e. demonic) scheculing.

### 2.1     Background and Suitability

Rabin has proposed a probabilistic mutual-exclusion algorithm [25] where the randomisation is used to achieve the following advantages over conventional algorithms:

- The size of the shared variable needed to ensure bounded waiting-time and absence of lockout is only $4 \lg N$ rather than $N+1$, where $N$ is the number of competing processes.

---

[2] There were many issues of *implementation* as well, which we do not discuss, such as convincing the $B$ software to accept real- rather than Boolean "predicates".

- The protocols of the processes are identical, and no single process ever becomes, even temporarily, controller of the computation.
- The entrance probability of a particular process is bounded below by a function of the number of processes actively attempting to enter, rather than by some function of the total number of processes (even "uninterested" ones) in the whole system.

Because Rabin's original algorithm was shown to have a subtle flaw [26] (subsequently corrected [14]), and because that flaw concerned the interaction of demonic choice (in the processes' assumed "adversarial" scheduling) with the probabilistic choices carried out by the processes themselves, and especially because Rabin's correctness arguments are informal (though still rigorous and mathematical), this seemed an ideal example for an attempted formalisation. Moreover, the algorithm in its original form [25] is not particularly simple (in detail); and the description of the error [26], and the correction [14] are truly complicated. Again, this suggests that a formal development could bring out (for the rest of us) the principal features of the design and how it actually functions.

## 2.2   Informal Description

Rabin's algorithm works roughly as follows. There are three shared variables: a single semaphore (one bit) that ensures safety; a lottery number used to resolve the competition between processes seeking entry to the critical section; and a round number which prevents multiple concurrent competitions from interfering.

To attempt entry to the critical section, a process chooses independently its own lottery number according to a certain distribution (in which higher values are less likely than lower ones); it then "maxes" that number (as an atomic action) with the shared lottery number; and finally (a separate and subsequent atomic action) it examines the shared variables again: if the semaphore says "critical section is free" and the process's own local lottery number is equal to the shared lottery number (thus is the largest), then it enters the critical section (setting the semaphore to "busy").

A remarkable feature of the algorithm is that the lottery-number generating distribution (Bernoulli, in which the probability of choosing $k$ is just $1/2^k$) has the property that the probability of a "tie", where more than one process has jointly chosen the maximum, is bounded below by a constant $c$ independent of the number of processes competing: even if a million processes compete, the probability of a tie for maximum is still no more than approximately $1/3$. Thus the probability of gaining entry is at least $1/N$ (by symmetry, the probability of having the highest lottery number) times $1-c$ (the constant reduction factor due to the possibility that the maximum might be shared with a competitor), that is about $2/(3N)$ where $N$ is the number of processes actually competing.

# 3   Results of the Case Study So Far

Our initial attempts to develop Rabin's algorithm threw up a number of interesting challenges, related to the integration of probability and Event $B$, beyond those mentioned earlier.[3] Here we look at a selection of them.

## 3.1   How Should Probability Be Specified?

Arguably the most natural way to indicate that an event occurs only with some probability is to annotate the guard of the event itself with that probability. Not only is this reminiscent of a similar (and successful) technique in process algebras, where a guard may combine a Boolean condition with a communication event, it also continues the Event $B$ tradition of making the events' internal structure as simple as possible. That latter is precisely the kind of intuition we hope to "import" from $B$, since it is based on practical experience of carrying out real system developments and so —we hope— will guide us away from trying to formalise very general interactions that we do not actually need.

In this case, the *Event B* style encourages us to write two separate events (with invented but —we hope— obvious syntax)

$$FlipH \quad = \quad SELECT\ 1/2\ THEN\ \ coin := H\ \ END$$
$$FlipT \quad = \quad SELECT\ 1/2\ THEN\ \ coin := T\ \ END$$

rather than for example the single event

$$Flip \quad = \quad PCHOICE\ 1/2\ THEN\ \ coin := H$$
$$ELSE\ \ coin := T$$
$$END\ .$$

(In both cases the Boolean portion *TRUE* of the guard is elided.)

In the theory [16] however we have transformer semantics only for the second form, and not for the first: that is, we do not (yet) have a semantics for "naked *probabilistically guarded* commands". Indeed, it's clear in any case that any set of mutually-exclusive probabilistic alternatives would have to be linked together somehow into groups: otherwise, a system comprising two coins (for example, each one specified in the first style above) would have a combined probability of two.

At the moment the best candidate for compromise here is to introduce extra variables, one per probabilistic group, with the "housekeeping" organised behind the scenes by the $B$ software. Thus two separate (biased) coins in the same system might be written

$$FlipHa \quad = \quad SELECT\ a{:}1/3\ \ THEN\ \ coinA := H\ \ END$$
$$FlipTa \quad = \quad SELECT\ a{:}2/3\ \ THEN\ \ coinA := T\ \ END$$
$$FlipHb \quad = \quad SELECT\ b{:}3/4\ \ THEN\ \ coinB := H\ \ END$$
$$FlipTb \quad = \quad SELECT\ b{:}1/4\ \ THEN\ \ coinB := T\ \ END\ ,$$

(1)

but would be treated as if it were in fact

---

[3] And we have not yet found an approach that is completely satisfactory!

$$
\begin{aligned}
FlipHa &= SELECT \ a=1 \ THEN \ coinA: = H \ END \\
FlipTa &= SELECT \ a=2 \ THEN \ coinA: = T \ END \\
\\
FlipHb &= SELECT \ b=1 \ THEN \ coinB: = H \ END \\
FlipTb &= SELECT \ b=2 \ THEN \ coinB: = T \ END
\end{aligned}
$$

and as part of the scheduling process there would be a new pair of events, viz.

$$
\begin{aligned}
SetA \quad = \quad & PCHOICE \ 1/3 \ THEN \quad a: = 1 \\
& \qquad\qquad\qquad\ \ ELSE \quad a: = 2 \\
& END
\end{aligned}
$$

and a similar *SetB*. These new events would be managed and reasoned about by the $B$ proof-engine without too much intervention by the developer explicitly.

Although this appears merely to "move the problem elsewhere", in fact the introduced events would always be concerned with simple assignments from among a small number of values; the possible complexity of the probabilistic choices is thus removed from the logic of the algorithm proper.

## 3.2 What Are the Rules for Probabilistic Refinement?

As we mentioned in Sec. 1.3, the Gries-Prins rules [7] for (data-) refinement (which $B$ uses) no longer work when probability is introduced. For example, the trivial refinement with coupling invariant $coin1 = coin2$ between

$$
\begin{aligned}
Flip \quad = \quad & PCHOICE \ 1/2 \ THEN \quad coin1: = H \\
& \qquad\qquad\qquad\ \ ELSE \quad coin1: = T \\
& END
\end{aligned}
$$

and

$$
\begin{aligned}
Flip \quad = \quad & PCHOICE \ 1/2 \ THEN \quad coin2: = H \\
& \qquad\qquad\qquad\ \ ELSE \quad coin2: = T \\
& END
\end{aligned}
$$

cannot be proved in the usual way: the couple is not maintained if, for example, the upper system chooses $H$ while the lower chooses $T$.

If we apply the technique of Sec. 3.1 then the issue only moves from the *Flip* events to the introduced events *SetA* and *SetB* which, in this case, are actually no simpler.

In general, the data-refinement formulations to which we must appeal (and which validate Gries and Prins [5]) are *second-order* —they involve quantification over predicates— and are often presented in two versions, so called *upwards-* (or *backwards-*) and *forwards-* (or *downwards-*) refinement [8]. (The Gries-Prins rule is forwards-refinement.) These more general rules do work for probabilistic systems, because they are the "bedrock" of the method and do not depend (for example) on conjunctivity for their validity.

To use the second-order rules within $B$, and in particular to allow the $B$ programs to carry out semi-automatic proofs concerning them, we will probably

$VARIABLES \quad x, z$
$INITIALLY \quad x: = 0$

| | | |
|---|---|---|
| $Init1$ | $=$ | $SELECT \quad x = 0 \quad THEN \quad x: = 1 \quad END$ |
| $Init2$ | $=$ | $SELECT \quad x = 0 \quad THEN \quad x: = 2 \quad END$ |
| $FlipA3$ | $=$ | $SELECT \quad a{:}1/2 \ \& \quad (x{=}1 \ OR \ x{=}2) \quad THEN \quad x, z: = 3, 3 \quad END$ |
| $FlipA4$ | $=$ | $SELECT \quad a{:}1/2 \ \& \quad (x{=}1 \ OR \ x{=}2) \quad THEN \quad x, z: = 4, 4 \quad END$ |
| $FlipB3$ | $=$ | $SELECT \quad b{:}1/2 \ \& \quad (x{=}1 \ OR \ x{=}2) \quad THEN \quad x, z: = 3, 3 \quad END$ |
| $FlipB4$ | $=$ | $SELECT \quad b{:}1/2 \ \& \quad (x{=}1 \ OR \ x{=}2) \quad THEN \quad x, z: = 4, 4 \quad END$ |

**Fig. 1.** Two-coin four-event system

$VARIABLES \quad y, z$
$INITIALLY \quad y: = 0$

| | | |
|---|---|---|
| $Init1$ | $=$ | $SELECT \quad i{:}1/2 \ \& \ y = 0 \quad THEN \quad y: = 1 \quad END$ |
| $Init2$ | $=$ | $SELECT \quad i{:}1/2 \ \& \ y = 0 \quad THEN \quad y: = 2 \quad END$ |
| $FlipA3$ | $=$ | $SELECT \quad y{=}1 \quad THEN \quad y, z: = 3, 3 \quad END$ |
| $FlipA4$ | $=$ | $SELECT \quad y{=}2 \quad THEN \quad y, z: = 4, 4 \quad END$ |
| $FlipB3$ | $=$ | $SELECT \quad y{=}2 \quad THEN \quad y, z: = 3, 3 \quad END$ |
| $FlipB4$ | $=$ | $SELECT \quad y{=}1 \quad THEN \quad y, z: = 4, 4 \quad END$ |

**Fig. 2.** Alternative two-coin four-event system

have to specialise them to simple events of the kind *SetA* above, where the number of values involved —just two (but twice, once for *A* and once for *B*)— is very small. In small cases of that kind, automatic proof may well be possible.

### 3.3   How Does Probability Interact with Demonic Nondeterminism?

This is the key theoretical question —we believe— in this area. And it is of great practical importance as well, being thrown up again and again in the case study.

Rabin's original formulation [25] of the mutual-exclusion algorithm was incorrect precisely because demonic choice (inherent in an adversarial scheduler) could exploit earlier probabilistic outcomes (for example, of whether lottery numbers drawn by competing processes led to success or failure). A simple "stand-alone" example of the potential difficulty is as follows.

We take a system analogous to the four-event two-system at (1) except that there is only one coin and the probabilities are equal, as shown in Fig. 1. There are two "initialisation" events: only one can be executed, and the choice between them is demonic. The system executes exactly one *Init* event and then exactly one *Flip* event; then it terminates. We regard variables $x$ and $y$ as internal: the "result" of executing the system will be found in $z$.

We compare Fig. 1 with the system of Fig. 2. It differs from Fig. 1 in that the *Flip* events have become deterministic: the probabilistic choice has been moved earlier, into the *Init* events. Internal variable $x$ has been replaced by $y$; external variable $z$ remains. (The $a, b, i$ are not variables we are concerned with directly: they are "linking" annotations, as we saw in Sec. 3.1, that identify the constituent members of a single probabilistic choice.)

Now the question is whether or not we should regard Fig. 2 as a refinement of Fig. 1. (Remember that ultimately we are concerned only with the value of the external variable $z$.)

An informal argument for "**YES**" is that we imagine a downwards refinement where the two state spaces are related with a coupling "invariant" as follows:

1. if $x = 0$ then $y = 0$;
2. if $x = 1 \vee x = 2$ then $y$ is 1 or 2 with probability $1/2$; and
3. if $x = 3 \vee x = 4$ then $y$ can be any value.

In addition we require that the two $z$'s — which formally we would call $z$ and $z'$ with a coupling conjunct $z = z'$ — are of course the same, since we have said that $z$ is to be an externally visible variable. The informal reasoning continues as follows:

– When $x = 0$ only the *Init* events are enabled in Fig. 1; from Item 1 above we have $y = 0$, so that only the *Init* events are enabled in Fig. 2 also. In Fig. 1 the choice between *Init1* and *Init2* is demonic; in Fig. 2 it is probabilistic; and probabilistic choice refines demonic choice.

  After the *Init* event has executed (in each of the two systems), the Fig. 1 state satisfies $x = 1 \vee x = 2$ and the Fig. 2 state satisfies "$y$ is 1 or 2 with probability $1/2$", just as Item 2 of the couple requires.
– If $x = 1$ then each *Flip* event is enabled with probability $1/2$ in Fig. 1. Then Item 2 of the couple tells us that $y$ is 1 or 2 with probability $1/2$, so that each *Flip* event is enabled with probability $1/2$ in Fig. 2 also. The effects of the events —whichever is chosen— are the same on $z$, and because of Item 3 of the couple, there is no requirement to link $x$ and $y$ after the *Flips* have executed.
– If $x = 2$ then we reason as for $x = 1$.
– If $x = 3 \vee x = 4$ then both systems have terminated.

Thus we conclude —perhaps— that Fig. 2 refines Fig. 1. Certainly it seems that our only control over $z$, which is all we can see externally, is to set it to either 3 or 4 with equal probability.

Yet there is also an argument for "**NO**: it is not a refinement", which depends on the demonic scheduler's being able to exploit its access to $y$. In Fig. 2 the scheduler could act to choose the *FlipA* events (whichever is enabled) when $y = 1$, but choose the *FlipB* events when $y = 2$. In this way it guarantees to set $z$ to 3 every time, which is *not* a refinement of the behaviour in Fig. 1, since the latter guarantees an unbiased probabilistic outcome between $z = 3$ and $z = 4$. [4]

---

[4] That might look like a refinement from $(z=3)$'s point of view — but it is not overall, since $z=4$ is being "unfairly treated".

# 4   Conclusion

We still have some way to go to achieve our goal of an *Event B*-style development of Rabin's algorithm. Yet our work so far has helped us to focus on what may turn out to be the crucial points in adapting adapting probability to this context.

What seems to be clear even at this stage is that a certain *style* of development is going to be the key to success: just sledgehammer mathematics is not enough. [5] That is, rather than tackling the entire issue of probabilistic/demonic transition systems, instead we adopt a "programming style" dictated by the issues we *can* resolve, and which actually occur in practice.

In this case it may be that an explicit treatment of demonic choice, so far implicit in the possibly overlapping guards of events in *Event B*, is what will help us make progress. There, all in one place, we find the interaction of demonic choice and probability, the gathering together of probabilistic choice into a single restricted space (which may allow first-order rules for refinement), and the mechanisms for allowing "probabilistically guarded" events.

# References

1. J.-R. Abrial. *The B Book: Assigning Programs to Meanings*. Cambridge University Press, 1996.
2. D. Bert, J.P. Bowen, S. King, and M. Waldén, editors. *Proc. 3rd Int. ZB Conference*, volume 2651 of *LNCS*. Springer Verlag, 2003.
3. M.J. Butler. *A CSP approach to action systems*. DPhil thesis, Computing Lab., Oxford University, 1992.
4. M.J. Butler and C.C. Morgan. Action systems, unbounded nondeterminism and infinite traces. *Formal Aspects of Computing*, 7(1):37–53, 1995.
5. Wei Chen and J.T. Udding. Towards a calculus of data refinement. In J.L.A. van de Snepsheut, editor, *Lecture Notes in Computer Science 375: Mathematics of Program Construction*. Springer Verlag, June 1989.
6. E.W. Dijkstra. *A Discipline of Programming*. Prentice Hall International, Englewood Cliffs, N.J., 1976.
7. D. Gries and J. Prins. A new notion of encapsulation. In *Symposium on Language Issues in Programming Environments*. SIGPLAN, June 1985.
8. Jifeng He, C.A.R. Hoare, and J.W. Sanders. Data refinement refined. In *Lecture Notes in Computer Science 213*, pages 187–196. Springer Verlag, 1986.
9. Jifeng He, K. Seidel, and A.K. McIver. Probabilistic models for the guarded command language. *Science of Computer Programming*, 28:171–92, 1997. Available at [15–key HSM95];
   dx.doi.org/10.1016/S0167-6423(96)00019-6.
10. Thai Son Hoang, Zhendong Jin, Ken Robinson, Annabelle McIver, Carroll Morgan, and Thai Son Hoang. Development via refinement in probabilistic B — foundation and case study. LNCS. Springer Verlag.
11. Thai Son Hoang, Zhendong Jin, Ken Robinson, Annabelle McIver, Carroll Morgan, and Thai Son Hoang. Probabilistic invariants for probabilistic machines. In Bert et al. [2].

---

[5] The etymology of "sledgehammer" has nothing to do with Santa Claus.

12. D. Kozen. Semantics of probabilistic programs. *Jnl. Comp. Sys. Sciences*, 22:328–50, 1981.

13. D. Kozen. A probabilistic PDL. *Jnl. Comp. Sys. Sciences*, 30(2):162–78, 1985.

14. Eyal Kushilevitz and M.O. Rabin. Randomized mutual exclusion algorithms revisited. In *Proc. 11th Annual ACM Symp. on Principles of Distributed Computing*, 1992.

15. A.K. McIver, C.C. Morgan, J.W. Sanders, and K. Seidel. Probabilistic Systems Group: Collected reports.
    web.comlab.ox.ac.uk/oucl/research/areas/probs.

16. Annabelle McIver and Carroll Morgan. *Abstraction, Refinement and Proof for Probabilistic Systems*. Technical Monographs in Computer Science. Springer Verlag, New York, 2004.

17. Annabelle McIver, Carroll Morgan, and Thai Son Hoang. Probabilistic termination in B. In Bert et al. [2].

18. Carroll Morgan. The generalised substitution language extended to probabilistic programs. In Didier Bert, editor, *Proc. 2nd Int. B Conference*, volume 1393 of *LNCS*. Springer Verlag, 1998. Also available at [15–B98].

19. C.C. Morgan. The specification statement. *ACM Transactions on Programming Languages and Systems*, 10(3):403–19, July 1988. Reprinted in [22];
    doi.acm.org/10.1145/44501.44503.

20. C.C. Morgan. Of wp and CSP. In W.H.J. Feijen et al., editor, *Beauty is Our Business*. Springer Verlag, 1990.

21. C.C. Morgan, A.K. McIver, and K. Seidel. Probabilistic predicate transformers. *ACM Transactions on Programming Languages and Systems*, 18(3):325–53, May 1996. doi.acm.org/10.1145/229542.229547.

22. C.C. Morgan and T.N. Vickers, editors. *On the Refinement Calculus*. FACIT Series in Computer Science. Springer Verlag, London, 1994.

23. J.M. Morris. A theoretical basis for stepwise refinement and the programming calculus. *Science of Computer Programming*, 9(3):287–306, December 1987.

24. G. Nelson. A generalization of Dijkstra's calculus. *ACM Transactions on Programming Languages and Systems*, 11(4):517–61, October 1989.

25. M.O. Rabin. $N$-process mutual exclusion with bounded waiting by $4 \log 2N$-valued shared variable. *Journal of Computer and System Sciences*, 25(1):66–75, 1982.

26. I. Saias. Proving probabilistic correctness statements: the case of Rabin's algorithm for mutual exclusion. In *Proc. 11th Annual ACM Symp. on Principles of Distributed Computing*, 1992.

# Requirements as Conjectures: Intuitive DVD Menu Navigation

Jemima Rossmorris and Susan Stepney

Department of Computer Science, University of York,
Heslington, York, YO10 5DD, UK
susan@cs.york.ac.uk

**Abstract.** In this paper we use Z to capture the requirements for an 'intuitive' menu navigation system as a series of conjectures that should hold. We use those requirements to investigate potential algorithms. The Z formalisation enables the somewhat fuzzy requirement of 'being intuitive' to be captured precisely, analysed, and critiqued, leading to possibly new requirements, and more intuitive algorithms.

**Keywords:** Z, requirements, conjectures, DVD.

## 1 Introduction

Interactive systems require some sort of input from the user to instruct the system on what behaviour is desired. One way of interacting is for the user to navigate around a menu system, selecting options as necessary to achieve the desired behaviour. Examples of this are navigating a TV menu to change the brightness and contrast, navigating a DVD menu to chose an episode or special feature, and navigating the links on a Web page. Normally Web page navigation is done using the mouse to control a cursor. However, blind and motion-impaired users may not be able to use a mouse, and are often restricted to using the tab key, or cursor keys, to navigate. Most TV and DVD controls are similarly restricted, and have some form of cursor that jumps between menu items.

The W3 guidelines on the use of the tab key state that web designers should "create a logical tab order through links, form controls, and objects" [WC3–checkpoint 9.4]. In practice, the order in which links are tabbed through on a web page is often taken to be the order in which the links are defined in the html code. This order may be the desired one, but it may not: it is left to the page designer to get it right.

For DVDs the situation is even worse. There is no standard or guidelines for how the cursor should react. As Donald Norman puts it: "Designers haven't figured out the cursor model yet either: In most DVDs, pushing the joystick (or arrow) control up will move the cursor up, but I have encountered some in which the cursor moves down." [Norman 2001].

H. Treharne et al. (Eds.): ZB 2005, LNCS 3455, pp. 172–186, 2005.

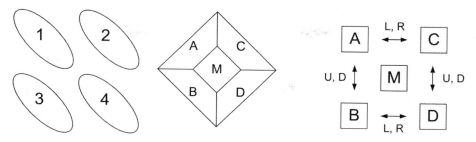

**Fig. 1.** Menu navigation: (a) two potentially ambiguous menu layout arrangements (taken from real DVD menus) (b) a navigation that misses the middle item

Ideally, cursor navigation should be 'intuitive', that is, predictable to the average user. Yet consider figure 1 (a layout seen on real DVD menus). In the oval layout, is item 2 or item 4 to the 'right' of item 1? In the diamond layout, is item C or item M to the 'right' of item A? If the cursor moves to C, how does it get to M? If it moves to M, where next, to C or to D? And so on.

The cursor navigation problem is a real, non-trivial, unsolved problem in set-top box,[1] DVD, and other interactive design. It is separate from the screen design problem. Individual screen designers layout their menu items in whatever manner they see fit; the screen display provider (for example, the set-top box manufacturer) then has to provide a general purpose 'intuitive' algorithm to navigate the cursor on any potential screen layout.

One selling point of formal methods is their ability to capture abstract requirements without being distracted by implementation detail. For example, a very abstract Z [ISO-Z 2002] specification would be written as the high level requirements specification, and then refined down to include more concrete implementation details. The usual approach is to write the Z specification in a 'state and operations' style. However, requirements are not always properties of single operations. In this paper we use Z to capture the requirements for an 'intuitive' menu navigation system as a series of conjectures that we want to hold on our (initially very underspecified) state and operations specification. We use those requirements to investigate potential operation specifications. In turns out that some obvious requirements (such as 'undo') put particularly strong constraints on the design, whilst others (such as the seemingly innocent 'right arrow moves the cursor right') are in fact very difficult to capture, not at all intuitive, and bear further investigation. The Z formalisation enables the somewhat fuzzy requirement of 'being intuitive' to be captured precisely, analysed, and critiqued, leading to possibly new requirements, and more intuitive algorithms.

---

[1] C. A. Whyte, private communication.

## 2    Basic Specification

We start by specifying the minimum necessary to capture the requirements. We simplify the problem by considering the screen to be tiled with squares, each of which may be a menu item.

The screen is $xSize$ units wide and $ySize$ units tall.

$$\mid\ xSize, ySize : \mathbb{N}_1$$

Positions on the screen are given by a pair of $(x, y)$ coordinates, each numbered from zero up to the maximum size. $x$ coordinates increase in the rightwards direction; $y$ coordinates increase in the downwards direction. We require there to be at least two screen positions, in order to exclude trivial menus.

$$position == 0\,..\,(xSize - 1) \times 0\,..\,(ySize - 1)$$
$$1 < \#position = xSize * ySize$$

The screen itself is then a set of (at least two) *menu* positions, and a *cursor* positioned on one of the menu items.

___ *Screen* _____
$menu : \mathbb{F}\ position$
$cursor : position$
_____
$1 < \#menu$
$cursor \in menu$
_____

The basic cursor movement does not change the *menu* items. (We do not provide any operations to change the menu items: it is assumed the screen is initialised with the desired items.)

$$BasicMove == [\ \Delta Screen \mid menu' = menu\ ]$$

The *MoveRight* operation moves the cursor 'rightwards'. We do not yet specify what that means, but we need to provide the declaration for use in the requirements conjectures. We can consider this specification to be parameterised by the *MoveRightPredicate*, which needs to be chosen such that it fulfils the requirements.

$$MoveRight == [\ BasicMove \mid MoveRightPredicate\ ]$$

Similar declarations are made for the other cursor directions. Then the general *Move* operation is a movement in one of the cursor directions.

$$Move == MoveRight \vee MoveLeft \vee MoveUp \vee MoveDown$$

# 3   Requirements as Conjectures

We now have enough machinery to capture the requirements. There are several requirements that the navigation system should 'clearly' fulfil. We analyse the consequences in the following section. We focus on *MoveRight*: the other directions follow by symmetry arguments.

## 3.1   Conjectures in Z

In ISO Standard Z [ISO-Z 2002], a conjecture paragraph has the following syntax:

$\vdash$? `Predicate`

In a well-formed specification, the `Predicate` must be well-typed in the context in which it appears, but it need not be *true*. If it is *true* (is implied by the properties of the specification) then it is said to be *valid*, and is then a *theorem* of the specification. (See [Valentine *et al.* 2004–chapter 5] for further explanation.)

In this paper, we use the following extension to the standard syntax in order to separate out declarations from the body of the conjecture:

`SchemaText` $\vdash$? `Predicate`

is equivalent to

$\vdash$? $\forall$`SchemaText` $\bullet$ `Predicate`

## 3.2   R1. Is Deterministic

The cursor's movement should be consistent with its historical behaviour. That is, whenever the cursor is on a particular menu item and you press a particular arrow key, the cursor should always move to the same next menu item.

This is captured by requiring each separate part of the *Move* operation to be deterministic, or functional.

$\vdash$? $\{$ *MoveRight* $\bullet$ *cursor* $\mapsto$ *cursor'* $\} \in$ *position* $\nrightarrow$ *position*

## 3.3   R2. All Reachable

Whichever menu item you start from, you should be able to reach any other menu item by a sequence of arrow key presses. (This might seem obvious, but there are web pages using frames where this does not hold, as it is not possible to tab between their frames.)

*Screen* $\vdash$? $\{$ *Move* $\bullet$ *cursor* $\mapsto$ *cursor'* $\}^* = $ *menu* $\times$ *menu*

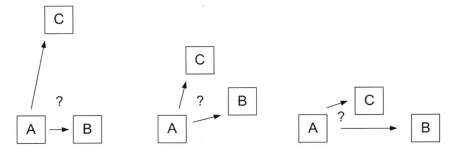

**Fig. 2.** What is right?

## 3.4    R3. Undo

Being able to undo one's actions is an important feature in any interactive system [Abowd & Dix 1992]. Undo in navigation is useful if you go past the link you want: you can go backwards, instead of having to scroll through all the links again.

So *MoveRight* followed by *MoveLeft* should leave you back where you started. (It is possible to consider the use of a 'shift' key, giving a separate *MoveLeft* and 'undo *MoveRight*', but that adds complexity to the user interface.)

*MoveRight* ⨾ *MoveLeft* ⊢? Ξ*Screen*

## 3.5    R4. Move Moves

Feedback is another important feature. If you press a key, something should happen. We capture this with the requirement that, no matter where the cursor is, if you press an arrow key, the cursor moves to another menu item. (We could alternatively require it to 'flash', say, if there was nowhere for it to sensibly move.)

*Move* ⊢? *cursor'* ≠ *cursor*

## 3.6    R5. MoveRight Moves Right

The previous requirements are all at a very basic level, that pressing a key does something sensible. This requirement captures a more detailed level of the intuition, that pressing a key does the 'correct' thing. So, no matter where the cursor is, if you press the right arrow key, the cursor should move to the next menu item to the right.

This requirement is surprisingly difficult to capture, and is where all the complexity, and most of the interest, lies.

We want the cursor to move to the 'nearest' 'rightward' menu item, including wrapping around when close to the right edge of the screen. (It is much easier to

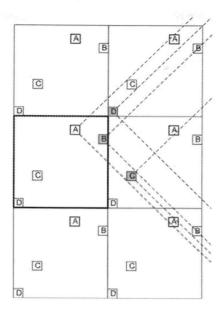

**Fig. 3.** Right-cones in the tiled plane, with the original screen shown in bold

specify if wrapping is not allowed, but that is considered to be a simplification too far, as real DVD menu navigation *does* wrap.)

Just what, however, is 'right' of the current position? Consider figure 2. In the lefthand pcture, should the cursor move from A to C (which has the smaller $x$-coordinate distance from A) or to B (which has the smaller Euclidean distance from A)? One feels that 'intuitively', the choice should be B. In the middle picture, B and C have the same Euclidean distance from A, and C has the smaller $x$-coordinate distance. One again feels that intuitively, the choice should be B, (although an argument might be made for C). B seems to be more 'rightward', and C more 'upward', as can be seen from the angle of the arrows pointing to them. However, it is not just the angle of the movement. In the righthand picture, B is definitely more rightward in terms of angle, yet in this case, C seems to be the intuitive 'right' choice. There is some combination of angle and distance. This is the intuition captured by the following requirement (which first needs a little machinery to be defined before it can be stated succinctly).

The definition is complicated by requiring wrapping when the cursor is at the far right. The usual way to model this is by modulo arithmetic. However, here it will be easier to visualise the effect by the isomorphic 'infinite tiling' approach. The entire plane is tiled with copies of the *Screen* rectangle, with corresponding menu positions and cursor (see figure 3). So each screen *position* is mapped to a corresponding set of tiled points in the plane:

$$tile == \lambda\, p : Point \bullet \{\; i, j : \mathbb{Z} \bullet (p.1 + i * xSize, p.2 + j * ySize)\; \}$$

*tile* takes a *Point* (defined in the appendix), and gives the set of all *Point*s resulting from tiling the plane in *xSize* * *ySize* tiles.

We then capture the difference between 'rightward' and 'upward' (or, symmetrically, 'leftward' and 'downward') directions, as a rightward viewing area subset of this tiled plane. The view to the right of a position is all those points within a right-pointing cone with 45 degree semi-angle, apex at the position of interest (see appendix for the definitions of *cos45* and *unitVector*), as shown in figure 3.

$$viewRight == \lambda\, p : Point \bullet$$
$$\{ \, q : Point \setminus \{p\} \mid cos45 \leq (unitVector(q -_v p)).1 \, \}$$

Now we define a screen of menu items, wrapped into this rightward view. *right-Menu* defines all rightward menu items as all the menu items in the infinite tiled plane, restricted to those in the rightward cone. *rightMenu1* picks out the one of these menu items in the rightward cone that is closest to the *cursor* (see appendix for the definition of the distance $d_R$). There may be more than one tiled menu item at the same distance from the cursor; we leave the definition loose at this stage.

```
┌─ WrapScreenRight ─────────────────────────────────────────────┐
│ Screen                                                         │
│ rightMenu : Point ↣ ℙ Point                                   │
│ rightMenu1 : Point ↣ Point                                    │
├───────────────────────────────────────────────────────────────┤
│ rightMenu = λ m : menu • tile m ∩ viewRight cursor            │
│                                                               │
│ ∀ m : menu •                                                  │
│     rightMenu1 m ∈ { p : rightMenu m |                        │
│                 ∀ q : rightMenu m • d_R(cursor, p) ≤ d_R(cursor, q) } │
└───────────────────────────────────────────────────────────────┘
```

Then the *nearest* menu item to the cursor, on the right, is the *rightMenu1* menu item that is no further from the cursor than any other. (Again, this is loose if there are several at the same closest distance.)

```
┌─ RightView ───────────────────────────────────────────────────┐
│ WrapScreenRight                                                │
│ nearest : position                                             │
├───────────────────────────────────────────────────────────────┤
│ nearest ∈ menu \ {cursor}                                      │
│ ∀ m : menu \ {cursor} •                                        │
│     d_R(cursor, rightMenu1 nearest) ≤ d_R(cursor, rightMenu1 m) │
└───────────────────────────────────────────────────────────────┘
```

So, finally, the requirement is that a *MoveRight* operation moves the cursor to the nearest right menu position:

$$MoveRight;\ RightView \vdash? \ cursor' = nearest$$

The corresponding requirements on the other direction operations follow by symmetry.

# 4    Satisfying the Requirements

## 4.1    Analysing the Requirements

We now consider the interactions of these five requirements.

R4 (Move moves) is subsumed by R5 (MoveRight moves right). Under R5, *MoveRight* does always move the cursor, because of the condition *nearest* ∈ *menu* \ {*cursor*}. (And the other direction operations also move it, by symmetry.) So, under this particular R5, we can ignore R4, but if we modify R5, we must remember to revisit R4.

R3 (Undo) in combination with R1 (Deterministic) implies that each direction operation is not just functional, but *injective*. It defines *MoveLeft* as the compositional inverse of the deterministic (functional) *MoveRight*, so implies *MoveRight* is in fact an injection. Undo injectivity requires that each menu be the closest left item of its closest right item. That is, under the current formulation of R5, if A has B as its nearest item in its 'right-cone', then B must have A as its nearest item in its 'left-cone'. In terms of figure 4, B is right-closest to A because there are no other items in the grey and hatched shaded areas. For A to be left-closest to B, there must also be no menu items in the dotted area of B's left-cone. This is a very strong constraint, and clearly not all screen layouts need meet it.

R2 (Reachable) puts some further strong constraints on *Move*. It is not clear at this point if this is compatible with the other requirements.

## 4.2    Implementing the Requirements

Ideally, the next step would be to calculate the weakest *MoveRight* predicate that satisfies all the requirements.

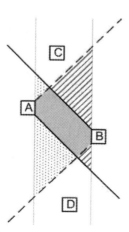

**Fig. 4.** Undo-consistent right-cone and left-cone, using the difference in *x*-coordinate metric

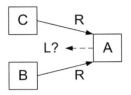

**Fig. 5.** Impossibility of injective undo under the 'right-cones' requirement

However, it is easy to see that this is not possible: consider a screen with two menu items in the first column, and one in the second (see figure 5). Whichever item the cursor is on in the first column, *MoveRight* will move it to the single unique item in the second; which clearly cannot be undone in an injective deterministic manner.

What to do? There are two possibilities: (a) strengthen *Screen* by putting more constraints on *menu* positions such that requirements do hold; (b) weaken (or change) some requirements conjectures so that they are implementable.

### 4.3    Constraining the Menu Layout

We discussed above how the undo requirement puts constraints on the menu layout (figure 4). If we were to enforce this constraint, would it be sufficient to satisfy all the requirements?

It is certainly not easy to see if such a constraint would guarantee reachability. Yet further constraints might be necessary. Before we expend effort in establishing such constraints, we should instead ask: is it reasonable to enforce this constraint? The answer is no, for two reasons. Firstly, it is very complicated: screen designers would not easily understand where they could place menu items in order to conform (particularly with Euclidean or Manhattan metrics, where the analogue of figure 4 is more complicated). Secondly, we actually cannot enforce it: screen designers can design whatever layouts they please, and we can make only recommendations.

So let us instead consider changing the requirements, to get an alternative 'intuitive' definition, but one that can be implemented.

### 4.4    Weakening the Requirements

Which requirement to weaken? R1 (Determinisim) and R2 (reachability) are non-negotiable. R3 (undo) is very strong – forcing injectivity on each *Move* function component, yet it does seem very desirable. Let us consider R5 *MoveRight*: it is certainly the most complicated requirement to specify and understand, so it seems an ideal candidate for weakening. (We must remember to check that R4 is still subsumed by the new R5′.)

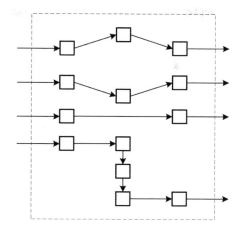

**Fig. 6.** A set of rightward chains covering all menu items on the screen

The existing requirements can actually help us formulate R5′. Consider plotting the path of a rightward moving cursor. Determinism means this path never splits; injectivity means no two paths ever join. So we can consider the *chain* of menu items described by this path. We want this chain to 'move right' across the screen, which we can specify by some predicate on the $x$ components of the menu items. What happens at the right-hand edge? The cursor wraps around to a left-edge menu item. If we were to consider the entire chain of rightward moves, including several possible wrappings, we would find it difficult to specify the desired property. But if we consider the rightward chains and the wrappings separately, we can get an elegant specification of the desired property. Moreover, we can specify different kinds of wrapping for different circumstances. Figure 6 shows one possible set of 'rightward' chains. Such chains do also allow purely downward movements (which were not allowed by the earlier 'rightward cone' formulation of R5), to allow for sensible behaviour with vertically stacked menu layouts.

An *LRChain* is an injective sequence of *positions* (injective, so all the positions are different), of length at least two (to remove trivial chains, and to ensure R4). In the chain the $x$ coordinates of the positions are increasing, or are the same with the $y$ coordinates increasing.

$$
\begin{aligned}
LRChain == \{ \ & s : \text{iseq } position \ | \\
& 1 < \#s \\
& \wedge \ (\ \forall m, n : \text{dom } s \ | \ m < n \ \bullet \\
& \quad (s \ m).1 < (s \ n).1 \\
& \quad \vee \ (s \ m).1 = (s \ n).1 \wedge (s \ m).2 < (s \ n).2 \ ) \ \}
\end{aligned}
$$

We augment the definition of *Screen* with a sequence of *LRChains*.

```
┌─ LRChains ──────────────────────────────────────────────┐
│ Screen
│ lrchain : seq LRChain
│ cl, cn : ℕ
├─────────────────────────────────────────────────────────
│ { l : dom lrchain • l ↦ ran(lrchain l) } partition menu
│ ¬ ChainsCross[lrchain/chain]
│ cl ∈ dom lrchain
│ cn ∈ dom(lrchain cl)
│ cursor = lrchain cl cn
└─────────────────────────────────────────────────────────┘
```

We require the positions in the set of chains to partition the *menu*: each menu position occurs in precisely one chain. The chains run from left to right across the screen by definition. We also require that the chains do not cross (see appendix for details). Finally, we define the position in the chains of the cursor.

There are (at least) two possibilities on wrapping: either the cursor moves back to the beginning of the same chain (a behaviour seen in simple DVD menues) or it moves to the beginning of the next chain (a kind of 'carriage-return/line-feed' behaviour suitable for text-based web pages). We capture each of these requirements in a separate conjecture.

**R5′a**: pressing the right arrow key causes the cursor to move to the next item in its chain, unless it is at the rightmost end, in which case it wraps to the beginning of the same chain. (See the appendix for the definition of the ++ operator.)

> *MoveRight*; *LRChains* ⊢?
> let $cn' == cn ++ \#(lrchain\ cl)$ • $cursor' = lrchain\ cl\ cn'$

**R5′b**: pressing the right arrow key causes the cursor to move to the next item in its chain, unless it is at the rightmost end, in which case it wraps around to the beginning of the next chain; if it is at the end of the last chain, it wraps to the beginning of the first chain.

> *MoveRight*; *LRChains* ⊢?
> let $cn' == cn ++ \#(lrchain\ cl)$ •
>      let $cl' ==$ if $cn' = 1$ then $cl ++ \#lrchain$ else $cl$ •
>          $cursor' = lrchain\ cl'\ cn'$

The new R5′ does seem to capture the move right requirement adequately. In addition R5′b satisfies R2 (reachable), as it directly scrolls through all menu items in the order specified by the chains. However, R5′a does not necessarily satisfy R2: see figure 7a for a counter-example. The chains may have to be chosen carefully to ensure reachability (figure 7b).

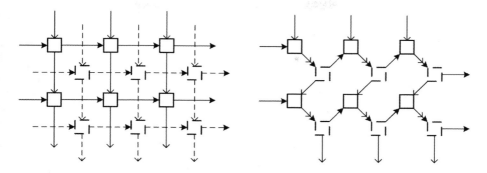

**Fig. 7.** Two possible patterns of right chains and down chains (a) mutually unreachable sub-regions under R5′a; (b) full reachability under R5′a

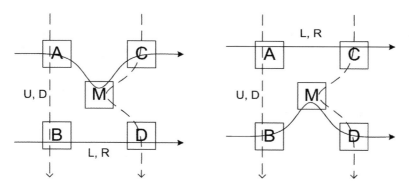

**Fig. 8.** Two possible patterns of right chains and down chains for the diamond menu of figure 1

So the diamond menu of figure 1 could be supplied with navigation chains as shown in figure 8.

# 5    Conclusions and Further Work

The implementation of the requirements is now reduced to developing an algorithm that can find suitable chains that obey the chain constraints, and provide reachability. (Recall, this is the responsibility of the screen navigation provider, not of the screen designer, because there is no standard facility in the screen design mark-up to include navigation information.) Developing such an algorithm is beyond the scope of this paper, but clearly requires further refinements of the requirements to capture 'good' chains.

However, the original problem has certainly been reduced to a much simpler one. The chains approach automatically ensures R1 and R3–R5, and shows a simple way to detect if R2 is fulfilled (a simple 'mark and sweep' algorithm is sufficient to test reachability). What is next required is a proof that it is always possible to find some set of chains that fulfil R2, and then an algorithm to find them.

The 'requirements as conjectures' approach has allowed us to write a 'state and operations' style Z specification, to explore the properties of the operations without having to specify them in any detail, to capture requirements that cannot be expressed as properties of single operations (such as reachability), and to analyse the impact and consequences of particular stated requirements.

It might be argued that we did end up with the rather algorithmic-looking requirement R5′; however the existence of the required chains is merely asserted, and no algorithm for finding them is (yet) provided. The process of getting to this point allowed us to understand what the seemingly simple 'move right' property really entailed.

This paper shows the route to a solution for simple menu layouts. The full problem is more complicated. Menu items may be non-rectangular, complicating the intuition of which other item should be visited next (figure 1). Menu labels may affect the intuitive navigation order (for example, if they are numbers). However, we believe the approach here is applicable in more general cases.

## Acknowledgements

We would like to thank Dr. Charles A. Whyte of ANT Ltd. for bringing the very real problem of DVD navigation menus to our attention, and the anonymous referees for helpful comments.

All the Z in this paper has been typechecked with Formaliser, and then undergone some minimal conversion to Standard Z syntax [ISO-Z 2002].

## References

[Abowd & Dix 1992]    Gregory D. Abowd and Alan J. Dix. Giving undo attention. *Interacting with Computers*, 4(3):317–342, 1992.

[ISO-Z 2002]    ISO/IEC 13568. *Information Technology – Z Formal Specification Notation – Syntax, Type System and Semantics: International Standard*, 2002. http://www.iso.org/iso/en/ittf/ PubliclyAvailableStandards/c021573_ISO_IEC_13568_2002(E).zip.

[Norman 2001]    Donald A. Norman. DVD menu design: The failures of web design recreated yet again. December 2001. http://www.jnd.org/dn.mss/DVDmenus.html.

[Valentine *et al.* 2004]    Samuel H. Valentine, Susan Stepney, and Ian Toyn. A Z patterns catalogue II: definitions and laws, v0.1. Technical Report YCS-2004-383, Department of Computer Science, University of York, October 2004.

[WC3]    WC3. *HTML Techniques for Web Content Accessibility: Guidelines 1.0, WC3 Note 6 November 2000*. http://www.w3.org/TR/2000/NOTE-WCAG10-HTML-TECHS-20001106/.

# A    Utility Functions and Predicates

We use real numbers and associated functions (including the extension of addition and multiplication to the reals, real division, square roots, and so on), to capture various vector operations on screen positions interpreted as vectors. We use the definitions in [Valentine $et$ $al.$ 2004].

A $Point$ is a pair of reals, representing a point in the infinite plane, or equivalently, as a vector from the origin to that point in the plane.

$$Point == \mathbb{R} \times \mathbb{R}$$

We define $(\_ +_v \_)$ as vector addition, $(\_ -_v \_)$ as vector subtraction, $(\_ \cdot_v \_)$ as vector dot product, and $(\_ *_v \_)$ as scalar multiplication on $Points$ in the obvious way (but omit the definitions here, for brevity).

$$\begin{array}{l} \_ +_v \_, \_ -_v \_ : Point \times Point \rightarrow Point \\ \_ \cdot_v \_ : Point \times Point \rightarrow \mathbb{R} \\ \_ *_v \_ : \mathbb{R} \times Point \rightarrow Point \end{array}$$

The definition of the rightward viewing cone uses the cosine of 45 degrees:

$$cos45 == 1 \div \sqrt{2}$$

A unit vector derived from a general non-zero vector $p$ is that unique vector that has unit length and points in the same direction as $p$.

$$unitVector == \lambda\, p : Point \mid \{p.1, p.2\} \neq \{0\} \bullet$$
$$( \ \mu\, u : Point;\ \alpha : \mathbb{R} \mid u._v u = 1 \wedge 0 < \alpha \wedge \alpha *_v u = p \bullet u \ )$$

We define the distance between points. We leave this loose, because we may want to use a Euclidean metric, a Manhattan metric, the difference between the respective $x$ coordinates, or some other measure. So we define the minimal constraints.

$$\begin{array}{l} d_R : Point \times Point \rightarrow \mathbb{R} \\ \hline \forall\, p, q : Point \bullet 0 \leq d_R(p, q) \\ \forall\, p, q : Point \bullet d_R(p, q) = 0 \Leftrightarrow p = q \\ \forall\, p, q : Point \bullet d_R(p, q) = d_R(q, p) \\ \forall\, p, q, r : Point \bullet d_R(p, r) \leq d_R(p, q) + d_R(q, r) \\ \forall\, p, q, r : Point;\ \alpha : \mathbb{R} \mid d_R(r, p) = d_R(r, q) \wedge 0 \leq \alpha \leq 1 \bullet \\ \quad d_R(r, (1 - \alpha) *_v p +_v \alpha *_v q) \leq d_R(r, p) \end{array}$$

The first four predicates capture the property of being a $metric$: it is positive, points are zero distance apart precisely when they are the same point, it is symmetric, and it satisfies the triangle inequality. The last predicate requires the metric to be $convex$: given two points $p$ and $q$ the same distance from a third point $r$, then any point on the straight line (defined in terms of the usual Euclidean metric on the plane) drawn between them is no further from $r$ (it may well be closer).

Given two line segments, one defined by end points $p$ and $q$, and the other by end points $p'$ and $q'$, the predicate *LineSegmentsCross* is true if they cross, that is, if they share a point in common.

$$
\begin{array}{|l}
\hline
\_\_ \textit{LineSegmentsCross} _____ \\
p, p', q, q' : position \\
\hline
\exists\, \alpha, \alpha' : \mathbb{R} \mid 0 \leq \alpha \leq 1 \wedge 0 \leq \alpha' \leq 1 \bullet \\
\quad \alpha *_v p +_v (1 - \alpha) *_v q = \alpha' *_v p' +_v (1 - \alpha') *_v q' \\
\hline
\end{array}
$$

A collection of chains of line segments cross if any segment from one crosses a segment from another.

$$
\begin{array}{|l}
\hline
\_\_ \textit{ChainsCross} _____ \\
chain : \text{seq iseq } position \\
\hline
\exists\, l, l' : \text{dom } chain \mid l \neq l' \bullet \\
\quad \exists\, m, n : \text{dom}(chain\ l); \ m', n' : \text{dom}(chain\ l') \bullet \\
\quad\quad \text{let } p == chain\ l\ m; \ p' == chain\ l'\ m'; \\
\quad\quad\quad\quad\quad\quad q == chain\ l\ n; \ q' == chain\ l'\ n' \bullet \\
\quad\quad\quad \textit{LineSegmentsCross} \\
\hline
\end{array}
$$

The infix operator $++$ increments its first argument, unless it equals its second, in which case it returns 1. (It is similar to addition of 1 modulo $n$, except that it is based from 1 rather than from 0.)

function 30 leftassoc($\_ ++ \_$)

$$
\begin{array}{|l}
\_ ++ \_ : \mathbb{Z} \times \mathbb{N}_1 \rightarrow \mathbb{Z} \\
\hline
\forall\, i : \mathbb{Z}; \ n : \mathbb{N}_1 \bullet i ++ n = \text{if } i = n \text{ then } 1 \text{ else } i + 1 \\
\end{array}
$$

# A Prospective-Value Semantics for the GSL

Frank Zeyda, Bill Stoddart, and Steve Dunne

School of Computing, University of Teesside,
Middlesbrough, TS1 3BA, UK
{f.zeyda, bill, s.e.dunne}@tees.ac.uk

**Abstract.** We present a prospective-value (pv) semantics for the Generalised Substitution Language. Whereas wp semantics captures the meaning of a computation in terms of the weakest precondition that must be fulfilled for a generalised substitution $S$ to establish any given postcondition $Q$, pv semantics expresses the meaning of a computation in terms of the value any expression $E$ would take were the computation to be carried out. To integrate non-termination we formulate improper bunch theory, an extended version of Hehner's bunch theory where each type is augmented with an improper bunch. Algebraic simplification laws for the pv expression transformer are presented, and proved to be sound. Iteration is treated as a fixed-point in *expressions*, and a corresponding theorem is presented allowing us to infer the pv effect of the while-loop construct.

**Keywords:** Generalised substitution, bunch theory, prospective-value semantics, expression transformers, wp calculus, B Method.

## 1 Introduction

The B Method is based on the use of predicate transformers and the wp calculus, with the transformation of predicates by programs being expressed in terms of the Generalised Substitution Language (GSL).

The substitution rules of the GSL can also be used to transform *expressions*. In previous work [7] we have used expression transformers to extend the expressive power of expressions in a programming language. In this paper we return to them with a different agenda; we would like to investigate the extent to which they can provide a more intuitive understanding and even perhaps, a semantic foundation for B. As before we use $S \diamond E$ to represent the values expression $E$ could take were it to be evaluated after the execution of program $S$. We call these its "prospective values". The current treatment will include a way of expressing the effect of non-termination, a problem which did not concern us previously but which we wish to consider now that we are concerned with more general semantic issues.

As motivation, consider a substitution $S$, assumed to act in the context of state variable(s) $s$. The characteristic predicate prd$(S)$ of $S$ is then a predicate on before-values $s$ and after-values $s'$ which expresses the effect of $S$. For example

H. Treharne et al. (Eds.): ZB 2005, LNCS 3455, pp. 187–202, 2005.

if $S$ is $x := x + 1 \; [\!] \; x := x + 2$ then $\mathrm{prd}(S)$ is $x' = x + 1 \lor x' = x + 2$. Using a predicate transformer formulation we have the general rule $\mathrm{prd}(S) = \neg \, [S]x \neq x'$ where the double negative is required to accommodate non-determinism.

In prospective-value terms we define $\mathrm{prd}(S)$ by saying $x'$ must be one of the values which $x$ could take after executing $S$. In the bunch theory formulation we use this is written as $x' : S \diamond x$. We hope the simplicity of this form will encourage the reader to bear with us in our forthcoming exposition.

The rest of the paper is organised as follows. In Section 2 we introduce "Improper Bunch Theory", an extension of bunch theory we have developed to capture the effect of non-termination. In Section 3 we introduce a bunch comprehension expression which intuitively captures the meaning of $S \diamond E$. We use it to provide proofs for a set of laws, defined over the syntactic constructs of GSL, which enable us to eliminate the diamond operator from expressions. We have already given, without proof, a restricted form of these laws in [7]. Here they are formulated in a way that expresses the effect of non-termination.

In Section 4 we present a fixed-point treatment of iteration. In Section 5 we draw our conclusions and indicate future work.

## 2     Bunch Theory and Improper Bunch Theory

Bunch theory is a simplification of set theory. Set theory in general allows one to build arbitrarily nested structures since sets are packaged, for example $\{1, \{2, \{3\}\}\}$. In contrast, bunches haven't got this packaging ability and therefore always remain flat. Accordingly, we don't write encapsulating brackets around bunches as we do with sets. The expressions $1$ and $1 , 2 , 3$ are both bunches (the first one only containing one element and hence called *elementary*). Note that bunch theory is defined in such a way that no distinction has to be made between the number 1 and the elementary bunch containing 1, in the same manner as there is no need to differentiate the rational number 1 and the complex number 1. In this paper our bunches are strongly typed, so that all the elements of a given bunch must be of the same type, and each type has its own distinct empty bunch.

Bunch theory was invented by Hehner [4, 5]. He argued that in most cases in computer science set theory is not required in its entire power, and for notational convenience we should aim for a simpler theory that has 'just the right' power for its purpose. Bunch theory has recently been used to notable effect by Morris and Bunkenburg [6]. Our particular reason for adopting bunch theory in our work here is that we believe it indeed does have 'just the right' expressive power we need to present our prospective-value semantics for the GSL.

### 2.1     Operators

The familiar set operators '$\cup$', '$\cap$' and '$-$' have their counterparts in bunch theory, namely bunch union '$,$', bunch intersection '$'$' and bunch subtraction '$\setminus$'. Enumerated elements of a bunch are simply separated by '$,$', and the comma also serves as the bunch union operator. Thus if $E$ and $F$ are bunches we may write $E$, $F$ for the bunch that contains both the elements of $E$ and $F$. The bunch that contains no elements is designated by **null**. For bunch inclusion the symbol ':' is used; since every single element is as well a bunch there is no need for a separate membership operator. Equality of bunches we define in terms of mutual inclusion, i.e. $E = F$ if, and only if $E : F \wedge F : E$.

Any operator defined on elementary values can be lifted to bunches in the obvious way, so that it distributes through bunch union and is strict with respect to **null**. For example, we can lift the addition operator '+' on naturals to be an operator on bunches of naturals, so that for instance

$$1 , 2 + 3 , 4 \;=\; 4 , 5 , 6 \quad \text{and} \quad 1 , 2 + \mathbf{null} \;=\; \mathbf{null}$$

## 2.2   The Improper Bunch

Conventional bunch theory isn't expressive enough to distinctively describe the outcome of a possibly non-terminating computation, e.g. the value of $2 + x$ after execution of the GSL program **abort**. To do so we extend bunch theory here with a new bunch for each type, called its *improper* bunch. We use the same symbol '$\perp$' for all these, relying on context to determine type. Note that $\perp$ is not some sort of improper elementary value, but a special bunch having the property of absorbing all other bunches, in the sense that bunch union and all bunch operators lifted from operators on underlying types are strict with respect to it. For example, for any bunch $E$ of natural numbers

$$E , \perp \;=\; \perp \quad \text{and} \quad E + \perp \;=\; \perp$$

## 2.3   The Bunch Refinement Lattice

In our improper bunch theory the two extreme bunches $\perp$ and **null** form respectively the bottom and top of the *inverted* inclusion ordering on the bunches of any given type, i.e. $E \sqsubseteq F \Leftrightarrow F : E$, which is moreover a complete lattice.[1] The motivation for this ordering is the reduction of non-determinism when moving up the lattice: as we will use bunches in what follows in Section 3 to describe the outcome of computations, less deterministic computations will yield bunches which are lower, and more deterministic computations ones which are higher in the lattice.

In our definitions, theorems and examples we use $E$ and $F$ for bunch expressions, $x$, $y$ for single variables and $z$, $w$ for arbitrary tuples of variables. $P$, $Q$ and $G$ will denote predicates, while $S$, $T$ denote generalised substitutions. We will

---

[1] In fact in ordinary bunch theory the proper bunches of a type also form a complete lattice, whose top is **null** and whose bottom is the carrier bunch of that type, for example for the naturals $\mathbb{N}_b = 1 , 2 , 3 , \ldots$   . In improper bunch theory we effectively extend the lattice by appending our improper bunch $\perp$ as a new bottom element below this.

often use corresponding lower-case letters to refer to the frame of a generalised substitution, for example $s$ may stand for the frame of the substitution $S$.

## 2.4    Bunch Comprehension

It is often useful to describe a bunch by means of a bunch comprehension expression. This is similar to a set comprehension. We introduce the following fundamental notation:

$$\S\, z \bullet E$$

where $z$ is a list of variables and $E$ is an expression. The types of the variables of $z$ must be inferable from $E$. The comprehension denotes the bunch of all values $E$ as each variable of $z$ ranges over the *elementary* values of its type. That the type(s) must be inferable from the syntax of $E$ usually means $E$ in practice will be a guarded bunch, as explained in the next subsection, whose guard will involve some type-constraining predicate for all the variables of $z$.

We note here as a general rule that quantified variables appearing in any universal or existential quantification range over the elementary values of a type.

**Degenerate Bunch Comprehension.** A degenerate case of a bunch comprehension arises when the list of range variables featuring in the comprehension is empty. Denoting such an empty list by $\emptyset$ we have

**Definition 1.** $\S\, \emptyset \bullet E \quad =_{df} \quad E$

## 2.5    Guarded and Preconditioned Bunches

We use the notation $G \longrightarrow E$ for a guarded bunch, and $P \mid E$ for a preconditioned bunch. The formal definitions (by means of a conditional expression) are given below.

**Definition 2.** $G \longrightarrow E \quad =_{df} \quad$ **if** $G$ **then** $E$ **else null end**

**Definition 3.** $P \mid E \quad =_{df} \quad E, \neg\, P \longrightarrow \bot$

Guarded and preconditioned bunches evaluate to the value of the expression $E$ when the guarding predicate is true, however degenerate respectively to **null** or $\bot$ if not so. Note that in particular we need the concept of a guarded bunch to express comprehension in its more familiar form involving a constraining predicate $P$ restricting the values of $E$ to be included[2]:

$$\S\, z \mid P \bullet E \quad \hat{=} \quad \S\, z \bullet P \longrightarrow E$$

---

[2] We used the notation $\S\, z \mid P \bullet E$ in [7], but in this paper we use the more fundamental alternative form $\S\, z \bullet P \longrightarrow E$.

## 2.6    Substitution

We will write $E[F/w]$, where $E$ is an expression, possibly denoting a bunch, $w$ is a list of variables and $F$ is a corresponding list of elementary-valued expressions of appropriate types, to denote the expression syntactically derived from $E$ by replacing each free occurrence of any of the variables of $w$ by the corresponding expression in $F$.

In particular, substitution distributes across bunch union. For example, if $E$ is a bunch such that $E = E_1$, $E_2$ then

$$E[F/w] \quad = \quad E_1[F/w], \ E_2[F/w]$$

# 3    Prospective-Value Semantics

In prospective-value semantics the meaning of a computation $S$, expressed in the Generalised Substitution Language, is given by the value an expression $E$ would take were $S$ to be carried out. We denote this value by $S \diamond E$, it is indeed the prospective value of $E$ after execution of $S$. Similarly to transforming a predicate in wp semantics, the application of $\diamond$ has no state changing side-effects. Note that variables occurring free in $S \diamond E$ refer to the state *before* executing $S$. The following closed form, involving the frame, trm and prd of a generalised substitution $S$, serves as a semantic definition for $S \diamond E$:

**Definition 4.** Let $S$ be a generalised substitution, and $E$ be an expression then

$$S \diamond E \quad =_{df} \quad \mathrm{trm}(S) \mid \S\, s' \bullet \mathrm{prd}(S) \longrightarrow E[s'/s]$$

where $s$ is the list of variables constituting the frame[3] of $S$, and $s'$ the list of respective primed variables.

Note that the predicates $\mathrm{trm}(S)$ and $\mathrm{prd}(S)$ have their usual meanings and can be inferred from the wp semantics of $S$. One might object that we aren't developing an independent and self-contained theory when building on the semantics of an existing one (the wp calculus for the GSL). There are however reasons for this: for one we have a sufficient conceptual understanding of the frame, trm and prd to confidently assert the correctness of Def. 4, and furthermore we will see that this definition allows us to prove elementary algebraic laws which would otherwise have to count as axioms. It is indeed a departure from our previous exposition [7], which presented pv semantics only for the terminating subset of the GSL, but in the light of incorporating non-termination soundly we feel a sensible one.

## 3.1    Example for Calculating $S \diamond E$

As an illustrating example for applying Def. 4 let us consider the following generalised substitution

---

[3] The theory of generalised substitutions incorporating frames is presented in [3].

$$S \;\hat{=}\; x > 0 \mid (x := x + 1 \;[\!]\; x := x + 2) \quad .$$

We first have to compute the frame, trm and prd of $S$. We can trivially see the frame of $S$ only consists of the variable $x$. Fig.2 contains a few laws we can use to infer the trm and prd.

$$
\begin{aligned}
\mathrm{trm}(S) \;&=\; x > 0 \wedge \mathrm{trm}(x := x + 1 \;[\!]\; x := x + 2) \\
&=\; x > 0 \\
\mathrm{prd}(S) \;&=\; x > 0 \Rightarrow \mathrm{prd}(x := x + 1 \;[\!]\; x := x + 2) \\
&=\; x > 0 \Rightarrow (x' = x + 1 \vee x' = x + 2)
\end{aligned}
$$

With these characteristic predicates we can now apply Def. 4. Let us decide to calculate the prospective value of the expression $2 * x$ after execution of $S$:

$$S \diamond 2 * x$$

$=$ "Applying Def. 4"

$$\mathrm{trm}(S) \mid \S\, x' \bullet \mathrm{prd}(S) \longrightarrow 2 * x[x'/x]$$

$=$ "Rewriting trm and prd"

$$x > 0 \mid \S\, x' \bullet x' = x + 1 \vee x' = x + 2 \longrightarrow 2 * x[x'/x]$$

$=$ "Splitting bunch comprehension into two cases"

$$x > 0 \mid (\S\, x' \bullet x' = x + 1 \longrightarrow 2 * x[x'/x]\,, \S\, x' \bullet x' = x + 2 \longrightarrow 2 * x[x'/x])$$

$=$ "One-point rule for bunch comprehension"

$$x > 0 \mid (2 * (x + 1)\,, 2 * (x + 2)) \quad .$$

Note that the result is an expression on the state before executing the computation $S$. The interpretation of it is that the value of $2 * x$ would be $x > 0 \mid (2 * (x + 1)\,, 2 * (x + 2))$ if we executed $S$. Since $S$ behaves non-deterministically we obtain a bunch of elementary results: $2 * (x + 1)\,, 2 * (x + 2)$. In particular if we invoke $S$ from a state where $x = 0$ holds the outcome for $2 * x$ after executing $S$ is $\bot$, indicating the possibility of non-termination.

## 3.2    Special Case for the Frame of $S$ Being Empty

To strengthen our confidence in Def. 4 we submit it to the boundary case where the frame of the generalised substitution $S$ is empty. Hence we let $S$ be the substitution Skip, and remind the reader that the trm and prd of Skip are both equivalent to true.

$$\mathbf{skip} \diamond E$$

$=$ "Applying Def. 4"

$$\mathrm{trm}(\mathbf{skip}) \mid \S\, \emptyset \bullet \mathrm{prd}(\mathbf{skip}) \longrightarrow E[\emptyset/\emptyset]$$

$=$ "$E[\emptyset/\emptyset]$ degenerates to $E$"

$$\mathrm{trm}(\mathbf{skip}) \mid \S\, \emptyset \bullet \mathrm{prd}(\mathbf{skip}) \longrightarrow E$$

$=$ "Rule for bunch comprehension: $\S z \bullet P \longrightarrow E = P \longrightarrow \S z \bullet E$ when $z \setminus P$"

  $\mathrm{trm}(\mathbf{skip}) \mid \mathrm{prd}(\mathbf{skip}) \longrightarrow \S \emptyset \bullet E$

$=$ "Degenerate case of bunch comprehension, see Sect. 2.4"

  $\mathrm{trm}(\mathbf{skip}) \mid \mathrm{prd}(\mathbf{skip}) \longrightarrow E$

$=$ "Rewriting $\mathrm{trm}(\mathbf{skip})$ and $\mathrm{prd}(\mathbf{skip})$, see Fig.2"

  $\mathrm{true} \mid \mathrm{true} \longrightarrow E$

$=$ "Simplifying preconditioned and guarded bunch"

  $E$

This coincides with our expectation because Skip always terminates having no state-changing effects, and hence doesn't alter the value of the expression $E$.

### 3.3  Algebraic Laws to Simplify $S \diamond E$

From the previous derivation we can immediately conclude that $\mathbf{skip} \diamond E$ may be replaced by $E$ wherever it occurs in our mathematical formalism (whereby the expression transformer $\diamond$ is eliminated). Knowing this has got practical advantages, e.g. that we don't need to appeal to the semantic definition Def. 4 anymore and carry out the cumbersome calculations involving the trm and prd of $S$. Moreover such algebraic laws exist for all other operators of the GSL, a comprehensive summary of them is given in Fig.1. Note that $s$ and $t$ designate the frames of the corresponding generalised substitutions $S$ and $T$. The notational conventions are as agreed in Section 2.3.

As we assume the reader is familiar with the Generalised Substitution Language, we won't explain the meaning of each individual construct given in Fig.1 in detail, but only make a few selected remarks where we think clarification could be beneficial. See [1,3] for a more detailed explanation of each GSL construct.

We follow [3] by incorporating frames into our pv semantics for the GSL. The frame of a generalised substitution is the list of state variables which the substitution potentially can affect. When using the GSL outside the context of a B machine, frames are essential to give a meaningful definition to all operators of the GSL - in particular parallel composition. We now present detailed remarks on some of the individual GSL constructors.

**Assignment.** One might wish to differentiate simple and multiple assignment, e.g. $x := 1$ and $x, y := 1, 2$. Such a distinction is however unnecessary since simple assignment can be regarded as a special case of multiple assignment. Hence in our rule for assignment $z$ always represents a tuple of variables, and $F$ a tuple of expressions. Both tuples nevertheless are required to have the same dimension, and the elements of the right-hand tuple have to be well-defined and of corresponding appropriate type. In case of $z$ being the empty tuple it is easy to show that such an assignment degenerates to Skip.

| Generalised Substitution Name | Syntax | Frame | $S \diamond E$ |
|:---:|:---:|:---:|:---:|
| Skip | **skip** | $\emptyset$ | $E$ |
| Assignment | $z := F$ | $z$ | $E[F/z]$ |
| Precondition | $P \mid S$ | $s$ | $P \; \mathbf{\mid} \; S \diamond E$ |
| Guard | $G \Longrightarrow S$ | $s$ | $G \longrightarrow S \diamond E$ |
| Frame extension | $S_y$ | $s \cup y$ | $S \diamond E$ |
| Choice | $S \mathbin{[\!]} T$ | $s \cup t$ | $S \diamond E \, , \, T \diamond E$ |
| Unbounded Choice | $@z \bullet S$ | $s - z$ | $\S\, z \bullet S \diamond E \quad$ if $z \setminus E$ |
| Sequential Composition | $S \, ; \, T$ | $s \cup t$ | $S \diamond T \diamond E$ |

**Fig. 1.** Simplification rules for $S \diamond E$ for all constructs of the GSL

**Precondition.** The precondition rule is one of the central contributions of this paper. In our previous approach of presenting an expression-transformer semantics for the GSL [7] we resolved the issue through neglect, e.g. restricting ourself to the terminating subset of the GSL. Here however we don't want to impose such an *a priori* restriction on the command syntax, and thereby give a meaning to the entire GSL in terms of its pv effect.

Preconditioning a substitution (thin bar '$\mid$') naturally translates into preconditioning an expression (thick bar '$\mathbf{\mid}$'). The latter is only meaningful in our extension of bunch theory to improper bunch theory.

**Guard.** Similarly, guarding a generalised substitution translates into guarding the respective bunch $S \diamond E$. Where the guard $G$ is false we consider the substitution $S$ to be infeasible, and hence don't expect any outcomes from an attempt to execute $S$. Note that both the Precondition and the Guard constructors could have been defined solely in terms of conditional expressions, without the aid of guarded and preconditioned bunches. We believe however that these render the theory more comprehensive.

**Frame Extension.** Frame extension is a constructor which is peculiar to Dunne's exposition of a theory of generalised substitutions [3]. It explicitly allows us to enlarge the frame of a substitution. Note that this has no effect on the prospective value $S \diamond E$ as the values of the variables in the residual frame $y - s$ are conserved and thus not altered.

**Iteration.** For an iteration $W$, or indeed more generally any recursively defined substitution $W$, we define $W \diamond E$ as the least fixed-point of a corresponding self-referential expression, having first established suitable orders on expressions of each given type. This will be discussed in Section 4 of the paper.

## 3.4    Proof of Algebraic Laws

As we already pointed out, using the closed form Def. 4 as a semantics definition for $S \diamond E$, the algebraic rules listed in Fig.1 become subject to validation via proof. Here we present three of the proofs in detail. We have selected proofs of moderate difficulty: namely, those for assignment, preconditioning and choice.

**Proposition 1.** $z := F \diamond E \;=\; E[F/z]$

*Proof.* $z := F \diamond E$

$=$ "Applying Def. 4"

$\quad \mathrm{trm}(z := F) \;|\; \S\, z' \bullet \mathrm{prd}(z := F) \longrightarrow E[z'/z]$

$=$ "Rewriting trm and prd, see Fig.2"

$\quad true \;|\; \S\, z' \bullet z' = F \longrightarrow E[z'/z]$

$=$ "One-point rule for bunch comprehension"

$\quad true \;|\; E[F/z]$

$=$ "Simplifying preconditioned bunch"

$\quad E[F/z]$ $\qquad\qquad\qquad\qquad\qquad\qquad\qquad\qquad\qquad\qquad\qquad$ $\square$

**Proposition 2.** $P \,|\, S \diamond E \;=\; P \;|\; S \diamond E$

*Proof.* $P \,|\, S \diamond E$

$=$ "Applying Def. 4, let $s$ be frame($S$)"

$\quad \mathrm{trm}(P \,|\, S) \;|\; \S\, s' \bullet \mathrm{prd}(P \,|\, S) \longrightarrow E[s'/s]$

$=$ "Rewriting trm and prd, see Fig.2"

$\quad P \wedge \mathrm{trm}(S) \;|\; \S\, s' \bullet P \Rightarrow \mathrm{prd}(S) \longrightarrow E[s'/s]$

$=$ "Eliminating preconditioned bunch"

$\quad \S\, s' \bullet P \Rightarrow \mathrm{prd}(S) \longrightarrow E[s'/s]\,,\; \neg(P \wedge \mathrm{trm}(S)) \longrightarrow \bot$

$=$ "Logic"

$\quad \S\, s' \bullet \neg P \vee \mathrm{prd}(S) \longrightarrow E[s'/s]\,,\; \neg P \vee \neg\mathrm{trm}(S) \longrightarrow \bot$

$=$ "Splitting bunch comprehension and guarded bunch"

$\quad \S\, s' \bullet \neg P \longrightarrow E[s'/s]\,,\, \S\, s' \bullet \mathrm{prd}(S) \longrightarrow E[s'/s]\,,\; \neg P \longrightarrow \bot\,,\, \neg\mathrm{trm}(S) \longrightarrow \bot$

$=$ "Reordering terms and applying Def. 4"

$\quad S \diamond E\,,\, \S\, s' \bullet \neg P \longrightarrow E[s'/s]\,,\; \neg P \longrightarrow \bot$

$=$ "Rule for bunch comprehension: $\S\, z \bullet P \longrightarrow E = P \longrightarrow \S\, z \bullet E$ when $z \setminus P$"

$\quad S \diamond E\,,\; \neg P \longrightarrow \S\, s' \bullet E[s'/s]\,,\; \neg P \longrightarrow \bot$

$=$ "Distribution of guarding through bunch union, absorptive property of $\bot$"

$S \diamond E , \neg P \longrightarrow \bot$

$=$ "Rewriting into preconditioned bunch"

$P \mid S \diamond E$ □

**Proposition 3.** $S \mathbin{[\!]} T \diamond E \;=\; S \diamond E , T \diamond E$

*Proof.* $S \mathbin{[\!]} T \diamond E$

$=$ "Applying Def. 4, let $s$ be frame$(S)$, $t$ be frame$(T)$, and $u = s \cup t$"

$\quad \mathrm{trm}(S \mathbin{[\!]} T) \mid \S\, u' \bullet \mathrm{prd}(S \mathbin{[\!]} T) \longrightarrow E[u'/u]$

$=$ "Frame extension law: $\mathrm{prd}(S \mathbin{[\!]} T) = \mathrm{prd}(S_t \mathbin{[\!]} T_s)$"

$\quad \mathrm{trm}(S \mathbin{[\!]} T) \mid \S\, u' \bullet \mathrm{prd}(S_t \mathbin{[\!]} T_s) \longrightarrow E[u'/u]$

$=$ "Eliminating preconditioned bunch"

$\quad \S\, u' \bullet \mathrm{prd}(S_t \mathbin{[\!]} T_s) \longrightarrow E[u'/u] , \neg\mathrm{trm}(S \mathbin{[\!]} T) \longrightarrow \bot$

$=$ "Rewriting trm and prd, see Fig.2"

$\quad \S\, u' \bullet \mathrm{prd}(S_t) \vee \mathrm{prd}(T_s) \longrightarrow E[u'/u] , \neg(\mathrm{trm}(S) \wedge \mathrm{trm}(T)) \longrightarrow \bot$

$=$ "Logic"

$\quad \S\, u' \bullet \mathrm{prd}(S_t) \vee \mathrm{prd}(T_s) \longrightarrow E[u'/u] , \neg\mathrm{trm}(S) \vee \neg\mathrm{trm}(T) \longrightarrow \bot$

$=$ "Splitting bunch comprehension and guarded bunch"

$\quad \S\, u' \bullet \mathrm{prd}(S_t) \longrightarrow E[u'/u] , \S\, u' \bullet \mathrm{prd}(T_s) \longrightarrow E[u'/u] , \neg\mathrm{trm}(S) \longrightarrow \bot ,$

$\quad \neg\mathrm{trm}(T) \longrightarrow \bot$

$=$ "Frame extension law: $\mathrm{trm}(S) = \mathrm{trm}(S_y)$"

$\quad \S\, u' \bullet \mathrm{prd}(S_t) \longrightarrow E[u'/u] , \S\, u' \bullet \mathrm{prd}(T_s) \longrightarrow E[u'/u] , \neg\mathrm{trm}(S_t) \longrightarrow \bot ,$

$\quad \neg\mathrm{trm}(T_s) \longrightarrow \bot$

$=$ "Reordering terms and applying Def. 4"

$\quad S_t \diamond E , T_s \diamond E$

$=$ "Frame extension law, see Fig.1"

$\quad S \diamond E , T \diamond E$ □

### 3.5    Some Characteristic Predicates

The characteristic predicates of a generalised substitution trm, fis and prd are already familiar from wp semantics. Fig.3 summarises how they can be calculated from the wp predicate transformer. In pv semantics we can provide a set of simple equations to do the same. Given any generalised substitution $S$, the following predicates allow us to characterise its trm, fis and prd directly from its pv semantics.

| $Sub$ | $\mathrm{trm}(Sub)$ | $\mathrm{fis}(Sub)$ | $\mathrm{prd}(Sub)$ | note |
|---|---|---|---|---|
| **skip** | true | true | true | |
| $z := E$ | true | true | $z' = E$ | |
| $P \mid S$ | $P \wedge \mathrm{trm}(S)$ | $P \Rightarrow \mathrm{fis}(S)$ | $P \Rightarrow \mathrm{prd}(S)$ | |
| $P \Longrightarrow S$ | $P \Rightarrow \mathrm{trm}(S)$ | $P \wedge \mathrm{fis}(S)$ | $P \wedge \mathrm{prd}(S)$ | |
| $S_y$ | $\mathrm{trm}(S)$ | $\mathrm{fis}(S)$ | $\mathrm{prd}(S) \wedge w = w'$ | $w$ is $y - s$ |
| $S \mathrel{[\!]} T$ | $\mathrm{trm}(S) \wedge \mathrm{trm}(T)$ | $\mathrm{fis}(S) \vee \mathrm{fis}(T)$ | $\mathrm{prd}(S_t) \vee \mathrm{prd}(T_s)$ | |
| $@z \bullet S$ | $\forall z \bullet \mathrm{trm}(S)$ | $\exists z \bullet \mathrm{fis}(S)$ | $\exists z, w' \bullet \mathrm{prd}(S)$ | $w$ is $s \cap z$ |
| $S \,;\, T$ | $[S]\,\mathrm{trm}(T)$ | $\neg\,[S]\,\neg\,\mathrm{fis}(T)$ | $\mathrm{trm}(S) \Rightarrow$ $(\mathrm{prd}(S_t)\,;\,\mathrm{prd}(T_s))$ | |

**Fig. 2.** Characteristic predicates of each basic substitution construct

**Proposition 4.** $\mathrm{trm}(S) \;=\; S \diamond \mathbf{null} : \mathbf{null}$

*Proof.* $S \diamond \mathbf{null} : \mathbf{null}$

$\equiv$ "Applying Def. 4, let $s$ be $\mathrm{frame}(S)$"

$\quad \mathrm{trm}(S) \;\mid\; \S\,s' \bullet \mathrm{prd}(S) \longrightarrow \mathbf{null}[s'/s] : \mathbf{null}$

$\equiv$ "Simplification of substitution: $\mathbf{null}[F/z] = \mathbf{null}$ for elementary $F$"

$\quad \mathrm{trm}(S) \;\mid\; \S\,s' \bullet \mathrm{prd}(S) \longrightarrow \mathbf{null} : \mathbf{null}$

$\equiv$ "Simplification of bunch comprehension: $\S\,z \bullet P \longrightarrow \mathbf{null} \;=\; \mathbf{null}$"

$\quad \mathrm{trm}(S) \;\mid\; \mathbf{null} : \mathbf{null}$

$\equiv$ "Logic, the above is exactly true when $\mathrm{trm}(S)$"

$\quad \mathrm{trm}(S)$ $\qquad\qquad\qquad\qquad\qquad\qquad\qquad\qquad\qquad\qquad\quad\square$

**Proposition 5.** $\mathrm{fis}(S) \;=\; \bot : S \diamond \bot$

*Proof.* $\bot : S \diamond \bot$

$\equiv$ "Applying Def. 4, let $s$ be $\mathrm{frame}(S)$"

$\quad \bot : \mathrm{trm}(S) \;\mid\; \S\,s' \bullet \mathrm{prd}(S) \longrightarrow \bot[s'/s]$

$\equiv$ "Simplification of substitution: $\bot[F/z] = \bot$ for elementary $F$"

$\quad \bot : \mathrm{trm}(S) \;\mid\; \S\,s' \bullet \mathrm{prd}(S) \longrightarrow \bot$

$\equiv$ "Rewriting bunch comprehension: $\S\,z \bullet P \longrightarrow E \;=\; (\exists z \bullet P) \longrightarrow E$ if $z \setminus E$"

$$\bot : \operatorname{trm}(S) \mid (\exists\, s' \bullet \operatorname{prd}(S)) \longrightarrow \bot$$

$\equiv$ "Eliminating preconditioned bunch"

$$\bot : \neg\, \operatorname{trm}(S) \longrightarrow \bot\,,\, (\exists\, s' \bullet \operatorname{prd}(S)) \longrightarrow \bot$$

$\equiv$ "Merging guarded bunches"

$$\bot : \neg\, \operatorname{trm}(S) \vee (\exists\, s' \bullet \operatorname{prd}(S)) \longrightarrow \bot$$

$\equiv$ "Logic, the above is exactly true when $\neg\, \operatorname{trm}(S) \vee \exists\, s' \bullet \operatorname{prd}(S)$"

$$\neg\, \operatorname{trm}(S) \vee \exists\, s' \bullet \operatorname{prd}(S)$$

$\equiv$ "Property of trm and prd: $\neg\, \operatorname{trm}(S) \Rightarrow \operatorname{prd}(S)$, see Prop. 2.1 in [3]"

$$\exists\, s' \bullet \operatorname{prd}(S)$$

$\equiv$ "$\exists\, s' \bullet \operatorname{prd}(S)$ is an alternative characterisation for the feasibility of $S$ since $S$ is feasible exactly where it has some behaviour"

$$\operatorname{fis}(S) \qquad\qquad\qquad \Box$$

**Proposition 6.** $\operatorname{prd}(S) = s' : S \diamond s$    *where $s$ is the frame of $S$.*

*Proof.* $s' : S \diamond s$

$\equiv$ "Applying Def. 4, let $s$ be frame$(S)$"

$$s' : \operatorname{trm}(S) \mid \S\, s' \bullet \operatorname{prd}(S) \longrightarrow s[s'/s]$$

$\equiv$ "Simplification of substitution $s[s'/s]$"

$$s' : \operatorname{trm}(S) \mid \S\, s' \bullet \operatorname{prd}(S) \longrightarrow s'$$

$\equiv$ "Elimination of preconditioned bunch, $\bot$ is a superbunch of any other bunch"

$$\neg\, \operatorname{trm}(S) \vee s' : \S\, s' \bullet \operatorname{prd}(S) \longrightarrow s'$$

$\equiv$ "Simplification of $s' : \S\, s' \bullet \operatorname{prd}(S) \longrightarrow s'$, generally $z : \S\, z \bullet P \longrightarrow z \equiv P$"

$$\neg\, \operatorname{trm}(S) \vee \operatorname{prd}(S)$$

$\equiv$ "Property of trm and prd: $\neg\, \operatorname{trm}(S) \Rightarrow \operatorname{prd}(S)$, see Prop. 2.1 in [3]"

$$\operatorname{prd}(S) \qquad\qquad\qquad \Box$$

| predicate name | in wp semantics | in pv semantics | note |
|---|---|---|---|
| $\operatorname{trm}(S)$ | $[S]$ true | $S \diamond \mathbf{null} : \mathbf{null}$ | |
| $\operatorname{fis}(S)$ | $\neg\, [S]$ false | $\bot : S \diamond \bot$ | |
| $\operatorname{prd}(S)$ | $\neg\, [S]\, s \neq s'$ | $s' : S \diamond s$ | where $s$ is the frame$(S)$ |

**Fig. 3.** Characteristic predicates trm, fis and prd in both wp and pv semantics

**Remark.** We proved the correctness of Proposition 4 - 6 under the assumption that $S$ is a computation expressed in the GSL. We could have indeed generalised here by permitting $S \diamond \_$ to be an arbitrary "meaningful" pv expression transformer, not necessarily one resulting from application of the closed form Def. 4. Then these three propositions would merely have intuitive justifications. More awkwardly we would have to explain what we mean by a meaningful expression transformer in the context pv semantics. Such a discussion is worthwhile but beyond the scope of this paper.

# 4    Iteration

The standard treatment of handling iteration in wp semantics is to define first a suitable ordering on substitutions, which has to be a complete partial order and each construct of the language has to be monotonic with respect it. The ordering used in total correctness is simply the refinement lattice of generalised substitutions. The meaning of a loop construct $W$ is then interpreted as the least solution of a fixed-point equation [2]. To write down this equation there are two possibilities, either we describe $W$ directly as a fixed-point in generalised substitutions, or we express for a given postcondition $Q$ the outcome of wp($W, Q$) as a fixed-point in predicates. Both approaches can be found in [2].

In pv semantics we express the meaning of $W \diamond E$ as a fixed-point in *expressions*. To do so we first have to agree on the ordering that is going to be employed. As explained in Section 2.3 we use the reverse inclusion ordering defined by $E \sqsubseteq F \Leftrightarrow F : E$ as a basis for a fixed-point treatment[4]. Like the inclusion ordering on sets over a given type yields a complete lattice, the inclusion ordering on bunches yields one too. In defining $\sqsubseteq$ we slightly modify the lattice by turning it upside down and giving it a new bottom, that is $\bot$. Note that this doesn't destroy the integrity of the original lattice. The second issue to be looked at is monotonicity. We won't present a proof here to show that in pv semantics all operators of the GSL are monotonic with respect to $\sqsubseteq$, however such can indeed be done with little effort.

Our satisfying the previous conditions justifies the application of Tarski's fixed-point theorem [8] and hence the assertion that $\mu Y \bullet S \diamond Y$ for a generalised substitution $S$ exists.

**Theorem 1.** *Let $W$ be a loop construct having the form* **WHILE** $G$ **DO** $S$ **END**. *Then the pv effect of $W$ for any expression $E$ is given by:*

$$W \diamond E \ = \ \mu Y \bullet \text{if } G \text{ then } S \diamond Y \text{ else } E \text{ end}$$

Before deriving the pv effect of $W$ and thereby proving Theorem 1 we will first establish a lemma which characterise the pv effect of the transitive opening

---

[4] Notice that the overloading of $\sqsubseteq$ as the refinement relation for generalised substitutions as well as the ordering relation for expressions isn't a problem as long as the context makes clear in what sense it is used.

$S^\wedge$ of a generalised substitution $S$. The transitive opening is the fundamental iteration construct introduced by Abrial [1]. Formally it is the least solution of the fixed-point equation $X = (S;\ X) \ [\!] \ \mathbf{skip}$. Operationally we can think of it as the choice of successively executing $S$ an arbitrary number of times (including the case of infinite repetition).

**Lemma 1.** *Let $S$ be a generalised substitution, and $E$ an expression. The pv effect of the transitive opening of $S$ is given by*

$$S^\wedge \diamond E \ = \ \mu\, Y \bullet S \diamond Y\,,\, E$$

*Proof.* $S^\wedge$ is the least solution of $X = (S;\ X) \ [\!] \ \mathbf{skip}$, thus

$$S^\wedge = (S;\ S^\wedge) \ [\!] \ \mathbf{skip}$$

$\Rightarrow$ "Leibniz law: $S = T \Rightarrow S \diamond E = T \diamond E$"

$$S^\wedge \diamond E = (S;\ S^\wedge) \ [\!] \ \mathbf{skip} \diamond E$$

$\equiv$ "Simplification of Choice (laws given in Fig.1)"

$$S^\wedge \diamond E = (S;\ S^\wedge) \diamond E\,,\, \mathbf{skip} \diamond E$$

$\equiv$ "Simplification of Sequential Composition and Skip (laws given in Fig.1)"

$$S^\wedge \diamond E = S \diamond S^\wedge \diamond E\,,\, E$$

$\equiv$ "Substituting $Y \,\hat{=}\, S^\wedge \diamond E$"

$$Y = S \diamond Y\,,\, E$$

We have now obtained a fixed-point equation for $S^\wedge \diamond E$ in expressions. $S^\wedge \diamond E$ shows indeed to be the weakest expression $Y$ that satisfies it. It has to be the weakest in order to render $S^\wedge$ in the least deterministic way (note that weaker expressions convey more behaviours under the $\sqsubseteq$-relation).

$$S^\wedge \diamond E \ = \ \mu\, Y \bullet S \diamond Y\,,\, E \quad \square$$

Equipped with the previous Lemma 1 we can conclude the proof of Theorem 1 by using Abrial's representation of a loop involving transitive opening:

$$\mathbf{WHILE}\ G\ \mathbf{DO}\ S\ \mathbf{END} \quad =_{df} \quad (G \Longrightarrow S)^\wedge\ ;\ \neg G \Longrightarrow \mathbf{skip} \tag{1}$$

$$W \diamond E$$

$=$ "Equation 1 characterising the while loop"

$$(G \Longrightarrow S)^\wedge\ ;\ \neg G \Longrightarrow \mathbf{skip} \diamond E$$

$=$ "Simplification of Sequential Composition (laws given in Fig.1)"

$$(G \Longrightarrow S)^\wedge \diamond \neg G \Longrightarrow \mathbf{skip} \diamond E$$

$=$ "Simplification of Guard and Skip (laws given in Fig.1)"

$$(G \Longrightarrow S)^\wedge \diamond \neg G \longrightarrow E$$

$= $ "Lemma 1"

$\quad \mu\, Y \bullet G \Longrightarrow S \diamond Y\,,\, \neg G \longrightarrow E$

$= $ "Simplification of Guard (laws given in Fig.1)"

$\quad \mu\, Y \bullet G \longrightarrow S \diamond Y\,,\, \neg G \longrightarrow E$

$= $ "Reformulating as a conditional expression"

$\quad \mu\, Y \bullet \mathbf{if}\ G\ \mathbf{then}\ S \diamond Y\ \mathbf{else}\ E\ \mathbf{end}$ $\qquad\qquad\qquad\qquad$ □

## 5  Conclusion and Future Work

We have developed a prospective-value semantics for the GSL by interpreting each basic command and constructor of the GSL as a pv expression transformer. We would contend $S \diamond \_$ captures the meaning of $S$ as least as well intuitively as wp($S$, $\_$) does. However a formal proof of isomorphism between these two semantics is beyond the scope of this paper.

To capture the effect of non-termination in pv semantics we have extended ordinary bunch theory with an improper bunch in order to describe the outcome of an abortive computation. A set of algebraic laws has been presented for each construct in terms of its pv semantics. With these the $\diamond$ operator can be eliminated from any expression by successive rewrites. We proved the correctness of each law, making the initial definition superfluous from a practical point of view. Nevertheless it played an important part in presenting the theory because it permitted us to prove facts which would otherwise have to count as axioms.

We incorporated the treatment of iteration into pv semantics by first arguing the existence of a suitable ordering, and then characterising the pv effect of a substitution as a fixed-point in expressions, which is an alternative to the familiar interpretation of it as a fixed-point in predicates or substitutions [1, 2].

Our future work will consist of investigating whether $S \diamond E$ can be incorporated into the expression syntax of the GSL, in contrast to our use of it in this paper only at a meta-level to reason *about* generalised substitutions. To avoid complications arising from the fact that $S \diamond E$ might not represent a single value but a bunch of such, we may have to restrict its occurrence within the GSL syntax so that it can only appear in set brackets (thus converting the bunch into a set). We are currently investigating this issue.

The question also naturally arises of how to express important constructions of the B Method in pv semantics such as invariants and data refinements. Our hope is thereby to obtain more elegant and intuitive formulations of their associated laws.

**Acknowledgements.** We would like to thank the anonymous reviewers for their valuable comments and encouraging remarks.

# References

1. J.-R. Abrial. *The B-Book: Assigning Programs to Meanings.* Cambridge University Press, 1996.
2. Ralph-Johan Back and Joakim von Wright. *Refinement Calculus: A Systematic Introduction.* Graduate Texts in Computer Science. Springer-Verlage, 1998.
3. S. Dunne. A theory of generalised substitutions. In *ZB 2002: Formal Specification and Development in Z and B*, volume 2272 of *Lecture Notes in Computer Science*, pages 270–290. Springer-Verlag, January 2002.
4. E. C. R. Hehner. Bunch theory: A simple set theory for computer science. *Information Processing Letters*, 12(1):26–30, February 1981.
5. E. C. R. Hehner. *A Practical Theory of Programming.* Texts and Monographs in Computer Science. Springer-Verlag, 1993.
6. J. M. Morris and Bunkenburg A. A theory of bunches. *Acta Informatica*, 37(8):541–561, May 2001.
7. W. J. Stoddart and F. Zeyda. Expression transformers in B-GSL. In *ZB 2003: Formal Specification and Development in Z and B*, volume 2651 of *Lecture Notes in Computer Science*, pages 197–215. Springer-Verlag, January 2003.
8. A. Tarski. A lattice-theoretical fixed-point theorem and its applications. *Pacific Journal of Mathematics*, 5:285–309, 1955.

# Retrenchment and the B-Toolkit

Richard Banach and Simon Fraser

Department of Computer Science, University of Manchester,
Manchester M13 9PL, UK
{banach, sfraser}@cs.man.ac.uk

**Abstract.** An experiment to incorporate retrenchment into the B-Toolkit is described. The syntax of a retrenchment construct is given, as is the proof obligation which gives retrenchment its semantics. The practical aspects of incorporating these into the existing B-Toolkit are then investigated. It transpires that the B-Toolkit's internal architecture is heavily committed to monolithic refinement, because of B-Method philosophy, and this restricts what can be done without a complete rebuild of the toolkit. Experience with case studies is outlined.

## 1   Introduction

The B-Method [2, 14, 19, 18, 17] has enjoyed what can only be called spectacular success in terms of vindicating the view that model based refinement, despite its theoretical depth, can, via the enabling effects of appropriate mechanisation, lead to highly significant benefits for the practical engineering of systems of the highest criticality. By now, B-engineered systems are widespread on the railways in France, and in other countries, where the French success has convinced the appropriate authorities [10, 9, 11].

It is well appreciated by practitioners of refinement, that for all its desirable properties, the technique displays a certain brittleness. The abstract and concrete models have to be in just the right relationship before the refinement proof obligations (POs) can be discharged. Unfortunately this state of affairs takes no account of the human-centred needs/requirements engineering that must contribute to system design, and depending on circumstances, can be a greater or lesser impediment to a transparent system construction process. In order to improve matters in this regard, retrenchment was introduced so that almost-but-not-quite-refinements could be described within a formal framework similar to that used for refinement [5, 6, 7, 4, 15, 16]. The ability to describe not-quite-refinements leads to the capacity to describe and analyse much more general system evolution scenarios [8, 3]. Needless to say this flexibility comes at a price; the guarantees offered by refinement are forfeit.

If refinement greatly benefits from mechanisation then so does retrenchment. The aim of this paper is to describe an experiment to incorporate retrenchment into the B-Toolkit [1], one of the two commercially available implementations of the B-Method, the other being Atelier-B. In fact retrenchment was first conceived

H. Treharne et al. (Eds.): ZB 2005, LNCS 3455, pp. 203–221, 2005.

in the context of the B-Method [5], precisely so that the impact of the issues surrounding mechanisation could be taken on board right at the outset.[1]

The rest of this paper is as follows. Section 2 covers the theoretical aspects of the integration, namely: the syntax and the PO it describes, a small example, and what it means for a syntactically correct retrenchment construct to be type correct. Section 3 covers the B-Toolkit's architecture, and how it interacts with the theoretical aspects of incorporating retrenchment. Section 4 covers evaluation, and Section 5 concludes.

**Acknowledgements and Note.** The authors are indebted to BCore (UK) Ltd. for access to the source of the B-Toolkit. According to the terms under which the access was granted, the IPR residing in the experimental tool described in this paper remains the property of BCore (UK) Ltd.

## 2    Extending the B-Method for Retrenchment

The B-Method [2, 17] is a methodology in which abstract models can be described and then refined all the way down to code; all this in a manner that lends itself to extensive and integrated machine checkability at all stages. As noted above, retrenchment was introduced to enable the benefits of formal decription and machine checkability to migrate beyond the confines mapped out by strict refinement. The original retrenchment proposal [5] employed a syntax that combined the syntax of abstract machines with the flavour of refinement machines. And while it is adequate for most theoretical investigations into the system engineering aspects of retrenchment, it proves less convenient for implementation within an existing toolkit, since it necessitates extensive modification to the code for processing abstract machines. So for the present experiment, a different syntactic strategy was employed.

### 2.1    Syntax, the POs, and an Example

In the B-Method, refinement characterises the target as an extension of the source abstraction [2]. Retrenchment however, is a relationship between two abstract machines, and so it was appropriate to introduce a new RETRENCHMENT construct, which refers to the relevant machines, but which (conveniently enough) does not impact their syntax and processing. Table 1 describes the syntax. The RETRENCHMENT keyword introduces the construct, and the FROM and TO keywords indicate the source and target abstract machines respectively of the retrenchment. The RETRIEVES predicate gives the desired retrieve relation between the machines, and the OPERATIONS clause lists the ramifications of the operations common to source and target abstract machines.

Since [5], a number of different flavours of retrenchment have been investigated, including the original or 'primitive' form, the 'sharp' form [6], and the

---

[1] The choice of the B-Toolkit was dictated principally by familiarity from its use in teaching the B-Method at Manchester.

**Table 1.** Syntactic Categories for Retrenchment Relationship

| Syntactic Category | Definition |
| --- | --- |
| *Retrenchment Relationship* | RETRENCHMENT<br>    *Identifier*<br>FROM<br>    *Identifier*<br>TO<br>    *Identifier*<br>RETRIEVES<br>    *Predicate*<br>OPERATIONS<br>    *Ramifications*<br>END |
| *Ramifications* | *Ramifications ; Ramification_Declaration*<br>*Ramification_Declaration* |
| *Ramification_ Declaration* | RAMIFICATIONS<br>    *Identifier*<br>LVAR<br>    *Id_List*<br>WITHIN<br>    *Predicate*<br>CONCEDES<br>    *Predicate*<br>OUTPUT<br>    *Predicate*<br>NEVERTHELESS<br>    *Predicate*<br>END |
| *Id_List* | *Id_List , Identifier*<br>*Identifier* |

'output' form [4]. All of these can be viewed as special cases of a common 'sharp output' form, and so the ramifications of the RETRENCHMENT construct were designed to cater for this more general variant. Thus for a given operation, the RAMIFICATIONS clause consists of an LVAR clause (allowing the introduction of 'logical variables' for remembering before-values in the context of the after-state), the WITHIN clause, for constraining the antecedent of the operation PO, and the CONCEDES, OUTPUT, and NEVERTHELESS clauses for use in the operation PO consequent. The operation PO itself is:

$$IC_f \wedge IC_t \wedge (Q_f \wedge R \wedge W) \Rightarrow Q_t \wedge [S_t] \neg [S_f] \neg (((R \wedge O) \vee D) \wedge E)$$

where $IC_f, IC_t$ are source/target static contexts, $Q_f, Q_t$ are source/target preconditions, $S_f, S_t$ are source/target predicate transformers, and $R, W, O, D, E$ are the retrieve, within, output, concedes, and nevertheless relations respectively.

Of the top level clauses, the RETRIEVES and OPERATIONS clauses are optional, whilst the RETRENCHMENT, FROM and TO clauses are mandatory. If an operation is ramified, then only the RAMIFICATIONS clause itself is mandatory, the remaining clauses are optional (although if an LVAR clause is present, then it is mandatory for a WITHIN clause to also be present that allows for the type checking of the variables declared).

Of course the operation PO is complemented by the intialisation PO:

$$IC_f \wedge IC_t \Rightarrow [I_t] \neg [I_f] \neg (R)$$

We give a small example of retrenchment in this syntax. The example shows how some of the clauses of the retrenchment may be omitted, and indirectly, how the more elaborate structures of the sharp or output forms can increase expressivity: the two conjuncts of the concession could justifiably be separated, putting the $TRUE$ case in an output clause.

| MACHINE | $abc$ | MACHINE | $def$ |
|---|---|---|---|
| VARIABLES | $aa, bb, cc$ | SEES | $Bool\_TYPE$ |
| INVARIANT | $aa \in \mathbb{N} \wedge$ | CONSTANTS | $MaxNum$ |
| | $bb \in \mathbb{N} \wedge$ | PROPERTIES | $MaxNum \in \mathbb{N}$ |
| | $cc \in \mathbb{N}$ | VARIABLES | $dd$ |
| INITIALISATION | $aa := 0 \parallel$ | INVARIANT | $dd \in \mathbb{N}$ |
| | $bb := 1 \parallel$ | INITIALISATION | $dd := 0$ |
| | $cc := 2$ | | |
| OPERATIONS | | OPERATIONS | |
| $my\_plus \mathrel{\widehat{=}} aa := bb + cc$ | | $resp \longleftarrow my\_plus(ee, ff) \mathrel{\widehat{=}}$ | |
| | | PRE $ee \in \mathbb{N} \wedge ff \in \mathbb{N} \wedge$ | |
| | | $ee \le MaxNum \wedge ff \le MaxNum$ | |
| | | THEN IF $ee + ff \le MaxNum$ | |
| | | THEN $dd := ee + ff$ | |
| | | $\parallel resp := TRUE$ | |
| | | ELSE $dd := 0 \parallel resp := FALSE$ | |
| | | END | |
| | | END | |
| END | | END | |

The abstract machines $abc$ and $def$

```
RETRENCHMENT abc_to_def
FROM            abc
TO              def
OPERATIONS

  RAMIFICATIONS my_plus
  WITHIN          bb = ee ∧ cc = ff
  CONCEDES        (resp = TRUE ∧ dd = aa) ∨
                  (resp = FALSE ∧ dd = 0)
  END

END
```

The retrenchment construct between the abstract machines $abc$ and $def$

**Table 2.** Source and Target Abstract Machines

| Source Machine | | Target Machine | |
|---|---|---|---|
| MACHINE | $M_f(X_f, x_f)$ | MACHINE | $M_t(X_t, x_t)$ |
| CONSTRAINTS | $C_f$ | CONSTRAINTS | $C_t$ |
| SETS | $S_f; T_f = \{a_f, b_f\}$ | SETS | $S_t; T_t = \{a_t, b_t\}$ |
| CONSTANTS | $c_f$ | CONSTANTS | $c_t$ |
| PROPERTIES | $P_f$ | PROPERTIES | $P_t$ |
| VARIABLES | $v_f$ | VARIABLES | $v_t$ |
| INVARIANT | $I_f$ | INVARIANT | $I_t$ |
| ASSERTIONS | $J_f$ | ASSERTIONS | $J_t$ |
| INITIALISATION | $U_f$ | INITIALISATION | $U_t$ |
| OPERATIONS | $o_f$ | OPERATIONS | $o_t$ |
| END | | END | |

## 2.2    Type Checking

The B-Method requires that, before a predicate involving set-theoretic variables
be proved, it must be type-checked. Here we show how the retrenchment construct can be type-checked by extending the 'check' predicate of [2]; we use the
same techniques as [2]. We assume that a retrenchment relationship as described
above[2] holds between a source machine $M_f$ and a target machine $M_t$ (see Table 2), with operations $op_f$ and $op_t$ (see Table 3).

Table 4, presents the type checking rule for a retrenchment construct. The
validity of three antecedents implies the validity of the 'check' predicate for
the whole construct. The first antecedent asserts the distinctness of the various

---

[2] The fields $R$, $W$, $D$, $O$ and $E$ refer to the RETRIEVES, WITHIN, CONCEDES,
   OUTPUT and NEVERTHELESS clauses respectively.

**Table 3.** Source and Target Operations

| Source Machine | Target Machine |
|---|---|
| $u_f \longleftarrow op_f(w_f) \mathrel{\hat{=}}$ PRE $\quad Q_f$ <br> THEN $\quad V_f$ <br> END | $u_t \longleftarrow op_t(w_t) \mathrel{\hat{=}}$ PRE $\quad Q_t$ <br> THEN $\quad V_t$ <br> END |

**Table 4.** Type Checking Rules for Retrenchment Constructs

| Antecedents | Consequent |
|---|---|
| $M_f,M_t,N,v_f,v_t,rmDup(c_f,c_t),$ <br> $rmDup(S_f,S_t),rmDup(T_f,T_t),rmDup(a_f,a_t),$ <br> $rmDup(b_f,b_t),X_f,X_t,x_f,x_t$ are all distinct <br><br> Operation names of $o_f$ are identical to operation names of $o$, and are all included in the operation names of $o_t$ <br><br> $given(X_f), given(X_t),$ <br> $given(S_f), given(S_t),$ <br> $given(T_f), given(T_t),$ <br> $a_f \in T_f, a_t \in T_t,$ <br> $b_f \in T_f, b_t \in T_t$ <br> $\vdash$ <br> $check(\forall x_f, x_t \bullet (C_f \wedge C_t \Rightarrow$ <br> $\quad \forall c_f, c_t \bullet (P_f \wedge P_t \Rightarrow \forall v_f, v_t \bullet (R \wedge o))))$ | check ( <br>   RETRENCHMENT <br>    $N$ <br>   FROM <br>    $M_f$ <br>   TO <br>    $M_t$ <br>   RETRIEVES <br>    $R$ <br>   OPERATIONS <br>    $o$ <br>   END <br> ) |

lexical elements listed. Note that $rmDup$ removes duplicates *prior to* distinctness checking, therefore *permitting* limited sharing of identifiers (more details are given below). The second antecedent checks the inclusion of source operation names in target operation names. The third antecedent succeeds provided: given the set parameters, and abstract and declared sets of the source and target machines, assuming the numerical parameters and the machine constraints, and assuming the constants and their properties, then the retrieve relation typechecks.

Table 5 presents the type checking rules for the ramifications of operations. The first rule allows lists of ramifications to be checked elementwise. The second rule infers the validity of the 'check' predicate for a ramification on the basis of five antecedents. The first two check the presence of the operation $op$ in the (previously typechecked) source and target machines, and extract their I/O types $(S_f, S_t, T_f, T_t)$. The next two check that I/O variables and logical variables are

**Table 5.** Type Checking Rules for Ramifications

| Antecedents | Consequent |
|---|---|
| $ENV \vdash \text{check}(o)$<br><br>$ENV \vdash \text{check}(q)$ | $ENV \vdash \text{check}(o \; ; \; q)$ |
| $S_f \longleftarrow op(T_f)$ occurs in $o_f$<br><br>$S_t \longleftarrow op(T_t)$ occurs in $o_t$<br><br>$l,u_f,u_t,op,w_f,w_t$ are all distinct<br><br>$l,u_f,u_t,op,w_f,w_t \setminus ENV$<br><br>$ENV,$<br>$u_f \in S_f, w_f \in T_f$<br>$u_t \in S_t, w_t \in T_t$<br>$\vdash$<br>$\text{check}(\forall l \bullet (W \Rightarrow D \wedge O \wedge E))$ | $ENV \vdash \text{check (}$<br>RAMIFICATIONS<br>$op$<br>LVAR<br>$l$<br>WITHIN<br>$W$<br>CONCEDES<br>$D$<br>OUTPUT<br>$O$<br>NEVERTHELESS<br>$E$<br>END<br>) |

**Table 6.** Visibility of Abstract Machine Variables

|  | $R$ | $W$ | $D$ | $O$ | $E$ |
|---|---|---|---|---|---|
| Machine Variables | $\checkmark$ | $\checkmark$ | $\checkmark$ | $\checkmark$ | $\checkmark$ |
| Logical Variables |  | $\checkmark$ | $\checkmark$ | $\checkmark$ | $\checkmark$ |
| Operation Inputs |  | $\checkmark$ | $\checkmark$ | $\checkmark$ | $\checkmark$ |
| Operation Outputs |  |  | $\checkmark$ | $\checkmark$ | $\checkmark$ |

distinct from each other and the environment. The final antecedent succeeds provided: given the environment, and the I/O variables in their types, assuming the logical constants and the within relation, then the concedes, output, and neverthless relations all typecheck.

Note that the rules outlined above take no account of the SEES, USES or INCLUDES mechanisms. These work in the standard way and are not discussed further here.

## 2.3    Visibility

The syntactic validation of a retrenchment necessitates the enforcement of a visibility discipline. Table 6 shows which clauses of a retrenchment can access which variables.

# 3    The B-Toolkit and Its Support for Retrenchment

The B-Toolkit is proprietary software of B-Core (UK) Ltd. Its architecture is shown in Fig. 1. The workhorse of the toolkit is the B-Platform (also known as the B-Tool or B-Kernel). This is a theorem proving assistant,[3] whose capabilities include various side effects such as the writing of files. Thus, although it maintains no state of its own, it can affect externally managed B-Toolkit state. To this end it is put to work for all sorts of B-Toolkit tasks such as parsing and typechecking ... which goes some way towards explaining the tool's sometimes eclectic responses to syntactic errors etc.

Maintaining a grip on the state of a B-Toolkit development is the job of the Construct Manager module. And acting as intermediary between the Construct Manager and the B-Platform is the Process Manager. So: users express their demands via the User Interface, these get digested by the Construct Manager, who translates them into a suitable series of commands for the B-Platform, which then get sent to it via the Process Manager. The B-Platform processes them one at a time, making appropriate reference to the B-Toolkit Libraries as necessary.

**Fig. 1.** Architecture of the B-Toolkit

## 3.1    The Machine Development Structure

A B-Toolkit construct is either an abstract machine (AM), a refinement machine (RM) or an implementation machine (IM). A B-Toolkit machine development is a collection of such constructs that provide different views of a single model. The B-Toolkit considers the development of one (main) abstract machine to proceed linearly from the abstract to the concrete (Fig. 2).

Incorporating retrenchment via a separate retrenchment construct (rather than a retrenchment machine), means that the B-Toolkit's mechanisms for refinement and implementation remain unaltered. However the B-Toolkit limits

---

[3] So it can perform inferences, but from user-supplied axioms and theories.

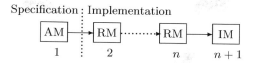

**Fig. 2.** B-Toolkit Development Structure

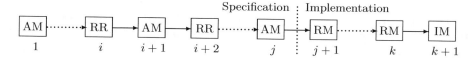

**Fig. 3.** Proposed Machine Development Structure

the use of abstract machines, allowing only one abstract machine per development, and restricting it to be only at the start. This raises some problems for the support of the retrenchment construct, as retrenchment fundamentally involves at least two abstract machines. (Typically, there is an 'idealised' abstract model, that undergoes one or more retrenchments until an abstraction refinable to code emerges.) A change to the structure of a machine development was thus required that allowed for at least the structure of machine development as just discussed. See Fig. 3, in which a retrenchment relation (RR) connects successive pairs of abstract machines until a machine refinable to an implementation is reached.

The B-Toolkit's limitations on the use of abstract machines turn out to be pervasive. The integration of the refinement relationship with the target machine is not just a syntactic convenience, but is maintained in all representations, internal and external. So the concept of a relationship distinct from (some flavour of) machine did not exist in the B-Toolkit, necessitating extensive redesign.[4]

## 3.2    Lifecycle of a Retrenchment Construct

Each construct under configuration control in the B-Toolkit has a state, recorded in the Construct Manager. This can be one of: uncommitted, unanalysed, analysed, unproved or proved. The state changes as the construct is moved through the construct lifecycle, and can be altered by changes occurring elsewhere in the development. This all applies equally to retrenchment constructs.

**Introduction.** The basic introduction of a retrenchment construct is a straightforward extension of the existing introduction mechanism; especially since the possibility to 'Introduce a retrenchment of Analysed Machines' was not pursued. The latter would have entailed a more extensive reworking of the introduction mechanism.

---

[4] For this reason the possibility of allowing the retrenchments to form an arbitrary (loop-free) directed graph between abstract machines was not entertained.

**Committing and Dependency Analysis.** The commit process basically has two phases. The first determines and resolves any dependencies on the construct, while the second verifies its syntactic correctness.

In the B-Method, a refinement machine is semantically an extension of the abstraction it refines. In the B-Toolkit therefore, when the abstraction is changed, any refinement of it can no longer be trusted, and it, and any further refinements are set to unanalysed and removed from the (B-Toolkit's internal view of the) state of the machine development.

By contrast, the target of a retrenchment is emphatically *not* an extension of its source machine. Both source and target machines need to be self contained consistent machines. Thus an alteration to the data of any retrenchment construct that connects them need affect neither the source or target machines themselves, nor the B-Toolkit's view of their state.

Fig. 4 illustrates a dependency chain starting with a series of retrenchments, and continuing with a series of refinements beyond machine $i + 2$. Fig. 5 shows what happens to this when retrenchment $i+1$ is altered. This relies on the simple development structure implemented during this experiment, which allows only for zero or more retrenchments followed by zero or more refinements.

We turn now to abstract machines. There are three distinct types of relationship that can cause dependency on an abstract machine – refinement, retrenchment and inclusion/importation. The refinement and retrenchment relationships are restricted to a single machine development, and are examined first. Fig. 6 shows the senarios we need to consider.

**Fig. 4.** A Retrenchment Construct in a Machine Development

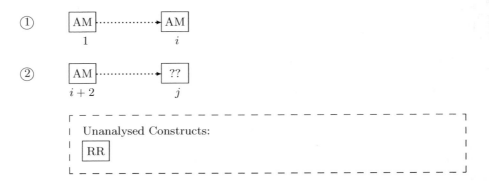

**Fig. 5.** Resolution of a Retrenchment Construct Commit

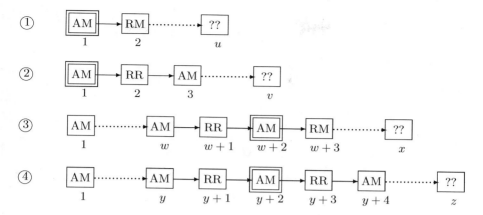

**Fig. 6.** Abstract Machines in Machine Developments

**Fig. 7.** Resolution of an Abstract Machine Commit ②

Development ① in Fig. 6 shows an abstract machine at the head of a (possibly empty) refinement chain. This is a standard B-Toolkit refinement picture, and needed no alteration in dependency analysis.

Development ② in Fig. 6 shows an abstract machine which is retrenched. Here the only construct dependent on the abstract machine is the retrenchment construct. When the machine is altered, it and the retrenchment construct become unanalysed, and the remainder of the chain forms a separate development. See Fig. 7

Development ③ in Fig. 6 shows an abstract machine which is the target of a retrenchment and the source of a refinement. It is clear that when the machine is altered, it, its parent retrenchment construct, and all its refinement descendants, must become unanalysed. Fig. 8 illustrates.

Finally, development ④ in Fig. 6 shows an abstract machine which is both the source and target of retrenchments. In this case, the development splits into two: the initial part up to the most concrete ancestot of the machine in question forms one piece, and the other part consists of the most abstract descendant of the machine in question up to the end. Fig. 9 illustrates.

An abstract machine can also be included in another (via the AMN IN-CLUDES clause), and although it can only be included in *one* other machine,

**Fig. 8.** Resolution of an Abstract Machine Commit ③

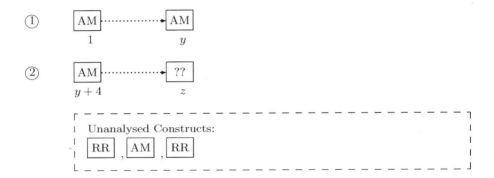

**Fig. 9.** Resolution of an Abstract Machine Commit ④

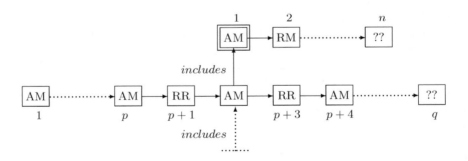

**Fig. 10.** Cross Machine Development Dependencies

that machine may itself be included in another ... and so on indefinitely. Fig. 10 shows a typical scenario.

The inclusion dependencies must be resolved before the refinement or retrenchment dependencies. The machine including the one at issue is located; then the one including that one, and so on until the end of the chain. All of these machines must become unanalysed. The last one has its refinement and retrenchment dependencies resolved according the rules above. Then its prede-

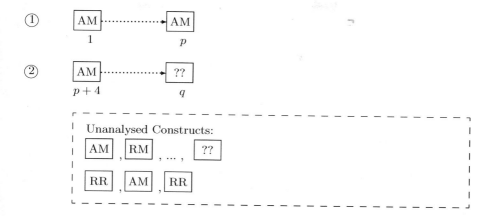

**Fig. 11.** Resolution of Inclusion Relationship

cessor, and so on until the original machine is unanalysed. For example, committing a change in the indicated machine in Fig. 10 would result in the state shown in Fig. 11.

Importation dependencies are handled in a way similar to this, the only difference being that an abstract machine may be imported by many different implementation machines.

Once the dependencies of a putative commit of a construct are resolved, the new definition of the construct is parsed. If it fails to parse, the changes remain uncommitted and of course any constructs set to unanalysed during dependency resolution remain unanalysed.

**Analysis.** The analysis phase consists of three stages: Normalisation, Syntax Checking and Type Checking. The aim is to ensure that the user's definition conforms to the rules of the B-Method, and to produce an internal representation of it.

Normalisation begins with a parse check of the user's construct. It should be noted that this parse check is different to the one in the commit phase, and can uncover different errors. The commit phase parse check simply determines whether the user's definition can be parsed by the B-Platform, and confirms that all keywords and operators have been used correctly. The parse check of the analyse phase determines whether the user's definition satisfies the restrictions encoded in the toolkit binaries.

It was necessary therefore, to create rules for the parsing of a retrenchment construct in the toolkit binaries, and to ensure that retrenchment keywords were not used in other constructs (and vice versa). For example, declaring a FROM clause in an implementation machine would cause an error as would using a VARIABLES clause in a retrenchment. Since the construct manager relies on the file extension of a construct to determine its type, checks were introduced to ensure that a .rmt extension corresponded to a retrenchment construct.

It was also necessary to introduce an acyclicity check into the normalisation stage. In principle, two machines can be retrenchments of each other. And while it is theoretically desirable to permit this and other pathologies, the resulting breaking of the linear development structure would have required a drastic re-design of the B-Toolkit due to its extensive internal dependence on linearity, so it was excluded.

After normalisation, a construct progresses to what the B-Toolkit calls syntax checking. In this stage, the B-Toolkit checks that the contents of each clause conform to the expected syntax. For example, each identifier is checked to ensure that its length is between two and sixty characters. Checks are also performed to ensure that the rules governing clause-use have been followed. For example, it is forbidden to have a CONSTANTS clause without a PROPERTIES clause.

Little of the latter is needed for retrenchments. The only clause in which new variables can be declared is the LVAR clause, and the identifiers of these variables must be checked in the same way as any other new identifier. If an LVAR clause is used however, it must have an associated WITHIN clause (so that the variables declared can be given some before-values and types). All the clauses consisting of predicates can be assumed to be well-formed (as they would not otherwise have passed the commit phase parse), but it is still necessary to check these clauses to ensure that typing errors have not occurred.

Once the basic checks described above have been performed, the list of constants, sets and variables of each construct is examined for duplication. When checking a machine, the B-Toolkit will fail with any duplication in any of these clauses. As a retrenchment construct inherits these lists from its source and target machines however, there is some scope for valid duplication. For example, both source and target abstract machine may see a common library machine which defines a constant used by both machines. Since seen constants are contained within the internal definition of the CONSTANTS clause, the retrenchment relationship will have two instances of this constant in its own list of constants. However, it is clear that this is not an error but a consequence of the difference in modelling machines and relationships. When examining the lists of sets and constants for a retrenchment construct therefore, the B-Toolkit will produce a warning when finding duplicate declarations. Any errors (where a constant has the same identifier, but different properties) will be caught in the type checking stage of the analysis. Duplications in the list of variables, however, will produce errors as it is necessary to be able to distinguish the variables of the source machine from those of the target.

For refinement and implementation machines, the B-Toolkit checks that the set of operation names matches that of their abstraction. For retrenchments, this is relaxed to an inclusion of source operation names in those of the target, requiring a slightly different check.

Having survived thus far, a construct passes to the type checking stage. For a retrenchment construct, the constants, sets, properties and variables clauses are derived from its source and target machines. The combined lists of sets and constants are each type checked against the combined properties clause, and it is at this stage that problems due to the duplication of constant or set identifiers can be uncovered. For example, if abstract machine $aa$ defines a constant $const$ with the property $const \in \mathbb{N}$, and abstract machine $bb$ also defines a constant $const$, but with the property $const \in \mathbb{N}1$, then an attempt to relate the two abstract machines via a retrenchment will cause type checking errors in the retrenchment as the constant cannot have both type $\mathbb{N}$ and $\mathbb{N}1$. Clearly, this type checking cannot guarantee that duplicate constants or sets are valid when their types do not disagree. For whilst two constants may have the same type, it is possible that they can have different values. Within the B-Toolkit's architecture there is no simple way to check that this is not the case. It was decided that the warnings given in the syntactic check and during type checking were sufficient for the purposes of this experiment, and it is left to the user to spot any erroneous duplication when attempting to prove their retrenchment relationship correct. Although this is not ideal, the framework of the B-Toolkit was designed for use with refinement, and a drastic reworking would have been needed to provide the complete checking required in this instance.[5]

The type checking stage results in the production of a file, stored in the TYP sub-directory of a development, that stores the type information for the variables and operations of an analysed construct. When type checking a retrenchment, the B-Toolkit uses the type files of source and target machines to ensure that all the variables used in the RETRIEVES clause have been defined (and typed) in the machines involved.

Likewise, for every operation, the ramifications are checked to ensure that the variables used, conform to the typing of that operation's inputs and outputs in source and target machines (any duplication of inputs and outputs between source and target machine will again cause errors). It is also necessary to check that the type of any logical variables declared in an LVAR clause can be derived from the associated WITHIN clause.

Once type checking is complete, the only task remaining is to add the analysed object to a machine development. For the existing constructs, this happens just as before. For retrenchment constructs, the only thing that needs to happen is to join up the development chains of the source and target machines. For example, Fig. 12 shows the state just before, and Fig. 13 shows the state just after, the moment when source machine $AM_x$ and target machine $AM_y$ get related via a retrenchment construct.

**Generation of Proof Obligations.** Once a construct has been analysed, proof obligations can be generated (since being in the analysed state is the only prerequisite for PO generation for any construct). The discharge of the POs will prove that the construct's definition is consistent. Of course, subsequent change to a construct discards any previously established proofs regarding it.

---

[5] The arguably preferable option of generating proof obligations to settle such unresolved issues was not pursued.

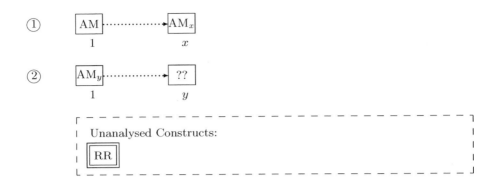

**Fig. 12.** Machine Developments Before Analysis of a Retrenchment Construct

**Fig. 13.** Resolution of Retrenchment Construct Analysis

In generating the POs for a retrenchment from a source to a target, there are three sets of obligations to create. Two sets concern the internal consistency of the source and target machines themselves, and the third concerns the validity of the claimed retrenchment relationship between them. Each of these PO generation activities is tied to the requisite syntactic construct; this must be in the analysed state as noted previously. For the retrenchment relationship, obviously all three participating constructs must be analysed.

The first stage in PO generation for a retrenchment construct is the creation of the initialisation PO. This is a simple task, and the form of the obligations depends only upon the presence of a RETRIEVES clause in the retrenchment construct. The second stage involves the generation of a PO for each ramified operation. The precise form of these proof obligations depends on which of the available clauses (see Table. 1) have been used in the ramifications for the operation.

Once the proof obligations have been generated, the GSL definitions of the initialisation and operations are used to replace the jokers within these obligations. The B-Toolkit then applies its special and implicit tactics to reduce these obligations to a number of predicates. Typically the substitution tactic will be used to reduce the proof obligation to a predicate, and then the deduction and conjunction tactics are used to break the PO into smaller chunks. These putative lemmas are then written to a file which contains all the obligations that must be discharged to validate the associated construct.

# 4    Evaluation

The development of the extended B-Toolkit described above involved the usual levels of functional and unit testing, which revealed that the basic ingredients were working satisfactorily. More extensive testing came via two case studies, one small the other larger.

The small case study was the little example that we saw in Section 2, involving machines $abc$ and $def$, and the retrenchment of the addition of unbounded numbers to the addition of finite numbers. The small size of this example meant that the extended toolkit dealt with all aspects of it unproblematically.

The larger case study was based on a case study focused on requirements engineering via retrenchment in the area of telecoms feature interaction [8]. Although, compared to the normal scale of things in real applications this was very much still a toy, as regards exercising the extended B-Toolkit it proved to be very much not a toy.

The case study centred on the operations of an atomic call model, with the inclusion or not of various additional features. Here is the most basic connect operation:

$$calls \text{ -}(i, connect_n, o)\text{-> } calls' \quad \texttt{iff}$$
$$free(n) \ \wedge$$
$$\texttt{if} \quad free(i) \ \wedge \ (n \neq i)$$
$$\texttt{then} \quad o = OK \ \wedge \ calls' = calls \cup \{n \mapsto i\}$$
$$\texttt{else} \quad o = NO \ \wedge \ calls' = calls$$

As is clear, this was written in a transition system notation, and its size is hardly enormous by today's standards (enhanced versions of the $connect_n$ operation typically had an additional clause).

A typical concedes relation from one of the retrenchments in [8] is reproduced below:

$$C_{CF,connect_n}(u, v, o, p; i, j, u, v) =$$
$$(busy(j) \ \wedge \ j \in dom(fortab) \ \wedge$$
$$fortab^+(j) = z \ \wedge \ free(z) \ \wedge \ z \neq n \ \wedge$$
$$u' = u \ \wedge \ v' = (calls \cup \{n \mapsto z\}, fortab) \ \wedge$$
$$o = NO \ \wedge \ p = OK)$$

(This concession captures the difference in behaviour between the connect operation in a simple system and in an enhance system incorporating call forwarding, with the forwarding data held in the $fortab$ function.) Again the size is hardly excessive, and there are a number of slightly more complicated models and more complicated retrenchments in [8].

For processing by the extended B-Toolkit, the above were hand translated into B syntax. After translation, and using the resources of a typical desktop machine, proving even the simplest of these retrenchments correct, turned out to be all but beyond the capabilities of the system. Upon closer investigation, the reason revealed itself to be that the B-Toolkit's prover took a rather naive approach to proving statements making heavy use of disjunctions (as retrenchment proof obligations invariably do). With a little bespoke optimisation, the toolkit was eventually persuaded to discharge the POs for the simplest of the retrenchments in [8] involving the concession above. When the more complex cases in [8] were attempted, it became clear that available machine resources were decidedly insufficient and the fully mechanised route was not pursued. Visual inspection confirmed however, that although it was unable to prove them, the toolkit had generated appropriate proof obligations, and that these were in fact true statements. A more extensive treatment of this case study can be found in [12] and is supported by [13].

## 5    Conclusions

In the preceding sections we described the essential tasks addressed in incorporating retrenchment into the B-Toolkit. We gave the syntax of the retrenchment construct and the proof obligation that that syntax represented, and then described how the data was processed within the toolkit's architecture. The latter details revealed that various aspects of the B-Toolkit's internal design were very heavily tied to its original objective of monolithic refinement, this being a result of the underlying B-Method philosophy that a refinement machine is really a kind of extension of its abstraction, rather than an independent entity. The consequences of this were principally that the development structure was restricted to linear as regards retrenchment/refinement dependencies. Moreover the feasibility of proving nontrivial retrenchments correct on today's typical desktop machines turned out to be heavily compromised by the relatively unsophisticated nature of some aspects of the B-Toolkit's prover.

Thus retrenchment was incorporated in a limited way, and it rapidly became clear that any attempt to extend this limited integration would yield very much diminishing returns. For this reason the implementation here described should be viewed principally as an experiment in the design of mechnical assistance for retrenchment, rather than an ideal solution. The experience gained quickly convinced us that addressing the full array of possibilities opened up by retrenchment would be much better served by a tool built from scratch. Such a tool is the objective of the second author's current doctoral work, for which the present experiment (described at greater length in [12]) provides valuable experience of course.

## References

[1] J.R. Abrial. *The B-Tool Reference Manual, Version 1.1.* B-Core (UK) Ltd.
[2] J.R. Abrial. *The B Book.* Cambridge University Press, 1996.
[3] R. Banach and R. Cross. Safety requirements and fault trees using retrenchment. In Heisel, Liggesmeyer, and Wittmann, editors, *Proc. SAFECOMP-04*, volume 3219 of *Lecture Notes In Computer Science*, pages 210–223. Springer, 2004.
[4] R. Banach and C. Jeske. Output retrenchments, defaults, stronger compositions, feature engineering. *Submitted*, 2002.
[5] R. Banach and M. Poppleton. Retrenchment: An engineering variation on refinement. *Lecture Notes In Computer Science*, 1393:129–147, 1998.

[6] R. Banach and M. Poppleton. Sharp retrenchment, modulated refinement and simulation. *Formal Aspects of Computer Science,* 11(5):498–540, 1999.

[7] R. Banach and M. Poppleton. Engineering and theoretical underpinnings of retrenchment. *Submitted,* 2001.

[8] R. Banach and M. Poppleton. Retrenching partial requirements into system definitions: A simple feature interaction case study. *Req. Eng. Journal,* 8:266–288, 2002.

[9] P. Behm, P. Desforges, and J-M. Meynadier. Meteor: An industrial success in formal development. In Bert, editor, *Proc. B-98,* volume 1393 of *Lecture Notes In Computer Science,* page 26. Springer, 1998.

[10] P. Desforges. Using the b-method to design safety-critical software for railway systems. *Recherche et Developpements - Fatis Marquant 97,* 1998.

[11] D. Essame. Handling safety critical requirements in system engineering using the b formal method. In Heisel, Liggesmeyer, and Wittmann, editors, *Proc. SAFECOMP-04,* volume 3219 of *Lecture Notes In Computer Science,* page 115. Springer, 2004.

[12] S. Fraser. *Mechanised Support for Retrenchment in the B-Toolkit,* 2004. Master's thesis, School of Computer Science, University of Manchester.

[13] S. Fraser. *Specifications, Proof Obligations and Proofs Supporting a Case Study of Retrenchment in the B-Toolkit,* 2004. Available online at http://www.cs.man.ac.uk/~frasers/casestudy.

[14] Haughton H. Lano, K. *Specification in B: An Introduction Using the B-Toolkit.* Imperial College Press, 1996.

[15] M. Poppleton and R. Banach. Retrenchment: Extending the reach of refinement. In *Proc. ASE-99,* IEEE, pages 158–165, 1999.

[16] M. Poppleton and R. Banach. Controlling control systems: An application of evolving retrenchment. In Bert, Bowen, Henson, and Robinson, editors, *Proc. ZB-02,* volume 2272 of *Lecture Notes In Computer Science,* pages 42–61. Springer, 2002.

[17] S. Schneider. *The B-Method: An Introduction.* Palgrave, 2001.

[18] E Sekerinski and K. Sere, editors. *Program Development by Refinement.* Springer, 1999.

[19] J.B. Wordsworth. *Software Engineering with B.* Addison-Wesley, 1996.

# Refinement and Reachability in Event_B

Jean-Raymond Abrial[1], Dominique Cansell[2], and Dominique Méry[3]

[1] ETHZ Zurich, Switzerland
jabrial@inf.ethz.ch
[2] LORIA, Université de Metz France
[3] LORIA, Université Henri Poincaré Nancy 1 France
{Dominique.Cansell, Dominique.Mery}@loria.fr

**Abstract.** Since the early 90's (after the seminal article of R. Back [4]), the refinement of stuttering steps [5] are performed by means of new actions (called here events) refining skip. It is shown in this article that such a refinement method is not always possible in the development of large systems. We shall instead use events refining some kind of non-deterministic actions maintaining the invariant (sometimes called keep). We show that such new refinements are completely safe. In a second part, we explain how such a mechanism can be used to express some reachability conditions that were otherwise expressed using some special temporal logic statements à la TLA [5] in a previous article [2]. Examples will be used to illustrate our proposals.

**Keywords:** Refinement, Stuttering, Reachability, B Method.

## 1 Introduction

In this article[1], we are addressing three problems, which occur in Event-B developments. The first one (section 2) deals with the proof rules concerning the introduction of new events in a refinement. The second one (section 3) is rather simple: it deals with the introduction of a new form of development step, which is different from refinement, it is a merging step. The third problem (section 4) deals with a simplification of the temporal logic statement that was proposed some years ago in [2]. Problems 1 and 3 will be illustrated by two examples (section 2.5 and sections 4.1 to 4.8).

## 2 First Problem: About New Events in a Refinement

Before explaining the nature of this first problem and the proposed solutions (sections 2.4 to 2.6), let us give a number of brief reminders on Event-B. These reminders deal with events (section 2.1), refinements (section 2.2) , and the special case of refinement consisting of introducing new events (section 2.3).

---

[1] This work has been partly supported by IST FP6 Rigorous Open Development Environment for Complex Systems (RODIN, IST-511599) Project.

H. Treharne et al. (Eds.): ZB 2005, LNCS 3455, pp. 222–241, 2005.

## 2.1    Reminder 1: Event Shape

**Events.** A *formal model* is made of a state defined by some variables $v$ and invariant $I(v)$. It is also made of various transitions (called actions or events). An event bears a unique name and it has the following form:

$$\textbf{when} \ \ G(v) \ \ \textbf{then} \ \ S(v) \ \ \textbf{end}$$

where $S(v)$ is a *generalized substitution* (next paragraph) defining the transition associated with the event, and where $G(v)$ denotes a conjoined list of predicates defining the guard of the event (we remind the reader that the guard of an event is the necessary condition for the event to occur). They are both parameterized by the variables $v$.

**Generalized Substitutions and Before-After Predicates.** We have three kinds of generalized substitutions: the deterministic multiple substitution, the empty substitution (skip), and the non-determinitistic multiple substitution.

The before-after predicate is supposed to denote the relationship holding between the state variables of the model just before (denoted by $v$) and just after (denoted by $v'$) "applying" a substitution. The before-after predicate is defined as follows for the three kinds of generalized substitutions:

| Generalized Substitution | Before-after Predicate |
|---|---|
| $v := E(v)$ | $v' = E(v)$ |
| skip | $v' = v$ |
| **any** $x$ **where** $P(x,v)$ **then** $v := F(x,v)$ **end** | $\exists x \cdot ( P(x,v) \wedge v' = F(x,v) )$ |

**Invariant Preservation.** Given a model with variables $v$, invariant $I(v)$ and an event with guard $G(v)$ and before-after predicate $R(v,v')$, the statement to prove in order to guarantee invariant preservation is the following:

$$I(v) \ \wedge \ G(v) \ \wedge \ R(v,v') \ \Rightarrow \ I(v') \quad \text{INV1}$$

## 2.2    Reminder 2: Event Refinement

So far, we have seen that a model was made of a number of state variables $v$, invariants $I(v)$ and finally some events. From a given model $M$, a new model $N$ can be built and asserted to be a refinement of $M$. Model $M$ will be said to be an *abstraction* of $N$ and model $N$ will be said to be a *refinement* of $M$ or a *concrete version* of it.

The concrete model $N$ has a collection of state variables $w$, which must be *completely distinct* (in first approximation) from the collection $v$ of variables in the abstraction. Model $N$ also has an invariant dealing with these variables $w$. But contrarily to the previous case where the invariant of $M$ exclusively depended on the local variables of this model, this time it is possible to have the invariant of $N$ also depending on the variables $v$ of its abstraction $M$. This is the reason why we collectively name this invariant of $N$ the *gluing invariant* $J(v, w)$: it "glues" the state of the concrete model $N$ to that of its abstraction $M$.

The new model $N$ has a number of events. For the moment, each event in the concrete model $N$ is supposed to refine a certain event in its abstraction $M$. Suppose we have an abstract event with guard $G(v)$ and before-after predicate $R(v, v')$ and a corresponding concrete event with guard $H(w)$ and before-after predicate $S(w, w')$. The latter is said to *refine* the former when the following holds:

$$I(v) \wedge J(v, w) \wedge H(w) \wedge S(w, w') \Rightarrow G(v) \wedge \exists v' \cdot (\, R(v, v') \wedge J(v', w') \,) \;\; \mathsf{REF1}$$

### 2.3    Reminder 3: Creation of New Events in a Refinement

**Constraints on a Simple Case.** Let us present a simple case to introduce the matter. We shall then generalize it.

Suppose we have an abstract model $M$ which only contains a single very primitive event $\mathsf{E}$, whose "execution" makes its own guard false. In other words, model $M$ immediately deadlocks after "executing" $\mathsf{E}$ only once. Now, event $\mathsf{E}$ might be realized, in a more concrete model $N$, by means of a collection of more elementary events $\mathsf{F_1}, \ldots, \mathsf{F_n}, \mathsf{F}$, where the $\mathsf{F_i}$s are *new events* which have no counterparts in the abstract model, while $\mathsf{F}$ is supposed to be a refinement of the more abstract event $\mathsf{E}$[2].

As an example, event $\mathsf{E}$ might be one yielding in one shot the maximum of a certain finite set $S$ of numbers, whereas event $\mathsf{F_1}$ might be computing the relative maximum of a subset $T$ of $S$ ($T$ being obtained by adding an element of $S \setminus T$ to its previous value). In that case, event $\mathsf{F}$ (the refinement of $\mathsf{E}$) just does nothing when $T$ is equal to $S$.

It is clear that the refinement we have just presented with events $\mathsf{F_i}$ and $\mathsf{F}$ is slightly different from a classical refinement as described in previous section. It contains three constraints, which are the following:

1. Each new event $\mathsf{F_i}$ should refine an implicit dummy event which does nothing (skip). This is so, precisely because event $\mathsf{F_i}$ is not part of the abstraction. Notice that this proposal of refining stuttering steps [5] by actions refining skip had first been proposed by R. Back in the early nineties in [4].

2. The new events should not together diverge (run for ever) since then the refinement could not be considered valid: remember, the abstraction immediately deadlocks after the "execution" of the single event $\mathsf{E}$ so that the refined model must also eventually deadlock after some finite elementary executions of the concrete events. More precisely, the refined model "execution" should be as follows: a *finite* (including zero) number of executions of events $\mathsf{F_i}$ (after this, no more $\mathsf{F_i}$ should be enabled), followed by a single executions of $\mathsf{F}$, possibly followed by a finite (in-

---

[2] Of course, the resulting model $N$ can be further refined in another model $P$ with each event $\mathsf{F_i}$ being now itself realized by means of a collection of more elementary *new events* $\mathsf{G_{ij}}$ and refined event $\mathsf{G_i}$, which is supposed to be a refinement of the more abstract event $\mathsf{F_i}$, and so on.

cluding zero) execution of events $F_i$ (again after this, no more $F_i$ should be enabled), finally followed by deadlock.

3. We have just seen that the refined model must eventually deadlock, but *it should not deadlock too early*. This means that it can only deadlock after the "execution" of event $F$. More precisely, *the concrete model should not deadlock before its abstraction*, otherwise the concrete model might not have achieved what the abstract model had previously required.

**Generalization.** The simple situation we have just described can now be generalized to more complicated cases. A first simple extension is one where we have several events like $E$ but still with a deadlock when each of them has been executed exactly once. The same constraints 1, 2, and 3 must clearly apply.

A more interesting generalization is one where we have no deadlock at the abstract level. In other words, the abstract model is supposed to run for ever. Constraint 1 above has no reason to be changed. Likewise, constraint 3 should not be changed either. Since the abstract model does not deadlock (this is part of its specification), it would certainly be an error for the concrete one to deadlock. Maintaining constraint 2 is more questionable however. Since the abstraction does not deadlock, a concrete version that run for ever (diverges) would seem to be correct. The problem is that the abstract model was able to execute, say, event $E$, which was thus an *achievable goal* that the model had to fulfill (it is part of the specification). As a consequence, it might then be incorrect to have (the refinement of) event $E$ being never executed (because the refined model diverge). We shall therefore also suppose that constraint 2 must be followed.

A final generalization is one where the abstract model might sometimes deadlock but not always: in certain circumstances it can run for ever. This mixed situation should also follow the three constraints above. When the refinement deadlocks then the abstraction must have deadlocked too (constraint 3). And the new events must not diverge (constraint 2). The justifications are exactly the same as in the previous case.

**Formalizing the Constraints.** We now formalize the three constraints we have just studied. Suppose we have an abstract model $M$ with variables $v$ and invariant $I(v)$. This model is refined to a more concrete model $N$ with variables $w$ and gluing invariant $J(v, w)$. In refined model $N$, we supposedly have a new event with guard $H(w)$ and before-after predicate $S(w, w')$. Constraint 1 (refining skip) leads to the following Law:

$$I(v) \ \wedge \ J(v, w) \ \wedge \ H(w) \ \wedge \ S(w, w') \ \Rightarrow \ J(v, w') \quad \text{REF2}$$

In order to prove that the new events do not diverge (constraint 2), it is necessary to exhibit a variant $V(w)$ (which, in first approximation, could be a natural number). And it is then necessary to prove that each new event decreases that variant. Here is the corresponding Law to be proved:

$$I(v) \ \wedge \ J(v, w) \ \wedge \ H(w) \ \wedge \ S(w, w') \ \Rightarrow \ V(w) \in \mathbb{N} \ \wedge \ V(w') < V(w) \quad \text{REF3}$$

Finally, constraint 3 about the relative deadlock freeness of the refined model with regards to the abstract one, can be formalized as follows:

$$I(v) \ \wedge \ J(v,w) \ \wedge \ \neg\,(\,H_1(w) \vee \cdots \vee H_m(w)\,) \ \Rightarrow \ \neg\,(\,G_1(v) \vee \cdots \vee G_n(v)\,)$$

Here the $G_i$s denote the abstract guards whereas the $H_i$s denote the concrete ones. The predicate $\neg\,(H_1(w) \vee \cdots \vee H_m(w))$ denotes the condition for the concrete model to deadlock (all concrete guards are false), whereas the predicate $\neg\,(G_1(v) \vee \cdots \vee G_n(v))$ denotes the condition for the abstract model to deadlock (all abstract guards are false). So that the law says that if the concrete model deadlocks then the abstract one does also (perhaps even before the concrete one, but never after). By contraposition, we obtain the following $n$ more tractable laws:

$$I(v) \ \wedge \ J(v,w) \ \wedge \ G_i(v) \ \Rightarrow \ H_1(w) \vee \cdots \vee H_m(w) \qquad \text{REF4}$$

### 2.4    Problem Raised by New Events Refining skip

**Coupling New Events with New Variables.** One of the main difficulties in developing event models is to find the *right order* in which to introduce details (by refinement) which represent some extensions in the problem analysis. When doing such a refinement, we might have two kinds of extensions: that of the state and that of the events. These extensions are clearly coupled. When extending the state with new variables (*superposition*), we might have to extend the events accordingly by adding new events which modify these variables. There is a strong coupling between the two because each new event must refine skip as we have seen in the previous section.

Suppose we introduce a new variable $v$ in a refinement $M$. We clearly cannot introduce in a subsequent refinement $N$ another *new* event, say E, which modifies $v$ and, at the same time, refines skip since it modifies a variable, which was already there in the abstraction. In other words, all events modifying variable $v$ must be introduced together with $v$.

The problem is that in large model development such a coupling is very difficult to achieve. Such cases happen quite frequently. For example, suppose we develop the model of a piece of software which controls a rotating device. At some stage, we might introduce a variable $m$ representing the state of a motor: working or stopped. And we define some new events controlling this variables: start_motor, stop_motor. Such events (and probably others) decrease a certain variant $V$. In a further refinement, we might be interested in the safety analysis of this system. This means that under certain emergency conditions we have to stop the motor. This situation can be handled by an event called emergency_stop, which certainly modifies variable $m$. Other emergency events might be introduced at this level, they all decrease a certain variant $W$. Because each new event must refine skip, then the emergency_stop event has to be introduced together with variable $m$ and events start_motor, stop_motor. This means that the safety analysis cannot be undertaken afterwards. It also probably means that some variables dealing with safety have also to be introduced earlier. So that, we sometimes end up in a situation where it is just impossible to gradually refine our analysis: we have to introduce every detail of the system at once.

**Coupling New Events with their Variant.** There is, in fact, another kind of coupling we might consider: that of new events with their corresponding variant. Remember from the last section that all new events introduced in a refinement must decrease a certain unique variant. It sometimes happen that a simple variant (say a natural number expression) is not feasible: one must exhibit a lexicographical variant. In other words, a certain group of new events all introduced at a certain refinement stage and collectively called GE, together decrease a certain quantity $V$, while another group of new events introduced at the same refinement stage and collectively called GF, keeps $V$ unchanged but decreases another quantity $W$.

When a situation like that occurs, this indicates that the development is probably not adequate: it might be better to introduce events GE in a certain refinement and events GF later in another subsequent refinement. But again, this is impossible because new events must refine skip.

Coming back to our previous example, it is probably the case that the variant associated with events start_motor and stop_motor is different from that associated with event emergency_stop as well as others events dealing with emergency conditions. That second variant might depend on variables dealing with emergency, while the first variant might depend on variables dealing with the main function of the system. The situation seems thus to be completely blocked.

## 2.5    The Solution

The idea of the solutions we present now is to have the new events *strongly coupled with their variant rather than with their variables*, so that no lexicographical variant will ever be needed in a refinement. In fact the lexicographical structure will be *implicit in the embedding of the refinement*. In order to explain the solution and have it coherent with the proof rules of previous section, we shall present two solutions in sequence. First a heavy (but fully correct) solution, and then a simpler one, from which the heavier one could always be mechanically reconstructed.

**A Heavy Solution.** The first solution we propose is one where we continue to have all new events refining skip. This solution, as we shall see, is rather heavy but it can always be used. The simpler solution we shall propose afterwards will be a kind of shorthand to the present solution.

Suppose we introduce a new variable $v$ and some new events at some refinement stage $M$. All such events refine skip. They can be divided into two groups: GE and GF. The new events of group GE all decrease a certain variant $V(v)$, which is defined on the newly defined variables and maybe on some other variables. The event of group GE are called the *genuine new events* of refinement $M$.

We have almost no information for the moment about the second group GF of new events. The only thing we know are the following two facts: (1) they all modify variable $v$ in a certain way which we do not know for the moment (it is thus non-deterministic at this stage), and (2) they keep the variant $V(v)$ unchanged. We call the events of groups GF the *anticipating new events* of refinement $M$.

In order, however, to be certain that *all new events* introduced in refinement $M$ indeed decrease a certain variant (this is a requirement from previous section), we have to introduce another (dummy) variable, say $d$, with the following constraints: (1) $d$ is a Natural Number, (2) $d$ is decreased (non-deterministically) by the events of group GF,

(3) $d$ might be modified (non-deterministically) by events of group GE. As a consequence, the global variant of refinement $M$ is the lexicographical variant: $<V(v), d>$

At some subsequent refinement stage $N$, a new variable $w$ is introduced. This is also the place where we are able to give full definitions to the previous events of groups GF. This is the case simply because we now have all the needed variables at our disposal. In order to simplify the presentation, we suppose that all new events introduced at this stage decrease a certain variant $W(w, v)$. And we suppose that the events refining the events of group GF also decrease that variant $W(w, v)$. We can thus now remove the (dummy) variable $d$ introduced in refinement $M$. In order to prove the refinement of the events in GF we have to introduce the gluing invariant $d = W(w, v)$. The anticipating events of group GF are now genuine events of refinement $N$ although they were introduced earlier (simply because they were modifying variable $v$).

The solution we have presented here although already complicated could have been made more complicated by having the events of group GF becoming genuine events in different refinement steps not just in one ($N$ here). And the situation described in refinement $N$ could have been made more complicated by having genuine new events and also other anticipating new events too.

**A Simpler Solution.** What makes the previous solution heavy concerns essentially the variable $d$, that is: (1) the introduction of $d$ in refinement step $M$, (2) the lexicographical variant $<V(v), d>$ in refinement step $M$, (3) the non-deterministic decreasing of $d$ by events of group GF, (4) the non-deterministic modification of $d$ by events of group GE, and (5) the removal of $d$ in refinement step $N$ by means of the gluing invariant $d = W(w, v)$. All this can be removed since it can be mechanically reconstructed. As a consequence, we shall never introduce such dummy variables like $d$ in this simpler solution.

But we keep the idea of the two groups of new events in a refinement like $M$: the group GE of genuine new events (with variants $V(v)$) and the group GF of anticipating events, which will be further refined to become genuine events in some refinement stage $N$. Notice that GF might be empty.

We shall proceed as follows. Whe developing refinement step $M$ (where variable $v$ is introduced), we introduce the genuine new event group GE. And we ignore for the moment the group GF simply because we have no idea at this stage of which events it may contain. When reaching subsequent refinement step $N$, we figure out that there are a number of "new" events GF which, with other genuine events of this refinement, decrease the variant $W(w, v)$, but which also modify variable $v$ introduced in refinement $M$.

We then modify refinement $M$ by introducing events of GF in $M$ as anticipating events. The constraints on these anticipating events in $M$ are simple: (1) they refine skip, (2) they modify non-deterministically the variable $v$, and (3) they do not modify the variant $V(v)$. All this can be defined in a simple manner in these events. In between refinements $M$ and $N$ exclusively, the refinements of these events pertaining to group GF should not modify the local variant if any. Most of the time these events remain unchanged between $M$ and $N$ exclusively. In section 4 we shall develop an example showing an illustration of this solution.

## 2.6    A Special Case

An interesting (and frequently encountered) special case is one where refinement stage $M$ is the first model of a formal development (it is not a refinement thus). In that case, the constraints on anticipating events of group GF are simpler than in the more general case since there is no variant $V(v)$. The only constraint on these events is that they maintain the local invariant. Later in refinement step $N$ (quite frequently the refinement step following $M$), the events of GF are refined and prove to decrease a local variant $W(w, v)$ built on the new variable $w$ introduced at this stage. Let us illustrate now this special case on an example.

**Initial Model.** Consider the following abstraction defining the sorting of a Natural Number array $f$ with $n$ distinct elements[3] :

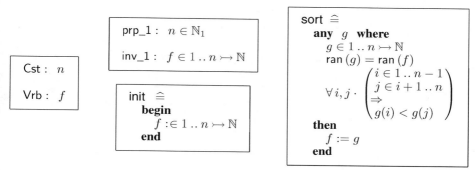

**First Refinement.** In the next refinement step, we introduce a new variable $k$ and a new event progress. Invariant inv_3 expresses that the array is sorted between indices 1 and $k - 1$ and that all members of the array situated between indices 1 and $k - 1$ are smaller than those situated between indices $k$ and $n$.

Cst : $n$

Vrb : $f, k$

$$\text{inv\_2}: \ k \in 1 .. n$$

$$\text{inv\_3}: \ \forall i, j \cdot \begin{pmatrix} i \in 1 .. k - 1 \\ j \in i + 1 .. n \\ \Rightarrow \\ f(i) < f(j) \end{pmatrix}$$

init $\ \widehat{=}$
  **begin**
    $f :\in 1 .. n \rightarrowtail \mathbb{N}$
    $k := 1$
  **end**

sort $\ \widehat{=}$
  **when**
    $k = n$
  **then**
    skip
  **end**

progress_1 $\ \widehat{=}$
  **any** $l$ **where**
    $k < n$
    $l \in k .. n$
    $f(l) = \min(f[k .. n])$
  **then**
    $f := f \lhd\mkern-14mu- \{k \mapsto f(l)\} \lhd\mkern-14mu- \{l \mapsto f(k)\}$
    $k := k + 1$
  **end**

---

[3] In the following events, conjunction symbols, $\wedge$, are omitted at the end of each line in an any condition. Likewise, parallel symbols, $\|$, are omitted at the end of the substitution part.

In event progress_1, the two array elements situated at indices $k$ and $l$ are swapped. The array element situated at index $l$ is the minimum of the array elements situated between indices $k$ and $n$ (this sorting model is rather simplistic!). As can be seen, event progress_1 modifies $f$ hence it cannot refine skip. It has thus to be introduced in the initial model as an anticipating event which simply maintains invariant inv_1:

$$
\begin{aligned}
&\text{progress\_1} \ \widehat{=} \\
&\quad \textbf{any} \ \ g \ \ \textbf{where} \\
&\qquad g \in 1\,..\,n \rightarrowtail \mathbb{N} \\
&\quad \textbf{then} \\
&\qquad f := g \\
&\quad \textbf{end}
\end{aligned}
$$

**Second Refinement.** We now refine one step further. For this, we introduce two more variables $j$ and $l$ and two more events progress_2 and progress_3. This time the new events are genuine events since they indeed refine skip. So there is no need to introduce them in the previous refinement as anticipating events. These events are used to compute the minimum envisaged in the previous section.

$$
\begin{aligned}
&\text{Cst}: \ n \\
&\text{Vrb}: \ f, k, j, l
\end{aligned}
$$

$$
\begin{aligned}
&\text{inv\_4}: \ \ j \in k\,..\,n \\
&\text{inv\_5}: \ \ l \in k\,..\,j \\
&\text{inv\_6}: \ \ \forall i \cdot \left( \begin{array}{l} i \in k\,..\,j \\ \Rightarrow \\ f(l) \leq f(i) \end{array} \right)
\end{aligned}
$$

$$
\begin{aligned}
&\text{init} \ \ \widehat{=} \\
&\quad \textbf{begin} \\
&\qquad f :\in 1\,..\,n \rightarrowtail \mathbb{N} \\
&\qquad k, j, l := 1, 1, 1 \\
&\quad \textbf{end}
\end{aligned}
$$

$$
\begin{aligned}
&\text{sort} \ \widehat{=} \\
&\quad \textbf{when} \\
&\qquad k = n \\
&\quad \textbf{then} \\
&\qquad \text{skip} \\
&\quad \textbf{end}
\end{aligned}
$$

$$
\begin{aligned}
&\text{progress\_1} \ \widehat{=} \\
&\quad \textbf{when} \\
&\qquad k < n \\
&\qquad j = n \\
&\quad \textbf{then} \\
&\qquad f := f \lhd\mkern-14mu- \{k \mapsto f(l)\} \lhd\mkern-14mu- \{l \mapsto f(k)\} \\
&\qquad k, j, l := k+1, k+1, k+1 \\
&\quad \textbf{end}
\end{aligned}
$$

$$
\begin{aligned}
&\text{progress\_2} \ \widehat{=} \\
&\quad \textbf{when} \\
&\qquad k < n \\
&\qquad j < n \\
&\qquad f(l) \leq f(j+1) \\
&\quad \textbf{then} \\
&\qquad j := j+1 \\
&\quad \textbf{end}
\end{aligned}
$$

$$
\begin{aligned}
&\text{progress\_3} \ \widehat{=} \\
&\quad \textbf{when} \\
&\qquad k < n \\
&\qquad j < n \\
&\qquad f(l) > f(j+1) \\
&\quad \textbf{then} \\
&\qquad j := j+1 \\
&\qquad l := j+1 \\
&\quad \textbf{end}
\end{aligned}
$$

**Generating Code.** Using a technique similar to the one presented in [3], it is now possible to mechanically generate the following straightforward sorting program, sorting an injective Natural Number array $f$ of size $n$.

$$
\begin{array}{ll}
\boxed{\text{k,j,l} := 1,1,1} \; ; & \text{init} \\
\textbf{while}\;\; k < n \;\; \textbf{do} & \\
\quad \textbf{while}\;\; j < n \;\; \textbf{do} & \\
\quad\quad \textbf{if}\;\; f(l) \le f(j+1) \;\; \textbf{then} & \\
\quad\quad\quad \boxed{j := j+1} & \text{progress\_2} \\
\quad\quad \textbf{else} & \\
\quad\quad\quad \boxed{\text{j,l} := \text{j+1,j+1}} & \text{progress\_3} \\
\quad\quad \textbf{end} & \\
\quad \textbf{end}\; ; & \\
\quad \boxed{\begin{array}{l} f := f \mathbin{\lhd\mkern-10mu-} \{k \mapsto f(l)\} \mathbin{\lhd\mkern-10mu-} \{l \mapsto f(k)\}; \\ k,j,l := k+1, k+1, k+1 \end{array}} & \text{progress\_1} \\
\textbf{end} &
\end{array}
$$

## 3    Second Problem: Merging Step

This problem is relatively simple and it will receive a straightforward solution. When doing large development, we figure out that it is sometimes convenient to introduce between refinement steps some, so-called, *merging steps*. It occurs in the special case where two or more events in a model are very close to each others. Given a model with variables $v$ and two events of the following forms

$$
\begin{array}{l}
\text{Alpha} \;\widehat{=} \\
\quad \textbf{any}\;\; x \;\; \textbf{where} \\
\quad\quad P(v,x) \\
\quad\quad Q(v,x) \\
\quad \textbf{then} \\
\quad\quad S(v,x) \\
\quad \textbf{end}
\end{array}
\qquad
\begin{array}{l}
\text{Beta} \;\widehat{=} \\
\quad \textbf{any}\;\; x \;\; \textbf{where} \\
\quad\quad P(v,x) \\
\quad\quad R(v,x) \\
\quad \textbf{then} \\
\quad\quad S(v,x) \\
\quad \textbf{end}
\end{array}
$$

The merging of these two events results in a single event, which is the following:

$$
\begin{array}{l}
\text{Alpha\_Beta} \;\widehat{=} \\
\quad \textbf{any}\;\; x \;\; \textbf{where} \\
\quad\quad P(v,x) \\
\quad\quad Q(v,x) \lor R(v,x) \\
\quad \textbf{then} \\
\quad\quad S(v,x) \\
\quad \textbf{end}
\end{array}
$$

Quite often, $R(v,x)$ is just $\neg\, Q(v,x)$. It makes $Q(v,x) \lor R(v,x)$ disappear. We shall give such a merging example in section 4.6.

# 4   Third Problem: Reachability

In this section we investigate the possibility to avoid having special constructs in the Event-B formalism for expressing some temporal logic statements. Such constructs were defined in an article [2] published some years ago. We now reduce such statements to the simpler statement of *reachability*. It seems for us that it is the main dynamic property we want to express and prove. Such a property, as we shall explain in what follows, is just a generalization (to ever running program) of the total correctness property (termination) of sequential programs.

As we know, *partial correctness* for a sequential program is the property which states that the program delivers the expected outcome (post-condition) *provided* it terminates. Whereas *total correctness* is the property which states that the program terminates *and* delivers the expected outcome. A sequential program which is made of a loop can be verified to be partially correct by proving that the loop invariant and the negation of the loop guard implies the post-condition. But it is not totally correct unless the loop terminates. Telling that a loop program terminates is clearly not enough: we have to *prove* it. This is done by exhibiting a variant expression (usually a Natural Number), which is then proved to be decreased by the loop body.

We can view an ever running program as containing an infinite number of tasks, where each such task is in fact a sequential program. Thus total correctness first looks like the one we had for individual sequential programs. Each task must deliver the expected outcome (post-condition) and also terminate if supposed to run alone. In other words, each task should first be a totally correct sequential program.

But we have another dimension of total correctness in an ever running program whose tasks are individually totally correct. We want that there does not exist any task, which, once started, cannot terminate (although it could have terminated if run alone) because it is indefinitely postponed by other running tasks, which always take priority over it. In other words, what has been expressed and proved to be individually achievable should always be achievable in the presence of other tasks. This is what we call *reachability*. In other words, the termination of each task must be reachable.

In order to prove such a reachability, the idea we might investigate in what follows is to define the task we are interested in as performed in *one shot* in a first model: it then indeed terminates because it is done at once. Other tasks thus cannot indefinitely postpone it since a single event executes the task: it terminates immediately after being called. This initial model is now refined and new events are added. But we know from section 2.3 that new events cannot take control for ever (a variant is exhibited) so that the task which was performed in one shot in the abstraction might not be done in one shot any more, but it will anyway be guaranteed to be done after a "finite time".

The question we study now is whether this approach is satisfactory. For this we shall take the example that was studied in the original paper [2]

## 4.1   Clients and Service: Initial Model

We are given a set $C$ of clients, which is finite (prp_1). Each such clients can ask for a certain service. Client which have asked for the service but have not yet been serviced are waiting in the set $p$ (inv_1). Thus, requesting the service puts a client (which is not yet requesting the service) in the waiting set $p$ (event Request_any), while servicing a client which is waiting in the set $p$, simply removes it from this set (event Serve_any).

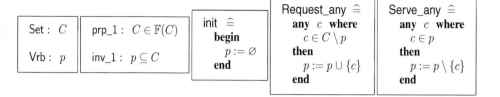

The property we would like to express is that no client can wait indefinitely in the waiting set $p$. In other words, every waiting client can eventually "reach" the service. At this stage we have no way to express this property.

### 4.2    Refinement: How to Express Non-starvation

The idea of this refinement is that each client is (magically) given a certain *unique* maximum non null waiting time $t$ when requesting the service. This means that the client is sure to wait no more than $t$ before being serviced (the "time" is a logical time expressed in terms of event execution). This is practically realized in this refinement by means of a partial injective function $w$ from $C$ to $\mathbb{N}_1$ (inv_2). The gluing invariant links the abstract variable $p$ to the domain of $w$ (inv_3). A client $c$ in the waiting set (in the domain of $w$) has thus to wait at most $w(c)$.

| Set : $C$ | inv_2 : $w \in C \rightarrowtail \mathbb{N}_1$ | init $\;\widehat{=}\;$ |
|---|---|---|
| Vrb : $w$ | inv_3 : $p = \mathrm{dom}\,(w)$ | **begin** $\quad w := \varnothing$ **end** |

The event Request_any is modified to be able to assign to a requesting client a certain waiting time which has not been given to any already waiting client. The event Serve_any chooses the client with the smallest waiting time and decreases all waiting times accordingly.

Request_any $\;\widehat{=}\;$
**any** $c, n$ **where**
$\quad c \in C \setminus \mathrm{dom}(w)$
$\quad n \in \mathbb{N}_1 \setminus \mathrm{ran}(w)$
**then**
$\quad w(c) := n$
**end**

Serve_any $\;\widehat{=}\;$
**any** $c$ **where**
$\quad c \in \mathrm{dom}(w)$
$\quad w(c) = \min(\mathrm{ran}(w))$
**then**
$\quad w := \{c\} \lhd (w\,;\,\mathrm{minus}(w(c)))$
**end**

At this stage we still have no way to *express and prove* that no client will wait indefinitely in the waiting set. In the mentioned paper [2] this was expressed by means of a special statement involving a proof obligation. What we would like to have is a way of expressing this reachability simply by means of the "standard" variant needed for new events as described in section 2.3.

### 4.3    Revisiting the Initial Model: Considering an Arbitrary Client $cl$

We then come back to our initial model and modify it. Since all clients are identical it suffices to do the proof for a single one that is chosen arbitrarily. This is close to what is done in classical logic when proving a predicate of the form $\forall x \cdot P(x)$: it is usually performed by simply proving $P(x)$ for an arbitrary $x$ (provided it is "fresh").

Here we choose a client $cl$ and split the Request and Serve events. The two events Request_cl and Serve_cl are dealing with client $cl$ exclusively. The two events Request_more and Serve_more are dealing with other clients, but only when $cl$ is not in the waiting set $p$. So that $cl$ is *immediately serviced* after being put into the set $p$.

---

Set :  $C$

Cst :  $cl$

Vrb :  $p$

---

prp_1 :  $cl \in C$

inv_1 :  $p \subseteq C$

---

init  $\widehat{=}$
**begin**
$\quad p := \varnothing$
**end**

---

Request_cl  $\widehat{=}$
**when**
$\quad cl \in C \setminus p$
**then**
$\quad p := p \cup \{cl\}$
**end**

---

Serve_cl  $\widehat{=}$
**when**
$\quad cl \in p$
**then**
$\quad p := p \setminus \{cl\}$
**end**

---

Request_more  $\widehat{=}$
**any**  $c$  **where**
$\quad c \in C \setminus (p \cup \{cl\})$
$\quad cl \notin p$
**then**
$\quad p := p \cup \{c\}$
**end**

---

Serve_more  $\widehat{=}$
**any**  $c$  **where**
$\quad c \in p$
$\quad cl \notin p$
**then**
$\quad p := p \setminus \{c\}$
**end**

---

The behavior of this model can be illustrated on the following diagram where the immediate service for client $cl$ can be seen (it can be formalized more carefully by showing that when $cl$ is in $p$, the only event that could be enabled is precisely Serve_cl).

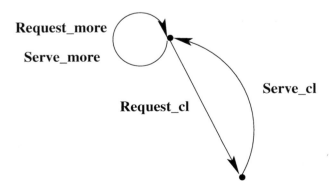

## 4.4     Refinement 1: Client *cl* Does Not Starve

We now revisit our previous refinement by implementing the set $p$ as before by means of a partial injective function $w$: the gluing invariant is exactly the same as above. We add a new event called Serve_others, which is supposed to serve clients that are waiting when $cl$ is also waiting. Note that this event is not genuinely new (it does not refine skip), it has thus to be an anticipating event in the previous model as indicated in section 2.5. We might illustrate the new situation with the following diagram, which could be considered a "refinement" of the previous one:

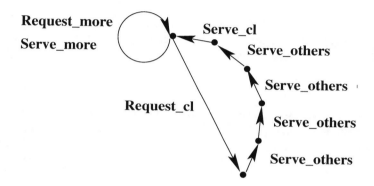

As you can see, the "old event" Serve_cl is not enabled immediately but only after a finite number of executions of event Serve_others. This is due to the presence of a variant that can be exhibited (namely $w(cl)$) and prove to be decreased by Serve_others.

---

Set :  $C$

Vrb :  $w$

---

inv_2 :  $w \in C \rightarrowtail \mathbb{N}_1$

inv_3 :  $p = \mathsf{dom}\,(w)$

vrt_1 :  $w(cl)$

---

init  $\widehat{=}$
**begin**
$w := \varnothing$
**end**

---

Request_cl  $\widehat{=}$
**any**  $n$  **where**
$cl \notin \mathsf{dom}(w)$
$n \in \mathbb{N}_1 \setminus \mathsf{ran}(w)$
**then**
$w(cl) := n$
**end**

---

Serve_cl  $\widehat{=}$
**when**
$cl \in \mathsf{dom}(w)$
$w(cl) = \mathsf{min}(\mathsf{ran}(w))$
**then**
$w := \{cl\} \lhd (w;$
$\mathsf{minus}(w(cl)))$
**end**

---

Serve_others  $\widehat{=}$
**any**  $c$  **where**
$cl \in \mathsf{dom}(w)$
$c \in \mathsf{dom}(w) \setminus \{cl\}$
$w(c) = \mathsf{min}(\mathsf{ran}(w))$
**then**
$w := \{c\} \lhd (w;$
$\mathsf{minus}(w(c)))$
**end**

Request_more $\widehat{=}$
  **any** $c, n$ **where**
    $cl \notin \mathrm{dom}(w)$
    $c \in C \setminus (\mathrm{dom}(w) \cup \{cl\})$
    $n \in \mathbb{N}_1 \setminus \mathrm{ran}(w)$
  **then**
    $w(c) := n$
  **end**

Serve_more $\widehat{=}$
  **any** $c$ **where**
    $cl \notin \mathrm{dom}(w)$
    $c \in \mathrm{dom}(w)$
    $w(c) = \min(\mathrm{ran}(w))$
  **then**
    $w := \{c\} \lhd (w \,; \mathrm{minus}(w(c)))$
  **end**

Notice that the variant $w(cl)$ is indeed decreased by the new event Serve_others since $w$ is an injection of range $\mathbb{N}_1$. As a consequence, the values of $w$ is indeed decreased by a positive number by means of the function minus $(w(c))$.

## 4.5   Refinement 2

In this refinement we introduce another new event Request_others (which must also be an anticipating event in the first model) dealing with clients requesting for service while client $cl$ is waiting in the waiting set. The corresponding variant is card $(C \setminus \mathrm{dom}(w))$. Notice that this event does not modify the previous variant, namely $w(cl)$. This is illustrated in the following diagram:

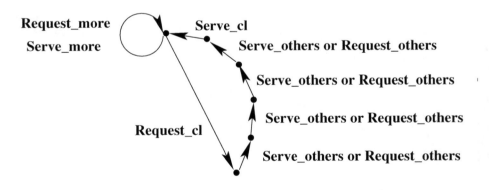

**Request_more**

**Serve_more**

**Serve_cl**

**Serve_others or Request_others**

**Serve_others or Request_others**

**Serve_others or Request_others**

**Request_cl**

**Serve_others or Request_others**

Notice that we slightly refine the various Request and Serve events so that it will be possible to merge them in the next step.

Set : $C$

Vrb : $w$

vrt_2 :  card $(C \setminus \mathrm{dom}(w))$

init $\widehat{=}$
  **begin**
    $w := \varnothing$
  **end**

Request_cl $\mathrel{\widehat{=}}$
  **any** $c, n$ **where**
    $c \in C \setminus \mathrm{dom}(w)$
    $n \in \mathbb{N}_1 \setminus \mathrm{ran}(w)$
    $c = cl$
  **then**
    $w(c) := n$
  **end**

Serve_cl $\mathrel{\widehat{=}}$
  **any** $c$ **where**
    $c \in \mathrm{dom}(w)$
    $w(c) = \min(\mathrm{ran}(w))$
    $c = cl$
  **then**
    $w := \{c\} \mathbin{\lhd} (w \,;\, \mathrm{minus}(w(c)))$
  **end**

Request_more $\mathrel{\widehat{=}}$
  **any** $c, n$ **where**
    $c \in C \setminus \mathrm{dom}(w)$
    $n \in \mathbb{N}_1 \setminus \mathrm{ran}(w)$
    $c \neq cl$
    $cl \notin \mathrm{dom}(w)$
  **then**
    $w(c) := n$
  **end**

Serve_more $\mathrel{\widehat{=}}$
  **any** $c$ **where**
    $c \in \mathrm{dom}(w)$
    $w(c) = \min(\mathrm{ran}(w))$
    $c \neq cl$
    $cl \notin \mathrm{dom}(w)$
  **then**
    $w := \{c\} \mathbin{\lhd} (w \,;\, \mathrm{minus}(w(c)))$
  **end**

Request_others $\mathrel{\widehat{=}}$
  **any** $c, n$ **where**
    $c \in C \setminus \mathrm{dom}(w)$
    $n \in \mathbb{N}_1 \setminus \mathrm{ran}(w)$
    $c \neq cl$
    $cl \in \mathrm{dom}(w)$
  **then**
    $w(c) := n$
  **end**

Serve_others $\mathrel{\widehat{=}}$
  **any** $c$ **where**
    $c \in \mathrm{dom}(w)$
    $w(c) = \min(\mathrm{ran}(w))$
    $c \neq cl$
    $cl \in \mathrm{dom}(w)$
  **then**
    $w := \{c\} \mathbin{\lhd} (w \,;\, \mathrm{minus}(w(c)))$
  **end**

## 4.6    Putting Together Requests and Services

It is now a simple matter to put together requests and services and thus obtain a model which is identical to the one of section 4.2. For this, we apply the merging rule that was given in section 3.

Set : $C$

Vrb : $w$

inv_2 : $w \in C \rightarrowtail \mathbb{N}_1$

inv_3 : $p = \mathrm{dom}(w)$

init $\mathrel{\widehat{=}}$
  **begin**
    $w := \varnothing$
  **end**

$$
\begin{array}{|l|}
\hline
\textsf{Request\_any}\;\;\widehat{=} \\
\quad \textbf{any}\;\; c, n \;\; \textbf{where} \\
\qquad c \in C \setminus \mathsf{dom}(w) \\
\qquad n \in \mathbb{N}_1 \setminus \mathsf{ran}(w) \\
\quad \textbf{then} \\
\qquad w(c) := n \\
\quad \textbf{end} \\
\hline
\end{array}
\qquad
\begin{array}{|l|}
\hline
\textsf{Serve\_any}\;\;\widehat{=} \\
\quad \textbf{any}\;\; c \;\; \textbf{where} \\
\qquad c \in \mathsf{dom}(w) \\
\qquad w(c) = \min(\mathsf{ran}(w)) \\
\quad \textbf{then} \\
\qquad w := \{c\} \mathbin{\lhd\mkern-9mu-} (w \,;\, \mathsf{minus}(w(c))) \\
\quad \textbf{end} \\
\hline
\end{array}
$$

We are now in a good position to propose two different refinement strategies implementing the "magic" behavior of the request event: the queue strategy and the ring strategy.

## 4.7    Refinement 3.1: The Queue Strategy

A queue strategy is obtained by imposing that the range of $w$ is exactly the interval $1 \mathbin{..} \mathsf{card}(\mathsf{dom}(w))$. The waiting times are then "dense", and the minimum waiting time (if any) is always 1. Notice that the queue is exactly the list obtained by inverting the injective function $w$.

$$
\boxed{\;\texttt{inv\_3}:\;\; \mathsf{ran}(w) \;=\; 1 \mathbin{..} \mathsf{card}(\mathsf{dom}(w))\;}
$$

$$
\begin{array}{|l|}
\hline
\textsf{init}\;\;\widehat{=} \\
\quad \textbf{begin} \\
\qquad w := \varnothing \\
\quad \textbf{end} \\
\hline
\end{array}
\quad
\begin{array}{|l|}
\hline
\textsf{Request\_any}\;\;\widehat{=} \\
\quad \textbf{any}\;\; c \;\; \textbf{where} \\
\qquad c \in C \setminus \mathsf{dom}(w) \\
\quad \textbf{then} \\
\qquad w(c) := \mathsf{card} \\
\qquad (\mathsf{dom}(w)) + 1 \\
\quad \textbf{end} \\
\hline
\end{array}
\quad
\begin{array}{|l|}
\hline
\textsf{Serve\_any}\;\;\widehat{=} \\
\quad \textbf{any}\;\; c \;\; \textbf{where} \\
\qquad c \in \mathsf{dom}(w) \\
\qquad w(c) = 1 \\
\quad \textbf{then} \\
\qquad w := \{c\} \mathbin{\lhd\mkern-9mu-} (w \,;\, \mathsf{pred}) \\
\quad \textbf{end} \\
\hline
\end{array}
$$

## 4.8    Refinement 3.2: The Ring (or Lift) Strategy

We suppose that the clients have a fixed setting forming a ring as indicated in the following figure:

The ring can thus be defined by means of a bijective function $nxt$ as indicated.

$$
nxt \;\in\; C \rightarrowtail\mkern-18mu\rightarrow C
$$

The problem with this bijective function is that it allows one to define several rings not a single one as we want:

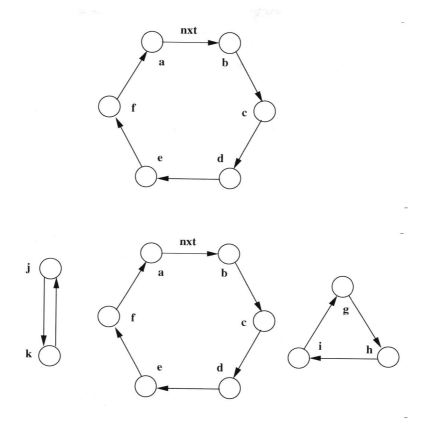

For solving this little difficulty, we first define a notion of interval $itv(x, y)$ on a ring between $x$ and $y$:

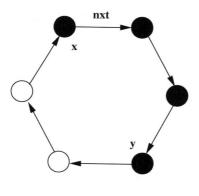

$$itv \in C \times C \to \mathbb{P}(C)$$

An interval can be defined first with a single element and then with more:

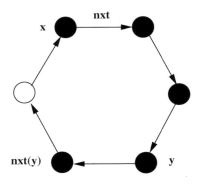

$$\forall x \cdot ( \, x \in C \; \Rightarrow \; itv(x,x) = \{x\} \, )$$

$$\forall x, y \cdot \left( \begin{array}{l} x \in C \\ y \in C \\ x \neq nxt(y) \\ \Rightarrow \\ itv(x, nxt(y)) = itv(x,y) \; \cup \; \{nxt(y)\} \, ) \end{array} \right)$$

Finally a single ring is defined if the interval from $nxt(x)$ to $x$ is exactly the entire set $C$ for any $x$, formally:

$$\forall x \cdot ( \, x \in C \; \Rightarrow \; itv(nxt(x), x) = C \, )$$

Besides the two constants $nxt$ and $itv$, we define a new variable $d$ which denotes the client which is next to the last serviced client ($d$ is initialized to the predefined constant client $cl$). All this can now be summarized as follows:

| | |
|---|---|
| Set : $C$ | |
| Cst : $cl, nxt, itv$ | |
| Vrb : $w, d$ | |

| | |
|---|---|
| prp_2 : | $nxt \; \in \; C \rightarrowtail C$ |
| prp_3 : | $itv \; \in \; C \times C \rightarrow \mathbb{P}(C)$ |
| prp_4 : | $\forall x \cdot ( \, x \in C \; \Rightarrow \; itv(x,x) = \{x\} \, )$ |
| prp_5 : | $\forall x, y \cdot \left( \begin{array}{l} x \in C \\ y \in C \\ x \neq nxt(y) \\ \Rightarrow \\ itv(x, nxt(y)) = itv(x,y) \; \cup \; \{nxt(y)\} \, ) \end{array} \right)$ |
| prp_6 : | $\forall x \cdot ( \, x \in C \; \Rightarrow \; itv(nxt(x), x) = C \, )$ |
| inv_4 : | $d \in C$ |
| inv_5 : | $\forall c \cdot ( \, c \in \mathsf{dom}(w) \; \Rightarrow \; w(c) = \mathsf{card}(itv(d,c)) \, )$ |

Notice invariant inv_5 which says that any client in the domain of $w$ is assigned a maximum waiting time which is equal to $\mathsf{card}(itv(d,c))$. Event Request_any is modified to assign a maximum waiting time to a requesting client $c$, which is equal to the cardinal of the interval between $d$ and $c$. Event Serve_any is also modified to move the variable $d$ to the client $nxt(c)$.

$$\boxed{\begin{aligned}&\text{init} \; \hat{=}\\ &\quad\textbf{begin}\\ &\qquad w := \varnothing\\ &\qquad d := cl\\ &\quad\textbf{end}\end{aligned}}$$

$$\boxed{\begin{aligned}&\text{Request\_any} \; \hat{=}\\ &\quad\textbf{any} \; c \; \textbf{where}\\ &\qquad c \in C \setminus \mathsf{dom}(w)\\ &\quad\textbf{then}\\ &\qquad w(c) := \mathsf{card}(itv(d,c))\\ &\quad\textbf{end}\end{aligned}}$$

$$\boxed{\begin{aligned}&\text{Serve\_any} \; \hat{=}\\ &\quad\textbf{any} \; c \; \textbf{where}\\ &\qquad c \in \mathsf{dom}(w)\\ &\qquad w(c) = \mathsf{min}(\mathsf{ran}(w))\\ &\quad\textbf{then}\\ &\qquad w := \{c\} \lhd (w;\\ &\qquad \mathsf{minus}(w(c)))\\ &\qquad d := nxt(c)\\ &\quad\textbf{end}\end{aligned}}$$

## 5 Conclusion

In this paper we have presented a new way of refining stuttering steps by means of events refining (a kind of) **keep** statement. We have shown that this new refinement aprroach is completely safe in that it "simulates" the more classical approach where stuttering steps are handled by refining **skip**. We have also tentatively shown how to use new events to express some reachability properties, without using special temporal logic statement.

**Acknowledgments:** We would like to thank L. Mussat for his very interesting comments.

## References

1. J.-R. Abrial. *The B Book - Assigning Programs to Meanings.* Cambridge University Press, 1996. ISBN 0-521-49619-5.
2. J.-R. Abrial and L. Mussat. Introducing dynamic constraints in B. In D. Bert, editor, *B'98 :Recent Advances in the Development and Use of the B Method,* volume 1393 of *Lecture Notes in Computer Science.* Springer Verlag, 1998.
3. J.R. Abrial. Event Based Sequential Program Development: Application to Constructing a Pointer Program. In Dino Mandrioli Keijiro Araki, Stefania Gnesi, editor, *FME 2003: Formal Methods,* volume 2805 of *Lecture Notes in Computer Science,* pages 51–74, Pisa, Sept 2003.
4. R. J. R. Back. Refinement calculus, part 2: Parallel and reactive systems. In J. W. De Roever, W. P. De Roever, and G. Rozenberg, editors, *Step Refinement of Distributed Systems Models, Formalisms, Correctness REX Workshop,* pages 67 – 93. EATCS, Springer Verlag, May-June 1989. LNCS 430.
5. L. Lamport. The temporal logic of actions. *ACM Transactions on Programming Languages and Systems,* 16(3):872–923, May 1994.

# A Rigorous Foundation for
# Pattern-Based Design Models

Soon-Kyeong Kim and David Carrington

School of Information Technology and Electrical Engineering,
The University of Queensland, St. Lucia, 4072, Australia
{soon, davec}@itee.uq.edu.au

**Abstract.** This paper presents a way to describe design patterns rigorously based on role concepts. Rigorous pattern descriptions are a key aspect for patterns to be used as rules for model evolution in the MDA context, for example. We formalize the role concepts commonly used in defining design patterns as a role metamodel using Object-Z. Given this role metamodel, individual design patterns are specified generically as a formal pattern role model using Object-Z. We also formalize the properties that must be captured in a class model when a design pattern is deployed. These properties are defined generically in terms of role bindings from a pattern role model to a class model. Our work provides a precise but abstract approach for pattern definition and also provides a precise basis for checking the validity of pattern usage in designs.

## 1 Introduction

In a model-driven development approach such as MDA [17], software systems are developed via model evolution. A model describing a problem is evolved to a model describing its solution from which code is generated. Problems are identified either from the business domain or during design. Since software design patterns describe solutions that can be used to solve general design problems [9], problems identified in design models can be readily solved by referencing design patterns.

While design patterns can provide an effective basis for model evolution, the current approaches to describing patterns fall short of what design patterns can offer for model evolution in the MDA context.

A pattern is described in terms of the problem that it addresses, the solution and its consequences. The solution component of a pattern description is often called a pattern specification and describes the structural and behavioural aspects of the participants in the pattern through their roles, relationships and collaborations.

Pattern specifications are typically defined imprecisely using natural language descriptions with graphical annotations. It is also common to describe patterns using a concrete design or a specific example of a pattern use, as is done in [7, 9]. In fact, the resulting pattern descriptions are not a pattern specification. They are particular examples of pattern use. This problem typically originates from the limitations of using object notations for describing patterns (e.g. OMT and UML). Object notations are basically designed to describe concrete design decisions and they are not appropriate

H. Treharne et al. (Eds.): ZB 2005, LNCS 3455, pp. 242–261, 2005.

for describing patterns in an abstract manner [5, 19]. Object notations lack precision in their notations. To enhance this situation, the following problems have to be solved:

- Patterns must be described in a precise manner. Thus a tool applying patterns can understand the properties of the patterns and a set of transformation rules can be applied to the patterns for model evolution.
- To use patterns in different applications, patterns must be described in an abstract manner focusing on their essential properties and omitting application-specific information from the pattern description.
- For modeling to be effective, efficient ways must exist to validate whether patterns are deployed in applications as intended.

To achieve these goals, this paper proposes a formal role-based metamodeling approach to describe patterns. By adopting a meta-modeling and formal approach, our work defines an innovative framework where generic pattern concepts based on roles are precisely defined as a formal role metamodel using Object-Z [2][1], and individual patterns are specified using these generic role concepts in terms of pattern role models[2]. Patterns described in this way are abstract, separating pattern realization information from the pattern description. Also they are sufficiently precise enough to be interpreted by a tool or a set of transformation rules. To support effective model evolution with design patterns, we formally define a set of properties that must be fulfilled by a design model when it deploys a pattern in terms of role bindings from a pattern role model to a design model. This formal definition provides a precise basis so that the validity of pattern usage in a design model can be checked.

The structure of the rest of this paper is as follows. Section 2 provides a review of related work. Section 3 presents a formal definition of the role concepts used in this paper using Object-Z. Section 4 shows how to specify patterns in an abstract, but precise manner using the role concepts defined in Section 3. Section 5 formalizes the properties that must be satisfied in a design model when it deploys a pattern. Section 6 draws some conclusions and discusses future work.

## 2 Related Work

Several researchers [8, 15, 19] use role-modeling techniques to describe patterns. Riehle [19] specifies patterns with three levels of abstraction: pattern, design template and concrete design. At the pattern level, he uses role diagrams to describe the distribution of responsibility and the interaction between objects playing specific roles in a pattern. At the design template level, he uses class diagrams to describe how a pattern specified by a role diagram can be made more concrete. Lastly, at the concrete design level, the design template is instantiated in an application.

---

[1] We use the UML Class diagram to show the model elements in our role metamodel and their relationships, but their definitions are given in Object-Z.
[2] Pattern role models can be viewed using different notations such as Object-Z and UML. Examples are presented in Section 4.

Lauder et al. [15] present similar work in which three layered models in terms of role, type and class level models are introduced as pattern specifications. A role level model expresses the pattern purely focusing on the essential elements of the pattern, a type level model refines the role model by adding usually-domain-specific refinements to the roles, and a class level model refines the type model by adding application-specific terms. Lauder et al. use different diagrams for different models, e.g., constraint diagrams for role models and modified UML-like class diagrams for both type and class models.

These works limit the role concepts mainly to objects and do not capture other roles played by different entities in a pattern such as classes, features of the classes and relationships between the classes and objects. Also type models in [15] or class templates in [19] do not reflect the full generality of patterns due to limitations of the object notations used to present them.

France et al. [8] reduce these problems by extending the role concepts beyond objects to classes, attributes, operations, associations and generalizations. They adopt a metamodeling approach to define a pattern generically. A pattern metamodel developed at the meta-level captures both role and type information. The properties that a UML class model should satisfy when it realizes a pattern are defined using OCL [18] as meta-level constraints. Nevertheless, this work discusses role concepts in the context of UML. Also utilizing role concepts in any UML model constructs makes the overall pattern description unnecessary complex. In contrast, our role-metamodel defines only core elements that are necessary to describe patterns and is not based on a specific modelling language. This makes our approach more flexible and extendable to apply to different modeling languages.

Soundarajan et al. [21] present a rigorous approach to specifying patterns based on roles and their responsibilities, but they neither formally define role concepts nor separate pattern definitions from their usage information, which, of course is our focus.

Not based on role concepts, but using object-notations (mainly UML), Fontoura and Lucena [7] define stereotypes and tagged values to improve the presentation of configuration design patterns. Dong [1] proposes annotation using tagged values to enhance pattern presentations with UML. Similarly, Sanada and Adams [20] define a UML profile for patterns that includes several stereotypes to support the presentation of design patterns. However pattern descriptions presented in these works inherit the limitations of using object notations discussed above. Another approach uses meta-modeling to define pattern concepts in the context of the UML metamodel. Guennec et al. [10] use meta-level collaborations to present design patterns and specify some pattern properties as a set of constraints using OCL. Mak et al. [16] present similar work to [10] using meta-level UML collaborations to present design patterns.

It should be also noted that there has been research to define pattern specifications precisely. Eden et al. [5] use a higher order language called LePUS to define patterns. Lano and Goldsack [14] formalize patterns using VDM++ and prove design patterns as refinement transformations using the Object Calculus. Flores et al. [6] use the RAISE Specification Language to formally specify properties of patterns. These approaches are however not role-based and do not provide an abstract view for pattern usage, so we do not discuss them further in this paper.

# 3 A Role Metamodel for Patterns

In this section, we present a metamodel for roles that are used to define design patterns. In defining the role metamodel, we first identify the underlying concepts that are commonly used to define existing design patterns and then abstract these concepts as meta-modeling elements in the role metamodel. Since the meta-modeling elements conceptualize common properties in patterns, we must be able to describe a pattern in terms of these modeling elements.

In this section, we use a UML class diagram to present the abstract syntax of our role modeling language, but we formalize the definition using Object-Z. We assume a basic understanding of UML and Object-Z. We have presented a preliminary overview of the role metamodel in [13] focusing on mainly class and their feature roles, but not considering occurrence properties and relationships. The role metamodel presented in this paper has significant extensions.

## 3.1 Role Concepts in Patterns

A pattern involves a set of roles that are played by participants in the pattern. We use roles and role models as first-class modeling concepts to define patterns. In our work, a role is defined to describe not only objects, but also their features and relationships with other objects or features of other objects in the context of a pattern. Fig. 1 presents a class diagram showing the role model elements defined in our work.

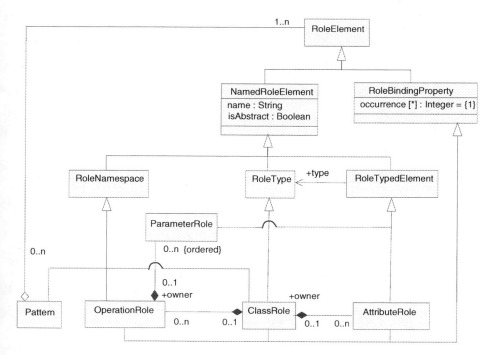

**Fig. 1.** A class diagram showing role model elements and their structure

The metaclass *RoleElement* is the top level model element from which all role concepts in our role modeling language are drawn. Inheriting from this class, we have two metaclasses: *NamedRoleElement* and *RoleBindingProperty*. *NamedRoleElement* is an abstract metaclass from which all role elements with a name are drawn. A *NamedRoleElement* has a name describing its intent or responsibility and has an attribute *isAbstract* defining whether the element is abstract or not[3] (e.g. the *Abstract-Factory* class role in the Abstract Factory pattern [9]). *RoleBindingProperty* defines the occurrence property of a role in a single pattern realization in a design model (e.g. the *ConcreteFactory* class role in the Abstract Factory pattern can occur multiple times in a single pattern realization). A formal definition of these metaclasses is presented below.

```
┌─RoleElement──────────────────────────────────────────────────┐
│                                                               │
└───────────────────────────────────────────────────────────────┘

┌─RoleBindingProperty──────────────────────────────────────────┐
│ RoleElement                                                   │
├───────────────────────────────────────────────────────────────┤
│ occurrence : ℕ                                                │
└───────────────────────────────────────────────────────────────┘

┌─NamedRoleElement─────────────────────────────────────────────┐
│ RoleElement                                                   │
├───────────────────────────────────────────────────────────────┤
│ name : Name                                                   │
│ isAbstract :B                                                 │
└───────────────────────────────────────────────────────────────┘
```

*Role Name space* is an element that can own other elements (such as class roles or operation roles). *RoleTypedElement* presents role elements with a type (e.g. attribute roles and parameter roles).

```
┌─RoleNamespace────────────────────────────────────────────────┐
│ NamedRoleElement                                              │
└───────────────────────────────────────────────────────────────┘

┌─RoleType─────────────────────────────────────────────────────┐
│ NamedRoleElement                                              │
└───────────────────────────────────────────────────────────────┘

┌─RoleTypedElement─────────────────────────────────────────────┐
│ NamedRoleElement                                              │
├───────────────────────────────────────────────────────────────┤
│ type: RoleType                                                │
└───────────────────────────────────────────────────────────────┘
```

By inheriting the *RoleTypedElement* metaclass, we define attribute roles. Since an attribute role may occur multiple times within its owning class role in a single pattern realization, it is also defined as a *RoleBindingProperty* element. Similarly we define parameter roles.

---

[3] At the pattern-level, it is enough to define whether a role participating in a pattern is abstract so that there are concrete roles realizing it. Whether the role is an interface or an abstract class is an implementation issue, which we do not consider in the pattern description.

```
┌─AttributeRole───────────────────────────────────────────────
│ RoleTypedElement    RoleBindingProperty
│ ┌──────────────────────────────────────────────
│ │ owner : ClassRole
│ ├──────────────────────────────
│ │ self ∈ owner.attributeRoles
│ └
```

```
┌─ParameterRole───────────────────────────────────────────────
│ RoleTypedElement
│ ┌──────────────────────────────────────────────
│ │ owner : OperationRole
│ ├──────────────────────────────
│ │ self ∈ ran (owner.parameterRoles)
│ └
```

An operation role owns an ordered set of parameter roles and can occur multiple times within its owning class role in a single pattern realization. Hence it inherits from both *RoleNamespace* and *RoleBindingProperty*.

```
┌─OperationRole───────────────────────────────────────────────
│ RoleNamespace    RoleBindingProperty
│ ┌──────────────────────────────────────────────
│ │ owner: ClassRole
│ │ parameterRoles: seq ParameterRole ©
│ ├──────────────────────────────
│ │ self ∈ owner.operationRoles
│ └
```

Using attribute roles and operation roles, we now define a class role. A class role owns feature roles such as attribute roles and operation roles, and it can occur multiple times in a single pattern realization, so it inherits from both *RoleNamespace* and *RoleBindingProperty*. A class role is a role type, so it also inherits from *RoleType*. Within a class role, attribute role names and operation role names should be unique. This property is formalized as a constraint in the Object-Z class *ClassRole* below.

```
┌─ClassRole───────────────────────────────────────────────
│ RoleNamespace  RoleBindingProperty   RoleType
│ ┌──────────────────────────────────────────────
│ │ attributeRoles: ℙAttributeRole ©
│ │ operationRoles: ℙOperationRole ©
│ ├──────────────────────────────
│ │ ∀a1, a2: attributeRoles • a1.name = a2.name ⇒ a1 = a2
│ │ ∀o1, o2: operationRoles • o1.name = o2.name ⇒ o1 = o2
│ └
```

## 3.2  Role Relationships in Patterns

Roles in a pattern may have relationships between them. These relationships are also role elements in the pattern. *RoleRelationship* is an abstract metaclass from which all types of relationships between role elements can be drawn (see Fig. 2).

```
┌─RoleRelationship───────────────────────────────────────────────
│ RoleElement
```

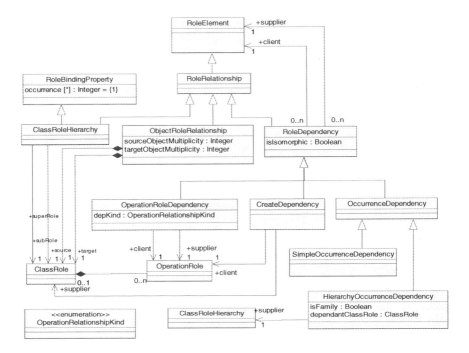

**Fig. 2.** A class diagram showing various role relationships in the role metamodel

One relationship often found in patterns is a hierarchical relationship between class roles. The metaclass *ClassRoleHierarchy* captures this relationship. Since a hierarchy relationship can appear several times in a single pattern realization (e.g. the hierarchy between *AbstractProduct* and *ConcreteProduct* class roles in the Abstract Factory pattern), it inherits from *RoleBindingProperty*. A hierarchy relationship has a super class role that defines abstract role features (e.g., operation roles) and a subclass role that realizes the abstract role features. In each class role hierarchy, the super class role is abstract and may occur only once, but the subclass role is not abstract and may occur multiple times, so its occurrence propriety remains undefined. A subclass role cannot be its own super class role. This property is formalized as a constraint.

---

─*ClassRoleHierarchy*───────────────────
*RoleRelationship*   *RoleBindingProperty*
────────────────────────────────────────
*superRole : ClassRole*
*subRole: ClassRole*
────────────────────────────────────────
*superRole.isAbstract* ∧ *superRole.occurrence* = *1*
¬ *subRole.isAbstract* ∧ *superRole* ≠ *subRole*
∀ *ao*: {*o*: *superRole.operationRoles* | *o.isAbstract*} •
    ∃₁ *co*: *subRole.operationRoles* • ¬ *co.isAbstract* ∧
        ∃₁ *d*: *OperationRoleDependency* •
            *d.client* = *ao* ∧ *d.supplier* = *co* ∧ *depKind* = *realize*

Patterns may capture relationships between objects (e.g. the relationship between a *Subject* object and a set of *Observer* objects in the Observer pattern [9]). These relationships between object roles are typically realized as associations in a class model. Most relationships between objects in patterns are a directed binary relationship between two class roles (source and target class roles). The metaclass *ObjectRoleRelationship* is defined as a binary relationship between two class roles. It has two attributes defining the multiplicity properties of these roles.

```
┌─ObjectRoleRelationship─────────────────────────────────────
│ RoleRelationship
│
│  source: ClassModel
│  target: ClassModel
│  sourceObjectMultiplicity: ℕ
│  targetObjectMultiplicity: ℕ
│
└────────────────────────────────────────────────────────────
```

Another type of relationship often found in patterns is a dependency relationship between various role elements (*RoleDependency*). This relationship is defined as a directed relationship from a client role to a supplier role. The relationship can be isomorphic (a total one-to-one relationship between the client and supplier roles).

```
┌─RoleDependency─────────────────────────────────────────────
│ RoleRelationship
│
│  isIsomorphic: Boolean
│  client: ↓RoleElement
│  supplier: ↓RoleElement
│ ───────────────────────────────────────────
│  isIsomorphic =>
│      #{d: RoleDependency | d.client= client ∧ r.supplier = supplier } = 1
│
└────────────────────────────────────────────────────────────
```

Role dependency relationships are further classified into: *BindingDependency*, *CreateDependency* and *OperationRoleDependency* and can be readily extended for different types of dependency in new patterns.

**OccurrenceDependency:** An occurrence dependency defines a binding relationship between role elements when they are realized in a design model. This property only applies to a situation where both the client and supplier roles have a multiple occurrence property. Occurrence dependencies can be used to check the integrity of pattern realizations in a design model.

```
┌─OccurrenceDependency───────────────────────────────────────
│ RoleDependency
│
│ ───────────────────────────────────────────
│  client.occurrence ≥ 1 ∧ supplier.occurrence ≥ 1
│
└────────────────────────────────────────────────────────────
```

A simple occurrence dependency example is drawn from the Visitor pattern [9]: the number of *Visitor* operation roles defined in the *AbstractVisitor* class role depends on the number of *ConcreteElement* class roles that exist in the Element hierarchy. For some patterns, however, occurrence dependencies can be more complex. For example, in the *Abstract Factory* pattern, two occurrence dependencies are identified:

- between the *CreateProduct* operation role defined in the *AbstractFactory* class role and the *AbstractProduct* class role in each Product hierarchy
- between the *ConcreteFactory* class role and a family of the *ConcreteProduct* class roles in the Product hierarchies

While the former can be readily captured by an isomorphic occurrence dependency between the *CreateProduct* operation role and the *AbstractProduct* class role because this relationship is between a single occurrence of the two role elements, the latter cannot be precisely captured by an isomorphic occurrence dependency because it involves a multiple occurrence of the role elements associated (e.g. a multiple occurrence of the *ConcreteProduct* class role in a multiple occurrence of the *Product* hierarchy role). To capture different types of occurrence relationships, we further classify the *OccurrenceDependency* into *SimpleOccurenceDependency* and *HierarchyOccurrenceDependency*.

A simple occurrence relationship can be defined between any role model elements. Each time a client role is realized in a design model, its supplier role must be realized as well in the same pattern realization. Thus, their occurrence properties must be the same.

┌─*SimpleOccurrenceDependency*─────────────────────────────────
│ *OccurrenceDependency*
│ ├─────────────────────────────────────────────────────────
│ │
│ │ *client.occurrence = supplier.occurrence*
│ └─────────────────────────────────────────────────────────
└──────────────────────────────────────────────────────────────

A hierarchy occurrence dependency is between a role element and a class role hierarchy. The supplier of the *HierarchyOccurrenceDependency* is restricted to *ClassRoleHierarchy*. It has two attributes, *dependentClassRole* and *isFamily*. The attribute *dependentClassRole* denotes the class role in the hierarchy that is restricted by the occurrence dependency.

┌─*HierarchyOccurrenceDependency*──────────────────────────────
│ *OccurrenceDependency*
│ ──────────────────────────────────────────────────────────
│ *dependentClassRole: ClassRole*
│ *isFamily: Boolean*
│ ──────────────────────────────────────────────────────────
│ *supplier ∈ ClassRoleHierarchy*
│ *dependentClassRole ∈ {supplier.superRole} ∪ {supplier.subRole}*
│ *dependentClassRole = supplier.superRole ⇒*
│      *client.occurrence = supplier.occurrence*
│ *dependentClassRole = supplier.subRole ⇒*
│      *client.occurrence = dependentClassRole.occurrence*
│ *isFamily ⇒ ¬ isIsomorphic*
└──────────────────────────────────────────────────────────────

When the dependent class role is the super class role of the hierarchy, the occurrence property of the client is the same as that of the supplier. This is because a super class role occurs only once in a class role hierarchy, thus the client occurrence depends on the occurrence of the hierarchy itself. In contrast, when the dependent class role is the subclass role of the hierarchy, the occurrence property of the client is the same as that of the dependent class role. This is because a subclass role may occur multiple times in a class role hierarchy, thus the client occurrence depends on the occurrence of the dependent class role in the hierarchy. The attribute *isFamily* denotes whether the occurrence dependency applies to the family of the dependent class role. In this case, the dependency cannot be isomorphic.

**CreateDependency:** A create dependency defines a create relationship between an operation role and a class role. For example, the *ConcreteProduct* operation role of the *ConcreteFactory* class role has a responsibility to create concrete products and this dependency is isomorphic.

```
┌─CreateDependency──────────────────────────────────
│ RoleDependency
│ ┌────────────────────────────────────
│ │
│ ├────────────────────────────────────
│ │ client ∈ OperationRole ∧ supplier ∈ ClassRole
│ └
└
```

**OperationRoleDependency:** Operation role dependency captures various relationships between operation roles. An operation role may have a responsibility to invoke another operation role. Also an operation role may realize another operation role. By the semantics of the *ClassRoleHierarchy* metaclass, operation roles defined in a subclass role realize the operation roles defined its super class role. The attribute *depKind* defines the kind of dependency and it has an enumeration type *OperationRelationshipKind*, which is readily extended when different types of dependencies are identified between operation roles.

We initially define three values for this type: *invoke, broadcast* and *realize*.

- The *invoke* value defines a dependency where the client operation role invokes the supplier operation role (e.g., the *Accept* operation role of the *Element* class role will invoke the *VisitConcreteElement* operation role of the *Visitor* class role in the Visitor pattern [9]).
- The *broadcast* value defines a dependency where triggering the client operation role is broadcast to all interested object roles so that the supplier operation role is triggered as a result (e.g. the *Notify* operation role of the *Subject* class role and the *Update* operation role of the *Observer* class role in the Observer pattern [9]).
- The *realize* value defines a dependency between an abstract operation role and its realizing concrete operation roles.

```
┌─OperationRoleDependency───────────────────────────
│ RoleDependency
│ ┌────────────────────────────────────
│ │ depKind: OperationRelationshipKind
│ ├────────────────────────────────────
│ │ client ∈ OperationRole ∧ supplier ∈ OperationRole
│ └
└
```

### 3.3 Patterns

Composing the Object-Z classes defined above, we define a formal description of a pattern. A pattern has a set of role elements. We define two secondary variables *classRoles* and *relationshipRoles* representing all class roles and all relationship roles in the pattern respectively.

---Pattern---

$roles$: $\mathbb{P}{\downarrow}RoleElement$
$\Delta$
$classRoles$: $\mathbb{P}\ ClassRole$
$relationshipRoles$: $\mathbb{P}{\downarrow}\ RelationshipRole$

---

$classRoles\ = \{cr: roles \mid cr \in ClassRole\}$
$relationshipRoles\ = \{rr: roles \mid rr \in\ {\downarrow} RelationshipRole\}$

---

# 4    Precise Pattern Descriptions

Specifying patterns using object notation has limitations in terms of generality. We address this problem by specifying patterns using the role concepts as defined in the previous section using the instantiation mechanism in Object-Z. Using the role meta-model, we can define patterns simply by assigning values for the features defined in the metamodel. Integrity consistency between role elements (e.g. role occurrence consistencies) are ensured by the properties defined at the meta-level. We use two design patterns from the Gang of Four's pattern book [9] as examples: Factory Method and Abstract Factory.

## 4.1    A Formal Role Model of the Factory Method Pattern

The following Object-Z class *FactoryMethod* is a formal role model of the Factory Method pattern. It is developed using the role concepts defined in the previous section. The Factory Method pattern has two class role hierarchies: *Creator* and *Product*.

**Creator role:** The *Creator* hierarchy has two class roles: *AbstractCreator* and *ConcreteCreator*.

---Creator---

[Creator Structure]
$creatorHierarchy$: $ClassRoleHierarchy$
$absCreator$: $ClassRole$
$absFactoryMethod$: $OperationRole$
$conCreator$:  $ClassRole$
$conFactoryMethod$: $OperationRole$
$absFactoryMethodConFactoryMethod$ : $OperationRoleDependency$

---

$creatorHierarchy.superRole = absCreator$
$creatorHierarchy.subRole = conCreator$
$absFactoryMethod \in absCreator.operationRoles$
$absFactoryMethod.isAbstract \wedge absFactoryMethod.owner = absCreator$
$conCreator.occurrence \geq 1$
$conFactoryMethod \in conCreator.operationRoles$
$\neg\ conFactoryMethod.isAbstract \wedge conFactoryMethod.owner = conCreator$
$absFactoryMethodConFactoryMethod.client = absFactoryMethod$
$absFactoryMethodConFactoryMethod.supplier = conFactoryMethod$

The *AbstractCreator* plays a super class role for the *ConcreteCreator* class role. The *ConcreteCreator* may occur multiple times but it depends on the occurrence of the Product families. The *AbstractCreator* class role has an operation role *Factory-Method* and the operation is realized in the *ConcreteCreator* class role. The creator class role hierarchy and the factory method operation roles can occur only once in a single pattern realization. However, we defer the definition of these properties to the pattern-level so as to make the role structure reusable in different patterns that might need to have a multiple occurrence of these roles (see the next section for composing patterns by reusing other patterns).

**Product role:** The *Product* hierarchy has two class roles: *AbstractProduct* and *ConcreteProduct*. The *AbstractProduct* plays a super class role for the *ConcreteProduct*. The *ConcreteProduct* may occur multiple times. The product hierarchy can occur multiple times. However, we again defer the definition of this property to the pattern-level for the same reason.

---
┌─*Product*────────────────────────────────────────

  [Product Structure]
  *productHierarchy :ClassRoleHierarchy*
  *absProduct*: *ClassRole*
  *conProduct*: *ClassRole*
  ─────────────────────────────────────────
  *productHierarchy.superRole = absProduct*
  *productHierarchy.subRole = conProduct*
  *conProduct.occurrence* $\geq 1$
---

**Role relationship:** There is an isomorphic occurrence dependency between *conCreator* and *conProduct* class roles (see the variable, *conCreatorConProduct*). Also there is an isomorphic create dependency from the *conFactoryMethod* operation role to the *conProduct* role (see the variable, *conFactoryMethodConProduct*). The invariants formalize the occurrence properties of the class role hierarchies and operation roles discussed above.

---
┌─*FactoryMethod*──────────────────────────────────
│ Creator  Product

  [Role Relationship]
  *conCreatorConProduct : SimpleOccurrenceDependency*
  *conFactoryMethodConProduct: CreateDependency*
  ─────────────────────────────────────────
  *conCreatorConProduct.client = conCreator*
  *conCreatorConProduct.supplier = conProduct*
  *conFactoryMethodConProduct.client = conFactoryMethod*
  *conFactoryMethodConProduct.supplier = conProduct*
  *conFactoryMethodConProduct.isIsomorphic*
  [Role occurrence properties at the pattern-level]
  *creatorHierarchy.occurrence = 1* $\wedge$ *productHierarchy.occurrence = 1*
  *absFactoryMethod.occurrence = 1* $\wedge$ *conFactoryMethod.occurrence = 1*
---

This Factory Method definition is generic and it allows parallel class hierarchies of creator and product class roles that are demonstrated as an example of the Factory Method pattern in [9].

## 4.2 Pattern Composition

Some patterns are strongly related. For example, the Abstract Factory pattern extends the Factory Method pattern. Using the inheritance and renaming mechanism in Object-Z, we can define patterns by composing other patterns (more precisely roles defined in the patterns). In this section, we show how to define the Abstract Factory pattern by composing the roles defined for the Factory Method pattern in the previous section.

Basically the Abstract Factory pattern has the same creator and product class role hierarchies defined in the Factory Method pattern, but with different occurrence properties. For example, the Abstract Factory pattern has multiple hierarchies for the product class roles and the creator operation role has a multiple occurrence. Also there are complex occurrence dependencies between the roles. For example, there is an isomorphic occurrence dependency between the abstract *CreateProduct* operation role and the *AbstractProduct* class role (see the variable, *absCreateProductAbsProduct*). There is also a complex occurrence dependency between the *ConcreteFactory* class role and a family of the *ConcreteProduct* class roles in the *Product* hierarchy (see the variable *conFactoryConProduct*).

The following Object-Z class *AbstractFactory* is a formal role model of the Abstract Factory pattern. It inherits from the Object-Z classes *Creator* and *Product*, and renames the variables defined in the class *Creator* according to those factory roles

---

┌─*AbstractFactory*─────────────────────────────────────────────

*Creator* [ *absFactory* / *absCreator*,
 *absCreateProduct* / *absFactoryMethod*, *conFactory* / *conCreator*,
 *conCreateProduct* / *conFactoryMethod*, *factoryHierarchy* / *creatorHierarchy*,
 *absCreateProductConCreateProduct* / *absFactoryMethodConFactoryMethod* ]
*Product*

─────────────────────────────────────────────

[Role Relationships]
*absCreateProductAbsProduct* : *SimpleOccurrenceDependency*
*conFactoryConProduct* : *HierarchyOccurrenceDependency*
*conCreateProductConProduct*: *CreateDependency*

─────────────────────────────────────────────

*absCreateProductAbsProduct.client* =*absCreateProduct*
*absCreateProductAbsProduct.supplier* =*absProduct*
*absCreateProductAbsProduct.isIsomorphic*
*conFactoryConProduct.client* = *conCreateFactory*
*conFactoryConProduct.supplier* = *productHierarchy*
*conFactoryConProduct.supplier.dependentClassRole* = *conProduct*
*conFactoryConProduct.supplier.isFamily*
*conCreateProductConProduct.client*  = *conCreateProduct*
*conCreateProductConProduct.supplier* = *conProduct*
*conCreateProductConProduct.isIsomorphic*
[Role occurrence properties at the pattern-level]
*factoryHierarchy.occurrenec* = $1 \wedge$ *productHierarchy.occurrence* $\geq 1$
*absCreateProduct.occurrence* $\geq 1 \wedge$ *conCreateProduct.occurrence* $\geq 1$

─────────────────────────────────────────────

defined in the Abstract Factory pattern (e.g., renaming *absCreator* to *absFactory, absFactoryMethod* to *absCreateProduct* and so on). This renaming is necessary because in a pattern, role names describe the intended responsibility of each role.

Since the product hierarchy can occur multiple times, the occurrence property of the product roles is defined as greater than or equal to 1. Also the two occurrence dependencies explained before and a create dependency between the *ConCreateProduct* operation role and the *ConProduct* class role are formalized.

Using Object-Z, we have significant power to define patterns in a compositional manner reusing existing patterns to define new patterns. In this way, we also can verify conflicts between patterns when their roles are combined.

### 4.3    A Visual Representation of the Abstract Factory Pattern

In this paper, we define the abstract syntax of a role modeling language as a metamodel. However, we do not propose a particular concrete syntax although we present an example pattern role model using Object-Z in the previous section. In fact, we can describe patterns using different concrete notations (e.g., UML) based on our role concepts as defined in the role metamodel. However, using UML we do not have the same power that Object-Z provides for defining patterns reusing existing pattern descriptions as shown in the previous section. Nevertheless, the diagrammatic presentation should enhance the readability of the pattern description.

An example of a visual representation of the Abstract Factory pattern in UML is presented in Fig. 3. The diagram is a meta-level UML object diagram and is

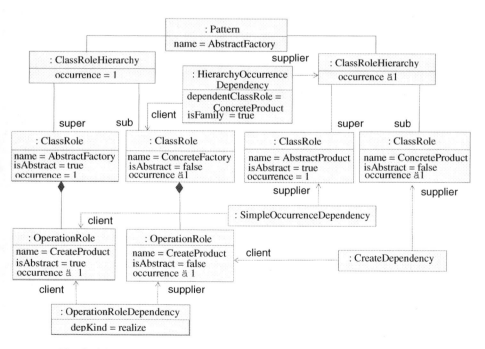

**Fig. 3.** A UML object diagram showing Abstract Factory pattern role model

developed using the same instantiation mechanism as we used for the Object-Z representation. We can also present the role model using a class diagram at the model-level, but we do not present this example in this paper for brevity.

# 5   Precise Pattern Usage Specifications

In the previous section, we introduced roles and role models as a more adequate means to describe the essentials of patterns. Patterns described in this way are abstract, separating pattern realization information from the pattern description. In this section, we provide a precise basis to validate pattern realizations in design models.

In our work, patterns are realized in a design model via a role binding. A role binding constitutes a model capturing all binding information from role elements defined in a pattern to class constructs defined in a design model. We can check validity of a pattern realization by checking the binding model. This separation of role binding information from design models has several advantages:

- It does not increase the complexity of the design model, which can occur when pattern usage information is provided within the same model (e.g. showing collaboration occurrences in a UML class diagram).
- After a design model evolves, pattern deployment information remains in the binding model. Any modifications of pattern use in the design model can be achieved by tracing the binding models at the individual pattern level, not at the whole design model level. This should help pattern-based design or refactoring approaches.
- The validity of the pattern realization can be checked using the binding model. When a role binding model is valid, its referenced design model is also valid in the context of the pattern.

Our role binding model is generic and does not restrict pattern usage in any particular way. Instead it defines common properties that must be preserved in pattern usage in terms of integrity constraints on the bindings. The role binding model should be used as a specification to develop tools that support the validation of pattern use.

Since patterns are realized mainly in class models, we restrict design models to class models in this paper. Prior to formalising the role binding model, we present a formal definition of a simple class model using Object-Z and use this definition to define the integrity constraints on the bindings formally.

## 5.1   A Simple Class Model in Object-Z

A class model consists of a set of classes and relationships between them. It should be noted that the class model presented in this section contains a minimum set of class constructs that are necessary to explain role bindings. For a full formal description of class models such as UML class diagrams, refer to [11, 12].

We assume that a given set, *Name*, is defined from which the names of all classes, attributes, operations, operation parameters, and associations are drawn. We also assume that a meta-type *Type* is defined from which all possible types used in a class model can be derived.

**Class:** A class has a name and contains a collection of features: attributes and operations. An attribute has a name, a type, and a multiplicity. Variable *multiplicity* in

*Attribute* describes the possible number of values for the attribute that may be held by an instance. An operation has a name and parameters. Each parameter of an operation has a name and a type.

```
┌─Attribute──────────────────────┐   ┌─Parameter──────────────────────┐
│ name: Name                     │   │ name: Name                     │
│ type   : Type                  │   │ type : Type                    │
│ multiplicity: ℙℕ₁              │   │                                │
└────────────────────────────────┘   └────────────────────────────────┘
```

$$\text{multiplicity}: \mathbb{P}\mathbb{N}_1$$

```
┌─Operation──────────────────────────────────────────────────────────┐
│ name: Name                                                          │
│ parameters: seq Parameter ©                                         │
│─────────────────────────────────────────────────────────────────── │
│ ∀p1, p2: ran parameters • p1.name = p2.name ⇒ p1 = p2              │
└─────────────────────────────────────────────────────────────────────┘
```

$$\forall p1, p2: ran\ parameters \bullet p1.name = p2.name \Rightarrow p1 = p2$$

Using these types we formally define a class. Attribute names defined in a class should be distinct and operations should have distinct signatures. The class invariant formalizes these properties. A circled , which models a containment relationship in Object-Z, is attached to the types of *attributes* and *operations* because an attribute or operation instance can belong to only one class. A class can inherit from other classes (the variable *superclass* and *subclass* capture this inheritance concept). Any circular inheritance is prohibited. To formalize this constraint, we define two secondary variable *allSupers* and *allSubs* representing all super classes and all sub classes of a class respectively and use these variables to exclude circular inheritance.

```
┌─Class──────────────────────────────────────────────────────────────┐
│ ┌─────────────────────────────────────────────────────────────────┐ │
│ │ name: Name                                                       │ │
│ │ attributes: ℙAttribute ©                                         │ │
│ │ operations: ℙOperation ©                                         │ │
│ │ superclass: ℙ Class                                              │ │
│ │ subclass: ℙ Class                                                │ │
│ │ Δ                                                                │ │
│ │ allSupers: ℙ Class                                               │ │
│ │ allSubs: ℙ Class                                                 │ │
│ │──────────────────────────────────────────────────────────────── │ │
│ │ ∀ a1, a2: attributes • a1.name = a2.name ⇒ a1 = a2              │ │
│ │ ∀ op1, op2: operations •                                         │ │
│ │   (op1.name = op2.name ∧ #op1.parameters = #op2.parameters ∧    │ │
│ │    ∀ i:1.. #op1.parameters •                                     │ │
│ │    op1.parameters(i).name = op2.parameters(i).name ∧            │ │
│ │    op1.parameters(i).type  = op2.parameters(i).type) ⇒ op1 = op2 │ │
│ │ allSupers = superclass ∪ (∪{ s: superclass • s.allSupers })     │ │
│ │ allSubs = subclass ∪ (∪{ s: subclass • s.allSubs })             │ │
│ │ self ∉ allSupers ∧ self ∉ allSubs                                │ │
│ └─────────────────────────────────────────────────────────────────┘ │
└─────────────────────────────────────────────────────────────────────┘
```

**Relationship:** In a class model, relationships between classes are represented as associations. In most cases, associations in a class model are between exactly two classes. For this reason, only binary associations are considered in this paper. A binary association has an association name, two association ends (source and target) each of which has a role name, a multiplicity constraint, and a class to which the end is attached. We first formalize the concept of association ends as Object-Z class *AssociationEnd*. The invariant states that a multiplicity cannot be $\{0\}$.

A binary association has a name and exactly two association ends. The invariant states the core properties of an association: each end name must be different, and the role name at an association end must be different from the attribute names of the class attached to the other end.

┌─*Association*──────────────────
│
│  *name*: *Name*
│  *source, target*: *AssociationEnd©*
│  ────────────────────────────
│  *source.name* ≠ *target.name*
│  *source.name* ∉
│  $\{a:target.class.attributes \bullet a.name\}$
│  *target.name* ∉
│  $\{a: source.class.attributes \bullet a.name\}$
│
└─────────────────────────────

┌─*AssociationEnd*───────────────
│
│  *name*: *Name*
│  *multiplicity* : $\mathbb{PN}$
│  *class*: *Class*
│  ────────────────────────────
│  *multiplicity* ≠ $\{0\}$
│
└─────────────────────────────

Using these definitions, we define a class model as a collection of classes and associations. Classes should have unique names within the class model. All superclasses of a class and all classes attached to an association end should also be classes in the class model. We also define a secondary variable *allConstructs* of type *ClassConstruct* to refer all class constructs defined in a class model. This variable is used when we discuss transformations from role models to class models in Section 5.2.

┌─*ClassModel*─────────────────────────────────────────
│
│  *class*: $\mathbb{F}$*Class*
│  *assoc*: $\mathbb{F}$*Association*
│  Δ
│  *allConstructs*: $\mathbb{P}$ *ClassConstruct*
│  ─────────────────────────────────────────────────
│  $\forall\ c1, c2: class \bullet c1.name = c2.name \Rightarrow c1 = c2$
│  $\bigcup \{c: class \bullet c.allSupers\} \subseteq class$
│  $\bigcup \{a: assoc \bullet \{source.class, target.class\}\} \subseteq class$
│  $allConstructs = class \cup assoc$
│       $\cup\ (\bigcup\{c: class \bullet c.attributes\}) \cup (\bigcup\{c: class \bullet c.operations\})$
│       $\cup\ (\bigcup \{o: \bigcup\{c: class \bullet c.operations\} \bullet o.parameters\})$
│
└─────────────────────────────────────────────────────

## 5.2  Role Binding Model

We define an Object-Z class *Binding* to describe mappings from a role element to a class model element. A binding has a client of type *RoleElement* and a supplier of type *ClassConstruct* representing all class constructs. A binding is directed from a role element to a class construct.

┌─*Binding*────────────────────────────────
│
│  *roleElement*: ↓ *RoleElement*
│  *classElement*: *ClassConstruct*
│
└──────────────────────────────────────────

A role binding model has a role model defining a pattern and a class model realizing the pattern, and a set of role bindings between role elements and class constructs.

```
┌─RoleBindingModel──────────────────────────────────────────────
│
│  classModel: ClassModel
│  pattern: RoleModel
│  bindings: ℙBinding
│ ─────────────────────────────────────────────────────────────
│  ∪{b: bindings • b.roleElement} ⊆ pattern.roles
│  ∪{b: bindings • b.classElement} ⊆ classModel.allConstructs
│  [1] ∀ r: { rr: pattern.Roles | rr ∉ RoleDependency } •
│            1 < #{b: bindings | b.roleElement = r } ≤ r.occurrence
│  [2] ∀ cr: pattern.classRoles •
│            ∀ c: {b: bindings | b.roleElement = cr ∧
│                              b.classElement ∈ Class • b.classElement } •
│              ∀ ar: cr.attributeRoles •  1 < #{b: bindings | b.roleElement = ar ∧
│                              b.classElement ∈ c.attributes} ≤ ar.occurrence
│              ∀ or: cr.operationRoles •  1 < #{b: bindings | b.roleElement = or ∧
│                              b.classElement ∈ c.operations} ≤ or.occurrence
│  [3] ∀ rr: pattern.relationshipRoles | rr ∈ ClassRoleHierarchy •
│            ∀ supc:{b: bindings | b.roleElement = rr.superRole ∧
│                   b.classElement ∈ Class • b.classElement },
│            ∀ subc: {b: bindings | b.roleElement = rr.subRole ∧
│                   b.classElement ∈ Class • b.classElement } • supc ∉ subc.allSubs
│  [4] ∀ od: {r : pattern.relationshipRoles | r ∈ SimpleOccurrenceDependency} •
│            #{ b: bindings | b.roleElement = od.client } =
│                              #{ b: bindings | b.roleElement = od.supplier }
│  [5] ∀ od :{r: pattern.relationshipRoles | r ∈ HierarchyOccurrenceDependency} •
│            od.dependentClassRole = od.supplier.superRole ⟹
│            #{ b: bindings | b.roleElement = od.client } =
│                              #{ b: bindings | b.roleElement = od.supplier}
│            od.dependentClassRole = od.supplier.subRole ⟹
│            #{ b: bindings | b.roleElement = od.client } =
│                              #{ b: bindings | b.roleElement = od.dependentClassRole }
│  [6] ∀ obr:{ r: pattern.relationshipRoles | r ∈ ObjectRoleRelationship } •
│            ∀ a: { b: bindings | b.roleElement = obr ∧ b.classElement ∈ Association •
│                   b.classElement } •
│            ∃₁ sb, tb: bindings •
│                sb.roleElement = obr.source  ∧ sb.classElement = a.source
│                tb.roleElement = obr.target  ∧ tb.classElement = a.target
│                obr.sourceObjectMultiplicity ∈ a.source.Multiplicity
│                obr.targetObjectMultiplicity ∈ a.target.Multiplicity
│
└───────────────────────────────────────────────────────────────
```

The properties of the role binding model are as follows:

[1] For each role in a pattern except dependencies (which will be realized by the bindings of their associated roles), there must be an element in the class model bound to the role. Otherwise, we assume that the role (except class role hierarchies) is bound to an empty element (a null value) meaning a new class construct needs to be created as a result of the pattern deployment. The occurrence property of each role must be preserved in the binding.

[2] When a class role is bound to a class, the feature roles of the class role must also be bound consistently with the class role (e.g. an operation role to a behavioural feature such as operation).

[3] When a class role hierarchy is bound to a class hierarchy, the class hierarchy in the class model must not conflict with the class role hierarchy in the role model, which means the class corresponding to the super class role must not appear in the set of subclasses of the class corresponding to the sub class role.

[4]  Simple occurrence dependencies must be consistent with the binding of their associated roles.
[5]  Hierarchy occurrence dependencies must be consistent with the binding of the dependent class role of the dependencies.
[6]  When an object role relationship is bound to an association, the multiplicity property of the dependency must be preserved in the association.

## 6   Conclusion and Future Work

In this paper, we have presented a formal metamodeling approach based on roles for pattern specification and application. We first formalized the role concepts used in our work as a role metamodel. Given this role metamodel, patterns are defined as a pattern role model in an abstract, but precise way using Object-Z and visualized using UML. Using Object-Z, we reuse existing pattern descriptions to define other patterns in a compositional manner. These features significantly increase the flexibility and extendibility of our work in describing patterns.

We also provide a precise basis to validate pattern usage in design models in terms of a role binding model. The role binding model generically defines the properties of patterns that must be fulfilled in pattern usage at the role binding-level. This is sound because patterns are a general solution for a well-known software problem but they must not restrict the pattern realization in a particular way. Once the role binding is valid satisfying all constraints on the role binding model, its design model is valid in the context of the pattern.

The pattern role models presented in this paper may not be directly understood by a tool. To support automatic model evolution in the MDA context, we are implementing our role metamodel using the Eclipse Modeling Framework (EMF) [3], a plug-in to the Eclipse Platform [4]. An editor of the role metamodel is automatically generated by EMF and is used to create and edit pattern role models. The pattern role models developed this way are in XMI and should be understood by MDA tools. We are currently investigating the use of model transformation techniques [22] for pattern-based model evolution and also checking that our techniques are consistent with MDA standards including UML 2.0 [18].

## Acknowledgments

This research is funded by an Australian Research Council Discovery grant, DP0451830: Formalizing Software Design Pattern Concepts and Pattern Specifications using Metamodeling.

## References

1.  Dong, J. UML Extensions for Design Pattern Compositions. In *Journal of Object Technology*, Vol. 1(5), 2002, pp. 149-161.
2.  Duke, R. and G. Rose. *Formal Object-Oriented Specification Using Object-Z*. 2000: Macmillan.
3.  Eclipse Modeling Framework. http://www.eclipse.org/emf/

4. Eclipse Project, Eclipse Foundation. http://www.eclipse.org/downloads/index.php
5. Eden, A., J. Gil, Y. Hirshfeld and Yehudai A. Towards a Mathematical Foundation For Design Patterns, Technical report 1999-004, Uppsala University.
6. Flores A., L. Reynoso and R. Moore. A Formal Model of Object-Oriented Design and GoF Patterns, *UNU/IIST Report No.200*, 2000.
7. Fontoura M. and C. Lucena. Extending UML to Improve the Representation of Design Patterns, *J. Object-Oriented Programming*, Vol. 13(11), 2001, pp. 12-19.
8. France, R., D.-K. Kim, G. Sudipto, E. Song. A UML-Based Pattern Specification Technique. In *IEEE Trans. Software Engineering*, Vol. 30(3), 2004, pp. 193-206.
9. Gamma E., R. Helm, R. Johnson and J. Vlissides. *Design Patterns: Elements of Reusable Object-Oriented Software*, 1995, Addison Wesley.
10. Guennec A., G. Sunye and J. Jezequel. Precise Modeling of Design Patterns, in *Proc. of UML 2000*, LNCS 1939, 2000, Springer-Verlag, pp. 482-496.
11. Kim, S. K. and D. Carrington. Formalizing the UML class diagram using Object-Z, in *Proc. UML 1999*, LNCS 1723, 1999, Springer-Verlag. pp. 83-98.
12. Kim, S. K. and D. Carrington. A Formal Denotational Semantics of UML in Object-Z. *l'Objet*, 2001, Vol. 7(1), pp. 323-362.
13. Kim, S. K. and D. Carrington. Using Integrated Metamodeling to Define OO Design Patterns with Object-Z. *Proc. APSEC 2004*, 2004, pp. 257-264.
14. Lano K., S. Goldsack, and J. Bicarrehui. Formalizing Design Patterns, in *Proc. the BCS-FACS*, 1996. http://www1.bcs.org.uk/DocsRepository/02700/2790/lano.pdf
15. Lauder A. and S. Kent. Precise Visual Specification of Design Patterns, in *Proc. ECOOP' 98*, LNCS 1445, 1998, Springer-Verlag, pp. 114-134.
16. Mak J., C. Choy, and D. Lun, Precise Modeling of Design Patterns in UML, *Proc. ICSE'04*, 2004, pp. 252 – 261.
17. OMG, MDA Guide Version 1.0.1 *OMG Document number omg/03-06-01*, 2003.
18. OMG, UML 2.0 superstructure specification, http://www.omg.org/uml/
19. Riehle D. Describing and Composing Patterns Using Role Diagrams, in *Proc. Ubilab Conference' 96*, 1996, pp. 137-152.
20. Sanada Y. and R. Adams. Representing Design Patterns and Frameworks in UML – Towards a Comprehensive Approach, *J. Object Technology*, Vol. 1(2), 2002, pp. 143-154.
21. Soundarajan N. and J. Hallstrom, Responsibilities and Rewards: Specifying Design Patterns, *Proc. ICSE'04*, 2004, pp. 666 – 675.
22. Tefkat: The EMF transformation engine. DSTC. http://www.dstc.edu.au/Research/Projects/Pegamento/tefkat/index.html

# An Object-Oriented Structuring for Z Based on Views

Nuno Amálio, Fiona Polack, and Susan Stepney

Department of Computer Science,
University of York, York, YO10 5DD, UK
{namalio, fiona, susan}@cs.york.ac.uk

**Abstract.** There is significant interest in the use of Z in conjunction with object-orientation. Here we present a new approach to structuring Z specifications in an object-oriented (OO) style. Our structuring is based on views, it uses the schema calculus, and it does not extend Z. The resulting OO Z specifications are comprehensible, modular, and conceptually clear. The modularity of the new approach supports a template-instantiation approach to expressing OO models in Z; practical formal verification and validation of the model can be undertaken using meta-proof, meta-lemmas, and formal snapshots.

**Keywords:** Z, object-orientation.

## 1   Introduction

For more than a decade, there has been interest in structuring Z specifications in an object-oriented (OO) style [1]. Researchers quickly realised that Z does not directly support object-orientation; fundamental OO concepts such as object and class are not Z language primitives. This has resulted in extensions, such as Object-Z [2], designed to facilitate the structuring of Z-based specifications in an OO style. However, this more natural way of expressing OO properties comes at a cost: a more complex language semantics, and reduced flexibility. This has implications in the language's proof and refinement theories, which also become more complex.

Z is a simple language based on typed set theory and first order logic with a simple structuring mechanism, the schema. It has a mathematical, rather than computational, semantics. This makes it flexible and extensible, allowing structuring based on different computational models.

Here we present a new approach to structuring Z specifications in an OO style, without extending the Z language. The approach has emerged in the context of developing a semantic model to represent abstract UML models [3, 4, 5], and the example used to illustrate the approach here is based on a simple UML class model. The full approach is not restricted to class models, to UML, or to any particular variant of OO semantics.

H. Treharne et al. (Eds.): ZB 2005, LNCS 3455, pp. 262–278, 2005.
© Springer-Verlag Berlin Heidelberg 2005

Our approach builds on existing research, reviewed in [6]. It has some novel features that enhance the comprehensibility, abstraction and modularity of the Z model:

- It separates concerns effectively by being based on views, following a views structuring approach for Z [7].
- It is very modular, which is achieved by being based on the schema calculus. This allows us to represent concepts as modules (schemas), that can be composed with other modules to form the whole.

## 2   The Structuring

This section introduces our structuring, explaining how the components of OO are represented and the views structure adopted, we also introduce our domain toolkit of templates, which allows the generation of models following this structuring by instantiating templates. In the following section, an example model is built up following this structuring.

### 2.1   Objects, Classes, Associations and Systems

OO models are structured around the concept of the *object*. Objects are characterised by an identity (distinguishing one object from all others) and observable properties. The building blocks of our models are object-based structures, namely *class*, which represents a set of objects; *association*, which represents relations between classes of objects; and *system*, which composes classes and their associations and represents global scope properties.

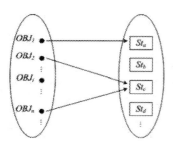

An OO class has a dual meaning. Class *intension* defines a class in terms of the properties shared by the objects of that class (for example, a class *Person* with properties *name* and *address*). Class *extension* defines a class in terms of the currently existing object instances of that class (for example, *Person* is $\{MrSmith, MrAnderson, MsFitzgerald\}$). This duality, inspired by the definitions of a set in set theory, is reflected in the way we represent classes: each class has one intensional and one extensional representation.

In our approach, Figure 1, objects are atoms (individuals represented in Z as elements of a given set). The class intension defines the set of all possible object states. A function maps the existing object atoms to their current states (the class extension). Representing objects as atoms ensures the identity property necessary for objects. Separation of concerns is achieved,

**Fig. 1.** The set of all object atoms *OBJ*, the set of all object states *St* (the class intension), and the mapping from existing objects to their current states (the class extension)

because objects, class intensions, and class extensions are all related, but separately represented.

Associations express relationships between classes. An association denotes a set of object tuples, where each tuple describes the objects being related (or linked). In our approach, associations are represented as a Z relation between objects.

Systems are used to assemble the local structures, classes, and associations into more global ones; systems also include invariants (or constraints) whose scope goes beyond local structures.

The representation of class intensions and extensions, associations and systems follows a Z state and operations style defined through the schema calculus. Each is represented as a Z abstract data type (ADT), comprising a state, initialisation, operations, and finalisation.

## 2.2   Views

A view [7] is a partial specification of a program consisting of a state space and a set of operations. A full specification is obtained by composing several views, linking them through their states and through their operations.

We use views because not all properties of OO models fit into a single representation. For example, we cannot capture the three representations of classes—atoms, intension, extension—in a single view. Also, views have proved to be an effective means of achieving clear separation of concerns in the specification. This conceptual clarity helps not only in writing and reading the Z models, but also in formal verification and validation. The clear separation of views allows, among other things, a simple solution to the frame problem in system operations (below).

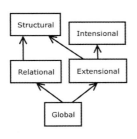

The views that we use are closely related to our basic OO structures. The *structural* view defines sets of object atoms, and captures properties of class structures from an atom perspective of classes. The *intensional* and *extensional* views represent, respectively, the intensional and extensional meanings of classes. The *relational* view represents associations. The *global* view represents systems. The structural view is the only one that does not follow a Z state and operations style; it is a conceptual view, enhancing the conceptual cohesion of the whole structuring. The other views are collections of ADTs, representing class intensions, class extensions, associations, and systems.

**Fig. 2.** The views of our structuring and dependency relationships (arrow means dependency)

Figure 2 shows the dependencies among these views. The structural view introduces global names that allow the relational and extensional views to be built independently whilst sharing the same vocabulary, and then to be linked in the global view. The intensional view defines the possible states of objects; these definitions are used in the extensional view to define the mapping between existing objects (atoms) and their current state.

We use different mechanisms to link views. The structural view defines global names, which are then used (directly or as a Z *parent* section) in the descriptions of the extensional, relational and global views. The extensional and intensional views are linked using Z promotion [8, 9]: a class extension includes a collection of state intensions (as a mapping from object atom to state), the intensional operations are then promoted to be applicable to all the objects of the class. Finally, the link between the description of the global view and the ones from the relational and extensional views is established through Z schema conjunction.

## 2.3    A Domain Toolkit of Templates

The use of views, and the resultant highly modular Z model, allows a systematic approach to constructing the model. We use *templates* to capture the structure of the Z model. Templates are pieces of instantiable Z, which we use to parameterise all sorts of Z phrases, such as axiomatic definitions, schemas and instantiations of Z generics. Template descriptions represent meta-level concepts, such as, class intension, class extension, association and global constraint. Templates are instantiated by reference to the labels of the equivalent concepts in conventional OO diagrams [3, 5] (e.g. the state definition of a class intension is obtained by instantiating the proper template with reference to the class name, and names of composing attributes), and by other model information not expressible in terms of diagrams (e.g. a state invariant of a class intension, which is not represented diagrammatically).

One particular interpretation of a modelling concept is represented by a set of templates. Alternative interpretations of a concept (e.g. association) can be defined by providing another set of templates. This allows us to construct Z models based on variant OO interpretations by selecting an appropriate alternative set of templates.

Standard conjectures, such as an initialisation conjecture, can also be expressed in template form. In our work, various template conjectures have been subject to formal analysis, leading to a number of meta-theorems and meta-lemmas. For correctly-instantiated specification templates, these reduce the proof of standard conjectures to a trivial exercise [10].

Our templates and associated meta-theorems constitute our domain toolkit for building OO Z specifications. Like the Z mathematical toolkit, they provide generic definitions and laws to construct and reason about Z specifications. Unlike the Z mathematical toolkit, which is based on Z generics, our toolkit is based, essentially, on templates; the use of templates allows us to increase the level of scope of generic definitions: we can generalise whole specifications and be closer the application domain. The Z model given below has been constructed and consistency-checked by using templates and meta-theorems from the domain toolkit. This strategy of building toolkits of generic definitions is based on the pattern application-oriented theory [11].

## 3    Example

We illustrate our OO structuring with the specification of a trivial bank system. The static structure is captured by a UML class diagram, figure 3.

- *Customer* represents the bank's customers; the attributes record the *name* of a customer, its *address*, and *type* (either *company* or *personal*).
- *Account* represents the accounts managed by the bank; the attributes record the account number (*accountNo*), the *balance*, and the *type* of account (either *current* or *savings*).
- The association *Holds* relates *Customers* and their *Accounts*; a *Customer* may have zero or more accounts; an *Account* must have one customer.

**Fig. 3.** The example UML model. See text for various Z annotations

The trivial bank system has the following constraints:

1. Savings accounts cannot have negative balances.
2. The total balance of all the bank's accounts must not be negative.
3. Customers of type *company* cannot hold savings accounts.

The system provides the following operations:

- *Open Account* : open a new account for an existing bank customer.
- *Deposit* : deposit some money into one account
- *Withdraw* : withdraw money from one account
- *Get Balance* : get the balance of one account
- *Get Customer Accounts* : get all the accounts of a certain bank customer
- *Get Accounts in Debt* : get all the accounts that are in debt
- *Delete Account* : delete one account from the system

We start the formal model of the trivial bank system by specifying the state space of the system, and define operations on the state. Only illustrative components are given; like components are specified in similar ways, instantiated from the same templates.

### 3.1    Specifying Z State

The Z state is constructed from the five views. We use systematic naming conventions, based on [12–chap. 8]. A name starting with the letter $\mathbb{S}$ designates a concept from the extensional view, and a name starting with the letter $\mathbb{A}$ designates a concept from the relational view.

**Structural View.** Z does not support subtyping; we define a single Z type to represent all object atoms, as this allows us to model OO specialisation hierarchies in a natural manner (not illustrated here).

[*OBJECT*]

Each class in the model has its own subset of object atoms. In addition, the object sets for the classes Customer and Account are disjoint, as these classes are not related by a specialisation relation:

$$
\begin{array}{|l}
\mathit{CustomerOs}, \mathit{AccountOs} : \mathbb{P} \; \mathit{OBJECT} \\
\hline
\mathrm{disjoint}\langle \mathit{CustomerOs}, \mathit{AccountOs}\rangle
\end{array}
$$

**Intensional View.** The state intension defines classes in terms of attributes, attribute types, and, where required, a class invariant. Attribute types are defined as appropriate. For example, for Account we define $ACCID$ as a given set, and $ACCTYPE$ as a Z free type:

[*ACCID*]                    $ACCTYPE ::= current \mid savings$

The state and initialisation of Account intension is given below. The state $Account$ defines the state attributes, and expresses the first system constraint (*savings accounts cannot have negative balances*). The initialisation makes an assignment of values to class attributes.

$$
\begin{array}{|l}
Account \\
\hline
accountNo : ACCID \\
balance : \mathbb{N} \\
type : ACCTYPE \\
\hline
type = savings \Rightarrow 0 \leq balance
\end{array}
\qquad
\begin{array}{|l}
AccountInit \\
\hline
Account\,' \\
accountNo? : ACCID \\
type? : ACCTYPE \\
\hline
accountNo' = accountNo? \\
balance' = 0 \\
type' = type?
\end{array}
$$

**Extensional View.** A class state extension defines the set of all *existing* objects (a subset of the class' object set), and a function that maps object atoms to their state intensions. The structure is expressed in a generic from our domain toolkit:

$$
\begin{array}{|l}
\mathbb{S}\mathrm{Gen}\,[OSET, OSTATE] \\
\hline
objs : \mathbb{P}\; OSET \\
objSt : OSET \rightarrowtail OSTATE \\
\hline
\mathrm{dom}\, objSt = objs
\end{array}
$$

Actual class state extensions are instantiations of this generic. For example, the Account state extension instantiates the generic and expresses the second system constraints (*the total of all the account balances must not be negative*):

$$\begin{array}{l} \underline{\text{S}Account} \underline{\phantom{xxxxxxxxxxxxxxxxxxxxxxxxxxxxxxxxxxxxxxxxxxxxxxxx}} \\ \quad \text{SGen}[AccountOs, Account][accounts/objs, accountSt/objSt] \\ \hline \quad 0 \leq \Sigma\{\ a : accounts \bullet a \mapsto (accountSt\ a).balance\ \} \end{array}$$

(See the appendix for the definition of $\Sigma$.) The instantiation, guided by a toolkit template, includes the renaming of generic components, to avoid name clashing when component schemas are composed to make the system schema.

The initialisation of the extension assigns both the set of existing objects and the set of object atoms to state mappings to the empty set; in the initial state there are no objects.

$$\text{S}AccountInit == [\ \text{S}Account\ ' \mid accounts' = \varnothing \wedge accountSt' = \varnothing\ ]$$

**Relational View.** In the relational view we define the association state as a Z relation between the object sets of the classes being associated.

The $\mathbb{A}Holds$ state definition defines the relationship between the object sets of the classes Customer and Account. The initialisation of the relationship states that the set of existing links is empty; in the initial state there are no objects, hence, no links between them.

$$\mathbb{A}Holds == [\ holds : CustomerOs \leftrightarrow AccountOs\ ]$$
$$\mathbb{A}HoldsInit == [\ \mathbb{A}Holds\ ' \mid holds' = \varnothing\ ]$$

At this stage, we do not constrain the *holds* relation to reflect the multiplicity of the association; multiplicities are defined on existing objects, which are defined in the extensional view and are not directly accessible from the relation view. An alternative modelling of associations that included extensions of the associated classes in the association state schema, to allow multiplicity constraints here, would break the separation that exists between relational and extensional views.

**Global View.** In the global view we compose classes and associations, and express properties of global scope, to form systems. The system state includes classes and association of the system, link invariants between associations and class extensions, and global scope constraints. The system initialisation is the initialisation of the system's components. In the illustration of the trivial bank system, the system has two classes and a single association between them; in general, however, the system is made up of subsystems comprising classes and their linking associations; invariants are added at the appropriate scope, to a subsystem or the full system, as appropriate.

In the global view, each association has a schema expressing the appropriate association link invariant. To maintain the modular structuring, global constraints are expressed in separate schemas, and then added to the predicate of the system schema (based on the Name Predicates pattern [11]).

$Link\mathbb{A}Holds$ expresses the link invariant of the association $Holds$:

```
┌─ Link𝔸Holds ──────────────────────────────────────
│ 𝕊Customer; 𝕊Account; 𝔸Holds
│ ────────────────────────────────────────────────
│ holds ∈ Rel₁,*[customers, accounts]
└────────────────────────────────────────────────────
```

The global view can use both the relational and extensional views, so the schema can include the extensions both of the participating classes and of the association. The predicate constrains the relation representing the association to be the correct multiplicity, using the appropriate association multiplicity generic from the toolkit (see Appendix); it says that the inverse of the relation must be a total function from the set of existing accounts to the set of existing customers. This ensures both the correct association multiplicity ($*\,..\,1$), and that the relation refers to existing objects only.

The third constraint of the system (*customers of type company cannot hold savings accounts*) involves concepts from multiple views. It is expressed in the global view as $ConstraintCompanyNoSavings$:

```
┌─ ConstraintCompanyNoSavings ──────────────────────
│ 𝕊Customer; 𝕊Account; 𝔸Holds
│ ────────────────────────────────────────────────
│ { oC : customers | (customerSt oC).type = company }
│     ◁ holds ▷ { oA : accounts | (accountSt oA).type = savings }
│ = ∅
└────────────────────────────────────────────────────
```

The system schema is defined by conjoining all the class extensions and associations, association link invariants, and global constraints:

```
┌─ System ──────────────────────────────────────────
│ 𝕊Customer; 𝕊Account; 𝔸Holds
│ ────────────────────────────────────────────────
│ Link𝔸Holds
│ ConstraintCompanyNoSavings
└────────────────────────────────────────────────────
```

The initialisation of the system consists of initialising the system's components. This is done by conjoining the component initialisations:

$$SysInit == System\,' \wedge \mathbb{S}CustomerInit \wedge \mathbb{S}AccountInit \wedge \mathbb{A}HoldsInit$$

Note that the after state of the $System$ is included in this conjunction, so that the constraints declared globally in $System$ are included. This ensures that all the constraints are taken into account in the system initialisation theorem.

## 3.2   Specifying Z Operations

A system operation in an OO system comprises operations on a number of classes. In modelling system operations in our Z style, we first decompose them into constituent class operations. For example, the operation to open a new account involves the creation of a new *Account* object and the addition of a link, between the new account and its customer, to the association *Holds*. The system operation is the composition of these two operations.

We specify operation components in the intensional, extensional and relational views, and then compose them in the global view to form system operations.

We introduce naming conventions to distinguish update (change state) from observe (do not change state) operations. Following Z conventions, names of update operations include the symbol $\Delta$ subscripted, whereas observe ones include the symbol $\Xi$.

**Intensional View.** The operations of the intensional view specify state transitions or observations on the state of a single class object.

We distinguish two kinds of operations. *Update operations* change the state of objects; they effect a state transition. *Observe operations* leave the state of objects unchanged, performing queries on the current state of objects. We may also need to specify the *finalisation*, which expresses a condition for objects of a class to cease their existence.

The system operations *Deposit* and *Withdraw* change the state of one account object: the *balance* is incremented or decremented by a certain amount. The intensional view is:

$$
\begin{array}{l}
\underline{\quad Account_\Delta\,Withdraw \underline{\hspace{3cm}}} \\
\Delta Account \\
amount? : \mathbb{N} \\
\hline
accountNo' = accountNo \\
type' = type \\
balance' = balance - amount?
\end{array}
\qquad
\begin{array}{l}
\underline{\quad Account_\Delta\,Deposit \underline{\hspace{3cm}}} \\
\Delta Account \\
amount? : \mathbb{N} \\
\hline
accountNo' = accountNo \\
type' = type \\
balance' = balance + amount?
\end{array}
$$

The system operation *GetBalance* observes the state of one *Account* object, specifically the *Account.balance* state attribute:

$$Account_\Xi\,GetBalance == [\ \Xi Account;\ balance! : \mathbb{Z} \mid balance! = balance\ ]$$

We want to be able to delete accounts, but only only when their balance is zero. This finalisation condition is specified on *Account* objects:

$$AccountFin == [\ Account \mid balance = 0\ ]$$

**Extensional View.** This view defines operations that are applicable to all existing objects of a class. Most operations of this view are defined by *promoting* operations from the intensional view.

Z Promotion uses *framing* schemas to promote local operations to a global state. Our approach provides framing schemas customised to our class state extensions, drawing on our work on promotion patterns [9, 11]. There is one framing schema for each kind of operation, the usual *new*, *update*, and *delete* framing schemas; in addition we introduce an *observe* framing schema. For example, the update and observe framing schemas for the class Account are:

$$
\begin{array}{l}
\_\varPhi\mathbb{S}AccountUpdate _____ \\
\Delta\mathbb{S}Account \\
\Delta Account \\
oAccount? : AccountOs \\
\hline
oAccount? \in accounts \\
\theta Account = accountSt\ oAccount? \\
accounts' = accounts \\
accountSt' = accountSt \oplus \\
\quad \{oAccount? \mapsto \theta Account'\}
\end{array}
\qquad
\begin{array}{l}
\_\varPhi\mathbb{S}AccountObserve _____ \\
\varXi\mathbb{S}Account \\
\varXi Account \\
oAccount? : AccountOs \\
\hline
oAccount? \in accounts \\
\theta Account = accountSt\ oAccount?
\end{array}
$$

The framing schemas are used to form promoted operations. For example, given the appropriate intensional view operations and framing schemas for the *Account* class, the extensional operations for initialisation, withdrawal, deposit, an account enquiry, and an account deletion are:

$$\mathbb{S}_\Delta AccountNew == \exists\ Account\ ' \bullet \varPhi\mathbb{S}AccountNew \land AccountInit$$

$$\mathbb{S}_\Delta AccountWithdraw ==$$
$$\qquad \exists\ \Delta Account \bullet \varPhi\mathbb{S}AccountUpdate \land Account_\Delta\ Withdraw$$

$$\mathbb{S}_\Delta AccountDeposit == \exists\ \Delta Account \bullet \varPhi\mathbb{S}AccountUpdate \land Account_\Delta Deposit$$

$$\mathbb{S}_\varXi AccountGetBalance ==$$
$$\qquad \exists\ \varXi Account \bullet \varPhi\mathbb{S}AccountObserve \land Account_\varXi\ GetBalance$$

$$\mathbb{S}_\Delta AccountDelete == \exists\ Account \bullet \varPhi\mathbb{S}AccountDelete \land AccountFin$$

We may also have operations in the extensional view that are not promotions. For example, the trivial bank may wish to identify all the accounts that are in debt. This is expressed in the extensional view without promotion of an intensional operation:

$$
\begin{array}{l}
\_\mathbb{S}_\varXi AccountGetDebtAccounts _____ \\
\varXi\mathbb{S}Account \\
osAccount! : \mathbb{P}\,AccountOs \\
\hline
osAccount! = \{\ a : accounts \mid (accountSt\ a).balance < 0\ \}
\end{array}
$$

**Relational View.** Operations in the relational view change or observe the state of associations. Association operations add and remove pairs from the tuples of the association relation, and perform queries on the state of associations.

In the trivial bank system, we need to associate bank customers with new accounts. This is done by adding tuples, consisting of one existing Customer object and one existing Account object, to the Holds association:

$$
\begin{array}{|l}
\underline{\mathbb{A}_\Delta HoldsAdd} \\
\Delta\mathbb{A}Holds \\
oCustomer? : CustomerOs \\
oAccount? : AccountOs \\
\hline
holds' = holds \cup \{oCustomer? \mapsto oAccount?\}
\end{array}
$$

When a bank account is removed, the link that exists between the account and its customer (association Holds) must also be deleted. The deletion of tuples of the association Holds, given a set of Account objects, is described by the operation $\mathbb{A}_\Delta HoldsDelAccount$ (below).

We also want to list all the accounts held by a customer, an observation on the state of *Holds*. The operation $\mathbb{A}_\Xi CustomerAccounts$ performs the required observation:

$$
\begin{array}{|l}
\underline{\mathbb{A}_\Delta HoldsDelAccount} \\
\Delta\mathbb{A}Holds \\
osAccount? : \mathbb{P}\ AccountOs \\
\hline
holds' = holds \rhd osAccount?
\end{array}
\qquad
\begin{array}{|l}
\underline{\mathbb{A}_\Xi CustomerAccounts} \\
\Xi\mathbb{A}Holds \\
oCustomer? : CustomerOs \\
osAccount! : \mathbb{P}\ AccountOs \\
\hline
osAccount! = holds (\!| \{oCustomer?\} |\!)
\end{array}
$$

**Global View.** The global view of operations defines system operations that act on the state of the system as a whole. These operations are defined by composition of the operations from the extensional and relational views. This is essentially schema conjunction (except where there is a necessary order of execution of component operations from the separate views). However, as the following example shows, we also need to maintain global constraints, and address the framing problem [13], by making explicit the effect of each operation on the whole system state.

When composing system operations using conjunction, some adjustments may be needed so that the elements of component operations relate correctly across the conjunction. This adjustment involves relating inputs and outputs of component operations.

These issues and their resolutions are explored using the example of a system operation to open a new account. This involves one operation from the extensional view (to create a new account), and one from the relational view (to associate the new account with an existing customer):

$$
SysOpenAccount == \mathbb{S}_\Delta AccountNew \wedge \mathbb{A}_\Delta HoldsAdd
$$

First, we need to make an adjustment, because $\mathbb{S}_\Delta AccountNew$ outputs an $oAccount!$ but the $\mathbb{A}_\Delta HoldsAdd$ requires an input $oAccount?$. This is resolved by renaming one (here the input of $\mathbb{A}_\Delta HoldsAdd$):

$$
SysOpenAccount == \mathbb{S}_\Delta AccountNew \wedge \mathbb{A}_\Delta HoldsAdd[oAccount!/oAccount?]
$$

This simple conjunction does not take into account the global scope constraint of the trivial bank system, that *customers of type company cannot hold savings accounts*, and the violation cannot be determined by formal analysis. To solve this, we need to *lift* component operations to system operations by conjoining $\Delta System$. (This follows the principle of *promotion*, but since promotion in Z refers to a concrete technical mechanism, we term this flavour of promotion *lifting*.)

However, this introduces a frame problem [13]. Component operations specify the change of state of their local components, but a system may include other components whose states should be unchanged by the operation. In this example, the operation should change the states of the Account extension and of Holds, but the extension of Customer, introduced by adding $\Delta System$, should remain unchanged. However, in Z, the state of any component that is not explicitly addressed is undetermined after the operation; any state of $\mathbb{S}\,Customer$ would satisfy the specification.

In our approach, we define *frames* for system operations. This makes explicit what is to change and what is to remain unchanged. The names of system operation frames are prefixed by $\Psi$ (by analogy to $\Phi$ promotion frames), and are formed by conjoining $\Delta System$ with the $\Xi$ (nothing changes) of every system component whose state is to remain unchanged. Thus, the frame for the above example is:

$$\Psi SysAccountHolds == \Delta System \wedge \Xi \mathbb{S}\,Customer$$

This simple solution is possible because views give the required separation of concerns. Components (classes and associations) are specified independently from each other; when we preceed a component with $\Xi$ we know that we are saying that only this component's state is to remain unchanged and nothing else[1].

The system operation to open an account can now be fully specified by schema conjunction:

$$SysOpenAccount == \Psi SysAccountHolds \wedge \mathbb{S}_\Delta\,AccountNew$$
$$\wedge\; \mathbb{A}_\Delta\,HoldsAdd[oAccount!/oAccount?]$$

In common with the constraints added to the global view of the system state, some operation preconditions can only be expressed in the global view. If, in our example, we want to add a precondition that the new account is associated with an existing bank customer, this is specified in a condition schema:

---

[1] A version of state extension modelling that included class extensions in the association state schema (for example, to allow the specification of association multiplicity constraints in the relational view) would preclude this simple solution, because $\Xi \mathbb{A}$ would mean that neither the association *nor* the included class extensions could change.

---
_CondIsCustomer_ _____

$\mathbb{S}$ _Customer_

$oCustomer? : CustomerOs$

---

$oCustomer? \in customers$

---

and conjoined in the system operation:

$$SysOpenAccount == \Psi SysAccountHolds \wedge \mathbb{S}_\Delta AccountNew$$
$$\wedge \mathbb{A}_\Delta HoldsAdd[oAccount!/oAccount?] \wedge CondIsCustomer$$

Other system update operations are similarly defined:

$$\Psi AccountOps == \Delta System \wedge \Xi \mathbb{S} Customer \wedge \Xi \mathbb{A} Holds$$

$$SysWithdraw == \Psi AccountOps \wedge \mathbb{S}_\Delta AccountWithdraw$$

$$SysDeposit == \Psi AccountOps \wedge \mathbb{S}_\Delta AccountDeposit$$

System observation operations do not require a specific frame; nothing changes in the system, so they can be simply conjoined with $\Xi System$. The system operations _get balance_, _get customer accounts_, and _get accounts in debt_ are:

$$SysGetBalance == \Xi System \wedge \mathbb{S}_\Xi AccountGetBalance$$

$$SysGetCustAccounts == \Xi System \wedge \mathbb{A}_\Xi CustomerAccounts$$

$$SysGetDebtAccounts == \Xi System \wedge \mathbb{S}_\Xi AccountGetDebtAccounts$$

The system operation to delete an account is defined in a similar way, but requires a rather more elaborate adjustment to the initial conjunction of the operations to delete the account from the set of existing accounts (operation $\mathbb{S}_\Delta AccountDelete$ from the extensional view) and the link to its customer (operation $\mathbb{A}_\Delta HoldsDelAccount$ from the relational view). $\mathbb{S}_\Delta AccountDelete$ takes as input one account object, however $\mathbb{A}_\Delta HoldsDelAccount$ expects a set of objects. The adjustment is made in a connector schema, _ConnAccountOs_, which transforms the single output of $\mathbb{S}_\Delta AccountDelete$ to a singleton set:

---
_ConnAccountOs_ _____

$osAccount? : \mathbb{P} AccountOs$

$oAccount? : AccountOs$

---

$osAccount? = \{oAccount?\}$

---

The connector is added to the system operation specification to form the correct composition:

$$SysDeleteAccount == \Psi SysAccountHolds \wedge \mathbb{S}_\Delta AccountDelete$$
$$\wedge ConnAccountOs \wedge \mathbb{A}_\Delta HoldsDelAccount$$

We could, of course, have avoided need for a connector schema by defining $\mathbb{A}_\Delta HoldsDelAccount$ to receive one input object rather then a set. However, the given specification is generated by instantiating our templates; we prefer to keep our operation templates generic and then adjust the connection in the global view; the forms of connection schema can also be provided as templates.

# 4    Discussion

We have described and illustrated an OO structuring for Z based on views and schema calculus. We are not aware of any other Z-only OO structuring approach that relies entirely on the schema calculus: other approaches all resort to Z axiomatic definitions to express state and operations in one way or another.

A consequence of exploiting the existing structuring mechanisms of Z, the schema and the schema calculus, is that we can systematically compose OO-structured Z specifications. In our approach, we select appropriate templates for each OO component, instantiate these to give named schemas, and then include or conjoin the instantiated components as appropriate to form the Z state and operations. Z schema conjunction is key in our structuring as it allows the propagation of system properties through the composition (a property satisfied by one schema is also satisfied by the conjunction of schemas).

Combined with the schema approach, views provide an effective means to separate concerns, and constituted a powerful conceptual tool. They allowed us to apply the principle of *divide and conquer* to design an aspect-focused structuring, where each individual aspect is conceptually clear and the collection of aspects is cohesive. This effective separation of concerns also allows a simple and elegant solution to the frame problem in the specification of system operations. Because of the basis in Z schemas, we can use Z promotion in the extensional view, to relate the class intension and extension, giving an elegant compositional approach.

The views and the schema approach also allow us to follow a modular approach towards proof. Elsewhere, we show our modular-based approach towards formal model analysis and validation. For example, our approach to consistency-checking [4] takes advantage of the modular structure of our specifications, and is based on the representation of our structures (class intensions and extensions, associations, and systems) as ADTs. To prove the consistency of our specifications, we prove initialisation theorems for the system's components, class intensions and extensions and associations (these are often trivial), and for the whole system; in proving the consistency of the whole system, we use the theorems establishing the consistency of the system's components, reducing the proof to show that the system's global constraints hold in the initial state [10].

To support writing Z models in our OO style, we have devised a domain toolkit of templates [5]. The collection of templates of the toolokit constitutes a meta-level representation of the structuring; the Z specification is created by instantiation of the relevant templates. For example, we can use templates to obtain formal representations, in Z, of UML diagrams; we can provide variant templates for different semantic interpretations of the UML notations. We use our template approach as the mechanism to support the development of *modelling frameworks* [5]: environments to build and analyse models of sequential software systems based on the combined use of UML and Z. In addition to the aspects covered in this paper, our structuring also supports the expression of specialisation (inheritance) hierarchies [5].

It is, of course, possible to write a Z specification following our structuring without instantiating our templates. However, the templates are the basis for *meta-proof* [10]: a set of meta-theorems and meta-lemmas that can be used to reduce the overhead of formal proof when consistency-checking and analysing Z specifications. Having pre-proved key theorems at the meta- or template level, correct instantiation of templates guarantees that the proofs will hold; further proof effort is restricted to local constraints; conversely, if a meta-proof cannot be discharged on an instantiated specification, then the instantiation or the underlying OO (for example, UML) model is wrong.

## 5    Related Work

Our OO structuring extends that of Hall [14, 15], who introduced the dual representation of classes, intension and extension, in the context of Z. We have introduced views, to achieve greater separation of concerns, and to make the structuring clearer. We have introduced the system structure, and the idea of representing our structures (class intensions and extensions, associations and systems) as ADTs. We have also presented an approach to compose structures: extensions are built from intensions by using promotion, and systems are built by composing class extensions and associations. We have eliminated the need for axiomatic definitions in the definition of operations; extensional class operations are defined by promoting intensional ones.

Our structuring uses the relational interpretation of associations. Alternatively, a representation where associations are interpreted as properties of a class could also be devised [6]. In this setting, a relational view would not be required, and associations would be represented as class attributes in the intensional view. We choose the relation interpretation because we consider it to be more abstract; our aim is to represent abstract UML models.

Utting and Wang propose an OO structuring for Z [16] where state and operations are defined by axiomatic definitions. Objects are atoms, and the relationship between atoms and state fields is given by axiomatically-defined functions, with one function per state field. Operations are also defined axiomatically, as a relation between an object and operation inputs and outputs. One problem with axiomatic-based descriptions in Z is that it is easy to introduce accidental contradictions (especially at the level of complexity of some operations); a contradictory description renders the whole specification unsatisfiable. We find this approach to be cumbersome and difficult to use in practice. We argue that the template support for specification and analysis would not be possible in this approach. Moreover, the resulting specifications are not succinct, and lack modularity; it is not as easy to compose axiomatic definitions as it is to compose schema-based ones.

Our model of objects can be compared to that of the formal specification language Alloy [17], which has a similar semantic basis as Z. Alloy's structuring mechanism, the signature, is inspired by the Z schema. Like schemas, a signature state definition includes the definition of state components (fields). The fundamental difference, however, is that a signature denotes a set of atoms, its fields are also atoms, and signature atoms and field atoms are linked through relations. Unlike Z schemas, this effectively gives identity to signature instances; instances of a Z schema with the same value for its fields denote the same schema object. To overcome this in Z we represent an object atom separately from the object state (a schema), and use a function to map object atoms to their state. In the end, our Z object-model and the Alloy one are not so different. Alloy has one relation between the object atom and each state field; our Z model has a function that relates the object atoms to the entire state schema.

# 6  Conclusions

We present an OO structuring for Z based on views that relies entirely on the schema calculus to describe both state and operations. The specifications resulting from our structuring are modular, abstract, and comprehensible, following a style that is familiar to and adopted by most Z users.

The OO structuring facilitates traceability (between diagrammatic models and Z models, for example), and supports template-based development and analysis. The approach is the basis for a practical framework for formal development, facilitating verification and validation checks of both formal and informal OO models. The approach is also flexible, as variant OO semantics can be represented simply by selecting the appropriate templates.

Future extensions based on the OO structuring include full support for key UML models (eg. class, state, and interaction diagrams); mutual model refinement, eventually via templates; and tool support for the templates themselves.

**Acknowledgements.** This research was supported for Amálio by the Portuguese Foundation for Science and Technology under grant 6904/2001.

# References

1. Stepney, S., Barden, R., Cooper, D., eds. *Object orientation in Z*. Workshops in Computing. Springer (1992)
2. Smith, G. P. *The Object-Z Specification Language*. Kluwer Academic Publishers (2000)
3. Amálio, N., Stepney, S., Polack, F. Modular UML semantics: Interpretations in Z based on templates and generics. In Van, H. D., Liu, Z., eds., *FACS'03*, 284, pp. 81–100. UNU/IIST Technical Report (2003)
4. Amálio, N., Stepney, S., Polack, F. Formal proof from UML models. In Davies, J., et al., eds., *ICFEM 2004*, volume 3308 of *LNCS*, pp. 418–433. Springer (2004)
5. Amálio, N., Polack, F., Stepney, S. A modelling and analysis framework for sequential systems I: Modelling. Technical Report YCS-2005, Department of Computer Science, University of York (2005)
6. Amálio, N., Polack, F. Comparison of formalisation approaches of UML class constructs in Z and Object-Z. In Bert et al. [18], pp. 339–358

7. Jackson, D. Structuring Z specifications with views. *ACM Transactions on Software Engineering and Methodology*, 4(4):365–389 (1995)
8. Woodcock, J., Davies, J. *Using Z: Specification, Refinement, and Proof.* Prentice-Hall (1996)
9. Stepney, S., Polack, F., Toyn, I. Patterns to guide practical refactoring: examples targetting promotion in Z. In Bert et al. [18], pp. 20–39
10. Amálio, N., Stepney, S., Polack, F. Modular meta-proof for structured specifications (2004). Available at http://www.cs.york.ac.uk/~namalio/publications.html
11. Stepney, S., Polack, F., Toyn, I. A Z patterns catalogue I, specification and refactoring. Technical Report YCS-2003-349, Department of Computer Science, University of York (2003)
12. Barden, R., Stepney, S., Cooper, D. *Z In Practice*. Practitioner Series. Prentice-Hall (1994)
13. Borgida, A., Mylopoulos, J., Reiter, R. On the frame problem in procedure specifications. *IEEE Transactions on Software Engineering*, 21(10):785–798 (1995)
14. Hall, A. Using Z as a specification calculus for object-oriented systems. In Hoare, C. A. R., Bjørner, D., Langmaack, H., eds., *VDM '90*, volume 428 of *LNCS*, pp. 290–318. Springer (1990)
15. Hall, A. Specifying and interpreting class hierarchies in Z. In Bowen, J., Hall, A., eds., *Z User Workshop, Cambridge*, Workshops in Computing, pp. 120–138. Springer (1994)
16. Utting, M., Wang, S. Object orientation without extending Z. In Bert et al. [18], pp. 319–338
17. Jackson, D., Shlyakhter, I., Sridharan, M. A micromodularity mechanism. In *ACM SIGSOFT Foundation of Software Engineering/ Europoean Software Engineering Conference* (2001)
18. Bert, D., et al., eds. *ZB 2003, Turku, Finland*, volume 2651 of *LNCS*. Springer (2003)

# A    OO Template Toolkit (Excerpt)

*Selected Association Multiplicity Generics*

$$\text{Rel}_{*,1}[X, Y] == X \to Y$$
$$\text{Rel}_{1,*}[X, Y] == \{\ r : X \leftrightarrow Y \mid r^\sim \in \text{Rel}_{*,1}[Y, X]\ \}$$

*Sum over a finite labelled set*

$$
\begin{array}{l}
\hline
[L] \\
\hline
\Sigma : (L \nrightarrow \mathbb{Z}) \to \mathbb{Z} \\
\hline
\Sigma \varnothing = 0 \\
\forall l : L;\ n : \mathbb{Z};\ f : L \nrightarrow \mathbb{Z} \mid l \notin \text{dom} f \bullet \Sigma(\{l \mapsto n\} \cup f) = n + \Sigma f \\
\hline
\end{array}
$$

# Component Reuse in B Using ACL2

Yann Zimmermann[1,2] and Diana Toma[3]

[1] KeesDA SA, 2 av. de Vignate 38610 Gières, France
yann@keesda.com
[2] LORIA, MOSEL team, 54506 Vandoeuvre-lès-Nancy Cedex, France
yann.zimmermann@loria.fr
[3] TIMA, 46 av. Félix Viallet, 38031 Grenoble Cedex, France
Diana.Toma@imag.fr

**Abstract.** We present a new methodology that permits to reuse an existing hardware component that has not been developed within the B framework while maintaining a correct design flow. It consists of writing a specification of the component in B and proving that the VHDL description of the component implements the specification using the ACL2 system. This paper focuses on the translation of the B specification into ACL2.

## 1 Introduction

Electronic systems are becoming more and more complex and they are now involved in a lot of products. Malfunction of an electronic circuit may have financial consequences or take a heavy toll in human life. Some standards, as IEC 61508 [12] or RTCA Do-254/EUROCAE ED-80 [17, 6], have been developed to address this. Our approach using the B method may be used in the parts relating to specifications and validations.

Formal methods are needed to ensure correctness of systems. Formal verification of circuits is often based on model-checking that is limited by the number of states of the system. Symbolic methods such as symbolic trajectory evaluation [10] may improve the efficiency of model-checking. Theorem proving is not limited by the size of the state space that may be sometimes unknown (or parameterised). Examples of successful applications of theorem provers for hardware verification include: ACL2 [21, 18], HOL [7] or PVS [20].

The PUSSEE project [16, 15] has defined a methodology to develop electronic systems by refinement from a very abstract model to its implementation at the register transfer level and translation to hardware description languages (HDL). Event-B [1, 2] is used as formal framework and BHDL®[1] is an implementation level for electronic circuits defined for B (as B0 is an implementation level for software). An example development of a circuit in B can be found in [9]. One

---

[1] BHDL is a registered trademark of KeesDA.

H. Treharne et al. (Eds.): ZB 2005, LNCS 3455, pp. 279–298, 2005.

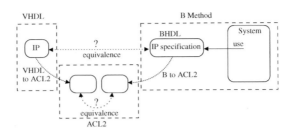

**Fig. 1.** Using ALC2 for IP reuse in B

issue of this development process is that it does not allow IP[2] reuse. To ensure correctness, components must be fully developed inside the B method and correctly translated into a HDL formalism. Reuse of existing components requires the opposite direction to be integrated into a formal B development. It is possible to translate the HDL description of the component in B, and perform proofs on the B model [4], but this is not the usual direction in B.

In this paper, we suggest using an intermediate approach (see figure 1) by specifying the circuit in B (actually in the sub-language BHDL) at a level of abstraction where the interface of the circuit corresponds to the interface of the IP. Then, this model is translated into ACL2. At the same time, the VHDL description of the IP is also translated into ACL2 [22] and we use ACL2 to prove the equivalence between both models.

This paper describes the translation from B to ACL2. The main step is to flatten the B model. It consists in building a B model where the evolution of each variable is specified using only references to inputs and registers of the circuit, without using any intermediate variable. This allows the construction of a compact model similar to the ACL2 model for a VHDL design. The advantage of doing this transformation in B and not in ACL2 is that we have proved that the flattening process is a B refinement (actually the flat model is equivalent to the original B model).

In the remainder of this paper, we first give a short introduction to circuits and to the three formalisms (VHDL, ACL2 and BHDL) of interest. The translation itself is presented in the next section by defining the notion of flat substitution, and flattening rules are explained. A sketch of the correctness of the transformation is given. We finish by summing up results obtained with case studies before the conclusion. Throughout the paper, we use the example of a simple counter to illustrate the theory.

## 2    Introduction to Synchronous Circuits

An electronic circuit is an assembly of elementary electronic components connected by wires. Wires carry electronic *signals* that can generally be in two

---

[2] Intellectual Property, this term refers to hardware sold by design companies. Usually a VHDL description is provided.

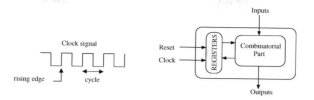

**Fig. 2.** The Clock signal and a schematic view of a syncthonous circuit

states: low-level or high-level. In this case, a signal can be modelled by Boolean values. When a signal may have more than two states, we use other logics. Electronic signals propagate in one direction on a wire; regarding the circuit as a black box, some signals enter the circuit, they are the *inputs* and some signals go out, they are the *outputs* of the circuit. Inputs and outputs taking boolean values, the circuit is modelled by a Boolean function that relates inputs to the outputs. According to the function that it defines, a circuit can be *combinatorial* (outputs are entirely defined by inputs at the same instant) or *sequential* (outputs may depends on the history of inputs). Sequential circuits include memory elements, and are called *synchronous* or *asynchronous* according to the kind of memories being used.

We only address synchronous circuits (or combinatorial circuits if there is no memory at all). A synchronous circuit is a circuit where memory elements are *flip/flops*. There are several kinds of flip/flop, the common principle is that they are driven by a *clock* signal. We call *registers* flip/flops that are sensitive to the rising edge of the clock: the stored value changes only when the clock signal changes from low-level to high-level. Between two rising edges of the clock, the register output does not change, and modifications on the input of the registers are not taken into account until a rising edge occurs. The *clock* signal is cyclic: the time interval between two rising edges is constant (see figure 2).

All registers are supposed to be loaded under to the same clock condition and so they all evolve at the same time, in a *synchronous* way. Some flip/flops can also have another input, called *asynchronous reset* that permits to reset the stored value independently of the clock signal. This signal is set by the environment of the circuit. It must be set to high-level to initialise the circuit when the whole system starts. When initialisation of the system is finished, it must remain indefinitely at low-level (unless the system needs to be reinitialised).

# 3   VHDL

One of the most used Hardware Description Language is VHDL[11]. We focus on the subset of VHDL that models hardware components at the register transfer level, this means the level where circuits are described using registers and signals.

A VHDL description consists of a list of concurrent processes. The basic process is the signal assignment $s \Leftarrow E$, $s$ is the name of the signal and $E$ is the

```
-- component interface
entity counter is
    port (
        clock : in std_logic;
        reset : in std_logic;
        rst : in std_logic;
        alm3 : out std_logic);
end;
-- component architecture
architecture tab of counter is
-- type of the register
    type tc_type is
    array (0 to 7) of std_logic;
-- declarations of signals
    signal gd : std_logic;
    signal tc_0 : tc_type; ...
begin
-- process that models registers
process (clock, reset) begin
    if reset = '1' then
        tc_0 ⇐ "1000 0000"
    elsif clock'EVENT and clock='1' then
        tc_0 ⇐ tc_1;
    end if;
end process;
```

```
-- Combinatorial part

-- the output alm3 is connected to
-- the last cell of the register tc_0
    alm3 ⇐ tc_0(7);

-- the first bit of tc_6 is '1', other bits '0'
    tc_6(0) ⇐ '1';
    GEN1 : for k in 1 to 7 generate
    tc_6(k) ⇐ '0';
    end generate;

-- gd is '1' if the maximum not reached
    gd ⇐ not (tc_0(7));

-- tc_10 is tc_0 right-shifted
    tc_10(0) ⇐ '0';
    GEN2 : for k in 1 to 7 generate
    tc_10(k) ⇐ tc_0(k - 1);
    end generate;

-- tc_8 is tc_10 unless maximum reached
    tc_8 ⇐ tc_10 when gd='1'
        else tc_0;
-- the register is
-- reinitialised (tc_6) if rst='1'
-- right-shifted if maximum not reached
-- unchanged otherwise
    tc_1 ⇐ tc_6 when rst='1'
        else tc_8;
end;
```

**Fig. 3.** A VHDL description of a counter

expression that is assigned to the signal. The semicolon ";" denotes concurrent composition: $t \Leftarrow s; s \Leftarrow E$ is the concurrent assignment of $s$ to $t$ and of $E$ to $s$. Compared to B, ";" has neither the same semantics as in B, nor the same semantics as $\parallel$ in B. It means that $t$ is connected to $s$ *and* $s$ is connected to $E$: so $t$ is also, indirectly, connected to $E$. Writting "A;B" or "B;A" is equivalent.

A more complex process is a block of sequential statements. Inside each process, statements are executed sequentially and it is possible to use local variables. Processes and signal assignments are concurrent. The semantics of concurrency are usually given using delta-delay (see [8] for example). The principle consists of applying assignments repeatedly until a fixed point is reached.

Notice that variables must not be confused with signals, they are two different kinds of objects. Signals usually correspond to wires in a circuit whereas variables are used in processes as a means of programming functionality. When a variable is assigned, its value changes immediately (as is usually the case in programming languages). When a signal is assigned, its value is not modified immediately, only the future value of the signal is modified. For example, we can write s $\Leftarrow$ '1' after 10ns, '0' after 30ns that means the value of the signal will be set to '1' (high-level) after a delay of 10ns, then set to '0' after 30ns (this means 20ns later). The modification of a signal may also depend on an event, for example we can write s $\Leftarrow$ '1' when t='0' else '0' that means the signal s will be set to '1' each time the signal t is equal to '0' and s is set to '0' in other cases.

The combinatorial part of the circuit is given by a list of concurrent signal assignments and a register is modelled by two signals and a process that is sensitive to *clock* and *reset* signals. One of these signals carries the current value of the register and the other one carries the next value of the register as specified by the combinatorial part.

As example, we give in Fig. 3 the VHDL code for a counter. The entity part is the interface of the circuit, the process corresponds to registers, and the part on the right corresponds to the combinatorial part of the circuit. In addition to the *clock* and *reset* signals, it has one input $rst$ and one output $alm3$. The signal $rst$ can be used to reinitialise the counter. If $rst$ is '0', the counter is incremented by 1 at each cycle. Here the counter is not implemented as an integer and an adder to increment it. We use a vector of bits ($tc$) that contains one token. At each cycle (unless $rst$ is set to '1'), the token moves to the next cell (GEN2 and tc_10(0) $\Leftarrow$ '0'). When the last cell is reached, it does not move anymore until the $rst$ signal is set to '1'. In this case, the token moves to the first cell (tc_6(0) $\Leftarrow$ '1' and GEN1). Signals tc_0 and tc_1 are respectively the output and the input of the register. Other signals tc_x are intermediate signals.

When the asynchronous *reset* is set to '1', the process specifies that the token moves to the first cell. The output $alm3$ is an alarm set to '1' when the counter has finished to count, that is why $alm3$ is connected to the last cell of $tc\_0$.

## 4    ACL2

ACL2 is a theorem prover based on a first order logic with equality and induction. We chose this theorem prover for its high degree of automation, and reusable libraries of function definitions and theorem proofs [13]. ACL2 is also a programming language based on Common Lisp. Therefore ACL2 models are both executable and provable. Before investing human time in a proof, it is thus possible to check the model on test vectors, a common simulation activity in design verification which helps debugging the formal model and gaining designer's confidence in it. ACL2 has already been used successfully for digital systems verification [14].

**ACL2 Model of VHDL.** The VHDL is automatically translated into a functional model using a method based on symbolic simulation developed by the VDS group, TIMA Laboratory [22]. The model is simulated symbolically for one clock cycle, actually corresponding to several VHDL simulation cycles, to extract the transition function for each output and state variable of the design. The body of a transition function is a conditional expression, an arithmetic or a

Boolean expression. The functions are translated into Lisp and used to define the Moore machine for the initial VHDL description. Standard VHDL operations on Boolean and bit vectors are replaced with corresponding operations defined and proved correct in ACL2.

Along with the functions above, information about inputs and state variables are translated to Lisp and two predicates are created: hyp-input (input), which states the type for each input element of the design, and hyp-st (st), which states the type for each state variable of the design.

A state of the Moore machine is the set of all internal memories and all the outputs of the design. A step is modeled as a function sim-step which takes as parameters the inputs of the design and the state of the machine at clock cycle k, and which produces the state of the machine at clock cycle k+1 (k is a natural number). The body of sim-step is the composition of the transition functions obtained by symbolic simulation.

Below, the corresponding sim-step function for the VHDL design implementing a counter.

```
(defun vhdl-sim-step (in st )
...
  (list (nextsig_tc_0 reset tc_1)
        (nextsig_tc_1 reset rst tc_1)
        (nextsig_tc_6)
        (nextsig_tc_8 reset tc_1)
        (nextsig_tc_10 reset tc_1)
        (nextsig_gd reset tc_1)
        (nextsig_alm3 reset tc_1))))
```

The nextsig_X function describes the behaviour of signal X during a clock cycle. For instance, here is the body of nextsig_alm3

```
(defun nextsig_alm3 (reset tc_1)
  (nth 7 (if (equal reset 1) (list 1 0 0 0 0 0 0 0)
         tc_1)))
```

The general state machine is defined as a recursive function system that takes a sequence of inputs *l-input* and an initial state *st* and returns the state obtained after consuming all inputs. *l-input* represents the list of symbolic or numeric values for the design's input ports at each clock cycle:

(*inputs_cycle*-1 *inputs_cycle*-2 ... *inputs_cycle*-k)

If the inputs list is empty (verified by the ACL2 function atom), the computation is finished and the function returns the state *st*. Otherwise, the next state is computed, and *st* is updated, by calling the step function sim-step. As we mentioned before, the model is also executable.

The funtion vhdl_counter below models the state machine function for the same VHDL design, over a time-sequence of inputs.

```
(defun vhdl-counter (l-input st )
  (if (atom l-input) st
    (vhdl-counter (cdr l-input) (vhdl-sim-step (car l-input) st ) )))
```

# 5    BHDL

The language BHDL [15–chapter 7] was defined during the PUSSEE project [16]. The goal of the project was to develop a methodology to elaborate systems (including electronic hardware) in B. Based on the same language of substitutions as B, BHDL can be used as a B implementation level for hardware, similar to B0 for software. During the project translators to SystemC and VHDL were also implemented using the logic solver of AtelierB.

We have extended the notion of frame introduced by Dunne [5] by defining for any substitution $S$ a *write frame* (denoted by $W_S$) and a *read frame* (denoted by $R_S$). They are respectively the sets of variables that are written and read by the substitution.

## 5.1    Development of Circuits in EventB

For developing a circuit in B, one may use refinement and formal verification of a system from a very abstract model to the implementation level. The development process is summed up on figure 4. Classically, the initial specification is provided in natural language. Since such a specification is not formal, it may be incomplete, inconsistent on some points or ambiguous. A first step consists in developing a B model that corresponds to this specification. This formal specification is not made in one shot but using the refinement process provided by B. A first abstract model specifies the more general view of the system, then details are added to the specification by refinement. Each element of the specification is introduced at the most abstract level possible, because it is easier to understand for the designer (there is less details) and proofs are easier to handle.

Particularly, abstraction permits to prove algorithms and protocols (see [3] for example) of the design before being overflowed by the details of a hardware implementation level.

When cycle accuracy is needed (as late as possible), it is modelled in an abstract way by synchronising components of the system. *Synchronisation* models the chain of cycles, concurrency and communications between components. The system is refined again to obtain an implementable model. Requirements of the implementation level are: implementable data types, each component is modelled separately and works only with its own state and input/output ports. Cycle accuracy is needed at the end of the development, it is the basis of the semantics of BHDL.

Once an implementable model is reached, the B model is translated in BHDL. An implementable model is fully deterministic, it uses only SELECT guards. The substitution WHILE is not used in BHDL, an implicit global loop corresponds to the succession of cycles. From an eventB model, the BHDL model is obtained by *recomposing* events of each components, implementing the synchronisation and specifying which variables are input and outputs ports.

Recomposition is based on two rules. The first one merges two events into one when their guards are complementary. The second one creates a sequential composition of two events when the first one establishes the guard of the second one.

SELECT $P \wedge Q$ THEN S END                    SELECT P THEN S POST Q END
SELECT $P \wedge \neg Q$ THEN T END                SELECT Q THEN T END
————————————————————                              ————————————————
SELECT P THEN                                     SELECT P THEN S; T END
       IF Q THEN S ELSE T END
END

The BHDL model has formal semantics[3] and can be translated to other formalisms. For example it can be translated to a hardware description language for simulation and synthesis or into a formalism that provides a better support than B for some verification activities, such as for temporal properties.

## 5.2   The BHDL Language

A BHDL design is an event-B model composed of only one event has no guard. An intuitive behaviour a BHDL design consists of:

- apply once the substitution of INITIALISATION, when the system starts
- then the substitution of the OPERATION clause is applied repeatedly

Relating this to synchronous circuits, the INITIALISATION clause specifies the initialisation of registers and the event specifies the combinatorial part of the circuit. Particularly, outputs of the circuit are specified by the operation clause even at the starting of the system: this means that the state between the initialisation and the first occurrence of the event is not observable. This corresponds to the fact that in a circuit, signals propagates inside the combinatorial part also during initialisation. Both signals *clock* and *reset* are not explicit in BHDL. The sequence of cycles is modelled by the repetitive application of the event.

Two kinds of objects carry values in a circuit: signals and registers. In a BHDL model, they are both modelled by variables. The distinction signal/register is not made explicitly, it is computed automatically using frames.

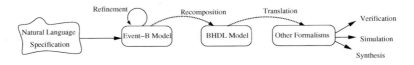

**Fig. 4.** Development Process

---

[3] Formal BHDL semantics are not yet published. They are based on before-after predicates: as a sub-language of B, BHDL inherits its semantics. These semantics has been used to ensure correctness of translations from BHDL to SystemC and VHDL.

BHDL uses a subset of B substitutions that is implementable by circuit at the RTL level. Below is a short grammar of substitutions used in this paper. The non-deterministic assignment ($x :\in Const$) is allowed only in the INITIALISATION clause and only constant set ($Const$) is allowed for this substitution. The term $BExp$ refers to B expression and $BoolExp$ to Boolean expressions.

$$Subst \leftarrow x := BExp \mid x :\in Const \mid Subst \parallel Subst \mid Subst \; ; \; Subst \parallel$$
$$\text{IF } BoolExp \text{ THEN } Subst \text{ ELSE } Subst \text{ END } \parallel$$
$$\text{IF } BoolExp \text{ THEN } Subst \text{ END}$$

### 5.3    Example of BHDL Design

We give the BHDL description of the counter (Fig. 5a). It has the same specification as the VHDL but the implementation differs. A register $compt$ stores the current value of the counter. The output $alm$ is set to $true$ when the counter reaches 7. In this case, the counter remains at 7 until the $rst$ input is set to $true$.

In the example of the counter, the register $compt$ is initialised to 0.

(a)    (b)

```
INITIALISATION
    compt := 0 ||
    rst :∈ BOOL || alm :∈ BOOL
OPERATIONS
    alm := bool(compt = 7)
    ;
    IF rst = true THEN
        compt := 0
    ELSE
        IF alm = false THEN
            compt := compt + 1
        END
    END
```

```
IF reset = true THEN
    compt := 0
END
;
alm := bool(compt = 7)
;
IF rst = true THEN
    compt := 0
ELSE
    IF alm = false THEN
        compt := compt + 1
    END
END
```

**Fig. 5.** (a) BHDL model of a 3-bit counter; (b) merging of initialisation and operation clauses

## 6    Translation from BHDL to ACL2

A BHDL design has two important parts, the INITIALISATION clause that specifies how registers are initialised when the $reset$ signal of the circuit is set, and the OPERATION clause that specifies the combinatorial part of the circuit.

The ACL2 circuit description used in our approach consists of one function per signal that computes the value of the signal at the end of a clock cycle. A function is also dedicated to simulate a clock cycle by calling all signal functions.

The translation process from BHDL to ACL2 is the following:

1. Convert the design into a design where the initialisation clause and the operation clause are merged into one substitution. A design with an initialisation clause $Init$ and an operation clause $Op$ is transformed into the substitution below. Moreover, the non-deterministic substitutions of $Init$ are removed.

$$\text{IF } reset = true \text{ THEN Init END ; Op}$$

The input signal $reset$ is introduced explicitly: if the signal $reset$ is set then $Init$ and $Op$ are applied. In the other case, only $Op$ is applied. This corresponds to the semantics of a BHDL model: the state between $Init$ and the first application of $Op$ is not observable. We give in Fig. 5b the event that corresponds to the BHDL description of Fig. 5a: the $reset$ signal is made explicit and the initialisation is directly introduced inside the event.

Notice that a requirement is that the signal $reset$ is set to $true$ when the system starts and then remains at $false$.

2. Flatten the resulting substitution
3. Translation of the flat substitution into ACL2.

## 6.1    Flat Form of a Substitution

The sequential substitution makes intermediate results available for reuse in some expressions. The ACL2 model is functional and, in our approach, the outputs are functions of inputs and registers, without any intermediate variables. To generate the ACL2 model, we first *flatten* the BHDL model to remove sequential substitutions. For example, the substitution $x := in + z; out := x + 1$ is first transformed into $x := in + z \| out := in + z + 1$.

In the definition of a flatten substitution, we only refer here to substitutions used in BHDL. A substitution is *flat* when :

- it contains no sequential composition,
- it is a parallel composition of substitutions, each one writing only one variable. Two of these substitutions cannot write the same variable and all variables must be written.

Notice that none of the composed substitutions can contain a parallel composition (because only one variable may be written), nor a sequential composition. So, according to the BHDL language, it can only be a tree of nested IF statements with simple substitutions of the form $v := E$ as leaves.

We can formalise this by giving the following grammar where $BoolExp$ is the grammar of predicates, $Exp$ of expressions and $var$ of identifiers. The predicate $card(W_S) = 1$ is a well-formedness side-condition to ensure that each substitution of the parallel composition only writes one variable. In particular, in the conditional substitution, $S^{(1)}$ and $S^{(2)}$ must write the same variable. The requirement that two substitutions cannot write the same variable is ensured by well-formedness of the parallel composition.

$$FlatS \leftarrow S \qquad\qquad card(W_S) = 1$$
$$| \ FlatS \parallel FlatS$$
$$S \leftarrow \text{IF } BoolExp \text{ THEN } S^{(1)} \text{ ELSE } S^{(2)} \text{ END}$$
$$| \ var := Exp.$$

**Example of Flat Substitution.** To illustrate how a BHDL model is transformed, we give on figure 6 the flat form of the counter given in section 5.3. It consists of two substitutions composed in parallel. The first one specifies the evolution of the variable $alm$ and the second one the variable $compt$. Each one depends only on inputs ($reset$ and $rst$) and registers ($compt$). In particular, the expression of $compt$ not longer depends on the variable $alm$.

```
IF reset = true THEN
    alm := bool(0 = 7)
ELSE
    alm := bool(compt = 7)
END

||

IF reset = true THEN                      ELSE
    IF rst = true THEN                        IF rst = true THEN
        compt := 0                                compt := 0
    ELSE                                      ELSE
        IF bool(0 = 7) = false THEN              IF bool(compt = 7) = false THEN
            compt := 0 + 1                           compt := compt + 1
        ELSE                                     ELSE
            compt := 0                               compt := compt
        END                                      END
    END                                      END
                                          END
```

**Fig. 6.** Flat substitution of the counter

## 6.2   Translation of the Flat Substitution into ACL2

The third step is easy after flattening, it just consists of rewriting the substitution using the ACL2 syntax. The syntax of the substitution respects the grammar given in previous section. Translation into ACL2 is done in this simple way by the operator $acl2$ defined below. This operator applies on flattened substitutions. Substitutions $S_1 \dots S_n$, $S$ and $T$ stand for substitutions that do not contain any parallel composition. They are simple substitutions or (flattened) conditional substitutions. We use $u_k$ to denote the name of the variable written by the substitution $S_k$, it is used to give a name to the ACL2 created function ($\text{B\_}u_k$).

$acl2(S_1\|...\|S_n) =$
for each substitution $S_k$, this ACL2 function is created:
(defun B_$u_k$ $acl2(S_k)$)
where $\{u_k\} = W_S$, $u_k$ is the variable written by $S_k$
$acl2($IF $C$ THEN $S$ ELSE $T$ END$) = ($if $acl2(C)$ $acl2(S)$ $acl2(T))$
$acl2(v := E) = ($ $acl2exp(E)$ $)$
where $acl2exp$ is the translation of a B expression into an ACL2 expression.

The translation of the counter given in sections 5.3 and 6.1 producesthe following ACL2 functions.

```
(defun B_alm (compt reset)
  (if (equal reset 1)
    (if (equal 0 7) 1 0)
      (if (equal compt 7) 1 0)))

(defun B_compt (compt rst reset)
  (if (equal reset 1)
    (if (equal rst 1)
      0
      (if (equal (equal 0 7) nil) (+ 0 1) 0 )
    )
    (if (equal rst 1)
      0
      (if (equal (equal compt 7) nil) (+ compt 1) compt )
    )))
```

# 7     Flattening

Flattening a substitution $S$ builds another substitution that has the same effect as $S$ but that is flat. The main transformation consists of removing sequential compositions $(S; T)$ by propagating effects of the first substitution $(S)$ inside the second one $(T)$. After the definitions of flattening rules, we give a sketch of the proof that the flattening process constructs a substitution that is equivalent to the original one.

## 7.1     Flattening Rules

The process is based on three operators. The main operator $flat$ flattens a substitution. It uses operators $extract$ and $integrate$. The operator $extract(v, S)$ gives a substitution that has the same effect as $S$ on the variable $v$ but that has exactly $\{v\}$ as the write frame. The operator $integrate(S, T)$ integrates the substitution $S$ inside the substitution $T$: if $T$ reads a variable $v$ that is written by $S$, it reads $v$ as it is after the application of $S$.

In this section, we use the notation $\|_{v \in E} S(v)$ to denote the parallel composition of substitutions $S(v)$ for each variable $v$ in the set of variables $E$. If $E = \{v_1, ..., v_k\}$ then $\|_{v \in E} S(v) = S(v_1)\|...\|S(v_k)$.

**Flattening of a Substitution.** A simple substitution $v := E$ is already flat and a parallel composition is flat if both composed substitutions are flat.

$$flat(v := E) = v := E$$
$$flat(A\|B) = flat(A)\|flat(B)$$

In a conditional substitution, both alternative substitutions may write several variables. A flat conditional substitution writes only one variable. In consequence, the transformation rule creates one conditional substitution for each written variable and composes them in parallel ($\|_{v \in W_A \cup W_B}$). In the expression $extract(v, flat(A)))$, $flat(A)$ is flat, it is a parallel composition of substitutions, each one writing only one variable. The operator $extract$ select the one that writes the variable $v$.

$flat(\text{IF } C \text{ THEN } A \text{ ELSE } B \text{ END}) =$
  $\|_{v \in W_A \cup W_B} \text{IF } C \text{ THEN } extract(v, flat(A)) \text{ ELSE } extract(v, flat(B)) \text{ END}$
$flat(\text{IF } C \text{ THEN } A \text{ END}) =$
  $\|_{v \in W_A \cup W_B} \text{IF } C \text{ THEN } extract(v, flat(A)) \text{ ELSE } v := v \text{ END}$

Sequential composition does not exists in the flat form. It must be transformed into an equivalent flat substitution. This is achieved by propagation of transformations specified by the first substitution inside the second substitution.

The principle for flattening the substitution $S; T$ is the following. For any variable $v$ written by $S$ and read by $T$, the value of $v$ used by $T$ is the value of $v$ after applying $S$, i.e. $v$ is substituted in $T$ by the expression specified by $S$. For example $x := E; x := x + 1$ is transformed into $x := E + 1$.

This transformation is achieved by the operator $integrate$, which is defined in the remainder of this section. It returns a flat substitution that has the same write frame as $T$. This means that variables that are written by $S$ but not by $T$ are not written by the result of the integration. So, we add the flat substitution $S_{/W_S - W_T}$ that have the same behaviour as $flat(S)$ on $W_S - W_T$ and for which the write frame is exactly $W_S - W_T$ (see operator $extract$ below).

$$flat(S; T) = S_{/W_S - W_T} \| integrate(flat(S), flat(T))$$

**Extraction from a Substitution.** The operator $extract(v, S)$ gives a substitution that has the same effect as $S$ on the variable $v$ and for which the write frame is exactly $\{v\}$. The operator $extract$ is defined here only on flat substitutions. This simplifies definitions because in a flat substitution, each substitution of the parallel composition writes only one variable. So, extraction simply consists of looking for the substitution that corresponds to the variable we want to extract.

$$extract(v, S) = v := v \text{ if } v \notin W_S$$
$$extract(v, S_1 \| ... \| S_n) = S_k \text{ where } W_{S_k} = \{v\}$$

**Integration.** The operator $integrate(S, T)$ propagates the effects of $S$ inside $T$: if a variable is modified by $S$ and used by $T$, $T$ is transformed and uses the new value of this variable as specified by $S$. The operator *integrate* is defined here only for flat substitutions, this allows some simplifications in the definition.

Integrate a simple substitution $x := E$ consists of applying this substitution on all expressions. For example, propagate the substitution $x := 2$ inside $x := x + 1$ leads to the substitution $x := 2 + 1$.

$$integrate(x := E, y := F) = y := [x := E]F$$
$$integrate(x := E, \text{IF } P \text{ THEN } S \text{ ELSE } T \text{ END}) =$$
$$\text{IF } [x := E]P \text{ THEN } integrate(x := E, S) \text{ ELSE } integrate(x := E, T) \text{ END}$$

If we integrate a substitution that writes some variables $v$ inside a substitution that does not use $v$ at all, the integration has no effect. For example, integrate $x := 2$ inside $x := y$ produces the substitution $x := y$.

$$integrate(S, T) = T \text{ if } W_S \cap R_T = \emptyset$$

Integrate a substitution $S$ in a substitution that is a parallel composition consists of integrating $S$ in all composed substitutions. For example, integration of $x := 2$ inside $x := x + 1 \| y := x - 2$ produces $x := 2 + 1 \| y := 2 - 2$.

$$integrate(S, A\|B) = integrate(S, A)\|integrate(S, B)$$

Integration of a parallel substitution $A\|B$ into a substitution $T$ consists of integrating $A$ and $B$. Since some variables modified by $B$ may be used by $A$ and vice versa, we cannot first integrate $A$ and then $B$. For example, if $B$ contains $x := E$ and $A$ contains $y := x$, integrating $A\|B$ in $z := y+x$ produces $z := x+E$. If we first integrate $A$, we obtain $z := x + x$ that produces $z := E + E$ after integrating $B$.

For confidentiality reasons, we do not give the exact rule we used to implement the integration of the parallel substitution. A possibility is to use transformation rules of the B Book [1] page 310 to transform $A\|B$ into a substitution in which only simple substitutions are composed in parallel ($x := E\|y := F$). The resulting substitution can be integrated using above rules (the case of the simple substitution can be easily generalised to multiple simple substitutions $x, y := E, F$).

For example, the integration of $S \equiv x := y + 1 \|\text{IF } x = y \text{ THEN } y := x + 2 \text{ ELSE } y := 1 \text{ END}$ inside $T \equiv x := x + y$ produces the substitution $\text{IF } x = y \text{ THEN } x := y + 1 + x + 2 \text{ ELSE } x := y + 1 + 1 \text{ END}$.

**Simplifications.** Flattening rules creates a lot of useless nested IF statements. This is because in B, except in the flat form, an IF substitution may contain several simple substitutions ($v := E$). The operator *flat* splits them into several IFs and *integrate* spreads and nests them. The result is a substitution that grows exponentially.

To simplify these substitutions, useless branches of an IF tree are cut and IF substitutions are simplified when both branches are equal. Substitution $S^s$ (resp. $T^s$) is the result of the simplification of $S$ (resp. $T$).

$$simpl(C, NC, \text{IF } P \text{ THEN } S \text{ ELSE } T \text{ END}) =$$
$$\quad \text{if } P \in C \text{ then } simpl(C, NC, S)$$
$$\quad \text{else if } P \in NC \text{ then } simpl(C, NC, T)$$
$$\quad \text{else}$$
$$\qquad \text{let } S^s = simpl(C \cup \{P\}, NC, S) \text{ and } T^s = simpl(C, NC \cup \{P\}, T) \text{ in}$$
$$\qquad \text{if } S^s = T^s \text{ then } S^s$$
$$\qquad \text{else IF } P \text{ THEN } S^s \text{ ELSE } T^s \text{ END}$$

The parameter $C$ is the set of conditions known to be true and $NC$ the set of conditions known to be false. They come from the fact that the substitution under simplification takes place in a branch of an IF tree. Initially $C = NC = \emptyset$.

**Implementation.** Flattening has been implemented in Prolog. Experiments have shown the usefulness of simplifications. Without it, constructed substitutions become larger and larger during the flattening process. To be useful, simplifications must be applied regularly during the flattening process, or be directly integrated inside the flattening rules.

Without any simplification, flattening of a design of about 200 lines, needs more that 100MB of RAM and the process takes several hours to complete. With simplifications, flattening of the same design takes about 1 second.

## 7.2    Flattening Is a Refinement

Flattening is an automatic refinement. Actually, the result of the flattening is a substitution that is equivalent to the original substitution. For any substitution $S$, and any predicate $Q$

$$[flat(S)]Q \Leftrightarrow [S]Q$$

For reasons of space, we cannot give the entire proof of this property here. However we give below a sketch of the proof for the interesting case $flat(S;T)$, based on the operator *integrate*.

Intuitively, the meaning of $integrate(S, T)$ is to produce a substitution that is consistent with $S;T$ but with the same write frame as T. With respect to the variables written by $T$, $integrate(S, T)$ is equivalent to $S;T$, but for the variables that are not written by $T$, $integrate(S, T)$ is equivalent to *skip*.

Let $S$ and $T$ be two flat substitutions. Let $x_t$ be a variable written neither by $S$ nor by $T$ ($x_t$ is a fresh variable) and $w_t$ a variable written by $T$ (possibly also written by $S$). We can prove the following property.

$$[S;T](x_t = w_t) \Leftrightarrow [integrate(S, T)](x_t = w_t) \tag{1}$$

The proof cannot be given here, it is based on a double recurrence on both arguments (on the structure of substitutions) of *integrate*.

Suppose there exists some variables written by $S$ but not by $T$, we choose a variable $w_{s-t}$. Let $x_{s-t}$ be a variable written neither by $S$ nor by $T$. The property below holds.

$$[S;T](x_{s-t} = w_{s-t}) \Leftrightarrow [S](x_{s-t} = w_{s-t}) \tag{2}$$

Let $Q$ be a predicate on variables written by $S$ or $T$, we denote it by $Q(w_t, w_{s-t})$ where $w_t$ is a variable written by $T$ and $w_{s-t}$ is a variable written by $S$ but not by $T$ (we make the assumption it exists). The predicate $Q(w_t, w_{s-t})$ may be rewritten $x_t = w_t \wedge x_{s-t} = w_{s-t} \wedge Q(x_t, x_{s-t})$, where $x_t$ and $x_{s-t}$ are two fresh variables. There is an implicit existential quantifier $\exists(x_t, x_{s-t}).(...)$ .

We know that

$$[S;T]Q(w_t, w_{s-t}) \Leftrightarrow [S;T](x_t = w_t) \wedge [S;T](x_{s-t} = w_{s-t}) \wedge [S;T]Q(x_t, x_{s-t}) \tag{3}$$

Suppose we have a substitution $S'$ such that its write frame is $W_S - W_T$ and that, for any predicate $P$ on the same frame,

$$[S']P \Leftrightarrow [S]P \tag{4}$$

For any substitution $A$ that has a disjoint frame from $S'$ ($W_T$ for example), we can say that $[S'\|A](x_t = w_t) \Leftrightarrow [A](x_t = w_t)$ because neither $x_t$ nor $w_t$ is written by $S'$. In particular, the following property holds.

$$[S'\|integrate(S,T)](x_t = w_t) \Leftrightarrow [integrate(S,T)](x_t = w_t) \tag{5}$$

In the same way, because variables $x_{s-t}$ and $w_{s-t}$ are not in the write frame of the substitution $integrate(S,T)$, we have to property below.

$$[S'\|integrate(S,T)](x_{s-t} = w_{s-t}) \Leftrightarrow [S'](x_{s-t} = w_{s-t}) \tag{6}$$

From (1) and (5), we deduce (7), and from (2), (4) and (6) we deduce (8).

$$[S;T](x_t = w_t) \Leftrightarrow [S'\|integrate(S,T)](x_t = w_t) \tag{7}$$

$$[S;T](x_{s-t} = w_{s-t}) \Leftrightarrow [S'\|integrate(S,T)](x_{s-t} = w_{s-t}) \tag{8}$$

Finally, from (3), (7), (8) and because there is no variable written by $S'\|integrate(S,T)$ in $Q(x_t, x_{s-t})$, we deduce the property (9).

$$[S;T]Q(w_t, w_{s-t}) \Leftrightarrow \begin{cases} [S'\|integrate(S,T)](x_t = w_t) \wedge \\ [S'\|integrate(S,T)](x_{s-t} = w_{s-t}) \wedge \\ [S'\|integrate(S,T)]Q(x_t, x_{s-t}) \end{cases} \tag{9}$$

From (9), we can recompose $Q$ to obtain the property below.

$$[S;T]Q(w_t, w_{s-t}) \Leftrightarrow [S'\|integrate(S,T)]Q(w_t, w_{s-t}) \tag{10}$$

The predicate $Q$ is on frame of $S;T$ (that is the same frame as $S'\|integrate(S,T)$). We can generalise to any predicate $Q$ because $S;T$ and $S'\|integrate(S,T)$ have no effect on other variables. The reasoning above uses a predicate $Q$ on two variables $w_t$ and $w_{s-t}$, it can be generalised to two sets of variables. We made the assumption that $W_S - W_T$ is not empty, the case where all variables written by $S$ are also written by $T$ is a simpler case that leads to the same result.

We also made the assumption of the existence of $S'$ that has $W_S - W_T$ as write frame and such that $[S']P \Leftrightarrow [S]P$ for any predicate $P$ on the same frame. These requirements are met by $S_{/W_S-W_T}$ used in the definition of $flat(S;T)$. In consequence, with $S' \equiv S_{/W_S-W_T}$ and (10), we can conclude that $flat(S;T)$ is equivalent to $S;T$.

$$[S;T]Q \Leftrightarrow [flat(S;T)]Q$$

## 8 Case Studies

We present two case studies. The first one illustrates the methodology on a non trivial example. The second one uses the example of the counter to explain how the verification is done in ACL2.

### 8.1 Controller for a Serial Bus

The first case study concerns a controller for a serial bus (standard SAE J1708 [19]): several components linked by a serial bus may send messages to other components using the bus. Each component has a controller that is responsible for sending messages bit by bit on the bus and for dealing with contentions (when two controllers attempt to send a message at the same time).

The B development [23] consisted of first modelling the whole system at a very abstract level to specify important properties. Refinement was used to derive a model of the protocol (so, proved by refinement) and finally the system was refined again to obtain the description of controllers at the register transfer level. This is the level of BHDL. From BHDL, the circuit was translated to VHDL, simulated and synthesised.

The goal of this case study is not to validate the VHDL description of the circuit but to confirm the methodology with a non trivial example that we know to be correct. It is also a chance to associate three translators developed separately. We started from the BHDL description of the circuit validated in B. This description was translated twice: into ACL2 (as described in this paper) and in VHDL (using the translator developed by KeesDA). The VHDL description has around 400 lines and uses 140 internal signals. Then, this VHDL description was translated to ACL2 using the translator developed by TIMA.

At this point we have two ACL2 descriptions of the same circuit and we want to verify that they are equivalent. Equivalence is expected because both ACL2 descriptions come from the same BHDL description. The three translators are based on three different approaches and they have been validated separately.

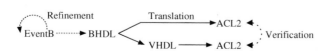

**Fig. 7.** Connection of translators

The fact that proof of equivalence can be done easily gives confidence in the implementation of these translators and confirms the methodology consisting of using ACL2 as an intermediary between B and VHDL.

The ACL2 model of the VHDL design has 148 functions and the ACL2 model of the BHDL description has 21 functions. For the equivalence proof we defined 65 theorems, and we used an already defined library about bit vectors and operations on bit vectors. The proof process was not difficult, it only took several hours of human time to complete it (against several weeks for the original B development). The proof itself is done in 17.23 minutes on a processor Ultra Sparc 3, 1.28 GHz, with 8GB memory.

Models were modified by hand to introduce some errors, particularly on types and arithmetic expressions. This permits one to check that not only purely functional errors are detected but also errors due to incompatible implementation of data (for example, an integer that may be valued to 8 cannot be implemented by a 3-bits vector). Errors were detected because some conjectures were shown to be false by ACL2.

## 8.2    Counter

We applied the ACL2 verification to the example of the counter. After the translation of the BHDL model to ACL2, the corresponding sim-step, system, hyp-input and hyp-st functions are defined.

We give below the sim-step and system functions for the BHDL model of the counter.

```
(defun b-sim-step (in st)
   (let ((reset (nth *b-reset* in)) (rst (nth *b-rst* in)) (compt (nth *b-compt* st)))
      (list (B_compt compt rst reset)
         (B_alm compt reset)))))
(defun b-counter (input st)
   (if (atom input) st (b-counter (cdr input) (b-sim-step (car input) st)))))
```

At this point, there are two ACL2 models : one corresponding to the VHDL design, and the other one to the BHDL model. Both models are cycle accurate.

To prove the bisimulation relation between the two models, a relation $Sim \subseteq ST_{VHDL} \times ST_{BHDL}$ is first defined, where $ST_{VHDL}$ is the set of VHDL design states, and $ST_{BHDL}$ is the set of BHDL model states. The proof that $Sim$ is a simulation relation is done in two steps: (1) starting from arbitrary states, after a clock cycle, when reset is 1, both models are in similar states, conform to $Sim$; (2) starting from similar states, st-b and st-vhdl, where $(st\text{-}vhdl,\ st\text{-}b) \in Sim$, after consuming the same inputs (taking into considerations the necessary type conversions), the two models are in similar states :

$$(vhdl\text{-}system(inputs, st\text{-}vhdl),\ b\text{-}system(inputs, st\text{-}b)) \in Sim$$

This is proved by induction on the number of clock cycles, i.e. the length of the list of inputs. The base case states that sim-step functions preserve the similarity.

A second relation $Sim^{-1} \subseteq ST_{BHDL} \times ST_{VHDL}$ is defined and proved to be the inverse of $Sim$. Likewise, $Sim^{-1}$ is proved to be a simulation relation between the BHDL model and the VHDL model.

Finally, $Sim$ is proved to be a bisimulation relation between the BHDL model and the VHDL design.

For the counter, $Sim$ is defined as follows:

$$(st\text{-}vhdl, st\text{-}b) \in Sim \Leftrightarrow ((alm3 = alm) \wedge (get\text{-}1\text{-}pos(tc\_1) = compt))$$

Where $st\text{-}vhdl = (tc\_0, tc\_1, tc\_6, tc\_8, tc\_10, gd, rst, alm3)$ and $st\text{-}b = (compt, alm)$. The function $get\text{-}1\text{-}pos$ takes a bit-vector as input and returns the position of 1 in the vector. For example, $get\text{-}1\text{-}pos((00100)) = 2$

$Sim^{-1}$ is defined as follows:

$$(st\text{-}b, st\text{-}vhdl) \in Sim^{-1} \Leftrightarrow$$
$$((alm = alm3) \wedge (tc\_1 = construct\text{-}table(compt)))$$

The function $construct\text{-}table$ takes a natural $n$ as input and returns a bit vector of size 8 with bit 1 on the $n$-th position, all other bits being 0.

The proof uses ACL2 libraries about naturals and lists included in the public distribution of the theorem prover. It also uses a library about bit-vectors that was previously developped for hardware verification.

# 9    Conclusion

We have presented a new methodology to reuse existing components that have not been developed within the B framework.

The principle consists of writing a specification of the component in B and proving that this specification corresponds to the component using ACL2. To achieve this, both BHDL and VHDL descriptions of the component are translated into ACL2. ACL2 is used to prove that both models are equivalent.

Translation of the BHDL into ACL2 needs to flatten the BHDL model. Translation rules have been explained and we have proved that this transformation leads to a model that is equivalent to the original one.

The methodology has been applied to a non trivial case study to verify its efficiency. It was also a chance to combine three translators that have been developed separately and with different approaches. Experiments have shown that non equivalence of models is detected by this methodology.

# References

[1]  J.-R. Abrial. *The B-Book – Assigning programs to meanings.* CUP, 1996.

[2]  J.-R. Abrial and L. Mussat. Introducing Dynamic Constraints in B. In D. Bert, editor, *B'98: Recent Advances in the Development and Use of the B-Method*, volume 1393 of *LNCS*, pages 83–128, 1998.

[3] Jean-Raymond Abrial, Dominique Cansell, and Dominique Méry. A mechanically proved and incremental development of ieee 1394 tree identify protocol. *Formal Aspects of Computing*, 14(3):215–227, Apr 2003.

[4] Ammar Aljer, Philippe Devienne, Sophie Tison, Jean-Louis Boulanger, and Georges Mariano. B-HDL: Circuit Design in B. In *ACSD 2003, International conference on Application of Concurrency to System Design*, pages 241–242, 2003.

[5] Steve Dunne. A Theory of Generalised Substitutions. In D. Bert, J. P. Bowen, M. C. Henson, and K. Robinson, editors, *ZB 2002*, volume 2272 of *LNCS*, pages 270–290, 2002.

[6] European Organisation for Civil Aviation Equipment. , http://www.eurocae.org/.

[7] A.C.J Fox. Formal specification and verification of ARM6. In D. Basin and B. Wolff, editors, *TPHOLs '03*, volume 2758 of *LNCS*, pages 25–40. Springer, 2003.

[8] Max Fuchs and Michael Mendler. A Functional Semantics for Delta-Delay VHDL Based on FOCUS. In C. D. Kloos and P. T. Breuer, editors, *Formal Semantics for VHDL*, pages 9–42. Kluwer Academic Publishers, 1995.

[9] Stefan Hallerstede and Yann Zimmermann. Circuit Design by refinement in EventB. In *Proc. of FDL'04*, 2004.

[10] Scott Hazelhurst and Carl-Johan H. Seger. Symbolic Trajectory Evaluation. In T. Kropf, editor, *Formal Hardware Verification: Methods and Systems in Comparison*, volume 1287 of *LNCS*, pages 3–78. Springer-Verlag, 1997.

[11] IEEE, editor. *Standard VHDL - Language Reference Manual*. IEEE Computer Society Press, USA, 1988.

[12] International Electrotechnical Commission. , http://www.iec.ch/61508/.

[13] M. Kaufmann, P. Manolios, and J S. Moore. *Computer-Aided reasoning: ACL2 An approach*, volume 1. Kluwer Academic Press, 2000.

[14] M. Kaufmann, P. Manolios, and J S. Moore. *Computer-Aided reasoning: ACL2 Case Studies*, volume 2. Kluwer Academic Press, 2000.

[15] J. Mermet, editor. *UML-B - Specification for Proven Embedded Systems Design*. Kluwer Academic Publishers, 2004. ISBN 1-4020-2866-0.

[16] PUSSEE project IST-2000-30103. http://www.keesda.com/pussee/, 2004.

[17] Radio Technical Commission for Aeronautics. , http://www.rtca.org/.

[18] D. M. Russinoff. A Case Study in Formal Verification of Register-Transfer Logic with ACL2: The Floating Point Adder of the AMD Athlon Processor. In *FMCAD 2000*, 2000.

[19] SAE International. SAE J1708 revised OCT93, serial data communication between microcomputer systems in heavy-duty vehicule applications, www.sae.org, 1993.

[20] M. Srivas, H. Rueß, and D. Cyrluk. Hardware Verification Using PVS. In T. Kropf, editor, *Formal Hardware Verification: Methods and Systems in Comparison*, volume 1287 of *LNCS*, pages 156–205. Springer-Verlag, 1997.

[21] D. Toma and D. Borrione. SHA formalization. In *ACL2 Workshop*, USA, 2003.

[22] D. Toma, D. Borrione, and G. Al-Sammane. Combining several paradigms for circuit validation and verification. In *CASSIS*, 2004.

[23] Yann Zimmermann, Stefan Hallerstede, and Dominique Cansell. Formal modelling of electronic circuits using event-B, case study : SAE J708 serial communication link. In Jean Mermet, editor, *UML-B - Specification for Proven Embedded Systems Design*. Kluwer Academic Publishers, 2004.

# GeneSyst: A Tool to Reason About Behavioral Aspects of B Event Specifications. Application to Security Properties[*]

Didier Bert, Marie-Laure Potet, and Nicolas Stouls

Laboratoire Logiciels Systèmes Réseaux - LSR-IMAG - Grenoble, France
{Didier.Bert, Marie-Laure.Potet, Nicolas.Stouls}@imag.fr

**Abstract.** In this paper, we present a method and a tool to build symbolic labelled transition systems from B specifications. The tool, called GeneSyst, can take into account refinement levels and can visualize the decomposition of abstract states in concrete hierarchical states. The resulting symbolic transition system represents all the behaviors of the initial B event system. So, it can be used to reason about them. We illustrate the use of GeneSyst to check security properties on a model of electronic purse.

## 1 Introduction

Formal methods, such as the B method [1], ensure that the development of an application is reliable and that properties expressed in the model are satisfied by the final program. However, they do not guarantee that this program fulfills the informal requirements, nor the needs of the customer. So, it is useful to propose several views about the specifications, in order to be sure that the initial model is suitable for the customer and that the development can continue on this basis. One of these important insights is the representation of the behavior of programs by means of diagrams (statecharts). Moreover, some particular views, if they are themselves formal, can provide new means to prove properties that cannot easily be checked in the first model.

In this paper, we present a method and a tool to extract a labelled transition system from a model written in event-B. The transition system gives a graphical view and represents symbolically all the behaviors of the B model. The method is able to take into account refinement levels and to show the correspondence between abstract and concrete systems, by means of hierarchical states.

We present also an application of this tool, namely, the verification of security properties. The security properties assert the occurrence or the absence of some particular events in some situation. They are a case of *atomicity property*

---

[*] This work was done in the GECCOO project of program "ACI : Sécurité Informatique" supported by the French Ministry of Research and New Technologies. It is also suported by CNRS and ST-Microelectronics by the way of a doctoral grant.

H. Treharne et al. (Eds.): ZB 2005, LNCS 3455, pp. 299–318, 2005.

of transactions. This is illustrated by an example of specification of an electronic purse, called Demoney[16, 15], developed in the SecSafe project [19]. This case study, written in Java Card [21], is an applet that has all the facilities required by a real electronic purse. Indeed, the purse can be debited from a terminal in a shop, credited by cash or from a bank account with a terminal in a bank or managed from special terminal in bank restricted area. Transactions are encrypted if needed and different levels of security are used depending on the actions. Demoney also supports to communicate with another applet on the card, for example, to manage award points on a loyalty plan. The specification of Demoney is public in version 0.8 [16], but the source code is copyrighted by Trusted Logic S.A.[1].

In Section 2, we recall the main features of event-B systems and refinements. We introduce a notion of behavioral semantics by the way of sequences of events. In Section 3, we define symbolic labelled transition systems (SLTS) and the links between SLTS and event-B systems are stated. In Section 4, we present the GeneSyst tool and an example of generation of SLTS dealing with the error cases in the Demoney case study. Section 5 presents security properties required in the application and shows how the GeneSyst diagrams can be used to check these properties. Then, we review related works, and we conclude the paper with some research perspectives in Section 6.

## 2     Event-B

### 2.1     General Presentation

Event-B was introduced by J.-R. Abrial [2, 3]. It is a formal development method as well as a specification language. In event-B, components are composed of constant declarations (SETS, CONSTANTS, PROPERTIES), state specification (VARIABLES, INVARIANT), initialisation and set of *events*. The events are defined by $e \triangleq eBody$ where $e$ is the name of the event and *eBody* is a *guarded* generalized substitution [1]. The events do not take parameters and do not return result values. They do not get preconditions and do terminate. Their effect is only to modify the internal state. If $\mathcal{S}$ is a component, then we denote by $Interface(\mathcal{S})$ the set of its events.

A well-typed and well-defined component is consistent if initialization *Init* establishes the invariant of the component and if each event preserves the invariant. So, using the notation $[S]R$ as the weakest precondition of $R$ for substitution $S$, the consistency of a component is expressed by the proof obligations: $[Init]I$ and $I \Rightarrow [eBody]I$ for each event.

In the paper, we use the notions of before-after predicate of substitution $T$ for variables $x$ ($\text{prd}_x(T)$) and the feasability predicate of a substitution as defined in the B-Book: $\text{fis}(T) \Leftrightarrow \neg[T]false$ [1]. Finally, the notation $\langle T \rangle R$ means $\neg[T]\neg R$, that is to say, there exists a computation of $T$ which terminates in a state verifying $R$.

---

[1] http://www.trusted-logic.fr/

## 2.2   Events and Traces

The events have the form "$e \ \widehat{=} \ G \Longrightarrow T$" where $G$ is a predicate, $T$ is a generalized substitution such that $I \wedge G \Rightarrow \mathsf{fis}(T)$. Predicate $G$ is called the *guard* of $e$ and $T$ is its *action*. They are respectively denoted by $Guard(e)$ and $Action(e)$. If the syntactic definition of an event $e \ \widehat{=} \ S$ does not fulfill this form, it can be built by computing $e \ \widehat{=} \ \mathsf{fis}(S) \Longrightarrow S$. Following the so-called *event-based* approach [10], the semantics of event-B systems can be chosen to be the set of all the valid sequences of event executions.

**Definition 1 (Traces of Event-B systems).** A finite sequence of event occurrences $e_0.e_1.e_2 \ldots e_n$ is a trace of system $S$ if and only if $e_0$ is the initialisation of $S$, $\{e_1, e_2, \ldots, e_n\} \subseteq Interface(S)$ and $\mathsf{fis}(e_0 \ ; \ e_1 \ ; \ e_2 \ ; \ \ldots \ ; \ e_n) \Leftrightarrow true$.

The set of all the finite traces of a system $S$ is called $Traces(S)$. For the initialisation, one can notice that $\mathsf{prd}_x(Init)$ does not depend on the initial values of the variables and that $Guard(Init) \Leftrightarrow true$. The following property characterizes traces by the existence of intermediary states $x_i$ in which the guard of $e_i$ holds and where the pair $(x_i, x_{i+1})$ is in the before-after predicate of event $e_i$:

**Property 1 (Trace characterization).** Let $x$ be the variable space of system $S$, then: $e_0.e_1 \ldots . e_n \in Traces(S) \ \Leftrightarrow$
$$\exists x_0, \ldots, x_{n+1} \cdot \bigwedge_{i=0}^{n}([x := x_i] Guard(e_i) \wedge [x, x' := x_i, x_{i+1}]\mathsf{prd}_x(Action(e_i))).$$

## 2.3   Event-B Refinement

In the event-B method, a refinement is a component called REFINEMENT. The variables can be refined (i.e. made more concrete) and a *gluing invariant* describes the relationship between the variables of the refinement and those of the abstraction. The events of refinement $\mathcal{R}$ must at least contain those of the abstraction $S$ (i.e. $Interface(S) \subseteq Interface(\mathcal{R})$). The other events are called *new* events.

We recall here the proof obligations of system refinements. Let $I$ be the invariant of the abstraction $S$ and $J$ be the invariant of refinement $\mathcal{R}$, then the gluing invariant is the conjunction $I \wedge J$. The refinement is performed elementwise, that is to say, the abstract initialisation is refined by the concrete initialisation and each abstract event is refined by its concrete counterpart. Proof obligations that establish the consistency of refinements are :

For initialisation $Init$ : $\quad\quad\quad\quad [Init^R]\langle Init^S\rangle J$
For events $e$ of $Interface(S)$ : $\quad I \wedge J \Rightarrow [e^R]\langle e^S\rangle J$
For the new events $ne^R$ : $\quad\quad\quad I \wedge J \Rightarrow [ne^R]\langle\mathsf{skip}\rangle J$

New events cannot indefinitely take the control, i.e. the refined system cannot diverge more often that the abstract one. So, a *variant* $V$ is declared in the refined system, as an expression on a well-founded set (usually the natural numbers), and the new events must satisfy ($v$ is a fresh variable) :

$V$ is a natural expression : $\quad\quad\quad\quad I \wedge J \Rightarrow V \in \mathbb{N}$
New events $ne^R$ decrease the variant : $\quad I \wedge J \Rightarrow [v := V][ne^R](V < v)$

Finally, a proof obligation of *liveness preservation* is usually required. If $\mathcal{S}$ contains $m$ events and $\mathcal{R}$ contains $p$ new events, then:

$$I \wedge J \Rightarrow (\bigvee_{i=1}^{m} Guard(e_i^S)) \Rightarrow (\bigvee_{i=1}^{m} Guard(e_i^R) \vee \bigvee_{i=1}^{p} Guard(ne_i^R)))$$

Traces associated to refinements are defined as for the systems.

# 3 Symbolic Labelled Transition Systems Associated to B Systems

## 3.1 Symbolic Transition Systems

We define *symbolic* labelled transition systems:

**Definition 2 (Symbolic Labelled Transition System).** A symbolic labelled transition system (SLTS) is a 4-uple $(N, Init, U, W)$ where

- $N$ is a set of states, and $Init$ is the initial state ($Init \in N$)
- $U$ is a set of labels of the form $(D, A, e)$, where $D$ and $A$ are predicates and
  $e$ is an event name
- $W$ is a transition relation $W \subseteq \mathbb{P}(N \times U \times N)$.

A transition $(E, (D, A, e), F)$ means that, in state $E$, the event $e$ is enabled if $D$ holds and, starting from state $E$, if event $e$ is enabled, then it reaches state $F$ if $A$ holds. Predicate $D$ is called the *enabledness* predicate and $A$ is called the *reachability* predicate.

States $N$ are interpreted as subsets of variable spaces on variables $x$. So, the interpretation of $N$ is given by a function $\mathcal{I}$ such that $\mathcal{I}(E)$ is a predicate on free variables $x$ which characterizes the subset represented by $E$. In the next definition, we determine the actual conditions to cross a transition from a particular state value $x_1$ of $E_1$ to $x_2$ of $E_2$ by an event $e$ which is defined in an event-B system $\mathcal{S}$. For that, $e$ must be enabled in $x_1$, $x_2$ must be reachable from $x_1$ by $e$, and $(x_1, x_2)$ must belong to the before-after predicate of $e$:

**Definition 3 (Transition Crossing).** Let $(E_1, (D, A, e), E_2)$ be a transition of a SLTS $\mathcal{T}$ on a system $\mathcal{S}$, and given $x_1$ and $x_2$ some values of the state variables $x$ which satisfy the invariant of $\mathcal{S}$, then a crossing from $x_1$ to $x_2$ by this transition is legal if and only if : 1. $[x := x_1](\mathcal{I}(E_1) \wedge D \wedge A)$
$\qquad\qquad\qquad\qquad$ 2. $[x, x' := x_1, x_2]\, \mathsf{prd}_x(Action(e))$
$\qquad\qquad\qquad\qquad$ 3. $[x := x_2]\mathcal{I}(E_2)$

Such a legal transition crossing is denoted by :

$$(E_1, x_1) \leadsto^{(D,A,e)}\!\leadsto (E_2, x_2)$$

Now, we introduce the notion of *path* in a symbolic labelled transition system. A path is a sequence of event occurrences, starting from the initial state, which goes over a transition system through legal transition crossings.

**Definition 4 (Paths).** Given a symbolic labelled transition system $T$ on a system $S$, a sequence of event occurrences $e_0 . . . . . e_{n+1}$ is a path in $T$ if there exists a list of states $E_0, \ldots, E_{n+1}$ of $N$, with $E_0 = Init_T$, and a list of transitions $(D_i, A_i, e_i), i \in 0..n$, such that :

$$\exists x_0, \ldots, x_{n+1} \cdot (\bigwedge_{i=0}^{n} ((E_i, x_i) \leadsto^{(D_i, A_i, e_i)}\leadsto (E_{i+1}, x_{i+1})))$$

The set of all the finite paths of $T$ is called $Paths(T)$.

## 3.2     Construction of States and Transitions

The aim of this section is to show how to compute a SLTS, from an event-B system $S$ and given a set of states $N$. First, to build the states $N$, consider a list of predicates $\{P_1, \ldots, P_n\}$ on the variable space. We require that this set is *complete* with respect to the invariant, i.e. all the states specified by the invariant are included in the states determined by the $P_i$ predicates, i.e.

$$I \Rightarrow \bigvee_{i=1}^{n} P_i$$

Then, the states of the SLTS are $N = \{Init_S, E_1, \ldots, E_n\}$ with the interpretation defined by:

$$\mathcal{I}(Init_S) = true \qquad\qquad \mathcal{I}(E_i) = P_i \wedge I, \quad i \in 1..n$$

We denote by $N1$ the set $N - \{Init_S\}$. From the completeness property above and the definition of $N$, we get: $I \Leftrightarrow \bigvee_{i=1}^{n} \mathcal{I}(E_i)$.

Now, we express the conditions to ensure that a symbolic labelled transition system $T$ represents the same set of behaviors as the associated system $S$. For that, in a starting state $E$, the enabledness condition must be equivalent to the guard of the event $e$, and if the target state is $F$, the reachability condition must be equivalent to the possibility to reach $F$ through $e$, when the enabledness predicate holds, so the condition:

**Condition 1 (Valid Transitions).** Let $S$ be a system, $E$ and $F$ two states in $N$ as defined above, and $e$ an event, then the transition $(E,(D,A,e),F)$ is valid if and only if predicates $D$ and $A$ satisfy :

$a)$     $\mathcal{I}(E) \Rightarrow (D \Leftrightarrow Guard(e))$
$b)$     $\mathcal{I}(E) \wedge Guard(e) \Rightarrow (A \Leftrightarrow \langle Action(e) \rangle \mathcal{I}(F))$

Notice that, by applying the definition of the conjugate weakest precondition, condition $b)$ is equivalent to :

$$\mathcal{I}(E) \wedge Guard(e) \Rightarrow (A \Leftrightarrow \exists x' \cdot (\mathsf{prd}_x(Action(e)) \wedge [x := x']\mathcal{I}(F)))$$

A SLTS with all the transitions valid with respect to a system $S$ is called a valid symbolic labelled transition system.

**Theorem 1 (Traces and Paths Equality).** Let $\mathcal{S}$ be an event-B system with invariant $I$ and events $Ev$ and let $\mathcal{T}$ be a valid symbolic labelled transition system built from $\mathcal{S}$, then:

$$Traces(\mathcal{S}) = Paths(\mathcal{T})$$

**Proof:** We prove that, for all $t$, $t \in Paths(\mathcal{T}) \Leftrightarrow t \in Traces(\mathcal{S})$.
The path $t \;\hat{=}\; e_0.e_1.\ldots.e_n$ is a path for the state sequence $E_0, E_1, \ldots, E_{n+1}$
iff (Definition 4): $\exists x_0, \ldots, x_{n+1} \cdot \bigwedge_{i=0}^{n}((E_i, x_i) \leadsto^{(D_i, A_i, e_i)} \leadsto (E_{i+1}, x_{i+1}))$.
By using Definition 3, we get:

$$\exists x_0, \ldots, x_{n+1} \cdot \bigwedge_{i=0}^{n}([x := x_i](\mathcal{I}(E_i) \wedge D_i \wedge A_i)$$
$$\wedge \; [x, x' := x_i, x_{i+1}]\mathsf{prd}_x(Action(e_i)) \; \wedge \; [x := x_{i+1}]\mathcal{I}(E_{i+1}))$$

By Condition 1, one can replace $D_i$ by $Guard(e_i)$ and $A_i$ by $\exists x' \cdot (\mathsf{prd}_x(Action(e_i))$ $\wedge \; [x := x']\mathcal{I}(E_{i+1}))$. The formula above is simplified and becomes:

(1) $$\exists x_0, \ldots, x_{n+1} \cdot \bigwedge_{i=0}^{n}([x := x_i](\mathcal{I}(E_i) \wedge Guard(e_i))$$
$$\wedge \; [x, x' := x_i, x_{i+1}]\mathsf{prd}_x(Action(e_i)) \; \wedge \; [x := x_{i+1}]\mathcal{I}(E_{i+1}))$$

We must prove that this formula is equivalent to the characterization of the traces (Property 1):

(2) $$\exists x_0, \ldots, x_{n+1} \cdot \bigwedge_{i=0}^{n}([x := x_i] \, Guard(e_i)$$
$$\wedge \; [x, x' := x_i, x_{i+1}]\mathsf{prd}_x(Action(e_i)) \; \wedge \; [x := x_{i+1}]I)$$

Implication (1) $\Rightarrow$ (2) is verified because states $E_i$ are such that $\mathcal{I}(E_i) \Rightarrow I$ (Section 3.2). To prove (2) $\Rightarrow$ (1), we must exhibit a list of states $E_0, E_1, \ldots, E_{n+1}$ such that these states satisfy (1). This follows from the fact that $\mathcal{I}(E_0) = true$ and from $I \Rightarrow \bigvee_{i=1}^{n} \mathcal{I}(E_i)$, which ensures that one of the states $\mathcal{I}(E_i)$ necessarily holds when $I$ hold. □

### 3.3     Labelled Transition Systems for the Refinements

We propose now the construction of a symbolic labelled transition system for the refinements. Our aim is to highlight the links between abstract and concrete transition systems, while preserving the overall structure of the abstract system. One aspect of the refinement is the change of the variable representation and redefinition of the events of the abstraction, according to the new representation. The point is taken into account by the notion of *state projection*.

In the following, $\mathcal{S}$ is a specification, $\mathcal{R}$ is its refinement with gluing invariant $L$, and $\mathcal{T}^S$ is a symbolic labelled transition system for $\mathcal{S}$. States $E^S$ and $F^S$ are states in $\mathcal{T}^S$. We assume that the variable set $x^S$ of $\mathcal{S}$ is disjoint to the variable set $x^R$ of the refinement. If some variables of the specification are kept in the refinement, they can be renamed and an equality between both variables is added to the invariant.

**Definition 5 (State Projection).** Let $\mathcal{S}$ be a system with variables $x^S$ and $\mathcal{R}$ be the refinement of $\mathcal{S}$ according to $L$. A state $E^R$ of $\mathcal{T}^R$, $E^R \neq Init_{\mathcal{R}}$ is the projection of $E^S$ of $\mathcal{T}^S$, denoted by $E^R = Proj_L(E^S)$, iff:

$$\mathcal{I}(E^R) \Leftrightarrow \exists x^S \cdot (L \ \wedge \ \mathcal{I}(E^S))$$

We propose to build a SLTS, called $Proj_L(\mathcal{T}^S)$, in which states are automatically deduced from abstract states and gluing invariant. The SLTS projection $Proj_L(\mathcal{T}^S)$ of the refinement $\mathcal{R}$ of system $\mathcal{S}$ with gluing invariant $L$ is such that: the initial state is any $q_0$ with $\mathcal{I}(q_0) = true$; the other states of the projection are the projections of abstract states, i.e. $N1^R = \{Proj_L(q) \mid q \in N1^S\}$. The transitions are $(E^R, (D', A', e^R), F^R)$ where $e^R \in \mathcal{R}$ and $D'$, $A'$ are such that Condition 1 is satisfied. A transition $(E^R, (D', A', e^R), F^R)$ is said a *projection of transition* $(E^S, (D, A, e^S), F^S)$ iff $E^R = Proj_L(E^S)$, $F^R = Proj_L(F^S)$ and event $e^R$ is the refinement of $e^S$. By construction, $Paths(Proj_L(\mathcal{T}^S)) = Traces(\mathcal{R})$. This equality can be proved in the same way as in Theorem 1.

**Property 2 (Transition Projection).** With   the definitions   above,   let $(E^R, (D', A', e^R), F^R)$ be the projection of transition $(E^S, (D, A, e^S), F^S)$, then we have:

$$\mathcal{I}(E^S) \ \wedge \ L \ \wedge \ D' \Rightarrow D$$

This property says that any transition enabled from a state $Proj_L(E^S)$ in a refinement $\mathcal{R}$ actually must be enabled in specification $\mathcal{S}$ (if the refinement is proved correct). Property 2 can make the computation of the transitions simpler. Indeed, if $e \in Interface(\mathcal{S})$, then, for all the transitions $(E^S, e, F^S)$ of the abstraction, it is only necessary to examine the transitions $(Proj_L(E^S), e, E')$ with $E' \in N1^R$. No other transition can be labelled by $e$ from this state.

Another key aspect of refinement is the refinement of behaviors. New events may be introduced that make the actions more detailed. These new events are not observable at the abstract level, as the stuttering in TLA [11]. Very often, new variables are introduced. Thus, it is useful to visualize the states referring to these variable changes. In order to preserve the structure of the abstract system, we choose to refine each abstract state in an independent way. So, the transitions, relative to events which belong to $Interface(\mathcal{S})$, are preserved by the introduction of hierarchical states.

**Definition 6 (Hierarchical States).** A set of sub-states $\{E_1^R, \dots, E_m^R\}$ can be associated to a super-state $Proj_L(E^S)$ of $\mathcal{R}$ if and only if

$$\bigvee_{i=1}^{m} \mathcal{I}(E_i^R) \Leftrightarrow \mathcal{I}(Proj_L(E^S))$$

In a refined system, the user must decide what projections of abstract states are decomposed and s/he must provide the predicates of the decomposition. If the abstract states are disjoint, then the transitions associated to the new events appear only between the sub-states of a hierarchical state. An example of refinement with decomposition of states is given in Section 4.4.

## 4     The GeneSyst Tool

### 4.1     Presentation

The GeneSyst tool is intended to generate a symbolic labelled transition system $T$ from an event-B system $S$ and a set of states $N$. Such a generated SLTS will be denoted by $T(S, N)$. The input of the tool is a B component, where the ASSERTIONS clause contains the formula $P_1 \vee \ldots \vee P_n$, which characterizes the list of predicates $\{P_1, \ldots, P_n\}$. By this way, the condition of completeness (section 3.2) is generated as proof obligation.

We give a sketch of the algorithm which computes the transitions of $T(S, N)$: it uses three main variables: the set of visited states, *visited*, the set of processed states, *processed*, and the set of computed transitions $tr$. First, the initial state is put in the *visited* set. Then each state $E$ in the *visited* set is processed: this consists in computing the transitions $(E, (D, A, e), F)$ with all events $e$ to all non-initial states $F$ of the system. Predicates $D$ and $A$ are determined following the algorithm defined in the following section. If $D$ or $A$ are not *false* then the transition $(E, (D, A, e), F)$ is added to $tr$, and if $F$ has not been processed, it is put in the *visited* set. After the processing of state $E$, $E$ is removed from *visited* and put in set *processed*. When *visited* is empty, then $tr$ contains all the computed transitions of $T(S, N)$ and *processed* contains the set of reachable states. The algorithm terminates, because the set of states to be visited is finite (bounded by the cardinal of $N$). This algorithm guarantees that the resulting SLTS is a valid transition system for $S$, with given states $N$.

### 4.2     Proof Obligations

A subprocedure of the algorithm is to determine effectively the enabledness predicate and the reachability predicate, given a triple $(E, e, F)$. For sake of usability of the resulting transition system, it is interesting to examine three cases: predicates are *true*, *false* or other. This information can be obtained by proof obligations. In Fig. 1, we give the conditions for the calculus of these predicates. Obviously, if $D$ and/or $A$ is *false*, then the transition is not possible.

In practice, the GeneSyst tool computes the proof obligations (POs) above and interacts with AtelierB to discharge the POs. For each triple $(E, e, F)$:

|     | Proof obligations | $D$ for $(E, e, F)$ |
|-----|-------------------|---------------------|
| (1) | $\forall x \cdot (\mathcal{I}(E) \Rightarrow Guard(e))$ | *true* |
| (2) | $\forall x \cdot (\mathcal{I}(E) \Rightarrow \neg Guard(e))$ | *false* |
| (3) | $\exists x \cdot (\mathcal{I}(E) \wedge Guard(e))$ | $Guard(e)$ |
|     | Proof obligations | $A$ for $(E, e, F)$ |
| (4) | $\forall x \cdot (\mathcal{I}(E) \wedge Guard(e) \Rightarrow \langle Action(e) \rangle \mathcal{I}(F))$ | *true* |
| (5) | $\forall x \cdot (\mathcal{I}(E) \wedge Guard(e) \Rightarrow [Action(e)] \neg \mathcal{I}(F))$ | *false* |
| (6) | $\exists x \cdot (\mathcal{I}(E) \wedge Guard(e) \wedge \langle Action(e) \rangle \mathcal{I}(F))$ | $\langle Action(e) \rangle \mathcal{I}(F)$ |

**Fig. 1.** Proof obligations for enabledness and reachability

1. if proof obligation (1) is automatically discharged then $D$ is *true*.
2. if proof obligation (2) is automatically discharged then $D$ is *false* and transition $(E, e, F)$ does not occur in the resulting $\mathcal{T}(\mathcal{S}, N)$.
3. otherwise, $D$ is $Guard(e)$ by default.

Then, after cases 1. and 3., GeneSyst computes the proof obligations for determining the reachability predicate $A$.

4. if proof obligation (4) is automatically discharged then $A$ is *true*.
5. if proof obligation (5) is automatically discharged then $A$ is *false* and transition $(E, e, F)$ does not occur in the resulting $\mathcal{T}(\mathcal{S}, N)$.
6. otherwise, the transition is kept with $\langle Action(e) \rangle \mathcal{I}(F)$ as $A$, by default.

We can notice that Condition 1 about the validity of the transitions is well satisfied by construction. The *by default cases* in 3. and 6. correspond to several possibilities. Either there exist values in state $E$ for which the transition is crossable (guard of $e$ is true and state $F$ is reachable), or there are not (the guard is false or state $F$ is not reachable). However, in both possibilities, these transitions are included in the resulting transition system. To manage this feature, we define the notion of *minimal* symbolic labelled transition system.

**Definition 7 (Minimal SLTS).** A minimal SLTS is a SLTS where all the transitions are valid, i.e. satisfy a) and b) of Condition 1, and also satisfy:
c)    $D \not\Rightarrow false$ and $A \not\Rightarrow false$

A SLTS built by GeneSyst is minimal if all the proof obligations of $D$ and $A$ have been effectively discharged in step 1. or 2. and step 4. or 5. in the algorithm above. To minimize the number of by-default transitionss, we have designed two variants of the algorithm. The first optional alternative of the algorithm is to change cases 3. and 6. into:

3'. if proof obligation (3) is automatically discharged, then $D$ is $Guard(e)$ by proof, otherwise, D is $Guard(e)$ by default.
6'. if proof obligation (6) is automatically discharged, then $A$ is $\langle Action(e) \rangle \mathcal{I}(F)$ by proof, otherwise, the transition is kept with $\langle Action(e) \rangle \mathcal{I}(F)$ as $A$ by default.

Another option of the tool allows the user to get the POs which have not been automatically discharged. Then, s/he can do an interactive proof to complete the work and return the information that the PO is discharged or not. However, the interactive mode is not very practicable when there are a great number of proof obligations that are not automatically discharged. It becomes useful to check actually the absence of some critical transitions (cases 2. and 4.).

## 4.3    Transition Systems Associated to the Demoney Case Study

In Fig. 2, we give an example of transition system generated from a subset of the abstract specification of the Demoney case study. The B machine is provided

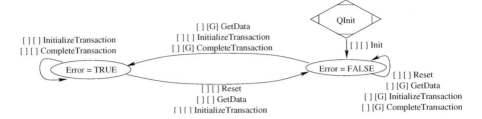

**Fig. 2.** Transition system associated to the error detection in the Demoney specification

in appendix. We just have represented four methods imposed by the Demoney specification [16]: *Initialize Transaction*, *Complete Transaction*, *Reset* and *GetData*. The two methods *Initialize Transaction* and *Complete Transaction* have to be executed in sequence. If they are called in the wrong order then an error must be returned. Moreover, any other methods cannot be invoked between them, except the method *Reset* which models the extraction of the card from the terminal. If it is called during a transaction, all the internal variables must be restored at their initial values. Finally, method *GetData* has been defined to represent any other method which plays a neutral rôle with respect to transactions.

Let us notice that our model has been expressed with events. In the applet Demoney, methods have neither parameters nor result, because they communicate through a global variable, named $APDU$, which allows the information transfer between the card and the terminal. An error can be returned by means of the same variable. Finally, methods have no precondition, because they are callable at any time. So the transformation of methods in events is straightforward.

In the diagrams generated by GeneSyst, transitions are prefixed by the information about predicates $D$ and $A$. A predicate denoted by "[ ]" means *true*, while "$[G]$" means that the transition is computed by cases 3. or 6. (see section 4.2).

Fig. 2 points out cases in which errors can occur. Transitions have no enabledness condition, because all the guards are *true* in the model. Some reachability conditions do not reduce to *true*, as for the event *GetData*, which is defined by:

$$GetData = \text{IF } EngagedTrans = \text{TRUE THEN}$$
$$Error := \text{TRUE} \parallel EngagedTrans := \text{FALSE}$$
$$\text{ELSE } Error := \text{FALSE END};$$

From state $Error = \text{FALSE}$, event *GetData* can reach the state $Error = \text{TRUE}$ with the condition $EngagedTrans = \text{TRUE}$ and stays in $Error = \text{FALSE}$ otherwise. Let us remark also that *GetData* is enabled in state $Error = \text{TRUE}$ and always reaches state $Error = \text{FALSE}$ because of the invariant $Error = \text{TRUE} \Rightarrow EngagedTrans = \text{FALSE}$.

### 4.4    Transition System Associated to a Refinement of Demoney

In our refinement of Demoney, the boolean variable $Error$ is changed into a value of a given set $StatusType$, which intends to describe error codes, as imposed by

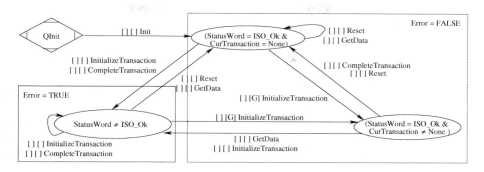

**Fig. 3.** Transition system associated to the refinement of the error detection

the specification [16]. In the same way, the boolean variable *EngagedTrans* is refined into a value of a given set *TransactionType*, which indicates the exact type of the current transaction. Finally, we have introduced the channel with two levels of security (FALSE and TRUE). All this information is declared in the invariant below (see also the refinement in appendix):

INVARIANT
$StatusWord \in StatusType \ \land \ CurTransaction \in TransactionType \ \land$
$ChannelIsSecured \in \textsf{BOOL} \ \land$
$((Error = \textsf{FALSE}) \Leftrightarrow (StatusWord = ISO\_Ok)) \ \land$
$((EngagedTrans = \textsf{FALSE}) \Leftrightarrow (CurTransaction = None)) \ \land$
$((CurTransaction \neq None) \Rightarrow (ChannelIsSecured = \textsf{TRUE})) \ \land$
$((StatusWord \neq ISO\_Ok) \Rightarrow (CurTransaction = None))$

Fig. 3 is built from this refinement. State *Error* = FALSE, which corresponds to $StatusWord = ISO\_Ok$, is split into two states according to that a transaction is engaged or not.

As expressed in Definition 6, the predicate given to GeneSyst to describe the states has to be a conjunction of equivalences between an abstract state and a disjunction of refined states. This predicate is written in the assertion clause. For example, the assertion below has been used to generate Fig. 3.

$((Error = \textsf{TRUE}) \Leftrightarrow ((StatusWord \neq ISO\_Ok \ \land \ CurTransaction = None)$
$\qquad\qquad\qquad\qquad \lor \ (StatusWord \neq ISO\_Ok \ \land \ CurTransaction \neq None)))$
$\land$
$((Error = \textsf{FALSE}) \Leftrightarrow ((StatusWord = ISO\_Ok \ \land \ CurTransaction = None)$
$\qquad\qquad\qquad\qquad \lor \ (StatusWord = ISO\_Ok \ \land \ CurTransaction \neq None)))$

With the splitting of the state *Error* = FALSE, transition conditions are simplified in *true* or *false* or, in the worst case, are unchanged. For example, in Fig. 2, the transition labelled by $[\,][G]CompleteTransaction$ and going from

$Error = $ FALSE to $Error = $ TRUE is, in Fig. 3, going from $StatusWord = ISO\_Ok \wedge$ $CurTransaction = None$ to $StatusWord \neq ISO\_Ok \wedge CurTransaction = None$ with the label $[][]CompleteTransaction$. So, its reachability has been made more precise. The same effect occurs on transition $[][G]CompleteTransaction$ going from $Error = $ FALSE to $Error = $ FALSE, which is refined by $[][]CompleteTransaction$ going from $CurTransaction \neq None$ to $CurTransaction = None$ in the super-state $Error = $ FALSE. These two specializations are directly due to the introduction of the $CurTransaction$ variable.

# 5    Verification of Security Properties on Demoney

In this section we propose a formalism to express properties relative to security aspects and we show how GeneSyst can be used to verify these properties. We will next give a concrete example relative to the Demoney case study.

## 5.1    Properties

Generally, security is designed and implemented through different levels of abstraction. Security policies are defined by a set of rules according to which the system can be regulated, in order to guarantee expected properties, as confidentiality or integrity. Security policies are then implemented through software and hardware functions, called security mechanisms. Such an approach has been adopted by the Common Criteria norm [8] which proposes, through the notion of assurance requirements, a catalogue of security policies and a hierarchy of mechanisms.

In this paper we focus on security properties relative to constraints on the global behavior of the system, as authentication procedures or access control. In this case, security requirements can be seen as constraints on the execution order of atomic actions, as operation calls. F. Schneider claims in [18] that automata are a well-adapted formalism which can, both, be used to specify some forms of security policies and to control implementations during their execution. On the other hand, K. Trentelman and M. Huisman [22] propose a logic that can be used also to express some forms of security properties, as temporal properties on JML specifications.

We adopt a formalism based on logic formulas, which allows us to point out expected behaviors either in specifying correct executions, or in specifying security violations. That offers a good flexibility and is suitable to describe as well open policies as closed policies, respectively relative to negative authorizations and positive authorizations [17].

## 5.2    Predicates of Security Properties

Security properties are often represented as a list of first order logic formulas that have to be verified. We want to define some predicates to make the expression of these formulas easier. Predicates that we introduce express the ability of an event to start from a state (*Enabled* and *AlwaysEnabled*) and the existence of a transition between two states (*Crossable* and *AlwaysCrossable*).

**Definition 8** (*Enabled*, *AlwaysEnabled*, *Crossable* **and** *AlwaysCrossable*).
Given $p_1$ and $p_2$ two state predicates and an event $ev$ from a system $\mathcal{S}$ with variables $x$, then:

$$
\begin{aligned}
Enabled(p_1, ev) &\mathrel{\widehat{=}} & \exists x \cdot (p_1 \ \wedge \ Guard(ev)) \\
AlwaysEnabled(p_1, ev) &\mathrel{\widehat{=}} & \forall x \cdot (p_1 \Rightarrow Guard(ev)) \\
Crossable(p_1, ev, p_2) &\mathrel{\widehat{=}} & \exists x \cdot (p_1 \ \wedge \ \langle ev \rangle p_2) \\
AlwaysCrossable(p_1, ev, p_2) &\mathrel{\widehat{=}} & \forall x \cdot (p_1 \Rightarrow [ev]p_2)
\end{aligned}
$$

Let us note that if $Enabled(p_1, ev) \Leftrightarrow false$, then, for each predicate $p_2$, $AlwaysCrossable(p_1, ev, p_2)$ will be *true* instead of *false*, which is the intuitive value expected. In the same way, if $p_1$ is equivalent to *false* then *AlwaysEnabled* and *AlwaysCrossable* are always *true*. Moreover, we can notice that:

$$Crossable(p_1, ev, p_2) \Rightarrow Enabled(p_1, ev)$$

From this definition we can deduce the properties below, relative to the implication:

**Property 3.** Given $p_1$, $p_2$ and $p_3$ three predicates and an event $ev$ then:

- if $p_1 \Rightarrow p_3$ and $Enabled(p_1, ev)$ then $Enabled(p_3, ev)$
- if $p_3 \Rightarrow p_1$ and $AlwaysEnabled(p_1, ev)$ then $AlwaysEnabled(p_3, ev)$
- if $p_1 \Rightarrow p_3$ and $Crossable(p_1, ev, p_2)$ then $Crossable(p_3, ev, p_2)$
- if $p_2 \Rightarrow p_3$ and $Crossable(p_1, ev, p_2)$ then $Crossable(p_1, ev, p_3)$
- if $p_3 \Rightarrow p_1$ and $AlwaysCrossable(p_1, ev, p_2)$ then $AlwaysCrossable(p_3, ev, p_2)$
- if $p_2 \Rightarrow p_3$ and $AlwaysCrossable(p_1, ev, p_2)$ then $AlwaysCrossable(p_1, ev, p_3)$

Here are two examples:

**Reactivity of a System.** The **JavaCard** specification imposes that any APDU instruction is callable at any time. Given $\mathcal{S}$ a system and $I$ its invariant, then this formula can be expressed as follows:

$$\forall ev \cdot (ev \in Interface(\mathcal{S}) \Rightarrow AlwaysEnabled(I, ev))$$

**Unicity of the Ways to Reach a State.** In some cases, like access control, we want to impose that the only way to reach a state $P$ is to execute a particular event *Begin*. If $I$ is the invariant of $\mathcal{S}$, then this property can be expressed as follows:

$$\forall ev \cdot (ev \in Interface(\mathcal{S}) \ \wedge \ ev \neq Begin \Rightarrow AlwaysCrossable(I, ev, \neg P)).$$

### 5.3   Property Checking Using GeneSyst **SLTS**

Security properties could be verified on B specifications, using definition 8. Nevertheless, in some cases, the SLTS produced by GeneSyst can be directly exploited. Then, the verification consists in using syntactic information relative to enabledness and reachability of transitions. Properties 4–7 list the different cases where the predicates above can be directly established from a symbolic labelled transition system.

Properties 4–7 share the following hypothesis: *Given an event $e$ and $q_1$, $q_2$ two states from a SLTS $\mathcal{T}$, such as $\mathcal{I}(q_1) \not\Leftrightarrow false$ and $(q_1, (D, A, e), q_2) \in W_{\mathcal{T}}$, then predicates Enabled, AlwaysEnabled, Crossable and AlwaysCrossable can be determined as follows:.*

## Property 4 (Enabledness Condition - General Case).

1. $D \equiv true$ $\quad\Rightarrow\quad Enabled(q_1, e)$
2. $D \equiv false$ $\quad\Rightarrow\quad \neg Enabled(q_1, e)$
3. $D \equiv true$ $\quad\Rightarrow\quad AlwaysEnabled(q_1, e)$
4. $D \equiv false$ $\quad\Rightarrow\quad \neg AlwaysEnabled(q_1, e)$

If the SLTS used to verify the property is minimal, then Property 4 can be enlarged: the conditions are necessary (and sufficient) and conditions 1 and 4 are refined.

## Property 5 (Enabledness for Minimal SLTS).

1. $D \not\equiv false$ $\quad\Leftrightarrow\quad Enabled(q_1, e)$
2. $D \equiv false$ $\quad\Leftrightarrow\quad \neg Enabled(q_1, e)$
3. $D \equiv true$ $\quad\Leftrightarrow\quad AlwaysEnabled(q_1, e)$
4. $D \not\equiv true$ $\quad\Leftrightarrow\quad \neg AlwaysEnabled(q_1, e)$

In the same way, syntactic conditions to check *Crossable* and *AlwaysCrossable* predicates are:

## Property 6 (Reachability Condition - General Case).

5. $A \equiv true$ $\quad\Rightarrow\quad Crossable(q_1, e, q_2)$
6. $A \equiv false \ \lor \ D \equiv false$ $\quad\Rightarrow\quad \neg Crossable(q_1, e, q_2)$
7. $A \equiv true \ \land$
   $\forall q_i \cdot (q_2 \not\equiv q_i \Rightarrow (q_1, (D, A_2, e), q_i) \notin W_{\mathcal{T}})$ $\quad\Rightarrow\quad AlwaysCrossable(q_1, e, q_2)$
8. $A \equiv false$ $\quad\Rightarrow\quad \neg AlwaysCrossable(q_1, e, q_2)$

Cases 7 and 8 are not symetric, as it would be expected, because, syntacticaly, we can just compare names of states, not the intersection of their interpretation. Just as for enabledness, the conditions can be enlarged, when the SLTS is minimal, as follow:

## Property 7 (Reachability for Minimal SLTS).

5. $A \not\equiv false$ $\quad\Leftrightarrow\quad Crossable(q_1, e, q_2)$
6. $A \equiv false \ \lor \ D \equiv false$ $\quad\Leftrightarrow\quad \neg Crossable(q_1, e, q_2)$
8. $A \not\equiv true$ $\quad\Rightarrow\quad \neg AlwaysCrossable(q_1, e, q_2)$

Cases 7 and 8 are just sufficient conditions because of the limitation of the syntactic verification. Case 7 is not present in Property 7 because it is the same as in Property 6 Finally, Property 3 allows the deduction of derived properties from the four properties above, by weakening or strenghtening the states.

## 5.4    Example of a Property Checking

In this section, we develop a real example of Demoney property and we do its verification by using the SLTS given in Figure 3. In the Demoney specification [16], the two APDU instructions *InitializeTransaction* and *CompleteTransaction* have to be executed in sequence, without any other instructions between them and without reaching any error state, to make a transaction. However, the card can be withdrawn at any time (modelled by the *Reset* event) without generating any error. Transaction atomicity property can be decomposed in five formulas given below, where $I$ stands for the invariant of the Demoney specification. Moreover, SLTS of Figure 3 is minimal and events are always enabled from all state of the SLTS. Finally, note than the invariant $I$ is equivalent to the union of all state predicates (Section 3.2).

**Formula 1:** There exists at least a value in $I$ such that the event *Initialize-Transaction* can reach *CurTransaction* $\neq$ *None*:

$$Crossable(I, InitializeTransaction, CurTransaction \neq None)$$

Predicate *CurTransaction* $\neq$ *None* directly corresponds to a state predicate. Since there exists a transition from *CurTransaction* = *None* $\land$ *StatusWord* = *ISO_Ok* to *CurTransaction* $\neq$ *None*, labelled with $[\ ][G]InitializeTransaction$, then we can use case 5 of Property 7 and conclude that the Formula 1 is *true*.

**Formula 2:** For all values, the event *InitializeTransaction* goes into the state *CurTransaction* $\neq$ *None* or into an error state:

$$AlwaysCrossable(I, InitializeTransaction,$$
$$CurTransaction \neq None \lor StatusWord \neq ISO\_Ok)$$

*CurTransaction* $\neq$ *None* and *StatusWord* $\neq$ *ISO_Ok* are two state predicates, and all the transitions labelled with *InitializeTransaction* go only in one of these states. Then, due to case 7 of property 6, this formula is *true*.

**Formula 3:** From *CurTransaction*$\neq$*None*, all events, but *CompleteTransaction* and *Reset*, go to an error state:

$$\forall e \cdot (e \in Interface(\mathcal{S}) \land e \neq CompleteTransaction \land e \neq Reset \Rightarrow$$
$$AlwaysCrossable(CurTransaction \neq None, e, StatusWord \neq ISO\_Ok)$$

The two predicates correspond to state predicates and the only events which go elsewhere than *StatusWord* $\neq$ *ISO_Ok* from *CurTransaction* $\neq$ *None* are *CompleteTransaction* and *Reset*. Thus Formula 4 is *true* (case 7 of Property 6).

**Formula 4:** eXCEPT *InitializeTransaction*, no event can reach *CurTransaction* $\neq$ *None*:

$$\forall e \cdot (e \in Interface(\mathcal{S}) \land e \neq InitializeTransaction \Rightarrow$$
$$AlwaysCrossable(I, e, CurTransaction = None))$$

Predicate $CurTransaction = None$ is the union of two existing state predicates. So, we have to check if there exists an event, different from $InitializeTransaction$, that can reach $CurTransaction \neq None$. Since it is not the case, this formula is *true* (case 7 of Property 6).

**Formula 5:** No transition labelled by $CompleteTransaction$ or $Reset$ is reflexive on state $CurTransaction \neq None$:

$$\neg Crossable(CurTransaction \neq None, CompleteTransaction,$$
$$CurTransaction \neq None)$$

and $\neg Crossable(CurTransaction \neq None, Reset, CurTransaction \neq None)$
$CurTransaction \neq None$ corresponds to a state predicate and no $Complete$-$Transaction$ or $Reset$ reflexive transition occurs. Thus this formula is *true* (case 5 of Property 7).

The model of Demoney is thus correct relatively to the atomicity security property of transactions. However, during the realisation of this example, which is a simplified Demoney applet, we found three errors due to an erroneous simplification of our complete model of Demoney.

The originality of this approach is to have brought back, under some hypotheses, the verification of security properties to a syntactic checking. However, it is important to be careful about the real value of the crossing conditions generated by GeneSyst. Indeed, if some proof obligations are not (automatically) discharged, the transitions system will have by-default transitions. Then, to properly exploit the information, we have to be sure that the property to be verify can be checked on a non-minimal SLTS.

# 6    Related Works and Conclusion

The work presented here is in line with the ideas presented in [5], itself inspired by [9]. In [5], the authors propose the construction of a labelled transition system which is a finite state abstraction of the behavior of an event-B system. The existence of transitions is determined by proof obligations, as here, but the resulting transition system does not contain any information about transition crossing. Moreover, the paper does not consider the refinement step in the diagram representation.

Other work is devoted to the translation of dynamic aspects described by statecharts in the B formalism (for instance [13, 20]). These approaches are inverse of ours, because they go from a diagrammatic representation to an encoding in a formal text. Their objective is to build a B model from UML descriptions. On our side, we suppose that the model has been stated and we are interested in representing the precise behavior of the system with respect to (a part of) variables, in order to check properties, or to validate the model against the requirements.

A similar approach has been envisaged for TLA [12] and extended in [6, 7] to take in account liveness properties and refinement. As in [5], the generated diagrams are abstractions of the system behavior.

Several tools are dedicated to the analysis of the behavior of B components by the way of the animation of machines [4] or by local exhaustive model checking [14]. Even if some of them allow the generation of symbolic traces, these tools can be considered as "testing" tools. They provide particular execution sequences of the system, not a static representation of all the behaviors. In [23], the authors describe the generation of statecharts from event-B systems, but their approach suffers from several restrictions and their diagrams are not symbolic.

In this paper, we have presented the GeneSyst tool, its logical foundations and its application to the verification of security properties. In the first part, we introduced the definition of traces of event-B systems and refinements. We formalized the notion of symbolic labelled transition systems, with transitions decorated by enabledness and reachability predicates. This gives a complete and precise view of the behavior of the system, which can be exploited for various objectives.

We described the algorithm that is implemented to generate a SLTS from a B system and a set of states, characterized by predicates. The computation of effective transitions between states is performed by proving proof obligations. Due to the indecidability of the proof process, we have the choice between two kinds of (non exclusive) results: the generation is automatic, but we can get more transitions than in the real system, or the user completes interactively the non-conclusive proofs and then, the resulting automaton reflects exactly the behavior of the system.

The user can take profit of the freedom degree achieved by the choice of the states, to obtain the best analyses useful for him/her purpose. Non classical verification techniques can be designed and implemented at this stage, to assess or to validate the model, as it was shown in the last part of the paper. This opens a large field of research in the domains of security properties, confidentiality, access control, validation of models with respect to the requirements, automatic documentation of specifications, etc. Our present research work is to develop a set of techniques in the GECCOO[2] project to express and to check security properties, as it was sketched in the paper. We want to investigate the extraction of states from the specification of property automata, the use of refinement to split states and achieve a suitable level of decomposition in order to check a property. Another work is to deal with complex B models (several refinement chains together with composition clauses SEES, INCLUDES, etc.), either by composing partial labelled transition systems, or by flattening a structured model before computing the whole associated SLTS.

# References

1. J.-R. Abrial. *The B Book - Assigning Programs to Meanings.* Cambridge University Press, August 1996.
2. J.-R. Abrial. Extending B without Changing it (for Developing Distributed Systems). In H. Habrias, editor, *First B conference*, Putting into Practice Methods and Tools for Information System Design, IRIN, pages 169–191, 1996.

---

[2] "Génération de Code Certifié Orienté Objet". Project of Program "ACI Sécurité Informatique", 2003.

3. J.R. Abrial and L. Mussat. Introducing Dynamic Constraints in B. In D. Bert, editor, *B'98: Recent Advances in the Development and Use of the B Method*, LNCS 1393, pages 83–128. Springer-Verlag, 1998.
4. F. Ambert, F. Bouquet, S. Chemin, S. Guenaud, B. Legeard, F. Peureux, M. Utting, and N. Vacelet. BZ-testing tools: A tool-set for test generation from Z and B using constraint logic programming. In *Formal Approaches to Testing of Software (FATES'02)*, pages 105–120. INRIA, 2002.
5. D. Bert and F. Cave. Construction of Finite Labelled Transition Systems from B Abstract Systems. In W. Grieskamp, T. Santen, and B. Stoddart, editors, *Integrated Formal Methods*, LNCS 1945, pages 235–254. Springer-Verlag, 2000.
6. D. Cansell, D. Méry, and S. Merz. Predicate Diagrams for the Verification of Reactive Systems. In W. Grieskamp, T. Santen, and B. Stoddart, editors, *Integrated Formal Methods*, LNCS 1945, pages 380–397. Springer-Verlag, 2000.
7. D. Cansell, D. Méry, and S. Merz. Diagram Refinements for the Design of Reactive Systems. *Journal of Universal Computer Science*, 7(2), 2001.
8. Common Criteria. *Common Criteria for Information Technology Security Evaluation, Norme ISO 15408 - version 2.1*, Aout 1999.
9. S. Graf and H. Saïdi. Construction of Abstract State Graphs with PVS. In *Computer-Aided Verification (CAV'97)*, LNCS 1254. Springer-Verlag, 1997.
10. C.A.R. Hoare. *Communicating Sequential Processes*. Prentice Hall, 1985.
11. L. Lamport. A Temporal Logic of Actions. *ACM Transactions on Programming Languages and Systems*, 16(3):872–923, may 1994.
12. L. Lamport. TLA in Pictures. *Software Engineering*, 21(9):768–775, 1995.
13. H. Ledang and J. Souquières. Contributions for Modelling UML State-charts in B. In M. Butler, L. Petre, and K. Sere, editors, *IFM*, LNCS 2335, pages 109–127. Springer-Verlag, 2002.
14. M. Leuschel and M. Butler. ProB: A Model Checker for B. In K. Akari, S. Gnesi, and D Mandrioli, editors, *FME 2003: Formal Methods*, LNCS 2805, pages 855–874. Springer-Verlag, 1997.
15. R. Marlet. DEMONEY: Java Card Implementation. Public technical report, SECSAFE project, 11 2002.
16. R. Marlet and C. Mesnil. DEMONEY : A demonstrative Electronic Purse - Card Specification -. Public technical report, SECSAFE project, 11 2002.
17. P. Samarati and S. De Capitani di Vimercati. Access Control: Policies, Models, and Mechanisms. In *Revised versions of lectures given during the IFIP WG 1.7 International School on Foundations of Security Analysis and Design on Foundations of Security Analysis and Design*, pages 137–196. Springer-Verlag, 2001.
18. F. B. Schneider. Enforceable security policies. *Information and System Security*, 3(1):30–50, 2000.
19. SecSafe. SecSafe Porject Home Page. http://www.doc.ic.ac.uk/ siveroni/secsafe/.
20. E. Sekerinski and R. Zurob. Translating Statecharts to B. In M. Butler, L. Petre, and K. Sere, editors, *IFM*, LNCS 2335, pages 128–144. Springer-Verlag, 2002.
21. SUN.                Java          Card        2.1        Platform        Specifications. http://java.sun.com/products/javacard/specs.html.
22. K. Trentelman and M. Huisman. Extending JML Specifications with Temporal Logic. In *Algebraic Methodology And Software Technology (AMAST '02)*, LNCS 2422, pages 334–348. Springer-Verlag, 2002.
23. J.-C. Voisinet and B. Tatibouet. Generating Statecharts from B Specifications. In *16th Int Conf. on Software and System Engineering and their applications (ISCEA 2003)*, volume 1, 2003.

# Appendix

Machine of the Demoney specification (diagram in Fig. 2, Section 4.3):

```
MACHINE Demoney
VARIABLES
    Error, EngagedTrans
INVARIANT
    Error ∈ BOOL ∧ EngagedTrans ∈ BOOL ∧
    (Error = TRUE ⇒ EngagedTrans = FALSE) ∧
    (EngagedTrans = TRUE ⇒ Error = FALSE)
ASSERTIONS
    /* The assertion provides the states for tool GeneSyst */
    /* Here, only two states are considered according to the Error values */
    Error = FALSE ∨ Error = TRUE
INITIALISATION
    Error := FALSE || EngagedTrans := FALSE
OPERATIONS
    = BEGIN EngagedTrans := FALSE || Error := FALSE END;
    GetData =
        IF EngagedTrans = TRUE THEN
            Error := TRUE || EngagedTrans := FALSE
        ELSE Error := FALSE
        END;
    InitializeTransaction =
        IF EngagedTrans = TRUE THEN
            Error := TRUE || EngagedTrans := FALSE
        ELSE
            ANY SW WHERE SW ∈ BOOL THEN
                Error := SW || EngagedTrans := bool(SW = FALSE)
            END
        END;
    CompleteTransaction =
        IF EngagedTrans = FALSE THEN
            Error := TRUE
        ELSE Error := FALSE || EngagedTrans := FALSE
        END
END
```

Refinement of the Demoney specification (diagram in Fig. 3, Section 4.4):

```
REFINEMENT Demoney_R1
REFINES Demoney
SETS
    TransactionType = {Credit, Debit, None};
    StatusType = {ISO_Error, ISO_Ok}
VARIABLES
    StatusWord, CurTransaction, ChannelIsSecured
```

INVARIANT

    $StatusWord \in StatusType \ \land \ CurTransaction \in TransactionType \ \land$

    $ChannelIsSecured \in \mathsf{BOOL} \ \land$

    $((StatusWord = ISO\_Ok) \Leftrightarrow (Error = \mathsf{FALSE})) \ \land$

    $((EngagedTrans = \mathsf{TRUE}) \Leftrightarrow (CurTransaction \neq None)) \ \land$

    $((CurTransaction \neq None) \Rightarrow ChannelIsSecured = \mathsf{TRUE}) \ \land$

    $((StatusWord \neq ISO\_Ok) \Rightarrow (CurTransaction = None))$

ASSERTIONS

    /* Each abstract state is decomposed in two concrete states */

    /* One of these states is not reachable */

    $((Error = \mathsf{TRUE}) \Leftrightarrow$

        $((StatusWord \neq ISO\_Ok \ \land \ CurTransaction = None)$

        $\lor \ (StatusWord \neq ISO\_Ok \ \land \ CurTransaction \neq None)))$

    $\land$

    $((Error = \mathsf{FALSE}) \Leftrightarrow$

        $((StatusWord = ISO\_Ok \ \land \ CurTransaction = None)$

        $\lor \ (StatusWord = ISO\_Ok \ \land \ CurTransaction \neq None)))$

INITIALISATION

    $StatusWord := ISO\_Ok \ || \ ChannelIsSecured := \mathsf{FALSE} \ ||$

    $CurTransaction := None$

OPERATIONS

    $Reset =$ BEGIN

        $StatusWord := ISO\_Ok \ || \ ChannelIsSecured := \mathsf{FALSE} \ ||$

        $CurTransaction := None$

    END;

    $GetData =$

    IF $CurTransaction \neq None$ THEN

        $StatusWord := ISO\_Error \ || \ CurTransaction := None$

    ELSE

        $StatusWord := ISO\_Ok$

    END;

    $InitializeTransaction =$

    IF $CurTransaction \neq None \ \lor \ ChannelIsSecured = \mathsf{FALSE}$ THEN

        $StatusWord := ISO\_Error \ || \ CurTransaction := None$

    ELSE

        $StatusWord :\in StatusType;$

        IF $StatusWord = ISO\_Ok$ THEN

          $CurTransaction :\in \{Debit, Credit\}$

        END

    END;

    $CompleteTransaction =$

    IF $CurTransaction = None$ THEN

        $StatusWord := ISO\_Error$

    ELSE

        $CurTransaction := None \ || \ StatusWord := ISO\_Ok$

    END

END

# Formal Verification of a Type Flaw Attack on a Security Protocol Using Object-Z

Benjamin W. Long

School of Information Technology and Electrical Engineering,
The University of Queensland,
Brisbane, Qld 4072, Australia
benl@itee.uq.edu.au

**Abstract.** We have identified a type flaw attack on the Amended Needham Schroeder Protocol with Conventional Keys due to a potential oversight at the presentation layer of the network architecture. Using Object-Z, a formal specification of the protocol is presented allowing us to state the assumed properties of the presentation layer explicitly. Object-Z's schema calculus is used to verify the attack we have found and the weaknesses upon which the attack depends, thus enabling us to minimise the effort required to prevent the attack and to specify this as part of the model accordingly.

## 1  Introduction

We have discovered a *type flaw attack* on the Amended Needham Schroeder Protocol with Conventional Keys [7]. Unfortunately, protocol analysis tools are not good at finding type flaw attacks [13]. For example, such tools have failed to reveal the type flaw attack we have discovered [7, 9, 4].

This is because security protocols are often specified purely at the *application layer* of the network architecture — the level at which the content of messages is determined — thus restricting the level of the corresponding analysis. However, the confusion that leads to a type flaw attack is due to the particular design decisions made at the *presentation layer* — the level at which the low-level representation of messages is determined.[1]

More specifically, type flaw attacks [1] result from misinterpretation of the bit strings used to encode messages. For example, a type flaw attack can occur when a message segment of one type is confused with a segment of another type, or when a message segment of one type is confused with the concatenation of two or more other segments of varying types.

In practice, simple type flaw attacks can be prevented by the use of 'tags' at a lower level of implementation [11], although, Meadows [13] has recently spoken of more complex type flaw attacks in which tags will not suffice. Nevertheless, it is

---

[1] We use terminology from the ISO OSI network architecture model as described by Tanenbaum [19].

H. Treharne et al. (Eds.): ZB 2005, LNCS 3455, pp. 319–333, 2005.
© Springer-Verlag Berlin Heidelberg 2005

never wise to apply countermeasures that may not even be required; in security-critical systems, we seek to find the *necessary* and not merely the *sufficient*. Hence, for a particular attack we want to prove the specific weaknesses upon which an attack depends in order to minimise the effort required to prevent it.

Over-protective tagging schemes can unnecessarily increase message sizes, complexity and other communication overheads. Battery-powered embedded systems such as PDAs, cell phones, networked sensors and smart cards require such overheads to be minimal [16]. In these systems, minimising the resources needed to prevent potential attacks is clearly beneficial.

We are in an age that requires us to follow rigorous development processes. For example, the Common Criteria [6], a standard for the development and evaluation of security systems, requires formal methods to be used in order to obtain the highest level of assurance (EAL7).

Our research aims to promote this level of assurance by providing a framework for

- formally specifying security protocols at the application layer with the capability to reason with message structures at the presentation layer; and
- deriving and proving the particular weaknesses upon which a given attack depends so we can minimise the effort required in order to prevent the attack.

In this paper we demonstrate our approach using the Object-Z specification language and its schema calculus for the specification of the Amended Needham Schroeder Protocol with Conventional Keys and verification of the attack we have discovered.

## 2   Related Work

Analyses of protocols susceptible to type flaw attacks have been attempted using various formalisms [9, 3, 2, 20, 18]. The attacks considered generally involve simple 'type confusion', in which message segments of one type are confused with segments of another type, or in the more advanced models, in which a segment of one type is confused with the concatenation of two or more other segments of varying types [13]. For instance, Figure 1 shows two identical bit string representations of a message at the presentation layer consisting of an agent identifier and a nonce, and for each, an alternative way of interpreting the message at the application layer.

Meadows [13] highlighted the further possibility of attacks in which sub-segments of one type may be confused with sub-segments of another type. This

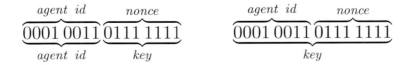

**Fig. 1.** Misinterpretation of message segments

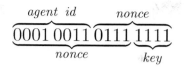

**Fig. 2.** Misinterpretation among message sub-segments

is particularly imaginable in the case where agents use different parsing algorithms for different protocols. In Figure 2, for instance, not only is the message interpreted at the application layer to consist of different types, but the segment lengths are not even the same. In response to this concern, Meadows devised a procedure specifically for determining whether or not type confusions of *any* kind are possible for a given protocol. Given two protocol messages of equal bit-string value, her approach involves an exhaustive search for all potential misinterpretations of those messages. A probability is then assigned to each misinterpretation to assess its likelihood.

Complementing this research, we devised a generic set of Z data structures to model messages at the presentation layer for reasoning with all such attacks, enabling us to determine whether potential type flaw attacks are, or are not, actually possible for a given specification of a protocol [12].

Based on our previous work, here we use Object-Z to formally specify and verify a type flaw attack we have recently discovered on the Amended Needham Schroeder Protocol with Conventional Keys. The object-oriented approach allows us to model protocol roles as individual classes, giving us the flexibility to assemble interesting scenarios from various roles played by agents for our analysis.

## 3    The Protocol

The original Needham Schroeder Protocol with Conventional Keys [14] uses conventional symmetric key encryption to establish a secure means of communication (establish a shared key) between two agents via a trusted third party. Denning and Sacco [8] found a vulnerability due to a lack of freshness in the third protocol message. They presented a solution based on timestamps that was rejected by Needham and Schroeder [15] on the grounds that "it required a good-quality time value to be universally available." Needham and Schroeder proposed an alternative amendment making use of an additional nonce. The resultant protocol as given by Clark and Jacob [7] is described in Figure 3 using the *standard notation* [5] with Alice $A$ playing the part of the initiator, Bob $B$ playing the part of the responder, and Sam $S$ playing the part of the trusted server.

Alice initiates the protocol by sending message 1 to Bob containing her identity $A$. Once Bob has received message 1, he replies with message 2 confirming his participation in the protocol. The message consists of Alice's identity and a nonce $N_B$ to let Bob identify future messages belonging to the current protocol

1. $A \longrightarrow B : A$
2. $B \longrightarrow A : \{A, N_B\}_{K_{BS}}$
3. $A \longrightarrow S : A, B, N_A, \{A, N_B\}_{K_{BS}}$
4. $S \longrightarrow A : \{N_A, B, K_{AB}, \{K_{AB}, N_B, A\}_{K_{BS}}\}_{K_{AS}}$
5. $A \longrightarrow B : \{K_{AB}, N_B, A\}_{K_{BS}}$
6. $B \longrightarrow A : \{N_0\}_{K_{AB}}$
7. $A \longrightarrow B : \{N_0 - 1\}_{K_{AB}}$

**Fig. 3.** The Amended Needham Schroeder Protocol with Conventional Keys

instance, and it is encrypted with the key $K_{BS}$ previously shared between Bob and Sam.

After receiving Bob's reply, Alice sends message 3 to Sam requesting a session key for herself and Bob. She also includes a nonce $N_A$ in order to identify that the next message she receives is fresh. Sam receives message 3 and decrypts the message using the key $K_{BS}$ shared between Bob and Sam. He responds by sending the new session key $K_{AB}$ encrypted for Alice with $K_{AS}$ in message 4 including a segment encrypted for Bob containing the key also.

On receipt of the session key in message 4, Alice checks the value of the nonce $N_A$ to ensure the key is fresh (that is, that it has not been replayed). Then she forwards the encrypted segment for Bob in message 5. Bob receives the session key and he also checks the nonce $N_B$ to ensure the key is fresh. However, as Bob is yet to authenticate Alice, he challenges Alice with a nonce $N_0$ encrypted using the new session key. Alice receives the challenge in message 6 and responds by sending this value decremented by one, in message 7. Finally, Bob checks this value received in message 7 and the protocol is complete.

## 4    A Type Flaw Attack on the Protocol

We have discovered a type flaw attack on the protocol (see Figure 4), requiring Alice $A$ to play the parts of both an initiator and a responder simultaneously in two concurrent instances of the protocol: she is the initiator of a protocol with an agent whom she thinks is Bob (but in fact is the intruder), and also the responder to a protocol initiated by the same intruder.

After Alice attempts to initiate a protocol with Bob (message 2.1), the intruder intercepts this message and sends an arbitrary encrypted segment $X$ to Alice (message 2.2). Alice will assume this message is from Bob as she cannot normally make sense of message 2, and she will generate message 2.3 according to the protocol using $X$ instead of $\{A, N_B\}_{K_{BS}}$.

Meanwhile, the intruder initiates a second protocol (message 2.1′) with Alice. He uses the composition of plaintext segments $N_A$ and $B$ sent by Alice in message 2.3, and a key chosen by him $K_{AB}$, as his identity ($I = N_A, B, K_{AB}$). Alice attempts to contact Sam accordingly in message 2.2′ not realising that the intruder's identity $I$ can be perceived as an alternate meaningful message.

$$
\begin{array}{llll}
2.1. & A \longrightarrow I(B) : A \\
2.2. & I(B) \longrightarrow A & : X \\
2.3. & A \longrightarrow I(S) : A, B, N_A, X \\
2.1'. & I \longrightarrow A & : I & (I = N_A, B, K_{AB}) \\
2.2'. & A \longrightarrow I & : \{I, N_{A_2}\}_{K_{AS}} \\
2.4. & I(S) \longrightarrow A & : \{N_A, B, K_{AB}, N_{A_2}\}_{K_{AS}} \\
2.5. & A \longrightarrow I(B) : N_{A_2} \\
2.6. & I(B) \longrightarrow A & : \{N_0\}_{K_{AB}} \\
2.7. & A \longrightarrow I(B) : \{N_0 - 1\}_{K_{AB}}
\end{array}
$$

**Fig. 4.** A type flaw attack on the protocol

In fact, the intruder sends message 2.2′ straight back to Alice in message 2.4 without modification, continuing the original protocol. Now, as Alice is expecting a message of a particular form, she will not recognise the intruder's identity $I$. Instead Alice will identify the nonce $N_A$ she sent in message 2.3, Bob's identity $B$, the key $K_{AB}$, and a forth segment $N_{A_2}$ assumed to be the encrypted segment ($\{K_{AB}, N_B, A\}_{K_{BS}}$) also expected in message 4. As Alice encrypted this message with the shared key $K_{AS}$ she will now believe that this message was sent to her by Sam, when it was actually redirected from herself via the intruder. It is at this point that Alice has been fooled by the intruder into accepting the intruder's chosen key as a key for secure communication between herself and Bob.

Following the protocol, Alice attempts to send the forth segment from message 2.4 to Bob in message 2.5. The intruder intercepts this message and proceeds to initiate a challenge (message 2.6) and response (message 2.7) with Alice whilst pretending to be Bob in order to finalise the protocol.

## 5   Modelling Messages

In previous work [12], we devised generic Z data structures for modelling messages at the presentation layer to reason about type flaw attacks. We can reuse these structures for the foundation of this verification.

We assume a given set of 'atoms' from which all messages and message parts are constructed at the presentation layer (for example, bits or bytes).

$[ATOM]$

The set of all messages or streams $STR$ is the set of all possible sequences of atoms.

$$STR == \text{seq } ATOM$$

Then we declare four subsets of $STR$ for the different types of data segments that exist at the application layer:

$$
\begin{array}{lr}
AID : \mathbb{P}\, STR & [\text{agent identifiers}] \\
NON : \mathbb{P}\, STR & [\text{nonces}] \\
KEY : \mathbb{P}\, STR & [\text{keys}] \\
ENC : \mathbb{P}\, STR & [\text{encrypted segments}]
\end{array}
$$

The subsets are not necessarily disjoint which means that individual segments may belong to one or more subsets of $STR$. Other segment types may also be added as required.

This is a detailed yet flexible specification of protocol messages allowing us to specify protocols at the application layer and yet reason with protocol messages at the presentation layer. Stronger constraints and assumptions can be introduced for the specification of a particular protocol as is shown in the following section.

## 6    Specification of the Protocol

In this section we specify the protocol using the data structures introduced in Section 5. We begin by adding assumptions regarding properties and functions of messages suitable for our particular analysis.

To allow for analyses of type flaw attacks, our data structures let different agents interpret the same message as consisting of different sequences of typed segments. However, when two agents 'speak the same language' or agree on the type structure of the message, there should be no ambiguity.

Instead of enforcing a specific correlation between the application and presentation layers, we assume the following global axiom which says that if two agents both interpret the initial part of a message to be an agent identifier, then the values they associate with this segment are identical.

$$
(\forall\, m, n : AID;\ o, p : STR \bullet m \,^\frown o = n \,^\frown p \Rightarrow m = n)
$$

Thus, if two identical message streams '$m \,^\frown o$' and '$n \,^\frown p$' begin with segments $m$ and $n$, both of which are interpreted to be of type $AID$, then $m$ and $n$ must be the same identifier. The same applies to the other segment types ($NON$, $KEY$ and $ENC$), however, we have omitted the corresponding predicates from this paper for brevity.

Our approach relies on unifying messages encrypted with the same key. To enable this, we specify a simple property of the encrypt function $enc$. This function maps every key to a function that will produce a unique encrypted segment for any given message stream.

$$
enc : KEY \rightarrow (STR \rightarrowtail ENC)
$$

Message 7 of the protocol was originally stated by Needham and Schroeder to be a reply related to message 6. They suggest the reply could be the value received in message 6 decremented by one, however, for our analysis we don't need to be this specific and choose to introduce a function *auth* to determine the related reply. Given a stream $s$, $auth(s)$ will produce a different and unique stream.

$$auth : STR \rightarrowtail STR$$
$$\forall\, s : STR \bullet auth(s) \neq s$$

## 6.1    Modelling Protocol Roles

The protocol describes three roles for interaction between three network agents: initiator, responder and server. For example, agent Alice may take on initiator roles, responder roles and depending on the topology of the network, even server roles, all at the same time.

Like Ryan et al. [17], we choose to model the protocol in terms of these roles and interactions between them, rather than modelling the behaviour of a given set of network agents. In doing this, we have the flexibility to assemble scenarios from various roles played by agents for the particular analyses we are interested in. Furthermore, our model is simplified because we can focus on one instance of the protocol at a time. For example, for a given instance, we only need to model the existence of one message in transit, and we can declare random values such as session keys and nonces as static variables for the lifetime of the roles.

Each role is captured within a single Object-Z class specification. Each class specification contains information and operations available to the role it is modelling. Instantiations of these classes, or role objects, may then interact with each other to simulate the protocol to which the roles belong. These interactions are specified within another class at a higher level. We do this in Sections 7 and 8 in order to perform our proofs.

The first class we model corresponds to the initiator role. Each role refers to the initiating agent as A, the responder as B and the server as S. A class representing the initiator will keep values for only those items used by that role. For example, in the protocol description, the initiator makes reference to A's identity $A$, B's identity $B$, A's nonce $N_A$, the final authentication nonce $N_0$, the key $K_{AS}$ shared between A and the server S, the new session key $K_{AB}$, and the current message *msg* in transit. These values are declared accordingly in the class state schema. (We assume that upon creation, keys and nonces are assigned a 'random' value from the corresponding sets *KEY* and *NON*.)

---

*Initiator*

$A, B : AID$
$N_A, N_0 : NON$
$K_{AS}, K_{AB} : KEY$
$msg : STR$

---

$$\boxed{\begin{array}{l} \underline{\;begin\;} \\ \Delta(msg) \\ \hline \\ msg' = A \end{array}}$$

$$\boxed{\begin{array}{l} \underline{\;requestKey\;} \\ \Delta(msg) \\ \hline \\ msg \in ENC \wedge msg' = A \frown B \frown N_A \frown msg \end{array}}$$

$$\boxed{\begin{array}{l} \underline{\;forwardKey\;} \\ \Delta(msg, K_{AB}) \\ \hline \\ msg = enc(K_{AS})(N_A \frown B \frown K_{AB}' \frown msg') \wedge msg' \in ENC \end{array}}$$

$$\boxed{\begin{array}{l} \underline{\;respond\;} \\ \Delta(msg, N_0) \\ \hline \\ msg = enc(K_{AB})(N_0') \wedge msg' = enc(K_{AB})(auth(N_0')) \end{array}}$$

Operation *begin* corresponds to the sending of message 1 in the standard notation description of the protocol shown in Section 3. Pre-state variables are undecorated and hold the value of the variables before execution of the operation, whereas post-state variables are decorated with a prime "'" and denote the value of the variables after execution of the operation. The Object-Z symbol '$\Delta$' declares pre-state and post-state variables for each of the named variables, indicating that these variables may be changed by the operation. The post-state variable $msg'$ updates the value of the message currently in transit. For this operation it holds the value of A's identity.

Operation *requestKey* corresponds to both A receiving message 2 from B and sending the request for a key to S (message 3). (We assume that intruders cannot interfere with operations internal to an agent.) The predicate $msg \in ENC$ requires that the incoming message is an encrypted segment, and the value of the outgoing message $msg'$ is the value of the incoming message prepended by $A$, $B$ and $N_A$.

Operation *forwardKey* corresponds to A receiving message 4 from S and forwarding the key to B (message 5). We use the post-state variable $K_{AB}'$ in the description of the incoming message to indicate that A is learning and updating this variable. The precondition on this operation is that the incoming message $msg$ is a segment encrypted with the key $K_{AS}$ shared between A and S, consisting of A's nonce $N_A$, B's identity $B$, the new session key $K_{AB}'$ and a remaining stream $msg'$ that becomes the value of the outgoing message.

Operation *respond* corresponds to A receiving message 6 and sending a related reply in message 7 using the function *auth* defined in Section 5.

A class for the responder role is constructed below in a similar way with three operations corresponding to the messages described in the standard notation description: *reply* corresponds to B receiving message 1 and responding to A's request in message 2; *challenge* corresponds to B receiving the key from A in message 5 and challenging A in message 6; and *check* corresponds to B receiving message 7 from A and checking the value for authentication purposes.

---

**Responder**

$A, B : AID;\ N_0, N_B : NON$
$K_{BS}, K_{AB} : KEY;\ msg : STR$

---

**reply**

$\Delta(msg, A)$

$msg = A' \wedge msg' = enc(K_{BS})(A' \frown N_B)$

---

**challenge**

$\Delta(msg, K_{AB})$

$msg = enc(K_{BS})(K_{AB}' \frown N_B \frown A) \wedge msg' = enc(K_{AB}')(N_0)$

---

**check**

$msg = enc(K_{AB})(auth(N_0))$

---

An agent in the server role determines which keys to use for decryption based on the identities of the agents received in the message. To capture this behaviour, the server requires a function *key* associating agent identifiers with keys. The server only requires one operation *giveKey* that corresponds to the receipt of message 3 and subsequent distribution of the session key in message 4.

---

**Server**

$A, B : AID;\ N_A, N_B : NON$
$key : AID \rightarrowtail KEY$
$K_{AB} : KEY$
$msg : STR$

---

**giveKey**

$\Delta(msg, A, B, N_A, N_B)$

$msg = A' \frown B' \frown N_A' \frown enc(key(B'))(A' \frown N_B')$
$msg' = enc(key(A'), N_A' \frown B' \frown K_{AB} \frown$
$\qquad\qquad enc(key(B'), K_{AB} \frown N_B' \frown A'))$

---

The intruder class *Intruder* specifies the operations required by the intruder to perform the type flaw attack described in Section 4.

```
┌─ Intruder ──────────────────────────────────────────────────────┐
│  ┌──────────────────────────────────────────────────────────┐   │
│  │ A, B : AID;  N_A, N_{A_2}, N_0 : NON                      │   │
│  │ X : ENC                                                   │   │
│  │ K_{AB} : KEY                                              │   │
│  │ msg : STR                                                 │   │
│  ├──────────────────────────────────────────────────────────┤   │
│  │  ┌─ intercept ──────────────────────────────────────────┐ │   │
│  │  │ Δ(msg, A)                                            │ │   │
│  │  ├──────────────────────────────────────────────────────┤ │   │
│  │  │ msg = A' ∧ msg' = X                                  │ │   │
│  │  └──────────────────────────────────────────────────────┘ │   │
│  │  ┌─ new ────────────────────────────────────────────────┐ │   │
│  │  │ Δ(msg, B, N_A)                                       │ │   │
│  │  ├──────────────────────────────────────────────────────┤ │   │
│  │  │ msg = A ⌢ B' ⌢ N_A' ⌢ X ∧ msg' = N_A' ⌢ B' ⌢ K_{AB} │ │   │
│  │  └──────────────────────────────────────────────────────┘ │   │
│  │  ┌─ challenge ──────────────────────────────────────────┐ │   │
│  │  │ Δ(msg, N_{A_2})                                      │ │   │
│  │  ├──────────────────────────────────────────────────────┤ │   │
│  │  │ msg = N_{A_2}' ∧ msg' = enc(K_{AB})(N_0)             │ │   │
│  │  └──────────────────────────────────────────────────────┘ │   │
│  │  ┌─ check ──────────────────────────────────────────────┐ │   │
│  │  │ msg = enc(K_{AB})(auth(N_0))                         │ │   │
│  │  └──────────────────────────────────────────────────────┘ │   │
│  └──────────────────────────────────────────────────────────┘   │
└──────────────────────────────────────────────────────────────────┘
```

Operation *intercept* corresponds to the intruder intercepting message 2.1 and sending a nonsense message consisting of an abitrary encrypted segment $X$ to A (message 2.2). The second operation *new* corresponds to the intruder intercepting message 2.3, and beginning a new protocol by sending message 2.1' to A consisting of the learned values $N_A'$ and $B'$, and a session key $K_{AB}$ chosen by the intruder. The third operation *challenge* corresponds to the intruder sending a challenge to A according to the protocol (message 2.6). The final operation *check* corresponds to the intruder checking that the value received in message 2.7 matches the value he sent previously in message 2.6. (We do not model the operation corresponding to the intruder's forwarding of message 2.2' in message 2.4 as this operation does not change the state in our model.)

## 7    Verification of the Protocol Model

Before verifying the attack, we need to confirm the correctness of our model by proving that under normal operation, the protocol achieves its desired goal. In order to do this, we first need to know how the operations specified in Section 6 relate to each other.

We define a class *Instance*1 to simulate an instance of the protocol. There are three roles required: the initiator played by Alice (*alice : Initiator*), the responder played by Bob (*bob : Responder*), and the server played by Sam (*sam : Server*).

We use a single communications medium for simplicity, specified by a state invariant that the agents' messages *msg* are always equal.

Initially, Alice must have the correct value for Bob's identity and Sam must have each agent's identity mapped to their corresponding key. These are reasonable assumptions and are specified within the initialisation schema *INIT*. (We also found that these were the minimal set of assumptions required for the proof to work.)

```
┌─ Instance1 ─────────────────────────────────────────────────────
│ ┌──────────────────────────────────────────────────────────────
│ │ alice : Initiator
│ │ bob : Responder
│ │ sam : Server
│ ├──────────────────────────────────────────────────────────────
│ │ alice.msg = bob.msg = sam.msg
│ └──────────────────────────────────────────────────────────────
│
│ ┌─ INIT ───────────────────────────────────────────────────────
│ │ alice.B = bob.B
│ │ sam.key(alice.A) = alice.K_AS ∧ sam.key(bob.B) = bob.K_BS
│ └──────────────────────────────────────────────────────────────
│
│ protocol ≙ alice.begin ⨾ bob.reply ⨾ alice.requestKey ⨾ sam.giveKey ⨾
│            alice.forwardKey ⨾ bob.challenge ⨾ alice.respond ⨾ bob.check
└──────────────────────────────────────────────────────────────────
```

Operation *protocol* specifies a complete instance of the protocol by appropriate composition of the agents' operations using Object-Z's schema composition '⨾' operator [10]. Simplification of schema composition is achieved by equating the post-state variables of each operation with the pre-state variables of the next, resulting in an operation schema equivalent to application of the operations one after the other. For example, composition of *alice.begin* with *bob.reply* gives the following predicate:

$$\exists\, alice.msg'', bob.msg'' : STR \bullet$$
$$alice.msg'' = alice.A \land bob.msg'' = bob.A'$$
$$bob.msg' = enc(bob.K_{BS}, bob.A' \frown bob.N_B)$$

Knowing that the invariant ensures $alice.msg'' = bob.msg''$ this predicate simplifies to:

$$bob.A' = alice.A \land bob.msg' = enc(bob.K_{BS}, bob.A' \frown bob.N_B)$$

The goal of the protocol is for agents Alice and Bob to receive the new key $K_{AB}$ from Sam, i.e., to have their values ($alice.K_{AB}$ and $bob.K_{AB}$) of the new key equal to the value of the key $sam.K_{AB}$ sent by Sam.

```
┌─ goal ───────────────────────────────────────────────────────────
│ alice.K_AB = sam.K_AB
│ bob.K_AB = sam.K_AB
└──────────────────────────────────────────────────────────────────
```

We can verify that the protocol actually achieves this goal by proving that the result of *protocol* implies the goal:

$protocol \Rightarrow goal'$ .

Assuming initialisation of *Instance*1, composition of the operations defining *protocol* results in the below schema.

---
**_protocol_**

$\Delta($ *alice.msg*, *bob.msg*, *sam.msg*, *sam.A*, *sam.B*, *sam.N_A*, *sam.N_B*,
   *bob.A*, *alice.K_{AB}*, *bob.K_{AB}*, *alice.N_0* $)$

---
$alice.K_{AB}' = sam.K_{AB} \wedge alice.N_0' = bob.N_0$
$bob.K_{AB}' = sam.K_{AB} \wedge bob.A' = alice.A$
$sam.A' = alice.A \wedge sam.B' = alice.B \wedge sam.N_A' = alice.N_A$
$sam.N_B' = bob.N_B$

---

We find that various of the agents' variables are updated, including Alice's and Bob's value of the session key $K_{AB}$. From the equalities $alice.K_{AB}' = sam.K_{AB}$ and $bob.K_{AB}' = sam.K_{AB}$, we can conclude that the intended sequence of protocol operations implies the goal.

## 8     Verification of the Type Flaw Attack

In order to perform verification of the attack, we need to specify another instance *Instance*2, this time including only the agents and trace of operations required to simulate the attack described in Section 4.

There are three roles: an initiator played by Alice ($alice_A$ : *Initiator*), a reponder also played by Alice ($alice_B$ : *Responder*), and the intruder. Note that Alice's identity is $alice_A.A$ when she is playing the initiator role, whereas her identity is $alice_B.B$ when she is playing the responder role. Initially, the key $alice_A.K_{AS}$ shared by the server and Alice in role A is equal to the key $alice_B.K_{BS}$ shared by the server and Alice in role B.

---
**_Instance2_**

---
$alice_A$ : *Initiator*
$alice_B$ : *Responder*
*intruder* : *Intruder*

---
$alice_A.msg = alice_B.msg = intruder.msg$

---
**_INIT_**

---
$alice_A.K_{AS} = alice_B.K_{BS}$

---
$attack \mathrel{\widehat{=}} alice_A.begin \,\fatsemi\, intruder.intercept \,\fatsemi\, alice_A.requestKey \,\fatsemi\,$
   $intruder.new \,\fatsemi\, alice_B.reply \,\fatsemi\, alice_A.forwardKey \,\fatsemi\,$
   $intruder.challenge \,\fatsemi\, alice_A.respond \,\fatsemi\, intruder.check$

---

A desirable secrecy property *secrectKey* of the protocol is that Alice and the intruder do not share a session key meant for Alice and Bob, i.e., the intruder's value of the key $intruder.K_{AB}$ is not the same as the value Alice has for the key $alice_A.K_{AB}$. This property is expressed by the following schema.

$$
\begin{array}{l}
\underline{\quad secretKey} \\
\hline
\quad alice_A.K_{AB} \neq intruder.K_{AB}
\end{array}
$$

Assuming that this secrecy property holds initially, insecurity of the protocol is proven by demonstrating that after the intrusion, the negation of the property holds:

$$(secretKey \wedge attack) \Rightarrow \neg \, secretKey' \; .$$

Assuming initialisation of *Instance*2, we evaluate the *attack* operation, again by simplification of the composition.

$$
\begin{array}{l}
\underline{\quad attack} \\
\hline
\Delta(alice_A.msg, alice_B.msg, intruder.msg, intruder.A, intruder.B, \\
\qquad intruder.N_A, alice_B.A, alice_A.K_{AB}, intruder.N_{A_2}, alice_A.N_0) \\
\hline
intruder.A' = alice_A.A \wedge intruder.B' = alice_A.B \\
intruder.N_A' = alice_A.N_A \wedge intruder.N_{A_2}' = alice_B.N_B \\
alice_B.A' = alice_A.N_A \frown alice_A.B \frown intruder.K_{AB} \\
alice_B.N_B \in ENC \\
alice_A.N_0' = intruder.N_0 \\
alice_A.K_{AB}' = intruder.K_{AB}
\end{array}
$$

Since the intruder's value for the key is unchanged by the *attack* operation (i.e., $intruder.K_{AB}' = intruder.K_{AB}$), it is evident that $alice_A.K_{AB}' = intruder.K_{AB}'$. So we can conclude that the attack implies the negation of the secrecy property, thus verifying the insecurity of the protocol.

# 9  Preventing the Attack

The predicate formed in the *attack* operation also reveals the following two application layer requirements in the precondition that must be preserved by the presentation layer for the attack to succeed:

$$\exists \, alice_B.A' : AID \bullet alice_B.A' = alice_A.N_A \frown alice_A.B \frown intruder.K_{AB}$$
$$alice_B.N_B \in ENC$$

Therefore, we know that the attack can be prevented by avoiding at least one of these conditions through implementable restrictions placed on the protocol.

The first condition states that an agent identity can be constructed from the concatenation of segments $alice_A.N_A$, $alice_A.B$ and $intruder.K_{AB}$. If this condition is not met, Alice will not accept message 2.1′ from the intruder and the protocol will be aborted. The first condition can be avoided by disallowing the multiple segments from being interpreted as the one. For example, each message could be prefixed with a tag identifying the number of segments contained within the message; a single reserved tag could identify the beginning of each message segment; or more simply, agent identifiers could have a single predetermined length.

The second condition states that Alice's nonce $alice_B.N_B$ can be interpreted as an encrypted segment. If this condition is not met, she will not accept message 2.4 and again the protocol will be aborted. The second condition can be avoided if agents are unable to confuse a nonce with an encrypted segment. For example, two tags could be introduced to uniquely identify nonces and encrypted segments only.

A specification of the protocol, secure against the type flaw attack we have presented, would simply include the negation of the precondition above as a special requirement as follows:

$$\neg(\exists\, alice_B.A' : AID \bullet alice_B.A' = alice_A.N_A \frown alice_A.B \frown intruder.K_{AB}) \lor$$
$$alice_B.N_B \notin ENC \ .$$

## 10    Conclusion

We have formally verified a type flaw attack we discovered on the Amended Needham Schroeder Protocol with Conventional Keys.

First, we used Object-Z to model the behaviour of the protocol at the application layer and verified the correctness of our model by proving that normal operation of the protocol satisfied its expected goal. Then we modelled the attack, verified its success, and in particular, the specific weaknesses at the presentation layer upon which the attack depends.

Knowing these weaknesses, we can derive minimal tagging options or other less expensive implementable restrictions that will secure the protocol without having to rely on over-protective tagging schemes.

## Acknowledgments

I would like to thank Colin Fidge for helpful discussions and comments on a draft of this paper, Peter Robinson and Graeme Smith for guidance with Z and Object-Z, and Brad Long, Philippa Hopcroft and the anonymous referees for useful feedback.

## References

1. C. Boyd. Hidden assumptions in cryptographic protocols. *IEE Proceedings, Part E*, pages 433–436, November 1990.

2. M. Bozzano. *A Logic-Based Approach to Model Checking of Parameterized and Infinite-State Systems.* PhD thesis, DISI, University of Genova, June 2002. http://www.disi.unige.it/person/BozzanoM/publications.html.

3. M. Bozzano and G. Delzanno. Automated protocol verification in linear logic. In *Proceedings of the Fourth ACM SIGPLAN Conference on Principles and Practice of Declarative Programming,* pages 38–49. ACM Press, October 2002.

4. S. H. Brackin. Evaluating and improving protocol analysis by automatic proof. In *Proceedings of 11th IEEE Computer Security Foundations Workshop (CSFW'98),* pages 138–152. IEEE Computer Society Press, 1998.

5. U. Carlsen. Generating formal cryptographic protocol specifications. In *Proceedings of the 1994 IEEE Computer Society Symposium on Research in Security and Privacy,* pages 137–146. IEEE Computer Society Press, 1994.

6. 1999. Common Criteria for Information Technology Security Evaluation. August, 1999. Version 2.1. CCIMB-99-031. http://csrc.nist.gov/cc/.

7. J. Clark and J. Jacob. A survey of authentication protocol literature: Version 1.0, 1997. http://www.cs.york.ac.uk/~jac/papers/drareviewps.ps. Accessed May 2003.

8. D. E. Denning and G. M. Sacco. Timestamps in key distribution protocols. *Communications of the ACM,* 24(8):533–536, 1981.

9. B. Donovan, P. Norris, and G. Lowe. Analyzing a library of security protocols using Casper and FDR. In *Proceedings of the Workshop on Formal Methods and Security Protocols,* Trento, Italy, 1999.

10. R. Duke and G. Rose. *Formal Object-Oriented Specification Using Object-Z.* Cornerstones of Computing. Macmillan Press Limited, UK, 2000.

11. J. Heather, G. Lowe, and S. Schneider. How to prevent type flaw attacks on security protocols. In *Proceedings of 13th IEEE Computer Security Foundations Workshop (CSFW'00),* pages 32–43. IEEE Computer Society Press, 2000.

12. B. W. Long. Formal verification of type flaw attacks in security protocols. In *Proceedings of the 10th Asia-Pacific Software Engineering Conference (APSEC) 2003,* pages 415–424. IEEE Computer Society, 2003.

13. C. Meadows. Identifying potential type confusion in authenticated messages. In *Proceedings of Workshop on Foundation of Computer Security (FCS'02),* pages 75–84, 2002. Published as a joint DIKU technical report, http://www.diku.dk/.

14. R. Needham and M. Schroeder. Using encryption for authentication in large networks of computers. *Communications of the ACM,* 21(12):993–999, 1978.

15. R. Needham and M. Schroeder. Authentication revisited. *Operating Systems Review,* 21(1):7, 1987.

16. N. R. Potlapally, S. Ravi, A. Raghunathan, and N. K. Jha. Analyzing the energy consumption of security protocols. In *Proceedings of the 2003 international symposium on Low power electronics and design,* pages 30–35. ACM Press, 2003.

17. P. Ryan, S. Schneider, M. Goldsmith, G. Lowe, and B. Roscoe. *The Modelling and Analysis of Security Protocols: The CSP Approach.* Addison-Wesley, 2000.

18. P. Syverson and C. Meadows. Formal requirements for key distribution protocols. In A. De Santis, editor, *Advances in Cryptology — EUROCRYPT '94,* volume 950 of *Lecture Notes in Computer Science,* pages 320–331. Springer-Verlag, 1994.

19. A. S. Tanenbaum. *Computer Networks.* Prentice Hall PTR, USA, 4th edition, 2003.

20. F. J. Thayer, J. C. Herzog, and J. D. Guttman. Strand spaces: Why is a security protocol correct? In *Proceedings of the 1998 IEEE Symposium on Security and Privacy,* pages 160–171. IEEE Computer Society Press, May 1998.

# Using B as a High Level Programming Language in an Industrial Project: Roissy VAL

Frédéric Badeau[1] and Arnaud Amelot[2]

[1] ClearSy, Europarc de Pichaury bat. C1 13856 Aix-en-Provence, France
frederic.badeau@clearsy.com
[2] Siemens Transportation Systems, 48-56 rue Barbès 92120 Montrouge, France
arnaud.amelot@siemens.com

**Abstract.** In this article we would like to go back on B used to design software, by presenting the industrial process established through years by Siemens Transportation Systems on a real project: the VAL shuttle for Roissy Charles de Gaulle airport. In this project, the logical core of an equipment located along the tracks and driving the shuttles is designed with B.

By confronting this B software development, with the historical context, we show that B can be used as a high-level programming language offering the feature of proving properties. We show how this process is used to build, by construction, a large size software with very few design errors ever since its first release, and for a predefined cost.

## 1   Introduction

Historically, the B Method was introduced in the late 80s' to design correctly safe software (see [BBook96]). A wider scope use of B appeared in the mid 90s', called *Event B*, to analyze, study and specify, not only software, but also whole systems (see [Abr96]). This article presents the results of using B in an industrial context, to produce the safety critical software WCU[1] for the Roissy VAL[2] system. The whole system is developed by Siemens Transportation Systems (formerly Matra Transport). The B development of the WCU, has been subcontracted to ClearSy, who applied Siemens B Method to produce software. This method has been first established for the development of Paris underground metro Line 14, called "Météor", and has been enhanced ever since (see [Behm99]). It consists in using B as a high-level programming language, including the feature of proving properties.

Controlling the development of safety critical software is a main concern for Siemens. They have to guarantee that the software complies to its requirements, and especially its safety requirements. They also need to control development costs and delays, especially for the development of a large project, where the size factor is a key issue.

To achieve this goal, Siemens designed a process for using B efficiently to build a correct piece of software by construction. That means that the first software release has already very few design errors. In this process Unit Tests are not performed, since more

---

[1] Wayside Control Unit.
[2] Véhicule Automatique Léger (Light Automated Train).

H. Treharne et al. (Eds.): ZB 2005, LNCS 3455, pp. 334–354, 2005.

effort is directed to the early specification phases, to build directly correct software. The next development steps remain basically the same: the software produced with B is integrated with the rest of the software and goes through host tests (simulation tests on a workstation). Then software is integrated in the hardware of the WCU and goes through target tests, and so on.

This article focuses on this process.

- Section 2 presents the Roissy VAL system.
- Section 3 introduces the principles of the B Method. This method is decomposed into two phases: formalizing detailed specification documents into a B *Abstract Model*, and then implementing this model into a *Concrete Model*.
- Section 4 details the *Abstract Model*.
- Section 5 details the *Concrete Model*.
- Section 6 analyzes the project statistics.
- Section 7 presents the maintenance of such a project.
- Section 8 concludes.

## 2    Roissy VAL Shuttle Presentation

A new VAL shuttle system is being developed by Siemens Transportation Systems to equip Roissy Charles de Gaulle airport for ADP (Aéroports De Paris). The first line, due in 2006, will connect Roissy terminal 1 to Roissy terminal 2, through Roissy Pole and two car parks. The VAL system is a driverless light train. Line 1, as shown in figure 1, is made up of 5 sections from CDG-1 to CDG-2, plus 2 technical sections to park and maintain trains. The line has two tracks. VAL trains usually drive on the right track, however they may drive on any direction and change direction at any time.

The Roissy VAL system is based on the VAL system of Chicago O'Hare airport. This system differs from the other VAL metros, like Orly-VAL (see [Dol03]). It offers higher functionalities thanks to a digital equipment called Wayside Control Unit (WCU). A WCU drives trains on a line section. Actually, a section has two redundant WCUs for availability issue. All the WCUs are linked by a safe Ethernet network, which also connects the Control Center. The Control Center manages traffic on the line by sending route orders to the WCUs. A WCU receives these orders and then safely commands and controls automatic trains on its section.

As shuttles are light trains, they are commanded by discrete speed programs. Every speed program is physically associated to an electric current loop located between the rails and covering some continuous part of the tracks. When it is powered, a speed program gives at any point of the loop a fixed speed order. Several speed programs may coexist at a certain point of the track. Examples of speed programs are cruise speed, low speed, departure speed and arrival speed. WCUs drive trains by selecting and powering the right loops. When the on-board train system detects a speed order, it adjusts the train speed according the order.

Before sending orders to trains, WCUs should be able to localize safely trains on the line. To do so, every section is decomposed into fixed blocks, which give the localization granularity. With the help of different sensors, WCUs should safely establish whether or not a train occupies a block.

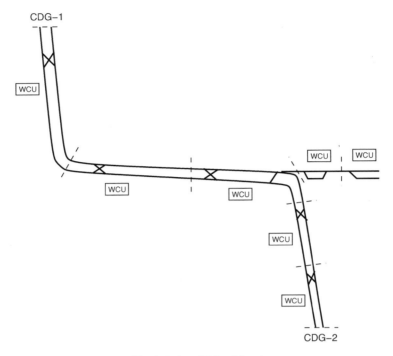

**Fig. 1.** Roissy VAL - Line 1

Those logical treatments are performed by a piece of software. The software is split into low-level modules that take care of input/output, task scheduling, as described into [Behm99], and into high-level modules, which handle the logical and functional treatments. The core of high-level modules, which contains Safety Critical Software, is called WCU-SCS[3]. It is designed in B and then translated into Digisafe-ADA. The rest of the software is directly designed in Digisafe-ADA. The Digisafe technique intends to insure safe runtime with only one processor and replaces architectures with redundant processors. It is complementary with the B Method, which avoids design software errors.

All the WCUs does not share the exact same ADA code, as configuration data are specific to each WCU. However, the core part designed in B is the same for all WCUs.

## 3    Principles of the B Method Used

We shall now introduce the principles of the B Method used in the project. This B Method is part of Siemens software development process. It describes step by step how to use B to build a piece of software. The whole process is made up of guidelines, of B

---

[3] Wayside Control Unit - Safety Critical Software

*generic* elements (which should be instantiated at each use in the project) and of tools also developed by Siemens.

The starting point of a project is low-level software specification documents, written in natural language and possibly using any formalism to help describing the system.

This method suits software mainly based on a discrete logic description, where basic types are Booleans, finite sets, integers or integers regarded as decimal numbers. It does not suit software based on continuous calculus or based on floating point numbers that cannot be regarded as decimal numbers.

The development process is split into two phases called *Abstract Model* and *Concrete Model*. These phases are named after the part of the B model they produce.

During the first phase, every functional piece of information or every requirement from the informal software specifications should be formalized into the Abstract Model. To make sure that the Abstract Model indeed matches its formal specification, we use inspections. A key feature of this Method is to offer the possibility of strengthening the abstract model by proving that some properties are established on the whole model.

Abstract Model data have abstract types since they are based on sets, relations and functions of scalars. Abstract data types make the Abstract Model compact and close from informal specifications. However, these data and their treatments cannot be directly implemented.

The goal of the second phase is to build the Concrete Model starting from the not implementable parts of the Abstract Model. This task is completely systematic and does not require any knowledge on the informal specifications. We have to prove that the Concrete Model is a correct implementation of the abstract model.

These two B development phases are now detailed in the next two sections.

## 4      The Abstract Model Phase

### 4.1      Informal Specifications

Informal software specification documents come as an output of the system development phase, performed by Siemens: system analysis. During system analysis, choices are made to design the system, so that it should meet its functional requirements, and more important, that it should meet them safely. System design produces an equipment architecture broken down into hardware and software specification documents. Software is also broken down into a safe part, where safety is concerned, and a part where it is not. In the case of the WCU equipment, the safe software part commands and controls driverless trains on a given line section.

The Safety Critical Software part (called WCU-SCS) is designed in B and will produce as an output Digisafe-Ada code. In order to ensure safety for the whole system, detailed choices have to be made for the safe software during this early phase. Actually the safe software requirements produced at the end of system analysis are very detailed. They describe a functional breakdown of the software into elementary functions with data flow charts. Most elementary functions are precisely specified in terms of input, output and pseudo-code to specify output computation. Sequencing of elementary functions is also specified.

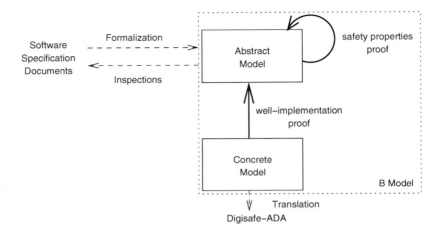

**Fig. 2.** Abstract and Concrete Models

In the case of the Roissy WCU-SCS project, informal specifications come as a collection of various, more or less old, documents. Three documents were written more than ten years ago for the Chicago VAL system, before B was used at Siemens. They describe the specification of the three main modules of the system (Block Logic, Route Logic, Mode Logic). They use functional breakdown, data flow charts and treatments are specified by pseudo-code. The top document is more recent. It was written just before the beginning of the B development. It uses a functional breakdown. It describes data directly in B and makes references to treatments covered by the three main modules documents. It also defines new treatments with the same kind of pseudo-code than the other documents.

We can point here, that having a specification document as close as possible from the B model is a key issue. Since no formal proof can be done between the informal specifications and the Abstract B Model, the closest the two are, the less formalization errors or misunderstanding of informal specifications are likely to appear.

In this project data were already described in B, which minimize the risk of errors when specifying data into the Abstract Model. Siemens made all the abstract data modelling choices. Sometimes choices are just mathematical or methodological choices, for example, a relation $A \leftrightarrow B$ can be used instead of a function of sets $A \nrightarrow \mathbb{P}(B)$. But most of the time choices come from knowledge of the system. For example, to model a relation between sets $A$ and $B$, should we use $A \leftrightarrow B$, $A \nrightarrow B$ or $A \rightarrow B$? It depends on the system properties.

Initializations and sequencing substitutions, which are quite simple, were also specified in B. Other operations were described by pseudo-code or in B. As they may lead to long B operations, their formalization requires to pay extra attention, to avoid any possible pitfall.

Formalizing software specifications into an abstract model is error prone since this cannot be covered by a formal proof. Informal specification are by nature liable to be incomplete, ambiguous and open to different understanding, especially when they are part of a 200-page document that has to be written in a reasonable time. Although they have flaws, informal specifications remain the best way to communicate specification. However, to handle this issue, a question/answer database on the software specification has been used to keep a trace of questions asked by ClearSy and answers provided by Siemens. This activity has been a key issue for ClearSy to understand every detail of the requirements. Sometimes questions led to explanations from Siemens and sometimes they led to precisions or adjustments of the specification documents. We can note here that updating regularly specification documents helped building a B model consistent with its informal specifications.

In order to check B models against the natural language specifications, we used inspections. Every B Language element of the model is read by a member of the modelling team who did not write it. Inspections should be as precise as possible. Every B symbol of the model should be checked. The reader has to be convinced that the related informal specification is correctly and completely formalized. Traceability between B models and specifications is achieved by giving explicit references, inside the quality-assurance comment at the beginning of each abstract operation. When a question arises during inspection, the B model may be changed, or the question might be forwarded to the project question/answer database.

## 4.2    Abstract Data

Data used to build the Abstract Model are abstract data. We are now going to detail those abstract data.

**Basic Types.** The basic types used are: Boolean (the BOOL predefined set), enumerated sets or deferred sets (declared in the SETS clause) and implementable integers (predefined B sets INT and NAT).

The Boolean set is used every time a data has two possible values.

An enumerated set is used when a data has strictly more than two possible values and when we need to name explicitly all the values. For example, a section, managed by a wayside control unit, is divided into fixed blocks. A block can be a normal block, a switch block or a station block. So we define:

> **SETS**
> $t\_block\_type = \{c\_normal\_block, c\_switch\_block, c\_station\_block\}$

A deferred set is used when a variable can take a finite number of values and we do not want to name explicitly the values in order to be generic. Most data of the project are typed with deferred sets. For example, all the blocks accessed by a WCU are gathered into the type $t\_block$. In the VAL system, beam sensors are used to detect the presence of a train at a certain point of a track. A train is detected when it cuts the beam. All the beam sensors are gathered into the type $t\_beam\_sensor$. So we define:

> **SETS**
> $t\_block$;
> $t\_beam\_sensor$

The only integer variables needed for the abstract model are delays. We define a concrete constant $t\_time$, as a renaming of NAT to declare delays regarded as decimal numbers. They express in milliseconds the time remaining before the delay expires. We define:

**CONCRETE_CONSTANTS**    $t\_time$ **PROPERTIES**    $t\_time = \mathrm{NAT}$

Those types bring strong typing, just like in a programming language such as ADA. This makes an efficient use of the type checking constraints of the B language, since, for example, wherever a block is expected, we cannot use anything else instead, like a beam sensor.

Those scalar data types are either used alone or they are combined with type constructors as shown in the following examples.

**Subsets of Scalar Types.** This type constructor was the most commonly used to type abstract data. For example, blocks accessed by a WCU are either occupied by a train or free. This information should be safely computed by the functional module "Block Logic". It is formalized by the abstract variable *occupied_blocks*, which is a subset of $t\_block$.

$$occupied\_blocks \subseteq t\_block$$

A block belongs to *occupied_blocks* if and only if it is considered to be occupied. We can point here, that another modelling choice could have been to use a total function from $t\_block$ to BOOL, associating to a block the value TRUE when the block is occupied and FALSE when it is not.

$$occupied\_blocks \in t\_block \rightarrow \mathrm{BOOL}$$

Actually this second choice suits less the proposed B Method, since it is more an encoding of the former (i.e., the use of a set characteristic function instead of the set directly). In this case using a subset of blocks is more abstract. Expressions, predicates and substitutions concerning this set are also more abstract and closest from informal specifications.

We also need to formalize block sensors, which are sensors detecting a train inside a block. We could have used a special deferred set to type the *occupied_block_sensors* abstract variable. However, as there is a strict mapping from one block to one block sensor, we typed it as we did for *occupied_blocks*.

$$occupied\_block\_sensors \subseteq t\_block$$

**Relations and Functions.** Let $t\_a$, $t\_b$ and $t\_c$ be scalar types. We also use the following relations, partial functions and total functions to type abstract data.

$$t\_a \leftrightarrow t\_bt\_a \nrightarrow t\_bt\_a \rightarrow t\_bt\_a \rightarrow \mathbb{P}(t\_b)t\_a \rightarrow (t\_b \nrightarrow t\_c)$$

For example, the abstract constant *ctx_next_block_up* associates to a block its next upward block. A block has at most one next block located in the upward direction. A terminal block in the upward direction has no next upward block. So *next_block_up* is a partial function from $t\_block$ to $t\_block$.

$$ctx\_next\_block\_up \in t\_block \nrightarrow t\_block$$

**Sequences.** We use sequences of a scalar type when we need to formalize a sequence of elements. For example, the abstract constant *ctx_block_occ_aut_up* gives in what order blocks have to be treated to compute block occupancy authorization in the upward direction. This abstract constant is formalized as a sequence of blocks.

$$ctx\_block\_occ\_aut\_up \in seq(t\_block)$$

**Read Operations.** The data types described above are used to type abstract data. However, in the end, concrete code should be produced, so in order to interface abstract data with concrete code, read operations are provided with abstract data. For example, to read the abstract variable *occupied_blocks*, we define the *read_occupied_blocks*, which returns as a Boolean value the fact that some block given as an input value is occupied.

$p\_bool \longleftarrow read\_occupied\_blocks(p\_block) \;\; \widehat{=}$
**PRE**
  $p\_block \in t\_block$
**THEN**
  $p\_bool := bool(p\_block \in occupied\_blocks)$
**END**


Read operations are defined for every variable that has an abstract data type. Sometimes, more than one read operation is given for a given variable. This is the case with partial functions where, before reading the value associated to some input value, one needs to know if the input value belongs to the domain of the partial function. All these read operations are defined as generic pieces of B model. A tool was used to generate automatically read operations for a given abstract machine, by instantiating the generic operations.

All the abstract data types presented here represent the basic elements of B regarded as a high-level language. During abstract modelling, only those types are used. Furthermore, after an abstract variable is defined in the abstract model, the variable will not be refined wherein. Abstract data will only be refined in the concrete model for implementation purpose. Actually in other B software projects we may refine some abstract variables with other abstract variables, but this was not used for Roissy WCU-SCS.

## 4.3    Abstract Model Architecture

The abstract model architecture is based on the functional breakdown provided by the informal specification documents. The B modules written at this stage are entirely part of the final B model. If we regard the final model as an importation tree (IMPORTS clause), then the abstract model is some higher part of this tree. The abstract model architecture looks like this.

The architecture is a tree of B modules. Two kinds of modules are used: modules with an abstract machine and an implementation and modules with only an abstract machine. Modules with an abstract machine and an implementation are called sequencing modules. They are used to specify sequencing of treatments inside operations implementation. An implementation imports modules defining the operations called by the implementation. Modules with only an abstract machine, named final modules, represent the leaves of the abstract model. They are used to specify data and to specify operations.

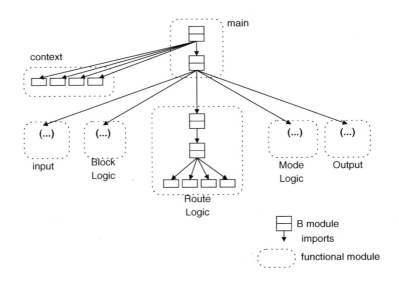

**Fig. 3.** Abstract Model Architecture

In the architecture, we recognize the main functional modules from the informal specifications:

**Main.** This is the starting point of the project. The main B module, which is the root of the import tree, contains an entry operation called *run_cycle* which is called at a regular pace, and which, as a sequencing operation, calls indirectly every operation of the B project.

**Input.** This functional module acquires input messages and filters them. Retrieving input data is carried on through basic machines, which have an abstract machine and handwritten ADA code to call low-level input procedures. Due to basic machines, the abstract model of this functional module differs slightly from the core functional modules. It will not be detailed any further in this paper.

**Block Logic.** This functional module computes, in a safe way, the occupation of blocks by trains.

**Route Logic.** This functional module establishes elementary routes, commands and controls switches positions on the tracks. It also contains a sub-function (command of route turnaround cycles) which is not classified as safety critical, but which is nevertheless specified in B as it is a high level function.

**Mode Logic.** This functional module manages train anti-collision. It computes, commands and controls selection and powers discrete train speed programs.

**Output.** This module gathers information computed by the previous modules to prepare the creation of output messages by basic machines.

**Context.** There is also on the far left a subpart called context, specific to the B project. The context defines enumerated and deferred sets (from the SETS clause), concrete and abstract constants. All these constants data are gathered, since they are highly shared inside the B project.

Abstract constants are used to make the final program independent from configuration data. Let's consider again the example of the abstract constant $ctx\_next\_block\_up$ that associates to a block its next upward block. The value of this constant may differ from one WCU to the other. But the properties describing the abstract constant in the PROPERTIES clause remain the same for all WCU. As the B model represents the core of the WCU software, it remains the same for all WCU. The constant values are thus given in ADA. They are specific to each WCU. As their valuation is performed outside the scope of the B process, a specific mechanism has to be used to check that actual constant values fulfill their B properties.

**Architecture.** In the abstract Model architecture, we may have columns of sequencing modules (one sequencing module importing another sequencing module and so on), to reflect that in specifications a treatment calls another treatment and so on. To avoid too many sequencing modules, we use local operations (see [MRefB02] LOCAL_OPERATIONS clause).

The abstract model importation tree is presented such that B modules are allowed to see (SEES clause) other modules located on their left. This rule corresponds to a data flow from the left to the right. Thus, input data are seen by the block logic whose results are seen by the route logic and so on. Context modules may be seen by any other module. Applying this rule makes this architecture valid as regards the constraints of the SEES clause (see [MRefB02]).

An abstract module with only an abstract machine contains abstract variables, their initialization and operations that formalize pseudo-code specifications. As discussed before, operation specifications are deterministic and feasible. Here is an example of a substitution inside an operation body where set-theoretical notation is useful.

$$occupied\_blocks := occupied\_blocks \cup$$
$$(ctx\_b2b\_up \cup ctx\_b2b\_down)^{-1}[obd] \cup$$
$$otd$$

Actually due to the size factor, an operation specification may be much larger.

When a functional module is modelled into a too large B module, we try to break it down since the tools are much more efficient on treating many small modules than few large ones, especially when it comes to proof and automatic refinement. Such an abstract model breakdown should respect B architecture rules, especially those concerning variable modifications (see [MRefB02]). So we try to gather operations modifying the same abstract variables in the same modules. When this cannot be performed, them we can still replace a variable by two variables representing the same entity at different moments of the execution cycle. Synchronization of the two variables can be achieved by a parent module, since it has the rights to modify both variables.

Operations traceability is achieved by placing references to informal specification inside the quality-assurance header of operations. This is helpful for inspection and maintenance.

## 4.4    Abstract Model Properties

The method described so far, can be summarized into formalizing the software functional specification, element by element, into a B abstract model. Each element is more or less independent from the others, which means that a modelling error in one particular element is unlikely to be discovered after the element has been formalized.

During the last stage of the abstract model phase, we insert properties, tying elements together, into the abstract model that has to be proved by the end of the abstract model phase. Those properties strengthen the abstract model since we have to prove that they hold when all elements of the abstract model are put together.

These properties are part of the specification documents. They come from system analysis and they all are safety critical properties. So proving that the software built through this process complies with those safety critical properties is of tremendous importance.

Abstract model properties are written inside the higher-level B module (called the main module), the one with the $run\_cycle$ operation. Properties could be either static or dynamic. Static properties are properties that can be expressed with abstract variables (and of course with constants). They are part of the main module invariant. Dynamic properties are properties that link the old values and the new values of some variables, before and after calling the $run\_cycle$ operation. So in the main abstract machine, the $run\_cycle$ operation is formalized as a "becomes such that" substitution containing dynamic properties. The old value of an abstract variable $x$ is expressed by $x\$0$ and the new value is expressed by $x$.

At runtime, the software developed in B is used by calling at a regular pace the $run\_cycle$ operation. As the B model should be entirely proved, thanks to invariant preservation and refinement consistency of the $run\_cycle$ operation, we are sure that static and dynamic properties hold at each call of this operation.

As an example, a property states that a block has to be regarded as occupied when its block detector is occupied or when a beam sensor located at one of the block borders is cut. A simplified predicate formalizing this property is given below.

$$\forall block \cdot (block \in t\_block \land$$
$$((ctx\_block\_bs\_up[\{block\}] \cup ctx\_block\_bs\_down[\{block\}])$$
$$\cap cut\_beam\_sensors \neq \varnothing \lor$$
$$ctx\_block\_detector[\{block\}] \subseteq occupied\_block\_detectors)$$
$$\Rightarrow$$
$$block \in occupied\_blocks)$$

In order to prove entirely the abstract model, those properties have to be handled through sequencing modules until they prop on final modules. This top down approach for properties along the abstract model is only useful for explanation purpose. Actually, we used a bottom up approach. The process of formalizing a property is described as follows. After analyzing a property we figure out on which operations the property is propped on. The property may come directly from the postcondition of one final operation or it may come from several operations. Sometimes, a more complex reasoning has to be carried on to convince oneself that the property holds. Usually in those cases, the property is cut into several smaller properties.

The actual B properties come at first from the postcondition of the relevant final operations. They are then spread in upper sequencing modules from the bottom to the top. The abstract variables dealing with properties are redefined in the upper sequencing abstract machines and properties are inserted inside operation specification. After each step, before spreading the property to the next upper level, we check if the lemmas are provable. In fact, at the beginning we do not have a completely clear idea on how the property should be formalized in B, so we first start with an initial version of the property and then we finalize it through proving. In case of non-provable lemma we check our alleged property against the informal property and against the called operations. Through this process, we found errors in the way properties were expressed in B but also inside final operations. We also asked for adjustments of a property from the software specification documents, when that property was not always true. For instance, the property could be true only in nominal mode, which was not initially stated explicitly in the informal specification documents.

The software specification documents contain 16 properties which had to be formalized in the abstract model. Although it seems to be a small number, some properties had to be cut into many actual properties. At the end, the size of the static and dynamic properties in the main abstract machine was more than 1,000 line long.

# 5    Concrete Model

## 5.1    Principles

The concrete Model phase consists in completing the Abstract Model to get to a completely implementable B project. As the operations of the final modules of the abstract model are deterministic, we do not need the specification documents any more. The only input of this phase is the abstract model and the goal is to implement it completely through refinement and importation breakdown. When the concrete model is fully proved, thanks to refinement proof, then we are sure that the concrete model complies with the abstract model.

Actually developing the concrete model is just a technical phase. Ideally, we could use a tool that would translate automatically the deterministic abstract model into ADA code in order to reduce drastically the development cost. However, as abstract model deals with abstract data types (see 4.2) such a tool is not obvious to implement and does not exist yet.

The concrete model was originally handwritten by Siemens (see [Behm99]). The process has been enhanced since. As the abstract model uses a limited number of abstract data types (see 4.2) and as terminal modules use set-theoretical substitutions working with these same data types, the refinement process is similar for all software developed with this method. So this process has been rationalized by developing semi-automatic refinement tools based on the application of refinement rules. These tools are called EDiTh B and Bertille (see [Burd99]).

During the automatic refinement process, abstract variables are either kept through refinement (see [MRefB02] homonymous abstract variable data refinement) or they are refined by a concrete variable with a complete gluing invariant. With this precaution, we are sure that proof refinement guaranties that the concrete model complies with the abstract model. So refinement tools do not require to be validated, since the process is fully covered by proof. In other words, refinement tools are just here to guess the refinement (hopefully a correct refinement), but if their guess is incorrect, proof will detect it.

The activity of automatic refinement by applying refinement rules is very similar to proving by applying proving rules. In both cases it is usually easier to treat a general case, than to treat a special case since it breaks down an initial, and possibly large problem, step by step into smaller problems described by rules with a limited complexity.

### 5.2    Semi-automatic Refinement

We are now going to describe the semi-automatic refinement. In practice, building the concrete model consists in refining independently every final abstract machine of the abstract model. We build an importation (clause IMPORTS) subtree for every such abstract machine.

**Manual Refinement Preparation.** In a first step we prepare manually the automatic refinement. This step aims to reduce the complexity of the automatic refinement by breaking down the starting point abstract machine into smaller abstract machines and by writing intermediate refinement levels to ease refinement of operations.

To break abstract machine $m$ down, we write an implementation that imports several abstract machines named $m\_a$, $m\_b$, $m\_c$,. The refinement of an operation is made by calling imported operations specified as a subpart of the original operation. Every abstract variable of $m$ is redeclared inside one of the imported abstract machine. Breaking down an abstract machine is not always easy since we have to comply with architecture rules, especially concerning abstract variables modification. However it was always at least possible to split an abstract machine into an abstract machine computing the conditions (of SELECT or IF substitutions) and an abstract machine computing the bodies of those substitutions, since a condition computation only returns a Boolean value and does not involve global variable modification.

This first step is not mandatory, however it was widely used in the project as we were dealing with very large terminal abstract machines.

**Semi-automatic Refinement.** In a second step we use automatic tools on the last B component of every leaf of the new import tree, which could be either an abstract machine or a refinement. In this case it operates on $m\_a$ and $m\_b$. The tool is made up of two passes. It calls once EDiTh B and then it calls Bertille till the concrete model is completed. In the project, automatic refinement may lead to a maximum of 7 levels of generated modules.

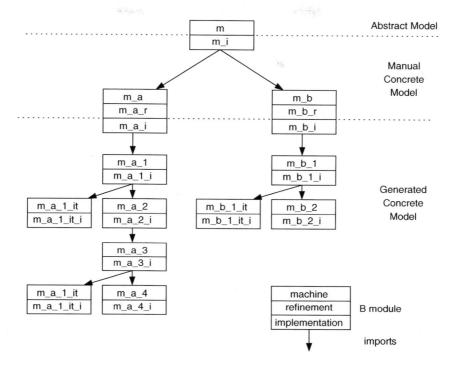

**Fig. 4.** Concrete Model of a Terminal Abstract Machine

EDiTh B is used to implement an abstract machine or a refinement with an implementation and a new sub-abstract machine (suffixed with _1) in which high level abstract substitutions (ANY, SELECT,"becomes such that",) are replace by low-level abstract substitutions (IF, CASE) that can be handled by Bertille.

Bertille implements an abstract machine that contains only low-level substitutions, and it may also produce a new sub-abstract machine (suffixed with _2, _3, _4,) and an abstract machine containing iterators (suffixed with _it). To refine abstract variables and substitutions, Bertille uses a refinement rule base. When Bertille produced a new abstract machine, then it is called again on this abstract machine, until the concrete model is complete or until it fails during refinement.

Abstract variables of an abstract machine are either kept in the next sub-abstract machine (see [MRefB02] homonymous refinement) when they are still needed in the sub-abstract machine or they are implemented by using a variable refinement rule. All the abstract data types described in 4.2 have a corresponding variable refinement. So variable refinement is an easy and complete process.

For example, the *occupied_blocks* abstract variable:

$$occupied\_blocks \subseteq t\_block$$

is refined by the *occupied_blocks_i* concrete variable:

$$occupied\_blocks\_i \in t\_block \rightarrow \text{BOOL} \wedge$$
$$occupied\_blocks = occupied\_blocks\_i^{-1}[\{\text{TRUE}\}]$$

Substitution refinement, however, is more complex. As a general principle, substitutions dealing with sets can be refined with the help of set iterators, as shown in the example below.

> **MACHINE** $m\_a\_1$
> $op\_1 \,\,\widehat{=}$
> $\quad a := bool(S \neq \varnothing)...$

> **IMPLEMENTATION** $m\_a\_1\_i$
> $op\_1 \,\,\widehat{=}$
> $\quad ...$
> $\quad a := \text{FALSE};$
> $\quad$ **WHILE** $continue = \text{TRUE}$ **DO**
> $\qquad continue, x \leftarrow iterate\_t\_a;$
> $\qquad y \leftarrow op\_1\_1(x);$
> $\qquad$ **IF** $y = \text{TRUE}$ **THEN**
> $\qquad\quad a := \text{TRUE}$
> $\qquad$ **END**
> $\quad ...$

> **MACHINE** $m\_a\_1\_it$
> $p\_bool, p\_elt \leftarrow iterate\_t\_a \,\,\widehat{=}$
> $...$

> **MACHINE** $m\_a\_2$
> $p\_y \leftarrow op\_1\_1(p\_x) \,\,\widehat{=}$
> **PRE**
> $\quad p\_x \in t\_a$
> **THEN**
> $\quad p\_y := bool(p\_x \in S)$
> **END**
> $...$

We have to implement here the set-theoretical substitution $a := bool(S \neq \varnothing)$ where $S$ is a subset of the deferred set $t\_a$. The idea is to initialize $a$ to FALSE and then to loop on each element $y$ of $t\_a$. If $y$ belongs to $S$ then $S$ is not empty, so $a$ is set to TRUE, otherwise $S$ is the empty set and $a$ remains equal to FALSE.

To do so, we use an abstract machine containing an iterator on type $t\_a$. This machine is available as a generic machine and offers services to perform efficiently a loop on a deferred set. The knowledge of this kind of iterators is integrated into Bertille, so that it generates automatically the loop variant and the part of the invariant related to the loop indexes. Bertille automatically generates the iterator abstract machine in which it instantiates generic parameters; in this case the $t\_a$ type. Bertille also generates the implementation of the iterator abstract machine.

We also use a new sub-machine containing an operation to test if some value $x$ belongs or not to $S$. As we can see, we have now another abstract machine to implement. However, this operation is this time quite easy to implement, since we just need to implement the abstract variable $S$ with the array $S\_i$ and them we can get the value of $y$ from $S\_i(x)$.

The refinement with those tools is only semi-automatic, since Bertille may fail during the refinement of a substitution. In this case, we have to examine the cause of the failure. Most of the time, we add a new rule, or we adapt an existing rule, in Bertille rule base, and that solves the problem. Them, Bertille should be rerun. This action may be repeated several times. At the end of the process, when everything is refined, the concrete B modules automatically produced should be type checked and one should check if the lemmas generated are provable. This is required to check that the code of new rules is correct. As proving easily is also a main issue, we should also check that the lemmas may be easily proved. That is why new rules may sometimes be completed by ASSERT substitutions.

## 5.3    ADA Code Produced

When the B model is complete and fully proved, it should be translated into ADA. Both the abstract and concrete models are translated. Actually the ADA code produced uses the Digisafe-ADA technology.

Automatic refinement lowers the cost of a software development but what about the efficiency of the code generated this way? According to Siemens studies, code produced through automatic refinement is 10% slower than hand written code, which is fully acceptable. However automatic refinement may lead to suboptimal algorithms which are not acceptable. To estimate code efficiency at runtime, a static tool was developed by Siemens. It requires, as an input, the dimensioning of types (for example the number of blocks of the $t\_block$ type) and gives as an output the estimated runtime of every operation. We spotted a half-dozen exponential-time algorithms where linear-time algorithms could be used instead. This was due to the automatic application of refinement rules. We corrected these points by writing new dedicated refinement rules applying appropriate linear-time algorithms.

As a final remark on the generated ADA code, it is interesting to note that when a member of the project development team took a look at some ADA code corresponding to an automatic refinement level, this person was lost and could hardly make the link with the software specification. Actually, it would be the same for a person who would compare the ADA code he wrote to the corresponding assembly code generated by a compiler. However, proof makes all the difference in our case. Although automatically generated B0 code may look meaningless, we can still be sure that it implements correctly its part of the abstract model.

## 6    Project Statistics

We shall now present and comment some project statistics.

## 6.1    B Model Size

| B Model | Lines | Rate |
|---|---|---|
| Grand total | 183,987 | 100% |
| Abstract Model without read operations and iterators (324 operations) | 28,163 | 15% |
| Abstract Model: read operations and iterators | 10,503 | 6% |
| Manual Concrete model without read operations | 27,756 | 15% |
| Automatic Concrete Model | 117,565 | 64% |

| Modules and Components | Number |
|---|---|
| Number of B modules | 532 |
| Number of basic modules | 28 |
| Number of intermediate refinements | 59 |
| Number of B componants | 1,093 |

The core of the abstract model is 28,000 line long. This is quite a large number that can be explained by the different kinds of sections (normal line sections, garage sections, switch section between the line and the garage). Though they share common principles, they have different software specification, since they have been specified at different times by different people. So they make the specification documents, as well as the abstract model, larger. The rest of the abstract model (10,000 lines) is generated automatically by instantiating abstract iterator machines or read operations.

Although the manual part of the concrete model is also 28,000 long, it does not cost much to produce since it is mostly written by applying simple transformations on a copy of the final abstract machines.

The rest of the concrete model is huge (118,000 lines) but it is automatically generated by tools.

## 6.2    ADA Code Size

| Translated ADA Code | |
|---|---|
| Lines number (without empty lines nor comments) | 158,612 |
| Number of procedures | 4,809 |

The number of ADA code lines is also huge. This is for three reasons:

– The use of Digisafe-ADA: data and instruction dedicated to Digisafe-ADA are automatically inserted during translation. We can also point out that Digisafe-ADA forbids complex expressions or conditions, which leads to an extra use of local variables and "becomes equal" substitutions.

- Every part of the concrete model is usually broken down into many intermediate levels, which produce a lot of code.

- Code is not shared through this process. For example, generic elements share a similar code, however the code is duplicated at each use.

The estimated size of the complete software without Digisafe-ADA and without so many intermediate levels would be 60,000 lines of ADA code.

## 6.3    Proof

| Proof of Lemmas | Lem. Nb | Rate | Lem. Nb | Rate |
|---|---|---|---|---|
| Grand total | 43,610 | 100% | | |
| Force 0 | 38,822 | 89% | | |
| Force 1 | 1,397 | 3% | | |
| Generic demonstrations (61 user pass) | 1,950 | 5% | | |
| - based on predicate prover | | | 1,272 | 3% |
| Total of automatic demonstrations | 42,169 | 97% | | |
| Interactive demonstrations (745) | 1,441 | 3% | | |

| Number of interactive demonstrations/day | 15 |
|---|---|

| Proof Rules | Nb | Rate |
|---|---|---|
| total | 290 | 100% |
| validated by the predicate prover | 243 | 84% |
| validated semi-automatiquely | 27 | 9% |
| validated manually | 20 | 7% |

The number of lemmas automatically generated is also high (43,000 lemmas). Thus performance of the tool concerning proof, and especially concerning automatic proof, is a major issue for the project cost. Force 0 of the automatic prover of Atelier B did most of the job, since it proved 89% of all lemmas. Force 1 proved 3%. Around 60 generic demonstrations, mainly based on the predicate prover, proved another 5%. This makes the automatic proof rate of 97%. The remaining 3% lemmas were demonstrated interactively with an average rate of 15 lemmas by man.day.

The concrete model was easier to prove than the abstract model; since everything which is done in the concrete model, is broken down into small steps repeating the same patterns optimized for proof. In the abstract model, the proof of safety properties leads to complex and long interactive demonstrations that cannot be easily reused.

The predicate prover was also very helpful for validating new proof rules.

### 6.4     Manpower Breakdown

| Manpower Cost Rate | | |
|---|---|---|
| Grand total | 100% | |
| Warmup | 5% | |
| Project management | 8% | |
| Abstract Model | 55% | |
| - questions/answers and documents analysis (267 questions, 4 questions/day) | | 18% |
| - inspections | | 5% |
| - proof | | 16% |
| Concrete Model | 24% | |
| - proof | | 11% |
| Finalization (configuration mngt,replay, doc, rules validation) | 8% | |

The cost ratio between abstract and concrete models is 2/3 for the abstract model and 1/3 for the concrete model.

Most of the time spent on building the abstract model was actually spent on analyzing the specification documents and tracing issues in the question/answer database.

Proof represents a high cost for abstract model (30%) but it is worthwhile, since this is the way to assure that the final code indeed fulfills the safety-critical properties.

The 10% of abstract model time spent in detailed inspections was also of interest, since it led to some corrections and raised new questions/answers.

### 6.5     Specification Documents Size

| Size of input documents (in pages) | |
|---|---|
| WCU Software Specification Document (84 functional modules) | 228 |
| Block Logic Software Specification Document (30 functional algo) | 51 |
| Route Logic Software Specification Document (37 functional algo) | 80 |
| Mode Logic Software Specification Document (50 functional algo) | 98 |

The size of the main input specification documents gives elements to measure the size of the project.

## 7     Maintenance

Whenever modifications or evolutions are performed on a piece of software developed through the method presented in this article, what are the consequences on the new software release?

First, we are sure that every release is still consistent, as long as it is again completely proved.

Then, modification cost is limited, if the software structure is not questioned and if the impact on the previous proof work, especially the proof of the abstract model properties, is limited because all the development environment is set up. In this case, refinement rules and proof rules are likely to be efficiently reused.

# 8   Conclusion

We have presented in this article, a straightforward process, summarized below, and based on reusable generic elements (read operations and iterators components) and on state of the art tools, especially automatic refinement tools.

The process is split into two phases, first software document specifications are formalized into an abstract model and then the abstract model is implemented into the concrete model.

The abstract B model manipulates high-level software data. Those data have a high-level aspect, since they use abstract data types such as sets of scalar types, relations, partial and total functions from an abstract data type into another abstract data type. However, they also have a concrete software aspect since every abstract data type is directly and systematically implemented by concrete data. This is the only data refinement used: an abstract variable defined in the B model is kept unchanged in lower imported modules (it is refined by an homonym abstract variable) until it is finally refined by its associated concrete variable(s) in the concrete model.

Sequencing treatments are formalized as sequencing calls of operations in the implementation of sequencing modules.

Core logical treatments are formalized in operation specifications by high-level software substitutions. They are high-level, since they use set-theoretical expressions and parallel substitutions. However these substitutions are deterministic and they can be implemented through automatic refinement rules. The refinement process to generate the concrete model starting from the abstract model is semi-automatic. Refinement rules implement step by step such a set-theoretical substitution by generating software loops going through every element of the set.

All these characteristics make the B Method used through this process, a high-level programming language. However, a key feature of this so-called language lies in its proof capabilities. The process offers the possibility of proving that some properties are indeed preserved by each call of the main software procedure. Obviously, in the case of safety critical software those properties shall be safety critical properties. The process also proves that the final code correctly implements its formal specification.

The process described here is suitable for any industrial domains, not only for railways command/control software. Actually this process deals with designing procedural software based on logical treatments, not based on real or floating-point numbers. It is all the more suitable that software specification can be easily formalized into set-theoretical expressions.

From the management point of view, the project went off according to the initial schedule, although the software produced is quite large, thanks to a straightforward process and efficient tools.

Every verification stage throughout the process was useful and led to early error detection: analysis of software document specification, type checking, inspections, proof of abstract model safety properties, refinement proof of correct implementation. The WCU-SCS is currently being integrated with the rest of the software.

**Acknowledgments.** We would like to thank Laurent Voisin for his very interesting comments.

# References

[Abr96]      Abrial, J.-R., Extending B Without Changing it (for Developing Distributed Systems), 1996

[BBook96]  Abrial, J.-R., The B-Book: Assigning Programs to Meanings, 1996

[Behm99]   Behm P., Benoit P., Faivre A. and Meynadier J.-M., Météor: A Successful Application of B in a Large Project, 1999

[Burd99]    Burdy L., Meynadier J.-M., Automatic Refinement; BUGM at FM'99, 1999

[Dol03]      Dollé D., Essamé D., Falampin J., B dans le transport ferroviaire, l'expérience de Siemens, Technique et science informatiques - volume 22, 2003

[MRefB02] Badeau F., B Language Reference Manual v1.8.5, 2002

# Development via Refinement in Probabilistic B — Foundation and Case Study

Thai Son Hoang[1,2], Zhendong Jin[1], Ken Robinson[1,2],
Annabelle McIver[3], and Carroll Morgan[1]

[1] School of Computer Science & Engineering, University of New South Wales,
NSW 2052, Australia
{htson, zjin, kenr, carrollm}@cse.unsw.edu.au
[2] National ICT, Australia
[3] Department of Computing, Macquarie University,
NSW 2109, Australia
anabel@ics.mq.edu.au

**Abstract.** In earlier work, we introduced probability to the *B-Method* (*B*) by providing a probabilistic choice substitution and by extending *B*'s semantics to incorporate its meaning [8]. This, a first step, allowed probabilistic programs to be written and reasoned about within *B*.

This paper extends the previous work into refinement within *B*. To allow probabilistic *specification* and *development* within *B*, we must add a probabilistic *specification* substitution; and we must determine the rules and techniques for its rigorous refinement into probabilistic code.

Implementation in *B* frequently contains loops. We generalise the standard proof obligation rules for loops giving a set of rules for reasoning about the correctness of probabilistic loops. We present a small case-study that uses those rules, the randomised Min-Cut algorithm.

**Keywords:** Probability, program correctness, generalised substitutions, weakest preconditions, *B*, randomised algorithms, refinement.

## 1 Introduction

Our overall aim is to extend the *B-Method* (*B*) to incorporate probability, with the aim of allowing its rigorous development techniques to apply to random algorithms, probabilistic distributed systems (via for example *Event-B*) and safety-critical applications (using fully quantitative judgments of the "cost" of program outcomes).

We have made a number of extensions already at what would be called a "low-level". For example, we have extended *B* to allow the deduction of probability-one conclusions about programs containing probability: this is called *qB* [11], and would apply to the final stages of an algorithm like the IEEE 1394 (FireWire) protocol [2, 6] where a potential livelock is resolved with probability one.

A second extension is the incorporation of full probabilistic reasoning into *B* (that is, not just probability-one) via the introduction of a probabilistic-choice

H. Treharne et al. (Eds.): ZB 2005, LNCS 3455, pp. 355–373, 2005.

substitution, with its associated semantics: this is called $pB$. Unlike $qB$, whose logic remains Boolean, the $pB$ logic is based on real numbers, necessary to be able to make judgments about probability.

The probabilistic-choice substitution is "code" in the sense that it can be (almost) directly translated into a programming language, and would typically be found in the last stages of a development. In that sense it can be considered "low-level".

Our aim in this paper is to begin to address the "higher-level" concerns of probabilistic development. Traditionally this involves some form of "specification", incorporating nondeterminism (interpreted as implementation freedom), together with an appropriate notion of "refinement" that leads from such specifications to the code that implements them.

We propose a probabilistic *specification* substitution (similar to the one proposed for $Z$ [21]), and we recall the definition of probabilistic refinement [16]. We prove the "fundamental theorem" for the new construct, in the $B$ context, by analogy with the fundamental theorem for the traditional specification statement [12] that shows the new statement's semantics properly interacts with refinement.

To illustrate and explore the extension, we extend the rules for partial and total correctness of standard loops to probabilistic loops, in the style of the probabilistic wp-logic [16]. Furthermore, the proof obligations for probabilistic loops can be separated so that we can prove standard (predicate) properties and probabilistic (quantitative) properties separately. The latter is especially important for a practical method, such as $B$, where we need to preserve as much as possible the facility and efficiency of dealing with a system's non-probabilistic components, limiting the new (and more complex) probabilistic reasoning to where it's required.

The new techniques mentioned are illustrated by a case study of a randomised algorithm. In the example, we go from specifying the algorithm, implementing it using a loop and reasoning about the correctness of the algorithm.

The paper is structured as follows: in Sec. 2 we briefly recall the details of the *probabilistic Generalised Substitution Language (pGSL)*, and illustrate the expectation logic by using simple examples; in Sec. 3 we first review the traditional specification substitution for standard systems and then introduce probabilistic specification substitution to describe probabilistic systems; in Sec. 4 we appeal to the expectation semantics from $pGSL$ and obtain the probabilistic fundamental theorem which is a generalised version of the corresponding standard theorem.

In Sec. 5 we discuss proof obligations for probabilistic loops, which is the generalisation of the variant and invariant technique for standard loops.

In Sec. 6 we first apply the fundamental theorem to the well-known example of "Min-Cut" algorithm, we also set out the proof obligations for maintaining the refinement; finally, we summarise the development, draw our conclusions and outline possible future work.

# 2    The Probabilistic-Choice Substitution

The probabilistic-choice substitution has been introduced into *probabilistic B* (*pB*) already [8]; as we noted in the introduction, it can be considered as a "low-level" extension.

The numeric logic *pGSL* necessary to accommodate the extension uses real- rather than Boolean-valued expressions for its "predicates", which we call "expectations": the numbers represent "expected values" rather than the normal predicates that definitely do, or do not hold. In other words, we replace certainty by probability.

We can give only a very brief description of *pGSL* in the space available here; the reader is referred to our earlier work for a full introduction [11].

The probabilistic-choice substitution is the only extension to standard *Generalised Substitution Language* (*GSL*). It has the form

$$prog_1 \;{}_p\oplus\; prog_2 \;,$$

which means that with probability $p$, the substitution $prog_1$ is executed, and with probability $1 - p$, the substitution $prog_2$ is chosen.

Implication-like relations between expectations are

$$
\begin{array}{lll}
exp_1 \Rrightarrow exp_2 & \;\widehat{=}\; & exp_1 \text{ is everywhere no more than } exp_2 \\
exp_1 \equiv exp_2 & \;\widehat{=}\; & exp_1 \text{ is everywhere equal to } exp_2 \\
exp_1 \Lleftarrow exp_2 & \;\widehat{=}\; & exp_1 \text{ is everywhere no less than } exp_2.
\end{array}
$$

The refinement relationship in *pB* is defined accordingly:

$$prog_1 \sqsubseteq prog_2 \quad \text{if and only if} \quad [prog_1]exp \;\Rrightarrow\; [prog_2]exp \quad \text{for all } exp$$

The semantics of the substitutions in *pGSL* are given in Fig. 1.

# 3    The Probabilistic-Specification Substitution

The probabilistic-specification substitution, and its properties, are the "high-level" subjects of this paper. Because our concern here is with larger-scale structures, we must turn to a specification construct, since that is the starting point for the refinement steps that are characteristic of *B* developments, whether standard or probabilistic. We begin by reviewing the "standard" specification that *B* already contains, where by *standard* we mean "without probability".

## 3.1    Standard Specification Substitution

In this section, we briefly review the interaction of specifications and so-called "specification substitutions" [1] for standard systems.

---

[1] For those familiar with the refinement calculus, these will correspond to pre-postcondition specifications [4], specification statements [13], and prescription [19]; we are going to treat the *B* version of those.

| | |
|---|---|
| $[v := E]\,exp$ | The expectation obtained after replacing all free occurrences of $v$ in $exp$ by $E$, renaming bound variables in $exp$ if necessary to avoid capture of free variables in $E$. |
| $[pre \mid prog]\,exp$ | $\langle pre \rangle * [prog]\,exp$, where $0 * \infty \;\widehat{=}\; 0$. |
| $[prog_1 \;\|\; prog_2]\,exp$ | $[prog_1]\,exp$ min $[prog_2]\,exp$ |
| $[prog_1 \,;\, prog_2]\,exp$ | $[prog_1][prog_2]\,exp$ |
| $[pre \Longrightarrow prog]\,exp$ | $1/\langle pre \rangle * [prog]\,exp$, where $\infty * 0 \;\widehat{=}\; \infty$. |
| $[skip]\,exp$ | $exp$ |
| $[prog_1 \;{}_p{\oplus}\; prog_2]\,exp$ | $p * [prog_1]\,exp \;+\; (1{-}p) * [prog_2]\,exp$ |
| $[@v \cdot pred \Longrightarrow prog]\,exp$ | (min $v \mid pred \cdot [prog]\,exp$), where $v$ does not occur free in $exp$. |
| $prog_1 \sqsubseteq prog_2$ | $[prog_1]\,exp \Rrightarrow [prog_2]\,exp$     for all $exp$ |

- $exp$ is an expectation (possibly but not necessarily $\langle pred \rangle$ for some predicate $pred$);
- $pre$ is a predicate (not an expectation);
- $\langle pred \rangle = 1$ when $pred$ holds, $\langle pred \rangle = 0$ when $pred$ does not hold;
- $*$ is multiplication;
- $prog, prog_1, prog_2$ are probabilistic generalised substitutions;
- $p$ is an expression over the program variables (possibly but not necessarily a constant), taking a value in $[0, 1]$; and
- $v$ is a variable (or a vector of variables).

$pGSL$ [15] acts over "expectations" rather than predicates: *expectations* take values in $[0, 1] \cup \{\infty\}$.
We give the definitions including infeasible or "miraculous" commands [13–Sec. 1.7], but omit them in the main text.

**Fig. 1.** $pGSL$ semantics

In the specification stage of a development, it is traditional to use pre- and post-conditions to describe the desired behavior of the system to be built. In general, there are many forms of this; one version is "Specification statements" [13]:

$$v : [P, Q]$$

where $v$ is the *frame*, a sub-vector of the program variables whose values may change. $P$ and $Q$ are predicates describing the initial state and the final state, respectively.

In $B$ [1], we find the same idea though with a different syntax. In this paper we will use the syntax

$$v : \{P, Q\} \; , \quad {}^2 \tag{1}$$

---

$^2$ In $B$ it could be written as

$$P \quad | \quad v : Q$$

with the meaning that the substitution will establish $Q$ under the precondition $P$, and change only the variables in $v$. In this form, we will always assume that $P$ and $Q$ are predicates over $x$ and over $x_0, v$. The variables $v$ are those that can be possibly changed by the substitution. The variables $x_0$ are distinct from $x$ and represent their original values.

## 3.2    Probabilistic Specification Substitution

We now show how the ideas of Sec. 3.1 can be generalised to the probabilistic context, that is, we will propose a probabilistic generalisation of (1) which will play the same role in probabilistic specification and refinement as the original (1) does in the standard case.

In the expectation logic of Sec. 2, we write

$$A \quad \Rightarrow \quad [S]B \ , \tag{2}$$

to mean that execution of $S$ must establish that the expected value of $B$ over final state distributions is bounded below by $A$'s value in the initial state. By analogy with the connection between Dijkstra-style specification and the specification statement, we propose a probabilistic specification substitution written as in the standard case, that is

$$v : \{A, B\} \ , \tag{3}$$

except that $A$ now is an expectation defined over the program variables, $B$ is an expectation that may additionally refer to $x_0$ and $v$ as before are variables that are allowed to change.

For example, if we want to specify a coin that with probability at least one-half comes up heads, then in the style of (2) we would write

$$\frac{1}{2} \quad \Rightarrow \quad [Flip] \langle c = H \rangle \ ,$$

where $c$ (for "coin") is the state variable with possible values $\{H, T\}$. In the style of (3), we would instead specify the substitution $Flip$ as the substitution

$$c : \left\{ \frac{1}{2}, \langle c = H \rangle \right\} \ , \tag{4}$$

for the following reason: it achieves $c = H$ (post-expectation $\langle c = H \rangle$) with probability at least $\frac{1}{2}$ (pre-expectation). Thus the *probabilistic specification substitution* generalises the traditional specification substitution into the probabilistic program domain.

We now give the semantic definition for (3) so that we can explain why the specifications like (4) have the meaning we claim for them.

**Definition 1.** *The semantics of the specification substitution $v : \{A, B\}$, with respect to arbitrary post-expectation $C$ (containing no $x_0$), is given by*

$$[v : \{A, B\}]\, C \quad \widehat{=} \quad A \quad * \quad [x_0 := x]\, (\sqcap x \cdot C \;\div\; B^w) \;, \tag{5}$$

*where $x$ is the vector of all variables appearing in $A, B$ or $C$; $w$ is the vector of unchanging variables, in $x$ but not in $v$; and $B^w$ is $B * \langle w = w_0 \rangle$. The symbols $*, \div$ denote multiplication, division respectively of real numbers.*

In general, $(\sqcap x \cdot D)$ means the greatest lower bound of the expression (expectation) $D$ over the possible values of $x$. We use explicit brackets to indicate the scope of the minimum, so in the definition, $(\sqcap x \cdot C \;\div\; B^w)$ means the minimum of $C \;\div\; B^w$ over all $x$.

We give the intuitive justification for Def. 1 as follows: it says that the specification takes an initial state to any one of a number of final state distributions, all of which satisfy the requirement that the expectation of $B$ over that final distribution is bounded below by $A$ evaluated on the initial state. Given that, the definition calculates the expected value of $C$ (instead of $B$), using algebraic properties of these substitutions.

Taking the example of (4), we can calculate the probability that the outcome is heads. From Def. 1 it is given as

$$
\begin{aligned}
&\;\; [c : \{\tfrac{1}{2}, \langle c = H \rangle\}]\, \langle c = H \rangle \\
\equiv &\;\; \tfrac{1}{2} \quad * \quad [c_0 := c]\, (\sqcap c \cdot \langle c = H \rangle \;\div\; \langle c = H \rangle) && \text{Def. 1} \\
\equiv &\;\; \tfrac{1}{2} \quad * \quad [c_0 := c]\, 1 && \text{arithmetic } ^3 \\
\equiv &\;\; \tfrac{1}{2} \;. && \text{arithmetic and simple substitution}
\end{aligned}
$$

So indeed the probability that (4) establishes $c = H$ is at least $\tfrac{1}{2}$.

If we calculate the probability that the outcome of the same program is tails, however, we have

$$
\begin{aligned}
&\;\; [c : \{\tfrac{1}{2}, \langle c = H \rangle\}]\, \langle c = T \rangle \\
\equiv &\;\; \tfrac{1}{2} \quad * \quad [c_0 := c]\, (\sqcap c \cdot \langle c = T \rangle \;\div\; \langle c = H \rangle) && \text{Def. 1} \\
\equiv &\;\; \tfrac{1}{2} \quad * \quad [c_0 := c]\, 0 && \text{minimum } 0 \div 1 \text{ occurs at } C = H \\
\equiv &\;\; 0 \;. && \text{arithmetic and simple substitution}
\end{aligned}
$$

The conclusion is that (4) does not give any guarantee at all that the outcome is tails. We address this point later, in Sec. 6.5.

## 4    The Fundamental Theorems for Specifications

In this section we justify the semantics given in Def. 1 by looking at a fundamental theorem that such semantics should satisfy. There is a standard fundamental theorem already; we propose a corresponding probabilistic fundamental theorem.

---

$^3$ We assume that $x \div 0$ is $\infty$ for any $x$ so that the $\sqcap$ ignores it.

## 4.1   The Standard Fundamental Theorem

This theorem comes from the refinement calculus [13, 12]; here we explain it in terms of $B$-style notation.

**Theorem 1.** *Let* $v : \{P, Q\}$ *be defined as in (1) and* $T$ *be any program written in* GSL *with state variables* $x$, *then* $v : \{P, Q\} \sqsubseteq T$ *if and only if*

$$P \quad \Rightarrow \quad [x_0 := x][T]Q^w ,$$

where $Q^w$ is $Q \wedge w = w_0$. Similar theorems and their proofs can be found in [17, 3]. The theorem states that if the before state satisfies $P$ then the substitution $T$ will guarantee to establish $Q$ in the after state, and change only variables in $v$. And therefore $T$ satisfies the specification $v : \{P, Q\}$.

## 4.2   The Probabilistic Fundamental Theorem

Now we return to the issue of the probabilistic fundamental theorem. It is Theorem 2 as follows:

**Theorem 2.** *Let* $v : \{A, B\}$ *be defined as in* **Def.** *1 and* $T$ *be any* pGSL *substitution and be free from variables* $x_0$. *Assume* $B$ *satisfies the assumption:* $\forall x_0 \cdot (\exists v \cdot (B \neq 0))$. *Then*

$$v : \{A, B\} \quad \sqsubseteq \quad T \quad \textit{iff} \quad A \quad \Rightarrow \quad [x_0 := x][T]B^w .$$

*Proof.* We now prove the theorem in each direction separately using **Lemma 1** and **Lemma 2** below.

**Lemma 1.** *Let* $v : \{A, B\}$ *and* $T$ *be the same as in Theorem 2. If* $v : \{A, B\} \sqsubseteq T$ *then we have*

$$A \quad \Rightarrow \quad [x_0 := x][T]B^w ,$$

*where as usual* $x$ *is "all variables", i.e. those occurring in* $A, B$ *or* $T$.

*Proof.* We begin the proof from the right-hand side. The first few lines for the proof is for the fact that the post-expectation in Def. 1 does not contain $x_0$. Also notice that the substitutions are right-associative:

$$[x_0 := x][T]B^w$$

$\equiv \quad [x_0 := x]([x' := x_0][T][x_0 := x']B^w) \qquad \qquad x'$ are fresh variables
$\qquad \qquad \qquad \qquad \qquad \qquad \qquad \qquad \qquad \qquad \qquad \qquad \qquad T$ contains no $x_0$

$\equiv \quad [x' := x][T]([x_0 := x']B^w) \qquad \qquad \qquad$ sequential substitution
$\qquad \qquad \qquad \qquad \qquad \qquad \qquad \qquad \qquad$ no $x_0$ in $[T][x_0 := x']B^w$

$\Leftarrow \quad [x' := x]([v : \{A, B\}][x_0 := x']B^w) \qquad \qquad$ monotonicity and assumption
$\equiv \quad [x' := x](A \ * \ [x_0 := x](\sqcap x \cdot [x_0 := x']B^w \ \div \ B^w)) \qquad \qquad$ from Def. 1

$\equiv$
$\qquad \qquad \qquad \qquad \qquad \qquad \qquad \qquad \qquad \qquad$ simple substitution $[x' := x]$
$A \ * \ [x' := x][x_0 := x](\sqcap x \cdot [x_0 := x']B^w \ \div \ B^w)$

$$\equiv \quad A \,*\, [x_0 := x][x' := x_0]\,(\sqcap x \cdot [x_0 := x']B^w \;\div\; B^w) \qquad\qquad [x_0 := x] \text{ is free of } x'$$
$$\equiv \quad A \,*\, [x_0 := x]\,(\sqcap x \cdot [x' := x_0][x_0 := x']B^w \;\div\; B^w) \qquad\qquad \text{properties of } \sqcap$$
$$\equiv \quad A \,*\, [x_0 := x]\,(\sqcap x \cdot B^w \;\div\; B^w) \qquad\qquad \begin{array}{l}\text{sequential substitution}\\ \text{no } x' \text{ in } B\end{array}$$

$$\equiv \quad A \,, \qquad\qquad\qquad\qquad \text{non-zero assumption on } B, \text{ arithmetic}$$

which completes the proof.

**Lemma 2.** *Let $v : \{A, B\}$ and $T$ be the same as in Theorem 2. If*

$$A \quad\Rightarrow\quad [x_0 := x][T]B^w \tag{6}$$

*then we have*

$$v : \{A, B\} \sqsubseteq T \;.$$

*Proof.* We begin by calculating the application of substitution $v : \{A, B\}$ to any expectation $C$ which is free from $x_0$:

$$\begin{array}{ll}
 & [v : \{A, B\}]\,C \\
\equiv \quad & A \,*\, [x_0 := x]\,(\sqcap x \cdot C \;\div\; B^w) & \text{Def. 1} \\
\Rightarrow \quad & [x_0 := x][T]B^w \,*\, [x_0 := x]\,(\sqcap x \cdot C \;\div\; B^w) & \text{Assumption (6)} \\
\equiv \quad & [x_0 := x]\,([T]B^w \,*\, (\sqcap x \cdot C \;\div\; B^w)) & \text{simple substitution } [x_0 := x] \\
\equiv \quad & [x_0 := x][T]\,((\sqcap x \cdot C \;\div\; B^w) * B^w) & T \text{ free from } x_0 \text{ and scaling } [T]; \text{ see below} \\
\Rightarrow \quad & [x_0 := x][T]((C \;\div\; B^w) \,*\, B^w) & \text{monotonicity} \\
 & & (\sqcap x \cdot C \;\div\; B^w) \Rightarrow C \;\div\; B^w \text{ as } C \text{ free from } x_0 \\
\equiv \quad & [x_0 := x][T]\,C & \text{non-zero assumption on } B \\
\equiv \quad & [T]\,C \;. & \text{both } T \text{ and } C \text{ free from } v_0
\end{array}$$

Since $C$ was arbitrary, we have that $v : \{A, B\} \sqsubseteq T$, which completes the proof.

For the deferred judgment, we using the scaling property of substitutions which states that multiplication by a non-negative constant distributes through substitutions [16].

# 5    Refining Probabilistic Specifications to Loops

We now turn to our second major topic, the development of loops in $pB$. In following section we will show how loops and specification substitutions fit together.

We will first recall the proof obligations for standard loops, then apply the theorems stated in Sec. 4 in order to set out the generalised proof obligations for probabilistic loops.

## 5.1    Proof Obligations for Standard Loops

For a standard loop, such as

$$\text{loop} \quad \widehat{=} \quad \text{WHILE } G \text{ DO } S \text{ INVARIANT } I \text{ VARIANT } V \text{ END} \,,$$

we recall the proof obligations for its correctness in the context of an initialisation which it occurs in a fragment: *init*; *loop*. Then we have that

$$P \Rightarrow [init; loop] Q$$

holds if the well-known variant-and-invariant rules are satisfied [7, 1].

*S1*: The invariant must hold before the while-test is made for the first time, which is formulated as: $P \Rightarrow [init] I$.

*S2*: The invariant is maintained by the loop body: $G \wedge I \Rightarrow [S] I$.

*S3*: When the loop ends, i.e. the while-test is false and the invariant is still true, the loop establishes the postcondition: $\neg G \wedge I \Rightarrow Q$.

*S4*: The invariant guarantees that the variant denotes a natural number, which is formulate as: $I \Rightarrow V \in \mathbb{N}$.

*S5*: The loop body decreases the variant: for some fresh variable $n$ we have: $G \wedge I \quad \Rightarrow \quad [n := V][S](V < n)$.

## 5.2   Proof Obligations for Probabilistic Loops

In setting up the proof obligations for *probabilistic loops*, we try to mimic the obligations for standard loops. We need to calculate the pre-expectation of a probabilistic substitution with respect to a particular post-expectation, which usually is a product of an embedded predicate[4] and another (general) expectation. The embedded predicate captures the normal invariant and the other deals with the quantitative property of the loop. We need to be able to separate them, for which we use "probabilistic conjunction operator".

Recall the *probabilistic conjunction operator* " & " defined over the expectation space [15]:

$$(E \ \& \ F).x \quad \hat{=} \quad (E.x + F.x - 1) \quad \sqcup \quad 0 \ , \quad [5]$$

for expectations $E, F$ and all $x \in X$. It is easy to see that " & " is monotonic with respect to $\Rightarrow$, and $\langle P \rangle * E \equiv \langle P \rangle \ \& \ E$, for predicate $P$ and general expectation $E$. Moreover, from an earlier work [15], we know that for any probabilistic substitution $S$ has the following *sub-conjunctivity* property:

$$[S](E \ \& \ F) \quad \Leftarrow \quad [S]E \ \& \ [S]F \ , \tag{7}$$

for all expectations $E, F$ (The properties of & operator can be seen in [16]).

We begin with a lemma that will allow us to deal with the standard and probabilistic expectations separately.

**Lemma 3.** *Let $S$ be a probabilistic substitution written in* pGSL*; let $P, Q$ be predicates; and let $A, B$ be expectations. If we have*

$$\langle P \rangle \quad \Rightarrow \quad [S] \langle Q \rangle \ , \quad and \tag{8}$$

$$\langle P \rangle * A \quad \Rightarrow \quad [S]B \ , \quad then \ we \ have \tag{9}$$

$$\langle P \rangle * A \quad \Rightarrow \quad [S](\langle Q \rangle * B) \tag{10}$$

---

[4]  Recall that an embedded predicate $\langle P \rangle$ is 1 if $P$ holds and 0 otherwise.
[5]  The definition of $\sqcup$ is: $a \sqcup b \ \hat{=} \ a \max b$.

*Proof.* We begin with the left-hand side:

$$
\begin{aligned}
&\langle P \rangle * A \\
\equiv\ &\langle P \rangle * \langle P \rangle * A && \text{arithmetic} \\
\equiv\ &\langle P \rangle\ \&\ (\langle P \rangle * A) && \langle P \rangle \text{ is standard} \\
\Rightarrow\ &[S]\langle Q \rangle\ \&\ [S]B && \text{(8), (9) and monotonicity of “ \&”} \\
\Rightarrow\ &[S](\langle Q \rangle\ \&\ B) && \text{sub-conjunctivity (7)} \\
\equiv\ &[S](\langle Q \rangle * B)\ , && \langle Q \rangle \text{ is standard}
\end{aligned}
$$

which completes the proof.

We now use probabilistic conjunction to explain the generalisation of Sec. 5.1 to probabilistic loops. In fact, we will just study one kind of probabilistic loops, whose partial correctness is probabilistic while its total correctness is absolutely trivial. Such loops can be written in *pGSL* as follows:

$$
\text{loop} \quad \widehat{=} \quad \text{WHILE } G \text{ DO } S \text{ INVARIANT } I \text{ EXPECTATION } E \text{ VARIANT } V \text{ END .}
$$

Assuming as before that the loop follows an initialisation, we will state and justify the proof obligations for its correctness with respect to the probabilistic implication

$$
\langle P \rangle * A \quad \Rightarrow \quad [init; loop](\langle Q \rangle * B)\ ,
$$

where $A, B$ are expectations and $P, Q$ are predicates [14, 16].

*P1*: The expectation $E$ together with the invariant $I$ must be bounded below by the pre-expectation $A$, with the precondition $P$, before the while-test is first made. This is precisely formulated as follows:

$$
\langle P \rangle * A \quad \Rightarrow \quad [init](\langle I \rangle * E)\ .
$$

According to Lemma 3, this can be achieved by the following two proof obligations:

*P1a*: The precondition $P$ must guarantee that the invariant $I$ is established before the while-test is made for the first time: $\langle P \rangle \Rightarrow [init]\langle I \rangle$, or equivalent to

$$
P \Rightarrow [init]\,I\ .
$$

*P1b*: The expectation $E$ must be bounded below by the pre-expectation $A$ with the precondition $P$ before the while-test is first made:

$$
\langle P \rangle * A \Rightarrow [init]E\ .
$$

*P2*: The loop body cannot decrease the expected value of $E$ with the invariant $I$ and the guard $G$:

$$
\langle G \wedge I \rangle * E \Rightarrow [S](\langle I \rangle * E)\ .
$$

According to Lemma 3, this is achieved by the following two proof obligations:

*P2a*: The invariant $I$ must hold within the loop body with probabilistic choice substitution being treated as demonic — this is called *demonic retraction*. If $\lfloor S \rfloor$ represents the demonic retraction of $S$ [6], then this rule can be formulated by $\langle G \wedge I \rangle \Rightarrow [S]\langle I \rangle$, or equivalent to

$$G \wedge I \Rightarrow \lfloor S \rfloor I \; .$$

*P2b*: The expectation $E$ must not decrease within the loop body , i.e. the operation within the loop body can not decrease the expectation $E$ by the invariant $I$ and the guard $G$:

$$\langle G \wedge I \rangle * E \Rightarrow [S] E \; .$$

*P3*: When terminating, the loop establishes the post-expectation $B$ with post-condition $Q$, i.e:

$$\langle \neg G \wedge I \rangle * E \Rightarrow \langle Q \rangle * B \; .$$

According to Lemma 3 this can be achieved by the following:

*P3a*: When terminating, the loop establishes the post-condition $Q$, that is we have: $\langle \neg G \wedge I \rangle \Rightarrow \langle Q \rangle$. We can rewrite this without embedding as:

$$\neg G \wedge I \Rightarrow Q \; .$$

*P3b*: When terminating, the loop establishes the post-expectation $B$:

$$\langle \neg G \wedge I \rangle * E \Rightarrow B \; .$$

*P4*: The standard invariant guarantees that the variant denotes a natural number as is the case in standard rule:

$$I \Rightarrow V \in \mathbb{N} \; .$$

*P5*: The loop body decreases the variant as is the case in standard rule, but the probabilistic choice within the body is treated as demonic retraction:

$$G \wedge I \Rightarrow [n := V] \lfloor S \rfloor (V < n) \; .$$

## 6    Case Study: Randomised Min-Cut

In this section, we show how to use the theorems of Sec. 4.2 and Sec. 5.2 in practice to develop a probabilistic algorithm. We will be using the well known technique of "probabilistic amplification".

---

[6] This demonic retraction is defined in [11] as $\lfloor S \rfloor I \equiv ([S]\langle I \rangle = 1)$. This is defined to take advantage of the fact that $[S]\langle I \rangle$ can only take values in $0, 1$, and can be easily calculated by replacing all probabilistic choice substitutions by non-deterministic ones.

In particular we take the example of finding a Min-Cut of a graph, the smallest number of edges whose removal would disconnect the graph. The algorithm contains two parts: the first part is to find a Min-Cut probabilistically, but at low probability; and the second part is to use probabilistic amplification to improve the probable correctness of the algorithm.

We will first briefly describe the Min-Cut algorithm and the probabilistic amplification technique; then we discuss how to code the Min-Cut algorithm in $B$, and we look in particular at the proof obligations required.

### 6.1    Informal Description of the Min-Cut Algorithm: Contraction

The Min-Cut algorithm operates on undirected and connected graphs. A *cut* is a set of edges such that if we remove just those edges, the graph will become disconnected.

Deterministic algorithms' complexities are often improved by randomisation, and Min-Cut is an example of that. The result for randomised algorithms is much better than for the deterministic one, especially for dense graphs [20].

The randomised algorithm consists of a number of "contraction" steps. In a *contraction*, two connected nodes are chosen randomly and merged together. The contracted graph then has one node less than the original one. It can be proved that the connectivity of the contracted graph is always no less than the original one and that any specific minimum cut in the original graph remains in the contraction with probability at least $\frac{N-2}{N}$ (where $N$ is the number of nodes of the graph). This contraction is done repeatedly until there are only two nodes left. At that point the only cut left is the (multiple) edges connecting the last two nodes. This will therefore be the cut that is chosen.

The above contraction procedure does not guarantee to find the minimum cut for the original graph, but there is a non-zero lower bound of probability that it will. By multiplying the probabilities for the successive stages, we see that probability is at least

$$p(N) \quad = \quad \frac{N-2}{N} * \frac{N-3}{N-1} * \dots * \frac{2}{4} * \frac{1}{3} \quad = \quad \frac{2}{N*(N-1)} \ ; \qquad (11)$$

Further, independent repetitions of the process can reduce the probability that a witness (solution to the problem) is not found on any of the repetitions, using the *probabilistic amplification* technique we describe below.

Full details of this algorithm are given by Motwani and Raghavan [20].

### 6.2    Probabilistic Amplification

Intuitively, because it is difficult to find solutions in a search space which contains a large number of witnesses, it often suffices to choose an element at random from the space. The randomly chosen element is likely to be a witness; further, independent repetitions of the process reduce the probability that a witness is not found on any of the repetitions. This improvement is known as *probabilistic amplification*.

$ans \longleftarrow$ **contraction**$( N )\ \widehat{=}$
**VAR** $n$ **IN**
   $n := N;\ ans := TRUE;$
   **WHILE** $2 < n$ **DO**
      $ans \longleftarrow merge(n, ans);$      /* Select two nodes and merge */
      $n := n$ - $1$
   **INVARIANT**   $n \in \mathbb{N}\ \wedge\ n \leq N\ \wedge\ 2 \leq n\ \wedge\ ans \in BOOL$
   **EXPECTATION**   $(2 \div (n * (n - 1)))\ *\ \langle ans \rangle$
   **END**
**END**

**Fig. 2.** Implementation of contraction in $pGSL$

As we saw at (11) above, the probability of finding the minimum cut in one test is quite small. For $N = 10$, it would be $\frac{2}{10*9}$, that is approximately 2%. In order to improve that, we use probabilistic amplification to find the minimum cut repeatedly. The probability that we find the right minimum cut is the probability that the minimum cut is found in any one of those tests, which for $M$ tests is at least is $P(N, M) = 1 - (1 - p(N))^M$, where $p(N)$ is as above.

For example, if we run the $N = 10$ case 120 times, the error probability would only be around 10%, that is, our probability of sucess is increased from 2% to $100 - 10 = 90\%$.

### 6.3 Formal Development of Contraction

In this section, we will see how the contraction steps are specified, and then implemented in $pGSL$; and we see the proof obligations for preserving the refinement relationship between the specification and the implementation.

**Specification of Contraction.** We look at the specification of the contraction, i.e. of the one test to find the minimum cut. Since the probability of the outcome for the test only depends on the number of nodes in the graph, we can take an abstract view for the specification. The machine (program) has one operation to model one test, with the input $N$ being the number of nodes for the original graph. The output $ans$ is $TRUE$ when we have found the right minimum cut, and $FALSE$ otherwise. In this specification, we want to state that for any input $N$, the probability that the output $ans$ is $TRUE$ on termination is at least $\frac{2}{N*(N-1)}$ (as at (11)). The specification is shown below:

$$ans \longleftarrow \textbf{contraction}( N )\ \ \ \widehat{=}\ \ \ ans : \{\langle N \in \mathbb{N} \wedge 2 \leq N\rangle * p(N), \langle ans \rangle\}$$

**An Implementation of Contraction.** A loop implementation of the contraction using $pGSL$ is given in Fig. 2. In this implementation, we have a local variable $n$ to keep the number of nodes in the current graph, and so we start with $n = N$ (original graph). At each stage, variable $ans$ is $TRUE$ just when the actual Min-Cut has not yet been destroyed by any merge so far. We keep merging while the number of nodes is greater than 2. The operation *merge(n, ans)* is specified in the machine **merge** as below.

$$ans \longleftarrow \mathbf{merge}\ (\ n\ ,\ a\ ) \quad \widehat{=} \quad n \in \mathbb{N} \wedge a \in BOOL \mid ans := FALSE\ _{\leq \frac{2}{n}} \oplus a$$

The operation says that with probability at most $\frac{2}{n}$, the minimum cut will be destroyed by the contraction. Otherwise, if the minimum cut has not been destroyed, it will be kept.

**Proof Obligations of Contraction.** We now will apply the generalised proof obligations for the probabilistic loop to prove the correctness of the implementation to the specification of the contraction process.

To prove the refinement relationship between the specification and the implementation in Fig. 2 of the contraction process, Theorem 2 is applied to those programs. We thus have to prove that

$$\langle N \in \mathbb{N} \wedge 2 \leq N \rangle * p(N)$$
$$\Rightarrow \quad [ans_0 := ans][contraction]\langle ans \rangle ,$$

which can be simplified to

$$\langle N \in \mathbb{N} \wedge 2 \leq N \rangle * p(N) \quad \Rightarrow \quad [contraction]\langle ans \rangle ,$$

where we have used the fact that there is no $ans_0$ on the right-hand side, so that the substitution $[ans_0 := ans]$ is redundant. Further more, we have used the fact that proving $\langle P \rangle * E \Rightarrow F$ is equivalent to prove $E \Rightarrow F$ under the assumption that $P$ holds, so it is necessary to prove: $p(N) \Rightarrow [contraction]\langle ans \rangle$, given that $N \in \mathbb{N} \wedge 2 \leq N$, which means that the implementation succeeds with probability (finding the right minimum cut) at least $p(N)$.

We first state all the components of the loop within our reasoning context. Referring to Sec. 5.2, we have the following information.

- The initialisation for the loop is: $init_1 \widehat{=} n := N; ans := TRUE$.
- The standard invariant is: $I_1 \widehat{=} n \in \mathbb{N} \wedge n \leq N \wedge 2 \leq n \wedge ans \in BOOL$.
- The guard for the loop is: $G_1 \widehat{=} 2 < n$.
- The body of the loop is: $S_1 \widehat{=} ans \longleftarrow merge(n, ans);\ n := n - 1$.
- The expectation (probabilistic invariant) is: $E_1 \widehat{=} \frac{2}{n*(n-1)} * \langle ans \rangle$.
- The precondition is: $P_1 \widehat{=} N \in \mathbb{N} \wedge 2 \leq N$.
- The pre-expectation is: $A_1 \widehat{=} p(N)$.
- The postcondition $Q_1$ is the constant predicate *true*.
- The post-expectation is $B_1 \widehat{=} \langle ans \rangle$.

From this information there are 14 proof obligations for the implementation of the contraction, all of which have been proved using the *B-Toolkit* with some extra proof rules.

$$ans \longleftarrow \mathbf{minCut}(\ N,\ M\ ) \ \hat{=}$$
$$ans : \{\langle N \in \mathbb{N} \wedge 2 \leq N \wedge M \in \mathbb{N}_1 \rangle * P(N, M), \langle ans \rangle\}$$

**Fig. 3.** Specification of probabilistic amplification

**Proving the Obligations.** The proofs of the obligations can be found in [9].

## 6.4    Formal Development of Probabilistic Amplification

In this section, we use probabilistic amplification in order to increase the probability of finding the minimum cut. We will again look at the specification and its implementation, and then look at the proof obligations for the refinement step. We will see that a slightly more specialised version of the probabilistic specification (and its fundamental theorem) is necessary for developments of this kind.

**Specification of Min-Cut Probabilistic Amplification.** The machine has only one operation, namely minCut. This operation has two inputs: they are $N$ for the number of nodes in the original graph and $M$ for the number of times that we do the amplification, i.e. the number of times that the contraction process is used. The output $ans$ of the operation abstractly models whether we find the right minimum cut or not after having done one amplification step. The specification states that the probability of finding the correct minimum cut should be at least $P(N, M) = 1 - (1 - p(N))^M$. The specification is shown in Fig. 3.

**Implementation of Min-Cut Probabilistic Amplification.** The implementation of the probabilistic amplification is shown in Fig. 4. In the implementation, we have two auxiliary variables $m$ and $a$, which represent the counter and the recent output from the contraction process, respectively. Initially, $m$ is assigned $M$ and $ans$ is assigned $FALSE$, which means that we intend to repeat the test process $M$ times and initially have not found the right minimum cut yet. In the body of the loop, the contraction process is taken and its result is returned in $a$; then $ans$ is the disjunction of the new result $a$ and the old $ans$ (since if we find the correct (least) cut once, we can never lose it); and finally, the counter decreases accordingly.

**Proof Obligations of Min-Cut Probabilistic Amplification.** Again, we will apply the generalised proof obligations for the probabilistic loop to prove the correctness of the implementation to the specification of probabilistic amplification. To prove the refinement relationship, Theorem 2 is applied between the programs in Fig. 3 and Fig. 4; it states that we must show

$$\langle N \in \mathbb{N} \ \wedge \ 2 \leq N \ \wedge \ M \in \mathbb{N}_1 \rangle * P(N, M)$$
$$\Rightarrow \ [ans_0 := ans][minCut]\langle ans \rangle \tag{12}$$

in order to establish the refinement. The implication (12) can be simplified to

$$\langle N \in \mathbb{N} \ \wedge \ 2 \leq N \ \wedge \ M \in \mathbb{N}_1 \rangle * P(N, M) \ \Rightarrow \ [minCut]\langle ans \rangle\ ,$$

$$ans \longleftarrow \mathbf{minCut}(\ N,\ M\ )\ \widehat{=}$$
$$\mathbf{VAR}\ m,\ a\ \mathbf{IN}$$
$$\quad m := M;\ ans := FALSE;$$
$$\quad \mathbf{WHILE}\ m \neq 0\ \mathbf{DO}$$
$$\qquad a \longleftarrow contraction(N);$$
$$\qquad ans := ans \vee a;$$
$$\qquad m := m - 1$$
$$\quad \mathbf{INVARIANT}\ m \in \mathbb{N} \wedge m \leq M \wedge ans \in BOOL$$
$$\quad \mathbf{EXPECTATION}\ \langle ans \rangle + \langle m \neq 0 \rangle * \langle \neg ans \rangle * P(N, m)$$
$$\quad \mathbf{END}$$
$$\mathbf{END}$$

**Fig. 4.** Probabilistic implementation of the specification in Fig. 3

by noting that there is no $ans_0$ on the right-hand side. Also, we again separate the standard predicate and expectation, i.e. we will prove $P(N, M) \Rightarrow [minCut] \langle ans \rangle$, under the assumption that $N \in \mathbb{N} \wedge 2 \leq N \wedge M \in \mathbb{N}_1$.

We first state all the components of the loop within our reasoning context. Referring to Sec. 5.2, we have the following information.

- The initialisation for the loop is: $init_2 \widehat{=} m := M; ans := FALSE$.
- The standard invariant is: $I_2 \widehat{=} m \in \mathbb{N} \wedge m \leq M \wedge ans \in BOOL$.
- The guard for the loop is: $G_2 \widehat{=} m \neq 0$.
- The body of the loop is

$$S_2 \quad \widehat{=} \quad ans \longleftarrow contraction(N);\ ans := ans \vee a;\ m := m - 1\ .$$

- The expectation (probabilistic invariant) is:

$$E_2 \widehat{=} \langle ans \rangle + \langle m \neq 0 \rangle \ * \ \langle \neg ans \rangle * P(N, m)\ .$$

- The precondition is': $P_2 \widehat{=} N \in \mathbb{N} \wedge 2 \leq N \wedge M \in \mathbb{N}_1$.
- The pre-expectation is $A_2 \widehat{=} P(N, M)$.
- The postcondition $Q_2$ is the constant predicate *true*.
- The post-expectation is: $B_2 \widehat{=} \langle ans \rangle$.

Here, we concentrate only on the proving of *P2b*; the other proofs can be seen elsewhere [9]. We find that the obligation *P2b* cannot be proved because of termination (details also can be seen in [9]). This is not surprising in retrospect, because for example a specification $v : \{p, \langle Q \rangle\}$ ensures termination in state satisfied $Q$ with probability $p$ only; with probability $1 - p$, abortion is possible. Here, we must ensure additionally that in the latter case, termination occurs although we do not care about the postcondition in that case. We address this briefly in the next section.

## 6.5     The "Terminating" Probabilistic Specification Substitution

In order to avoid the problem revealed in the last section, we would have to introduce the concept of "terminating probabilistic specification substitution" and a corresponding fundamental theorem for it as well.

To do that we would consider a special case of the probabilistic substitution, where the post-expectation $B$ is standard, i.e is $\langle Q \rangle$ for some predicate $Q$, and the pre-expectation $A$ is the probability — still a function of the state — that $Q$ will be achieved. For consistency with probability elsewhere, we use lower-case $p$ for pre-expectation.

**Definition 2.** *Let $p$ be a probabilistic expression over $x$ and free from $x_0$; $Q$ a predicate defined over $x_0, v$ and satisfying $\forall x_0 \cdot (\exists v \cdot Q)$. The specification $v : \{\!|\, p, \langle Q \rangle \,|\!\}$ is defined by:*

$$v : \{\!|\, p, \langle Q \rangle \,|\!\} \quad \hat{=} \quad v : \{1, \langle Q \rangle\} \ {}_p\!\oplus\ x : \{1, 1\} \ . \tag{13}$$

And accordingly, we introduce the fundamental theorem for the above substitution as follows.

**Theorem 3.** *Let $p$ be an expression over $x$ and let $Q$ be a predicate defined over $x_0, v$, and satisfying $\forall x_0 \cdot (\exists v \cdot Q)$; and $T$ a program written in pGSL. For all such programs $T$, if $x : \{1, 1\} \sqsubseteq T$ and $v : \{p, \langle Q \rangle\} \sqsubseteq T$ then $v : \{\!|\, p, \langle Q \rangle \,|\!\} \sqsubseteq T$.*

With the new terminating version of the specification and fundamental theorem, we can reconstruct and prove all the proof obligations for the implementation of probabilistic amplification, which can be seen in [9].

We now can prove the correctness of the refinement for the contraction steps and the probabilistic amplification technique, both containing probabilistic specification substitution.

# 7     Conclusion and Challenges

We have taken a "second step" into the probabilistic-B world, by adding above our earlier work [8] the "superstructure" required for following the specify-refine-code path embodied in the *B-Method*. We have been successful in the sense that the new constructs are shown to be well defined, and interact properly with each other. In addition, the case-study is not completely trivial.[7]

Neil White in his MSc thesis at Oxford [21] presented similar ideas expressed in $Z$.

The $B$ context however provides a number of new challenges, some of which we have addressed here. The issue of *separation* of standard reasoning from probabilistic reasoning is (or will be) of crucial importance if the probabilistic $B$ is to handle developments of anything like the same size and scope as standard $B$. And the "terminating" specification substitution (mentioned here in the case study) will probably become the one used in practice.

---

[7] It was suggested to us by a case-study of the same algorithm done in the theorem-proving environment Coq [10] by Christine Paulin of the *LRI* in Paris.

# Acknowledgments

We wish to acknowledge the assistance of B-Core [5] for the modification of the B-Toolkit.

The authors at University of New South Wales gratefully acknowledge the support of the Australian Research Council under the large grant A00103115.

We wish to thank anonymous reviewers for their comments, which have been used to improve the paper.

# References

1. Jean-Raymond Abrial. *The B-Book*. Cambridge University Press, 1996.
2. Jean-Raymond Abrial, Dominique Cansell, and Dominique Mery. A mechanically proved and incremental development of IEEE 1394 firewire tree identify protocol. *Formal Aspects of Computing*, 14(3):215–227, 2003.
3. Ralph-Johan Back. *On the correctness of refinement in program development*. PhD thesis, Department of Computer Science, University of Helsinki, 1978. Report A-1978-4.
4. Ralph-Johan Back and Joakim Von Wright. *Refinement Calculus, a Systematic Itroduction*. Springer-Verlag New York, Inc., 1998.
5. B Core(UK) Ltd. B Toolkit. http://www.b-core.com.
6. Colin J. Fidge and Carron Shankland. But what if I don't want to wait forever? *Formal Aspects of Computing*, 14(3):281–294, 2003.
7. David Gries. A note on a standard strategy for developing loop invariants and loops. *Science of Computer Programming*, 2:207–214, 1984.
8. Thai Son Hoang, Zhendong Jin, Ken Robinson, Annabelle McIver, and Carroll Morgan. Probabilistic Invariants for Probabilistic Machines. In D. Bert, J. P. Bowen, S. King, and M. Waldén, editors, *ZB2003: Formal Specification and Development in Z and B, Proceedings of the 3rd International Conference of B and Z Users*, volume 2651 of *LNCS*, Turku, Finland, June 2003. Springer-Verlag.
9. Thai Son Hoang, Zhendong Jin, Ken Robinson, Annabelle McIver, and Carroll Morgan. Proofs of the Min-Cut development. http://www.cse.unsw.edu.au/~htson/b/minCutProofs.pdf, April 2004.
10. INRIA. The Coq proof assistant. http://coq.inria.fr/.
11. Annabelle McIver, Carroll Morgan, and Thai Son Hoang. Probabilistic termination in B. In D. Bert, J. P. Bowen, S. King, and M. Waldén, editors, *ZB2003: Formal Specification and Development in Z and B, Proceedings of the 3rd International Conference of B and Z Users*, volume 2651 of *LNCS*, Turku, Finland, June 2003. Springer-Verlag.
12. Carroll Morgan. The specification statement. *ACM Transactions on Programming Languages and Systems*, 10(3), July 1988. Reprinted in [18].
13. Carroll Morgan. *Programming from Specifications*. Prentice-Hall, second edition, 1994. At web.comlab.ox.ac.uk/oucl/publications/books/PfS.
14. Carroll Morgan. Proof rules for probabilistic loops. In He Jifeng, John Cooke, and Peter Wallis, editors, *Proceedings of the BCS-FACS 7th Refinement Workshop*, Workshops in Computing. Springer-Verlag, July 1996.
15. Carroll Morgan. The Generalised Substitution Language extended to probabilistic programs. In *Proceedings B'98: the 2nd International B Conference*, volume 1393 of *LNCS*, Montpelier, April 1998.

16. Carroll Morgan and Annabelle McIver. *Abstraction, Refinement and Proof for Probabilistic Systems*. Monographs in Computer Science. Springer-Verlag, 2004.
17. Carroll Morgan and Ken Robinson. *On the Refinement Calculus*, chapter Specification Statements and Refinements, pages 23–45. Springer-Verlag, 1992.
18. Carroll Morgan and Trevor Vickers, editors. *On the Refinment Calculus*. FACIT Series in Computer Science. Springer-Verlag, Berlin, 1994.
19. J.M. Morris. A theoretical basis for stepwise refinement and the programming calculus. *Science of Computer Programming*, 9(3):287–306, December 1987.
20. Rajeev Motwani and Prabhakar Raghavan. *Randomized Algorithms*. Cambridge University Press, 1995.
21. Neil White. Probabilistic Specification and Refinement. Master's thesis, Keble College, September 1996.

# Formal Program Development with Approximations

Eerke A. Boiten[1] and John Derrick[2]

[1] Computing Laboratory, University of Kent at Canterbury
[2] Department of Computer Science, University of Sheffield
`E.A.Boiten@kent.ac.uk, J.Derrick@dcs.shef.ac.uk`

**Abstract.** We describe a method for combining formal program development with a disciplined and documented way of introducing realistic compromises, for example necessitated by resource bounds. Idealistic specifications are identified with the limits of sequences of more "realistic" specifications, and such sequences can then be refined in their entirety. Compromises amount to focusing the attention on a particular element of the sequence instead of the sequence as a whole.

This method addresses the problem that initial formal specifications can be abstract or complete but rarely both. Various potential application areas are sketched, some illustrated with examples. Key research issues are found in identifying metric spaces and properties that make them usable for refinement using approximations.

**Keywords:** Refinement, approximations, metric spaces.

## 1 Introduction

In formal program development, one starts with a complete formal statement of the problem to be solved, and then develops a program by gradually adding detail to the solution. In practical program development, one starts with an incomplete informal problem statement, and then develops a program by adding detail to the solution (and implicitly also to the specification). The difference between the two approaches thus appears immediately in two aspects: *formality* and *completeness* of the initial specification. Just using a *formal* initial specification is a definite[1] improvement on the practical development process; however, insisting that the initial specification be *complete* requires a radical change in the process.

Indeed, it is sometimes argued that this assumption of completeness makes formal development inadequate in practice. Initial specifications often *cannot* be complete and abstract at the same time. Consider, for example, a garbage collector for a programming language. An idealistic specification would say that it collects all memory cells that have become inaccessible whenever they become

---

[1] Disregarding issues of communication – assume a specification language is used which transliterates to English or the diagrammatic notation *du jour*.

H. Treharne et al. (Eds.): ZB 2005, LNCS 3455, pp. 374–392, 2005.

so. As this is unrealistic and probably not desirable, one might specify it as: *"periodically* collects *some* memory cells which have become inaccessible". Unfortunately, without quantifying "some" and "periodically", such a specification is likely to be inadequate, also satisfied by a program which collects no cells on a yearly cycle. Replacing "some" and "periodically" by explicit values makes the specification less abstract; worse, it may only be evident much later in the development process which values are realistic or optimal. An informal incomplete specification which can *avoid* using either "all" or "some" appears to be at an advantage here.

This paper presents an approach which addresses this issue through using *chains* of specifications, which are considered equivalent to their limits. Different examples may be based on different limits for the chain, based on measures of distance between specifications (i.e., metrics), or orderings such as degree of fairness or randomness, machine integer size, floating point precision, memory space, etc. The limits represent idealised behaviour, such as unbounded integers, infinite floating point precision, etc. Elements in the chain represent approximations to the limits, which for sensible orderings behave "correctly" within boundaries which can be characterised precisely. Metrics measure the distance between specifications, and thus provide a notion of convergence to idealised behaviour from approximations which might be realisable as implementations.

The corresponding development process starts with an initial "optimistic" specification. At some stage, this is replaced by a chain of specifications whose limit it represents. Further development then refines[2] the chains uniformly in their entirety for as long as possible. This implies that "the position in the chain" – often a resource constraint – is treated as a parameter of the specification. The, a specific member of the chain is selected for further development – this step represents a *compromise* with respect to the limit specification, and will generally *not* preserve correctness. However, by postponing this step for as long as possible, any further development which relies on the specific choice of compromise is isolated from the more "generic" development up to that point, which could later be reused for a *different* choice. In this way, the development trail clearly documents where resource constraints were first taken into consideration, and most importantly: at which point the resource constraint's impact on the specification forced a compromise. One might call this process "approximate refinement", but it is actually refinement interspersed with isolated and highlighted approximation steps.

This process addresses the "incompleteness vs. abstraction" issue by allowing initial specifications to be optimistic, assuming for example unbounded resources. For as long as any *mention* of resource bounds can be avoided, it *is*; then, we introduce the resource bound but continue to develop independently of its value for as long as possible. This may go all the way to a code level constant,

---

[2] This paper will use the term "refinement" to describe any formal development process, without implying the post-hoc verification bias sometimes associated with "refinement".

that is later instantiated on the basis of empirical information such as testing or profiling.

Apart from the issue of limited resources, a number of other areas which traditional refinement does not cover in a satisfactory way are addressed by this approach. One of these is *probabilistic algorithms* which can come arbitrarily close to the exact solution but are not guaranteed to ever reach it. Floating point precision was already mentioned above; in general, any system which should be dealing with real numbers (e.g. hybrid systems) at some stage should be dealing with the approximation by floating point numbers. Also, the notion of *urgency* in real-time formalisms, i.e., actions that happen instantaneously once they are enabled, is often an unsatisfactory way of describing "as soon as possible"; approximation is useful in this context as well.

No particular specification notation or refinement relation has been assumed so far – indeed, apart from the specific notions of metrics and limits, the approach described here applies independently of such choices. However, examples in this paper will mostly use relational refinement [5, 6] using Z [14] as a concrete syntax. This is briefly described in Section 2.

Section 3 presents sequences of specifications, identified with their limits, and describes a formal development method using sequences. The rich mathematics of chains and convergence leads to a number of foundational questions. Some of these are discussed in Section 4 which considers limits defined by metrics over the space of specifications. We discuss possible approaches to defining metrics for use with refinement, and sketch a number of these. Section 4.3 discusses open issues concerning metrics, limits and their induced topology. Section 5 considers the relationship between refinement of limits and element-wise refinement of chains.

Various ways of addressing limitations of refinement have been published previously; these are discussed in Section 6, and we conclude in Section 7.

## 2     Refinement

Although the approach described in this paper is independent of the choice of specification notation, we fix a notation and notion of refinement for use in examples. Our basic formalism is that of alphabetised relations [9], characterised by predicates, using Z as a concrete syntax.

Where we consider a single operation on a fixed state, we may give its frame directly, e.g., $\Delta[x : \mathbb{N}]$, rather than define an explicit state schema.

Refinement for Z is described in the monograph [6]; we omit many of the more general definitions and technical details here. For the examples in this paper, algorithmic or *operation* refinement mostly suffices. We first recap on the basic definition of refinement.

A Z specification defines a data type consisting of partial relations, $D = (\mathsf{State}, \mathsf{Init}, \{\mathsf{Op}_i\}_{i \in I}, \mathsf{Fin})$, where $I$ is the alphabet of the data type (its set of operations). Each such data type induces a number of potential programs, each program being a relation over some global state $G$ (the final element $\mathsf{Fin}$ is the finalisation which details what is observable, its technicalities need not concern us here). In the context in which we are working, a program will be characterised by a sequence of operation indices (i.e., elements of I), and each such sequence defines a program. E.g., if $p = \langle p_1, ..., p_n \rangle$ then $p_D = \text{Init} \mathbin{\S} \text{Op}_{p_1} \mathbin{\S} ... \mathbin{\S} \text{Op}_{p_n} \mathbin{\S} \text{Fin}$.

We use the standard definition of refinement [5], defined in terms of these potential programs. The relational inclusion ensures that the observations produced by data type C must be consistent with those produced by data type A for the same sequence of inputs.

**Definition 1 (Data Refinement).** *For data types* A *and* C, C *refines* A, *written* A $\sqsubseteq_{data}$ C, *iff for each program p over I, $p_C \subseteq p_A$. Further, we write $=_{data}$ to denote data refinement in both directions.* □

In general two methods are used to verify such refinements: downward and upward simulations. In this paper they coincide because we will use retrieve relations which are the identity. Thus we use the following.

**Definition 2 (Operation Refinement).** *Operation COp is an operation refinement of the operation AOp on the same state, using the same inputs and outputs, iff*

$$\text{pre } AOp \Rightarrow \text{pre } COp$$
$$\text{pre } AOp \wedge COp \Rightarrow AOp$$

*hold for all states, inputs and outputs.* pre *Op denotes the "domain" of Op: those before-states and inputs for which related after-states and outputs are defined by Op.*

This definition is extended operation-wise to abstract data types of the form $(State, Init, \{Op_i\}_{i \in I})$ (both using the same state) with sets of operations and initialisation (as an operation with an irrelevant before-state). The same conditions hold for operation refinement when the abstract state is a subset of the concrete one.

However, in a real development it could be argued that this ideal is not always obtained. Consider the following two examples.

## 2.1   Example - Bounded Buffer

Part of an abstract specification might specify an abstract buffer:

```
┌─ Buffer ─────────────────        ┌─ Remove ──────────────
│ cont : seq Item                  │ ΔBuffer
                                   │ out! : Item
┌─ EmptyBuf ───────────────        ├───────────────────────
│ Buffer'                          │ cont = ⟨out!⟩ ⌢ cont'
├──────────────
│ cont' = ⟨ ⟩
```

$$\begin{array}{|l}
\underline{\;Insert_\infty\;}\\
\Delta Buffer\\
in? : Item\\
\hline
cont' = cont \frown \langle in? \rangle
\end{array}$$

However, this might be implemented by a bounded buffer of a particular size, e.g., $n = 256$. In this implementation, $Insert_\infty$ is replaced by $Insert_n$, where this is defined as:

$$\begin{array}{|l}
\underline{\;Insert_n\;}\\
\Delta Buffer\\
in? : Item\\
\hline
(\#cont < n \land cont' = cont \frown \langle in? \rangle) \lor (\#cont \geq n \land cont' = cont)
\end{array}$$

This bounded buffer is only an approximate refinement (in some sense) of the abstract infinite buffer – it certainly does not meet the requirements of the definition of operation refinement.

### 2.2   Example - Add

We could also imagine a development involving several steps that include an approximation at the end. One that starts with $Add_\infty$, replaces it by $Add_n$, refines that to $ModAdd_n$ and finally instantiates $n$ to $\texttt{maxint}$. Here the specifications are:

$$\begin{array}{|l}
\underline{\;Add_\infty\;}\\
\Delta [\, x : \mathbb{N} \,];\; add? : \mathbb{N}\\
\hline
x' = x + add?
\end{array}
\qquad
\begin{array}{|l}
\underline{\;Add_n\;}\\
\Delta [\, x : \mathbb{N} \,];\; add? : \mathbb{N}\\
\hline
x' = x + add? \land x' < n
\end{array}$$

$$\begin{array}{|l}
\underline{\;ModAdd_n\;}\\
\Delta [\, x : \mathbb{Z} \,|\, -n \leq x < n \,]\\
add? : \mathbb{N}\\
\hline
x' \bmod (2 * n) = (x + add?) \bmod (2 * n)
\end{array}$$

The final result is not a correct implementation of the original specification, but it can be formally traced back to it, recording the approximations needed in its development.

## 3   Refinement and Approximation with Chains

To model these types of approximate refinements we consider chains of specifications $(S_n)$, where we will identify a chain with its limit:

**Definition 3.** *A sequence of specifications* $(S_n)_{n \in \mathbb{N}}$ *is considered equivalent to its limit.*

Sequences which do not have a limit are not considered meaningful. Different approximations give different notions of a limit, and we consider examples of these in section 4. In this section, we describe an envisaged formal development process using chains of specifications. (For simplicity, we do not mention sequences with multiple indices, although they are definitely not excluded.)

The development process contains four kinds of steps:

**Element-Wise Refine.** A refinement step is a normal development step of the notation at hand, applied to the current specification. When we are dealing with a sequence $(S_n)$, we apply such a step uniformly to each of its elements.

**Introduce Sequence.** At any time, we may replace a specification $S$ with a sequence of specifications $(S_n)$ such that $S$ is the limit of $(S_n)$.

**Replace Sequence.** A sequence $(S_n)$ may be replaced by a sequence $(T_n)$ whose limit is identical to, or a refinement of, the limit of $(S_n)$.

**Compromise.** We replace a sequence $(S_n)$ with one of its elements $S_n$.

Sequence introduction and replacement are correct steps, this follows directly from our interpretation of sequences. Conditions for the correctness of refinement steps applied element-wise are discussed below, where we also explain what we mean by the "uniform" application of such steps. A compromise step generally does not preserve correctness, and for that reason forms a central part of the development documentation.

Example 2.2 uses sequence introduction when we replace $Add_\infty$ by the sequence $(Add_n)$ and element-wise refinement in the refinement to $(ModAdd_n)$, and the final step is a compromise, i.e., when we instantiate $n$ to `maxint`.

A variation on the bounded buffer example given previously might start development from the unbounded buffer, replace it by $(Buf_n)$ (sequence introduction), then by $(Buf_{2*n})_{n \in \mathbb{N}}$ (sequence replacement, the limit of even-sized buffers is still the infinite buffer), implement that by serial composition of two copies of $Buf_n$ (element-wise refinement), and finally instantiate $n$ to 256 (compromise).

The definition of refinement between sequences is inherited from their identification with limits. Thus, we have:

**Theorem 1.** *The sequence* $(S_n)$ *with limit* $S_\infty$ *is refined by the sequence* $(T_n)$ *with limit* $T_\infty$ *iff* $S_\infty$ *is refined by* $T_\infty$.

Clearly our main objective in refining chains should be to use element-wise refinement as much as possible. Sequence replacement is complete by definition for sequence refinement (assuming a complete rule for refinement of their limits), but defeats the purpose of moving to sequences. Its use is probably best limited to replacing sequences which converge "at different speeds", such as in the even-sized buffer example above. However, element-Wise refinement does *not* necessarily lead to refinement between sequences; this is discussed further in Section 5 below.

# 4    Metrics and Limits

The above discussion on orders and limits is the precursor to a discussion on alternative approaches to limits in terms of metrics (and hence topologies). We first recap on the standard definitions. Limits are defined in terms of convergence, which is relative to a particular distance function: a *metric*.

**Definition 4 (Metric).** *A metric on a space $A$ is a function $d : A \times A \to \mathbb{R}$ such that $\forall\, x, y, z \in A$:*

$$d(x, y) \geq 0$$
$$d(x, y) = d(y, x)$$
$$d(x, y) = 0 \ \textit{iff} \ x = y$$
$$d(x, y) \leq d(x, z) + d(z, y) \qquad \qquad \square$$

The limit of a sequence is defined as the point of convergence with respect to a metric.

**Definition 5 (Limit of a Sequence).** *A sequence $s_n$ converges to $s$, denoted $s_n \to s$, whenever:*

$$\forall\, \epsilon > 0 \bullet \exists\, N \bullet \forall\, n > N \bullet d(s_n, s) \leq \epsilon \qquad \qquad \square$$

There are several approaches to defining metrics and topologies for specifications, to understand what is relevant in terms of refinement we return to its definition. This was defined as consisting of program observation, expressed as $p_C \sqsubseteq p_A$, where $p_C$ is a finite sequential composition of operations from $C$. From this there are two immediate parameters which can be used to define metrics: the consistency of observations as represented by $\sqsubseteq$, and the programs themselves. We discuss each of these in turn.

## 4.1    Program Length

Data refinement asks for consistency of observations for all programs. We can define a metric by assigning a distance to specifications which agree on observations up to a certain length. This is easiest if phrased in terms of equivalence (i.e., data refinement in both directions). Thus we define

**Definition 6 (Program Length Metric).** *We define the metric $d_l$ on specifications as follows:*

$$d_l(A, C) = \begin{cases} 0 & \textit{if } A =_{data} C \\ 2^{-n} & \textit{if } n = min\{m : \mathbb{N} \mid \exists\, p \bullet p_C \neq p_A \wedge \#p = m\} \end{cases}$$

*where the length of a program is the number of operations plus one (for the initialisation).* $\qquad \square$

It should be clear that this defines a metric on the set of equivalence classes (with respect to $=_{data}$) of specifications. The basis of this metric, see [4], is the idea that two specifications are close if it takes a long time to tell them apart, where a 'long time' is the length of the program before the difference is observed.

Limits with respect to this metric are characterised as follows. The sequence $S_n$ converges to $S$ whenever, $d_l(S_n, S) \to 0$, i.e., $2^{-n} \to 0$ where $n$ is the minimum length of program needed to distinguish $S_n$ from $S$.

**Buffer Example.** This metric works well on the buffer example. The shortest program that can observe that $Buf_n$, a buffer of size $n$, does not have infinite capacity has size $2n + 2$: first $n + 1$ elements are inserted (the last of which is the first one to be ignored), then $n$ *Remove* operations are successful, and the next *Remove* operation fails[3].

Thus $d_l(Buf_n, Buf) = 2^{-(2n+3)}$ and so $Buf_n \to Buf$.

This metric has thus here correctly formalised our intuition that $Buf_n$ gets closer to its idealised behaviour as $n$ gets larger. The metric quantifies this closeness numerically.

Notice that the definition of the metric is, as one would hope, not sensitive to small changes. For example, if we consider finite and infinite stacks (i.e., inserting and removing from the same end) we can observe the difference more quickly than in the buffer example (since we do not have to remove all the elements first). However, the distance is $2^{-(n+1)}$, and thus we still get convergence to the infinite stack as one would expect.

Although its definition seems to assume observations being characterised by outputs, it also works for specification styles that use other notions of observability [7]. This is because there will always be a minimum length program where any difference can be observed – whether that be due to an output of an operation, or an explicit finalisation after the last operation.

**Add Example.** Applying this metric to the second example results in the following. First, note that as it stands the specifications are data refinement equivalent (for any $n$) since no difference can be *observed*. So let us add an observer to both:

---
*Obs*
_____
$\Xi\,[\,x : \mathbb{N}\,];\ out! : \mathbb{N}$
_____
$out! = x$
---

Denoting the two specifications by $A_n$ and $A_\infty$, we find that $d_l(A_n, A_\infty) = 2^{-3}$ since the sequence *Init*; *Add*; *Obs* will observe a difference for any input

---

[3] The standard semantics of applying *Remove* outside its precondition allows for any result including the "correct" one and a completely undefined one; however, we are looking for *equality* of semantics of programs rather than *inclusion*.

bigger than $n$. Thus, with respect to this metric, we do not get convergence. This is despite the sequence $(Add_n)$ being ordered by refinement:

$$\text{pre } Add_n = x + add? < n \Rightarrow \text{pre } Add_{n+1} = x + add? < n + 1$$

and

$$\text{pre } Add_n \wedge Add_{n+1}$$

$$\equiv$$

$$x + add? < n \wedge x' = x + add? \wedge x' < n + 1$$

$$\equiv$$

$$x + add? < n \wedge x' = x + add? \wedge x' < n$$

$$\equiv$$

$$Add_n$$

The use of this metric on this example could be criticised because, although $d_l(A_n, A_\infty) = 1/2^3$, the behaviour is correct for some inputs. That is, this definition stresses quantification over programs at the expense of quantification over inputs and outputs. Consider, for example,

$$
\begin{array}{|l|}
\hline
Op_N \\
\hline
\Delta[x : \mathbb{N}] \\
x? : \mathbb{N} \\
y! : \mathbb{B} \\
\hline
x? \neq N \Leftrightarrow y! \\
\hline
\end{array}
\qquad
\begin{array}{|l|}
\hline
Op \\
\hline
\Delta[x : \mathbb{N}] \\
x? : \mathbb{N} \\
y! : \mathbb{B} \\
\hline
y! \\
\hline
\end{array}
$$

then (assuming each specification is completed in an obvious way) $d_l(Op_N, Op) = 1/4$ despite the fact that $Op$ and $Op_N$ have identical behaviour for all but one input. The metric in Section 4.2 tackles this issue.

**Metrics via Probability Distributions.** It should be noted that the program length metric is a worst case analysis. The shortest program that one can observe the difference on is used to determine the difference, irrespective of whether that program is likely to appear in practice. Such a worst case analysis is useful in, for example, safety analysis. However, it might well be that other analyses are useful on occasion, and this would involve the use of a different metric. To determine the correct measure, a probability distribution would have to be assigned to the possible programs occurring, and this probability would be reflected in the distance calculated.

For example, let $\pi : \mathsf{P} \to [0, 1]$ be a probability distribution on the space of all finite programs $\mathsf{P}$ (which is countable). Thus $\pi(\mathsf{p})$ represents the probability that $\mathsf{p}$ will occur. At this moment we abstract away from any discussion of time intervals over which programs may be invoked, but assume they occur in some unspecified interval, kept finite (along with the program length) to avoid any issues of fairness.

**Definition 7.** *We say a probability distribution $\pi$ is observationally consistent over a set of specifications $S$ if, for all $A, C \in S$ we have $A \neq_{data} C \Rightarrow \exists\, \mathsf{p}.\pi(\mathsf{p}) > 0 \wedge \mathsf{p_A} \neq \mathsf{p_C}$.*  □

This is needed to ensure that we can observe the non-equivalent specifications. It is a natural requirement to seek, since $A \neq_{data} C$ means we can observe a difference in behaviour, and this will only be the case if there is a non-zero probability of a program being invoked which exhibits that difference. We can now define a metric with respect to such a probability distribution as follows.

**Definition 8.** *Let $\pi$ be an observationally consistent probability distribution over a set of specifications $S$. Define $d_\pi$ by*

$$d_\pi(A, C) = \begin{cases} 0 & \text{if } A =_{data} C \\ p & \text{if } p = \Sigma\{\pi(\mathsf{p}) \mid \mathsf{p} : \mathsf{P} \wedge \mathsf{p_C} \neq \mathsf{p_A}\} \end{cases}$$

□

Thus $d_\pi$ measures the distance in terms of a probability that the non data-equivalence will be observed by one of the programs.

**Theorem 2.** *$d_\pi$ is a metric on the set of equivalence classes (with respect to $=_{data}$) of specifications.*

**Proof:**

1. Non-negativity and symmetry are obvious.

2. $d_\pi(A, C) = 0$ iff $A =_{data} C$ follows from $\pi$ being observationally consistent.

3. For the triangle equality, given non-equivalent specifications $A, B, C$. Let $\mathsf{p}$ be a program with $\mathsf{p_C} \neq \mathsf{p_A}$ and $\pi(\mathsf{p}) = p$; then either $\mathsf{p_B} \neq \mathsf{p_A}$ or $\mathsf{p_C} \neq \mathsf{p_B}$ (or indeed both), thus $p$ will be in the sum of probabilities in the measure $d_\pi(A, B)$ or $d_\pi(B, C)$. This holds for all elements in the sum $\Sigma\{\pi(\mathsf{p}) \mid \mathsf{p} : \mathsf{P} \wedge \mathsf{p_C} \neq \mathsf{p_A}\}$, and thus

$$\Sigma\{\pi(\mathsf{p}) \mid \mathsf{p} : \mathsf{P} \wedge \mathsf{p_C} \neq \mathsf{p_A}\} \leq$$
$$\Sigma\{\pi(\mathsf{p}) \mid \mathsf{p} : \mathsf{P} \wedge \mathsf{p_B} \neq \mathsf{p_A}\} + \Sigma\{\pi(\mathsf{p}) \mid \mathsf{p} : \mathsf{P} \wedge \mathsf{p_C} \neq \mathsf{p_B}\}$$

as required.  □

Other variants of such a metric are clearly feasible and this approach needs to be assessed against practical as well as theoretical relevance.

## 4.2    Input/Output Metrics

An alternative to a metric based around program length is one that 'counts' the inputs/outputs for which the concrete specification correctly refines the abstract one. Due to the issue of counting over an infinite domain such as $\mathbb{N}$, we first consider bounded data types before generalising to unbounded ones.

**Bounded Data Types.** Consider a simplification of the *Add* example given as follows.

$Set_n$

$\Delta\,[\,x : 0..m\,]$
$set? : 0..m$

$x' = set? \wedge x' < n$

$Set_\infty$

$\Delta\,[\,x : 0..m\,]$
$set? : 0..m$

$x' = set?$

$Obs$

$\varXi\,[\,x : 0..m\,];\ y! : \mathbb{N}$

$y! = x$

We want to define a metric which counts the values for which $(Init, Set_n, Obs)$ differs from $(Init, Set_\infty, Obs)$. This time we will base our metric on the simulation rules (i.e., operation refinement as in Definition 2), in contrast to the metric in Section 4.1, which used the basic definition of data refinement.

First note that the temptation to just count the outputs (i.e., observations) is not sufficient: *Obs* in the concrete is clearly a correct refinement of *Obs* in the abstract. Thus if we are to base a metric on the simulation rules we will clearly need to consider both inputs and outputs. This means we will consider refinement of both preconditions and postconditions. Again we will define a metric $d$ that is zero on data refinement equivalent specifications, this will be defined in terms of the maximum distance between the constituent operations:

$$d(A, C) = max_{i \in I}\, d(AOp_i, COp_i)$$

and the distance between two operations in terms of an asymmetrical distance based on applicability and correctness:

$$d(AOp, COp) = max\{\rho(AOp, COp), \rho(COp, AOp)\}$$
$$\rho(AOp, COp) = \rho_a(AOp, COp) + \rho_c(AOp, COp)$$

Here $\rho_a$ will measure distance in preconditions, and $\rho_c$ distance in correctness. Both will count values where failure occurs, and return the ratio of this to the size of the input/output domain as the distance. Thus we define (with suitable generalisation):

**Definition 9 (Input/Output Metric).** $\rho_a(AOp, COp) = \frac{(\#Y - \#T)}{\#Y}$ *where $Y$ is the type of the input $x?$ and $T$ is the largest set $T \subseteq Y$ such that*

$$\forall\, x? : T \bullet \forall\, State \bullet pre\, AOp \Rightarrow pre\, COp$$

$\rho_c(AOp, COp) = \frac{(\#Z - \#T)}{\#Z}$ *where $Z$ is the type of the output $y!$ and $T$ is the largest set $T \subseteq Z$ such that*

$$\forall\, y! : T \bullet \forall\, State;\ State';\ x? : Y \bullet pre\, AOp \wedge COp \Rightarrow AOp \qquad \square$$

Limits, and convergent sequences, with respect to this metric are characterised as follows. The sequence $S_n$ converges to $S$ whenever the number of inputs and outputs for which $S_n$ and $S$ are not equivalent tends to zero.

We can calculate the distance between $A_n = (Init, Add_n, Obs)$ and $A_\infty = (Init, Add_\infty, Obs)$:

$$
\begin{aligned}
d(A_n, A_\infty) &= d(Add_n, Add_\infty) && \text{since } Obs \text{ is identical in } A_n \text{ and } A_\infty \\
&= \rho(Add_\infty, Add_n) && \text{since } Add_n \sqsubseteq Add_{n+1} \\
&= \rho_a(Add_\infty, Add_n) && \text{since there are no outputs} \\
&= (m + 1 - \#T)/(m + 1)
\end{aligned}
$$

where $T$ is the largest $T \subseteq 0..m$ for which $add? : T \bullet add? < n$, hence

$$
d(A_n, A) = \begin{cases} (m + 1 - (n - 1))/(m + 1) & \text{if } n < m \\ 0 & \text{otherwise} \end{cases}
$$

Hence $A_n \to A_\infty$ with respect to this metric. In a similar way with the $Add$ example from Section 2.2 we also get $A_n \to A_\infty$. The following proposition follows directly.

**Proposition 1.** *$d$ is a metric on the set of equivalence classes (with respect to refinement) of specifications.*

**Proposition 2.** *If $S_i \sqsubseteq S_{i+1}$ and $S$ is the least upper bound in the refinement ordering (i.e., $S_i \sqsubseteq S$ and no other $S_i \sqsubseteq T \sqsubseteq S$ with $T \neq_{data} S$), then $d(S_i, S) \to 0$.*

**Proof**

It suffices to consider one operation $Op_i$. Since $S_i \sqsubseteq S_{i+1}$ we have

$$
\text{pre } S_i \Rightarrow \text{pre } S_{i+1}
$$
$$
\text{pre } S_i \wedge S_{i+1} \Rightarrow S_i
$$

and the distance will depend upon convergence of the following

$$
\text{pre } S_{i+1} \Rightarrow \text{pre } S_i
$$
$$
\text{pre } S_{i+1} \wedge S_i \Rightarrow S_{i+1}
$$

Now since the sequence $(S_i)$ is bounded above and the types are bounded, the preconditions must eventually converge, i.e., $\exists N \bullet \forall n > N \bullet \text{pre } S_n = \text{pre } S$.

Similarly, correctness will allow reduction of non-determinism in output and after-state. With the bounded output type, once the preconditions have converged, the correctness must do so also, i.e., $\exists M > N \bullet \forall m > M \bullet S_m =_{data} S$. $\square$

Notice that this proposition is also true for the metric in Section 4.1.

In order to calculate a ratio $\frac{\#Y - \#T}{\#Y}$ the input and output types must obviously be bounded, however, the state does not have to be bounded. However, a non-finite state can lead to differences in the distance calculated as the following example shows.

$\underline{\quad State_1\quad}$
$x : 0..m$

$\underline{\quad State_2\quad}$
$x : \mathbb{N}$

$\underline{\quad Add_n[S]\quad}$
$\Delta S$
$add? : 0..m$
──────────
$x' = x + add? \land x' < n$

$\underline{\quad Add_\infty[S]\quad}$
$\Delta S$
$add? : 0..m$
──────────
$x' = x + add?$

We can calculate $d(Add_n[State_1], Add_\infty[State_1]) = 1 - \#T/(m+1)$, where, similarly to before, we find that

$$T = \begin{cases} \varnothing & \text{if } n \le m \\ 0..m & \text{if } n > 2m \\ 0..(n-m) & \text{if } m < n \le 2m \end{cases}$$

so again $d(Add_n[State_1], Add_\infty[State_1]) \to 0$, indeed the distance is zero after $n = 2m$.

However, if we calculate $d(Add_n[State_2], Add_\infty[State_2])$, this also comes to $1 - \#T/(m+1)$, but $T = \varnothing$ since for no input values can we guarantee that $x' < n$ for all state. And this sequence does not converge, correctly reflecting our intuition that we can never force $Add_n$ to behave like $Add_\infty$ no matter what input values are chosen.

A similar situation occurs when we apply this metric to the buffer example. In *Insert*, the value of the input chosen is immaterial thus $d(Buf_n, Buf) = 1$ since it is the size of the state that forces convergence or otherwise.

**Arbitrary Input/Output Types.** How do we generalise the above metric to arbitrary input/output types such as $add? : \mathbb{N}$? The approach we take is to avoid the problem and recognise the nature of approximation of implementation. The observation is that in any real implementation approximations will be made to data types such as $\mathbb{N}, \mathbb{Z}, \mathbb{R}$ etc. For example, $\mathbb{N}$ will usually be implemented as $0..maxint$ and so forth, $\mathbb{R}$ as a certain precision of float.

As an example, consider our original addition example:

$\underline{\quad Add_n\quad}$
$\Delta[x : \mathbb{N}]$
$add? : \mathbb{N}$
──────────
$x' = add? + 1 \land x' < n$

$\underline{\quad Add_\infty\quad}$
$\Delta[x : \mathbb{N}]$
$add? : \mathbb{N}$
──────────
$x' = add? + 1$

$Add_n$ is a correct refinement of $Add_\infty$ whenever $x' < n$. Now, the maximum range of a realistic implementation for $\mathbb{N}$ is $0..maxint$, so when $n$ exceeds $maxint$, $Add_n$ should correctly refine the implementation of $Add_\infty$.

We thus use the same definition for $d$ and $\rho$, and adapt the definition of $\rho_a$ and $\rho_c$ to take into account the implementation range. Then to adapt Definition 9 we take $Y_{imp}$ (and resp. $Z_{imp}$) to be the actual implementation of $Y$ (and resp. $Z$), and then find $\frac{(\# Y_{imp} - \# T)}{\# Y_{imp}}$ where $T$ is the largest set $T \subseteq Y_{imp}$ such that

$$\forall x? : T \bullet \forall State \bullet \operatorname{pre} AOp \Rightarrow \operatorname{pre} COp$$

and similarly for $\rho_c$. (Notice we do not change the calculation of the precondition.)

With this metric should be a description of how each infinite type has been implemented, e.g., $\mathbb{N}$ as $0..maxint$.

Applying this to the example above gives us:

$$\operatorname{pre} Add_\infty = true$$
$$\operatorname{pre} Add_n = (add? + 1 < n)$$
$$= add? : 0..n - 2$$

So we find the largest $T$ with $\forall add? : T \bullet \forall State \bullet add? : 0..n - 2$, we then calculate $\frac{(\# Y_{imp} - \# T)}{\# Y_{imp}}$ which is

$$\begin{cases} \frac{(maxint+1-(n-1))}{maxint+1} & \text{if } n < maxint + 2 \\ 0 & \text{otherwise} \end{cases}$$

which tends to zero as $n \to \infty$.

**Discussion.** Although this metric has the pleasing characteristic that it is defined via the simulation rules, and this is tractable, it is open to criticism in a number of respects. Firstly, it is somewhat ad hoc, and one must wonder whether a better characterisation can be obtained by beginning with the definition of downward simulation instead of the definition of data refinement. Second, the fudge to deal with unbounded data types is indeed a fudge. Whilst it deals satisfactorily with an infinite data type such as $\mathbb{N}$, it is less clear how effective it would be with $\mathbb{R}$ where the subset of values actually represented in a programming language varies more wildly depending on implementation strategy.

There are a number of ways these issues could be tackled. For example, one could embed the input/output in the state (in the standard fashion [6]) in order to derive the simulation rules from the data refinement definition. The metric could also take account of the complexity of constructing a particular input as its characterisation of how often this would occur (as opposed to a ratio as above). Such a complexity measure is akin to using a probability distribution, and this perhaps is the most promising avenue to explore. Instead of returning a ratio of failures to all possible values, we should construct a distance in terms of the probability of a particular input/output occurring that is a witness to the non-equivalence of $A$ and $C$. This could then be combined with the approach to probability distribution discussed in Section 4.1. How a simulation based characterisation could be derived from this definition would be a challenging problem.

## 4.3   Open Questions

The purpose of this paper was to provide an initial articulation of the problem of approximate refinement, and sketch an approach based on metrics, chains and their limits. The use of metrics as a semantic basis in computer science is not new [4, 1, 11], however, the emphasis here has been on using the measure of distance and characterisation of limits rather than interest in the induced topological structure. In addition to the questions raised in the discussions above, there are a number of open questions which need addressing, including:

**What is the relationship of the metrics outlined in this paper to work on metric space approaches to semantics?** Metric spaces used for denotational semantics have principally been used where concurrency is an issue, however, the metric defined in Section 4.1 is based upon that in [4], and this could be the starting point for such an exploration. It is less obvious what the relation is between the metric in Section 4.2 and those used as the basis for the semantics of concurrency.

**What are the topological characteristics of the metrics?** Some will be inherited from their derivation, e.g., the metric used in [4]. For others, such as that in Section 4.2, an understanding of completeness, compactness and when they induce known topologies would be interesting.

**What is their basis in terms of data refinement?** The metric defined in Section 4.1 is based upon the definition of data refinement, how does this interact with the normal definition of simulation rules? On the one hand, the metric from Section 4.2 adapts the definition of operation refinement, rather than going back to the basic definition (Definition 1). This is rather unsatisfactory, and a better characterisation would derive the definition from that of data refinement. How should this be done, and how do these metrics relate to the finalisations (which determine what is visible). How do the results generalise to non-identity retrieve relations, and what topological properties do the retrieve relations induce?

**What alternative metrics are there?** Do the ones defined here capture all the intuitive properties of approximation? Which, if any, is the most attractive from a theoretical or practical viewpoint? How do notions of approximate refinement relate to work on implementing programming language data types such as [10]?

## 5   Metrics and Chains

The previous section has discussed possible metrics at some length. We now briefly discuss how they fit into the use of chains as an approach to development. Four kinds of development steps were proposed. The metric chosen will have a direct relevance to the limits in *introduce sequence* and *replace sequence*. It is also worth noting that our discussion above has revealed there is no single canonical notion, thus the choice of metric is down to practical considerations: it depends on what aspects one considers important for a particular application. Similarly the choice of *compromise* depends on practical considerations, that is, how close an approximation is needed in particular circumstances.

In *element-wise refinement*, metrics and refinement are closely intertwined. What is needed is a way of refining each element in such a way that the refined sequence converges (hopefully to a refinement of the original limit).

A simple example shows that arbitrary refinement does not always have this property. Consider the following specifications together with the program length metric of Section 4.1.

Consider the sequence of ADTs consisting of an observer operation together with $Inc_n$, where each $Inc_n$ is defined by

$$\begin{array}{|l}
\hline
\rule{0pt}{1em}\_\ Inc_n \underline{\hspace{7cm}} \\
\Delta\left[\,x : \mathbb{N}\,\right] \\
\hline
x \leq x' \leq x + 2 \\
\hline
\end{array}$$

This sequence is constant (its elements are independent of $n$), so it converges. However, the individual operation $Inc_n$ is refined by the operation $EvenInc_n$, defined as

$$\begin{array}{|l}
\hline
\rule{0pt}{1em}\_\ EvenInc_n \underline{\hspace{6cm}} \\
\Delta\left[\,x : \mathbb{N}\,\right] \\
\hline
\textbf{if } even(n) \textbf{ then } x' = x + 2 \textbf{ else } x' = x \\
\hline
\end{array}$$

but the sequence $(EvenInc_n)$ does not converge.

This proves the following (counter-)theorem:

**Theorem 3.** *Element-wise refinement does not guarantee sequence refinement, i.e., a refinement relation $\sqsubseteq$ and sequences $(S_n)$ and $(T_n)$ exist such that*

$$\forall\, n : \mathbb{N} \bullet S_n \sqsubseteq T_n$$

*and $(S_n)$ converges, but $(T_n)$ does not.*

This example shows that non-determinism cannot, in general, be resolved without losing uniformity. To preserve it one would have to ensure that the non-determinism was resolved in the same way in each element of the sequence. Further, with this metric, preconditions cannot be weakened, even if the weakening is the same in each element in the sequence.

Consider the following diagram, which shows the effect of one operation after another. There is no discernible difference, however, this does not hold if we weaken the precondition of the first operation (this is represented by the dotted line), and the distance has increased with this element-wise refinement.

$$Op_1 \qquad\qquad Op_2 \qquad\qquad\qquad\qquad Op_1 \qquad\qquad Op_2$$

In order to achieve element-wise refinement we clearly need the refinement to be uniformly convergent in the following (usual) sense. Letting $f(x)$ denote a refinement of $x$, we need

$$\forall\, \epsilon > 0 \bullet \exists\, \delta > 0 \bullet d(x,y) < \delta \Rightarrow d(f(x), f(y)) < \epsilon$$

which might be achieved, for example, in the following ways.

One possibility is to use the refinement calculus to refine each element in the sequence uniformly. This would involve not weakening the preconditions and resolving the non-determinism in a uniform way.

Another similar idea is to use calculational approaches. In particular, one can calculate the weakest downward or upward simulation of a specification (with respect to a retrieve relation which might change the state), and the result is equivalent to the original. Thus calculation could be applied element wise to a sequence, and convergence would be preserved (as required by element-wise refinement).

An alternative is to perform the refinement independently of $n$ in such a way that element-wise refinement is obtained. Details of this are left for the future.

## 6    Related Work

The observation that idealised specifications correspond to "realistic" specifications with resource bounds tending to infinity is not new. In particular, in his PhD thesis [12], Neilson defined $\infty$-refinement $\sqsubseteq_\infty$ in terms of ordinary refinement $\sqsubseteq$ as follows:

$$A \sqsubseteq_\infty B$$
$$\Leftrightarrow$$
$$\exists\, c_1, c_2, \ldots, c_n : ResourceLimit \bullet \lim_{c_1, c_2, \ldots, c_n \to \infty, \infty, \ldots, \infty} (A \sqsubseteq B)$$

where the resource constraints $c_i$ appear free in $B$ and not at all in $A$. Such a refinement step establishes resource limits as constants in the specification; Neilson implicitly indicates that subsequent refinement may fix the values of these constants. Thus, these constants act as existential rather than universal parameters of the specification [3]: they may be arbitrarily constrained as long as the specification remains satisfiable. In our view, the use of underspecified constants obscures the distinction between the introduction of resource constraints, refinement, and the actual approximation that occurs by specialising their values. Another difference to our approach is that after the $\infty$-refinement step, there is no further mention (let alone development) of chains.

Banach and Poppleton have defined and investigated a generalisation of refinement called "retrenchment" [2]. They add "within" and "concedes" relations to every refinement step, indicating where preconditions are strengthened and postconditions weakened. These allow for developments which are not quite correctness preserving to be documented. However, this documentation refers to the internals of a specification at any given point in the development trace, and is thus hard to relate to external behaviour. Clearly, by taking a strong enough "within" relation, retrenchment holds between any pair of specifications – its value is in the documentation of where and how refinement has been relaxed. Taking that interpretation, our main objection to retrenchment as a development relation is that it encourages inexact development steps throughout, rather than localising them as we do here. Similar ideas are explored by Smith [13] for real-time specification – importantly, this work concentrates on the properties that are preserved by development steps which are not quite refinement steps but so-called "realisations".

Approximate refinement has been listed in a number of contexts as being desirable. In the UK Grand Challenge for Non-Classical Computation [15], it is mentioned as necessary for non-classical models such as quantum computation. Researchers at Berkeley [8] suggested its use for hybrid systems, although offered no means to do so.

## 7    Concluding Comments

This paper has set out an approach which we believe might be useful for combining formal program development in a disciplined way with the inevitable compromises required by the bounded resources of implemented programs. The underlying mathematics is very rich, and we have hardly begun to explore it, even in the context of relational specification languages – but we hope that the examples presented give a flavour of what might be possible, and some indication that a further exploration of these ideas would be worthwhile.

**Acknowledgements.** Thanks are due to members of the EPSRC RefineNet network (www.refinenet.org.uk), whose feedback on an earlier presentation substantially improved some of the above ideas, to Dan Grundy who commented on the draft, and to the reviewers for their useful suggestions.

## References

1. P. America and J. Rutten. Solving reflexive domain equations in a category of complete metric spaces. In J. W. de Bakker and J. J. M. Rutten, editors, *Ten Years of Concurrency Semantics: Selected Papers of the Amsterdam Concurrency Group*, pages 131–163. World Scientific, Singapore, 1992.
2. R. Banach and M. Poppleton. Retrenchment, refinement and simulation. In J.P. Bowen, S. King, S. Dunne, and A. Galloway, editors, *ZB 2000*, volume 1878 of *Lecture Notes in Computer Science*, pages 304–323. Springer-Verlag, 2000.

3. E.A. Boiten. Loose specification and refinement in Z. In D. Bert, J.P. Bowen, M.C. Henson, and K. Robinson, editors, *ZB 2002*, volume 2272 of *Lecture Notes in Computer Science*, pages 226–241. Springer-Verlag, 2002.

4. J. W. de Bakker and J.-J. C. Meyer. Metric semantics for concurrency. In J. W. de Bakker and J. J. M. Rutten, editors, *Ten Years of Concurrency Semantics: Selected Papers of the Amsterdam Concurrency Group*, pages 104–130. World Scientific, Singapore, 1992.

5. W.-P. de Roever and K. Engelhardt. *Data Refinement: Model-Oriented Proof Methods and their Comparison.* CUP, 1998.

6. J. Derrick and E.A. Boiten. *Refinement in Z and Object-Z: Foundations and Advanced Applications.* FACIT. Springer Verlag, May 2001.

7. J. Derrick and E.A. Boiten. Relational concurrent refinement. *Formal Aspects of Computing*, 15(2):182–214, 2003.

8. A. Ghosal, M. Jurdzinski, R. Majumdar, and V. Prabhu. Approximate refinement for hybrid systems. Berkeley EECS Research Summary for 2003, http://buffy.eecs.berkeley.edu/ResearchSummary/03abstracts/vinayak.1.html.

9. C.A.R. Hoare and He Jifeng. *Unifying Theories of Programming.* Prentice-Hall, 1998.

10. B. Jacobs. Java's integral types in PVS. In Elie Najm, Uwe Nestmann, and Perdita Stevens, editors, *FMOODS'03*, pages 1–15, Paris, November 2003. Springer.

11. Marta Kwiatkowska and Gethin Norman. A fully abstract metric-space denotational semantics for reactive probabilistic processes. In Abbas Edalat, Achim Jung, Klaus Keimel, and Marta Kwiatkowska, editors, *Electronic Notes in Theoretical Computer Science*, volume 13. Elsevier, 2000.

12. D.S. Neilson. *From Z to C: Illustration of a Rigorous Development Method.* PhD thesis, Oxford University Computing Laboratory, 1990.

13. G. Smith. From ideal to realisable real-time specifications. In N. Leslie, editor, *Fifth New Zealand Formal Program Development Colloquium*, number 99-1 in IIMS Technical Report. Institute of Information and Mathematical Sciences, Massey University at Albany, 1999.

14. J. M. Spivey. *The Z Notation: A Reference Manual.* International Series in Computer Science. Prentice Hall, 2nd edition, 1992.

15. Susan Stepney, John A. Clark, Colin G. Johnson, Derek Partridge, and Robert E. Smith. Artificial immune systems and the grand challenge for non-classical computation. In Jon Timmis, Peter Bentley, and Emma Hart, editors, *Proceedings of the 2003 International Conference on Artificial Immune Systems*, LNCS 2787, pages 204–216. Springer, September 2003.

# Practical Data Refinement for the Z Schema Calculus

Lindsay Groves

School of Mathematics, Statistics and Computer Science,
Victoria University of Wellington,
Wellington, New Zealand
lindsay@mcs.vuw.ac.nz

**Abstract.** It is well known that the principal operators in the Z schema calculus are not monotonic with respect to either operation or data refinement. This is generally regarded as limiting their usefulness in software development, and has lead to proposals to redefine the schema calculus and/or the notion of refinement so that monotonicity is established. We examine this issue more closely, to demonstrate just how non-monotonicity arises, and identify various conditions under which components of schema expressions can be safely replaced by their refinements. This shows that in a wide range of practical situations, refinement of such components can be justified by checking fairly simple conditions.

## 1 Introduction

Two important features of Z — perhaps the most important — are the *schema calculus* [1], which allows specifications to be composed by combining partial specifications of operations and/or states, and the *refinement theory* [1, 2, 3],[1] which allows specifications to be made progressively more concrete in preparation for being turned into code. Unfortunately, these features do not blend together as well as might be hoped, because certain key operators of the schema calculus are not *monotonic*, which means that refining a component of a specification does not (in general) automatically give a refinement of the whole specification. Thus, one must either remove schema operators before performing refinements, or prove explicitly each time a component is refined that this gives a refinement of the whole specification.

In response to this lack of monotonicity, some authors (e.g. [4]) have sought to redefine the schema calculus (e.g. by adding explicit preconditions) and/or the notion of refinement so that monotonicity is obtained. Others have abandoned Z in favour of alternative formalisms, such as B or the refinement calculus. All of these responses mean sacrificing some of the more appealing aspects of Z,

---

[1] We use the general term *refinement* to encompass both data refinement and operation refinement, and use the more specific terms where appropriate, unless it is clear from the context which is meant.

H. Treharne et al. (Eds.): ZB 2005, LNCS 3455, pp. 393–413, 2005.

most notably the simple and intuitive definitions of its schema operators and refinement.

In this paper we look more closely at the interaction between the schema calculus and refinement, extending the results presented in [5] to include data refinement. We focus mainly on schema conjunction, disjunction and composition, since these have the most interesting properties and are the most widely used,[2] and also give results for schema override [7]. We show that monotonicity of these schema operators can be guaranteed by discharging fairly simple proof obligations which appear to be applicable in a wide range of practical situations. Some of these conditions are simple syntactic checks, some involve only computing preconditions of components, and some are equivalent to feasibility conditions that would still be required in a modified Z or another formalism. In the case of data refinement, they impose additional constraints upon the kinds of abstraction relation that can be used.

Section 2 reviews key aspects of the schema calculus to establish some notation and introduce some basic results required later. Sections 3 and 5 give basic definitions of operation and data refinement, and some important special cases. Section 4 summarises the main results on monotonicity for operation refinement (taken mainly from [5]), providing a basis for Section 6, which presents our new results on monotonicity for data refinement, and Section 7, which examines the calculation of data refinements for composite specifications. Section 8 then concludes by discussing the significance of our results and possible extensions.

## 2    The Schema Calculus

We are concerned with using the Z schema calculus to specify operations that modify some state, as described for example in [1].

Simple operations are defined as schemas, with the general form:

$$[\Delta S; x? : X; y! : Y \mid P]$$

where $\Delta S$ is an abbreviation for $S; S'$, denoting the sets of *pre-state* $(S)$ and *post-state* $(S')$ variables, $x?$ are the input variables and $y!$ are the output variables. Such schemas are interpreted as defining operations that can exhibit various behaviours described by bindings for variables in $\Delta S$, $x?$ and $y!$ that satisfy $P$.

In discussing operation refinement, we restrict our attention to operations that act only on the state and have no input or output variables (and no unusual decorations), and thus consider schemas of the form:

$$[\Delta S \mid P]$$

The ensuing results can be adapted systematically to handle input and output variables, by treating input variables in the same way as pre-state variables and output variables in the same way as post-state variables.

---

[2] Early empirical evidence is given in [6]; my experience suggests that this is still the case.

Complex operations can be defined by combining operations using various schema operators. When combining schemas in this way, their declarations must first be standardised so that they can be merged; we will usually assume that declarations have already been standardised is such a way that operations being combined have the same signature.

In addition to the standard schema operators, we will also consider schema override [7], which is defined so that $A \oplus B$ behaves like $A$ except where a behaviour is specified by $B$ (pre is defined below):[3]

**Definition 1.** $A \oplus B = (\neg \text{ pre } B \wedge A) \vee B$

Given an operation $A = [\Delta S \mid P]$, we write $Vars(A)$ for the set of state variables (declared in $\Delta S$) that occur in $P$.[4]

The *precondition* of an operation in Z characterises the pre-states (and values of input variables) for which the operation is defined.

**Definition 2.** (*Precondition*) *For an operation* $A = [\Delta S; x?:X; y!:Y \mid P]$,

$$\text{pre } A = \exists S'; y! : Y \bullet A$$
$$\equiv [S; x?:X \mid \exists S'; y! : Y \bullet P]$$

Ignoring input and output variables, this reduces to $\exists S' \bullet A$ or $[S \mid \exists S' \bullet P]$.

We will need the following properties of preconditions:

**Law 1.** *For any operations $A$ and $B$ on the same state:*[5]

 (i) $A \Rightarrow \text{pre } A$

 (ii) $\text{pre } (A \vee B) \equiv \text{pre } A \vee \text{pre } B$

 (iii) $\text{pre } (A \wedge B) \Rightarrow \text{pre } A \wedge \text{pre } B$

 (iv) *If* $Vars(A) \cap Vars(B) = \varnothing$, *then* $\text{pre } (A \wedge B) \equiv \text{pre } A \wedge \text{pre } B$

 (v) *If $A$ does not constraint its post-state variables (i.e. no variable in $S'$ occurs in $A$), then* $\text{pre } A \equiv A$ *and* $\text{pre } (A \wedge B) \equiv \text{pre } A \wedge \text{pre } B \equiv A \wedge \text{pre } B$

 (vi) $\text{pre } (A \oplus B) \equiv \text{pre } A \vee \text{pre } B$

 (vii) $\text{pre } (A \, \mathbf{\mathring{,}} \, B) \equiv (\exists S'' \bullet A[S''/S'] \wedge \text{pre } B[S''/S]) \equiv \text{pre } (A \, \mathbf{\mathring{,}} \, \text{pre } B)$

We say that two operations are *consistent* if their conjunction is defined whenever they are both defined; i.e. that $A \wedge B$ terminates whenever $A$ and $B$ both terminate.

---

[3] We use $=$ to denote syntactic equality (including definitions) and $\equiv$ to denote semantic equivalence of schemas.

[4] A semantic definition would be less sensitive to minor syntactic variations, but a syntactic definition is easier to use in practice.

[5] When there is no confusion, we often omit universal quantification over the state.

**Definition 3.** (*Consistency*) *Two operations, A and B, on the same state, S, are* consistent *iff* $\forall\, S \bullet \text{pre } A \wedge \text{pre } B \Rightarrow \text{pre } (A \wedge B)$ *holds.*

Since pre $(A \wedge B) \Rightarrow$ pre $A \wedge$ pre $B$ always holds (see Law 1(iii)), the added condition means that when $A$ and $B$ are consistent we have pre $(A \wedge B) \equiv$ pre $A \wedge$ pre $B$.

## 3    Operation Refinement

An operation, $A$, is *refined* by another operation, $B$, if $B$ produces a valid result whenever $A$ does, and any behaviour exhibited by $B$ is permitted by $A$ [1].

**Definition 4.** (*Operation Refinement*) *Let A and B be operations with state S, input variables* $x? : X$ *and output variables* $y! : Y$, *then B is an* operation refinement *of A, written* $A \sqsubseteq B$, *iff the following conditions hold:*

*Applicability:*
$$\forall\, S;\, x? : X \bullet \text{pre } A \Rightarrow \text{pre } B \tag{1}$$

*Correctness:*
$$\forall\, \Delta S;\, x? : X;\, y! : Y \bullet \text{pre } A \wedge B \Rightarrow A \tag{2}$$

Ignoring input and output variables, these reduces to:

$$\forall\, S \bullet \text{pre } A \Rightarrow \text{pre } B \tag{3}$$

$$\forall\, \Delta S \bullet \text{pre } A \wedge B \Rightarrow A \tag{4}$$

Operation refinement can be understood as having two possible effects, which we often describe using more operational terminology:

- Refinement can increase the domain over which an operation is defined (i.e. weaken preconditions or increase termination).
- Refinement can reduce nondeterminism (i.e. strengthen postconditions).

Note that the applicability condition limits the extent to which nondeterminism can be reduced. If nondeterminism is reduced so much that no possible outputs (i.e. post-state values) are left for some inputs (i.e. pre-state values), those inputs no longer satisfy the precondition, so the applicability condition fails.

It will be useful later to distinguish refinements that only modify an operation in one of the ways described in Definition 4. We say that $A$ is *pre-refined* by $B$, if $B$ can only modify $A$ by increasing its precondition, i.e. by adding new behaviours for inputs not in the precondition of $A$, and that $A$ is *post-refined* by $B$, if $B$ can only modify $A$ by reducing nondeterminism, i.e. by removing some (but not all) behaviours for inputs in the precondition of $A$.

**Definition 5.** (*Pre-refinement*) $A$ *is* pre-refined *by* $B$, *written* $A \sqsubseteq_{pre} B$, *iff* $B$ *refines* $A$, *but does not reduce nondeterminism for any initial state in the precondition of* $A$; *i.e.* $A \sqsubseteq_{pre} B$ *iff* $A \sqsubseteq B$ *and* $\forall \Delta S \bullet A \Rightarrow B$, *which simplifies to* $A \sqsubseteq_{pre} B$ *iff* $\forall \Delta S \bullet \text{pre } A \wedge B \equiv A$.

**Definition 6.** (*Post-refinement*) $A$ *is* post-refined *by* $B$, *written* $A \sqsubseteq_{post} B$, *iff* $B$ *refines* $A$, *but is only defined for initial states where* $A$ *is defined; i.e.* $A \sqsubseteq_{post} B$ *iff* $A \sqsubseteq B$ *and* $\forall S \bullet \text{pre } B \Rightarrow \text{pre } A$, *which simplifies to* $A \sqsubseteq_{post} B$ *iff* $\forall S \bullet \text{pre } A \equiv \text{pre } B$ *and* $\forall \Delta S \bullet B \Rightarrow A$.

# 4    Monotonicity for Operation Refinement

This section defines monotonicity with respect to operation refinement, and presents some results regarding monotonicity of schema operators with respect to operation refinement. These results are presented without proofs or examples, since most of them were presented in [5].[6] They are included here as they provide helpful background for understanding the results for data refinement in Section 6, and can be used in concert with the calculations discussed in Section 7.

A schema operator is *monotonic* with respect to operation refinement in a given argument position if refining that argument gives a refinement of the entire operation. This means that a component of a composite specification can safely be refined independently of the rest of the specification.

**Definition 7.** ($\sqsubseteq$-*Monotonicity*) *An* $n$-*ary schema operator* $\mathcal{F}$ *is* monotonic *with respect to operation refinement in its* $k$th *argument, for* $1 \leq k \leq n$, *iff* $S \sqsubseteq S'$ *implies* $\mathcal{F}(a_1, \cdots, a_{k-1}, S, a_{k+1}, \cdots, a_n) \sqsubseteq \mathcal{F}(a_1, \cdots, a_{k-1}, S', a_{k+1}, \cdots, a_n)$.

With operation refinement it is sufficient to consider refinement in just one argument position, since refinements in several arguments can be performed one at a time, in any order. For example, if binary operator $\mathcal{F}$ is monotonic in both argument positions, then $S_1 \sqsubseteq S_1'$ and $S_2 \sqsubseteq S_2'$ implies $\mathcal{F}(S_1, S_2) \sqsubseteq \mathcal{F}(S_1', S_2) \sqsubseteq \mathcal{F}(S_1', S_2')$ and $\mathcal{F}(S_1, S_2) \sqsubseteq \mathcal{F}(S_1, S_2') \sqsubseteq \mathcal{F}(S_1', S_2')$. We will see in Section 6 that this is not the case for data refinement.

Although many of the Z schema operators are not monotonic, it is often possible to find fairly simple conditions under which component replacement is safe. Our aim is to find rules that are useful in practice, so we are interested in finding a range of conditions that make the operators monotonic, rather than just finding the most general conditions.

We present results for conjunction, disjunction, override and composition, since they have the most interesting properties, and are also used frequently in composing specifications. Universal and existential quantification (and hiding)

---

[6] More specifically, [5] presents detailed proofs and examples for conjunction and disjunction (except for Law 13); results for composition were mentioned only briefly.

have similar properties to conjunction and disjunction, respectively, and piping is effectively the same as composition in this context. Precondition and renaming are straightforward monotonic, while negation, implication and equivalence are pathologically non-monotonic, so don't have many interesting properties. Conjunction and disjunction are both commutative, so we don't need to consider the two argument positions separately. Override and composition are not commutative, so we do need to consider the two argument positions separately.

## 4.1   Conjunction

Reducing nondeterminism in the components of a conjunction can leave the operation with no choices for some input(s), thereby reducing the precondition of the operation and violating the applicability condition of Definition 4. This is the *only* way in which refining the components of a conjunction can lead to non-monotonicity. We can therefore guarantee that the components of a conjunction can be refined safely, by ensuring that this does not remove all possible behaviours for any input in the precondition of the conjunction.

First, we observe that refining the components of a conjunction cannot violate the correctness condition of Definition 4, so we only need to consider the applicability condition. This gives us (by Definition 3) a very general law:

**Law 2.** *If* $A \sqsubseteq A1$, $B \sqsubseteq B1$, *and* $A1$ *and* $B1$ *are consistent whenever* $A$ *and* $B$ *are, then* $A \wedge B \sqsubseteq A1 \wedge B1$.

While very general, this condition may be too difficult to check because it involves computing pre $(A1 \wedge B1)$, and possibly also pre $(A \wedge B)$.[7] We would prefer to avoid this, since it usually involves computing $A1 \wedge B1$, which defeats the aim of refining components independently.

We can obtain a simpler condition by observing that we can safely refine the components of a conjunction in a way that only increases termination, i.e. is a pre-refinement (see Definition 5), since this cannot reduce nondeterminism in a conjunction and thus cannot lead to non-monotonicity. Moreover, since this cannot reduce nondeterminism, the resulting refinement is a pre-refinement.

**Law 3.** *If* $A \sqsubseteq_{pre} A1$ *and* $B \sqsubseteq_{pre} B1$, *then* $A \wedge B \sqsubseteq_{pre} A1 \wedge B1$.

Note that $A \sqsubseteq_{pre} A1$ holds if $A \sqsubseteq A1$ and $A$ is deterministic; similarly for $B$ and $B1$. Thus, we can always safely refine a component of a conjunction if we know that that component is deterministic.

Finally, the components of a conjunction can be refined safely if they (and their refinements) act on disjoint parts of the state, or if the refinement of one of them does not constrain its post-state variables (see Laws 1(iv) and 1(v)).

---

[7] The condition that $A1$ and $B1$ are consistent whenever $A$ and $B$ are holds if $A1$ and $B1$ are always consistent, so we only need to compute pre $(A \wedge B)$ if pre $(A1 \wedge B1)$ can be falsified.

**Law 4.** *If $A \sqsubseteq A1$, $B \sqsubseteq B1$, $Vars(A) \cap Vars(B) = \emptyset$, $Vars(A1) \subseteq Vars(A)$ and $Vars(B1) \subseteq Vars(B)$, then $A \wedge B \sqsubseteq A1 \wedge B1$.*

**Law 5.** *If $A \sqsubseteq A1$, $B \sqsubseteq B1$, and $A1$ does not constrain its post-state variables, then $A \wedge B \sqsubseteq A1 \wedge B1$.*

Thus, we have a range of conditions that suffice to show that components of a conjunction can be refined safely, ranging from the most general condition in Law 2 to the very simple syntactic conditions in Laws 4 and 5. The simple syntactic conditions in Laws 4 and 5 will hold for a wide range of practical uses of schema conjunction, which is often used to extend the state and/or outputs (e.g. to add a result indicator) or to add a test on the inputs/pre-state (e.g. when distinguishing a success case from a fail case of an operation or adding an authorisation condition).

Law 3 gives a weaker condition that can be used in more general cases. This can often be checked by calculating preconditions of individual components, by noting that $B$ is a pre-refinement of $A$ iff $B$ can be written as a disjunction of $A$ and another operation $C$ whose precondition is disjoint from that of $A$, i.e. $B = A \vee C$, where pre $A \Rightarrow \neg$ pre $C$.

It seems that the more general Law 2 is seldom likely to be needed in practice. However, it is worth noting that the condition in Law 2 corresponds to checking for feasibility in the refinement calculus [8, 9], and cannot in general be completely avoided. Unlike in the refinement calculus, checking for feasibility cannot be deferred, since in Z, if each of the components of a conjunction undergoes a sequence of refinements, say $A \sqsubseteq A1 \sqsubseteq A2$ and $B \sqsubseteq B1 \sqsubseteq B2$, the fact that $A2$ and $B2$ are consistent does not ensure that $A1$ and $B1$ were consistent.

## 4.2   Disjunction

Weakening the precondition of one component of a disjunction can add behaviours for initial states in the precondition of the other component, thereby admitting previously excluded behaviours and violating the correctness condition of Definition 4. This is the *only* way in which refining the components of a disjunction can lead to non-monotonicity. We can therefore guarantee that the components of a disjunction can be refined safely, by ensuring that this does not add new behaviours for initial states in the precondition of the other component.

First, we observe that refining the components of a disjunction cannot violate the applicability condition of Definition 4, so we only need to consider the correctness condition. This can be specialised (and simplified) to obtain the following very general law:

**Law 6.** *If $A \sqsubseteq A1$, $B \sqsubseteq B1$, pre $A \wedge \neg$ pre $B \wedge B1 \Rightarrow A$ and pre $B \wedge \neg$ pre $A \wedge A1 \Rightarrow B$, then $A \vee B \sqsubseteq A1 \vee B1$.*

This can be understood as saying that any behaviour of $B1$ for inputs that are in the precondition of $A$ but not of $B$ must be permitted by $A$, and any behaviour of $A1$ for inputs that are in the precondition of $B$ but not of $A$ must be permitted by $B$.

While Law 6 provides a general way of showing that components of a disjunction are refined safely, it is quite complex to apply, because it involves reasoning about the effects of the two operations not just their preconditions. Situations requiring this complexity, however, seem unlikely to arise in practice, so the law will usually be more complex than we really need.

One way to obtain a simpler and more useful law is to require that if the preconditions of $A$ and $B$ (and thus of $A1$ and $B1$) overlap, then $A1$ only adds behaviours for states that are not in the precondition of $B$, and $B1$ only adds behaviours for states that are not in the precondition of $A$.

**Law 7.** *If $A \sqsubseteq A1$, $B \sqsubseteq B1$, pre $A1 \wedge$ pre $B \Rightarrow$ pre $A$ and pre $B1 \wedge$ pre $A \Rightarrow$ pre $B$, then $A \vee B \sqsubseteq A1 \vee B1$.*

This only involves reasoning about preconditions, so is considerably simpler than Law 10, but still allows refinements that are unlikely to arise in practice. It is far more likely (and should probably be regarded as good practice) that the refinement of one component is only defined outside the precondition of the other (original) component, and vice versa. This also requires the preconditions of the original components to be disjoint, but allows the preconditions of the refinements to overlap outside of the preconditions of original components.

**Law 8.** *If $A \sqsubseteq A1$, $B \sqsubseteq B1$, pre $A \Rightarrow \neg$ pre $B1$ and pre $B \Rightarrow \neg$ pre $A1$, then $A \vee B \sqsubseteq A1 \vee B1$.*

This can be simplified further by requiring that the refined components have disjoint preconditions, in which case the preconditions of the original components must also be disjoint.

**Law 9.** *If $A \sqsubseteq A1$, $B \sqsubseteq B1$ and pre $A1 \Rightarrow \neg$ pre $B1$, then $A \vee B \sqsubseteq A1 \vee B1$.*

We can obtain a still simpler law by observing that, since increasing termination is the *only* way in which refining the components of a disjunction can lead to non-monotonicity, we can safely refine the components of a disjunction in a way that only decreases nondeterminism; i.e. is a post-refinement.

**Law 10.** *If $A \sqsubseteq_{post} A1$ and $B \sqsubseteq_{post} B1$, then $A \vee B \sqsubseteq_{post} A1 \vee B1$.*

Note that $A \sqsubseteq_{post} A1$ holds if $A \sqsubseteq A1$ and $A$ is total; similarly for $B$ and $B1$. Thus, we can always safely refine a component of a disjunction if we know that that component is total.

A special case of Law 9 arises when the components of the disjunction (and their refinements) act on disjoint parts of the state. This situation is unlikely to arise in practice, because whichever disjunct is chosen, the variables in the other disjunct are completely unconstrained.

**Law 11.** *If $A \sqsubseteq A1$ and $B \sqsubseteq B1$, $Vars(A) \cap Vars(B) = \emptyset$, $Vars(A1) \subseteq Vars(A)$ and $Vars(B1) \subseteq Vars(B)$, then $A \vee B \sqsubseteq A1 \vee B1$.*

We also note that refining both components to the same operation is safe.

**Law 12.** *If* $A \sqsubseteq C$ *and* $B \sqsubseteq C$, *then* $A \vee B \sqsubseteq C \vee C \equiv C$.

Finally, we observe that any refinements of the components of a disjunction can be adapted to obtain safe refinements, by restricting their preconditions to ensure that they do not add behaviours in the precondition of the other component.

**Law 13.** *If* $A \sqsubseteq A1$ *and* $B \sqsubseteq B1$, *then* $A \vee B \sqsubseteq$ pre $A \wedge A1 \vee$ pre $B \wedge B1$.

The conditions in this law can be weakened, at the expense of added complexity, by replacing pre $A$ by pre $A \vee \neg$ pre $B1$ and pre $B$ by pre $B \vee \neg$ pre $A1$.

Again, we have a range of conditions that suffice to show that components of a disjunction can be refined safely, ranging from the most general conditions in Law 6 to the very simple syntactic condition in Law 11. In this case, the simple syntactic condition of Law 11 is unlikely to be useful in practice. However, the conditions in Laws 9 and 10 are likely to cover most practical situations, since in most practical uses of disjunction the preconditions of the components are disjoint and are likely to remain so under refinement. Law 9 only requires computing the preconditions of the refined components, which is standard practice in developing Z specifications in any case (e.g., see [2, 10]). Law 10 can also often be checked easily by noting that $B$ is a post-refinement of $A$ iff $B$ can be written as a conjunction of $A$ and another operation $C$ whose precondition is contained in that of $A$ and is consistent with $A$; i.e. $B = A \wedge C$, where pre $C \Rightarrow$ pre $A$, and $A$ and $C$ are consistent. Finally, Law 13 provides a more constructive approach which allows any refinements of the components of a disjunction to be adapted in a way that guarantees monotonicity.

## 4.3   Override

It is easy to see that schema override is monotonic in its first argument, but not in its second argument. We can prove properties of override using our laws for conjunction and disjunction.

**Law 14.** *If* $A \sqsubseteq A1$, *then* $A \oplus B \sqsubseteq A1 \oplus B$.

*Proof.* We first observe that $\neg$ pre $B$ does not constrain its post-state variables, so $A \sqsubseteq A1$ implies $\neg$ pre $B \wedge A \sqsubseteq \neg$ pre $B \wedge A1$ by Law 5, and pre $(\neg$ pre $B \wedge A1) \equiv \neg$ pre $B \wedge$ pre $A1$ by Law 1(v).

$A \oplus B$

$\equiv$   $\langle$ Definition of $\oplus$ $\rangle$

$\neg$ pre $B \wedge A \vee B$

$\sqsubseteq$   $\left\langle \begin{array}{l} \text{Law 9, since } \neg \text{ pre } B \wedge A \sqsubseteq \neg \text{ pre } B \wedge A1 \text{ and} \\ \text{pre } (\neg \text{ pre } B \wedge A1) \Rightarrow \neg \text{ pre } B \end{array} \right\rangle$

$\neg$ pre $B \wedge A1 \vee B$

$\equiv$   $\langle$ Definition of $\oplus$ $\rangle$

$A1 \oplus B$

Override is not monotonic in its second argument for the same reason that disjunction is not monotonic, so we can thus guarantee safe refinement of the second argument in similar ways to those presented in Section 4.2. For example, we can refine the second argument of an override provided that its precondition is not increased.

**Law 15.** *If* $B \sqsubseteq_{post} B1$, *then* $A \oplus B \sqsubseteq A \oplus B1$.

*Proof.* Follows immediately from Law 10, since $A \sqsubseteq_{post} A$.

### 4.4    Composition

Composition is not monotonic in its first argument because reducing nondeterminism in the first component can exclude the only behaviours that "link" the two components, and is not monotonic in its second argument because increasing definedness in the second component can admit previously excluded behaviours.

Since non-monotonicity in the first argument arises from reducing nondeterminism, we can guarantee safe refinement of the first component in ways similar to those for conjunction. We can get a quite general result by observing that reducing nondeterminism is the *only* way in which refining the first component of a composition can lead to non-monotonicity, and is safe provided that it does not remove all behaviours that "link" the two components for any input. This is equivalent to saying that the refinement of the first component must be able to establish the precondition of the second component, provided that the original first component could also.

**Law 16.** *If* $A \sqsubseteq A1$, *and* $\mathrm{pre}\,(A \,\raise.5ex\hbox{$\scriptscriptstyle\circ$}\kern-.25em\raise-.5ex\hbox{$\scriptscriptstyle\circ$}\, B)$ *implies* $\mathrm{pre}\,(A1 \,\raise.5ex\hbox{$\scriptscriptstyle\circ$}\kern-.25em\raise-.5ex\hbox{$\scriptscriptstyle\circ$}\, B)$, *then* $A \,\raise.5ex\hbox{$\scriptscriptstyle\circ$}\kern-.25em\raise-.5ex\hbox{$\scriptscriptstyle\circ$}\, B \sqsubseteq A1 \,\raise.5ex\hbox{$\scriptscriptstyle\circ$}\kern-.25em\raise-.5ex\hbox{$\scriptscriptstyle\circ$}\, B$.

Note that pre $(A \,\raise.5ex\hbox{$\scriptscriptstyle\circ$}\kern-.25em\raise-.5ex\hbox{$\scriptscriptstyle\circ$}\, B)$ is equivalent to $(\exists\, S'' \bullet A[S''/S'] \wedge \mathrm{pre}\, B[S''/S])$ (see Law 1(vii)). We would usually be able to prove pre $(A1 \,\raise.5ex\hbox{$\scriptscriptstyle\circ$}\kern-.25em\raise-.5ex\hbox{$\scriptscriptstyle\circ$}\, B)$ (i.e. $(\exists\, S'' \bullet A1[S''/S'] \wedge$ pre $B[S''/S])$) without having to calculate pre $(A \,\raise.5ex\hbox{$\scriptscriptstyle\circ$}\kern-.25em\raise-.5ex\hbox{$\scriptscriptstyle\circ$}\, B)$ or $A1 \,\raise.5ex\hbox{$\scriptscriptstyle\circ$}\kern-.25em\raise-.5ex\hbox{$\scriptscriptstyle\circ$}\, B$. For example, pre $(A \,\raise.5ex\hbox{$\scriptscriptstyle\circ$}\kern-.25em\raise-.5ex\hbox{$\scriptscriptstyle\circ$}\, B)$ reduces to pre $A$ if $B$ is total, and to pre $B$ if $A$ is total.

We can obtain a simpler law by observing that increasing termination in the first component, without reducing nondeterminism, cannot lead to non-monotonicity.

**Law 17.** *If* $A \sqsubseteq_{pre} A1$, *then* $A \,\raise.5ex\hbox{$\scriptscriptstyle\circ$}\kern-.25em\raise-.5ex\hbox{$\scriptscriptstyle\circ$}\, B \sqsubseteq_{pre} A1 \,\raise.5ex\hbox{$\scriptscriptstyle\circ$}\kern-.25em\raise-.5ex\hbox{$\scriptscriptstyle\circ$}\, B$.

As with Law 3, we note that $A \sqsubseteq_{pre} A1$ holds if $A \sqsubseteq A1$ and $A$ is deterministic.

Since non-monotonicity in the second argument arises from increasing definedness, the conditions under which the first component of a composition can be refined safely are similar to those for disjunction. We can get a quite general result for the second argument by observing that increasing definedness in the second component will only add new behaviours to the composition if it adds behaviours for states that can be reached by the first component.

**Law 18.** *If* $B \sqsubseteq B1$ *and* $(\forall S'' \bullet A[S''/S'] \wedge \text{pre } B1[S''/S] \Rightarrow \text{pre } B[S''/S])$, *then* $A \mathbin{\raise.3ex\hbox{$\scriptstyle\S$}} B \sqsubseteq A \mathbin{\raise.3ex\hbox{$\scriptstyle\S$}} B1$.

We can obtain a simpler law by observing that decreasing nondeterminism in the second component, without increasing termination, cannot lead to non-monotonicity.

**Law 19.** *If* $B \sqsubseteq_{post} B1$, *then* $A \mathbin{\raise.3ex\hbox{$\scriptstyle\S$}} B \sqsubseteq_{post} A \mathbin{\raise.3ex\hbox{$\scriptstyle\S$}} B1$.

As with Law 10, we note that $B \sqsubseteq_{post} B1$ holds if $B \sqsubseteq B1$ and $B$ is total.

Finally (and somewhat uninterestingly), we observe that both components of a composition can be refined safely if they (and their refinements) act on disjoint parts of the state.

**Law 20.** *If* $A \sqsubseteq A1$, $B \sqsubseteq B1$, $Vars(A) \cap Vars(B) = \varnothing$, $Vars(A1) = Vars(A)$ *and* $Vars(B1) = Vars(B)$, *then* $A \mathbin{\raise.3ex\hbox{$\scriptstyle\S$}} B \sqsubseteq A1 \mathbin{\raise.3ex\hbox{$\scriptstyle\S$}} B1$.

Once again, we have a range of conditions that can be used to show that components of a composition can be refined safely, ranging from the general conditions in Laws 16 and 18 to the simpler Laws 17 and 19 which will suffice in most practical situations.

# 5    Data Refinement

A *Z data type specification* (cf. [3]) is a triple $(State, Init, Ops)$, where $State$ is a schema describing the set of values the type may assume, $Init$ is an initialisation schema over $State$ describing the possible initial states, and $Ops$ is a set of operation schemas over $State$ describing the operations that may be performed. Two Z data type specifications are *compatible* if there is a one to one mapping between their sets of operations, and corresponding pairs of operations have the same inputs and outputs. Spivey [1] builds this mapping into the operation names, so $AddBirthday1$ is the concrete version of $AddBirthday$, etc.

Let $A = (S_A, Init_A, Ops_A)$ and $C = (S_C, Init_C, Ops_C)$ be compatible Z data type specifications.

**Definition 8.** (*Data Refinement*) $C$ *is a* data refinement *of* $A$, *with respect to a given abstraction relation Abs, written* $A \sqsubseteq_{Abs} C$, *iff:*

- *Every initial state of $C$ corresponds to some initial state of $A$.*[8]

$$\forall S'_C \bullet Init_C \Rightarrow (\exists S'_A \bullet Init_A \wedge Abs') \tag{5}$$

---

[8] We assume that initial states are define in terms of post-state variables. If initial states are defined in terms of pre-state variables, as in [1], the condition is: $\forall S_C \bullet Init_C \Rightarrow (\exists S_A \bullet Init_A \wedge Abs)$.

- *For every corresponding pair of operations, $Op_A$ and $Op_C$, we have:*

Applicability:

$$\forall S_A; S_C; x? : X \bullet \\ \text{pre } Op_A \wedge Abs \Rightarrow \text{pre } Op_C \tag{6}$$

*Correctness:*

$$\forall S_A; S_C; S_C'; x? : X; y! : Y \bullet \\ \text{pre } Op_A \wedge Abs \wedge Op_C \Rightarrow (\exists S_A' \bullet Op_A \wedge Abs') \tag{7}$$

Since we are primarily interested in the relationship between two operations, we introduce the notation $Op_A \sqsubseteq_{Abs} Op_C$ to mean that conditions (6) and (7) hold for operations $Op_A$ and $Op_C$ and abstraction relation $Abs$.

If the abstraction relation is a total function from concrete states to abstract states (i.e. if $\forall S_C \bullet \exists_1 S_A \bullet Abs$ holds), condition (7) becomes:

$$\forall S_A; S_A'; S_C; S_C'; x? : X; y! : Y \bullet \\ \text{pre } Op_A \wedge Abs \wedge Abs' \wedge Op_C \Rightarrow Op_A \tag{8}$$

## 6    Monotonicity for Data Refinement

This section defines monotonicity with respect to data refinement, and presents some results regarding monotonicity of schema operators with respect to data refinement. We can adapt the definition of monotonicity with respect to operation refinement, to define monotonicity with respect to data refinement, as follows.

**Definition 9.** ($\sqsubseteq_{Abs}$-*Monotonicity 1*) *An n-ary schema operator $\mathcal{F}$ is monotonic with respect to data refinement with abstraction relation Abs in its kth argument, for $1 \leq k \leq n$, if $S \sqsubseteq_{Abs} S'$ implies $\mathcal{F}(a_1, \cdots, a_{k-1}, S, a_{k+1}, \cdots, a_n) \sqsubseteq_{Abs} \mathcal{F}(a_1, \cdots, a_{k-1}, S', a_{k+1}, \cdots, a_n)$.*

It only makes sense to data refine a single component of a specification if its state is disjoint from the states of the other components, in which case it is easy to demonstrate monotonicity. We will prove the case for conjunction; the proofs for disjunction and composition are similar.

**Law 21.** *Let $A$, $B$ and $C$ be operations on pairwise disjoint states $S_A$, $S_B$ and $S_C$, and let Abs be an abstraction relation between $S_A$ and $S_B$ such that $A \sqsubseteq_{Abs} B$, then $A \wedge C \sqsubseteq_{Abs} B \wedge C$.*

*Proof.*

| *Applicability:* | *Correctness:* |
|---|---|

$$\text{pre}\,(A \wedge C) \wedge Abs$$

$$\equiv \Big\langle \text{Law 1(iv)};\ S_A \text{ and } S_C \text{ disjoint} \Big\rangle$$

$$\text{pre}\,A \wedge \text{pre}\,C \wedge Abs$$

$$\Rightarrow \Big\langle \text{Applicability of } A \sqsubseteq_{Abs} B \Big\rangle$$

$$\text{pre}\,B \wedge \text{pre}\,C$$

$$\equiv \Big\langle \text{Law 1(iv)};\ S_B \text{ and } S_C \text{ disjoint} \Big\rangle$$

$$\text{pre}\,(B \wedge C)$$

$$\text{pre}\,(A \wedge C) \wedge Abs \wedge B \wedge C$$

$$\equiv \Big\langle \text{Law 1(iv)};\ S_A \text{ and } S_C \text{ disjoint} \Big\rangle$$

$$\text{pre}\,A \wedge \text{pre}\,C \wedge Abs \wedge B \wedge C$$

$$\Rightarrow \left\langle \begin{array}{l} \text{Correctness of } A \sqsubseteq_{Abs} B; \\ \text{Definition of pre } C \end{array} \right\rangle$$

$$(\exists\,S'_A \bullet Abs' \wedge A) \wedge (\exists\,S'_C \bullet C)$$

$$\equiv \left\langle \begin{array}{l} S'_A \text{ not free in } C; \\ S'_C \text{ not free in } Abs' \text{ or } A \end{array} \right\rangle$$

$$(\exists\,S'_A;\ S'_B \bullet Abs' \wedge A \wedge B)$$

A more interesting case is the where two or more components have the same state and are data refined in the same way. This is captured in the following definition for binary schema operators, but can easily be extended to operators of higher arity.

**Definition 10.** ($\sqsubseteq_{Abs}$-*Monotonicity 2*) *A binary schema operator $\mathcal{F}$ is monotonic with respect to data refinement with abstraction relation Abs, iff $A_1 \sqsubseteq_{Abs} B_1$ and $A_2 \sqsubseteq_{Abs} B_2$ implies $\mathcal{F}(A_1, A_2) \sqsubseteq_{Abs} \mathcal{F}(B_1, B_2)$.*

We now consider the situations under which the principal schema operators are monotonic with respect to data refinement. We only consider conjunction, disjunction and override in detail. Data refinement of sequential compositions will be discussed further in Section 7; similar comments apply to the other operators as noted in Section 4

In the rest of this section, we assume that an abstract operation $A$ is defined in terms of two partial operations $A_1$ and $A_2$, defined on state $S_A$, and that $A_1$ and $A_2$ are data refined by $C_1$ and $C_2$, respectively, defined on state $S_C$, via abstraction relation $Abs$. Expanding the assumptions that $A_1 \sqsubseteq_{Abs} C_1$ and $A_2 \sqsubseteq_{Abs} C_2$, we get (omitting outer universal quantifiers):

$$\text{pre}\,A_1 \wedge Abs \Rightarrow \text{pre}\,C_1 \tag{9}$$

$$\text{pre}\,A_1 \wedge Abs \wedge C_1 \Rightarrow (\exists\,S'_A \bullet A_1 \wedge Abs') \tag{10}$$

$$\text{pre}\,A_2 \wedge Abs \Rightarrow \text{pre}\,C_2 \tag{11}$$

$$\text{pre}\,A_2 \wedge Abs \wedge C_2 \Rightarrow (\exists\,S'_A \bullet A_2 \wedge Abs') \tag{12}$$

## 6.1    Conjunction

Suppose $A$ is defined as the conjunction of $A_1$ and $A_2$, i.e. $A = A_1 \wedge A_2$. We want to determine under what additional conditions $A$ is refined by $C = C_1 \wedge C_2$. In order for $A \sqsubseteq_{Abs} C$ to hold, we must be able to show:

$$\mathrm{pre}\,(A_1 \wedge A_2) \wedge Abs \Rightarrow \mathrm{pre}\,(C_1 \wedge C_2) \tag{13}$$

$$\mathrm{pre}\,(A_1 \wedge A_2) \wedge Abs \wedge C_1 \wedge C_2 \Rightarrow (\exists\, S'_A \bullet A_1 \wedge A_2 \wedge Abs') \tag{14}$$

First, consider (13):

$$\mathrm{pre}\,(A_1 \wedge A_2) \wedge Abs$$
$$\Rightarrow \quad \Big\langle\, \mathrm{Law}\ 1\mathrm{(iii)} \,\Big\rangle$$
$$\mathrm{pre}\,A_1 \wedge \mathrm{pre}\,A_2 \wedge Abs$$
$$\Rightarrow \quad \Big\langle\, \mathrm{Assumptions}\ (9)\ \mathrm{and}\ (11) \,\Big\rangle$$
$$\mathrm{pre}\,C_1 \wedge \mathrm{pre}\,C_2$$

We can deduce $\mathrm{pre}\,(C_1 \wedge C_2)$ if we can infer $\mathrm{pre}\,C_1 \wedge \mathrm{pre}\,C_2 \Rightarrow \mathrm{pre}\,(C_1 \wedge C_2)$ from $\mathrm{pre}\,(A_1 \wedge A_2) \wedge Abs$, i.e. if $C_1$ and $C_2$ are consistent whenever $A_1$ and $A_2$ are consistent for corresponding states.

Now, consider (14):

$$\mathrm{pre}\,(A_1 \wedge A_2) \wedge Abs \wedge C_1 \wedge C_2$$
$$\Rightarrow \quad \Big\langle\, \mathrm{Law}\ 1\mathrm{(iii)} \,\Big\rangle$$
$$\mathrm{pre}\,A_1 \wedge \mathrm{pre}\,A_2 \wedge Abs \wedge C_1 \wedge C_2$$
$$\Rightarrow \quad \Big\langle\, \mathrm{Assumptions}\ (10)\ \mathrm{and}\ (12) \,\Big\rangle$$
$$(\exists\, S'_A \bullet A_1 \wedge Abs') \wedge (\exists\, S'_A \bullet A_2 \wedge Abs')$$

In order to deduce $(\exists\, S'_A \bullet A_1 \wedge A_2 \wedge Abs')$, we must now show that the two existential quantifiers can have the same witness. This can be inferred if we assume that $Abs$ is functional, or if $A_1$ and $A_2$ act on disjoint parts of the state.

Thus, we have the following laws.

**Law 22.** *If $A_1 \sqsubseteq_{Abs} C_1$, $A_2 \sqsubseteq_{Abs} C_2$, $C_1$ and $C_2$ are consistent whenever $A_1$ and $A_2$ are consistent for corresponding states, and $Abs$ is functional, then $A_1 \wedge A_2 \sqsubseteq_{Abs} C_1 \wedge C_2$.*

**Law 23.** *If $A_1 \sqsubseteq_{Abs} C_1$, $A_2 \sqsubseteq_{Abs} C_2$, $C_1$ and $C_2$ are consistent whenever $A_1$ and $A_2$ are consistent for corresponding states, and $Vars(A_1) \cap Vars(A_2) = \varnothing$, then $A_1 \wedge A_2 \sqsubseteq_{Abs} C_1 \wedge C_2$.*

We can simplify these law as we did in Section 4.1, by replacing the consistency condition by the requirement that $C_1$ and $C_2$ act on disjoint parts of the state, or that either $C_1$ or $C_2$ does not constrain its post-state variables (cf. Laws 4 and 5). The former condition will hold if $A_1$ and $A_2$ act on disjoint parts of the abstract state and this disjointness is preserved by the abstraction relation.

Data refining a conjunction can violate both of the data refinement conditions. The additional conditions required to ensure applicability are similar to those discussed in Section 4.1, and the same comments apply about their practicality. To ensure correctness, we need to guarantee that the same abstract value can represent the result of both concrete components. We can do this if the abstraction relation is function, which is quite common in practice, or if the concrete components act on disjoint parts of the state, which is common in many uses of conjunction.

## 6.2    Disjunction

Suppose $A$ is defined as the disjunction of $A_1$ and $A_2$, i.e. $A = A_1 \vee A_2$. We want to determine under what additional conditions $A$ is refined by $C = C_1 \vee C_2$. In order for $A \sqsubseteq_{Abs} C$ to hold, we must be able to show:

$$\text{pre}\,(A_1 \vee A_2) \wedge Abs \Rightarrow \text{pre}\,(C_1 \vee C_2) \tag{15}$$
$$\text{pre}\,(A_1 \vee A_2) \wedge Abs \wedge (C_1 \vee C_2) \Rightarrow (\exists\, S'_A \bullet (A_1 \vee A_2) \wedge Abs') \tag{16}$$

Now, (15) follows from (9) and (11) above:

$$\text{pre}\,(A_1 \vee A_2) \wedge Abs$$
$$\equiv \quad \Big\langle\, \text{Law 1(ii); Logic} \,\Big\rangle$$
$$(\text{pre}\,A_1 \wedge Abs) \vee (\text{pre}\,A_2 \wedge Abs)$$
$$\Rightarrow \quad \Big\langle\, \text{Assumptions (9) and (11); Law 1(ii)} \,\Big\rangle$$
$$\text{pre}\,(C_1 \vee C_2)$$

To see under what conditions (16) holds, let us calculate:

$$\text{pre}\,(A_1 \vee A_2) \wedge Abs \wedge (C_1 \vee C_2)$$
$$\equiv \quad \Big\langle\, \text{Law 1(ii); Logic} \,\Big\rangle$$
$$(\text{pre}\,A_1 \wedge Abs \wedge C_1) \vee (\text{pre}\,A_1 \wedge Abs \wedge C_2) \vee$$
$$(\text{pre}\,A_2 \wedge Abs \wedge C_1) \vee (\text{pre}\,A_2 \wedge Abs \wedge C_2)$$
$$\Rightarrow \quad \Big\langle\, \text{Assumptions (10) and (12); Logic} \,\Big\rangle$$
$$(\exists\, S'_A \bullet (A_1 \vee A_2) \wedge Abs') \vee (\text{pre}\,A_1 \wedge Abs \wedge C_2) \vee (\text{pre}\,A_2 \wedge Abs \wedge C_1)$$

Since we cannot proceed further without additional assumptions, we have the following law.

**Law 24.** *If $A_1 \sqsubseteq_{Abs} C_1$, $A_2 \sqsubseteq_{Abs} C_2$, and* pre $(A_1 \vee A_2) \wedge Abs \wedge (C_1 \vee C_2)$ *implies* (pre $A_1 \wedge Abs \wedge C_2$) $\vee$ (pre $A_2 \wedge Abs \wedge C_1$), *then* $A_1 \vee A_2 \sqsubseteq_{Abs} C_1 \vee C_2$.

The extra assumption ensures that the data refined components do not add new behaviours starting from concrete states related by $Abs$ to a state in the precondition of the abstract version of the other component. This can be simplified in ways similar to those discussed in Section 4.2. For example, we can simply disallow this kind of overlap between the preconditions of operations (cf. Law 8).

**Law 25.** *If $A_1 \sqsubseteq_{Abs} C_1$, $A_2 \sqsubseteq_{Abs} C_2$,* pre $A_2 \wedge Abs \Rightarrow \neg$ pre $C_1$, *and* pre $A_1 \wedge Abs \Rightarrow \neg$ pre $C_2$, *then* $A_1 \vee A_2 \sqsubseteq_{Abs} C_1 \vee C_2$.

Or we can require that the data refined components have disjoint preconditions, in which case the preconditions of the original components must also be disjoint (cf. Law 9).

**Law 26.** *If $A_1 \sqsubseteq_{Abs} C_1$, $A_2 \sqsubseteq_{Abs} C_2$, and* pre $C_1 \Rightarrow \neg$ pre $C_2$, *then* $A_1 \vee A_2 \sqsubseteq_{Abs} C_1 \vee C_2$.

As with operation refinement, data refinement a disjunction can only violate the correctness condition. The additional conditions required to ensure applicability are similar to those discussed in Section 4.1, but with the additional effect of the abstraction relation. The condition for Law 25 can be guaranteed if the abstraction relation preserves disjointness of the preconditions of the components of disjunction, which we would always expect in practice. For example, if the abstract operation chooses between two components according to whether a set is empty or whether a given element belongs to a set, we must be able to make the same choice on the basis of the representation of the set. The condition for Law 26 is also like to hold in many practical situations. It thus appears than data refinement of disjunction will be safe in most cases.

## 6.3    Override

Suppose $A$ is defined as the override of $A_1$ by $A_2$, i.e. $A = A_1 \oplus A_2$. We want to determine under what additional conditions $A$ is refined by $C = C_1 \oplus C_2$. In order for $A \sqsubseteq_{Abs} C$ to hold, we must be able to show:

$$\text{pre } (A_1 \oplus A_2) \wedge Abs \Rightarrow \text{pre } (C_1 \oplus C_2) \tag{17}$$

$$\text{pre } (A_1 \oplus A_2) \wedge Abs \wedge (C_1 \oplus C_2) \Rightarrow (\exists S'_A \bullet (A_1 \oplus A_2) \wedge Abs') \tag{18}$$

Now, (17) follows from (9) and (11) above:

$\text{pre}\,(A_1 \oplus A_2) \wedge \textit{Abs}$

$\equiv \quad \Big\langle \text{Law 1(vi)} \Big\rangle$

$(\text{pre}\,A_1 \vee \text{pre}\,A_2) \wedge \textit{Abs}$

$\Rightarrow \quad \Big\langle \text{Logic; Assumptions (9) and (11)} \Big\rangle$

$\text{pre}\,C_1 \vee \text{pre}\,C_2$

$\equiv \quad \Big\langle \text{Law 1(vi)} \Big\rangle$

$\text{pre}\,(C_1 \oplus C_2)$

To see under what conditions (18) holds, let us calculate:

$\text{pre}\,(A_1 \oplus A_2) \wedge \textit{Abs} \wedge (C_1 \oplus C_2)$

$\equiv \quad \Big\langle \text{Law 1(vi); Definition of } \oplus \Big\rangle$

$(\text{pre}\,A_1 \vee \text{pre}\,A_2) \wedge \textit{Abs} \wedge (\neg\,\text{pre}\,C_2 \wedge C_1 \vee C_2)$

$\equiv \quad \Big\langle \text{Logic; Assumption (11) excludes pre}\,A_2 \wedge \textit{Abs} \wedge \neg\,\text{pre}\,C_2 \wedge C_1 \Big\rangle$

$(\text{pre}\,A_1 \wedge \textit{Abs} \wedge \neg\,\text{pre}\,C_2 \wedge C_1) \vee (\text{pre}\,A_1 \wedge \textit{Abs} \wedge C_2) \vee (\text{pre}\,A_2 \wedge \textit{Abs} \wedge C_2)$

$\Rightarrow \quad \Big\langle \text{Assumptions (10) and (12)} \Big\rangle$

$(\neg\,\text{pre}\,C_2 \wedge (\exists\,S_A' \bullet A_1 \wedge \textit{Abs}')) \vee (\text{pre}\,A_1 \wedge C_2 \wedge \textit{Abs}) \vee (\exists\,S_A' \bullet A_2 \wedge \textit{Abs}')$

$\equiv \quad \Big\langle \text{Logic; } S_A' \text{ not free in } \neg\,\text{pre}\,C_2 \Big\rangle$

$(\exists\,S_A' \bullet (\neg\,\text{pre}\,C_2 \wedge A_1 \vee A_2) \wedge \textit{Abs}') \vee (\text{pre}\,A_1 \wedge C_2 \wedge \textit{Abs})$

$\equiv \quad \Big\langle \text{Definition of } \oplus \Big\rangle$

$(\exists\,S_A' \bullet (A_1 \oplus A_2) \wedge \textit{Abs}') \vee (\text{pre}\,A_1 \wedge C_2 \wedge \textit{Abs})$

Since we cannot proceed further without additional assumptions, we have the following law.

**Law 27.** *If* $A_1 \sqsubseteq_{Abs} C_1$, $A_2 \sqsubseteq_{Abs} C_2$, *and* $\text{pre}\,(A_1 \oplus A_2) \wedge \textit{Abs} \wedge (C_1 \oplus C_2)$ *implies* $\text{pre}\,A_1 \wedge C_2 \wedge \textit{Abs}$, *then* $A_1 \oplus A_2 \sqsubseteq_{Abs} C_1 \oplus C_2$.

As in Section 6.2, we can simplify this law in several ways. For example, we can exclude the case where $\text{pre}\,A_1 \wedge C_2 \wedge \textit{Abs}$ holds, i.e. where $\textit{Abs}$ maps a state in the precondition of $A_1$ to a state from which $C_2$ can be satisfied with the following law (cf. conditions for Law 25).

**Law 28.** *If* $A_1 \sqsubseteq_{Abs} C_1$, $A_2 \sqsubseteq_{Abs} C_2$, *and* $\text{pre}\,A_1 \wedge \textit{Abs} \Rightarrow \neg\,\text{pre}\,C_2$, *then* $A_1 \oplus A_2 \sqsubseteq_{Abs} C_1 \oplus C_2$.

# 7    Calculating Data Refinements

It is well known that when the abstraction relation is a total surjective function from concrete states to abstract states, we can calculate the least refined data refinement of a specification, and that any data refinement of the abstract specification is an operation refinement of the calculated data refinement (see [1, 2, 3]). We will now consider what happens when we attempt to calculate the least refined data refinement of a specification defined using the principal schema operators.

Suppose $A$ and $Abs$ are defined as follows, where $f$ is a total surjective function from $S_C$ to $S_A$:

$$A = [\Delta S_A \mid a]$$
$$Abs = [S_A; S_C \mid \theta S_A = f(\theta S_C)]$$

Then the least refined data refinement of $A$ with respect to $Abs$ is given by $Abs \mathbin{\fatsemi} A \mathbin{\fatsemi} Abs'$.[9] From the above assumptions, we have:

$$Abs \mathbin{\fatsemi} A \mathbin{\fatsemi} Abs' \equiv [\Delta S_C \mid a[f(\theta S_C), f(\theta S_C')/\theta S_A, \theta S_A']] \tag{19}$$

Now, also suppose that $A_1$ and $A_2$ are defined as:

$$A_1 = [\Delta S_A \mid a_1]$$
$$A_2 = [\Delta S_A \mid a_2]$$

We can calculate the least refined data refinements of $A_1 \wedge A_2$, $A_1 \vee A_2$ and $A_1 \mathbin{\fatsemi} A_2$, by calculate the least refined data refinements of $A_1$ and $A_2$.

**Law 29.** $Abs \mathbin{\fatsemi} (A_1 \wedge A_2) \mathbin{\fatsemi} Abs' \equiv (Abs \mathbin{\fatsemi} A_1 \mathbin{\fatsemi} Abs') \wedge (Abs \mathbin{\fatsemi} A_2 \mathbin{\fatsemi} Abs')$

*Proof.*

$\quad Abs \mathbin{\fatsemi} (A_1 \wedge A_2) \mathbin{\fatsemi} Abs'$

$\equiv \quad \Big\langle$ Definitions of $A_1$ and $A_2$; Schema calculus $\Big\rangle$

$\quad Abs \mathbin{\fatsemi} [\Delta S_A \mid a_1 \wedge a_2] \mathbin{\fatsemi} Abs'$

$\equiv \quad \Big\langle$ From (19); Schema calculus $\Big\rangle$

$\quad [\Delta S_C \mid a_1[f(\theta S_C), f(\theta S_C')/\theta S_A, \theta S_A']] \wedge [\Delta S_C \mid a_2[f(\theta S_C), f(\theta S_C')/\theta S_A, \theta S_A']]$

$\equiv \quad \Big\langle$ From (19); Definitions of $A_1$ and $A_2$ $\Big\rangle$

$\quad (Abs \mathbin{\fatsemi} A_1 \mathbin{\fatsemi} Abs') \wedge (Abs \mathbin{\fatsemi} A_2 \mathbin{\fatsemi} Abs')$

---

[9] To simplify this result and the ensuing calculations, we abuse the definition of $\mathbin{\fatsemi}$, to allow schemas to be composed other than via their pre- and post-state variables. If $U$ and $V$ are schemas, with signatures $X; Y$ and $Y; Z$, then $U \mathbin{\fatsemi} V$ is $\exists Y \bullet U \wedge V$.

**Law 30.** $Abs \, \raisebox{0.3ex}{\(_9^9\)} \, (A_1 \vee A_2) \, \raisebox{0.3ex}{\(_9^9\)} \, Abs' \equiv (Abs \, \raisebox{0.3ex}{\(_9^9\)} \, A_1 \, \raisebox{0.3ex}{\(_9^9\)} \, Abs') \vee (Abs \, \raisebox{0.3ex}{\(_9^9\)} \, A_2 \, \raisebox{0.3ex}{\(_9^9\)} \, Abs')$

*Proof.* Almost identical to the proof for Law 29.

**Law 31.** $Abs \, \raisebox{0.3ex}{\(_9^9\)} \, (A_1 \, \raisebox{0.3ex}{\(_9^9\)} \, A_2) \, \raisebox{0.3ex}{\(_9^9\)} \, Abs' \equiv (Abs \, \raisebox{0.3ex}{\(_9^9\)} \, A_1 \, \raisebox{0.3ex}{\(_9^9\)} \, Abs') \, \raisebox{0.3ex}{\(_9^9\)} \, (Abs \, \raisebox{0.3ex}{\(_9^9\)} \, A_2 \, \raisebox{0.3ex}{\(_9^9\)} \, Abs')$

*Proof.*

$$Abs \, \raisebox{0.3ex}{\(_9^9\)} \, (A_1 \, \raisebox{0.3ex}{\(_9^9\)} \, A_2) \, \raisebox{0.3ex}{\(_9^9\)} \, Abs'$$
$$\equiv \quad \Big\langle \text{ Definitions of } \raisebox{0.3ex}{\(_9^9\)}, A_1 \text{ and } A_2; \text{ Schema calculus } \Big\rangle$$
$$Abs \, \raisebox{0.3ex}{\(_9^9\)} \, [\Delta S_A \mid \exists S''_A \bullet a_1[S''_A/S'_A] \wedge a_2[S''_A/S_A]] \, \raisebox{0.3ex}{\(_9^9\)} \, Abs'$$
$$\equiv \quad \Big\langle \text{ From (19) } \Big\rangle$$
$$[\Delta S_A \mid (\exists S''_A \bullet a_1[S''_A/S'_A] \wedge a_2[S''_A/S_A])[f(\theta S_C), f(\theta S'_C)/\theta S_A, \theta S'_A]]$$
$$\equiv \quad \Big\langle \text{ Distribute substitution; Schema calculus } \Big\rangle$$
$$\exists S''_A \bullet [\Delta S_A \mid a_1][f(\theta S_C), f(\theta S'_C)/\theta S_A, \theta S'_A] \wedge$$
$$[\Delta S_A \mid a_2][f(\theta S_C), f(\theta S'_C)/\theta S_A, \theta S'_A]$$
$$\equiv \quad \Big\langle \text{ From (19); Schema calculus } \Big\rangle$$
$$(Abs \, \raisebox{0.3ex}{\(_9^9\)} \, A_1 \, \raisebox{0.3ex}{\(_9^9\)} \, Abs') \, \raisebox{0.3ex}{\(_9^9\)} \, (Abs \, \raisebox{0.3ex}{\(_9^9\)} \, A_2 \, \raisebox{0.3ex}{\(_9^9\)} \, Abs')$$

This can be proved more easily if $Abs$ is also injective, since then we have $Abs' \, \raisebox{0.3ex}{\(_9^9\)} \, Abs = \text{id}$, and the result follows since $\raisebox{0.3ex}{\(_9^9\)}$ is associative in this case.

Thus, when the abstraction relation is a total surjective function, we can perform a component-wise refinement by calculating the least refined data refinement of a composite specification. We can then perform operation refinement on the resulting specification using the techniques presented in Section 4.

## 8    Discussion

One of the most appealing aspects of Z is the way that the schema calculus can be used to compose specifications by combining fragments describing different aspects of the system being described. It is often desirable to be able to preserve this structure when specifications are refined to more concrete forms in preparation for being turned into code, but our ability to do so is limited by the non-monotonicity of the principal schema calculus operators. The operators that matter most are conjunction and disjunction, and to a lesser extent composition, since these are the ones most heavily used [6], and most of the others are either trivially monotonic or pathologically non-monotonic.

Modifying the definitions of these operators so that they are monotonic generally leads to operators that do not have the same intuitive appeal as the existing ones, and are thus more likely to lead to errors in specifications. Modifying the definition of refinement leads to similar problems.

We have examined the way in which the principal schema calculus operators fail to be monotonic, and identified additional conditions under which they are monotonic. The most general conditions are quite complicated, but there are a range of simpler conditions which are easier to test if they are applicable. Our results for data refinement rely on those for operation refinement. In some cases we also required abstraction relations to be functional, or total, or to preserve aspects of the structure of the abstract specification. These conditions deserved further investigation, since they may provide additional insight into the nature of data refinement.

The question remains as to how widely applicable these conditions are. They certainly cover the majority of examples found in Z text books and other published specifications, where conjunctions are mostly used to combine partial specifications relating to different parts of the state and disjunctions are used almost exclusively to combine partial specifications with disjoint preconditions. Likewise, most practical uses of data refinement do use functional abstraction relations, and in any case the restriction to functional abstraction relations may be able to be overcome by using history variables. The requirement that abstraction relations should preserve the consistency of components of conjunctions and the disjointness of the preconditions of disjunctions seem quite reasonable — indeed, failure of such conditions would usually reveal an inadequacy in the proposed data representation. There are, of course, always going to be cases where the simpler conditions do not apply, but as long as there are sufficiently few of them, using the more general conditions for these cases should not be too onerous.

It remains to examine larger examples and case studies to see how often the various cases we have identified do occur, and to extend our results to common patterns of use of the schema calculus, especially promotion to see how they compare to the results presented in [11] and [2]. It would be interesting to define counterparts of pre- and post-refinement for data refinement, which might allow additional laws and/or simpler proofs of existing laws. Finally, it would also be interesting to attempt to extend the results for data refinement to include backward simulation [2, 3].

## Acknowledgements

I wish to thank Martin Henson and Steve Reeves for many fruitful discussions, the anonymous referees for their detailed and helpful comments, and the Foundation for Research, Science and Technology for financial support.

## References

1. Michael Spivey. *The Z Notation: A Reference Manual.* Prentice-Hall International, 1988. Second edition, 1992.
2. Jim Woodcock and Jim Davies. *Using Z: Specification, Refinement and Proof.* Prentice-Hall International, 1996.

3. John Derrick and Eerke Boiten. *Refinement in Z and Object-Z: Foundations and Advanced Applications*. Springer-Verlag, 2001.
4. Martin C. Henson and Steve Reeves. Program development and specification refinement in the schema calculus. In J.P. Bowen, S. Dunne, A. Galloway, and S. King, editors, *Proceedings of ZB2000: Formal Specification and Development in Z and B*, number 1878 in LNCS, pages 344–362. Springer, September 2000.
5. Lindsay Groves. Refinement and the Z schema calculus. In Jim Woodcock, John Derrick, Eerke Boiten, and Joakim von Wright, editors, *Proc. REFINE'02, Copenhagen, July 20-21, 2002*, volume 70, number 3 of *Electronic Notes in Theoretical Computer Science*, 2002. (See http://www.mcs.vuw.ac.nz/~lindsay/Papers.).
6. Rosalind Barden, Susan Stepney, and David Cooper. The use of Z. In J. E. Nicholls, editor, *Proc. 6th Z User Meeting, York 1991*, Workshops in Computing, pages 99–124. Springer-Verlag, 1992.
7. Ian Hayes. *Specification Case Studies*. Prentice-Hall, second edition, 1993.
8. Carroll Morgan. *Programming from Specifications*. Prentice Hall, second edition, 1994.
9. Ralph-Johan Back and Joakim von Wright. *Refinement Calculus: A Systematic Introduction*. Graduate Texts in Computer Science. Springer-Verlag, 1998.
10. John Wordsworth. *Software Development with Z*. Addison-Wesley, 1992.
11. J. C. P. Woodcock. Implementing promoted operations in Z. In Cliff B. Jones, Roger C. Shaw, and Tim Denvir, editors, *Proceedings of the 5th BCS Refinement Workshop*, pages 367–378. Springer-Verlag, 1992.

# Slicing Object-Z Specifications for Verification[*]

Ingo Brückner[1] and Heike Wehrheim[2]

[1] Universität Oldenburg, Department für Informatik, 26111 Oldenburg, Germany
`ingo.brueckner@informatik.uni-oldenburg.de`
[2] Universität Paderborn, Institut für Informatik, 33098 Paderborn, Germany
`wehrheim@uni-paderborn.de`

**Abstract.** Slicing is the activity of reducing a program or a specification with respect to a given condition (the slicing criterion) such that the condition holds on the full program if and only if it holds on the reduced program. Originating from program analysis the entity to be sliced is usually a program and the slicing criterion a value of a variable at a certain program point. In this paper we present an approach to slicing Object-Z specifications with temporal logic formulae as slicing criteria and show the correctness of our approach. The underlying motivation is the goal to substantially reduce the size of the specification and subsequently facilitate verification of temporal logic properties.

## 1 Introduction

Program slicing has been introduced by Weiser [18, 19] as a technique for reducing programs with respect to some criteria under interest. The title of his first article already suggests what the main idea of slicing and its main application was (and partly still is): "programmers use slices when debugging". Whenever a variable turns out to have a wrong value at a certain program statement programmers are interested in finding out what the part (slice) of the program is which influences this variable value, and for debugging they just want to look at that part. This is exactly what slicing is doing for them. Ever since this first article a huge number of publications on slicing have appeared, introducing slicing techniques in various flavours and for various types of programs (with procedure calls, pointers, concurrency etc.). For a general survey see [15]. Recently, slicing techniques have been transferred to the area of model checking [10, 8] where the slicing criterion is no longer a variable value but a temporal logic formula. In these works slicing should guarantee that the property specified by the formula holds on the reduced program/specification if and only if it holds on the full program/specification. This is similar to the technique of cone-of-influence reduction used in hardware verification [3].

---

[*] This work was partly supported by the German Research Council (DFG) as part of the Transregional Collaborative Research Center "Automatic Verification and Analysis of Complex Systems" (SFB/TR 14 AVACS). See `www.avacs.org` for more information.

H. Treharne et al. (Eds.): ZB 2005, LNCS 3455, pp. 414–433, 2005.

In this paper, we suggest a method for slicing Object-Z specifications with respect to formulas of an interval based temporal logic over states and events. To this end a dependence graph of the specification is build which precisely reflects data and control dependencies. Starting from the atomic propositions in the formula this graph is traversed in a backward direction thus determining the part of the specification which potentially influences these atomic propositions. We show that the remaining part of the specification can safely be omitted when checking for the holding of the formula since the formula holds on the full specification iff it holds on its slice. This can substantially reduce the size of the Object-Z specification and thus the state space during verification of temporal logic properties.

A related approach has been presented in [17, 16] where slicing techniques have been used to determine whether changes of a specification might influence already proven properties. In contrast to the work there we will here build a dependence graph with a much finer granularity. Dependencies will be determined on the level of *predicates* not complete schemas. This allows to omit some predicates in a schema while keeping other necessary parts. Moreover, we will use a state- and event-based temporal logic for property specification instead of ordinary LTL. The logic is inspired by the Duration Calculus (DC) [21], however, omitting the time. The reason for choosing a logic talking about events for a state-based formalism lies in our ultimate goal of extending this work to CSP-OZ [7], a combination of Object-Z with the process algebra CSP, and finally to CSP-OZ-DC [9] which additionally adds Duration Calculus formulae (for specifying timing constraints) to CSP-OZ. Properties will in the final setting be expressed in DC (which is one of the reasons for choosing a timeless variant of DC here).

The paper is structured as follows. In the next section we introduce Object-Z (or more precisely, the Object-Z part of CSP-OZ) by means of a small example which we later use for slicing. Furthermore, following Winter and Smith [20] we define a Kripke structure semantics for Object-Z. This is used as the basis for interpreting the temporal logic (SE-IL) formulae. Section 3 will then present the construction of the dependence graph and the slicing algorithm, and illustrate both on the running example. The slicing algorithm will be proven correct with respect to preservation of the SE-IL property under interest in section 4. The last section concludes.

## 2   Background

This section sets the background for our work on slicing Object-Z specifications. We briefly describe Object-Z [13, 6] by means of an example that we will later use for slicing. Furthermore we introduce the temporal logic and explain how to give a Kripke structure semantics to Object-Z so that the holding of formulae for Object-Z specifications can be defined. Finally, we give a definition of projection, which is the relation used to compare full and reduced specification.

*Example.* The example is inspired by the Tic-Tac-Toe specification of [5], but has been slightly modified to serve as a good example for slicing. Tic-Tac-Toe is a game involving two players (called black and white) and a board with 9 positions in a 3-by-3 array.

| 0 | 1 | 2 |
|---|---|---|
| 3 | 4 | 5 |
| 6 | 7 | 8 |

The players take turns to move. A move consists of choosing a free position and adding it to the players owned positions. The goal (in our modified version) is to obtain as many diagonal, vertical or horizontal lines with three positions as possible[1]. The game ends when all positions are occupied.

$$Posn == 0..8$$

The function *inLine* determines whether a set of positions contains a line with three positions, the function *lines* counts the number of three-position lines.

$$inLine : \mathbb{P}\,Posn \to \mathbb{B}$$

$$\forall ps : \mathbb{P}\,Posn \bullet$$
$$inLine(ps) \Leftrightarrow$$
$$\exists s : \{\{0,1,2\},\{3,4,5\},\{6,7,8\},\{0,3,6,\}$$
$$\{1,4,7\},\{2,5,8\},\{0,4,8\},\{2,4,6\}\} \bullet s \subseteq ps$$

$$lines : \mathbb{P}\,Posn \to \mathbb{N}$$

$$\forall ps : \mathbb{P}\,Posn \bullet$$
$$lines(ps) = \#\{x,y,z : Posn \mid \{x,y,z\} \subseteq ps \wedge inLine(\{x,y,z\}) \bullet \{x,y,z\}\}$$

The game has three possible outcomes:

$$Result ::= black\_wins \mid white\_wins \mid draw$$

The following is the specification of the class *TicTacToe*. It is not exactly Object-Z but the Object-Z part of a CSP-OZ [7] specification[2]. The difference can be found in the schemas for methods: in CSP-OZ a method $m$ can be specified by giving an *enable* schema defining a guard to the execution of the method plus an *effect* schema defining the actual execution.

---

[1] This is the difference to the usual Tic-Tac-Toe where the player with the first line of three positions wins.

[2] Note in particular that no object references are present due to the communications that are used in CSP-OZ. Therefore the aliasing problem does not occur.

┌─ *TicTacToe* ──────────────────────────────────────────

| ┌──────────────────────────── | ┌─ Init ─────────────── |
| --- | --- |
| $bposn, wposn, free : \mathbb{P}\, Posn$ | $bposn = \varnothing$ |
| $over, turn : \mathbb{B}$ | $wposn = \varnothing$ |
| $moves : \mathbb{N}$ | $\neg over$ |
| ───────────────────────── | $turn$ |
| $free = Posn \setminus (bposn \cup wposn)$ | $free = Posn$ |
| $over \Leftrightarrow (moves = 9)$ | $moves = 0$ |

| ┌─ enable_*white* ──────────── | ┌─ enable_*black* ──────────── |
| --- | --- |
| $turn$ | $\neg turn$ |
| $\neg over$ | $\neg over$ |

| ┌─ effect_*white* ──────────── | ┌─ effect_*black* ──────────── |
| --- | --- |
| $\Delta(wposn, moves, free, over, turn)$ | $\Delta(bposn, moves, free, over, turn)$ |
| $p! : Posn$ | $p! : Posn$ |
| ──────────────────────── | ──────────────────────── |
| $p! \in free$ | $p! \in free$ |
| $wposn' = wposn \cup \{p!\}$ | $bposn' = bposn \cup \{p!\}$ |
| $\neg turn'$ | $turn'$ |
| $moves' = moves + 1$ | $moves' = moves + 1$ |

┌─ enable_*result* ────────────────────────
| $over$ |
| --- |

┌─ effect_*result* ────────────────────────

$r! : Result$

────────────────────────────────────────

$lines(bposn) > lines(wposn) \Rightarrow r! = black\_wins$
$lines(wposn) > lines(bposn) \Rightarrow r! = white\_wins$
$lines(wposn) = lines(bposn) \Rightarrow r! = draw$

This class specification will later be sliced with respect to some temporal logic properties.

*Kripke Structure Semantics.* The temporal logic will be interpreted on Kripke structures, therefore we will next define a Kripke structure semantics for Object-Z classes. The temporal logic will talk both about states *and* events (viz. methods). In contrast to ordinary Kripke structures transitions are thus labelled with events.

**Definition 1.** *Let AP be a nonempty set of atomic propositions, E an alphabet of events (or methods names).*

*An (event-)labelled Kripke structure $K = (S, S_0, \rightarrow, L)$ over AP and E consists of a finite set of states S, a set of initial states $S_0 \subseteq S$, a transition relation $\rightarrow \subseteq S \times E \times S$ and a labelling function $L : S \rightarrow 2^{AP}$.*

*An infinite sequence of events and states* $s_0 e_1 s_2 e_3 s_4 \ldots$ *is a* path *of the Kripke structure iff* $s_0 \in S_0$ *and* $(s_i, e_{i+1}, s_{i+2}) \in \longrightarrow$ *holds for all* $i \geq 0, i$ *even.*

*A path is* fair *with respect to a set of events* $E' \subseteq E$ *(or* $E'$*-fair) iff* $inf(\pi) \cap E' \neq \varnothing$ *where* $inf(\pi) = \{e \in E \mid \exists \text{ infinitely many } i \in \mathbb{N} : e_i = e\}.$

By convention we assume that paths are always infinite. This can be achieved by augmenting states $s$ with no outgoing transitions by an extra transition $s \xrightarrow{\tau} s$, where $\tau$ is an internal event (e.g. as in the process algebras CSP and CCS). We furthermore will in the following only consider paths that are fair with respect to some $E'$. This fairness requirement can be seen as an assumption on an environment which infinitely often has to call methods (viz. events) from $E'$. Since an Object-Z class is not executing methods without a client calling them anyway such fairness requirements are reasonable assumptions.

The Kripke structure semantics for an Object-Z class is obtained by taking all possible valuations of variables as states and state changes via execution of methods as transitions. The set of atomic propositions $AP$ are the predicates over the class' variables, e.g. for class $TicTacToe$ predicates $moves = 3$ and $free \neq \varnothing$ are possible atomic propositions. The set of events $E$ are those which can be built from the methods by filling in values for inputs and outputs, e.g. the method $white$ gives rise to events $white.3$, $white.4$, etc.. For convenience we will not make an explicit distinction between methods and events here and will not treat inputs and outputs. Thus we say that each class has a set of events $E$ and for every such event there might be an *enable* and an *effect* schema.

**Definition 2.** *The* Kripke structure semantics *of an Object-Z class* $C = (State, Init, (\texttt{enable\_e})_{e \in E}, (\texttt{effect\_e})_{e \in E})$ *is the labelled Kripke structure* $K = (S, S_0, \rightarrow, L)$ *over* $AP$ *and* $E$ *with*

- $S = State,$
- $S_0 = \{s \in S \mid Init(s)\}$ *a set of initial states,*
- *the transition relation* $\rightarrow = \rightarrow' \cup \{(s, \tau, s) \mid \nexists s' \; \nexists e : s \xrightarrow{e}' s'\}$ *where*

$$\rightarrow' = \{(s, e, s') \mid \texttt{enable\_e}(s) \wedge \texttt{effect\_e}(s, s')\},$$

- $L(s) = \{p \mid p \in AP \wedge s \Rightarrow p\}.$

In the following we only consider Object-Z classes that satisfy the following two further assumptions: First, we assume the set of initial states to be nonempty ($\exists State \bullet Init$) and second, we assume for any *enable* schema to imply the pre-condition of its *effect* schema ($\forall e \in E : \texttt{enable\_e} \Rightarrow \text{pre} \texttt{effect\_e}$).

*Logic.* The logic for expressing temporal properties is inspired by the Duration Calculus (DC), and allows us to reason about events and states but (for suiting our purposes) not about time and can therefore be regarded as an untimed projection of DC. There are two reasons for choosing this logic: first of all, our ultimate goal is to apply slicing to integrated specifications which in addition to Object-Z contain parts specifying the dynamic behaviour (in CSP) and timing constraints (in DC). The logic for expressing properties of this type of specifications will be the full DC. As a second reason, we are interested in a logic which can precisely express orderings between events and state propositions (e.g. like "when event $e$ happens then immediately afterwards variable $x$ has the value 5"). Since we are interested in reducing the specification it should, however, on the other hand not be able to precisely speak about *steps* of the system (e.g. like "the 10th operation of the system is event $e$"). The paths of the reduced specification will be projections of the paths of the full specification (omitting some events), and thus a preservation of properties under slicing does only make sense for logics which do not talk about particular steps.

The following grammar describes formulae of the state/event interval logic SE-IL (where $ev \in E$ is an event and $p \in AP$ an atomic proposition).

$$\varphi ::= \begin{array}{l} \lceil p \rceil \\ ev \\ \neg \varphi \\ \varphi \wedge \psi \\ \Diamond \varphi \\ \\ \varphi \, ; \, \psi \end{array}$$

- phase ($p$ holds in all states of the given interval)
- event ($ev$ occurs in the given interval)
- negation
- conjunction
- eventually operator with liveness ($\varphi$ holds inside or beyond the given interval)
- chop operator (divides the given interval into two parts where $\varphi$ holds on the first and $\psi$ holds on the second part)

We use the abbreviation $\Box \varphi$ to stand for $\neg \Diamond \neg \varphi$. For a formula $\varphi$ we let $E(\varphi)$ denote the set of events occurring in it and $V(\varphi)$ the set of variables of atomic propositions in it.

In order to define when a Kripke structure satisfies an interval logic formula we first define path-satisfaction. Duration Calculus is used to reason about continuous time models, and the validity of formulas is defined via a quantification over all time intervals: a formula holds iff it is true in all intervals (starting at time 0). This definition is now transferred to the discrete setting of paths: a path satisfies a formula iff the formula holds on all intervals $[0, e]$, $e \in \mathbb{N}$. Let $\pi = s_0 e_1 s_2 e_3 s_4 \ldots$ be a path and $\pi[i]$ the $i$-th component of $\pi$: $\pi[i]$ can either be an event or a state.

1. $\pi, [b, e] \models \lceil p \rceil$ iff $\exists\, m, b \leq m \leq e : \pi[m] \in S$
   and $\forall\, m, b \leq m \leq e : \pi[m] \in S \Rightarrow p \in L(\pi[m])$,
2. $\pi, [b, e] \models ev$ iff $b = e$ and $\pi[b] = ev$,
3. $\pi, [b, e] \models \neg \varphi$ iff not $\pi, [b, e] \models \varphi$,
4. $\pi, [b, e] \models \varphi \wedge \psi$ iff $\pi, [b, e] \models \varphi$ and $\pi, [b, e] \models \psi$,
5. $\pi, [b, e] \models \Diamond \varphi$ iff $\exists\, m_1, m_2 \geq b : \pi, [m_1, m_2] \models \varphi$,
6. $\pi, [b, e] \models \varphi \, ; \, \psi$ iff $(\exists\, m, b \leq m \leq e : \pi, [b, m] \models \varphi$ and $\pi, [m, e] \models \psi)$
   $\vee \, (\pi[b] \in S$ and $\pi[b, b-1] \models \varphi$ and $\pi[b, e] \models \psi)$
   $\vee \, (\pi[e] \in S$ and $\pi[e, e-1] \models \psi$ and $\pi, [b, e] \models \varphi)$

Some explanations for this unusual definition are at place. Item 1: the decision taken here is that during execution of an event we do not know what atomic propositions hold, thus the formula $\lceil p \rceil$ evaluates to false on an interval with an event only. This reflects the fact that events may invalidate atomic propositions which hold in the state before their execution and make others become true in the state after their execution. In order to be able to say that an event causes a state change we can neither assume that atomic propositions in pre-states still hold while the event takes place nor that those of post-states already hold. Item 2,3 and 4 should be as expected. Item 5: The eventually operator has to reason about positions outside the current interval since we want to achieve real liveness, not just bounded liveness. This operator is taken from the DC with liveness [12]; the standard DC does not allow to reason about unbounded liveness. Item 6: The first part of the disjunction captures the case where the interval is divided into two parts such that $\varphi$ holds on the first part and $\psi$ on the second. The second and third part of the disjunction mimic the phenomenon that in continuous time one can chop off an empty interval from every interval. The empty interval is denoted by $[b, b-1]$ (or $[e, e-1]$). In an empty interval neither $\lceil p \rceil$ nor $ev$ holds. Note that for instance $ev \mathbin{;} ev \equiv ev^3$ but $\neg\lceil p \rceil \not\equiv \lceil \neg p \rceil$[4].

A Kripke structure then satisfies a formula if all of its paths do (and an Object-Z class satisfies a property when its Kripke structure does).

**Definition 3.** *Let $K = (S, S_0, \to, L)$ be a Kripke structure and $\varphi$ an SE-IL formula. A path $\pi$ satisfies $\varphi$ if $\pi, [0, e] \models \varphi$ holds for all $e \in \mathbb{N}$. $K$ satisfies $\varphi$ $(K \models \varphi)$ iff $\pi \models \varphi$ holds for all paths of $K$. $K$ fairly satisfies $\varphi$ w.r.t. a set of events $E' \subseteq E$ $(K \models_{E'} \varphi)$ iff $\pi \models \varphi$ holds for all $E'$-fair paths of $K$.*

As an example consider the following Kripke structure $K$:

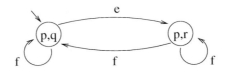

For $K$ we for instance have $K \models \boxed{L}\,p$ ($p$ always holds), $K \models \neg\Diamond(e \mathbin{;} \lceil \neg r \rceil)$ ($r$ holds after $e$, formulated as a counter-example: there is no interval in which $\neg r$ holds immediately after $e$) but $K \not\models \Diamond e$ (event $e$ will eventually happen is not true since there are paths with event $f$ only) and $K \not\models \boxed{L}\,\lceil q \rceil$.

For class *TicTacToe* we are interested in the following two properties:

$$\varphi_1 := \boxed{L}\,\lceil moves = 9 - \#free \rceil$$
$$\varphi_2 := \neg\Diamond(black \mathbin{;} (\lceil true \rceil \wedge \neg(\lceil true \rceil \mathbin{;} white \mathbin{;} \lceil true \rceil)) \mathbin{;} black)$$
$$\wedge \neg\Diamond(white \mathbin{;} (\lceil true \rceil \wedge \neg(\lceil true \rceil \mathbin{;} black \mathbin{;} \lceil true \rceil)) \mathbin{;} white)$$

---

[3] The formula $ev$ only holds on a zero interval $[b, e]$ with $b = e$. The chop operator can divide this interval into two zero intervals that both satisfy $ev$.

[4] From the fact that $\lceil p \rceil$ does not hold on an interval one cannot conclude that $\lceil \neg p \rceil$ holds on this interval.

Property $\varphi_1$ states an invariant between two variables of the class and $\varphi_2$ states that moves are taken in turn. The second property is again formulated as a counter-example: there should not be an interval in which an event *black* is followed by a nonempty interval in which no *white* happens which is then followed by another *black* (and similar for *white*). Nonemptiness of the middle interval is achieved by conjunction with $\lceil true \rceil$.

*Projection of Event-Labelled Kripke Structures.* The task of slicing is to compute a reduced specification which satisfies a certain property if and only if the full specification satisfies it. For proving this we will show that the reduced specification is a *projection* of the full specification onto some relevant subset of the atomic propositions and events, i.e. they only differ on atomic propositions and events that the formula does not mention.

The projection relation is again first defined on paths and then lifted to Kripke structures. Intuitively, when computing the projection of a given path onto a set of atomic propositions and a set of events one divides the path into blocks such that all states inside a block are "projection-equivalent" (i.e. they coincide on the given set of atomic propositions) and all events inside a block are "irrelevant" events (i.e. events not from the given set of events) except for the last event in the block which is a "relevant" event (i.e. an event from the given set of events). The projection of the original path contains then any path such that for each of the blocks of the original path all states and irrelevant events are mapped onto one single state of the new path while the "relevant" event remains in the new path as illustrated in the following sketch of a projection of a path:

| | Block 0 | Block 1 | Block 2 | Block 3 |
|---|---|---|---|---|
| $\pi =$ | $s_0\ e_0\ s_1\ e_1$ | $s_2\ e_2$ | $s_3\ e_3\ s_4\ e_4$ | $\ldots$ |
| $Pr(\pi) \ni$ | $r_0\ e_1$ | $r_1\ e_2$ | $r_2\ e_4$ | $\ldots$ |

**Definition 4.** *Let* $\pi = s_0 e_0 s_1 e_1 s_2 e_2 s_3 \ldots$ *be an* $E'$*-fair path over a set of atomic propositions* $AP$ *and a set of events* $E \supseteq E'$*. The projection of* $\pi$ *onto a set of atomic propositions* $AP'$ *and a set of events* $E'$ *($Pr_{AP',E'}(\pi)$) contains any* $E'$*-fair path* $\rho = r_0 f_0 r_1 f_1 r_2 f_2 r_3 \ldots$ *such that there is a sequence of indices* $0 = i_0 < i_1 < i_2 < \ldots$ *(that divides* $\pi$ *into blocks) with*

- $\forall k \geq 0: L(s_{i_k}) \cap AP' = L(s_{i_k+1}) \cap AP' = \cdots = L(s_{i_{k+1}-1}) \cap AP' = L(r_k) \cap AP'$
  *(relevant atomic propositions do not change within a block and are the same in the correspondent state of* $\rho$*),*
- $\forall l \in \mathbb{N}, \forall k : i_l \leq k < i_{l+1} - 1 : e_k \in E \setminus E'$
  *(no relevant events occur inside a block),*
- $\forall l \geq 1 : e_{i_l-1} = f_{l-1} \in E'$
  *(transitions between blocks are labelled with the same relevant event as the correspondent transition of* $\rho$*).*

For comparing the Kripke structures we restrict the definition to fair paths since we are only considering satisfaction of formulae on fair paths.

**Definition 5.** *Let* $K_i = (S_i, S_{0,i}, \rightarrow_i, L_i)$, $i \in \{1, 2\}$, *be labelled Kripke structures over a set of atomic propositions* $AP$ *and a set of events* $E$, $AP' \subseteq AP$ *a subset of the atomic propositions and* $E' \subseteq E$ *a subset of the events.*

*$K_2$ is in the* projection *of $K_1$ onto $AP'$ and $E'$ ($K_2 \in Pr_{AP',E'}(K_1)$) iff the following holds:*

1. *For each $E'$-fair path $\pi$ in $K_1$ there exists an $E'$-fair path $\pi'$ in $K_2$ such that $\pi' \in Pr_{AP',E'}(\pi)$,*
2. *and vice versa, for each $E'$-fair path $\pi'$ in $K_2$ there exists an $E'$-fair path $\pi$ in $K_1$ such that $\pi' \in Pr_{AP',E'}(\pi)$.*

Such a projection relation between two Kripke structures guarantees that formulae which only mention propositions from $AP'$ and events from $E'$ hold for either both or none of the Kripke structures.

**Theorem 1.** *Let $\varphi$ be an SE-IL formula over $AP'$ and $E'$, and $K_1$, $K_2$ labelled Kripke structures over a set of atomic propositions $AP$ and a set of events $E$ with $AP' \subseteq AP$ and $E' \subseteq E$. If $K_2 \in Pr_{AP',E'}(K_1)$ then the following holds:*

$$K_1 \models_{E'} \varphi \quad \textit{iff} \quad K_2 \models_{E'} \varphi .$$

Due to space restrictions we omit the proof that can be found in appendix 1 of the full version of the paper [1].

## 3    Slicing

Slicing means reducing a program or a specification such that the reduced program/specification only contains those parts of the full specification which can influence a certain property called the slicing criterion. At the beginning slicing criteria have usually been of the form "what is the value of variable x at statement n?". The task of the slicing algorithm was to find the (smallest) part of the program/specification sufficient for correctly answering this question.

In the context of model checking slicing criteria have become more complex and are usually temporal logic formulae. Nevertheless, techniques similar to ordinary slicing can be used for slicing with respect to temporal logic formulae since the essence of slicing has remained the same: slicing needs precise information about dependencies between different parts of a program/specification. Such dependencies are represented in a *program (or system) dependence graph*[5]. This section explains the construction of program dependence graphs for Object-Z classes and their slicing with respect to SE-IL formulae.

---

[5] We stick to the word program although we treat specifications.

*Program Dependence Graph.* We start with some notational conventions. We assume $V$ to be the set of variables of the class, $E$ to be its methods (or events) and *Pred* to be predicates over $V$.

For a predicate $p$ over a set of variables $vars(p)$ standing in some schema we define $mod(p)$ to be those variables which occur in primed form and are in the $\Delta$-list of the schema, and $ref(p)$ to be the variables occurring in unprimed form. For input and output variables we use the following convention: output variables of a predicate $p$ are in $mod(p)$ and input variables in $ref(p)$. This effect could alternatively be achieved by embedding inputs and outputs into the state as in [14]. For the initialisation schema *Init* we assume the $\Delta$-list to be $V$ and $ref(p)$ to be $\varnothing$ for all predicates $p$ in *Init* (although variables appear in unprimed form they are actually set in the *Init* schema). For an effect schema `effect_e` and variables $u, v$ we say that $u$ *constrains* the value of $v$ in `effect_e` ($constrains^{\texttt{effect\_}e}(u, v)$) if there is a predicate $p$ in `effect_e` such that both $u$ and $v$ are in $mod(p)$. The relation *constrains* is thus symmetric.

The construction of the program dependence graph (PDG) starts with the construction of the control flow graph (CFG) (depicted in fig. 1). It contains

- one node $n_{Init}$ labelled *Init*,
- one node $n_{DO}$ labelled *DO* (nondeterministic choice),
- for every method/event $e$ two nodes $n_{en\_e}$ and $n_{eff\_e}$ labelled `enable_e` and `effect_e`.

These nodes also appear in the PDG where they are supernodes, i.e. nodes that contain a number of ordinary nodes. This hierarchical relation corresponds to the relation between predicates (ordinary nodes) that occur inside schemas (supernodes). The control flow between nodes is used to determine dependencies in the PDG.

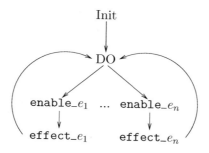

**Fig. 1.** Control flow graph of a class

The construction of the PDG then proceeds in two steps. The first step is a kind of normalisation (although not as complete as the ordinary one) on the specification; the second step builds the graph.

1. First step: Class normalisation.
   - The state invariant is attached to every effect schema in primed form.
   - For every variable $v$ of type $T$ occurring in the $\Delta$-list of some schema but not in primed form in a predicate we add a predicate $v' \in T$ to the schema (in order to make it explicit that the variable might change).

2. Second step: Graph construction.
   From the CFG we build a hierarchical graph in which the supernodes are those of the CFG and the predicates of the schemas occur as subnodes. Furthermore, we add *control dependencies* between two nodes $n$ and $n'$ if the evaluation of the predicate of $n$ may influence the execution of $n'$, and *data dependencies* if $n$ modifies a variable that $n'$ references.
   More formally, for a class $(State, Init, (\texttt{enable\_}e)_{e \in E}, (\texttt{effect\_}e)_{e \in E})$ we build a hierarchical graph $G = (K, P, l, \leadsto, \rightarrowtail)$ with

   - $K = \{n_{Init}, n_{DO}\} \cup \{n_{en\_e} \mid e \in E\} \cup \{n_{eff\_e} \mid e \in E\}$ a set of *supernodes*,
   - $P = \{p_x \mid p$ is a predicate in a schema named $x\}$, a set of *ordinary nodes*[6],
   - $l$ a *labelling function* defined as

   $$l : n_{Init} \mapsto Init$$
   $$n_{DO} \mapsto DO$$
   $$n_{en\_e} \mapsto \texttt{enable\_}e$$
   $$n_{eff\_e} \mapsto \texttt{effect\_}e$$
   $$p_x \mapsto p$$

   - $\leadsto \subseteq P \times P$ the *data dependence* edges defined by $p_x \leadsto q_y$ iff
     - directed data dependencies exist, i.e.

     $$mod(p_x) \cap ref(q_y) \neq \varnothing \text{ and } y \neq Init,$$

     - or symmetric data dependencies exist, i.e.

     $$mod(p_x) \cap mod(q_y) \neq \varnothing \text{ and } y = x,$$

   - $\rightarrowtail \subseteq P \times P$ the *control dependence* edges defined by

   $$p_x \rightarrowtail q_y \text{ iff } \exists e \in E : x = \texttt{enable\_}e \text{ and } y = \texttt{effect\_}e.$$

The program dependence graph of the class *TicTacToe* can be found in fig. 2. Control dependencies between two supernodes (of an enable and an effect schema) stand for dependencies between every predicate in the first and in the second node. It can be seen that due to normalisation the effect schemas have two extra predicates which appeared in the original specification as the state invariant.

---

[6] The hierarchical relation between an ordinary node and its associated supernode is implicitly present in an ordinary node's index that refers to the schema the predicate comes from, i.e. its supernode.

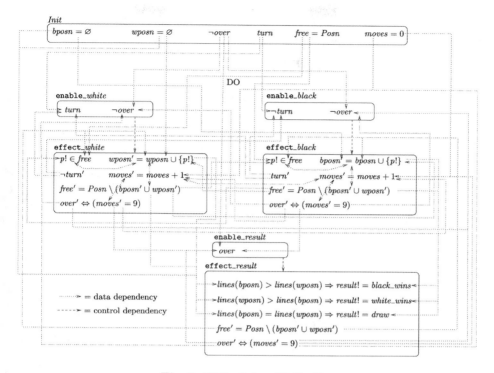

**Fig. 2.** PDG of class TicTacToe

*Backward Slice.* The construction of the program dependence graph is independent of the actual SE-IL formula. The formula comes into play when the slicing is carried out. In ordinary slicing the slicing criterion is the value of a variable at a certain program statement. In order to construct the slice of a program w.r.t. this criterion the node representing the statement is determined and then all nodes are included in the slice which are backward reachable (via dependencies) from this particular node. In this way the part of the program which might influence the slicing criterion is obtained.

When slicing w.r.t. SE-IL formulae this is less easy. We first have to find out what the "start nodes" for slicing are, i.e. which nodes represent the slicing criterion. From the formula $\varphi$ we can derive a set of events $E_\varphi$ and a set of variables $V_\varphi$ under interest (those appearing in the formula). From these we can determine the nodes $N_\varphi$ (predicates) in the PDG which directly manipulate these variables or influence the execution of these events:

$$E_\varphi = E(\varphi)$$
$$V_\varphi = V(\varphi) \cup \{v \mid \exists\, e \in E_\varphi, \exists\, p_{en\_e} : v \in vars(p)\}$$
$$N_\varphi = \{p_x \mid \exists\, v \in V_\varphi : v \in mod(p)\} \cup \{p_y \mid \exists\, e \in E_\varphi : y = en\_e\}$$

The nodes in $N_\varphi$ are those from which the slicing is then started. All nodes in the *backward slice* of $N_\varphi$ might potentially influence execution of events in $E_\varphi$ or values of (and thus atomic propositions over) $V_\varphi$.

$$bs(N_\varphi) = \{n' \in P \mid \exists n \in N_\varphi : n'(\rightsquigarrow \cup \rightarrowtail)^* n\}$$

The backward slice contains the set of nodes which influence the truth value of $\varphi$ and thus gives us the events, predicates and variables which still have to be in the reduced class specification.

$$N' = bs(N_\varphi)$$
$$V' = \bigcup_{p_x \in N'} vars(p)$$
$$E' = \{e \mid \exists p : p_{en\_e} \in N' \vee p_{eff\_e} \in N'\}$$

There are, however, some variables in $V'$ whose values cannot influence the holding of the formula since they are never referenced (i.e. never occur in unprimed form in predicates of $N'$). Thus we define a second set of variables

$$\overline{V} = V_\varphi \cup \{v \in V' \mid \exists p_x \in N' : v \in ref(p)\}$$

which are those actually referenced. Variables out of $V' \setminus \overline{V}$ are still needed in the reduced specification since there might be predicates referring to their primed version. As an example, consider an effect schema with predicates $u' = v'$ and $v' = 5$ where $u \in V(\varphi)$. Since the value of $u$ in the post-state is constrained by that of $v$ both predicates and variables are needed in the reduced specification. The value of $v$ in some state is however never used, it cannot influence the value of $u$. Thus $v$ would be in $V'$ but not in $\overline{V}$. We let $\overline{AP}$ denote the set of atomic propositions over $\overline{V}$.

*Reduced Specification.* Given the set $N'$, $V'$ and $E'$ it is then straightforward to construct the reduced specification. The class $C^{red}$ contains a state schema with variables from $V'$ only (same type as in $C$), with schemas only for events in $E'$ (plus *Init*), and in these schemas only the predicates from nodes in $N'$. We refer to the schemas in this class specification as $State^{red}$, $Init^{red}$, $\texttt{enable\_}e^{red}$, $\texttt{effect\_}e^{red}$ and in order to properly distinguish it from the original specification this will in the following be called $C^{full}$.

*Examples.* When slicing the class *TicTacToe* with respect to the formula

$$\varphi_1 := \boxed{L} \lceil moves = 9 - \#free \rceil$$

the result is the following:

$$N' = N \setminus \{(lines(bposn) > lines(wposn) \Rightarrow result! = black\_wins)_{\texttt{effect\_result}},$$
$$(lines(wposn) > lines(bposn) \Rightarrow result! = white\_wins)_{\texttt{effect\_result}},$$
$$(lines(wposn) = lines(bposn) \Rightarrow result! = draw)_{\texttt{effect\_result}}\}$$
$$V' = V = \overline{V}$$
$$E' = E$$

Thus the slice w.r.t. $\varphi_1$ exhibits only one difference in comparison to the original specification, namely only the predicates are removed that determine the final result that is communicated by schema *result*. This is sensible, of course, since the communicated result does not influence the given property.

When slicing the class *TicTacToe* with respect to the formula

$$\varphi_2 := \neg \diamondsuit^{\!\!\textit{l}} (black \,;\, (\lceil true \rceil \wedge \neg (\lceil true \rceil \,;\, white \,;\, \lceil true \rceil)) \,;\, black)$$
$$\wedge \neg \diamondsuit^{\!\!\textit{l}} (white \,;\, (\lceil true \rceil \wedge \neg (\lceil true \rceil \,;\, black \,;\, \lceil true \rceil)) \,;\, white)$$

the result is the following:

$$
\begin{aligned}
N' = N \setminus \{ & (bposn = \varnothing)_{Init}, (wposn = \varnothing)_{Init}, (free = Posn)_{Init}, \\
& (p! \in free)_{\textsf{effect\_white}}, (wposn' = wposn \cup \{p!\})_{\textsf{effect\_white}}, \\
& (free' = Posn \setminus (bposn' \cup wposn'))_{\textsf{effect\_white}}, \\
& (p! \in free)_{\textsf{effect\_black}}, (bposn' = bposn \cup \{p!\})_{\textsf{effect\_black}}, \\
& (free' = Posn \setminus (bposn' \cup wposn'))_{\textsf{effect\_black}}, \\
& (lines(bposn) > lines(wposn) \Rightarrow r! = black\_wins)_{\textsf{effect\_result}}, \\
& (lines(wposn) > lines(bposn) \Rightarrow r! = white\_wins)_{\textsf{effect\_result}}, \\
& (lines(wposn) = lines(bposn) \Rightarrow r! = draw)_{\textsf{effect\_result}}, \\
& (free' = Posn \setminus (bposn' \cup wposn'))_{\textsf{effect\_result}} \} \\
V' = V \setminus & \{bposn, wposn, free\} = \overline{V} \\
E' = E &
\end{aligned}
$$

This leads to the following specification slice:

---

**TicTacToe**

----

$over, turn : \mathbb{B}$
$moves : \mathbb{N}$

----

$over \Leftrightarrow (moves = 9)$

**Init**

$\neg over$
$turn$
$moves = 0$

----

**enable_white**

$turn$
$\neg over$

**enable_black**

$\neg turn$
$\neg over$

----

**effect_white**

$\Delta(moves, over, turn)$

$\neg turn'$
$moves' = moves + 1$

**effect_black**

$\Delta(moves, over, turn)$

$turn'$
$moves' = moves + 1$

----

**enable_result**

$over$

**effect_result**

$\Delta()$

true

Thus, additional to the difference that we saw in the previous example, this slice has another difference in comparison to the original specification: All predicates have been removed that determine the sets of free and occupied fields. This difference is sensible since the given property expresses only that there is a strict alternation between the players' moves. In order to analyze the sequence of moves the players can perform, the exact occupation of fields during the course of the game is irrelevant and all related predicates can safely be removed together with the variables that store the associated information about free and occupied fields.

This example shows that slicing can substantially reduce the size of the specification and hence the state space of the associated Kripke structure. Verification of temporal logic properties can thus be facilitated.

## 4   Correctness

In this section we show correctness of the slicing algorithm, i.e. we show that the Kripke structure of the reduced specification is a projection of that of the full specification. As a consequence the property (and slicing criterion) $\varphi$ then holds on the full specification if and only if it holds on the reduced specification. In the proofs we use the notation of the last section, i.e. let $N'$, $E'$, $V'$ denote the nodes, events, variables which remain in the specification or PDG after slicing and $\overline{V}$, $\overline{AP}$ are the variables and atomic propositions, respectively, on which the full and reduced specification should agree.

We start the correctness proof with two lemmas showing the relationships between events, predicates and variables which remain in the specification.

**Lemma 1.** *Let $e \in E'$ be an event and $p$ a predicate out of the schema* enable_e. *Then $p_{en\_e} \in N'$.*

**Proof:** Take some $e \in E'$. Then by definition of $E'$ there is some predicate $q$ such that either $q_{en\_e} \in N'$ or $q_{eff\_e} \in N'$.

- Assume $q_{en\_e} \in N'$. Then either $q_{en\_e} \in N_\varphi$ or it is not in $N_\varphi$ but in the backward slice of $N_\varphi$. In the first case $e \in E_\varphi$ and hence $p_{en\_e} \in N_\varphi$ and thus in $N'$. Or $q_{en\_e}$ is in the backward slice of $N_\varphi$. Since $q$ is coming from an enable schema the outgoing dependencies are only control dependencies. Hence there is some predicate $r$ in effect_e such that $r$ is in the backward slice. The control dependency is going from $q$ to $r$ but also from $p$ to $r$ and therefore $p$ is in $N'$ as well.
- Assume $q_{eff\_e} \in N'$. Then $p_{en\_e}$ is in the backward slice since there is a control dependency from $p_{en\_e}$ to $q_{eff\_e}$.

As a consequence, either all or none of the predicates of an enable schema are in the backward slice.

**Corollary 1.** $\forall e \in E'$ : enable_$e^{red}$ = enable_$e^{full}$.

The next lemma shows that events not in $E'$, i.e. omitted in the reduced specification, have no influence on the variables in $\overline{V}$.

**Lemma 2.** *Let* $e \notin E'$ *be an event. For all predicates* $p$ *appearing in* `effect_e` *we then have* $mod(p) \cap \overline{V} = \varnothing$.

**Proof:** Assume there is some $\overline{v} \in \overline{V}$ with $\overline{v} \in mod(p)$. Then one of the following two cases hold:

1. $\overline{v} \in V_{\varphi}$
   $\Rightarrow p_{eff\_e} \in N_{\varphi}$
   $\Rightarrow p_{eff\_e} \in N'$
   $\Rightarrow e \in E'$ (Contradiction!)
2. $\overline{v} \in \{v \in V' \mid \exists\, q_x \in N' : v \in ref(q)\}$
   $\Rightarrow$ data dependency from $p_{eff\_e}$ to $q_x$
   $\Rightarrow p_{eff\_e} \in N'$
   $\Rightarrow e \in E'$ (Contradiction!)

Next, we state the main theorem of the paper which is the correctness of slicing with respect to the interval logic property. This is proven by showing that the Kripke structure of the reduced specification is a projection of that of the full specification.

**Theorem 2.** *Let* $C^{full}$ *be a class specification,* $\varphi$ *an SE-IL formula and* $C^{red}$ *the class obtained when slicing* $C^{full}$ *with respect to* $\varphi$. *Let* $E'$ *and* $\overline{AP}$ *be the set of events and atomic propositions, respectively, which the slicing algorithm delivers as those of interest (in particular* $E(\varphi) \subseteq E'$ *and* $V(\varphi) \subseteq \overline{V}$*).*

*Let furthermore* $K^{full}$ *and* $K^{red}$ *be the corresponding Kripke structures. Then the following holds:*

$$K^{red} \in Pr_{\overline{AP}, E'}(K^{full})$$

**Proof:**

1. Let $\pi = s_0 e_1 s_2 e_3 \ldots$ be an $E'$-fair path of $K^{full}$. We construct a sequence $\rho' = t_0 f_1 t_2 f_3 \ldots$ with

   $t_i : s_i|_{V'}$
   $f_i : e_i$ if $e_i \in E', nop$ else

   Out of $\rho'$ we construct a sequence $\rho$ by eliminating all subsequences of the form $nop\ t_j$.
   We have to show that $\rho$ is an $E'$-fair path of $K^{red}$.
   (a) Fairness: $\rho$ contains infinitely many events from $E'$ since $\pi$ contains them and they are preserved by the construction.
   (b) Path: Since $K^{red}$ contains fewer predicates than $K^{full}$ in the schemas, there are fewer restrictions on values of variables. Hence

   $$Init^{full}(s_0) \Rightarrow Init^{red}(s_0|_{V'})$$
   $$\texttt{enable\_}e^{full}(s_i) \Rightarrow \texttt{enable\_}e^{red}(s_i|_{V'})$$
   $$\texttt{effect\_}e^{full}(s_i, s_{i+2}) \Rightarrow \texttt{effect\_}e^{red}(s_i|_{V'}, s_{i+2}|_{V'})$$

Furthermore by Lemma 2 we know that $e_i \notin E'$ implies $s_{i-1}|_{\overline{V}} = s_{i+1}|_{\overline{V}}$. If there is now a transition $s_{i-1} \xrightarrow{e_i} s_{i+1}$ in $K^{full}$ with $e_i \in E'$ then a transition $t_j \xrightarrow{e_i} t_{i+1}$ with $j \leq i-1, \forall k : j < k < i-1 : e_k \notin E'$ and $e_{j-1} \in E'$ is possible in $K^{red}$ since 1) $t_j|_{\overline{V}} = s_j|_{\overline{V}} = s_{i-1}|_{\overline{V}}$ and $t_{i+1}|_{\overline{V}} = s_{i+1}|_{\overline{V}}$ and 2) $\mathtt{enable\_}e_i{}^{red}$ only references variables from $\overline{V}$ and 3) $\mathtt{effect\_}e_i{}^{red}$ only references unprimed variables from $\overline{V}$ and moreover makes no or the same restrictions as $\mathtt{effect\_}e_i{}^{full}$ on primed variables in $V'$ (and hence the value in $s_{i+1}$ is ok, since it coincides with the value in $t_{i+1}$).

Thus $\rho$ is a path of $K^{red}$.

By construction $\rho$ is in the projection of $\pi$ onto $\overline{AP}$ and $E'$.

2. Let $\rho = t_0 f_1 t_2 f_3 \ldots$ be a (by definition) $E'$-fair path of $K^{red}$. We inductively construct a sequence $\pi = s_0 e_1 s_2 e_3 \ldots$ by

$$s_i : s_i \xrightarrow{e_{i+1}}{}_{full} s_{i+2}$$
$$e_i : f_i$$

We have to show the well-definedness of this construction (by induction), i.e. show that a transition $s_i \xrightarrow{e_{i+1}}{}_{full} s_{i+2}$ is indeed possible in $K^{full}$. Furthermore we have to show that $s_{i+2}|_{\overline{V}} = t_{i+2}|_{\overline{V}}$ (note that $s_{i+2}$ and $t_{i+2}$ might differ on variables in $V' \setminus \overline{V}$).

(a) Induction base: $s_0$

We know that $Init^{red}(t_0)$ holds. We have to show that there is some $s_0$ with $Init^{full}(s_0)$ and $s_0|_{\overline{V}} = t_0|_{\overline{V}}$. To this end we show that $Init^{red}$ contains all predicates of $Init^{full}$ which directly or indirectly influence the variables of $\overline{V}$.

   i. Directly: let $\overline{u} \in \overline{V}$ and $q$ a predicate in $Init^{full}$ such that $\overline{u} \in mod(q)$. Then $q_{Init} \in N'$ since either 1) $\overline{u} \in V_\varphi$ and then $q_{Init} \in N_\varphi$ and hence in $N'$, or 2) $\overline{u} \in \{v \in V' \mid \exists p_x \in N' : v \in ref(p)\}$ and then there is data dependency from $q_{Init}$ to $p_x$ and hence $q_{Init} \in N'$.

   ii. Indirectly: let $\overline{u} \in \overline{V}$ and assume there is a chain of variables $u_1, u_2, \ldots, u_n$ such that $u = u_1$, $\overline{u} = u_n$ and $constrains(u_i, u_{i+1}), 1 \leq i \leq n-1$. Due to symmetric dependencies all predicates $q$ causing the $constrains$-relationships are in $N'$.

(b) Induction step: assume we have constructed the sequence up to some state $s_i$ and $s_i|_{\overline{V}} = t_i|_{\overline{V}}$.

We have to show that $e_{i+1}$ is enabled in $s_i$ and its execution leads to some state $s_{i+2}$ such that $s_{i+2}|_{\overline{V}} = t_{i+2}|_{\overline{V}}$. By Corollary 1 we get $\mathtt{enable\_}e_{i+1}{}^{red} = \mathtt{enable\_}e_{i+1}{}^{full}$, and thus there is some $s'_{i+2}$ with $s_i \xrightarrow{e_{i+1}}{}_{full} s'_{i+2}$. Now we choose $s_{i+2} = s'_{i+2} \oplus t_{i+2}|_{V''}$ with

$$V'' = \bigcup_{p_{\mathtt{effect\_}e_{i+1}{}^{full} \in N'}} mod(p) \cup \overline{V}.$$

This choice ensures that $s_{i+2}|_{\overline{V}} = t_{i+2}|_{\overline{V}}$ holds since $\overline{V} \subseteq V''$. Furthermore this choice is admissible since each predicate in $\mathtt{effect\_}e_{i+1}{}^{full}$ falls into one of the following cases:

– $p_{\text{effect}\_e_{i+1}{}^{full}} \in N'$: Then $mod(p) \subseteq V''$ and due to the construction of the slice $ref(p) \subseteq \overline{V}$. Since $s_i|_{\overline{V}} = t_i|_{\overline{V}}$, $s_{i+2}|_{V''} = t_{i+2}|_{V''}$ and $\text{effect}\_e_{i+1}{}^{red}(t_i, t_{i+2})$, we know that predicate $p$ holds for the transition from $s_i$ to $s_{i+2}$.

– $p_{\text{effect}\_e_{i+1}{}^{full}} \notin N'$: Then $mod(p) \cap V'' = \varnothing$ holds, since otherwise there would be some variable $v \in mod(p)$ inducing a dependence such that $p_{\text{effect}\_e_{i+1}{}^{full}} \in N'$. From $mod(p) \cap V'' = \varnothing$ we know that $s_i|_{mod(p)} = s'_{i+2}$. Together with $\text{effect}\_e_{i+1}{}^{full}(s_i, s'_{i+2})$ this leads finally to $\text{effect}\_e_{i+1}{}^{full}(s_i, s_{i+2})$.

By construction $\pi$ is thus an $E'$-fair path of $K^{full}$ and furthermore $\rho$ is in the projection of $\pi$ onto $\overline{AP}$ and $E'$.

As a consequence of theorem 1, the formula $\varphi$ holds on the reduced specification if and only if it holds on the full specification.

## 5    Conclusion

This paper is concerned with reducing Object-Z specifications for the verification of temporal logic properties. Given a formula the technique presented in this paper computes a reduced specification on which the formula holds if and only if it holds for the full specification. The technique can substantially facilitate verification of specifications since the preparatory construction of the program dependence graph is only linear in the size of the original specification while its state space is usually much larger (or infinite) and might therefore not be amenable for an analysis. Slicing can thus be seen as one method for fighting the state explosion problem in verification, along with other techniques like abstraction (for Z for instance by combining the work of [14] and [4]), symmetry reduction, compositional verification (like e.g. [20]) and partial order reductions.

*Related Work.* Slicing in formal specifications, in particular in Z, has been proposed in [2,11]. These works carry out slicing with respect to a "standard" slicing criterion, which are the values of variables. Slicing with respect to temporal logic formulae is usually done either in the context of hardware verification [3], therein known as cone-of-influence reduction, or in software model checking, most notably in the Bandera project [8] where it is applied to Java programs.

*Future Work.* So far, this technique considers a single class only. It could be extended to larger systems either by combining it with compositional verification techniques (e.g. for Object-Z [20]), or by constructing a program dependence graph of the whole system. The latter could be achieved by combining program dependence graphs of the individual objects through a special new dependency arc reflecting the call structure between objects (possibly following approaches for slicing programs with procedures).

The development of tool support for slicing is another important issue. Our small example already revealed the necessity for a program computing program dependence graphs and backward slices and the presented algorithms for these computations clearly suggest such an automation. This is envisaged in the research project AVACS which forms the overall context of this work.

Our main focus for future work is, however, an extension of this technique to an integrated specification formalism combining Object-Z with CSP and Duration Calculus.

**Acknowledgement.** We would like to thank Jochen Hoenicke for numerous discussions on the definition of a state- and event-based interval logic and for a careful reading of the paper.

# References

1. I. Brückner and H. Wehrheim. Slicing Object-Z specifications for verification. Technical Report 3, SFB/TR 14 AVACS, http://www.avacs.org/, 2005.
2. D. Chang and D. Richardson. Static and Dynamic Specification Slicing. In *ACM SIGSOFT international symposium on Software testing and analysis*, pages 138–153. ACM, 1994.
3. E. Clarke, O. Grumberg, and D. Peled. *Model checking.* MIT Press, 1999.
4. J. Derrick and G. Smith. Linear temporal logic and Z refinement. In C. Rattray, S. Maharaj, and C. Shankland, editors, *Algebraic Methodology and Software Technology (AMAST 2004)*, volume 3116 of *Lecture Notes in Computer Science*, pages 117–131. Springer, 2004.
5. R. Duke and G. Rose. *Formal object-oriented specification using Object-Z.* Macmillan, 2000.
6. R. Duke, G. Rose, and G. Smith. Object-Z: A specification language advocated for the description of standards. *Computer Standards and Interfaces*, 17:511–533, 1995.
7. C. Fischer. CSP-OZ: A combination of Object-Z and CSP. In H. Bowman and J. Derrick, editors, *Formal Methods for Open Object-Based Distributed Systems (FMOODS '97)*, volume 2, pages 423–438. Chapman & Hall, 1997.
8. J. Hatcliff, M. Dwyer, and H. Zheng. Slicing software for model construction. *Higher-order and Symbolic Computation*, 13(4):315–353, 2000.
9. J. Hoenicke and E.-R. Olderog. Combining Specification Techniques for Processes, Data and Time. In M. Butler, L. Petre, and K. Sere, editors, *Integrated Formal Methods*, volume 2335 of *Lecture Notes in Computer Science*, pages 245–266. Springer-Verlag, May 2002.
10. L. Millett and T. Teitelbaum. Issues in slicing PROMELA and its applications to model checking, protocol understanding, and simulation. *Software Tools for Technology Transfer*, 2(4):343–349, 2000.
11. T. Oda and K. Araki. Specification slicing in formal methods of software development. In *Proceedings of the Seventeenth Annual International Computer Software & Applications Conference*, pages 313–319. IEEE Computer Society Press, 1993.
12. J. U. Skakkebæk. Liveness and fairness in duration calculus. In B. Jonsson and J. Parrow, editors, *CONCUR'94*, volume 836 of LNCS, pages 283–298. Springer-Verlag, 1994.
13. G. Smith. *The Object-Z Specification Language.* Kluwer Academic Publisher, 2000.

14. G. Smith and K. Winter. Proving Temporal Properties of Z specifications Using Abstraction. In *ZB2003: Formal Specification and Development in Z and B*, number 2651 in LNCS, pages 260–279. Springer, 2003.

15. F. Tip. A survey of program slicing techniques. *Journal of programming languages*, 3(3), 1995.

16. H. Wehrheim. Inheritance of Temporal Logic Properties. In *FMOODS 2003: Formal Methods for Open Object-based Distributed Systems*, number 2884 in LNCS, pages 79–93. Springer, 2003.

17. H. Wehrheim. Preserving Properties under Change. In F.S. de Boer, M. Bonsague, S. Graf, and W.P. de Roever, editors, *Formal Methods for Components and Objects*, volume 3188 of *LNCS*, pages 330–343. Springer, 2004.

18. M. Weiser. Programmers use slices when debugging. *Communications of the ACM*, 25(7):446–452, 1982.

19. Mark Weiser. Program slicing. In *Proceedings of the 5th international conference on Software engineering*, pages 439–449. IEEE Press, 1981.

20. K. Winter and G. Smith. Compositional Verification for Object-Z. In *ZB2003: Formal Specification and Development in Z and B*, number 2651 in LNCS, pages 280–299. Springer, 2003.

21. Zhou Chaochen, C.A.R. Hoare, and A.P. Ravn. A Calculus of Durations. *Information Processing Letters*, 40/5:269–276, 1991.

# Checking JML Specifications with B Machines[*]

Fabrice Bouquet, Frédéric Dadeau, and Julien Groslambert

Laboratoire d'Informatique (LIFC),
Université de Franche-Comté, CNRS - INRIA,
16, route de Gray - 25030 Besançon cedex, France
Tel.: (33) 381 666 664, Fax: (33) 381 666 450
{bouquet, dadeau, groslambert}@lifc.univ-fcomte.fr

**Abstract.** This paper presents a solution to the lack of tool-support for the JML models verification. We propose an approach for expressing JML specifications within the B abstract machines notation. The B machines generated from the JML can then be checked to ensure their correctness. Thus, we deduce the correctness of the original JML specification, ensured by rewriting rules which give the semantical equivalence of the two models. More generally, this translation can be applied to object-oriented specification languages using before-after predicates.

**Keywords:** Java Modeling Language, JML, object-oriented, B method, specifications, abstract machines.

## 1    Introduction

Formal models is a widely spread practice in the software engineering process. Specification languages are used to formally describe the systems to study, leading to safer implementations. The B method [Abr96] is an incremental software engineering process, starting from the building of an abstract system which is later on refined to reach an implementation. For each step, properties have to be checked to ensure the correctness of the specification. In the case of B abstract machines, the specifier has to ensure that the invariant is established by the initialization and preserved by the execution of an operation. This is the *verification process* which aims at checking the correctness of the specification.

In recent years, The Java Modeling Language –JML– [LBR99] has been introduced to act as a behavioral interface specification language to formally describe Java programs. JML is presented as an alternative to UML [RJB99] with OCL [WK98] for the formal description of object programs. Since its syntax is close to Java, this specification language may even be used by non-specialists of modeling. Indeed, JML is presented as annotations embedded within Java comments so that only specific compilers may recognize them. As for B, JML makes it pos-

---

[*] This work has been realized within the GECCOO project of program "ACI Sécurité Informatique" supported by the French Ministry of Research and New Technologies.

H. Treharne et al. (Eds.): ZB 2005, LNCS 3455, pp. 434–453, 2005.

sible to describe properties on the system. These properties, applied on a class, are supposed to hold at every state of the system.

Whereas the B method is well tool-supported –the AtelierB [Cle01], the B-Toolkit [NS99], B4Free [B4F03], or experimental work around the verification of the B invariance proof obligations with different provers such as haRVey [CDD+03]– the verification of JML models suffers from the lack of tool-support. Indeed, most of the JML-related tools [BCC+03] were developed to ensure the conformity of the Java code with regard to the JML annotations. Thus, JML is not really considered as a modeling language but is more of an annotation language in which it is possible to express assertions for the Java code. We want to use JML as a modeling language. For that, we would like to be able to easily prove the correctness of the JML model.

This paper presents a solution to the verification of JML specifications, by rewriting them into equivalent B machines. Although these two specification languages present relatively close semantics, the expression of JML within B machines is not straight-forward, due to the presence of objects, inheritance, and especially the difficulty of building generalized B substitutions from JML before-after predicates. Therefore, we introduce the theoretical grounds for expressing JML specifications in B, providing an original approach for the expression of JML within a B framework. This model-based approach is not exhaustive in the sense that the whole JML specification clauses can not be expressed with the B notation. Nevertheless, our translation covers an interesting subset of JML and presents, at our knowledge, an original proposal for the verification of JML models.

The paper is organized as follows. Section 2 presents the Java Modeling Language and introduces the example we use throughout the remainder of the paper. Section 3 shows how we express Java concepts within a B machine. Section 4 presents the expression of JML specifications within B machines. Section 5 presents how the expression of inheritance can be realized within our framework. Section 6 presents the experimental results we obtained with the example. Section 7 presents the related work, and finally Section 8 concludes and introduces the future work.

# 2   Java Modeling Language

The Java Modeling Language was introduced by Leavens et al. at the Iowa State University. This specification language, describing Java modules behavior, aims at being used by developers as well as by specifiers. The JML annotations are embedded within Java comments by using //@ for a single-line annotation and /*@ ... @*/ for multiple-lines annotations. Moreover, the JML syntax is based on the Java syntax for expressing predicates, enriched with several new operators and keywords.

## 2.1   Overview of JML Specifications

JML describes the behavior of Java modules, i.e., classes or interfaces, using first-order logic predicates written with a Java-based syntax. New operators, such as ==> for implication, <==> (resp. <=!=>) for equivalence (resp. non-equivalence), or \forall (resp. \exists) for the universal (resp. existential) quantifier, are added to the usual Java syntax. These predicates are used within specification clauses, which can be applied to the class or to methods. Classical boolean operators of Java are still used, such as && for the conjunction, || for the disjunction, and ! for the negation.

The invariant is a class specification clause, which represents properties that should hold at each state of the system. In the same context, history constraints, which are written with before-after predicates, describe properties that are supposed to hold after each method call, linking the resulting state with its predecessor. In order to express before-after predicates, a new functional symbol, \old, designates the evaluation of an expression in the before state. In a before-after predicate, an attribute or a method call which is not under the scope of \old is by default considered to be evaluated in the after state. Obviously, history constraints do not have to hold after an instance creation, since the instance does not have any previous state.

Method specifications are written within annotations above the method declaration, as described in Fig. 1, which also presents the principal method specification clauses. In this figure, $X$ represents the set of class attributes in the before state and $X'$ the corresponding attributes in the after state. $Param$ designates the set of input parameters of the method. The return value, represented by the JML \result keyword, is expressed by $result$ in the figure.

The requires clause presents the requirements $P(X, Param)$ that the system must fulfill for the method to be executed. This principle is called Design By Contract, and was introduced in Eiffel [Mey97] from which JML is inspired. The diverges clause exhibits a condition $D(X, Param)$ under which the execution of the method may not terminate (e.g. loops forever). Unfortunately, there is no guarantee that the method will diverge if the predicate is established when the method is invoked. This corresponds to the Hoare notion of *partial correctness*. The assignable is used to specify a list of attributes $A$, $A \subseteq X$, that are modified by the method execution. A special keyword, \nothing (resp. \everything) symbolizes that no attributes (resp. all the attributes) are modified by the execution of the method. The when clause makes it possible to delay the execution of the method until the system satisfies the specified predicate

```
/*@   requires  P(X, Param);
 @    diverges  D(X, Param);
 @    assignable A;
 @    when  W(X);
 @    ensures  Q(X, X', Param, result);
 @    signals (Exception₁) R₁(X, X', Param);
 @    ...
 @    signals (Exceptionₙ) Rₙ(X, X', Param);
 @*/
returnType methodName(Type₁ Param₁, ...) { ... }
```

**Fig. 1.** The principal JML method specification clauses

```
class Purse {

    //@ invariant balance >= 0;
    protected short balance;

    /*@ public normal_behavior
      @   requires amount >= 0;
      @   assignable balance;
      @   ensures balance == amount;
      @*/
    public Purse(short amount) {...}

    /*@ public behavior
      @   requires amount >= 0;
      @   assignable balance;
      @   ensures
      @       balance == \old(balance) - amount;
      @   signals (NoCreditException E1)
      @       balance == \old(balance)
      @       && amount > balance;
      @*/
    public void withdraw(short amount)
                throws NoCreditException {...}

    /*@ public normal_behavior
      @   assignable \nothing;
      @   ensures \result == balance;
      @*/
    public /*@ pure @*/ short getBalance() {...}

    /*@ public normal_behavior
      @   requires p != null && p != this
      @   assignable balance;
      @   ensures balance == p.getBalance();
      @*/
    public void transfer(Purse p) {...}
```

```
    /*@ public normal_behavior
      @   requires amount >= 0;
      @   assignable balance;
      @   ensures
      @       balance == \old(balance) + amount;
      @*/
    public void credit(short amount) {...}

}

class LimitedPurse extends Purse {

    //@ invariant balance <= max_amount;
    //@ constraint \not_modified(max_amount);
    static short max_amount = 10000;

    /*@ public normal_behavior
      @   requires b >= 0 && b <= max_amount;
      @   assignable balance;
      @   ensures balance == b;
      @*/
    public LimitedPurse(short b) { ... }

    /*@ also
      @   public normal_behavior
      @       requires
      @           max_amount - balance >= amount
      @           && amount >= 0;
      @       assignable balance;
      @       ensures
      @           balance==\old(balance)+amount;
      @*/
    public void credit(short amount) { ... }

}
```

**Fig. 2.** JML specification of a simplified Purse with inheritance

$W(X)$. The **ensures** and **signals** clause are both used to express the post-conditions established after the execution of the method. The **ensures** clause describes the *normal postcondition* $Q(X, X', Param, result)$, established when the method does not throw any exception during its execution. The **signals** clauses describes the *exceptional postconditions* $R_i(X, X', Param)$, which are established when the specified exception is thrown by the method. The method specification clauses may involve method parameters, with the restriction that they should not be modified by the method. Indeed, the evaluation of method parameters in the postconditions systematically refers to their before value, without having to use the \old keyword.

JML also introduces new kind of modifiers, the most interesting being the notion of **purity** applied to a method. A **pure** method is a method that does not modify any class attribute. Only the pure methods may be called within JML predicates, in order to prevent from side-effects.

## 2.2   An Example of JML Specification

The example presented in Fig. 2 specifies a simplified electronic purse. The **Purse** class describes a basic purse, managing only one attribute named **balance** representing the amount of money available in the considered purse. A constructor creates an instance of Purse and initializes its balance. The credit(short) method is used to add money to the purse, whereas the withdraw(short) method removes money from the purse. Notice that the latter may possibly throw an exception named NoCreditException where there is not enough money in the purse. A *pure* method named getBalance() returns the value of the balance, without modifying any class attribute. Finally, the transfer(Purse) method makes it possible to transfer the amount contained in the purse in parameter into the current purse.

In order to illustrate the notion of inheritance in JML, we describe the specification of the LimitedPurse class, which extends the previously described Purse class, by introducing a limitation to the amount contained in the purse. Therefore, this specification inherits the balance attribute and invariant clause from class Purse. It also inherits the withdraw(short), getBalance() and transfer(Purse) method and their method specifications, since these methods are not redefined in the subclass. The credit(short) method is redefined so that the addition of the amount to the balance does not exceed a maximal value. The invariant is enriched to specify that the balance should not exceed the maximum defined by the max_amount static attribute.

## 3    Expressing Java/JML Classes with B Machines

The expression of objects in B has already been studied with UML class diagrams [LP02]. The main difference between expressing JML classes and UML classes resides in the interactions between objects. In UML, they are defined through associations, which create a link between classes. Thus, UML classes only contain data that are not typed as objects, since associations exists, and only built-in types are expressed inside UML classes. This makes it possible to express each UML class within a different B machine, and to describe the associations within a specific machine. In Java/JML, object interactions are described through object-typed attributes. Unfortunately, the B method does not support cyclic references in the machine inclusions, and therefore, it is not possible to declare one machine per Java class, and to use machine inclusion to reference and modify another class' attributes. Indeed, this would induce a too strong restriction on our framework.

The representation of JML classes is thus done through one single machine, in addition to an independent machine destined to handle global items.

This section defines the translation of Java/JML class structures in B. First, we define the heap and instances management in a global machine. Second, we define the expression of classes and objects with a B machine. Then we describe the translation of class attributes, and finally, we present how instance creation is realized within our representation.

```
MACHINE
      global
SETS
      EXCEPTIONS; INSTANCES
CONSTANTS
      null, no_exception
PROPERTIES
      null ∈ INSTANCES ∧
      no_exception ∈ EXCEPTIONS
VARIABLES
      exception, instances, diverges
INVARIANT
      exception ∈ EXCEPTIONS ∧
      instances ⊆ INSTANCES ∧
      null ∉ instances ∧ diverges : BOOL
INITIALISATION
      exception := no_exception ||
      instances := ∅ || diverges := FALSE
OPERATIONS
      diverge ≙
        PRE diverges = FALSE
        THEN diverges := TRUE
        END;
```

```
throw(exc) ≙
  PRE   exc ∈ EXCEPTIONS ∧
        exception = no_exception ∧
        exception ≠ exc
  THEN exception := exc
  END;

catch(exc) ≙
    PRE   exception ≠ no_exception ∧
          exc = exception
    THEN exception := no_exception
    END;

new(inst_set) ≙
  PRE inst_set ⊆ INSTANCES - instances
      ∧ inst_set ≠ ∅
      ∧ null ∉ inst_set
  THEN
      instances := instances ∪ inst_set
  END
END
```

**Fig. 3.** The `global` abstract machine

## 3.1   One Machine to Rule Them All...

In order to express JML specification functionalities, we have identified three different Java mechanisms, which are not related to classes but to the language itself. Therefore, we manage these mechanisms within a specific machine named `global`, which is independent from the JML specifications. The code of the `global` machine is given in Fig. 3.

The first mechanism is the object management. An abstract representation of the heap is handled by a B abstract set of addresses named `INSTANCES`. In addition, we consider a variable, named `instances`, subset of `INSTANCES` designating the addresses that are used in the heap. We also consider a constant named `null`, representing a null pointer, and we specify that `null` should not belong to the set of object-assigned addresses.

The second Java mechanism is the management of exceptions, which may be thrown during the execution of methods, but which may also be caught to continue the execution of the program. Exceptions described in the specifications are referenced in an abstract set, named `EXCEPTIONS`. This set contains an additional constant, named `no_exception` to express that no exception has been thrown. A variable named `exception` specifies which exception is currently thrown. Two operations represent the throwing or the catching of exceptions.

The last mechanism to consider is the divergence of method, which indicates whether an executed method may terminate or not. In this case, the system is locked and no more methods may be executed. We define a boolean variable named `diverges` specifying whether or not the system is executing a method that loops forever. A corresponding operation makes it possible to modify this variable during a method execution.

## 3.2     Classes and Objects Representation

On the same principle as an UML to B translation, we need to consider the Java classes used as a whole set of classes. Therefore, we start with a gathering of all the JML classes referenced from the considered specification. For the reasons previously explained, we have to express all the classes within a single B machine. This machine includes the `global` machine. In order to avoid any identifier names conflicts, we prefix the identifiers extracted from the class by `b_ClassName_` to obtain distinct B identifiers, where `ClassName` is the name of the class. On the same principle, we prefix by `b_ClassName` the variables we introduce. For each class, a set variable, subset of the abstract addresses set, named `b_ClassNameInstances` represents the objects that have already been created. In order to be able to express JML history constraints, we need to represent the system state preceding the current state. Thus, we duplicate the variables designating the instances, since the creation of an instance induces a difference between the set of instances before and after the constructor invocation. Since we do not consider the garbage collector which retrieves the unused addresses, we consider that the set of instances in the previous state is a subset of the current set of instances.

In addition, we declare constants to represent each exception that may be thrown in the JML specification.

*Example 1 (Illustration of the Classes Structures).* We illustrate the expression of class structures with our example. Considering the Java/JML classes `Purse` and `LimitedPurse`, described in Fig.2, the corresponding part of the B machine concerning class translation and instances management is the following:

```
MACHINE
    system
INCLUDES
    global
CONSTANTS
    exc_NoCreditException
PROPERTIES
    exc_NoCreditException ∈ EXCEPTIONS ∧ exc_NoCreditException ≠ no_exception
VARIABLES
    b_PurseInstances, b_Purse_oldInstances
    b_LimitedPurseInstances, b_LimitedPurse_oldInstances
INVARIANT
    b_PurseInstances ⊆ Instances ∧ b_Purse_oldInstances ⊆ b_PurseInstances ∧
    b_LimitedPurseInstances ⊆ Instances ∧
    b_LimitedPurse_oldInstances ⊆ b_LimitedPurseInstances ∧ ...
INITIALISATION
    b_PurseInstances,b_LimitedPurseInstances := ∅,∅ ||
    b_Purse_oldInstances,b_LimitedPurse_oldInstances := ∅,∅ || ...
```

## 3.3     Types Translation and Attributes Representation

Most of the Java types can be expressed with integers only. This is the case of the integers types (such as `byte`, `short`, `int` and `long`). Distinction is made between all these types by specifying their range of values in the machine invariant. Restrictions are put onto the `long` type, whose range of value may exceed the maximal and minimal integer value of the verification tools. Characters are

| Type | Range of values |
|------|-----------------|
| byte | -128..127 |
| short | -32768..32767 |
| int | -2147483648..2147483647 |
| char | 0..65535 |
| Object of class $C$ | b_$C$Instances $\cup$ {null} |
| Type[ ]...[ ] | NAT $\nrightarrow$ (... (NAT $\nrightarrow$ $Range$(Type))...) |

**Fig. 4.** Range of values for supported types

expressed by their unsigned short value. Floating types (`float` and `double`) are prohibited since they cannot be expressed in B notation.

Object references are typed as addresses, element from the set of created objects of the corresponding class/machine, which is itself a subset of the common INSTANCES set. Moreover object references may be `null`. This way, we simulate the principle of aliasing, since several references can be made onto the same object.

Arrays are also managed and considered as a partial function from naturals to the corresponding type values.

Figure 4 presents the *Range* function that is used to compute the range of values for each type.

We express class attributes using machine variables, which are declared, typed and initialized in the corresponding B machine clauses. Depending on the static modifier of the attribute, we may have two different cases. Either the attribute is non-static and the variable is typed as a total function mapping created instances to their corresponding value. Otherwise, if the attribute is static –it has the same value for all the class instances– its value does not depend of any instance, and it can directly be typed.

Since we both need before and after values of the class attributes in order to express history constraints, we duplicate each attribute to keep the value in the previous state. Inspired from the principle of JML, we distinguish before values by prefixing the variable name by `old_`. In the rest of the paper, this set is designated by $X_{B_{old}}$.

**Proposition 1 (Expression of Class Attributes).** *Let $att_1$ be a non-static attribute from class $C_1$ whose Java type is $T_1$ and whose initial value is $val_1$, and let $att_2$ be a static attribute from class $C_2$ whose Java type is $T_2$ and whose initial value is $val_2$. We assume that $T_1$ and $T_2$ are supported and we define the representation of $att_1$ and $att_2$ in a B machine as follows.*

```
VARIABLES
     ... b_C₁_att₁, b_C₁_old_att₁, b_C₂_att₂, b_C₂_old_att₂
INVARIANT
     ... b_C₁_att₁ ∈ b_C₁Instances → Range(T₁) ∧
         b_C₁_old_att₁ ∈ b_C₁_oldInstances → Range(T₁) ∧
         b_C₂_att₂ ∈ Range(T₂) ∧ b_C₂_old_att₂ ∈ Range(T₂)
INITIALISATION
     ... b_C₂_att₂, b_C₂_old_att₂ := val₂, val₂
END
```

Unlike the non-static attributes, which are initialized at the creation of an instance, the static attribute values are directly assigned in the INITIALISATION clause. Thus, Java expressions such as $C_2.att_2$ can be evaluated without having to create an instance.

*Example 2 (Attributes Expression).* Considering the example in figure 2, the non-static attribute `balance` of class `Purse`, and the static attribute `max_amount` of class `LimitedPurse` are expressed in the B machine as follows.

```
VARIABLES
    ... b_Purse_balance, b_Purse_old_balance,
        b_LimitedPurse_max_amount, b_LimitedPurse_old_max_amount, ...
INVARIANT
    ... b_Purse_balance ∈ b_PurseInstances → -32768..32767 ∧
        b_Purse_old_balance ∈ b_Purse_oldInstances → -32768..32767 ∧
        b_LimitedPurse_max_amount ∈ -32768..32767 ∧
        b_LimitedPurse_old_max_amount ∈ -32768..32767 ∧ ...
INITIALISATION
    ... b_LimitedPurse_max_amount, b_LimitedPurse_old_max_amount := 10000, 10000 ...
END
```

### 3.4    Instance Creation

In the semantics of Java [GJS00], it is possible to express initial values of class attributes by two different ways - either the value is specified in the attribute declaration, or it is assigned by the constructor. The latter overrides any value given at the declaration. If no value has been defined in the attribute declaration and if the constructor does not assign a value to the attribute, a default value is substituted - either 0 for numerical-derived types, or `null` for object types.

In the JML specifications, we have the possibility to know which attributes are affected by the execution of a method by consulting the `assignable` clause. Thus, we deduce which fields are assigned with an initial value given at the declaration. The expression of the constructor is based on the method specifications expressions. The following example presents a glimpse of this technique, detailed in Section 4.2.

*Example 3 (Constructor representation).* In the class `Purse`, the B operation `b_Purse_constructorPurse_short` representing the constructor `Purse(short)`, is described as follows. The precondition of the operation is used to firstly type the parameters and secondly to express the JML precondition. Notice that the operation requires that no diverging method is being executed, and that no exceptions have been thrown unless they have been previously caught.

```
b_Purse_constructorPurse_short(this, b_amount) ≜
    PRE
        this ∈ INSTANCES - instances ∧ this ≠ null ∧ b_amount ∈ -32768..32767 ∧
        exception = no_exception ∧ diverges = FALSE ∧ b_amount ≥ 0
    THEN
        ANY assigned_balance WHERE
            assigned_balance ∈ -32768..32767 ∧ assigned_balance = b_amount
        THEN
            new({this}) || b_PurseInstances := b_PurseInstances ∪ {this} ||
            b_Purse_balance := b_Purse_balance ∪ {this ↦ assigned_balance}
        END
        || b_Purse_oldInstances := b_PurseInstances
        || b_Purse_old_balance := b_Purse_balance
    END
```

Notice that this operation realizes a call to the **new** operation of the **global** machine to register the newly created instance.

# 4  Expressing JML Specifications in a B Machine

This section presents the representation the JML specifications, i.e., the expression of the invariant, the history constraints, and the method specification which describe the behavior of the Java method, composed of method specification clauses given in Fig. 1.

In this section, we first describe the invariant and history constraints expression within our framework. Then, we describe the expression of the pre- and postconditions of the method specification clauses, before describing how more exotic clauses such as **when** and **diverges** are expressed in our framework. Finally, we present how to express the **pure** method calls, which may be used to write JML predicates.

For this section and the followings, we assume we have a function $[\![-]\!]_B$ which traduces first order JML predicates into B first order predicates inside our framework. This function traduces syntacticly all JML operators into B operators, and replaces all the JML variables – including JML pre-state variables– by their corresponding B variables, as explained in Section 3.

## 4.1  Invariant and History Constraints Expression in B

In order to check invariant and history constraints, we express them both within the machine **INVARIANT** clause. These properties depend on the instances, and therefore their expression has to be prefixed by an universal quantification on the created instances of the considered class.

**Proposition 2 (Expression of the JML Invariant).** *Let $I(X)$ be the predicate of the JML invariant of class $C$. The expression of $I(X)$ in the B machine INVARIANT clause is the following.*

$$\forall xx_{inv}.(xx_{inv} \in b\_CInstances \Rightarrow [\![I]\!]_B(X_B(xx_{inv})))$$

Notice that the quantified variable representing the instances, is suffixed with **inv** to express that this predicate corresponds to the JML invariant of the source specification.

*Example 4 (Invariant of the Purse Class).* Considering the example of Fig. 2, the expression of the class invariant adds the following predicate to the INVARIANT clause.

```
INVARIANT
     ... ∧ ∀ xx_inv . (xx_inv ∈ b_PurseInstances ⇒ b_Purse_balance(xx_inv) ≥ 0)
```

Contrary to the JML class invariant which only applies on a single state, the history constraints are expressed with both current and previous state. Therefore we have introduced in the JML attributes representation, a copy of previous state value of each attribute. Thus, we are able to express the JML history constraints within the INVARIANT clause of the B machine.

**Proposition 3 (Expression of the JML History Constraints).** *Let $H(X_{old}, X)$ be the predicate of the JML history constraint of class $C$. The expression of $H(X_{old}, X)$ in the B machine INVARIANT clause is the following.*

$$\forall\, xx_{hc}.(xx_{hc} \in b\_C\_oldInstances \Rightarrow [\![H]\!]_B(X_{B_{old}}(xx_{hc}), X_B(xx_{hc}))$$

Syntactically, when translating an history constraint, we replace all attributes of the predicate in the scope of a \old symbol by the corresponding variables of the B set $X_{B_{old}}$. This set represents the values of the attributes in the previous state of the execution. An history constraint does not have to hold after the call of the constructor. Indeed, there is no previous state for the instance, so the constraint can not be evaluated. Thus, the predicate representing the history constraints is quantified on the instances that were already created in the previous state.

*Example 5 (History Constraints of the LimitedPurse Class).* Considering the example of figure 2, the expression of the history constraints adds the following predicate to the INVARIANT clause.

```
INVARIANT
    ... ∧ ∀ xx_hc . (xx_hc ∈ b_LimitedPurse_oldInstances ⇒
                     b_LimitedPurse_old_max_amount = b_LimitedPurse_max_amount)
```

## 4.2    Method Specification Expression

JML methods makes it possible to change the value of the private attributes. Therefore, we describe a translation scheme for each method.

**Proposition 4 (Expressing a JML Method in B).** *A JML non-static method is expressed as a B operation, which takes as an input parameter named* this, *which is the instance to which the method is applied. On the contrary, a JML static method does not need such an input parameter. Each method parameter is expressed as an operation input parameter. If the method is non-void, an output parameter named* result *is used to describe the return value.*

The main difficulty is to express a generalized substitution starting from a predicate which holds after the execution of the method. In order to help us in this task, we take into account the assignable indicating which attributes are modified by the method. The idea of the translation described hereafter is to introduce local variables in the substitution that will represent the values of the attributes in the after state. These variables are constrained so that the postcondition (normal or exceptional) established by the method execution holds. After that, the attributes of the assignable clause are assigned with these new values.

We assume that the method specifications are composed by the clauses described in Fig. 1. The unspecified clauses are considered as their default value, i.e., `true` for `requires`, `ensures` and `when`, `false` for `diverges` and `signals` and `\everything` for `assignable`.

**Proposition 5 (Expressing Pre- and Postconditions).** *Given a JML specification of a non-static method m of class C. This method and its specification are equivalent to the following B operation* $b\_C\_m\_TypeParam_B$:

```
result ← b_C_m_TypeParamB(this, ParamB) =
   PRE [[P]]B(XB, ParamB) ∧ this ∈ b_CInstances
       ∧ Type(ParamB) ∧ exception = no_exception ∧ diverges = FALSE
   THEN
        CHOICE
           ANY LA, L̄A, lr
           WHERE Type(LA) ∧ Type(L̄A) ∧ Type(lr) ∧ [[Q]]B(XB(this), LA ∪ L̄A, ParamB, lr)
           THEN AB(this) := LA ‖ result := lr
           END
        OR
           ANY LA, L̄A, lr
           WHERE Type(LA) ∧ Type(L̄A) ∧ Type(lr) ∧ [[R1]]B(XB(this), LA ∪ L̄A, ParamB, lr)
           THEN AB(this):=LA ‖ throw(E1) ‖ result := lr
           END
        OR ... OR
           ANY LA, L̄A, lr
           WHERE Type(LA) ∧ Type(L̄A) ∧ Type(lr) ∧ [[Rn]]B(XB(this), LA ∪ L̄A, ParamB, lr)
           THEN AB(this):=LA ‖ throw(En) ‖ result := lr
           END
        END
        ‖ Vold := V
   END
```

*Where $L_A$ is the set of local variables representing the after values of the assignable attributes, $\overline{L_A}$ is the complementary to $L_A$ in $X_B(this)$, $l_r$ is a local variable representing the returned value, $V$ is the set of all the B variables that exist in an* `old_` *version, and Type is a function which returns the typing predicate of a variable according to the definitions given in 3.1.*

Following the semantics of JML, our translation can be informally justified as follows:

- The precondition $P$ must hold when the method is invoked. We represent this by a precondition on an operation. We strengthen this precondition coming from the JML specification by four other predicates. First the operation assume that the variable `this`, which represents the current instance, belongs to the set of the created instances. Second, the operation also check the type of the parameters. Third, we check that no exception is being thrown. Finally, we ensure that no other method is diverging.
- If the method terminates, it is either normally or exceptionally. This is modeled this by a non-deterministic choice between a substitution which implies a normal termination and substitutions which imply exceptional terminations.
- Only the variables included in the `assignable` clause may change during the invocation of the method, this is the *frame condition* in JML. That is why in

our model, only the variables included in set $A$ are substituted. Thus, only these variables may have changed after the termination of the operation. $\overline{L_A}$ is introduced to avoid errors which may appear when the `assignable` clause is not complete (e.g. unchanged attributes may be expressed within the postcondition predicates, but may not appear in the `assignable` clause). This makes it possible to express the after values for all the attributes within the B predicate representing the postconditions.

- When the method terminates normally, the postconditions introduced by the keyword `ensures` must hold. We represent that by a bounded choice of local variables which have the same type as the modifiable variables and which establish the postconditions $Q$. The *assignable* variables of the current instance – denoted by the parameter `this` – are assigned with their corresponding local variable.
- We represent the exceptional termination of the method by the same kind of substitution. To represent an exceptional postcondition, we assign to the exceptional variable the type of the generated exception by calling the `throw` operation located in the `global` machine.
- As we keep the values of fields and instances (the $V$ set) in the previous state, we update the old values after each operation.

*Example 6 (Translation of a Method into B).* Considering the JML method `credit(short)` located in the `Purse` class described in Fig. 2. The corresponding B operation is the following.

```
b_Purse_credit_short(this,b_amount) ≜
    PRE
        this ∈ b_PurseInstances ∧ b_amount ∈ -32768..32767 ∧
        b_amount ≥ 0 ∧ exception = no_exception ∧ diverges = FALSE
    THEN
        ANY assigned_balance WHERE
            assigned_balance ∈ -32768..32767 ∧
            assigned_balance = (b_Purse_balance(this)+b_amount)
        THEN
            b_Purse_balance(this) := assigned_balance
        END
        || ... /* update of the old variables */
    END
```

Notice that the translation of the JML precondition `amount >= 0` appears in the precondition of the B operation. Moreover, only variables specified in the `assignable` clause are updated. The postcondition `balance == \old(balance) + amount` is now expressed by the `ANY` substitution. Moreover, the translation of the $Q$ predicate appears in the `WHERE` clause.

## 4.3    Methods Call

However JML predicates and B predicates are both expressed in first-order logic, the translation is not a simple operator translation since JML allows `pure` method calls – without side-effects – into predicates. We propose a method to translate these predicate in cases without recursive structure in calls of methods.

The idea is to introduce local variables to designate the return value of the method call and the input parameters. The predicate corresponding to the normal postcondition is locally rewritten, and substitutions are performed on it in order to instantiate the method parameters with their value as the method is called. In the case of method calls in postconditions, the new local variables are introduced within an ANY substitution, otherwise, they are introduced using an existential quantifier.

*Example 7 (Postcondition of the Transfer Method).* The predicate of the postcondition of the `transfer` method is `balance == p.getBalance()`. It includes a call to the pure `getBalance()` method, which is translated as follows.

```
ANY assigned_balance, res_getBalance WHERE
    assigned_balance ∈ -32768..32767 ∧ res_getBalance ∈ -32768..32767 ∧
    res_getBalance = b_Purse_balance(b_p) ∧ assigned_balance = res_getBalance
THEN
    b_Purse_balance(this) := assigned_balance
END
```

As explained above, a new local variable `res_getBalance` is introduced. In the WHERE clause, notice that `res_getBalance` is typed and `assigned_balance` is equal to this new variable representing the result of `p.getBalance()`. The expression `res_getBalance = b_Purse_balance(b_p)`, is the translation of the postcondition predicate of the method `getBalance()`.

### 4.4    Expressing the Diverges Clause

When the `diverges` clause of a method is satisfied on the state preceding the invocation of a method, it means that this method *may* diverges, *i.e.*, loops forever. To model a diverging state, we have introduced a `diverges` B variable in our model (see 3.1). In the method model, we have to take care that an operation representing a JML method cannot be called when the machine is in a diverging state. To do that, we strengthen all precondition of the operation modeling a method by the predicate `diverges = FALSE`.

Moreover, we modify the model of a method to introduce the behavior of the method, which may diverge. This is modeled as follows.

```
PRE ⟦P⟧_B (X_B, Param_B) ∧ this ∈ b_CInstances ∧ Type(Param_B) ∧
    exception = no_exception ∧ diverges = FALSE
THEN
    IF ⟦D⟧_B (X_B, Param_B) THEN
        CHOICE
            diverge
        OR
            ANY L_A, L̄_A, l_r
            WHERE ...        ELSE
        CHOICE
            ANY L_A, L̄_A, l_r
            WHERE ...        END
    || ... /* update of the old variables */
END
```

This introduces an conditional choice in the B operation. If the $D$ predicate is satisfied, then we have a nondeterministic choice between termination – the ANY substitutions introduced in Section 4.2 – and non-termination – the `diverges` variable is set to `TRUE` by calling the `diverge` operation located in the `global` machine.

### 4.5    Expressing the `When` Clause

To model the JML `when` clause of a method $m$, we introduce a new variable `m_wait` which has the type $b\_C$Instances $\rightarrow$ `BOOL`. This variable indicates that the method $m$ is delayed. This variable is initialized as `FALSE` when an instance is created.

In the translation framework, we represent the method $m$ by an operation $b\_C\_m\_TypeParam_B$(`this`, $Param_B$) and an event $b\_C\_m\_$`when` as follows.

| | |
|---|---|
| $b\_C\_m\_TypeParam_B$(`this`, $Param_B$) $\hat{=}$ <br>   PRE $[\![P]\!]_B(X_B, Param)$ $\wedge$ <br>     `this` $\in$ b$\_C$Instances $\wedge$ <br>     $Type(Param_B)$ $\wedge$ <br>     exception = no_exception $\wedge$ <br>     diverges = FALSE <br>   THEN <br>     m_wait(this) := TRUE <br>   END | $b\_C\_m\_$`when` $\hat{=}$ <br>   ANY xx WHERE <br>     xx $\in$ INSTANCES $\wedge$ <br>     m_wait(xx) = TRUE $\wedge$ $[\![W]\!]_B(X_B)$ <br>   THEN <br>     ANY $L_A$, $\overline{L_A}$ WHERE ... <br>     THEN $A_B(xx)$ := $L_A$ $\parallel$ <br>       m_wait(this) = FALSE <br>   END <br>   $\parallel$ ... /* update of the old variables */ <br>   END |

Informally, the action of the operation representing $m$ does not establish the postcondition of $m$ but sets the variable `m_wait` to `TRUE` for the current instance. The B event we have introduced, has as a guard the translation of the JML $W$ predicate and the predicate `m_wait = TRUE`. It means that the B event is automatically executed when its guard is true. This leads to the same results as the JML `when` clause. Of course, the action of the event $b\_C\_m\_$`when` establishes the postcondition of $m$.

## 5    Expressing Inheritance

This section details how inheritance is handled within our framework. First, we describe the handling of instances and attributes. Second, we present the expression of method inheritance.

### 5.1    Instances and Attributes

According to the concept of inheritance, the instances of subclasses are also instances of the superclass. This property is added to the invariant as described below.

**Proposition 6 (Specifying Subclass Instances).** *Let $C$ be a Java class, and $C_{Sub}$ be a Java class extending $C$. The following code is added to the invariant.*

$$b\_C_{Sub} Instances \subseteq b\_C Instances$$

In the Java/JML semantics, inheritance can be seen as a recopy of the superclass fields -attributes and specifications- within the subclasses. In practice, we do not recopy fields in the subclasses. Attributes are named with respect to the class in which they are declared. Since all the classes are declared within the same machine, the fields can be accessed from any operation representing a method from any class.

When a subclass instance is created, the corresponding B operation of our framework adds the instance to the set of the class instances, in addition to adding the instance to the set of the superclass instances.

*Example 8.* Considering the `LimitedPurse` class described in figure 2, the B operation representing the constructor `LimitedPurse(amount)` is the following.

```
b_Purse_constructorLimitedPurse_short(this, b_amount) ≜
    PRE
        this ∈ INSTANCES - instances ∧ this ≠ null ∧ b_amount ∈ -32768..32767 ∧
        exception = no_exception ∧ diverges = FALSE ∧
        b_LimitedPurse_max_amount = b_LimitedPurse_old_max_amount ∧
        b_amount ≥ 0 ∧ b_amount ≤ b_LimitedPurse_max_amount
    THEN
        ANY assigned_balance WHERE
            assigned_balance ∈ -32768..32767 ∧ assigned_balance = b_amount
        THEN
            new({this}) ‖ b_PurseInstances := b_PurseInstances ∪ {this} ‖
            b_LimitedPurseInstances := b_LimitedPurseInstances ∪ {this} ‖
            b_Purse_balance := b_Purse_balance ∪ {this ↦ assigned_balance}
        END
        ‖ ... /* update of the old variables */
    END
```

## 5.2    Method Inheritance

In the Java/JML semantics, inheritance of method can be seen either as a new method if the method of the subclass overrides the method of the superclass, or a recopy of the superclass method within the subclasses otherwise.

Whereas the second case does not lead to a recopy of the corresponding B operations, as for the attributes, the first case is reduced to the introduction of a new operation, named $b\_C_{Sub}\_m\_TypeParam_B$, specifying the new method $m$ as described in 4.2.

*Example 9 (Translation of an inherited method).* Considering the example described in Fig. 2, the redefined method `credit(short)` in the `LimitedPurse` class is expressed as follows.

```
b_LimitedPurse_credit_short(this,b_amount) ≜
    PRE
        this ∈ b_LimitedPurseInstances ∧ b_amount ∈ -32768..32767 ∧
        b_amount ≥ 0 ∧ amount ≤ b_LimitedPurse_max_amount ∧ exception = no_exception
    THEN
        ANY assigned_balance WHERE
            assigned_balance = -32768..32767 ∧
            assigned_balance = (b_Purse_balance(this)+b_amount)
        THEN
            b_Purse_balance(this) := assigned_balance
        END
        ‖ ... /* update of the old variables */
    END
```

This operation used both inherited fields like **b_Purse_balance** and fields of the subclass like **b_LimitedPurse_max_amount**.

To disallow the call of a method of the superclass overridden in the subclass on a instance of the subclass, we strengthen the precondition of the operation representing such a method by the predicate **this** $\notin$ **b_$C_{Sub}$ Instances**. For example, **b_Purse_credit_short** has the precondition **this** $\in$ **b_PurseInstances - b_LimitedPurseInstances** instead of **this** $\in$ **b_PurseInstances**.

# 6     Experimental Results

This section presents the experimental results we obtained using our translation on the example presented in Fig. 2. These experiments were realized with the AtelierB 3.6.

## 6.1     From Failed B Proof Obligations to JML Model Errors

If the prover fails to establish the validity of the invariant preservation, several clues may be used to indicate which part of the original JML invariant is responsible.

In order to illustrate this principle, an error is introduced within the JML invariant of class **Purse**, specifying **balance > 0** instead of **balance >= 0**. The rest of the JML specification is left unchanged. The AtelierB fails to prove the four operations corresponding to the four JML methods **Purse(short)**, **withdraw(short)**, **credit(short)**, and **LimitedPurse(short)**. Each time, the message displayed is the same:

```
"'Check that the invariant (!xx_inv.(xx_inv: b_PurseInstances => b_Purse_balance(xx_inv)>0))
is preserved by the operation - ref ...'" &
=>
1<=(b_Purse_balance\/{this|->assigned_balance})(xx_inv)
```

Using this error message and remarking the **xx_inv** constant used in the expression, we deduce that the error comes from the JML invariant clause. The failing B invariant can be easily understood, and transposed back into the JML syntax to identify which part of the JML invariant cannot be checked.

In this case, there are two possibilities to correct the error, either to weaken the invariant, or to strengthen the preconditions of the operations.

## 6.2     Detecting a Tricky Error

The experienced readers may have surely noticed that an error has been – voluntarily– introduced within the JML specification of the LimitedPurse. Indeed, the attempts for proving the method **transfer(Purse)** fails, indicating an error induced by the invariant. The corresponding error message is the following.

```
"'Check that the invariant
      (!xx_inv.(xx_inv: b_LimitedPurseInstances => b_Purse_balance(xx_inv)>=0
                       & b_Purse_balance(xx_inv)<=b_LimitedPurse_max_amount))
 is preserved by the operation - ref ...'" &
=>
 (b_Purse_balance<+{this|->assigned_balance})(xx_inv)<=b_LimitedPurse_max_amount
```

This error concerns the preservation of the invariant of the JML LimitedPurse class by the execution of the transfer method. The prover claims that the application of the method may violate the invariant of class LimitedPurse ... which is effectively true! The reason is the following. Since the transfer method is not redefined in the LimitedPurse class, it may be applied to an instance of Purse and LimitedPurse. It is then possible for the method to be invoked on an instance of LimitedPurse with a Purse as parameter. Given that no upper limitation on the balance attribute in the Purse class is defined, there is no guarantee that the transferred balance is less or equal to max_amount. To correct this error, the method transfer(Purse) and its specification have to be redefined in the subclass.

After the correction of this error, the resulting B machine generates 72 nonobvious proof obligations, which are all proved by the AtelierB in *Automatic (force 1)* mode.

## 7   Related Work

The expression of object concepts in the B notation have already been studied in the past. A large majority of these works used UML/OCL as an objectoriented modeling language, as in [LP02]. At our knowledge, no investigations have been proposed around JML, or any object-oriented language using pre- and postconditions.

Several tools work on JML annotations. Krakatoa [MPMU04] has been developed to generate proof obligations to be checked with interactive provers. This tool is used to check that a Java implementation is compliant with a JML specification, but it does not aim at verifying the consistency of the model. The LOOP project [HJ00] is originally exploring the Java semantics, and particularly the object-oriented concepts. The main goal of this tool is to verify the correctness of Java programs, using the JML annotations. As for Krakatoa, the LOOP tool considers JML as an independent formal language.

The most related work to ours is the JACK (Java Applet Correctness Kit) tool [BRL03], provided by Gemplus and INRIA Sophia-Antipolis. This tool performs static verification of a JML model, by generating proof obligations for different automated provers. To the best of our knowledge, it does not formalize inheritance concept, and moreover, JACK is currently not publicly available.

Contrary to these tools which check Java code against JML, our approach aims at considering JML specifications by themselves, and to prove class invariant and history constraints preservation. As for every formal method verification, the more informations the JML model contains, the more accurate results we get. Indeed, it is better to force a JML specification to be as precise as possible –

a good practice for any model-based approach, whatever the purpose is: checking model properties or checking implementation.

## 8    Conclusion and Future Work

In this paper[1], we have described an approach for expressing JML specifications with B abstract machines, and therefore use all the B verification tools to prove the model described in the JML specification. We have shown a translation scheme for Java classes and object concepts, such as inheritance, and we have proposed a mechanism for expressing JML before-after predicates in postconditions using B generalized substitutions.

We have also illustrated how our translation provides human-readable B specifications, whose unchecked proof obligations messages may easily be transposed back into the original JML specifications to provide an assistance for the writing of correct JML models. Moreover, this representation can also be used for object-oriented specification languages expressed with before-after predicates.

Our work for the future is the following. First, we plan to implement a compiler to automatically generate B machines that may later on be checked with automatic proof tools for B. This implementation can be based on the parsing technology of the JML-Testing-Tools specification animator [BDLU05] which already converts JML annotations into a B-like language.

Second, according to the principles described by Back et al. [BMvW00], we would propose to use the B refinement to verify correct object substitutability.

Finally, based on the translation exposed in this paper, we plan to develop the translation of JML specifications into B event systems. This will make it possible to check temporal properties and especially liveness properties [BGH+04].

## References

[Abr96]     J.-R. Abrial. *The B-book: assigning programs to meanings*. Cambridge University Press, 1996.

[B4F03]     The B4free web site. http://www.b4free.com, 2003.

[BCC+03]    L. Burdy, Y. Cheon, D. Cok, M. Ernst, J. Kiniry, G.T. Leavens, K.R.M. Leino, and E. Poll. An overview of JML tools and applications. In Th. Arts and W. Fokkink, editors, *Eighth International Workshop on Formal Methods for Industrial Critical Systems (FMICS 03)*, volume 80 of *ENTCS*, pages 73–89. Elsevier, 2003.

[BDLU05]    F. Bouquet, F. Dadeau, B. Legeard, and M. Utting. JML-Testing-Tools: a Symbolic Animator for JML Specifications using CLP. In *Proceedings of 11th Int. Conf. on Tools and Algorithms for the Construction and Analysis of Systems, Tool session (TACAS'05)*, Lecture Notes in Computer Science, Edinburgh, United Kingdom, April 2005. Springer-Verlag. To appear.

---

[1] An extended version of this paper is available at http://lifc.univ-fcomte.fr/publis/

[BGH$^+$04]   F. Bellegarde, J. Groslambert, M. Huisman, O. Kouchnarenko, and J. Julliand. Verification of liveness properties with JML. Technical Report RR-5331, INRIA, 2004.

[BMvW00]   R-J. Back, A. Mikhajlova, and J. von Wright. Class refinement as semantics of correct object substitutability. *Formal Aspects of Computing*, 12:18–40, 2000.

[BRL03]   L. Burdy, A. Requet, and J.-L. Lanet. Java applet correctness: A developer-oriented approach. In K. Araki, S. Gnesi, and D. Mandrioli, editors, *FME 2003: Formal Methods: International Symposium of Formal Methods Europe*, volume 2805 of *Lecture Notes in Computer Science*, pages 422–439. Springer-Verlag, 2003.

[CDD$^+$03]   J.-F. Couchot, F. Dadeau, D. Déharbe, A. Giorgetti, and S. Ranise. Proving and debugging set-based specifications. In *Electronic Notes in Theoretical Computer Science, proceedings of the Sixth Brazilian Workshop on Formal Methods (WMF'03)*, volume 95, pages 189–208, May 2003.

[Cle01]   Clearsy, Europarc de Pichaury 13856 Aix-en-Provence Cedex 3 - France. *Atelier B Technical Support version 3*, May 2001. http://www.atelierb.societe.com.

[GJS00]   J. Gosling, B. Joy, and G. Steele. *The Java Language Specification*. Java Series. Sun Microsystems, 2000. Second edition.

[HJ00]   Marieke Huisman and Bart Jacobs. Java program verification via a Hoare logic with abrupt termination. *Lecture Notes in Computer Science*, 1783:284–303, 2000.

[LBR99]   G.T. Leavens, A.L. Baker, and C Ruby. JML: A notation for detailed design. In Haim Kilov, Bernhard Rumpe, and Ian Simmonds, editors, *Behavioral Specifications of Businesses and Systems*, pages 175–188. Kluwer Academic Publishers, Boston, 1999.

[LP02]   R. Laleau and F. Polack. Coming and going from UML to B: a proposal to support traceability in rigorous IS development. In *Proceedings of the International Conference on Formal Specification and Development in Z and B (ZB'02)*, volume 2272 of *LNCS*, pages 517–534, Grenoble, France, January 2002. Springer Verlag.

[Mey97]   B. Meyer. *Object-Oriented Software Construction*. Prentice Hall, 2 edition, 1997.

[MPMU04]   C. Marché, C. Paulin-Mohring, and X. Urbain. The Krakatoa tool for certification of Java/JavaCard programs annotated in JML. *Journal of Logic and Algebraic Programming*, 58(1-2):89–106, 2004.

[NS99]   D. Neilson and I.H. Sorensen. *The B-Technologies: a system for computer aided programming*. B-Core (UK) Limited, Kings Piece, Harwell, Oxon, OX11 0PA, 1999. http://www.b-core.com/btoolkit.html.

[RJB99]   J. Rumbaugh, I. Jacobson, and G. Booch. *The Unified Modeling Language Reference Manual*, addison-wesley edition, 1999.

[WK98]   J. Warmer and A. Kleppe. *The Object Constraint Language: Precise Modeling with UML*. Addison-Wesley, 1998.

# Including Design Guidelines in the Formal Specification of Interfaces in Z

Judy Bowen and Steve Reeves

Department of Computer Science,
University of Waikato, New Zealand
{jab34, stever}@cs.waikato.ac.nz

**Abstract.** For any sort of computer system, the problems of being sure you have asked for the right thing and then being sure you are implementing the right thing are important and hard problems. For systems with a graphical user interface there are the analogous additional problems of making sure that the interface allows any interaction that is required, and works in a usable way. Design guidelines are used in both the design and evaluation of user interfaces to try and ensure that the systems we build are both usable and conform to specific requirements. This paper discusses practical ways in which we can use formal methods to model guidelines for interface design and then use these as a basis for the formal proof that a specified system has the desired properties described in the guidelines.

## 1 Introduction

We are familiar with the idea of formally specifying systems before we build them and with the benefits that this brings us, such as the ability to verify the system behaviour prior to implementation. Software engineers and formal methods researchers have also worked on different ways of including the interface to a system in the specification. Such works typically cover important areas such as ensuring reachability, ensuring desired interactive behaviour and proving temporal properties, and are typified by the abstract interactive system model known as PIE [6], and its derivatives, as well as structure-based formalisms such as interactors [8] [9].

While this work is comprehensive, it is generally concerned with the interactive nature of the interface in terms of its behaviours and properties and not with the graphical aspect of the interface. Specification of the graphical aspect of the interface includes not only interactive behaviour, but also issues such as the visual or layout properties of the user interface. Considerations around layout properties have included work on automatic generation and/or evaluation of interfaces, and are often based on layout constraint rules [4] [15]. Our focus for this paper was to find a way of including graphical interfaces as part of a system specification in a useful and informative way, and which allowed us to incorporate design guidelines.

H. Treharne et al. (Eds.): ZB 2005, LNCS 3455, pp. 454–471, 2005.

By useful and informative we mean that we wish to provide enough information about the interface to allow us to be able to relate design guidelines directly to our specification, whilst at the same time keeping our specification to a manageable size so that it remains readable. We aim to show that by incorporating design guidelines at the specification stage we will assist the designers who have to interpret and use the guidelines when they build the interface.

We also aim to ensure that changes made to the interface during an iterative design cycle do not cause these guidelines to become broken or forgotten at a later stage. We use the formal specification language Z for this project as it is a well-established language which allows us to reason about the behaviour of a system and has a number of tried and tested methods and support tools which allow us to perform proofs of this behaviour. We use the proof assistant Z/EVES [17] to perform our proofs.

The first part of this paper looks at a particular way of describing graphical user interfaces in Z, and how we integrate this into our system specification. We then discuss design guidelines and how we can both describe them formally and incorporate them into our specification. Next we present two examples of these methods and show how they enable us to both refine our specification as well as identify, and fix, potential design choice problems at the specification stage. Finally we present our conclusions and discuss the future of this work.

## 2    Specifying the Interface

In formalising the Graphical User Interface (GUI) our aim was to include the GUI specification as part of an overall system specification and describe it in a way which would embody not only behavioural aspects but could also describe visual aspects.

In previous research where a formal specification of an interface has been done, it is not unusual to see the interface uncoupled from the underlying system functionality and described separately [16]. This is true at both the specification stage and the design stage. Consider the use of UIMS tools [7] whose purpose is to make that distinction.

We were interested in having an entire system specification which included both the underlying system and the GUI, not only because we believe they are inherently connected and should be related together at the earliest possible stage, but also because of our wish to incorporate guidelines into the specification. When we are considering introducing the guidelines we are aware that there are different categories of guidelines: those relating to the system functionality as well as those relating to the interface (although our work focuses on interface guidelines). Because of this it was important to treat the whole system as one entity, which allows us to include guidelines of any type. If we have two separate models which have been separately validated and verified, then once we have completed the process of bringing the two specifications together, which may not be a straightforward task, we have to reverify our whole system, or risk introducing errors in the whole implementation.

Specifying user interfaces in a formal language such as Z can lead to something which is inherently much more complex than other design models. For example paper-based designs and prototypes are relatively straightforward artefacts which a designer and potential future user can interact with or view with a reasonable level of understanding and so may seem preferable to using a formal notation. However informal prototypes can hide many problems: while they are generally easy to interpret and can show that a GUI can do what is required, they may also hide unwanted behaviour and do not necessarily expose underlying problems.

Many different approaches have been taken to the specification of user interfaces. Earlier work is often more focused on the interactivity and behaviour of the interface and is concerned with interfaces in general rather than graphical user interfaces specifically [10][21]. We looked at a wide range of different methods, including model-based methods such as [13] and [11], algebraic methods such as [23] and different ways of using Z such as [12] and [5]. One major difference from much of the other work in what we were hoping to achieve with our interface specification was the ability to describe not only the behaviour and interactive properties of the interface, but also visual elements. We were mindful, however, that by incorporating visual elements and their detail into our specification we would increase the complexity of our specification and there were dangers that it would become simply too large and unwieldy to be of any practical use.

We decided, therefore, to describe our interfaces at a widget level in a manner similar to the work of Systä [22]. We use the general understanding of the term widget to describe a physical item on an interface, such as a button or scroll-bar, and also to include things such as windows or non-interactive items like borders or graphical items. Our interface is described as a collection of widgets, some of which will have a relationship with system operations, some of which will have relationships with each other, and which will be combined to create the overall GUI.

Note that while we talk about the GUI as a single entity, it is in reality often made up of a number of different views which are produced in relation to the current state of the system and events generated by user actions. A user can move through different views and interact with different parts of the GUI either through new primary windows, or via sub-windows such as dialogue boxes which appear in conjunction with the primary window. We therefore consider our GUI to be a collection, or set, of windows. Each window is itself described by its collection of widgets.

In our overall specification, the initialisation of our system will define the first thing we see by describing the first visible window via its widget set, and what we can see subsequently via the operations of the system when the window changes. We effectively map each individual view of the interface to a particular system state.

Part of our work has been to create a hierarchy of windows and widgets which allows us to break down the GUI into widget categories based on their particular behaviours. A section of this hierarchy is shown here:

- Controls
  - Event Generators
  - Selection Controls
  - Event Responders
  - Event Generators and Responders
  - Entries
- Displays
  - Containers
  - Static

When we consider interface design guidelines we can similarly categorise them. We therefore have guidelines that apply to all parts of the interface, guidelines that apply to certain categories of widgets and guidelines that apply to specific widgets only. By using the same categorisation within both the specification and the guidelines we make it easier to decide which guidelines are applicable. Our intention is not only to have a specification of the interface, but also to have specifications of sets of guidelines. While there are large bodies of work which provide a specific set of guidelines, such as the Apple Design Guidelines [1] and GNOME interface guidelines [2], we recognise that software designers will often make use of these in conjunction with their own in-house requirements, or may combine several different groups of guidelines for their own purposes. Our intention is that they specify their personal sets of guidelines which can then be used in conjunction with the specification of their systems.

Of course in order for the specified guidelines to be useful within the system specification we need to describe some relationship between them. The fact that we have formally specified a set of guidelines in Z does not mean there is an automatic link between them and a system specification. We needed to find a way to link the two things together and make it easy for others to follow this link. We found that having a shared vocabulary between the system specification and the guidelines allowed us to incorporate the guidelines without having to re-write them for each new system specification. This relies on two things: firstly we need a standard way of describing the interface which we can re-use across different system specifications; secondly, we need a similar standard for describing our guidelines so that any set of guidelines suitably specified can be used in conjunction with any system specification.

Following the work of Stepney *et al.* in [19] [20] we have devised a model for interface specification which is not only widget-based but which relies on particular conventions for naming and relating both interface items and system operations. We extend these conventions to our guideline specifications and find that it provides the consistent link we require. Not only does it allow us to incorporate the guidelines into our specifications as predicates which we can later prove or disprove, it allows us to do it at different levels of abstraction. Where we have a high-level specification with just a notion of operations and some sort of interface control we can relate the guidelines with a similar level of abstraction. Similarly as we refine our specification to a more concrete description, so we can start to incorporate more concrete guidelines. We have also found that this notion of abstraction within the GUI specification and guidelines allows us to use the guidelines to assist with our refinement. This is discussed further in the next section.

## 3    Formalising Guidelines

Graphical user interfaces are complex systems which have a number of difficult-to-satisfy requirements. They must not only present the user with the ability to interact with an underlying system fully, *i.e.* allow the user to perform all required actions, but they must also themselves interact with the underlying system functionality. In addition, there are usability issues which require that the design of the GUI enables the user to be able to interact with it in a reasonably intuitive manner and without constant reference to manuals or help files. That this issue of usability has turned out to be a growing area within the field of human computer interaction (HCI) shows what a large and difficult problem it is. The use of design guidelines is an important part of the work included in this discipline, but one which, nevertheless, can give a substantial benefit in the design of interfaces.

Guidelines are the product of filtering and combining the knowledge and experience gained from user-testing of interfaces over a number of years. They can be seen as a 'best-practice', or 'how-to', which helps us in our goal of designing better GUIs. While the use of guidelines alone does not guarantee that the GUIs we design will be usable, they do ensure that we avoid some of the common, known pitfalls and allow us to concentrate our user-testing efforts on finding new and unexpected problems. As such we can consider guidelines to be additional requirements of our system, as they are properties that we expect our final implementation to have.

Our intention was to find a way to formalise guidelines so that they could be used in conjunction with a system specification in order to be able to prove certain desirable properties about the GUI of that system. Our hope is that the process of formalising the guidelines will not only assist with clarifying their meaning and making them unambiguous, but will also allow designers to ensure that exactly the right set of appropriate guidelines are used in each particular case.

One early consideration was how to deal with the varying levels of abstraction within a set of guidelines. For example, some of the guidelines may be described in very general terms, such as:

> *Provide displayed feedback for all user actions* [18]

or, conversely, they may be very specific, as in:

> *Don't use metal buttons in dialogs. Dialogs should never use the brushed metal look* [1].

It may appear at first glance that guidelines as general as the first one cannot be used in any useful way within our specification. However, if we consider how we may start by specifying a system at an abstract level and then through a process of refinement move toward a more concrete implementation then we can perform a similar process with the guidelines themselves. We have stated that we provide a breakdown of widgets into a hierarchy. This can also be viewed as a model that moves from the general to the specific in that we start with things we identify only as controls, and then by a process of examining the desired behaviour of the controls we get more and more specific until we can decide on a particular widget or widget type as the correct option. If we model our guidelines using the same widget breakdown then we have a relationship between levels of hierarchy in our guideline specification and system specification. So when our system specification is at an abstraction level where we are just referring to *userControls* with no notion of what these may actually be, we can include the very general guidelines such as *Provide displayed feedback for all user actions* in the form of a predicate such as

$$\forall\, uc : userControl \bullet providesFeedback$$

At this stage we can do nothing useful with this predicate since we cannot prove it in any formal way, but when we begin to refine our *userControls* to more specific widgets we can similarly refine this general guideline. We can give it a specific meaning for the widgets we refine to. For example if we refine a *userControl* to a Slider, we can refer to our guidelines and discover that providing feedback for a Slider means that we must give the user a visible indication of the value as the Slider is moved, either by providing valued tick-marks along the line of the Slider, or by displaying a value label next to the Slider. In this way we treat the very general level guidelines as placeholders within our specification which can be refined to specific properties during our refinement process.

Another issue we need to consider is that the differing terminology used within different sets of guidelines means that it could be difficult to know when and how the guidelines should be used and it is not immediately clear when two guidelines refer to the same type of thing.

We began by applying the same categorisation of widgets we had used in our GUI specification work to some sample sets of guidelines, starting with sections from the Smith and Mosier guidelines [18] and the GNOME guidelines [2]. We wanted to see how well the widget categorisation could be applied to the levels of abstraction within the guidelines themselves. With some adjustments to our initial categorisation we found that it was relatively straightforward to structure the sample guideline sets we were considering in this way. At the same time we had begun specifying some very simple GUIs (windows with just two or three widgets) and we used these to ensure that we used the same vocabulary in our guideline specifications as we were using in our specification of the GUIs.

For example, at an abstract level we would describe a widget which the user interacts with as a *control*. A guideline which describes a less abstract *control* widget, for example one which generates an event to cause an underlying system operation to occur, will describe that widget as an *action control* which is a subset of the *event generator* widgets. We now had a direct relationship between our GUI specification and our guideline specification whatever the current level of abstraction. If our GUI specification was at a high level of abstraction and referring only to *controls* then we could use the guidelines relating to all *controls*, whereas a more refined specification describing, for example, *binary selection controls* would use only the guidelines describing *binary selection controls*. By describing and structuring our guidelines in a hierarchical manner reflecting the widget categorisation hierarchy we have found it easy to identify the correct parts of the guideline specification.

During the process of relating the guidelines to the specification, we found that we could use the guidelines in two different ways. When we are trying to refine our specification we can use the guidelines to assist us in making choices about the sorts of widgets we should refine to. When used in this way we incorporate the desired properties given to us in the guidelines into our specification directly, *i.e.* the way we propose the widget be described is informed by some of the guidelines. For example, if our guidelines state that all *Buttons* must have a label, then our framework for describing a *Button* will include an observation called *ButtonLabel*, so we have satisfied this guideline by following our framework and no further work is required. In this way some of the guidelines can become incorporated into our specification by showing us what additional information we need to include in our widget descriptions.

We can also include guidelines as predicates in our specification and subsequently try to prove that our specification has these properties during verification. The relationship between the way we formalise the guidelines and the way we describe the interface is what brings them together and allows us to use them in these ways. In the next section of this paper we will provide examples of these two uses. The examples we will be presenting in this paper may, at first reading, appear trivial. They deal with very simple cases of guidelines and can be resolved by inspection. Our purpose however in choosing these particular examples is to demonstrate the general process which we are proposing, and in order to be able to do this within this paper it has proved necessary to choose simple examples. It is important, therefore, when following the examples to concentrate on the generality of the process we are presenting rather than the specifics of the particular example.

## 4    Making Refinement Choices

We have discussed how using the guidelines in conjunction with a system specification may assist us to refine the interface description into more concrete widgets. We now present an example of this. Consider the following specification segment which relates to a dialogue window where a user can set certain options for the way their text is displayed in an application.

$[FONTTYPE, FONTSTYLE]$
$CONTROLSTATE ::= Active \mid NotActive$
$FONTSIZE ::= Small \mid Medium \mid Large$
$EVENT ::= ChangeFontSizeEvent \mid ChangeFontTypeEvent \mid$
$\qquad\qquad ChangeFontStyleEvent \mid None$
$SELECTION ::= Selected \mid NotSelected$
$[CHAR]$

```
┌─ TextDisplay ──────────────────────────────────────
│  text : seq CHAR
│  fsize : FONTSIZE
│  ftype : FONTTYPE
│  fstyle : ℙ FONTSTYLE
└────────────────────────────────────────────────────
```

```
┌─ ChangeFontSize ───────────────────────────────────
│  Δ TextDisplay
│  eventValue? : FONTSIZE
│  event? : EVENT
├────────────────────────────────────────────────────
│  event? ≠ ChangeFontSizeEvent ⇒ fsize' = fsize
│  event? = ChangeFontSizeEvent ⇒ fsize' = eventValue?
│  text' = text
│  ftype' = ftype
│  fstyle' = fstyle
└────────────────────────────────────────────────────
```

Before we can describe the type of control that will cause the *ChangeFontSize* operation to occur we need to consider the behaviour that we wish the control to exhibit, and from this infer the type of the control using our widget hierarchy. In this example there are three possible font sizes which we describe as *Small*, *Medium* or *Large*. We want the user to be able to change the size of the text font by selecting a new value from the control, so we will require a selection control. Next we consider whether it is a binary selection control or a selection control with a value. Given that there are a number of different choices the user can make we decide on a selection control with a value. Finally we need to consider whether the control will produce a single value when activated or whether it will produce several values. In the case of setting the text to a font size we need to consider only a single value at any given time, so we can refine our choice to that of a single-value selection control. We describe this by first considering each individual selection choice as a binary choice control, and then grouping these together (this mirrors the actual way in which we create, for example, button groups when we design an interface).

```
┌─ SmallSizeSelector ────────────────────────────────
│  sselected : SELECTION
```

$$
\begin{array}{|l}
\underline{\ MediumSizeSelector\ \rule{0pt}{0pt}}\\
\quad mselected : SELECTION \\
\end{array}
$$

$$
\begin{array}{|l}
\underline{\ LargeSizeSelector\ \rule{0pt}{0pt}}\\
\quad lselected : SELECTION \\
\end{array}
$$

$$
\begin{array}{|l}
\underline{\ ChangeFontSizeControl\ \rule{0pt}{0pt}}\\
SmallSizeSelector \\
MediumSizeSelector \\
LargeSizeSelector \\
cstate : CONTROLSTATE \\
event! : EVENT \\
eventValue! : FONTSIZE \\
\hline
sselected = Selected \wedge cstate = Active \Rightarrow \\
\quad event! = ChangeFontSizeEvent \wedge eventValue! = Small \\
mselected = Selected \wedge cstate = Active \Rightarrow \\
\quad event! = ChangeFontSizeEvent \wedge eventValue! = Medium \\
lselected = Selected \wedge cstate = Active \Rightarrow \\
\quad event! = ChangeFontSizeEvent \wedge eventValue! = Large \\
sselected = Selected \Leftrightarrow mselected = NotSelected\ \wedge \\
\quad lselected = NotSelected \\
mselected = Selected \Leftrightarrow sselected = NotSelected\ \wedge \\
\quad lselected = NotSelected \\
lselected = Selected \Leftrightarrow sselected = NotSelected\ \wedge \\
\quad mselected = NotSelected \\
\end{array}
$$

$$
ActiveChangeFontSize \;\widehat{=}\; ChangeFontSizeControl \gg ChangeFontSize
$$

We now use our guidelines to assist with a further refinement. The guidelines used in this example are taken from [1]. There are seven possible widget types within the single-value selection control set. For this example we will consider two of them and show how we can make a correct decision regarding their appropriateness in this situation. Let us suppose we are considering refining our *ChangeFontSizeControl* to either a RadioButtonGroup or a CheckBoxGroup, which would appear as in figure 1.

Our guideline contains the following information (these are from the Apple guidelines [1]):

*Use radio buttons for a set of mutually exclusive choices*

*Use checkboxes to indicate one or more options that must be either on or off*

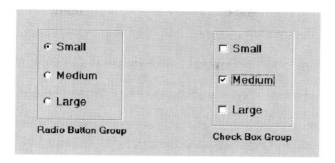

**Fig. 1.** Widget Options for FontSizeControl

Our two widget types can then be expressed by:

```
┌─ RadioButtonGroup ──────────────────────────────────────────
│ radiobuttons : 𝔽 RadioButton
├──────────────────────────────────────────────────────────────
│ 2 ≤ #radiobuttons ≤ 8
│ ∃₁ a : RadioButton • a ∈ radiobuttons ∧ a.selected = Selected
└──────────────────────────────────────────────────────────────
```

$$2 \leq \#radiobuttons \leq 8$$
$$\exists_1\, a : RadioButton \bullet a \in radiobuttons \land a.selected = Selected$$

```
┌─ CheckBoxGroup ─────────────────────────────────────────────
│ checkboxes : ℙ CheckBox
├──────────────────────────────────────────────────────────────
│ 2 ≤ #checkboxes ≤ 8
│ ∃ a : CheckBox • a ∈ checkboxes ∧ a.selected = Selected
└──────────────────────────────────────────────────────────────
```

$$2 \leq \#checkboxes \leq 8$$
$$\exists\, a : CheckBox \bullet a \in checkboxes \land a.selected = Selected$$

*Note: we have simplified the information shown in our actual guideline specifications for the purpose of this example.*

In our *ChangeFontSizeControl* specification, the observations labelled *Small-SizeSelector, MediumSizeSelector* and *LargeSizeSelector* represent the sets *radiobuttons* or *checkboxes* in the guidelines. If we inspect the predicate part of *ChangeFontSizeControl* we see that we describe the *selected* behaviour of the individual selection controls such that exactly one, and one only, is selected at any given time. If we compare this with the *RadioButtonGroup* and *CheckBox-Group* schemas from our guidelines we can see that we have exactly the same constraints on the *RadioButtonGroup*, whereas the selection behaviour of the *CheckBoxGroup* is unconstrained. In this example we would therefore choose to refine our *ChangeFontSizeControl* to something which includes a *RadioButton-Group* based on the information provided by the guidelines. Further, using the association between observation names as above, we can prove that the system requires the use of radio buttons rather than check boxes.

Another benefit of what we are doing also becomes apparent at this point. We had intended to use the GNOME guidelines for this example, however whilst they are very specific about the use of radio buttons, stating:

*Exactly one radio button should be set in the group at all times.*

they are not so specific regarding check boxes, rather the examples they give imply the usage of check boxes without directly stating that any number of check boxes in a group may be selected at the same time. So, needing to formalise the guidelines means we are very likely to find gaps or, perhaps even, inconsistencies in them, and if required (to convince the writers of their mistakes, perhaps) we can prove that these gaps or inconsistencies exist (relative, of course and as ever, to our formalisation).

## 5   Proving Properties of the Interface

In our second example we look at ways of using our specified guidelines to prove that an interface has particular desirable properties or does not have undesirable properties. The following example uses the Find dialogue window from Windows95. A full critique of this dialogue appears in [3]. We will provide a partial specification of the Find dialogue and then show how we can find guideline violations by including guideline predicates in our specification and trying to prove properties of the dialogue.

Our guidelines come from the GNOME Human Interface Guidelines(1.0) [2]. In using this example from Windows95 we do not imply that the designers intended to follow the guidelines that we are using and no suggestion about the quality of their interface design is intended, we merely provide it by way of an example of how our work may be applied. Also, notice that in this case we are reverse-engineering an existing interface rather than specifying a new one. There are a couple of points that are worth making regarding this. Firstly, the principles and methods used in this reverse-engineered example are exactly the same as those we would use if we provided the example the other way around, *i.e.* if we described a dialogue that did not already exist. By choosing this method for our example we show how real-world applications may benefit from this work.

Secondly, the notion of reverse-engineering interfaces and then applying the guidelines is something which may prove to be useful and not uncommon in real-world situations. As software engineers we would hope that prior to the design of our systems and interfaces a full and rigorous specification, verification and validation process would take place. However, we also recognise that in many instances this is not the case. Interface design in particular is an iterative process, often starting with prototypes and developing through various forms of user-testing and refinement. It may be that the starting point for the interface is based on our specifications, but after many iterations and changes we also want to be sure that the properties we were able to prove at the prototype stage still hold true at the implementation stage. If the design cycle has not followed a specification refinement then we cannot be certain of this unless we are able to re-test these properties on the final interface. Methods of making this reverse-

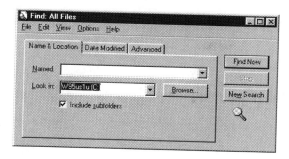

**Fig. 2.** Windows95 Find Dialogue

engineering both practical and workable are discussed in our conclusions and future-work section.

We start by presenting the dialogue interface and then a partial specification of that interface. We present only a partial specification for the sake of brevity and do not expand or elaborate on items which have no bearing on the point of our example. In keeping with our format for specifying interfaces, our DialogueWindow is described in terms of a collection of its components. We provide the specification of one of the components to assist with the reader's understanding of the example.

First we can look at the specification of just one button on this interface, the button labelled with the _ symbol which serves to minimise the window when the user clicks on it.

$$
\begin{array}{l}
\rule{1em}{0.4pt}\ MinimiseWindowButton \rule{6cm}{0.4pt} \\
\quad buttonName : BUTTONNAME \\
\quad buttonlabel : BUTTONLABEL \\
\quad minwbevent! : EVENT \\
\quad cstate : CONTROLSTATE \\
\rule{7.5cm}{0.4pt} \\
\quad buttonName = Minimise \\
\quad buttonlabel = NoLabel \\
\quad cstate = Active \Rightarrow event! = MinimiseWindowEvent \\
\quad cstate = NotActive \Rightarrow event! = NoEvent
\end{array}
$$

Notice that in keeping with our GUI specification framework and exemplified by the font size changing example, we give the widget an output called *minwbevent!* which will synchronise with a system operation based on its value. We would then describe each other part of the *FindDialogue* in a similar manner, with each of the widgets that cause system operations to occur having a *nameevent!* output of its own. When we describe the total interface for *FindDialogue*, we describe it as a collection of its component widgets, these will be schemas themselves which will have been previously described.

```
┌─ FindDialogue ──────────────────────────────────────────────
│  FindNowButton
│  StopButton
│  NewSearchButton
│  SearchFunctionWindow
│  FileMenu
│  EditMenu
│  ViewMenu
│  OptionsMenu
│  HelpMenu
│  MinimiseWindowButton
│  MaximiseWindowButton
│  CloseWindowButton
│  fdeventset : ℙ EVENT
├──────────────────────────────────────────────────────────────
│  fdeventset = {fnbevent!} ∪ {sbevent!} ∪ {nsbevent!}∪
│              {sfwineventset} ∪ {fmenuevent!} ∪ {emenuevent!}∪
│              {vmenuevent!} ∪ {omenuevent!} ∪ {hmenuevent!}∪
│              {minwbevent!} ∪ {maxwbevent!} ∪ {clswbevent!}
└──────────────────────────────────────────────────────────────
```

Each of the individual widget *event!* outputs are unioned to create *FindDialogue*'s *fdeventset*. The elements of *eventset* at any given time are determined by the value of each component's *controlstate*. If it has a *controlstate* value *Active* then its *event!* value will be present in *eventset*, otherwise the value *NoEvent* will be present. For example in the state of the system where the *controlstate* observation of *MinimiseWindowButton* is *Active*, then *MinimiseWindowEvent* will be present in *fdeventset*. Describing each of the component schemas of *FindDialogue* in full to show what their *event!* values are is too long a process for the purposes of this paper. However, in order to fully understand the application of the guidelines to this example, we do need to know what the possible values for *fdeventset* are. We therefore now provide a simplified view of what *fdeventset* would look like if it contained every possible *event!* value provided by its component widgets. This is done for reader convenience only and is not a part of our general process.

$$fdeventset = \{FindNowEvent, StopFindEvent, NewSearchEvent,$$
$$FileMenuEvent, EditMenuEvent, ViewMenuEvent,$$
$$OptionsMenuEvent, HelpMenuEvent, MinimiseWindowEvent,$$
$$MaximiseWindowEvent, CloseWindowEvent, BrowseEvent\}$$

We will refer to this as the maximum possible value for *fdeventset*. Notice that the value *NoEvent* does not appear in this maximum set as it will only be present if one of the components widgets is not active.

The following guidelines are those that we wish to adhere to when designing our interface in this example. We provide them first in their original form and then how they appear in our specification of the GNOME guidelines [2].

*Dialogues :*
*Provide all dialogues with the following window command: Minimise.*

*Provide all dialogues with a Cancel Button. This provides an escape route for users to stop an action. Clicking the Cancel button closes the dialogue box and reverts the application to its state prior to the user action.*

These appear in our guideline specification as:

*Identify all schemas describing Dialogues, these will be all schemas called xDialogue, where x is a parameter representing the actual name given to the dialogue. The following predicate must then apply, again you must replace x with the actual dialogue name:*

$$\exists\, dw : xDialogue \bullet MinimiseWindowEvent \in dw.eventset$$
$$\exists\, dw : xDialogueWindow \bullet CancelDialogEvent \in dw.eventset$$

*Notice that we are reliant on the naming conventions that we propose in our interface specification instructions. We expect that all Dialogue boxes described will follow the xDialogue naming convention, and that all events generated will follow the actionEvent naming convention, where action is the behaviour indicated by the event.*

We now set about trying to prove that both of these existentially quantified predicates hold true in our example, *i.e.* can we prove them of *FindDialogue*? For this we need to examine our maximum possible value for *eventset*. Our first guideline requires that:

$$\exists\, dw : FindDialogue \bullet MinimiseWindowEvent \in dw.eventset$$

The maximum possible set for *dw.eventset* where *dw.eventset* is actually *fdeventset* is:

$\{FindNowEvent, StopFindEvent, NewSearchEvent, FileMenuEvent,$
$\quad EditMenuEvent, ViewMenuEvent, OptionsMenuEvent,$
$\quad HelpMenuEvent, MinimiseWindowEvent, MaximiseWindowEvent,$
$\quad CloseWindowEvent, BrowseEvent\}$

This satisfies our predicate as it gives us an instance which does contain the *MinimiseWindowEvent*, so we can state that *FindDialogue* exhibits the property required of our first guideline. Moving on to the second guideline, we require that

$$\exists\, dw : FindDialogue \bullet CancelDialogEvent \in dw.eventset$$

Again we examine the maximum possible value of *fdeventset*, but in this case there is no *CancelDialogEvent* so our predicate is false. We have therefore identified a problem with our specification. It does not adhere to our required guidelines. We would expect that the next step would be to fix this problem prior to further refinement or implementation of the specification. Notice that the two guidelines used are specific to all dialogue windows, so any other dialogues in the interface would also be expected to adhere to these rules and would be tested in the same way.

In these simplified examples we have been able to prove or disprove properties by inspection of our specification, whereas in larger examples this would not be the case. Consider the following guideline which is taken from [18]:

> *Be consistent in command names. If a command refers to the same action as another, both should use the same command name.*

In a large and complex system the interface may be made up of many different views leading to a long and detailed specification. In order to prove that the above guideline is adhered to throughout the specification we would need additional predicates as constraints on the interface schemas which would have to be discharged at the refinement stage.

## 6     Conclusions

We have presented our method for incorporating design guidelines into the formal specification of interfaces and discussed how this may form part of a whole system specification. We have described how we use a particular framework for the formal description of interfaces based on the categorisation of widgets, and the notion of the interface as a collection of these widgets. We have noted that the process of formalisation can lead to the identification of mistakes in informal guidelines.

By using this framework and adopting a shared vocabulary between the GUI description and the sets of guidelines we wish to use we can also incorporate design guidelines into our specification. The guidelines can then be used to assist with the refinement of our specification into a more concrete collection of widgets, as well as proving that a described interface has particular desirable properties. We believe that this may encourage software engineers to incorporate the interface into their system specifications as an integral part of that specification. It may also assist GUI designers in their work by removing some of the burden of monitoring ever-changing prototypes with reference to guidelines, trying to work out how they should be interpreted or incorporated into the design of their interface.

We have proposed a specific framework and vocabulary for our interface and guideline descriptions using Z which is based on what we have found to be a clear and helpful way for doing this. Our aim throughout was to ensure that we described the GUI in as concise a way as possible to prevent the specification from exploding in size and becoming unreadable and unmanageable. We recognise that there may be other ways of describing the GUI and linking it to the underlying system behaviour which would also work, provided the interface description and the guideline specification both use the same structure and terminology and their model follows a shared hierarchy which supports the abstraction problem.

Our aim here was to show how we have undertaken this work so that others may follow our framework or devise their own methods based on it.

## 7  Future Work

In our second example we discussed the notion of reverse-engineering an existing interface (or prototype). We are mindful that in an iterative design process where incremental prototypes are used and changed regularly, the overhead of this sort of work may lead to a reluctance to perform it. With this in mind we propose the development of tools which can be used by interface designers to aid them in this task. Rather than suggest brand-new GUI design tools and then hope people adopt them, we suggest finding ways to use the existing tools which are commonly used in the early design stage. These may be RAD (rapid application design) tools, or full implementation suites and include such things as VisualBasic, JBuilder, Glade etc.

Rather than propose that the users of these tools abandon them for some new tool we suggest that we build tools and systems which can be used in conjunction with these existing tools. We have already developed some prototypes of such tools. We have created a VisualBasic component which can be imported into any VisualBasic project and which will interrogate an interface form and produce an output file which contains the widget breakdown for that interface form in a set of basic Z schemas. Similarly we have looked at ways of parsing Java class files to extract the interface elements described using the SWING toolkit and produce a similar widget hierarchy output. We believe that there is much work that could be done in this area. A separate research group at the University of Waikato is currently looking at automating design guidelines in the Glade development environment using XML descriptions, and we are interested in working more closely with this group to see what possible collaboration there may be between our projects.

In the near future we aim to publish the full framework we propose for describing interfaces along with the widget hierarchy and breakdown and refinement assistance documents. In conjunction with this we would like to fully describe some of the commonly used sets of guidelines such as the Gnome Human Interface Guidelines(1.0) [2], the Apple Human Interface Guidelines [1] and Smith and Mosier's Guidelines for Designing User Interface Software [18]. We also hope to produce a full system and interface specification for a large "real-world" system and examine some applications of our work in conjunction with this.

## References

1. Apple Human Interface Guidelines (2004), available at `http://developer.apple.com/documentation/UserExperience/Conceptual/OSXHIGuidelines/index.html`
2. GNOME Human Interface Guidelines (1.0) (2002), available at `http://developer.gnome.org/projects/gup/hig/1.0/`

3. Isys Information Architects Inc., Interface Hall of Shame,
   `http://digilander.libero.it/chiediloapippo/Engineering/iarchitect/`
   `target.htm`
4. Bodard, F., Hennebert, A., Leheureux, J., Vanderdonckt, J.: Towards a Dynamic Strategy for Computer-Aided Visual Placement, In Catarci, T., Costabile, M., Levialdi, S., and Santucci, G., eds. Proceedings of Advanced Visual Interfaces. pp.78–87.(1994)
5. Bowen, J.: Formal Specification and Documentation Using Z, A Case Study Approach. International Thomson Computer Press.(1996)
6. Dix, A., Runciman, C.: Abstract models of interactive systems. People and Computers: Designing the Interface, Ed.P.J. and S.Cook, Cambridge University Press. pp.13–22.(1985)
7. Dix, A., Finlay, J., Abowd, G., Beale, R.: Human-Computer Interaction, second edition. Prentice Hall Europe. (1997)
8. Duke, D., Harrison, M.: Abstract Interaction Objects. Computer Graphics Forum, 12(3):C-25–C-26.(1993)
9. Duke, D., Harrison, M.: Interaction and task requirements. In Palanque, P. and Bastide, R., eds. DSV-IS'95: Eurographics Workshop on Design, Specification and Verification of Interactive Systems, pp.54–75. Springer-Verlag.(1995)
10. Harrison, M., Dix, A.: A state model of direct manipulation in interactive systems. In Formal Methods in Human-Computer Interaction, eds. Harrison, M. and Thimbleby, H.Cambridge University Press. (1990)
11. Horrocks, I.: Constructing the User Interface with Statecharts. Addison Wesley. (1999)
12. Jacky, J.: The Way of Z: Practical programming with formal methods. Cambridge University Press. (1997)
13. Jacquot, J.-P., Quesnot, D.: Early Specification of User-Interfaces: Toward a Formal Approach. Proceedings of the 19th International Conference on Software Engineering, pp.150–160, ACM Press. (1997)
14. Knight, J., Brilliant, S.: Premliminary Evaluation of a Formal Approach to User Interface Specification. Proceedings of the 10th International Conference of Z Users on the Z Formal Specification Notation, pp.329–346. (1997)
15. Lok, S., Feiner, S., Nga, G.: Evaluation of Visual Balance for Automated Layout, Proceedings of the 9th International Conference on Intelligent User Interface, ACM Press.(2004)
16. Took, R.: Putting Design into Practice: Formal Specification and the User Interface. In Formal Methods in Human-Computer Interaction, eds. Harrison, M. and Thimbleby, H.Cambridge University Press, 1990.
17. Saaltink, M.: The Z/EVES System. In Bowen, J., Hinchey, M., Till, D., eds. Proceedings of the 10th International Conference on the Z Formal Method (ZUM), vol.1212 of Lecture Notes in Computer Science, pp. 72–88. Springer Verlag.(1997)
18. Smith, S., Mosier, J.: Guidelines for designing user interface software. Report EDS-TR86 -278. The MITRE Corporation, Bedford. (1986)
19. Stepney, S., Polack, F., Toyn, I.: An outline pattern language for Z. In: ZB2003: Formal Specification and Development in Z and B: Third International Conference of B and Z Users, Turku, Finland, June 2003. Proceedings, Springer-Verlag Heidelberg, pp 2–19.(2003)
20. Stepney, S., Polack, F., Toyn, I.: A Z patterns catalogue I: specification and refactoring, v0.1. Technical Report YCS-2003-349, York. (2003)

21. Sufrin, B., He, J.: Specification, analysis and refinement of interactive processes. In Formal Methods in Human-Computer Interaction, eds. Harrison, M. and Thimbleby, H.Cambridge University Press, 1990.
22. Systä, K.: Adding user interface to a behavioral specification. In Engineering for Human-Computer Interaction, pp 227–244. Chapman and Hall.(1995)
23. Thimbleby, H.: User interface design with matrix algebra. ACM transactions, Computer-Human Interaction, vol.11,2, pp181–236. (2004)

# Some Guidelines for Formal Development of Web-Based Applications in B-Method

Abdolbaghi Rezazadeh and Michael Butler

School of Electronics and Computer Science,
University of Southampton,
Highfield, Southampton SO17 IBJ, United Kingdom
{ar02r, mjb}@ecs.soton.ac.uk

**Abstract.** Web-based applications are the most common form of distributed systems that have gained a lot of attention in the past ten years. Today many of us are relying on scores of mission-critical Web-based systems in different areas such as banking, finance, e-commerce and government. The development process of these systems needs a sound methodology, which ensures quality, consistency and integrity. Formal Methods provide systematic and quantifiable approaches to create coherent systems. Despite this there has been limited work on the formal modelling of Web-based applications. In this paper our aim is to provide researchers with some guidelines based on results from ongoing work to model a Web-based system using the B-Method. Session and state management, developing formal models for complex data types, abstraction of distributed database systems and formal representation of communication links between different components of a web-based system are the main issues that we have examined.

## 1   An Introduction to Web-Based Systems

Web-based applications are distributed systems that can be accessed using a Web browser. During recent years the extent and scope of their use has grown rapidly, significantly affecting all aspects of our lives. Industries such as manufacturing, travel and hospitality, banking, education, and government are Web-enabled to improve and enhance their operations. E-commerce has expanded quickly, cutting across national boundaries. Even traditional legacy systems have migrated to the Web. The scope and complexity of current Web applications varies widely: from small-scale, short-lived services to large-scale enterprise applications distributed across the Internet and corporate intranets and extranets.

Although numerous Web-based systems are in use now and many of us rely on them, the manner in which they are developed raises serious concerns [1, 2, 3]; they need to be reliable and perform well. To build such systems, Web-based system developers need a sound methodology, a disciplined process and a set of good guidelines. Due to the high amount of new demands, Web applications are evolving continually and the complexity of these systems is increasing rapidly. Therefore the use of a rigorous method becomes more important.

H. Treharne et al. (Eds.): ZB 2005, LNCS 3455, pp. 472–492, 2005.

Formal methods use mathematical notation to describe systems in a clear and rigorous manner. Abstraction and stepwise refinement employed by formal methods is a valuable approach for developing complex Web-based systems. The B-Method is a well-known formal method [4] which has been applied to several software development missions including academic and industrial projects [5, 6, 7].

Our aim in this paper, through the modelling of this specimen Web-based system, is to identify some challenging aspects of these types of systems and propose an approach to their formal representation. We hope to provide a set of guidelines which could serve as a basis for further work. In the rest of this paper we present the travel agency case study and briefly discuss its initial aims and objectives. The chosen case study has been selected to be inclusive enough to represent the main properties and functionality of typical Web applications. By developing formal models in B we have extracted some generic and essential patterns. These patterns are considered to model some common properties and functionality shared by a broad category of Web applications. In the next step we have tried to find some appropriate formal refinements for these abstract patterns which could be provable within the framework of the B prover tool [8, 9, 10]. As Web applications are distributed systems, the decomposition of primary refinement models into subsystems and introducing suitable formal models for communication links are other objectives. The last section concludes the paper with recommendations for further work and discussions.

## 2 Informal Representation of the Case Study

Here we outline the main requirements and sketch the overall architecture of the system. The aim is to develop a Web-based Travel Agency system to enable potential users to access it through an Internet connection using a standard Web browser to perform one or more of the following tasks:

- Book a flight or Cancel a booked flight
- Book a room or or Cancel a booked room
- Hire a car or Cancel a hired car

The Travel Agency Web-based system is hosted on the Travel Agency Server which is responsible for processing the Web-clients' requests. These messages are produced and sent by the client browser through Internet links and based on HTTP or other similar standards. The travel agency system relies on a group of secondary agencies' servers like flight agencies to accomplish the client requests. The travel agency system uses Internet links to communicate with the secondary servers. A simple architecture of this system is depicted in Figure 1.

In Figure 1 we see that more than one client could communicate with the travel agency system simultaneously. The travel agency system will manage the status of different sessions using state variables, stored in a local database. For booking requests like flight booking, a message which includes details about the request will be broadcast to all related agencies' servers by travel agency system.

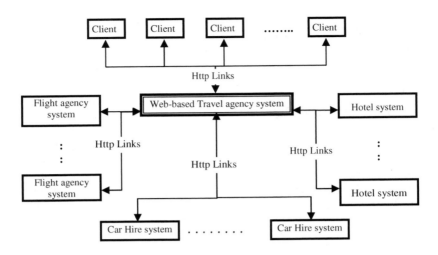

**Fig. 1.** A Simple Architecture of the System

Responses which the travel agency should expect could vary from zero to the number of all secondary agencies in the best situation. The collected response will be sent by the travel agency system to the appropriate client. In other cases, like cancelling a booked flight, the request will be sent directly to the related flight agency. Also it is quite convenient to assume a local database in the travel agency server for representing all booked services. This database could reduce the amount of communication and complexity of un-booking process.

## 3   An Overview of Formal Development Process

As we mentioned previously our main objective, in applying formal method to this case study, was to identify some common challenging issues and propose some formal models for them. Therefore instead of detailed presentation of formal models, in this section we have summarised the formal development process.

This work is based on Event-B style for development of distributed systems [11, 12]. Unlike standard B, which is used to specify and develop software modules in B, Event-B was introduced for modelling of distributed systems. In the Event-B style operations are called "events" which may occur spontaneously rather than being invoked. Those events are no longer pre-conditioned, but guarded by a predicate, which express the condition under which the event can be enabled. When we refine a model, we either refine an existing event by strengthening the guard or/and the before-after predicate (removing non-determinism or applying data refinement), or add a new event which is supposed to refine the skip event. The introduction of new events is supported by superposition method [13, 14]. In superposition, new functionality is added to an existing model in the form of additional variables and assignments to these variables as new operations, while the original computation is preserved.

In the first stage of formal process an abstract model based on Event-B style has been produced. The abstract model is a single B-machine which encloses some operations to model the main functionality of the travel agency system from the viewpoint of the users. In the second step we have refined the abstract specification by introducing client side operations based on the superposition methodology. Operations of the abstract model have been classified as the server side operations at this stage. Some operations of the abstract model which are influenced by the introduction of client operations have been refined by adding extra guards and removing non-determinism.

Operations of the secondary agencies servers have been introduced in the second refinement model. In this stage some formal definitions for distributed databases have been added. Each secondary server has a local database which is contains information about available service that this agency can offer to its customers. Data distribution among secondary servers and the travel agency system leads to distribution of processing between servers. In other words, introducing new operations which finally reside on secondary servers for manipulating distributed data resulted in further refinement of the travel agency operations in this stage. In the second refinement we have operations of the clients, the travel agency system and the secondary servers.

Decomposition is the main strategy to tackle the complexity of the model in Event-B style. Introducing communication links between different parts is a pre-stage to the decomposition process. Therefore in the third refinement stage we have introduced communication links. The main challenging questions which we have identified during the above mentioned development processes are:

- Session and State Management in Both Client and Server side
- Inter-Server Interactions
- Refinement of Complex Data types
- Abstraction of Distributed Databases
- Formal Modelling of Communications Links

In the following sections we have examined these issues in detail and we have presented some solutions for them. Although we have used the travel agency case study to discuss the main properties of a Web application and to clarify the key issues in developing a B-model for them, the identified aspects and proposed solutions could be applied to a wide range of Web applications.

# 4    State Representation in Web-Based Systems

The Web started as a means for sharing documents among scientists. Its designers have built the underlying technology (e.g., HTTP and HTML) with these goals in mind. Since then, people have realised the Web's potential as an application delivery medium and have started to exploit it. With the growth of e-business applications, the Web is rapidly being transformed into an application-intensive environment. In Web-based application the core functionality of system, the business logic, is handled by the server. Most web applications need to maintain communication sessions with their client, and monitor each client's individual status and activities. Unfortunately, the communication protocol between web browser and web server (HTTP) is stateless and it does not provide the functionality on session control. Therefore it is not trivial to maintain information about each client interaction with server. The server-centric architecture of current Web applications makes a server-side session the natural choice. In the following sections we have examined this subject in detail.

## 4.1    Session Handling and State Management in Server Side

State maintenance is one of the major issues in many applications, such as e-commerce and banking applications. As transactions between Web clients and Web servers occur in a stateless environment, state must somehow be passed from one transaction to the next in a Web application. Keeping state data on the server side is generally considered the safest and most appropriate technique when handling information of a sensitive nature.

The server uses a session's state variables to identify a user, process the input data provided by a client and determine user rights or the type of access to be offered to a user. Furthermore, based on the information which has been provided by the client, the server can set state variables to determine the next possible execution path.

**Challenge:** How do you represent the state information related to a user's interaction with a Web application?

**Guideline:** We have used explicit state variables to represent sessions state information on the server side. By defining two reference sets for state and sessions ID and a mapping function from a session ID to session state we can manage each session in the server side identically. So each session has a session identifier *"sid"* which could be used as an index to access session information on the server side. A new *"sid"* could be allocated to a new client as soon as it establishes a connection with server and afterward the client can use this *"sid"* on subsequent interactions.

To clarify the guideline we have presented a snapshot of the specification machine for the Travel agency case study in Figure 2. We have introduced the set *"STATE"* and *"SESSION"*. The first definition represents the possible states for a client session and the second one serves as a typing reference for sessions' ID. The *"session_state"* variable maps each client session to its related state. The variable *"session"* represents the set of all current active sessions. The operation *"StartNewSession"* models the creation of a new session by the travel agency system. This operation allocates a free session ID for the newly created session and sets the necessary environmental variables for it. Any changes in a session's state variable could enable a operation and execution of an operation could resulted in some changes in a state variable. For example, the *"SelectService"* operation is enabled when the session state is *"fresh"* and its execution changes the state of related session to one of *"booking"*, *"unbooking"* or *"signed_in"* state.

```
MACHINE TravelAgency
SETS
  SESSION;
STATE={fresh,booking,unbooking,service_selct,options_ret,choice_made,
        signed_in,certified,valid,invalid,booking_ret,unbooked_sel};
DEFINITIONS
  freshSESSION ≙ SESSION - session;
VARIABLES
  session, session_state,
INVARIANT
  session ⊆ SESSION ∧
  session_state∈ session → STATE ∧ ...
INITIALISATION
  session := ∅ ‖ session_state := ∅ ‖ ...
OPERATIONS
 StartNewSession ≙
  ANY sid WHERE  sid∈ freshSESSION  THEN
    session := session ∪ {sid} ‖
    session_state(sid) := fresh
  END;
 SelectService ≙
  ANY sid  WHERE sid∈session ∧ session_state(sid)=fresh  THEN
    SELECT (....... ) THEN
      session_state(sid):= booking
    WHEN (.......) THEN
      session_state(sid):= unbooking
    WHEN (.......)THEN
        session_state(sid):= signed_in
    END ‖ ...
  END;
 FlightRequest ≙
  ANY sid WHERE sid∈ session ∧ session_state(sid)= booking THEN
    session_state(sid):= service_selct
  END;
```

**Fig. 2.** Abstract model of the travel agency system

The *"SelectService"* operation models the interaction of the clients with the system, when they select an available service.

## 4.2    State Management in Client Side

In Web based application Web clients generally are classified as thin clients. This implies that processing in the client side usually is not significant. Web clients take input from users, perform type checking and simple data validation and in some cases carry out data encryption if necessary. Web clients use the application through Web browsers, over the Internet. They interact with system concurrently, independently, in an asynchronous manner. You can't control what they're doing and when they do it. Although the browser and underling mechanism do not support sate handling, still some coordination mechanism and state passing between server and client operations is necessary.

**Challenge:** How do you maintain the state information in the client side and perform coordination between different clients and the Web server.

**Guideline:** We have used a message-based mechanism for this purpose. Each message is mapped to a session ID which relates the message to a specific client session. The message-based mechanism could be considered as an implicit state representation in the client side. Therefore from this viewpoint we can assume that two different approaches have been taken for state representation in the server and the client side. We have found that the main advantage of this approach is to avoid shared state variables among clients and the Web server which in its turn could lead to further complication.

We have presented some operation of the clients along with the server's operations from first refinement of the case study in Figure 3 to illustrate the guideline. We have used comments to make a distinction between the server and newly introduced client's operations. The server operations use explicit state variables for state representation. On the other hand, the client operations employ an implicit message-based method for state representation and coordination with the server operations.

The session ID, *"sid"*, plays a central role to convey state information between client and server. However there is a situation that a client has triggered a new session but it has not obtained a session ID yet. In this step the client should use a temporary identification mechanism which could be the IP address or any other similar mechanism. The *"Client_ReqSession"* operation in Figure 3 depicts this situation. We have defined a new variable named *"handle"* to use it as temporary index to represent a client request for a new session. When in the *"StartNewSession"* operation the server has processed this request it allocates a new session ID for this specific client session and replies to the client by placing the new session ID in the *"new_client"* message buffer. In the *"Get_SessionID"* operation the client receives this allocated *"sid"* and it will use it through the rest of session to communicate with the travel agency server. For example in the *"PicService"* operation we have a message buffer named *"reqsevice_buf"* which has been defined as a mapping from *"session"* to *"REQUEST"* to carry the client's requests to the Server.

As we have mentioned in section 3, we have used superposition refinement to introduce client operation. This means that we retain the variables and operations of the abstract specification and introduce new operations which have no effect on the pervious variables. Some new variables which can be exploited by both the clients' operations as well as the Web server have been introduced in this stage. New variables are used as message buffers to exchange data between client and server operations. The introduction of these new variables has some implication on the Web server's operations.

```
SETS
  HANDLE
DEFINITIONS
 freshHANDLE ≙ HANDLE - dom(new_client)
INVARIANT
 /* Client Variables */
  new_handle ⊆ HANDLE ∧
  new_client ∈ HANDLE ⤀ SESSION ∧
  token ⊆ SESSION ∧
  fresh_session ⊆ SESSION ∧
  reqsevice_buf ∈ SESSION ⤀ REQUEST
OPERATIONS
 Client_ReqSession ≙      /* Client Operation */
  ANY handle WHERE handle ∈ freshHANDLE THEN
   new_handle:= new_handle ∪{handle}
  END;
 StartNewSession ≙     /* Server Operation */
  ANY sid, handle WHERE sid ∈ freshSESSION ∧ handle ∈ new_handle THEN
   session:= session ∪ {sid} ‖
   session_state(sid) := fresh ‖
   new_client(handle):= sid ‖
   new_handle:= new_handle - {handle}
  END;
 Get_SessionID ≙      /* Client Operation */
  ANY sid WHERE sid ∈ SESSION ∧ sid ∈ ran(new_client) THEN
   token:= token ∪ {sid} ‖
   fresh_session:= fresh_session ∪ {sid} ‖
   new_client:= new_client ⩥|{sid}
  END;
 PicService ≙       /* Client Operation */
  ANY sid, req WHERE sid ∈ fresh_session ∧ req ∈ REQUEST THEN
   reqsevice_buf(sid):= req ‖
   fresh_session:= fresh_session - {sid}
  END;
```

**Fig. 3.** Some operation of the first refinement

In the abstract model some operations use nondeterministicly chosen values which need to satisfy just some typing and basic state conditions. In the refinement model some changes have been made in these operations' guard. This is to refine the nondeterministic choices to the available values in the related message buffers which are provided by clients. By using superposition refinement instead of more general Event B refinement in this stage, we do not require any gluing invariant which implies an easier set of prove obligations.

## 4.3 Conducting Inter-server Interactions

Coordination and communication management is an important issue in modelling interactions between two or more servers. In the case of inter-server communications, unlike client and server communication, both parties which are involved in a session are providing some services. Interaction between the travel agency system and secondary servers is an example of such inter-server communication. For example the travel agency system can ask a flight Agency server for available flight options and the flight agency server will reply with available options.

**Challenge:** What is the best way to model inter-server interactions?

**Guideline:** Considering the fact that the servers are independent, any approach to modelling their interaction, should provide a solution with minimum possible cohesion between these subsystems. Using the message-based approach seems to be a good candidate for this purpose and furthermore it complies with common web services technologies. The messages are defined as mapping from a session ID to the requested information.

---

**INVARIANT**
/* Server's New Variables */
reqflight_buf $\in$ FLIGHT_AGENCY $\rightarrow$ (SESSION $\rightarrow$ FLIGHT_REQUEST) $\wedge$
/* Flight Agency Variables */
respflight_buf $\in$ SESSION $\rightarrow$ (FLIGHT_AGENCY $\rightarrow$ $\mathbb{P}$(FLIGHT_DETAIL))
**OPERATIONS**
**Request_Flight** $\cong$     /* Server Operation */
 **ANY** sid,fr **WHERE** sid $\in$ SESSION $\wedge$ fr $\in$ FLIGHT_REQUEST **THEN**
  reqflight_buf:= $\lambda$ fa . (fa$\in$ FLIGHT_AGENCY | reqflight_buf(fa) $\cup$ {sid$\mapsto$fr})
 **END**;
**Resp_FlightReqs** $\cong$     /* Flight Agency Server Operation */
 **ANY** sid,fa,fr **WHERE** sid $\in$ session $\wedge$ fa $\in$FLIGHT_AGENCY $\wedge$
                        fr $\in$ FLIGHT_REQUEST   **THEN**
  **ANY** xx **WHERE** xx$\in$ $\mathbb{P}$(FLIGHT_DETAIL) $\wedge$ xx $\subseteq$
                        Matchflight(fr $\mapsto$ flight_db1(fa)) **THEN**
   respflight_buf(sid):= respflight_buf(sid) $\cup$ {fa $\mapsto$ xx}
  **END**  ‖
  reqflight_buf(fa):= reqflight_buf(fa)- {sid $\mapsto$ fr}
 **END**;

---

**Fig. 4.** Some operations of the secondary servers

The message-based approach could be exploited to exchange both data and state information between servers. Regarding the fact that server to server communications are mostly asynchronous, the message-based communication is an appropriate candidate.

Some operations of the secondary servers and the travel agency system which involve communication are presented in Figure 4. In this model, *"reqflight_buf"* is used to transmit requests from the travel agency to flight agencies. Flight agencies use *"respflight_buf"* message buffer to send responses to the travel agency.

# 5    Abstraction and Refinement of Complex Data-Types

In many Web applications frequently we need to represent some complex data types in different abstraction levels. For example this data could be a record with many fields containing all necessary information for a booking request. Refining abstract data types in a single step, especially when we do not need all details in this step, is not a good approach to refinement; because it swiftly turns our simple abstract model into an over-complicated refined model. Therefore we need to find a mechanism for stepwise refinement of the abstract data types.

**Challenge:** What is a proper abstraction for data structures like records and how we can refine an abstract representation of a record in a step-wise manner?

**Guideline:** We found that most details could be abstracted away by defining some simple data types in the form of set definitions in the specification level. In refinement stage to overcome the problem of unnecessary detail we found that, instead of direct refinement of abstract data types, some constant mapping could be used. A mapping defines a relation from an abstract data type to the required additional detail. By employing this method we introduce fields into refined model when it is necessary.

The abstract data types make operations very simple and understandable at specification level and help us to have a clearer picture of overall functionality of system. But we need to introduce the necessary details into these abstract data types in the refinement level. Using constant mappings to introduce new fields of a previously defined abstract type could help to avoid unnecessary complication in the early stage of refinement and postpone the detailed refinement of abstract data types to after decomposition.

Using constant mapping to refine an abstract record may present some ambiguity to the reader. So we will try to make some clarification here. Let assume that we have an abstract record, *"REC"* in the specification level. We want to refine this abstract record by introducing two new fields of it, namely *"afield"* and *"bfield"*. We can define these two fields as a constant mapping from *"REC"* to two arbitrary types *"SETA"* and *"SETB"* respectively. Now we can assert that for any *"aa"* and *"bb"* that *"aa"* belong to *"SETA"* and *"bb"* belong to *"SETB"* we can define a record that belongs to *"REC"*. Performing record refinement with a constant mapping rather than a variable mapping simply means that this information is global to all subsystems. Using constant mapping has not any restrictive impact on records manipulation. To clarify this issue we have presented an example operation in Figure 5 that adds a record to a database.

Here is An example from the case study is provided in Figure 6. We have two abstract data types; the first one is an abstraction for a record which contains all the necessary information for a flight request and the second one is the abstraction of a record which contains all details about an offered flight by a flight agency. We have used two abstract set definitions *"FLIGHT_REQUEST"* and *"FLIGHT_DETAIL"* for these two abstract records respectively. In the re-

**MACHINE** Database
**SETS**
   REC; SETA; SETB
**CONSTANTS**
 afield, bfield
**PROPERTIES**
 afield $\in$ REC$\rightarrow$SETA $\land$ bfield $\in$ REC$\rightarrow$SETB $\land$
 $\forall$ (aa, bb$\cdot$((aa $\in$ SETA $\land$ bb $\in$ SETB)$\Rightarrow$
 $\exists$ rr. (rr $\in$ REC $\land$ afield(rr) = aa $\land$ bfield(rr) = bb))
**VARIABLES**
 db
**INVARIANT**
 db $\in$ $\mathbb{P}$(REC)
**INITIALISATION**
  db:=$\varnothing$
**OPERATIONS**
**Add_Database** $\hat{=}$
**ANY** af,bf,rn **WHERE** af $\in$ SETA $\land$ bf $\in$ SETB $\land$ rn $\in$ REC $\land$
                         afield(rn)=af $\land$ bfield(rn)= bf
   **THEN**
    db:= db $\cup$ {rn}
   **END**
**END**

**Fig. 5.** An example of constant mapping

**CONSTANTS**
 flightagency
**PROPERTIES**
 flightagency $\in$ FLIGHT_ DETAIL $\rightarrow$ FLIGHT_AGENCY
**SETS**
 FLIGHT_REQUEST; FLIGHT_DETAIL; FLIGHT_AGENCY;

**Fig. 6.** An example of constant mapping from the case study

finement stage we need to access the flight agency that has provided a flight. We assume that the flight agency identifier is a part of the *"FLIGHT_DETAIL"* record. Instead of direct refinement of the abstract data type, we have defined a constant mapping from *"FLIGHT_DETAIL"* to *"FLIGHT_AGENCY"* which could satisfy our requirement in this stage. The definition of this constant mapping is presented in Figure 5. The use of a constant function provides a way of modelling a record's field in B. By using similar techniques we are able to introduce any extra detail which might be necessary in successive refinement steps. Obviously at the implementation stage we have to replace these constant mapping with an actual data field; but the fact that we could postpone this step until after decomposition is helpful.

# 6  Abstraction and Refinement of Distributed Databases

Data that is shared between Web components and persistent between invocations of a Web application is usually maintained by one or more databases. These databases generally are distributed over different servers. Developing a formal abstract model and refinement for them is another challenge that we examine in this section. This issue has a close relation with process distribution; therefore we consider the process distribution and distributed databases together. We can assume different functionality for a database system. For example the simplest case is a database which allows its contents to be viewed by different parts of the Web application. On the other hand a complex database could support different type of queries and permits updating current information or removing some records from it. As the system is distributed it means that when a server makes some changes in its database which could affects another part of the Web application, it takes some time for the other part to know about it.

**Challenge:** How we can represent a proper abstraction and refinement of certain distributed database operations?

**Guideline:** In a distributed setting involving multiple clients, the high level specification of a transaction such as confirming a flight booking needs to include the possibility of failure. Also query operations involving multiple databases should be specified very loosely at the abstract level.

To understanding the complicate relation of process and Database refinement we need some examples. In the travel agency system as depicted in Figure 1 we have a set of secondary servers which store some information about their available services. Based on web clients' requests the travel agency server occasionally initiates and sends a distributed query to these secondary servers for information lookup. Later it should collect and send available services to related Web clients. Obviously in the specification level we need an abstract formal representation of these distributed processes and databases.

The first abstract model is presented in Figure 7. In this specification *"Match-flight"* is a constant function type definition. It takes *"FLIGHT_REQUEST"* as an abstraction for user request and an abstract database which contains some *"FLIGHT_DETAIL"* records and returns a set of *"FLIGHT_DETAIL"* records which match the user request. In this abstract model we have defined the virtual database, *"flight_db"*, as an abstract representation for a set of distributed databases which reside on secondary servers. As we mentioned earlier the content of these distributed databases could change independently from the travel agency system. Based on the above assumption we have defined the operation *"Retrieve_FlightOptions"* which is an abstraction for collecting secondary servers' responses to a distributed query for a service. Obviously we have not introduced secondary servers and their related databases in the abstract model to avoid making the model over-complicated.

```
CONSTANTS
 Matchflight
PROPERTIES
 Matchflight∈ FLIGHT_REQUEST × ℙ(FLIGHT_DETAIL)→ℙ(FLIGHT_DETAIL)
INVARIANT
 flight_db ∈ ℙ(FLIGHT_DETAIL)
Retrieve_FlightOptions≙     /* Server Operation */
 ANY sid, fr WHERE sid ∈ session ∧ fr ∈ FLIGHT_REQUEST THEN
  ANY xx WHERE xx ∈ ℙ(FLIGHT_DETAIL) ∧ xx ⊆ Matchflight(fr ↦flight_db)
 THEN
  flight_options(sid) := xx
 END
END;
```

**Fig. 7.** An abstract model of the database operation

A refinement of the abstract model is presented in Figure 8. In this refinement based on the superposition technique we have introduced some new operations. The *"Request_Flight"* operation models the travel agency side event that initiates a query broadcast to a set of secondary servers. Equally when a secondary server receives a query for a service, it responds if it has any available option(s). This is demonstrated in *"Resp_FlightReqs"* operation. The virtual database definition has been replaced by actual databases which are distributed among secondary servers and we have defined these by a mapping form *"FLIGHT_AGENCY"* to power set of *"FLIGHT_DETAIL"*. The *"Retrieve_FlightOptions"* has been refined in response to the introduction of the new operations and now clearly reflects the fact that it should collect the secondary servers' responses to reply the initial service query. Our intention is that the abstract database is an abstraction of the union of all of the distributed databases. The response to a client request is formed from the union of the responses from each of the agencies so this may seem like a reasonable abstraction. However, we faced some difficulties when we tried to prove that the model in Figure 8 is a valid refinement of the abstract model in Figure 7. The problem is that the abstract specification of *"Retrieve_FlightOptions"* is based on the value of (the abstraction of) all the flight agency databases at the point at which the results are collated by the travel agency. But the results collated in the refined version will have been generated by the individual flight agencies at earlier points in time. If the flight agency databases did not change in between the point at which they respond to a flight request and the point at which those responses are collated by the travel agency, then our refinement would be valid. However, this is clearly an unrealistic restriction. The fact that the user gets information about an available flight is no guarantee that that flight will still be available when they try to book it. In principle the value of a flight agency database at the point of generating a response might be completely different to its value at the point at which that response is collated with other responses.

```
CONSTANTS
  Matchflight
PROPERTIES
  Matchflight ∈ FLIGHT_REQUEST × ℙ(FLIGHT_DETAIL) → (FLIGHT_DETAIL)
INVARIANT
  flight_db ∈ FLIGHT_AGENCY ⇸ ℙ(FLIGHT_DETAIL)
OPERATIONS
  Request_Flight ≙          /* Server Operation */
  ANY sid,fr WHERE sid ∈ SESSION ∧ fr ∈ FLIGHT_REQUEST THEN
    reqflight_buf:= λfa . (fa ∈ FLIGHT_AGENCY | reqflight_buf(fa) ∪ {sid↦fr})
  END;
  Resp_FlightReqs ≙        /* Flight Agency Server Operation */
  ANY sid,fa,fr WHERE sid ∈ session ∧  fa ∈FLIGHT_AGENCY ∧
                                fr ∈ FLIGHT_REQUEST
    THEN
    ANY xx WHERE xx∈ ℙ(FLIGHT_DETAIL) ∧ xx ⊆
                                Matchflight(fr ↦ flight_db1(fa))
      THEN
      respflight_buf(sid):= respflight_buf(sid) ∪ {fa ↦ xx}
    END
  END;
  Retrieve_FlightOptions ≙       /* Server Operation */
  ANY sid WHERE sid ∈ session THEN
    flight_options(sid):= ⋃ fa.(fa ∈ FLIGHT_AGENCY ∧
                    fa∈ dom(respflight_buf(sid)) | respflight_buf(sid)(fa))
  END;
```

Fig. 8. A refinement of the database operations

```
Retrieve_FlightOptions ≙       /* Server Operation */
ANY sid WHERE sid ∈ session  THEN
  VAR xx IN
   xx : ( xx ∈ ℙ(FLIGHT_DETAIL)) ‖
   flight_options(sid):= xx
  END
END;
```

Fig. 9. A valid abstraction of the database operation

One possible abstract specification for this kind of distributed database query is presented in Figure 9. Although it appears to be a very loose specification but it is the strongest specification that we could introduce in the abstract level. In this specification we do not use definitions like "Matchflight" and virtual database "flight_db". As we mentioned earlier data and process distribution have a reciprocal effect on each other. We present another scenario from the travel agency case study to clarify this issue further. During the booking process when

**Flight_Booking** $\widehat{=}$
   **ANY** sid,fd **WHERE** sid $\in$ session $\wedge$ fd $\in$ FLIGHT_DETAIL $\wedge$
       session_state(sid)= valid $\wedge$ sid $\mapsto$ fd $\in$ selctflight_buf **THEN**
   CHOICE
     flight_booking := flight_booking $\cup$ {session_user(sid) $\mapsto$ fd} $\parallel$
     selctflight_buf := {sid} $\lhd$ selctflight_buf $\parallel$
     session_state(sid):= fresh $\parallel$ session_request(sid):= none
   **OR**
     selctflight_buf:= {sid} $\lhd$ selctflight_buf $\parallel$
     session_state(sid) := fresh $\parallel$ session_request(sid):= none
   **END**
   **END**;

Fig. 10. Modelling the possibility of failure

a web client receives some available options from the travel agency system, it can select one of them and send back its selected service to the travel agency system. Now the travel agency system will know which secondary server has offered this service and then send a booking request to this specific secondary server. In the meantime this service could have been offered to another Web client and is no longer available. Therefore in general the travel agency system could expect either a successful or a failed response for a requested service booking. If the travel agency system receives a confirmation for service booking it will add an appropriate record to it local database for booked services. In either case of success or fail, it should reply to the related Web client with a suitable response.

Developing an abstract formal specification for this case is not a straightforward task. In the abstract level we have not introduced secondary servers, just to avoid complication, but we have to find a mechanism to model the system behaviour. Using nondeterministic "choice" could be an acceptable approach to model this case in the abstract level. This solution is depicted in Figure 10. It should be emphasised that in the actual system the booking process is a two stage process. If the requested service is still available on a specific secondary server, then the first stage takes place on that secondary server. In the second stage, when the travel agency system receives a message from this specific secondary server denoting successful booking in the first stage, then the travel agency system will add this booking to its database. Therefore the booking database on each secondary server just stores booked services which have been offered by this specific server. On the other hand the booking database on the travel agency system stores all booked services of its users. The *"Flight_Booking"* operation in Figure 10 demonstrates the booking process in the travel agency system. This operation is defined as the nondeterministic choice of two outcomes. In cases, the request is processed. In the first case it results in a successful booking, while in the second (failed) case, no booking is made. In the refined model when we introduced databases in the secondary servers, now the booking process in the Travel agency system is no longer nondeterministic and it depend on the state

```
CONSTANTS
  flght_agency
PROPERTIES
  flght_agency ∈ FLIGHT_DETAIL → FLIGHT_AGENCY
Agency_flight_booking ≙        /* Flight_agency Server Operation*/
  ANY fa,sid,fd WHERE fa ∈ FLIGHT_AGENCY ∧
                     sid ∈ SESSION ∧ fd ∈ FLIGHT_DETAIL
  THEN
   SELECT fd ∈ flight_db1(fa) THEN
    ANY fdb WHERE fdb ∈ ℙ(FLIGHT_DETAIL) ∧ fdb ⊆ flight_db1(fa) THEN
     /* Updating original Database that maybe affected by booking */
     flight_db1(fa):= fdb
    END ||
     fa_booking(fa):= fa_booking(fa) ∪ {(fd ↦ session_user(sid))} ||
     flightbookingresp(sid) := success
    WHEN fd ∉ flight_db1(fa) THEN
     flightbookingresp(sid) := failed
   END
  END;
Flight_Booking ≙        /* Server Operation */
  ANY sid,fa,fd WHERE sid ∈session ∧ fd ∈ FLIGHT_DETAIL ∧
     fa∈ FLIGHT_AGENCY
  THEN
   SELECT sid↦success∈ flightbookingresp THEN
    taf_booking:= taf_booking ∪ {(session_user(sid) ↦fd ↦fa)} ||
    suc_session:=suc_session ∪ {sid}
   WHEN sid↦failed∈ flightbookingresp THEN
    selectflight_buf(fa):= selectflight_buf(fa) - {sid ↦fd} ||
    unsuc_session:=unsuc_session ∪ {sid}
   END
  END;
```

**Fig. 11.** Refined model after introduction of secondary servers

of these databases. Therefore the refined operation could be modelled as we presented in Figure 11. Here the *"Agency_flight_booking"* shows the first stage of booking in the secondary server and the *"Flight_Booking"* has been refined accordingly.

# 7    Developing Formal Models for Communication Links

Communication links are the medium for interaction between different parts of distributed systems. In Web-based systems communication links connect a client to a Web server or a Web server to another Web server or a data server. Although communication in different levels could be based on different protocols and standards, but in general a message-based approach is a widely accepted method in Web based application. This approach is flexible and general enough to be implemented in the context of available standards like XML based technologies and tools. In Event-B developments introducing communication is an important stage before decomposition of a single model to several sub-models. In the following sections we discuss the process of developing a formal model for communication links.

## 7.1    Formal Models of Synchronised Communication Links

Synchronised communication is a common pattern of communication between Web clients and Web servers. In other words generally the communication between clients and the Web sever follows the send-process-receive pattern.

**Challenge:** What is an appropriate abstract model and refinement for communication links between clients and the Web Server?

**Guideline:** At the abstract level it is convenient to model communication link a one-place buffer. But this causes problems with model decomposition. So we present a pattern for refining a communication link involving a one-place buffer by an unbounded buffer.

To exemplify this issue we have presented some operation of the travel case study in Figure 12. We have used a function definition to present a single place buffer for data communication between each client and the travel agency server. In this model the *"reqsevice_buf"* and *"resp_buf"* define a single-place buffer from *"session"* to *"REQUEST"* and *"RESPOSE"* respectively. The *"PicService"* is a client operation which puts a request in the *"reqsevice_buf"*. The client then waits for the server response, i.e., the first client operation is no longer enabled for this session and the second client operation is enabled when a response appears in the response buffer. On the server side the *"SelectService"* operation takes the request from the buffer and then produces a response for the client by placing a response in the *"resp_buf"*. Later the client's operation *"Submit_Servic_Dtail"* can take this response from buffer when received it.

Before the decomposition step we have to refine each buffer by splitting it to three buffers and distribute them between the client, the communication and the server machines. But when we replace a single-place buffer with three single-place buffers we face difficulty. We should be able to demonstrate that all buffers are empty when for example a web client's operation produces a new message to put a in the buffer. Clearly this is not a practical solution since, for example, a client cannot see whether or not a buffer on the server side is empty. To overcome this difficulty we consider the refinement of the one-place buffers with unbounded buffers based on using sequence definition in B-method.

This intermediate refinement would help to split the buffers between different machines and without too much restriction discharges prove obligations associated with this distribution. Using unbounded buffers resolves the need for condition that distributed buffers should be empty when we add a new message.

The intermediate refinement for the above model is presented in Figure 13. Here the single-place buffers of Figure 12 have been replaced by unbounded

```
INVARIANT
  reqsevice_buf ∈ SESSION ⇸ REQUEST ∧
  resp_buf∈ SESSION ⇸ RESPOSE
OPERATIONS
 PicService ≙        /* Client Operation */
 ANY sid, req WHERE sid ∈ fresh_session ∧ sid∉dom(reqsevice_buf) ∧
                                    req∈ REQUEST ∧ req≠ none THEN
   reqsevice_buf(sid):= req ‖
   fresh_session:= fresh_session - {sid}
 END;
 SelectService ≙        /* Server Operation */
 ANY sid,req WHERE sid ∈ session ∧ req ∈ REQUEST ∧ resp ∈ RESPONSE ∧
                                    sid∈dom(reqsevice_buf) THEN
   session_request(sid):= req ‖
   reqsevice_buf:= {sid} ⩤ reqsevice_buf ‖
   resp_buf(sid):= resp
 END;
 Submit_Servic_Dtail ≙        /* Client Operation */
 ANY sid,resp WHERE sid ∈dom(resp_buf) ∧ resp ∈ RESPONSE ∧
                                    resp_buf(sid):= resp THEN
   resp_buf(sid):= {sid} ⩤ resp_buf(sid)
 END;
```

**Fig. 12.** Abstract model with one-place buffers

buffers. Part of the necessary gluing invariant are illustrated as well. The gluing invariant was constructed using an iterative approach in combination with the B prover as described in [15]. We first considered the case of a single implicit session. This simplification means that the invariant has no universal quantifiers and the proof is much more automatic. We start with a trivial invariant contains type information. We then generate and attempt to prove the refinement proof obligations. Those that cannot be proved lead to a clause in the invariant. The additional invariant clauses result in further proof obligations which may in turn lead to further invariant clauses. In this case a sufficient invariant was constructed in three iterations and the proof was completely automatic (for the case without universal quantification). The invariant is then generalised to multiple sessions and the proof goes through, though not completely automatically. The above refinement indicates that single-place buffers could be refined by multi-places buffers.

The refinement works because the request-response protocol that the client and server follow. Multi-place buffers allow having more than one message at the same time in different buffers. Although in this model message duplication is impossible but due to error and delay in communication links, message duplication is very likely and it could be taken in to account in later refinements. The next step refinement involves splitting each unbounded buffer into three unbounded buffers and introducing new operations for communications between these. These three buffers will be distributed between client, communication and

INVARIANT
  sreq_buf∈ SESSION ⇸ seq(REQUEST) ∧
  sresp_buf∈ SESSION ⇸ seq(RESPOSE) ∧
  /* Gluing Invariant */
  ∀sid.(sid ∈ fresh_session ⇒ reqsevice_buf(sid) =∅ ) ∧
  ∀sid.(sid ∈dom(sreq_buf) ∧ sreq_buf(sid)≠[] ⇒
     first(sreq_buf(sid))∈ reqsevice_buf(sid) ) ∧
OPERATIONS
PicService ≘      /* Client Operation */
 ANY sid, req WHERE sid ∈ fresh_session ∧ sid ∉ dom(sreq_buf) ∧
              req ∈ REQUEST ∧ req≠ none THEN
   sreq_buf (sid):= sreq_buf ⌢ [req] ‖
   fresh_session:= fresh_session - {sid}
 END;
SelectService ≘      /* Server Operation */
 ANY sid,req WHERE sid ∈ session ∧ req ∈ REQUEST ∧ resp ∈ RESPONSE ∧
      sid ∈dom(sreq_buf) ∧ sreq_buf(sid)≠[] ∧ first(sreq_buf(sid)) = req THEN
   session_request(sid):= req ‖
   sreq_buf:= tail(sreq_buf) ‖
   sresp_buf(sid):= sresp_buf(sid) ⌢ [resp]
 END;
Submit_Servic_Dtail ≘         /* Client Operation */
 ANY sid,resp WHERE sid∈dom(resp_buf) ∧ resp ∈ RESPONSE ∧
               sresp_buf(sid)≠ [] First(sresp_buf(sid)):= resp THEN
  sresp_buf(sid):=  tail(sresp_buf(sid))
 END;

Fig. 13. Refined model with unbounded buffers

server respectively. This decomposition process is a straightforward task with a simple gluing invariant which states that the order concatenation of the sub-buffers should be equal to the original buffer. Due to space restriction we have not presented this refinement here.

Using sequences to represent communication buffers imposes the order of messages. In other words it assumes that the communication link should guarantee message delivery in the order which they been sent out by sender. This implication could be considered as a restriction and in some cases it might be necessary to use a more general model to represent communication buffers. Therefore a different model based on using unordered multi-place buffers which is defined in [16] can be used. This unordered buffer had been named as a "Bag" which is a collection of elements that may have a multiple occurrences of any element. Due to space restriction we have not presented this solution here.

## 8    Summary of Results, Conclusions and Further Work

We have identified some key issues in formal modelling of Web-based systems like state representation in server and client side, distributed database system abstraction and refinement, handling complex data types and formal model for communication links. We have proposed some solutions for these aspects which have been exemplified with event-b models of a Travel agency case study.

In formal modelling we have considered only the safety properties and we have not tackled the liveness issue. Although our work has been influenced by mainstream work in Web-based system modelling and implementation, our models require further refinement to implementation level.

Furthermore Web-based systems are constructed from distributed subsystems which could operate concurrently. The fact that complicated nature of such systems could not be completely enclosed by a single B machine, reveals the importance of decomposition as a next step in formal development process. Decomposition is also an essential strategy for tackling the rapid growth of system complexity. Decomposition strategy could be based on CSP style value passing channels which has been developed in [16] and applied to other types of distributed systems [17].

# References

1. Murugesan, S., Deshpande, Y., eds.: Web Engineering, Software Engineering and Web Application Development. Lecture Notes in Computer Science 2016, Springer (2001)
2. S. Murugesan, et al.: Web Engineering: A New Discipline for Development of Web-based Systems. In: Proceedings of the First ICSE Workshop on Web Engineering. LNCS 1189, Los Angeles (1999)
3. Y. Deshpande, et al.: Web Engineering: Beyond CS, IS and SE. In: Proceedings of the First ICSE Workshop on Web Engineering, Los Angeles (1999) 171–176
4. J. R. Abrial: The B book - Assigning Programs to Meanings. Cambridge University Press (1996)
5. E. Sekerinski and K. Sere (eds.): Program Development by Refinement  Case Studies Using the B Method. SpringerVerlag (1998)
6. P. Luigia et al.: A Methodology for Integrating of Formal Methods in a Healthcare Case Study. Technical Report 436, TUCS (2001)
7. M. Butler and M. Waldén: Distributed system development in B. In: Proceedings of the 1st Conference on the B Method, Nantes, France (1996) 155–168
8. J.-R. Abrial and D. Cansell: Click'n'Prove- Interactive Proofs Within Set Theory, Version 23 (2003) http://www.loria.fr/~cansell/cnp.html.
9. : (Atelier B Web Page) http://www.atelierb.societe.com/.
10. : (B4free Web Page) http://www.b4free.com/.
11. J.-R. Abrial: Extending B without changing it (for developing Distributed Systems). In Abrias, H., ed.: Proceedings of the 1st Conference on the B Method. (1996) 169–191
12. J.-R. Abrial and L. Mussat: Introducing Dynamic Constraints in B. In: B'98 : The 2nd International B Conference, Recent Advances in the Development and Use of the B Method. (1998) 83–128
13. M. Waldén and K. Sere: Reasoning About Action Systems Using the B-Method. Formal Methods in Systems Design **13** (1998) 5–35
14. R. Back and K. Sere: Superposition Refinement of Reactive Systems. Formal Aspects of Computing **8** (1996) 324–346

15. C. Ferreira and M. Butler: Using B Refinement to Analyse Compensating Business Processes. In: ZB 2003: Formal Specification and Development in Z and B: Third International Conference of B and Z Users. LNCS 2651, Turku, Finland, Springer (2003)

16. M. J. Butler: Stepwise Refinement of Communicating Systems. Science of Computer Programming **27** (1996) 139–173

17. A. Rezazadeh and Michael Butler: Event-Based Modelling and Refinement of Distributed Monitoring and Control Systems. In: Refinement of Critical Systems (RCS'03), Turku (2003)

# Author Index

# Lecture Notes in Computer Science

For information about Vols. 1–3347

please contact your bookseller or Springer

Vol. 3397: T.G. Kim (Ed.), Artificial Intelligence and Simulation. XV, 711 pages. 2005. (Subseries LNAI).

Vol. 3396: R.M. van Eijk, M.-P. Huget, F. Dignum (Eds.), Agent Communication. X, 261 pages. 2005. (Subseries LNAI).

Vol. 3395: J. Grabowski, B. Nielsen (Eds.), Formal Approaches to Software Testing. X, 225 pages. 2005.

Vol. 3394: D. Kudenko, D. Kazakov, E. Alonso (Eds.), Adaptive Agents and Multi-Agent Systems III. VIII, 313 pages. 2005. (Subseries LNAI).

Vol. 3393: H.-J. Kreowski, U. Montanari, F. Orejas, G. Rozenberg, G. Taentzer (Eds.), Formal Methods in Software and Systems Modeling. XXVII, 413 pages. 2005.

Vol. 3391: C. Kim (Ed.), Information Networking. XVII, 936 pages. 2005.

Vol. 3390: R. Choren, A. Garcia, C. Lucena, A. Romanovsky (Eds.), Software Engineering for Multi-Agent Systems III. XII, 291 pages. 2005.

Vol. 3389: P. Van Roy (Ed.), Multiparadigm Programming in Mozart/OZ. XV, 329 pages. 2005.

Vol. 3388: J. Lagergren (Ed.), Comparative Genomics. VII, 133 pages. 2005. (Subseries LNBI).

Vol. 3387: J. Cardoso, A. Sheth (Eds.), Semantic Web Services and Web Process Composition. VIII, 147 pages. 2005.

Vol. 3386: S. Vaudenay (Ed.), Public Key Cryptography - PKC 2005. IX, 436 pages. 2005.

Vol. 3385: R. Cousot (Ed.), Verification, Model Checking, and Abstract Interpretation. XII, 483 pages. 2005.

Vol. 3383: J. Pach (Ed.), Graph Drawing. XII, 536 pages. 2005.

Vol. 3382: J. Odell, P. Giorgini, J.P. Müller (Eds.), Agent-Oriented Software Engineering V. X, 239 pages. 2005.

Vol. 3381: P. Vojtáš, M. Bieliková, B. Charron-Bost, O. Sýkora (Eds.), SOFSEM 2005: Theory and Practice of Computer Science. XV, 448 pages. 2005.

Vol. 3380: C. Priami, Transactions on Computational Systems Biology I. IX, 111 pages. 2005. (Subseries LNBI).

Vol. 3379: M. Hemmje, C. Niederee, T. Risse (Eds.), From Integrated Publication and Information Systems to Information and Knowledge Environments. XXIV, 321 pages. 2005.

Vol. 3378: J. Kilian (Ed.), Theory of Cryptography. XII, 621 pages. 2005.

Vol. 3377: B. Goethals, A. Siebes (Eds.), Knowledge Discovery in Inductive Databases. VII, 190 pages. 2005.

Vol. 3376: A. Menezes (Ed.), Topics in Cryptology – CT-RSA 2005. X, 385 pages. 2005.

Vol. 3375: M.A. Marsan, G. Bianchi, M. Listanti, M. Meo (Eds.), Quality of Service in Multiservice IP Networks. XIII, 656 pages. 2005.

Vol. 3374: D. Weyns, H.V.D. Parunak, F. Michel (Eds.), Environments for Multi-Agent Systems. X, 279 pages. 2005. (Subseries LNAI).

Vol. 3372: C. Bussler, V. Tannen, I. Fundulaki (Eds.), Semantic Web and Databases. X, 227 pages. 2005.

Vol. 3371: M.W. Barley, N. Kasabov (Eds.), Intelligent Agents and Multi-Agent Systems. X, 329 pages. 2005. (Subseries LNAI).

Vol. 3370: A. Konagaya, K. Satou (Eds.), Grid Computing in Life Science. X, 188 pages. 2005. (Subseries LNBI).

Vol. 3369: V.R. Benjamins, P. Casanovas, J. Breuker, A. Gangemi (Eds.), Law and the Semantic Web. XII, 249 pages. 2005. (Subseries LNAI).

Vol. 3368: L. Paletta, J.K. Tsotsos, E. Rome, G.W. Humphreys (Eds.), Attention and Performance in Computational Vision. VIII, 231 pages. 2005.

Vol. 3367: W.S. Ng, B.C. Ooi, A. Ouksel, C. Sartori (Eds.), Databases, Information Systems, and Peer-to-Peer Computing. X, 231 pages. 2005.

Vol. 3366: I. Rahwan, P. Moraitis, C. Reed (Eds.), Argumentation in Multi-Agent Systems. XII, 263 pages. 2005. (Subseries LNAI).

Vol. 3365: G. Mauri, G. Păun, M.J. Pérez-Jiménez, G. Rozenberg, A. Salomaa (Eds.), Membrane Computing. IX, 415 pages. 2005.

Vol. 3363: T. Eiter, L. Libkin (Eds.), Database Theory - ICDT 2005. XI, 413 pages. 2004.

Vol. 3362: G. Barthe, L. Burdy, M. Huisman, J.-L. Lanet, T. Muntean (Eds.), Construction and Analysis of Safe, Secure, and Interoperable Smart Devices. IX, 257 pages. 2005.

Vol. 3361: S. Bengio, H. Bourlard (Eds.), Machine Learning for Multimodal Interaction. XII, 362 pages. 2005.

Vol. 3360: S. Spaccapietra, E. Bertino, S. Jajodia, R. King, D. McLeod, M.E. Orlowska, L. Strous (Eds.), Journal on Data Semantics II. XI, 223 pages. 2005.

Vol. 3359: G. Grieser, Y. Tanaka (Eds.), Intuitive Human Interfaces for Organizing and Accessing Intellectual Assets. XIV, 257 pages. 2005. (Subseries LNAI).

Vol. 3358: J. Cao, L.T. Yang, M. Guo, F. Lau (Eds.), Parallel and Distributed Processing and Applications. XXIV, 1058 pages. 2004.

Vol. 3357: H. Handschuh, M.A. Hasan (Eds.), Selected Areas in Cryptography. XI, 354 pages. 2004.

Vol. 3356: G. Das, V.P. Gulati (Eds.), Intelligent Information Technology. XII, 428 pages. 2004.

Vol. 3355: R. Murray-Smith, R. Shorten (Eds.), Switching and Learning in Feedback Systems. X, 343 pages. 2005.

Vol. 3354: M. Margenstern (Ed.), Machines, Computations, and Universality. VIII, 329 pages. 2005.

Vol. 3353: J. Hromkovič, M. Nagl, B. Westfechtel (Eds.), Graph-Theoretic Concepts in Computer Science. XI, 404 pages. 2004.

Vol. 3352: C. Blundo, S. Cimato (Eds.), Security in Communication Networks. XI, 381 pages. 2005.

Vol. 3351: G. Persiano, R. Solis-Oba (Eds.), Approximation and Online Algorithms. VIII, 295 pages. 2005.

Vol. 3350: M. Hermenegildo, D. Cabeza (Eds.), Practical Aspects of Declarative Languages. VIII, 269 pages. 2005.

Vol. 3349: B.M. Chapman (Ed.), Shared Memory Parallel Programming with Open MP. X, 149 pages. 2005.

Vol. 3348: A. Canteaut, K. Viswanathan (Eds.), Progress in Cryptology - INDOCRYPT 2004. XIV, 431 pages. 2004.